D1345421

INTRODUCTION TO ITALIAN LAW

General Editors of the Series: Tuğrul Ansay and Don Wallace, Jr.

Introduction to the Law of the United States (1992)
Introduction to Greek Law (second edition 1993)
Introduction to the Law of Israel (1995)
Introduction to Swiss Law (second edition 1995)
Introduction to German Law (1996)
Introduction to Turkish Law (fourth edition 1996)
Introduction to Hungarian Law (1998)
Introduction to Belgian Law (2001)
Introduction to the Law of the United States (second revised edition 2002)
Introduction to Italian Law (2002)

Introduction to Italian Law

Edited
by

Jeffrey S. Lena, Esq.
California Bar

Ugo Mattei
Professor of Civil Law, University of Turin, and
Alfred and Hanna Fromm Professor of International and Comparative Law,
U. C. Hastings

2002

KLUWER LAW INTERNATIONAL
THE HAGUE – LONDON – NEW YORK

Published by:
Kluwer Law International
P.O. Box 85889, 2508 CN The Hague, The Netherlands
sales@kli.wkap.nl
http://www.kluwerlaw.com

Sold and Distributed in North, Central and South America by:
Kluwer Law International
101 Philip Drive, Norwell, MA 02061, USA
kluwerlaw@wkap.com

Sold and Distributed in all other countries by:
Kluwer Law International
Distribution Centre, P.O. Box 322, 3300 AH Dordrecht, The Netherlands

A CIP Catalogue record for this book is available from the Library of Congress

Printed on acid-free paper.

ISBN 90-411-1707-5

© 2002 Kluwer Law International

Kluwer Law International incorporates the imprint of Martinus Nijhoff Publishers.

To Adele N. D'Alessandro

— JSL

To FGS

— JSL, UM

Preface

We are pleased to offer to our readers the *Introduction to Italian Law*, a volume in our series of Introduction books to the laws of different countries.

Italy has a particular place among contemporary Civil Law countries. She is a member of the European Union, which has its inception in the Rome Treaty of 1958. But the significance of Italy goes back much further, being the home of Roman Law and the root of the unification of law centuries ago. The spirit of modern Civil Law comes from those days and became the inspiration of our age. World renowned scholars such as Cappelletti during the last decades, as well as a brilliant new generation of lawyers are putting strong emphasis on comparative law and unification of law. Italy is the host country to various international institutions such as UNIDROIT as well as other institutes of law. She is currently engaged in intensive efforts to modernize her legal structure. Nevertheless, there have not been many books in the market in English covering the whole legal system, and those which do are now outdated.

We are grateful to Professor Mattei, Mr. Lena, and to the authors who contributed their respective chapters, for preparing this Introduction to Italian Law.

In this book on Italian law, readers will find not only descriptions of different institutions of present Italian law, prepared by experts on the topics, but they will get something not present in other volumes in our series – trends in the development of the contemporary Italian law, enriched with many references to court decisions and scholarly publications. We, as general editors share the view of Professor Mattei and Mr. Lena that such a book on Italian law will be appreciated by our readers, and we hope that the book will serve the needs of both beginners and practitioners and scholars, who do not have direct access to the Italian law in the original Italian.

Prof. Tuğrul Ansay

Prof. Don Wallace, Jr.

Introduction

What is the value of an English language introduction to Italian law?

In the increasingly global environment of legal practice, there is a basic need to know something about the legal systems of different countries. International practice requires an essential understanding of the legal minds of colleagues operating outside of one's own legal system. We are still far from achieving a common taxonomy and a common conceptual framework for comparative work of this nature. It is possible that we will never achieve it, but because English has become the lingua franca of Western international legal culture, it follows that such basic knowledge should at least be disseminated in English.

There is surprisingly little written in English on Italian law. The classic work of Cappelletti, Merryman, and Perillo published in 1967 is more than thirty years old, and is unfortunately out of print. And though other work has been produced in the interim, there remains a gap to be filled. This book aims to fill that gap.

Although one could argue that the "Italian Style," as captured in John Henry Merryman's groundbreaking work,[1] cannot be changed by the stroke of the legislator's pen, changes in Italian law have been substantial indeed since Professor Merryman first wrote. Italy has an entirely new code of criminal procedure. Civil procedure has been fundamentally transformed. A new body of family law is in place. The encroachment of European legislation has redrawn the map of the sources of law. Private international law is new. Administrative law has undergone recent reform. The changes are such that even an Italian lawyer who attended school twenty years ago and who has not kept abreast of recent developments would find it hard to recognize the system – let alone someone whose knowledge is based on the presently available English-language literature.

---

[1] J.H. Merryman, "The Italian Style: Doctrine," *18 Stanford Law Review* 39 (1965); The "Italian Style II: Law," *18 Stanford Law Review* 396 (1966); "The Italian Style III: Interpretation," *18 Stanford Law Review* 583 (1966).

Some English-language materials reflecting the evolution of Italian law have been published, and have attracted unprecedented international interest. The Italian Association of Comparative Law has attempted publication of a yearbook in English patterned after the Scandinavian Studies in Law. Specific yearbooks are also available for Civil Procedure and International Law. These initial efforts notwithstanding, much more needs to be done. The work on legal transplants in the area of Criminal Procedure has not led to further examination of the law-in-action in its new legal-cultural context. The *Italian Studies in Law* have been discontinued. The *Civil Procedure Yearbook* reflects the highly technical and formalisitic jargon of Italian proceduralists and is therefore unusable by non-Italians. Finally, studies of international law are not the place to look for changes in national legal culture.

It therefore seemed useful to offer scholars and practitioners an updated introduction for those who do not have the time or ability to search specialized libraries or consult Italian language texts, but who still need to know something about current Italian law. The motivation behind this project, however, was not merely practical. Introductions to foreign legal systems written in English have an impact that extends beyond international legal practice to reach the structure of legal taxonomies – a task that lies at the very core of the comparative legal profession. Such introductions, indeed, are usually major reference sources for comparative law work. They are the new materials from which comparative generalizations can be developed and new taxonomic structures are theorized.

As in every collaborative work, one of the most important tasks is careful selection of the contributors. We determined early on that we wanted comparativists to undertake the work because they are accustomed by training and habit of mind to step outside of the internal legal frame and think broadly about fundamental operative principles. We felt this was essential to produce accounts of Italian law helpful to foreign jurists engaged in trying to understand a legal system different from their own.

Fortunately, following the lead of scholars such as Sacco, Gorla, Cappelletti, Denti, and Verrucoli, an exceptionally strong comparative law community has developed in Italy (despite the many hurdles that the ministry of Higher Education, and other conservative academic establishments have placed in its path). These scholars have developed the seeds of a useful critical approach to comparative law as an instrument for challenging deeply embedded assumptions of local legal cultures often still dominated by legal positivism. As a result, today's Italian legal culture now includes an emerging vanguard of scholars whose work is worthy of world-wide discussion. We searched for our contributors among this group, often enjoying the luxury of selecting from among several strongly qualified colleagues.

It is also important to note that in the balance between scholarly quality and practical interest, we thought to privilege the former, with the understanding that an introduction offering only the most recent black-letter enactment or the most recent court decision would be less useful to both scholars and practitioners. Consequently, the contributing authors were invited to discuss major trends in their areas primarily to illustrate legal principles and how an Italian lawyer might think about them. At times, this tradeoff has resulted in contributions that are more interesting and topical than they are elementary. Still, after reading this book, the non-Italian lawyer should be able to engage in fruitful conversation with an Italian colleague and have a sense of what he or she is talking about. The reader should also be able to use this book as a point of departure for further exploration of either a scholarly or practical sort in most areas of Italian law.

A word about structure and coverage: our grouping of contributors attempts to capture the law in a dynamic context. We avoided the use of locally loaded taxonomies such as "public law vs. private law" or "civil law vs. commercial law." We also avoided the use of a formal theory of sources of law as a structural point of departure since many aspects of legal systems function as sources of law without being recognized as such. In sum, we tried to make our material accessible to anyone who comes to it with an open mind, without requiring him or her to grapple with the technicalities of a particular legal system.

Of course, the coverage is not complete. There are areas of commercial law that are very important in practice – bankruptcy, insurance, intellectual property – which are not covered. There is no section on tax law, and the American reader might wonder about the absence of systematic treatment of the law of evidence. Also, we have not provided, with some regret, chapters on substantive criminal law, or a systematic view of the legal profession. Beyond the standard space constraints imposed by the publisher, we had good reason to omit certain areas. Taxation law in Italy, for example, is a disparate array of contingent enactments. Intellectual property is mostly covered by European Union law, and the law of evidence does not exist as a unitary body common to civil and criminal processes. These lacunae notwithstanding, we offer the present work as a sound introduction to the Italian legal system and trust that it will help the reader build a bridge between the Italian legal system and his or her own.

Finally, the editors wish to thank Ted Jang and Stephen Lothrop of Hastings College of the Law; Christine Robben, Elize Plink, and Steve Lambley of Kluwer; Tuğrul Ansay and Don Wallace, our general series editors; and Jen Scappettone of the University of California, Berkeley. Each improved the volume or facilitated its production, or both.

Jeffrey S. Lena, Esq.
jlena@attglobal.net

Ugo Mattei
matteiu@uchastings.edu

Berkeley, California

31 October 2001

Presentation

This interesting and authoritative new book on the Italian legal system is an important contribution to the English language literature of comparative law. I know of only three earlier works that attempt to deal comprehensively with the Italian legal system. The first, by Cappelletti, Merryman and Perillo, was published in 1967 and is now out of print.[1] The second, by Certoma, appeared in 1985,[2] and the third, by Watkin, in 1997.[3] This new collective work, written by a number of distinguished Italian academics and jointly edited by Professor Ugo Mattei and American Attorney Jeffrey Lena, will at once displace its predecessors and dominate the field.

It is a small, thinly populated field, at least on this side of the Atlantic. When I started to become a comparative lawyer in the early 1960's, Joseph M. Perillo of Fordham and I were the only American academics who appeared to display any interest in Italian law. The situation has since improved, partly due to transatlantic commuting by a number of Italians, notably including Mauro Cappelletti (of Firenze and Stanford) and one of the Editors of this volume, Ugo Mattei (of Torino and Hastings). Interest in Italian law has of course also been fostered by an increase in transatlantic commercial activity requiring a familiarity with foreign legal systems. Still, the attention paid to Italy by comparative lawyers in the English-speaking world continues to be modest.

Someone has said that all Western lawyers are Roman lawyers. I take this to mean that all of us are beneficiaries of the record of legal experience and scholarship that, beginning in ancient Rome, was preserved in Justinian's compilation and the early Canon law of the Church of Rome, was revived and nourished in the Italian universities in the early Renaissance and spread throughout what came to be called the "civilized world" in succeeding centuries. The suggestion, as I understand it, is

---

[1] M. Cappelletti, J.H. Merryman and J.M. Perillo, *The Italian Legal System: an Introduction*, Stanford, The Stanford University Press, 1968.

[2] G. Leroy Certoma, *The Italian Legal System*, London, Butterworths, 1985.

[3] T.G. Watkin, *The Italian Legal Tradition*, Aldershot/Brookfield USA/Singapore/Sydney, Ashgate Dartmouth, 1997.

that the deep structure of our modern law – Common Law as well as Civil Law – is a distillate of that historical experience.

Argument about such a proposition, while endlessly fascinating to some, is bound to be inconclusive, although Civil lawyers may be expected to find it more congenial than Common lawyers. Some will relate it to a different but comparably attractive idea: the thesis that the medieval *jus comune*, fractured by the rise of the nation-state, was in some profound empirical sense socially and culturally *valid*. It was a natural legal state of affairs to which the West now finds itself returning by way of the European Union and other international institutions.[4]

Consciousness of such a Romanic presence in modern law is nowhere more immediately felt than in Italy. Nowhere does one find a more vital and productive community of legal scholars actively engaged in comparative scholarship. The volume, variety and quality of Italian legal publications – journals, monographs, treatises, encyclopedias – astonishes those who first encounter them.

Young comparative lawyers, I encourage you to look to Italy, the source of the Civil Law tradition. This important new book provides an excellent place to begin such a voyage. Other readers, who may have only an occasional need to deal with specific questions of Italian law, will find this book a convenient and reliable place to begin to learn how such questions are phrased and addressed by thoughtful Italian lawyers.

My compliments and congratulations to the Editors and Authors of this important work.

John Henry Merryman

Stanford, 19 November 2001

---

[4] Compare the interesting discussion by Professor Monateri in chapter 2 of this book. I address a variation of this thesis in *The French Deviation*, originally published in *Studi in memoria di Gino Gorla*, vol. I, p. 619 (Milano, Giuffrè, 1994), republished in 44 *American Journal of Comparative Law* 109 (1996) and in my essay collection *The Loneliness of the Comparative Lawyer,* p. 160 (The Hague/London Boston, Kluwer Law International, 1999).

Table of Abbreviations

Codes

ABGB — Codice Austriaco del 1811

C. Nap. – Codice Napoleone

BGB — Codice Civile Tedesco del 1900

CC — Codice Civile

CPC — Code di procedura Civile

CCrPr — Code di Procedura Penale

Courts

Cass. – Corte di Cassazione

Cass. S.U. — Cassazione Sezioni Unite

Corte Cost. – Corte Costituzionale

T.A.R. — Tribunale Amministrativo Regionale

Encylopedias

Dig. IV Disc. Priv. Sez. Civ. — Digesto IV Discipline Privatistiche Sezione Civile

Enc. Dir. — Enciclopedia del Diritto

Enc. Giur. Del Lavoro — Enciclopedia Giuridica del Lavoro

Noviss. Dig. It. — Novissimo Digesto Italiano

Law Reviews

Am J Comp L — American Journal of Comparative Law

Arch. Civ. — Archivio Civile

BBTC — Banca Borsa e Titoli di Credito

Cass. Pen. — Cassazione Penale

Colum L Rev — Columbia Law Review

Contr. Impresa — Contratto e Impresa

Corriere Giur. — Corriere Giuridico

Dir. Eccl. — Diritto Ecclesiastico

Dir. Fam. — Diritto di Famiglia

DL — Diritto del Lavoro

ECJ Report — European Court of Justice Report

Fam. E Dir. — Famiglia e Diritto

Foro Amm. — Foro Amministrativo

Foro It. (or *FI*) — Foro Italiano

Gazzetta Giur. — Gazzetta Giuridica

Giur. Comm. — Giurisprudenza Commerciale

Giur. Cost. — Giurisprudenza Costituzionale

Giur. It. (or *GI*) — Giurisprudenza Italiana

Giur. Pugliese — Giurisprudenza Pugliese

Giust. Civ. — Giustizia Civile

Guida al Dir. — Guida al Diritto

Harv. Env. L Rev. — Harvard Environment Law Review

Hastings LJ — Hastings Law Journal

J Leg. Studies — Journal of Legal Studies

Mass. Foro It. — Massimario del Foro Italiano

Michigan L Rev. — Michigan Law Review

MLR (or *Mod L Rev.*)— Modern Law Review

NGCC — Nuova Giurisprudenza Civile Commentata

Notre DameLRev. — Notre Dame Law Review

Nuova Giur. Civ. — Nuova Giurisprudenza Civile

Pol. Dir. — Politica e Diritto

Quadr. — Quadrimestre

Rass. Giur. Umbra — Rassegna di Giurisprudenza Umbra

Rass. Locaz. e Condominio — Rassegna Locazioni e Condominio

RDCo (or *Riv. Dir. Comm.*)— Rivista di Diritto Commerciale

RDI — Rivista Diritto Industriale (or Internazionale)

Rep. Foro It. — Repertorio Foro Italiano

Resp. Civ. e Prev. — Responsabilità Civile e Previdenza

Riv. Crit. Dir. Priv. — Rivista Critica del Diritto Privato

Riv. Dir. Agr. — Rivista di Diritto Agrario

Riv. Dir. Civ. — Rivista di Diritto Civile

Riv. Dir. Eur. — Rivista di Diritto Europeo

Riv. Giur. Amb. — Rivista giuridica dell'Ambiente

Riv. Società — Rivista delle Società

Riv. Trim. Dir. e Proc. Civ. — Rivista Trimestrale di Diritto e Procedura Civile

Riv. It. Dir. pubbl. — Rivista Italiana di diritto pubblico

Società e Dir. — Società e Diritto

Stan L Rev – Stanford Law Review

U Chi L Rev — University of Chicago Law Review

Vita Not. — Vita Notarile

Yale J Int'l Law — Yale Journal of International Law

Yale LJ — Yale Law Journal

Treatises

Giur. Sist. Civ. e Comm. diretta da W. Bigiavi — Giurisprudenza Sistematica Civile e Commerciale diretta da W. Bigiavi

Trattato di Dir. Civ. Cicu – Messineo — Trattato di Diritto Civile diretto da Cicu e Messineo

Trattato di Dir. Priv. Rescigno — Trattato di Diritto Privato diretto da Rescigno

Trattato di Dir. Civ. Vassalli — Trattato di Diritto Civile diretto da Vassalli

Miscellaneous

C.S.M. — Consiglio Superiore della Magistratura

CGIL — Confederazione Generale Italiana lavoratori

CISL — Confederazione Italiana Sindacati dei Lavoratori

CONSOB — Commissione Nazionale per le Società e la Borsa

DM — Decreto Ministeriale

DPR — Decreto del Presidente della Repubblica

EC — European Community

ECSC — European Coal and Steel Community

EU — European Union

EURATOM — European Atomic Energy Community

GU — Gazzetta Ufficiale

ILO — International Labor Organization

L. (or *l.*) — Legge

R.D. — Regio Decreto

UIL — Unione Italiana Lavoratori

WS — Workers' Statute

Table of Contents

PART FIVE: Legal Research

CHAPTER ONE

A Sketch of Legal History

Antonio Padoa-Schioppa [1]

I. Introduction

Our preliminary question is this: does a history of Italian law exist? We cannot answer "yes" unconditionally, because the political unity of Italy was achieved only in 1860, and we must determine how to regard what occurred in the domain of law in the preceding centuries. In fact, when the "History of Italian Law" became part of the study at the law schools in 1876, it was natural for scholars to ask what the significance of this new discipline was. Debate over the subject was lively and prolonged, because the recent unification of the Peninsula into the nation-state of Italy called for the search for a pre-existent national identity, if it did not actually postulate the existence of such an identity.

While inquiring into the nature and existence of an Italian national identity in the legal history of Italy, we will aim our sketch in two directions. On the one hand, we shall try to examine the major phases in the historical development of law on the Peninsula (part II), and to underscore those distinctive characteristics of law – in the crucial period from the late eleventh to the early sixteenth centuries – which assumed such importance that they have a significance not just for Italy, but for Europe as a whole (part III). On the other hand, we will deal with the question of whether Italy prior to the unification had experienced, in its institutions, legal scholarship, legislation, customs, and judicial decisions, not only specific local developments in law, but also some common developments in the legal system along the whole Peninsula (part IV). Finally, we will sketch a few aspects of Italian legal development after 1860 (part V).

---

[1]   Professor of Italian Legal History, University of Milan. Translated from the Italian original by Jeffrey S. Lena.

Jeffrey S. Lena and Ugo Mattei (eds.), *Introduction to Italian Law*, 1-20
©2002 Kluwer Law International. Printed in the Netherlands.

II. The Historical Development of Law on the Peninsula

The main phases of historical development on the Peninsula may be delineated in six phases, as follows.

A *first phase* stretches from the fourth to the sixth centuries; this phase saw the transition from the ancient world to the early medieval period. The late Roman Empire, from the rule of Constantine to Justinian, experienced a series of basic legal transformations, both in the public institutions (as occurred with the new hierarchy of local and central authorities, the separation between civil and military authority, and the entrusting of civil and criminal process exclusively to imperial and public judges and civil servants), and in the various branches of private law. This resulted partially from the increasing influence of Christianity and the impact of Greek law, but mainly from the novel historical conditions and needs of the late Roman Empire.

The whole system of the sources of law was modified in this period, in that the source of authority that produced new law was only the imperial power, which acted through judicial decisions (*rescripta*) and general constitutions (*edicta*). These were gathered together in private and public collections, the latter by Teodosius II (438 AD) and by Justinian (529-534 AD). By that time, legislative power had been divided into the western and the eastern parts of the Roman Empire. Though originating in Constantinople, both codifications had a deep influence throughout medieval as well as (in the case of the Justinian Code) modern Italy and Europe.

It is important to note that the final centuries of the ancient world witnessed the creation of some ecclesiastical institutions and doctrines that are to be counted among the very foundations of Western European civilization. At the end of the fourth century, the principle of the separation between the areas of competence and functions of the secular authority and those of religious authority was underscored by Bishop Ambrose of Milan, among others; Ambrose was a strong supporter of the Church's autonomy even with respect to the imperial authority of Teodosius the Great. A century later, Pope Gelasius I elaborated the theory of the two "distinct dignities" in the figures of the Pope and the Emperor. In the sixth century, Benedictus, a monk from Norcia, wrote the Benedictine Monastic Rule. Soon after, in 590, a high civil official in Rome who had become a Benedictine monk was elected Bishop of Rome under the name of Gregory. His writings would form a lasting contribution to western canonical law.

A *second phase* covers the early medieval period, from the seventh to the eleventh centuries. The descent of the Lombards into Italy initiated a reign with its capital in Pavia, that extended from the north through the middle sections of the Peninsula and lasted two hundred years (from 568 to 774). It introduced a body of rules of German stamp codified in the Edicts of Rotari and Liutprand. These rules remained in force alongside the Roman law, which had survived thanks to the German legal rule of the "personal laws," which allowed the Latin population to conserve and rely on its own Roman laws, though in simplified and vulgar form, while the Lombards followed their own legal traditions and customs. Areas covered by Lombard law included the rules regarding inheritance, the legal status of women, the forms of litigation, and a criminal law based upon the payment of monetary penalties even in cases of homicide. Their influence remained strong, even after the fall of the Lombard kingdom, through the early and late Middle Ages. The Carolingian period (774-888) was marked by the introduction into Italy of new laws and customary rules which were mostly of Frankish origin. Among these were the feudal institutions of vassalage and benefice, whose impact was to become particularly vital from the tenth century forward. In southern Italy, the Byzantine influence remained dominant, and Greco-Roman sources of law continued to hold sway. Sicily, by contrast, was under Islamic domination from the ninth to the eleventh centuries.

Throughout this long period, the basic legal source was customary law much more than written law (one need only recall that feudal institutions were born and flourished as customary law). This complex of unwritten rules assumed a great variety of forms in different regions, boroughs and towns, whether in contracts, property rights, inheritance and family law, procedure, or criminal sanctions. Nevertheless, they shared many features that were born of common socioeconomic conditions and religious convictions prevalent throughout Italy and Europe. The continuity of the Roman legal tradition in the area of private law was also based upon its preservation as a set of customs, largely through the perpetuation of notarial forms and traditions.

A *third phase* runs from the late eleventh century to the early sixteenth century, when Italy demonstrated an extraordinary vitality and renewal in such different areas as economy, urban institutions, ecclesiastical life, monastic orders, literature, arts, theology, and law. This period saw the development of agriculture as well as economic production and exchange through artisanal and mercantile guilds. It also witnessed the flowering of communal institutions with jurisdictional and legislative authority exercised by elected consuls and judges, both in cities and in the country.

A new science of the law developed in Bologna and spread quickly across the Alps into Europe, eventually forming a vast system of common law which did not depend upon, and was not limited by, national or linguistic boundaries. This new science was founded upon Roman texts and was the result of the work of several generations of university scholars. Over the course of time, it took on the form of a "republic of legal culture" throughout most of continental Europe.

At the same time, the Church developed a fully articulated legal structure in the vast field of Canon Law. And certain political formations, as the Norman kingdom of Sicily and later the duchy of the Visconti in northern Italy, prefigured the centralized modern state in some of its aspects. These are, in other words, the centuries in which the legal history of Italy is the history of Europe as well: we will devote some pages (part III, *infra*) to a sketch of various aspects of the Italian legal history of these centuries. Over such a long span of time, one has to distinguish various specific periods.

With respect to political institutions, the first to arise was the commune ruled by elected citizens, who were called "consuls," after the Roman term. From the early thirteenth century on, the consuls were replaced by an elected *podestà* at the head of the commune; this position was deliberately conferred upon a foreigner in order to try to ensure impartiality among the turbulent factions of the city. Finally came the *comune del popolo* and of the arts or guilds, commencing around the middle of the same century. These institutional developments led, in the fourteenth century, to the crisis of communal liberty, the beginnings of the *signorie*, and the formation of the local and regional principalities that that would characterize the centuries to follow. But it is important to underscore that every commune had its own unique history. Only a few cities – such as Venice, Genoa, and Lucca – survived as aristocratic republics beyond the Middle Ages and into the modern era.

As for the schools of law, the Glossators from Irnerius to Accursius – five generations of professors at the newly born University of Bologna – were active between the early years of the twelfth century and the middle of the thirteenth century. Accursius' great *Glossa magna* to the whole *Corpus Iuris Civilis* was used throughout Europe until the close of the eighteenth century. During the same period, in the area of canon law, legal experts known as the *decretistae* studied, analyzed and summarized the *Decretum* of Gratian according to the same exegetical methods introduced by the Glossators, while toward the end of the twelfth century the Popes' decretals gave form to a *ius novum* that quickly became the object of study by the *decretalistae*. A second major school of law, whose exponents came to be known as the Commentators, originated in France at Orléans in the second half of the thirteenth century, and then flourished over the course of the fourteenth and fifteenth centuries, with its greatest exponents in Italy; Bartolus of Sassoferato and Baldus de Ubaldis, to name the two most famous jurists of the fourteenth century, were read and cited in Europe well beyond the Middle Ages. The developing humanistic culture of fifteenth-century Italy was later to encourage new approaches to the study of law that bore fruit particularly in the teachings of Andrea Alciatus and in the works of the great French scholars of Roman law of the sixteenth century.

At the core of this lengthy historical trend in legal culture was the doctrinal work of scholars, manifest in the production of legal commentaries and treatises as well as in their *consilia*, which were legal opinions rendered in specific cases at the request of either the judge or one of the litigants. Both sources were regarded as bearing great weight, not just on the academic level, but in the realm of legal practice as well: in a legal case discussed in a court, a lawyer often quoted with success the opinion expressed by a law professor who had written as early as a century or more beforehand, either in a commentary or in a *consilium*. The same role and prestige enjoyed by the English Royal Judges of Common Law were enjoyed by some celebrated university scholars on the European continent.

A *fourth phase* occurred from the beginning of the sixteenth century to the beginning of the eighteenth century, an epoch known in Italy as the Age of Spanish Domination due to the hegemony exercised on the Peninsula by the Spanish crown throughout almost the entire period: the duchy of Milan, the kingdoms of Naples, Sicily, and Sardinia, and other Italian regions were all directly subjected to Spanish rule.

With regard to the legal system, this period maintained a marked dualism between the *ius commune* and the local statutes of medieval origin which remained in place, only partly substituted by or integrated into an overlay of royal ordinances. Civil society was characterized by the strong presence of an aristocracy (*patriziato*) of feudal or communal origin. The aristocrats maintained an almost total monopoly over civic affairs, as all the responsibilities for the town administration were reserved to their families. The need to preserve intact, generation after generation, the social authority and the economic standing of their families explains the success of such legal institutions as primogeniture and *fideicommissum*, which prevented the risk of splintering the family patrimony among several sons. The exercise of commerce was generally forbidden to members of the nobility.

Legal scholarship developed in new directions in this period. Along with the traditional method of the *commentum* (now called *mos italicus*, and particularly praised in the Italian universities and courts), there flourished the humanistic *scuola culta*, called *mos gallicus*; the latter was transplanted to France by Alciatus and later developed there by a group of great scholars, including François Duaren, Hugues Doneau, and Jacques Cujas. Beyond these doctrinal tendencies, one finds a huge production of treatises designed to assist practicing lawyers and the courts in Italy. The spread of printed books multiplied the quantity (if not always the quality) of legal texts in circulation many times over. Through these developments, legal scholarship took on a renewed importance: any specific point of law upon which scholarly opinion was relatively settled – among either ancient or more recent scholars (*communis opinio doctorum*) – came to be recognized as so important in the practice of law as to almost take on the quality of legislative authority. In the same period, the high courts of the Italian states began to exercise not only vast jurisdictional authority, but legislative and administrative authority as well.

Between the sixteenth and the seventeenth centuries, Italy continued to witness the production of legal scholarship of importance throughout Europe. One need only think of the influential works of Julius Clarus and Prosper Farinaccius, who wrote authoritative works on criminal law very often referenced across the continent; or of the treatises in the area of commercial law produced by Bartolomeus Stracca, Ansaldus de Ansaldis, and Benvenuto Scaccia; or of important jurists such as Jacobus Menochius or Johannes Baptista de Luca. Yet from the sixteenth century on, the center of legal culture in Europe gradually shifted from Italy to other European countries. In the second half of the sixteenth century, a new direction was taken at the Theological School in Salamanca in Spain. Here, for the first time, the shaping of legal principles and rules began to depart from the sources derived from the Justinean *Corpus iuris*. Then in the Low Countries, and soon after in Germany, the modern school of natural law was born, thanks to the contributions of scholars such as Hugo Grotius, Samuel Pufendorf, Christian Thomasius, and Christian Wolff.

A *fifth phase* began in the second half of the eighteenth century and concluded a century later with the unification of the Italian Peninsula into a nation-state. Enlightenment thought, which germinated in and grew out of seventeenth-century natural law theory, subjected the whole system of legal institutions to rationally based criticism, and proposed radical reforms. Enlightenment legal thought, beginning with Montesquieu and Voltaire, had some very important exponents in Italy, particularly in Milan and Naples. In 1764, Cesare Beccaria authored a short critical work entitled *Dei delitti e delle pene* on the system of criminal law, and in particular on the death penalty, which met with immediate and widespread success throughout Europe. Twenty years later, a Neapolitan patrician, Gaetano Filangieri, produced a work of scholarship entitled *La scienza della legislazione* that was destined to be translated and read even outside of Italy. From the middle of the eighteenth century onward, rulers in Vienna undertook a series of reforms in the domains of the Hapsburg monarchy concerning a wide range of institutions and rules of law: the role of the state in relation to the Church (as in the area of matrimonial law), crimes and punishments, court organization, criminal and civil procedure, taxation, local administration, limitations on patrician privileges, and reorganization of the universities, among others. In Lombardy, Maria Teresia of Austria and Joseph II (but his brother Leopold in Tuscany as well) modified the traditional legal order with sovereign provisions inspired by methods of enlightened absolutism.

The coming of the French and the years of Napoleonic domination (1796-1814) constituted a sharp break from the past for Italy, but also witnessed a convergence of the various regions of Italy in many respects. The lively debate of the Jacobin period (1796-1799) generated a new spirit animated by the prospects of independence that the young Bonaparte had initially encouraged on the Peninsula. The unified legal order achieved in the three areas of Italy subject to Napoleonic influence – the Kingdom of Italy in the northern part of the Italian Peninsula, the northern and central portions of Italy directly annexed by France, and the Kingdom of Naples – added to the stirrings of the new European culture of romanticism among a circle of intellectuals to impel the formation of a still-embryonic national consciousness, giving life to the concept of a nation-state that would comprise the entire Peninsula for the first time. Without the Napoleonic period, there probably would not have been a *Risorgimento*, and perhaps not even a national unification at all.

With the Hapsburg reforms and the new Napoleonic Codes (these last derived in part from the great wave of reforms associated with the French revolution), the legal system and the traditional order of the *ancien régime* were radically altered in Italy. The legislation produced by the state, inspired by organic and systematic programs of reform, became the engine of the law's change and evolution. The most significant result of this process was the elaboration of civil, commercial, criminal and procedural Codes. With a single blow, the whole edifice of the common law of continental Europe, which had been in place and functioning for seven hundred years, fell – and along with it fell the teachings of the Doctors, the authority of the courts, and the plurality of normative levels (local law, feudal law, guild law, and *ius commune*). The Codes and state laws thus became the sole official source of every legal and judicial decision, even though, and this is an important point to note, the Codes took on this role through, and thanks to, the very techniques of legal reasoning that had been developed by the medieval law which the modern Codes replaced. A major part of the specific rules of law, as they were put down in the Codes, derives from the tradition of the Roman, medieval and early modern law as developed in the centuries of the *ius commune*. But other rules, mainly in family law, property law, commercial law, and criminal law and procedure, were new. Here began the era of codifications with which Italy and the rest of Europe would live for the next two centuries.

In the decades following the fall of Napoleon, continuity prevailed, even if Italy was again divided into distinct states. Such was the case for the Neapolitan Civil Codes, as well as those of Parma and Piedmont, each inspired in varying measure by the French model of the *Code civil*. The only exception to this is the Lombardy-Venetian Civil Code, which was a translation of the Austrian Code of 1811 (ABGB). The French influence is even more evident in the Napoleonic Commercial Code, which was transmitted directly from the French model or through codifications substantially identical to it, as occurred in Naples, in the Vatican state, and in Piedmont. Tuscany produced well-known and highly regarded scholars in the area of criminal law and produced an important Penal Code in 1853. Most importantly, in the decades following the Restoration until the decisive turn of events in 1848, Italy witnessed the emergence of a culture that made the relationship between history, nation and state the fundamental basis of a great political project. One crucial aspect of this project was a careful consideration of the relationship between law, constitution, and civil society. On this topic, one need only think of the ideas of the jurist Giandomenico Romagnosi related to "etnicarchia" (which tried to give a constitutional basis to the links between state and nation), or of the theses set forth in 1851 by Pasquale Stanislao Mancini, a Neapolitan lawyer exiled in Piedmont, who attempted to erect an entire edifice of both private and public international law on the cardinal principle of national identity.

The *sixth phase* coincided with the unification of Italy that followed in 1860, and is sketched below in part V.

III. The Late Eleventh to the Early Sixteenth Centuries

The decades of the late eleventh and early twelfth centuries witnessed the beginning of a long period (described above as the "third phase") in which more than a few of the enduring and important concepts in European law originated in Italy. We will limit ourselves here to listing just a few aspects of particular importance.

Ecclesiastical reform was achieved through the struggle for investiture with the Empire, the liberation from feudal bondage, the affirmation of the hierarchy and unity of the Church culminating in the Roman Papacy, the vindication of the superiority of the Church with respect to secular powers, and finally, the exercise by the Pope, on both a local and far-reaching scale, of jurisdictional and then legislative powers throughout the Christian West. It is this knot of doctrines and of events which had their germ in Italy in the second half of the eleventh century, with the determining contribution provided by the monk Hildebrandus of Soana, who went on to become Pope Gregory VII, that led a scholar such as Harold Berman to describe this as the historical phase in which modern Western legal culture was born.

The formation of townships and *communal institutions* in the twelfth and thirteenth centuries, with their complex and articulated legal systems, was only partially derived from the models of antiquity, though the terminology employed was often derived from Roman law. Among the salient changes witnessed in this period, we may highlight the crucial shift towards the creation of a collective body of local authorities, the electoral rules for the appointment of judges, the elaboration of a decision-making system by majorities, the control over public officials (*syndacatus*), and the development of legislative autonomy through local statutes in both the cities and in the country. Modern democracies and modern constitutionalism were born later, elsewhere, and in an entirely different historical context, yet the Italian communal city-states undeniably acted as a laboratory for several institutions, both public and private, which ultimately developed in the modern period.

The birth of the *new legal science*, founded upon the methods put into practice in Bologna by Irnerius and his school in the twelfth century, constituted one of the most decisive events in the history of the Western Legal Tradition. The new method was founded on an exegetic study and systematic use of a single written source of law considered supreme and binding – that is, the Justinian compilation – which was rediscovered, explained and turned to modern uses by the Glossators in order to resolve every problem (both in theory and daily practice) of public, private, criminal, and procedural law. The techniques of reasoning and argumentation used by the Glossators were inspired by the great Roman models, but were also innovative in some of their basic aspects, such as their constant reference to one and only one "omnicomprehensive" source, the Justinian *Corpus iuris*, in which every single legal precept is interpreted in the context of all the others. The method introduced by the Glossators abides at the basis of the modern science of law. It diffused rapidly from Italy throughout most of continental Europe.

This superior legal formation was made possible by the institution of the new school for the study of law, set up in the form of an association between students and teachers, that took the technical name of "university." Universities spread from Bologna (or in the case of theology, from Paris) throughout Italy and Europe, and were attended by thousands of students. For centuries, from Padua to Orléans, from Heidelberg to Prague, from Oxford to Coimbra, the teaching model that originated in Bologna, based upon the *Corpus iuris*, was adopted everywhere. This was a highly specialized technique of teaching and study designed to mold the professional jurist as an expert technician in the interpretation and application of legal rules, a technique that early medieval society had not needed. From the twelfth century to the present, this would be the university formation characterizing jurists trained on the Continent.

The coexistent *ius commune* based on Roman law, statutes governing towns and guilds, local and class customs, and canonical law, comprised a functional system thanks to a series of interconnections among various categories of norms – interconnections forming a legal system theorized by the Italian jurists of the thirteenth and fourteenth centuries. This system consisted of entrusting the priority to statutory and "particular" law (*ius proprium*) with respect to the common law (*ius commune*), such that the legislator of local statutes could introduce new rules and have them applied. But the common law's strength nevertheless remained essential because it acted in three fundamental ways: first, it served to fill the numerous gaps in local and particular law; secondly, it was applied in the interpretation of statutory rules; and thirdly, it was considered the basis to which the local statutes were exceptions, and therefore served as the source of analogical application.

In the twelfth and thirteenth centuries, alongside the civil law *ius commune*, *Canon Law* developed as a legal order universal to the whole of Western Christendom. From its beginnings, inspired by the methods of the civil Glossators from Gratian forward, Canon Law acquired a complex and mature scholarship and systematization with the law schools of the decretists, who studied and interpreted the texts of the *Decretum Gratiani*, and the decretalists, who dealt with the papal decretals. These schools did exist outside of Italy – since the twelfth century we find, in fact, outstanding canonical works in Germany, England, France, and elsewhere – but their center was undoubtedly in Italy. The *ius novum* of papal origin was also born in Italy, and was soon diffused throughout Europe, between the end of the twelfth century and the first half of the thirteenth century. Born of the legal decisions of the Roman papal *Curia* thanks to certain great jurist-popes, above all the Sienese Rolandus Bandinelli (under Alexander III) and the Roman Lotarius Segni (under Innocent III), the decretals were quickly gathered in a series of collections, among them the fundamental *Liber Extra* of 1234, which shaped the law of the Roman Catholic Church until the codification of 1917. The analytical and synthetic works of authors such as Henricus of Susa from Piedmont (under Cardinal Hostiensis) and Sinibaldus Fieschi from Genoa (serving Pope Innocent IV) signaled the high point of canonical scholarship in the West, toward the middle of the thirteenth century. It is important to note that several legal rules which became part of modern law were born in the classic Canon Law, in large part elaborated (as noted) by Italian jurists from the twelfth century to the fifteenth century: among these we may note, for example, the notion of direct agency, the liability of a *pactum nudum*, the notion of *officium*, the rules concerning evidence and legal presumptions, marriage law, the theory of "legal person," and the legal development of the concept of "person."

Commencing in the twelfth century, civil law and canonical scholars elaborated the body of *civil and criminal procedure* through a new type of literary genre, the *ordo iudiciorum*. Through this genre, thanks to the works of many scholars as well as Church legislation and statutes of the Italian cities, many rules developed regarding jurisdiction, witnesses and documentary evidence, "indicia" and presumptions, accusatory and inquisitorial procedure, the rights of appeal, the government of post-judgment execution orders, controls over the judges, summary procedures, and many others. This complex set of norms took the name of the "Roman-canonical process" and existed throughout Europe for centuries, well beyond the medieval period, until the period of the modern Codes.

We can also detect the genesis of the *public notary* from the Italian matrix. In the civil life of the communes, the notary was present at every economic, legal, or institutional transaction from the twelfth century forward; at the end of the thirteenth century in Bologna, about 300 new notaries were appointed every year. The transition from the early medieval "*charta*" to the notarial *instrumentum* – that is, a document that functioned as conclusive proof of a public act, without the necessity of calling the parties or the witnesses to testify as to the act – constitutes a fundamental step in the establishment of legal relationships based upon writings. The theory and use of notarial forms was accomplished in Italy by jurists and notaries who drafted formulas and treatises in the notarial arts, culminating in the middle of the thirteenth century with the *Ars notaria* and the *Formularium* of Rolandinus Passeggeri of Bologna, which were used throughout Europe for centuries thereafter.

Alongside the *ius commune* of the *Corpus iuris* of civil law scholars, the legal system of the late medieval period and the modern era also comprised *local laws* (statutes and customs) and particular laws concerning social status and orders. Among these last, an important role was played by feudal law, which was born out of customary law outlined in written form around the middle of the twelfth century in Lombardy thanks to the work of jurists and experts such as Obertus de Orto of Milan. The *Consuetudines* (later: *Libri*) *feudorum* were employed throughout Europe as the source of *ius commune feudale*, though they never received formal legislative recognition as such. The text of the *Libri feudorum* became part of the *Libri legales* used to teach law at many universities.

In the economic realm of the same period, important legal rules were elaborated out of the *guilds* that governed every profession, art, and craft. The guilds were granted broad autonomy, though the amount differed in degree according to each guild's economic and political strength within the town, as well as the monopoly over its profession and control over the entry of new members. Through the mechanism of corporation and the autonomous exercise of judicial and statutory powers, the guild system was essential for the development of artisanship, commerce, and professions. Guilds were also an important source of law in the economic field both at both the legislative and judicial levels. The guild system survived throughout Europe until the end of the eighteenth century.

The customs born in the world of Italian merchants, crystallized in legal formulas by notaries of the Italian townships of the thirteenth and fourteenth centuries, gave form to *commercial law* – a new branch of law. The bill of exchange, the *accomandita* (limited partnerships) and other forms of business organization, insurance on transport, bankruptcy, and commercial registers and volumes containing specific rules of evidence were some of the institutions that were born of the needs of commercial exchange and then rendered actionable under the jurisdiction of the guilds. These institutions were rapidly diffused through the same roads of commerce from Provence to Catalonia, from Burgundy to Rhine, from Flanders to England. Thus, even the English Normans, who rejected the Romanist model and developed their own judicial and legal system, did not reject the commercial law developed in the Italian city-states; it was embraced as the Law Merchant in special courts and remained active throughout the eighteenth century when it was grafted by Lord Mansfield and others onto the trunk of the English common law.

Italians were also the greatest exponents of the school of the *Commentators* of the fourteenth and fifteenth centuries, from the great Bartolus of Sassoferrato to his former student Baldus de Ubaldis, from Bartolomeus de Saliceto to Paulus de Castro, from Alexander Tartagna to Franciscus de Arezzo, from Philippus Decius to Jason de Majnus, and many other professors whose works were well-known and widespread in continental Europe, and whose fame attracted thousands of students to Bologna, Padua, Perugia, Pavia, Pisa, and other universities on the Italian Peninsula from every part of the continent.

Lastly, it was in Italy that the study of the sources of Roman law with historical and philological tools originated; this study aimed to set these texts and the rules they stated into their original historical contexts. This was a stream of the legal humanism that was an offshoot of the general growth of humanistic culture in the fifteenth century, aided by Laurentius Valla, Alexander d'Alessandro, Ludovicus Bolognini, Cato Sacco, and others. Later, in the sixteenth century, the work of the Milanese Andrea Alciatus permitted it to penetrate the world of university legal scholars that had long been hostile to such study. Here we may divine the origins of humanistic jurisprudence, which saw its greatest moments in France in the wake of Alciatus, professor at Bourges, over the course of the sixteenth century.

We have listed some highlights to make clear what an outstanding contribution the Italian Peninsula made to the legal history of continental Europe from the twelfth through the sixteenth centuries. After that time, as noted above, the primacy in new ideas passed gradually over to other regions of Europe: the late scholastic school in Spain in the late sixteenth century, the natural law school in Holland, Germany and England during the seventeenth century, the great French Royal *ordonnances* of the seventeenth and eighteenth centuries, the Enlightenment doctrines of Montesquieu, Voltaire, and Rousseau (but in this case Italy, through the works of Beccaria and Filangieri, would again assume a Europe-wide role), the French and Austrian rulers of the late eighteenth and early nineteenth centuries, the historical school and the Pandectist German school of the nineteenth century, the scientific positivism and the multifaceted approaches of the legal sciences of the twentieth century in both Europe and the United States.

IV. Developments in the Legal System along the Whole Peninsula

It is appropriate to inquire whether the fundamental contributions to legal culture and legal institutions which flowered on the Peninsula from the eleventh to the sixteenth centuries may be considered expressions of Italy as a whole, and of Italy alone. That raises the problem, mentioned above, of the national identity of Italian legal history. In fact, faced with the *a priori* assertion by many legal historians of the late nineteenth and early twentieth centuries who were convinced that an "Italian Law" existed prior to the birth of a politically and legally unified Italy, the most recent historiography has cast light on two further aspects: on the one hand, the legal history of medieval and modern Italy is also the history of Europe and therefore cannot be considered as isolated from Europe. On the other hand, it is a municipal and regional history rather than a national history.

Italian legal history means *European* legal history because, above all of the local and guild or class legal systems, Italy has experimented and participated for seven centuries in a common law that must be considered meta-national and supra-national, founded on the Justinian sources and teachings of the Doctors. Even if the Italian Glossators and Commentators had a definitive impact, one cannot deny that the legal system of the continental *ius commune* was not, in large measure, linked to a state, or territorial or political identity. The common law, born in Italy, grew and asserted itself as a European phenomenon in which, after the initial phase, the impact of men, works, and ideas proceeded from many different areas of the European continent.

Italian legal history means *municipal and regional* history because the study of urban and rural customs, examination of municipal statutes, and investigations into the deeds of the notaries shows, through common tendencies and recurring exchanges of models, that each city, and not infrequently even borough and village, developed specific rules for organizations, business practices, contracts, property law, family law, and inheritance law. The variety of local systems combined with a high degree of instability in written local statutes. Later, with the formation of late medieval and early modern states and principalities, a certain degree of unity and homogeneity was produced at the regional level – in Piedmont, in the Duchy of Milan, in Venice and its Terrafirma domains, in Tuscany, in the Papal State, in the Kingdom of Naples, and elsewhere – though local legal specificity was never eliminated. And this was the case as late as the end of the eighteenth century.

Here begins, then, the moment of the creation of regional identities in the legal history of Italy. It is evident to anyone who knows Italy that the "Sardinian," the "Sicilian," the "Ligurian," the "Tuscan," the "Friulan," the "Piedmontese" (and so on), but also the citizens of Bergamo, Pisa, or Naples (and so on), represent not just different dialects and linguistic inflections, but also varying types of personal character. These cannot fail to be reflected in the law of the city or region, and therefore in the history of law in Italy. Such local and regional identities are in fact affirmed and still survive today: different agricultural contracts and uses, different customs related to inheritance and family law (including dowry, hereditary strategies, and the power of parents over children and between the husband and wife), different application of the same rules of criminal law (due to the fact that certain crimes are viewed differently in the various parts of the Peninsula), different rules in labor law, different habits in the exercise and deontology of the legal profession, and so on. All this survives in the form of customs and uses underlying statutory law, and an examination of contracts and wills and sometimes of judicial or administrative decisions alone can detect them. Significant in this direction are also the valuable elements of the knowledge of legal mentality and ideas as evinced by literary sources that reflect positions in civil society: we might cite the works of Matteo Bandello (XV century), Carlo Goldoni (XVIII century), Giuseppe Gioacchino Belli (XIX century), or Giuseppe Tomasi di Lampedusa (XX century), to limit ourselves to a few among the many writers who help shed light on the actual application of law in historical and regional contexts that manifest a strong and distinct identity. This province of legal history has remained largely unexplored.

All this said, our original question remains: does a common identity exist in the historical development of law on the Peninsula? One must highlight the distinctions among the communal city-states of northern and central Italy, the Papal state, and the southern Sicilian-Neapolitan kingdom. Thus, at least three different Italys coexisted, each with its own institutional system, its own method of producing rules and regulations, and its own civil and criminal judicial processes. There are in fact other Italian regions which had specific identities in legal history: in Venice, for example, the *ius commune* was not officially recognized.

Communal Italy has undoubtedly witnessed many shared tendencies in the legal system. One need only think of the frequent transplantations of statutory forms and models from one city to another, the contemporary growth of certain constitutional developments (as occurred with the transition from the consuls to the *podestà* in the early thirteenth century, up until the crisis of urban democracies) and the coming of the *signorie* in the fourteenth century. Often the same men, mainly professional jurists, acted successively in their role as jurists and *podestà* in different cities. On the contrary, the early centralization of the Norman-Sveve Kingdom of Sicily constitutes a world in which the cities found themselves having to deal with sovereign powers that severely limited the local powers.

And yet important exchanges and interrelations took place between these two Italys. Exchanges of men: professors of law who taught successively in Bologna and Naples, in Pavia and Ferrara, in Pisa and in Rome. Transmigration of laws and legal institutions, not just through the migration of that part of customary law which knows no frontiers, as in the area of commercial law, but also through the adoption of similar or identical norms, as occurred with the adoption of capital punishment in the early thirteenth century to replace the use of pecuniary sanctions for homicide – a system that had been prevalent in the earlier statutes of the communes. Or the rules that excluded daughters from paternal inheritances that were in force almost everywhere on the Peninsula (but often beyond the Alps as well). Even if Latin was the language of the law throughout Europe, the fact that Italian was the common literary language on the Peninsula made frequent exchanges of men and institutions much easier there.

A study of the rules and legal institutions diffused throughout the entire Peninsula, and eventually to other regions or states of Europe, remains to be written. The warp and weft of Italian identity is shown in the organization of law students at Bologna in the thirteenth and fourteenth centuries. We find distinct organizations for each group of students coming from each region of Europe: next to the *nationes* of the French, the German, and the Helvetian, we also find distinct *nationes* of Lombards, Campani, and Siculi. But all of these "nations" came together in the two *universitates* of the "Ultramontane" and of the "Citramontani," each of which elected its own rector. The Citramontani included all (and only) the students of the distinct *nationes* of the Italian Peninsula and Sicily, gathered together primarily on the basis of language. In this, it is clear that the term *natio* was not reserved for Italy as a whole, but rather for single historical regions (as the term *patria* refers to a single municipality) of the Peninsula. But it is also clear that in the context of persons coming from other parts of Europe, an Italian cultural identity did exist at this time.

Even the High Courts of law of the modern age – as the *Rote* of Genoa, Florence, Rome, the *Senati* of Milan and Turin, the *Sacro Consiglio* of Naples, and other Courts – frequently counted jurists who came from other parts of Italy among their members. This is another chapter in Italian legal history on which recent investigations have focused their attention. From the fifteenth to the eighteenth century, in fact, notwithstanding the division of Italy into distinct states and principalities, the collections of decisions from each of these Courts circulated on the Peninsula, sharing common features and several common rules of law.

V. Italian Legal Development after 1860

In the period following the unification of 1860, the political class of the Kingdom of Italy had to select a model upon which to construct the legal order of the new state. The conflict between a federal model, which preserved the specificity and legal traditions of the pre-unification states (supported by intellectuals like Carlo Cattaneo) and a unitary, centralized model (fashioned essentially along the lines of the French model) was ultimately resolved in favor of the latter. The constitution of the Kingdom of Sardegna (the "Statuto Albertino" approved in 1848) was maintained as the constitutional text of the new Kingdom of Italy, and it remained in force until the approval of the republican Constitution in 1948.

Following unification, the debate and approval of new civil and commercial codes, along with new Codes of civil and criminal procedure, was quick: each was adopted in 1865, largely inspired by the Piedmontese model, which had in turn been inspired by the Napoleonic codes. Work on the Penal Code, however, was protracted, mostly due to the difficulty in overcoming the contrast between the Piedmontese-Napoleonic model and the Tuscan model of 1853 on the question of the death penalty, which only Tuscany had abolished. The new version of the Penal Code was not ultimately adopted until 1889, followed by a new Code of Criminal Procedure in 1913. A new Commercial Code was adopted in 1882. Also innovative was the statutory organization of administrative justice which had been part of the ordinary civil jurisdiction for all harms to "subjective rights" by the Public Administration since 1865; and then, from 1889 forward, a specific jurisdictional power was given to the *Consiglio di stato* in matters for which harms by the Public Administration to *interessi legittimi* (legitimate interests) of the citizen were at stake.

The law that emerged from the new nation-state of Italy was the product of a collective effort in which jurists belonging to all of the legal traditions found on the Italian Peninsula contributed, even if those contributions were made with and through vigorous debate and as the result of differing positions. To give just one example, in the new Commercial Code of 1882, men working together for several years on the preliminary drafts included Tuscan scholars (Tommaso Corsi, reformer of the law of corporations), Genoese lawyers (Antonio Caveri and Cesare Cabella), Piedmontese jurists (Matteo Pescatore), Lombards (Giuseppe Zanardelli, Ercole

Vidari), Venetians (Felice Lampertico, Francesco Piccoli, Giovanni Battista Varè), Romans (Luigi Maurizi), Neapolitans (Pasquale Stanislao Mancini, Nicola Alianelli), and Sicilians (Giuseppe Carnazza Puglisi).

After political unification, Italian legal scholarship went through a period of creative growth. The contact with nineteenth-century German culture – a contact which had become constant from the 1880s – resulted not in a merely imitative legal culture, but in original developments. One recalls important intellectual figures such as Vittorio Emanuele Orlando, Santi Romano, and Costantino Mortati for constitutional law; Oreste Ranelletti and Federico Cammeo for administrative law; Cesare Vivante, Gustavo Bonelli, Angelo Sraffa, Mario Rotondi, and Tullio Ascarelli for commercial law; Giacomo Venezian, Francesco Ferrara, and Gino Gorla for private law; Giuseppe Chiovenda, Piero Calamandrei, Francesco Carnelutti, Salvatore Satta, Enrico Redenti, and Enrico Tullio Liebman for civil procedure; Vittorio Scialoja, Pietro Bonfante, and Vincenzo Arangio Ruiz for Roman law; Lodovico Barassi for labor law; Francesco Ruffini, Mario Falco, and Arturo Carlo Jemolo for ecclesiastical law; Giacomo Delitala for criminal law; and Francesco Schupfer, Nino Tamassia, Enrico Besta, Federico Patetta, and Francesco Calasso for medieval legal history. And yet this list fails to include many very distinguished professors worthy of mention.

Between the two World Wars, Italian legal scholarship achieved international renown even beyond the shores of Europe. The best scholarship of this period had some qualities not easily reducible to formulas. It drew upon, but remained distinct from, both the German and the French models, and often managed to synthesize the profundity of the Germans with the clarity of the French.

The fascist period (1922-1942) witnessed legislative innovations derived from the authoritarianism of a regime guided by a corporativist theory of society. Nevertheless, legislation was only in part affected by the political ideology. This resistance at the legislative level is attributable to the fact that, appearances and compromises aside, the exceptional intellectual foundations of scientific positivism upon which Italian leading legal scholarship had been based for half a century allowed it to resist the vicissitudes of political life. Significantly enough, it was precisely this legal scholarship that the regime charged with the task of drafting the new Codes. And though it is undeniable that certain rules of the criminal Codes of 1930 (prepared mainly by Alfredo Rocco) bear the marks of an authoritarian state, these aspects would be easily removed in the post-war period through legislative revision and decisions by the Constitutional Court.

The same is truer still of the 1942 Code of Civil Procedure (which benefited from the contributions of Calamandrei, a figure certainly not sympathetic to fascism), and particularly of the area of private law. In fact, the Civil Code of

1942, a text approved after twenty years of preparation, and carried out principally by the efforts of Vittorio Scialoja, Filippo Vassalli, and Alberto Asquini, united the civil and the commercial law in a single text, and handled several areas of the private legal system – persons, family law, inheritance, property rights, law of obligations, single contracts, labor law, corporate and partnership law, and other areas such as the registration of legal acts and protection of the rights – in a way that proved to be modern and sound. Notwithstanding the modifications of great importance which have been introduced in the last quarter-century, particularly in the areas of family law and (due to the integration of Europe and the single European market) commercial and industrial law, the 1942 Civil Code remains in force, and no global revision is foreseen.

Today, rather, what is being discussed is the very idea of the Codes, due to increasing and chaotic legislative activity affecting areas of the law covered by them. This tendency obviously raises the issue of the importance of legal certainty, which is in a period of deep crisis. The Italian legal system has also endured an increasingly negative involution: court cases, both criminal and civil, take an extremely long time to resolve. This is due to the absence of organizational and logistical strategies adequate to guarantee a functioning judicial system. It is also due to the inertia not just of the politicians but also of the legal profession; both judges and attorneys – not as individuals but as professional groups – are responsible in this respect.

Legal scholarship has in recent years significantly increased the knowledge of foreign legal systems and the best products of European and American legal scholarship in Italy, not just passively but often with original contributions of international standing. The role of Italy has also been significant in creating the rules established in the European treaties of 1957 (Rome), 1975, 1986 (Single Act), 1992 (Maastricht), and 1998 (Amsterdam), in particular those concerning the institutional framework of the European Union.

Bibliographic Note

The following works in English, though generally devoted to the study of European legal history, are nevertheless largely concerned with Italy and Italian law: H. J. Berman's, *Law and Revolution, The Formation of the Western Legal Tradition*, Cambridge Mass. and London, 1983, offers an interpretation of the history of law in Europe characterized by a special accent on the role played by the Church in the eleventh century; J. P. Dawson, *The Oracles of the Law*, Ann Arbor, 1968, covers the history of the role of the judge in the civil law system as compared to the common law system; A. Watson, *The Making of the Civil Law*, Cambridge Mass.,

1981; R. C. van Caenegem, *Judges, Legislators and Professors, Chapters in European Legal History*, Cambridge, 1987; P. Stein, *Legal Institutions, The Development of Dispute Settlement*, London, 1984, describe some basic institutions of the European legal tradition in historical perspective; *see also* P. Steinand J. Shand, *Legal Values in Western Society*, Edinburgh, 1974. A synthetic and well-documented introduction to the history of European private law in the medieval and modern period is available in R. C. van Caenegem, *An Historical Introduction to Private Law*, Cambridge, 1992. Also important is the vast and systematic reconstruction provided by R. Zimmermann, *The Law of Obligations, Roman Foundations of the Civilian Tradition*, Cape Town-Deventer-Boston, 1992, in which the author draws attention to the historico-legal connections between the law of obligations in the European civil law tradition and in the English common law tradition. *See also* A. Padoa Schioppa (ed.), *Legislation and Justice*, Oxford, 1997 ("The Origins of the Modern State in Europe, XIII-XVIII Centuries").

CHAPTER TWO

Shifting Frames: Law and Legal "Contaminations"

Professor P. G. Monateri & F. A. Chiaves [1]

I. Introduction

The aim of this chapter is to try to describe the two main turning points in the modern history of Italian legal culture.[2] The first was a transplant of French legal sources, and a general framing of the national law after a French pattern. The second was a global shift toward German paradigms that had a dramatic influence on legal discourse and the mode of approaching and utilizing legal sources. In this account, we maintain a critical and comparative view of the law in which formal sources are to be viewed as authorities to which the legal profession attaches a meaning, in which meaning is therefore not rooted in, but instead is produced by the legal community. In the process, we may observe how much a legal system may constitute not a coherent unit, but rather a bundle of foreign traits cobbled together by lawyers.

---

[1] Pier Giuseppe Monateri, Professor of Comparative Law, University of Turin; Dott. Riceratore F.A. Chiaves, University of Turin.

[2] A recent masterful work that should be consulted in this area is P. Grossi, *Scienze Giuridiche Italiane – un profilo storico*, Giuffrè Milan, 2001. The classic treatment of the materials discussed in this chapter remains the triad by John Henry Merryman "The Italian Style I: Doctrine," 18 *Stanford Law Review* 39 (1965); "The Italian Style II: Law," 18 *Stanford Law Review* 396 (1966); "The Italian Style III: Interpretation," 18 *Stanford Law Review* 583 (1966). These materials were republished in J.H. Merryman, *The Loneliness of the Comparative Lawyer, and Other Essays Foreign and Comparative Law*, The Hague, Kluwer (1999).

Jeffrey S. Lena and Ugo Mattei (eds.), *Introduction to Italian Law*, 21-30

II. Italian Legal Culture: A Portrait of Italy as a "Weak" Tradition

A. The Love Affair with the French

This chapter sketches the formation of Italian legal culture, which, from the early nineteenth century forward, has evolved as a bundle of borrowed traits.

In the first decades of the nineteenth century, Italy was taken over by the French army, and the French Civil Code of 1804 was introduced throughout the country: the northwest (Piedmont and Liguria) was annexed to France, and thus the French Civil Code was directly put in force in those regions; the Kingdom of Italy (northeast and center) received an Italian translation of the French Code (1805), and the same occurred in the Kingdom of Naples, which comprised the southern regions (1808).

After the collapse of the French administration and the Congress of Vienna (1815), Italy was divided into a number of small states, each with its own legal system,[3] for the first half of the century. These small states can be grouped into four main regions: the northwest, the northeast, the center, and the south.

A slight revision of the French Code was maintained in the northwest (the Kingdom of Sardinia, including Piedmont, Liguria, and Sardinia) (1837) and in the south (the Kingdom of Sicily, including Naples and Sicily) (1819). The northeast, in which Milan, Venice, and Trieste formed a single realm within the Austro-Hungarian Empire, was governed by the Austrian Civil Code. The center of Italy was split into two main states: Tuscany, under an Austrian Grand Duke, and the Regions of Rome and Bologna, under the Papal administration. After the French experience, both areas returned to the *ius commune*, a form of uncodified modern Roman law based on Justinian's Compilation as developed in the case law.

As a result of the aggressive foreign policy of the Savoy family, which ruled in the northwest, Italy was unified in 1861, with its capital at Turin. This policy was backed by the French government in opposition to Austria, which had formerly possessed a prodigious influence in Italy. Later, however, Napoleon III refused any further aid and decided to support the Pope in Rome to avoid a unification of the country. Thus it was only in 1870, when the Germans defeated the French, that the Italians were finally able to conquer Rome and dethrone the Pope; in the meantime, the Holy City became the capital of the Kingdom of Italy.

There was a complex relationship of rivalry and friendship between France and

---

[3] *See* S. Santoro Passarelli, "*Dai codici preunitari al codice civile del 1865,*" in *Studi A. Torrente,* Giuffrè, Milan (1968), p. 1029.

the Italian states.[4] Certainly Piedmont, which enacted the forced unity of the country, was largely indebted to French culture, and French was still spoken by the ruling elites as well as by the royal family, who were in fact of French origin.

From the legal perspective, the northwest adopted a Constitution (*Statuto Albertino*) in 1848 (that had been transplanted from the French Constitution of 1830), which took the throne away from the Bourbons and handed it to Louis Philippe d'Orléans. In 1861, the *Statuto* was subsequently extended to apply to all of Italy.

In 1865, the government decided to entirely re-shape the legal features of the new Kingdom and the 1865 Act, still in force, tailored public administration to the French pattern.

In the field of public law there was, in our view, no real alternative to this French model. First, the unity was achieved by Piedmont, which was within the French area of influence, and which indeed became "Italianized" only after 1870. Secondly, unity was achieved *against* the "others" (the Pope, the Austrians from Milan and Venice, and the southern Kingdom of Sicily), and it would really have been inconceivable to adopt their "patterns." Finally, the French model was perceived as a "liberal" model: France was the country of liberty and reform, and the elites promoting the unification process all shared this "liberal" culture.

In the field of private law, a choice existed among three possible alternatives: the French Civil Code; the Austrian Code, which ruled the entire northeast, the more economically advanced region of the new country; and the renewed Roman law, which was certainly felt to be rooted in a "national" legal culture. A fourth alternative could have been the elaboration of a newer "Italian" pattern.

For the purpose of the above-sketched "strategic" model, we can consider the adoption of a Code and the elaboration of a model, or the importation of such a complicated system as the case law system developed from Roman law, as separate items. Because the purpose of the government was to frame national unity in the short term, the alternatives were, in reality, the French Civil Code and the Austrian Civil Code.

We maintain that this was a question of "self-definition," much more than a matter of policy. Indeed, both of the above Codes had been designed to cope with a market-based society,[5] and thus no peculiar political issue was at stake in choosing one or the other. Both Codes were based on the following principles:

---

[4] *See* N. Valeri (ed.), *Storia d'Italia*, IV, Utet, Turin (1965), pp. 89-191.

[5] *See* A. Gambaro, *Codice civile*, in 2 *Digesto italiano* 442, 4th ed., Turin (1988), at 447.

1. Abolition of the caste system based on status, and the general legal capacity of all citizens (general citizenship) (art. 1 C.Nap.; para. 17, ABGB);

2. Definition of property rights in land stated in "absolute" terms, and abolition of perpetuities and feudal incidents (arts. 537 and 544 French Civil Code; para. 308, Austrian Civil Code);

3. Freedom of contract and marketable property rights;

4. Right of enclosures (art. 552, French Civil Code; para. 362, Austrian Civil Code);

5. Egalitarian inheritance law coupled with freedom in the disposition of property at death.

The Austrian Civil Code is indeed widely credited as being just as "liberal" as the French.[6] But "French culture" was much more widespread than its Austrian counterpart among the ruling elites, and the choice was in fact imposed by the "winning state" over other Italian states. In much the same way, the Code of Commerce and the Criminal Code were tailored after French liberal conceptions. Thus, cultural *sentimenti* played an important role in the choice: Italy had to become a "Latin sister" of France in southern Europe.

The adoption of a revised French Code also implied the adaptation of French legal methods and court organization.[7] The method of Italian lawyers was styled after the prevailing French "exegetic" school.[8] The court system was arranged according to French pattern of the *Cour de Cassation*, but because the Italian Peninsula had only been recently united, five Supreme Courts were created – in Turin, Florence, Naples, Palermo, and Rome. A unique Supreme Court was created only in 1923 (Act 601 (1923)), after the fascist regime came to power.

Due to the lack of a unified case law, legal education played a major role in Italy and was based heavily on works and translations of French authors. We can measure the impact of French legal culture on Italy by the volume of translations of French law books. Merlin's *Commentaries* on the French Code were translated in Naples (1824-28), and even in Venice (1834-44), notwithstanding the fact that part of the Peninsula was still ruled by the Austrian Code. The major French textbooks were

---

[6] *See* R. Sacco, *Introduzione al diritto comparato*, 5th ed., Utet, Turin (1992), at 224 & 256.

[7] *See* A. Gambaro & A. Guarneri, "*Italie*," in *La circulation du modele juridique francais*, 14 *Travaux de l'Association Henri Capitant* 17, Litec, Paris (1993), at 78 ff.

[8] *See* G. Tarello, "*La scuola dell'esegesi e la sua diffusione in Italia*," in *Scritti per il XL della morte di Bensa*, Giuffrè, Milan (1969).

also translated into Italian: Duranton in 1852-54; Zachariae in 1862; Aubry and Rau in 1841-49. The last French work translated was the massive, multi-volume work of Baudry-Lacantinerie, translated in 1900. The close of the century marked an end to the process of translation and also, as we shall see, to the impact of French culture on Italy. In the new century, the works of Planiol, Josserand, Gény, and so on were also studied, but never translated.

Thus, the Constitution, Codes, courts, legal education, and public administration were all created on a French template, but the most influential *formant* was undoubtedly French *doctrine*. French case law had been derived only through the citations of professors in their books;[9] there was no direct knowledge of, nor real interest in, French decisions. Italian books made reference to the conceptions of French professors rather to than the French decisions themselves. As an example, we can examine a widely distributed law book of the period, Emilio Pacifici-Mazzoni's work on wills: in the first fifty pages of the volume, Demolombe is cited sixty-eight times, followed closely by Marcadé, Aubry and Rau, and Toullier, whereas only one citation of a French case appears. This is quite interesting because the role of case law, and in particular the role of the *Cour de Cassation*, has been overwhelming in France. Indeed, the Italian judicial style in writing opinions was modeled after that of the courts of the old *ius commune* (mainly the courts of Florence and Rome), and was not influenced by the concise style of French judges, who wrote opinions of just one sentence.[10] From this standpoint there was a split between the "culture of judges" and the "culture of professors." The literary style of the former preserved a national pattern, whereas the style of the latter introduced French exegetics.

Thus we can see that Italian legal culture borrowed much more from French legislation and French *scholarship* than it did from case law. Borrowing is a selective activity, and it would be quite misleading to say that the "French model" has been transplanted into Italy, because the transplanted model happened to become quite different from the original over time. Once again, it is the theory of *formants* that assists us in understanding that "models" are made up of different traits, and that, in the process of appropriation, original traits can be mixed up and even twisted to produce a different model. In fact, in transplanting the French model into Italy, foreground and background exchanged positions, since the role of the courts certainly became secondary to that of *scholarship*, to produce quite the opposite of

---

[9] *See* A. Gambaro & A. Guarneri, *supra* note 5, at 82.

[10] Writing a one-sentence opinion is the traditional French style, but the *Circulaire du 31 Janvier 1977* allowed judges to frame their opinions in two or more sentences (!).

the French power relation between these *formants*. In the next section, we discuss how this increased role of intellectuals gave birth to a major shift from the French toward the German "style" of legal thought within the legal profession.

B. The "Coming of the Germans"

In the previous section, we saw how the French model was received in Italy, with an emphasis on the role of intellectuals. Now we will examine how, after national unity was achieved in 1870, Italian universities were reorganized[11] according to new standards. In particular, the law schools were entrusted to a "first generation" of professional legal scholars.[12] From the beginning, the best-developed department within the new legal academy was that of Roman law. All the leading figures of this first generation of scholars were professional Romanists. It is quite evident that they were interested in theory and in Roman law, and that they could find both in Germany. In a few decades, Italy became one of the areas in which German studies exercised a strong influence.[13] The shift away from French legal culture was widespread, and began because of the perceived prestige of German academic studies in the field of Roman law.[14] Italian professors began to borrow the German "theoretical" approach to law, which had a strong impact on the law schools in comparison with the now-discredited French method, and new lawyers and judges began to be educated in the new German mode. Thus, the "style" of legal discourse changed dramatically, and a new legal jargon was styled after German templates.[15]

As we have noted, the "professionalization" of Italian academia was a major factor in this shift. The leading figure in this process was Vittorio Scialoja (1856-1933). Scialoja was a great mentor, with a number of disciples in all academic fields of law: Bonfante and Segré in Roman law, Filippo Vassalli, and De Ruggiero in private law, and Chiovenda in civil procedure. He was also one of the most active borrowers of German legal culture, together with Filippo Serafini (1831-97), Fadda (1853-1931), and Bensa (1858-1928). Professional academics found German scholarship excellent fuel for their legitimacy within the schools and even

---

[11] *See* N. Valeri, *supra* note 2, at 657-89.

[12] *See* A. Gambaro & A. Guarneri, *supra* note 7, at 82.

[13] For German influences in America, *see* M. Reimann (ed.), *The Reception of Continental Ideas in the Common Law World, 1820-1920*, Duncker & Humboldt, Berlin (1993).

[14] *See* R. Sacco, *supra* note 6, at 259-63.

[15] *See id.* at 261.

the legal process. Once again, we can trace the translations of German works to measure their impact. At mid-century, Serafini and Colgiolo translated the immense Gluck's Pandects. Vittorio Scialoja, in 1886, published a version of Savigny's "System." Fadda and Bensa translated Windscheid's work between 1903 and 1905, and it was subsequently reprinted in the thirties. All the major Italian jurists of the time adopted the German approach: Nicola and Leonardo Coviello; Francesco Ferrara Sr., Giuseppe Messina, Ettore de Ruggiero, Vittorio Polacco, and Giovanni Pacchioni.

In order to contrast the old French approach with the newer German style, it is useful to cite a biographical narrative by one of the leading authors of the thirties, Giovanni Pacchioni:

> [I] remember the teachings of my two main professors: Piero Cogliolo and Pasquale Melucci. The latter, since he was a disciple of Pacifici Mazzoni, followed the French style, and that of Laurent in particular. The former having been a student of Filippo Serafini followed the methods and theories of Savigny, and of the other great German scholars as Windscheid, Brinz, Becker *et al.* ... The two modes of teaching were strikingly opposed. Melucci was conducting classes on the basis of an article of the code. He would construe the meaning of it, then through an exercise of logic, try to derive all the possible consequences; when these were difficult to arrive at, his usual *memento* to the young students was: *dura lex, sed lex.*
>
> On the contrary, Cogliolo gave lectures which began with old Roman law, reconstructing the historical evolution of legal conceptions up to the present Code, and discussing solutions on the basis of analytical as well as sociological doctrines ... Even if I had been very young at the time, I could have easily perceived that the German approach was superior. Thanks to Filippo Serafini and Vittorio Scialoja, this approach has prevailed ... I could never suffer the *dura lex sed lex.*[16]

This narrative captures the felt difference between "passive interpretism" and "active theory" that was a key factor of the German success in Italy. The new German approach placed intellectuals in a new context within the legal process. Intellectuals and professors of law, more than the judges, now had to lead the process, because theory was the realm of intellectuals, and law was essentially conceived of as

---

[16] G. Pacchioni, *Il diritto civile italiano*, I, Cedam, Padua (1937), vii. *See also* A. Gambaro & A. Guarneri, *supra* note 7, at 86.

theory. The role of courts would have to become that of merely "applying" professors' theories to particular cases. Law had to be conceived as a bundle of conceptions, not rules. Rules were to be derived from the former, which were to be refined by professors. It was quite evident, in addition, that statutory provisions could only have the meaning and scope permitted them by academics. In the beginning, the prestige of professors induced lawyers and judges to accept their roles and to imitate the academic way of writing; the "theoretical" tone of legal discourse became a dominant paradigm even among practitioners. It is quite clear that this strategy of dominance succeeded because Italy lacked a single Supreme Court and a weak organization of the bar.

The shift away from French culture became so prevalent that when, in the twenties, the Italian and French governments decided to adopt a common code of contract, the project was aborted because of the opposition of academic elites to a project based on "outdated" French patterns.[17]

The 1920s represented the height of German prestige in Italy. In the 1930s, a new generation occupied the chairs and began to challenge the German paradigm from within. Two leading authors, Fr. Ferrara, Sr., and G. Messina, fueled a new wave of "critique" of the prevailing German paradigm by way of the same German formalism. Salvatore Pugliatti and Mario Allara became the major representatives and proponents of this approach. In their view, "intellectual honesty" almost always required a global re-thinking of the law to produce new theories, giving up received truths and categories to build new systems, and even developing a new vocabulary when needed. They cultivated "mere brilliance"[18] as the proper academic standard and the proper approach to law. The unintended impact of their efforts was that each professor engaged in developing new theories, with new attendant concepts, categories, and vocabulary. The "common enterprise" of the German pandectists became an individualistic effort to propose the "best" personal system of law. Because this occurred when the different courts were unified into one Supreme Court, the unintended consequence was that the role of professors rapidly declined while that of judges increased. The Supreme Court was entrusted to a leading figure, Mariano D'Amelio, who succeeded in reorganizing the previous case law in a coherent way, imposing the practice of *stare decisis*, which heightened the impact of the Court. Having followed this history, we can see how academic

---

[17] R. Sacco, *supra* note 6, at 262.

[18] *See* J. Gordley, *Mere Brilliance: The Recruitment of Law Professors in the United States*, 41 *Am J Comp L* 367 (1993).

intellectuals lost their position of preeminence when split into different schools, each of which cultivated its own "system," while the judiciary, by contrast, was reorganized around one Supreme Court. Thus, from the standpoint of cultural strategy, the overemphasis of "theory" and "brilliance" proved to be disadvantageous and led to a universal discrediting of intellectuals in favor of an increased judicial role in the legal process.

All this had a further impact when the fascist regime decided to adopt a new Code. This project was entrusted to law professors, but they were no longer the "oracles" of a common legal culture, but rather the divided exponents of different schools. It was impossible to unify their disparate definitions, categories, and vocabularies. The story ended with a unified Code of private and commercial law enacted in 1942,[19] and influenced in a limited manner by the German Civil Code,[20] mainly in the fields of corporations, partnerships, and the law of inheritance.[21] Consequently, the new Italian Code was by and large a rewording of the previous Codes. Indeed, not all the major features of the German Code embodied in the *"Allgemeiner Teil"* of the BGB were transplanted, because the *querelles de chapelle* about "general conceptions" were too strong in the drafting committee. Thus, the French pattern of legislation resisted change because of the disharmony within the academy, engendered by the exaggerations of "theory and brilliance."

Once again, in borrowing legal concepts and methods, the Italian system realized a unique amalgam of French and German patterns, unthinkable in its countries of origin. Italian legal culture is thus a product of "contamination" based on the peculiar selectivity of appropriation. From a broader perspective, such a "contamination" of legal cultures is the key feature of transplants and appropriations of legal patterns, one which we shall try to sketch in the conclusion.

III. Conclusion: Convergence, Divergence, and "Contamination"

Is there any theory to be drawn from the history here presented? We maintain, first, that the process of importing and exporting rules and institutions is an almost "unconscious" process of plugging them into the ideology of the borrowing system. Thus, the meaning of the borrowed institutions will depend upon the struggle among the *legal elites* of the receiving system, a struggle that will almost always produce

---

[19] L. Ghisalberti, *La codificazione del diritto in Italia*, Bari (1985).

[20] P. Rescigno, *"Fondazione,"* in *Enciclopedia del Diritto*, Giuffrè, Milan (1968).

[21] *See* A. Gambaro & R. Sacco, *Sistemi Giuridici Comparati*, Utet, Turin (1996), 381-383.

something different from the original. But we also believe that the ideology of a system is very often not a product of local and inner developments, but rather a contamination of different traits derived from the outside. In more general terms, the actual legal world is to be seen more as a world of "contaminations" than a world divided into discrete families. The widespread cross-diffusion of French and German patterns[22] within the civil law, and the transplant of American models in the present,[23] shape a similar legal landscape across the western world, with a wide variety of local variants. We do not think that these contaminations are something new, or strictly linked to globalization. We think that, with the eventual exclusion of peculiarly insulated legal systems, such as the old "classical" English common law, rooted in a peculiar organization of the legal profession, nearly every system, even in antiquity, has grown through "contaminations." We maintain that the practice of borrowing has always been a normal practice and, above all, that it has never been, nor will it be, the peculiar activity of "comparative" lawyers alone. It is a purposeful practice, to be carried on by municipal lawyers, and to be studied especially from the perspective of "weak" borrowing systems, responding to inner strategies of governance and the need to legitimate legal elites, and involving the conventional process of blanketing cases with authorities, and producing meaning.

Notably, a "comparativist" is one who is *not* involved in these ideological processes, because the comparativist has made a "move out," to deconstruct and critique. He is one who has decided to *wander about*.

What a comparative lawyer can do is to reveal the unofficial, and to critique those processes of meaning production as social and political realities, peculiarly in a world of "contaminations."

---

[22] *See* A. Gambaro & R. Sacco, *Sistemi Giuridici Comparati*, Utet, Turin (1996), 367-370.

[23] *See* U. Mattei, "Why the Wind Changed: Intellectual Leadership in Western Law," 42 *Am J Comp L* 195 (1994).

Constitutional Law

Mario Comba [1]

I. Introduction

This overview of Italian constitutional law outlines the main features of the constitutional system and provides the reader with an up-to-date description of both the political and legal situation in Italy. It also describes the main actors in the system and their principal roles.

After a brief historical sketch in part II, this chapter follows the divide in the Constitution itself between fundamental rights and the frame of government. In the Italian Constitution, after the first 12 articles setting forth the *Fundamental Principles*, Part 1 (arts. 13-54) addresses Constitutional Rights and Duties, while Part 2 (arts. 55-139) describes the Organization of the Republic.[2]

Part 1 of the Italian Constitution divides the Constitutional Rights and Duties into four categories: Civil Rights (arts. 13-28), Ethical and Social Relations (arts. 29-34), Economic Relations (arts. 35-47), and Political Rights (arts. 48-54). In part III of this chapter these rights were regrouped to follow the more familiar distinction between liberty rights and welfare rights, leaving a specific sub-paragraph for constitutional duties. The jurisprudence of the Constitutional Court has shaped the definition and the level of protection of constitutional rights such that they are now, in a certain sense, what the Constitutional Court wants them to be. This is particularly true with respect to welfare rights, which the Constitutional Court has held to be justiciable in some cases, but not others.

Part IV of this chapter focuses on the present Italian form of government, based as it is upon the relationship between Parliament (*rectius*: the parliamentary

---

[1]   Professor of Public Comparative Law, University of Torino, Faculty of Political Sciences (comba@cisi.unito.it).

[2]   All citations are to articles of the Italian Constitution unless otherwise noted.

Jeffrey S. Lena and Ugo Mattei (eds.), *Introduction to Italian Law*, 31-62
©2002 Kluwer Law International. Printed in the Netherlands.

majority) and the Government expressed through Parliament's vote of confidence. Because the Constitution does not clearly spell out the procedure nor the substance of this bond, it is necessary to use other tools borrowed from political science and public choice analysis to understand the behavior of political actors (political parties, politicians, interest organizations, and voters) in the game of government formation and survival.

The centrality of Parliament to the Italian form of government also influences the system of the sources of law, which can be defined, according to the framer's notion, as monistic. That is to say, only Parliament can produce national sources of law or authorize others (such as the Executive) to produce them. Part V will describe how this design is rooted in the Constitution, and how it was changed first with a shift from monism to dualism – represented by the huge governmental trend toward issuing *decreti legge* (law decrees) and *decreti delegati* (delegated decrees) – and then through the increasing importance of European sources of law (directives and regulations) for the Italian legal system.

As we broaden the picture to examine other institutions of the Italian constitutional system, most lucid approach is to view all of them as checks and balances the framers placed upon the power held by the parliamentary majority in connection with its Government.[3] From this perspective, part VI analyzes the Judiciary, the Referendums, the Constitutional Court, and the Regions as devices that counterbalance the power of Parliament/Government. In fact, all of these institutions can manipulate existing sources of law with a certain degree of autonomy from the national Parliament and Government, whose centrality is therefore effectively limited and counterbalanced.

Recent developments in Italian constitutional law are considered in part VII. Due to space limitations, it was necessary to select only a few representative topics. The work of the *Commissione bicamerale per le Riforme istituzionali* (the Bicameral Commission for Institutional Reform) appointed by Parliament in 1997, offers a good opportunity for a complete overview to the most current proposals of amendments to Part 2 of the Italian Constitution, which deals with the Organization of the Republic (the Bicameral Commission was not given the power to reform Part 1 of the Constitution). After the failure of the Commission, however, the process of federalization was fostered by the approval of a Constitutional law (no. 1 of 22 November 1999, hereinafter "Constitutional law no. 1/99"), which introduced the direct popular election of the Presidents of the Regions and modified the approval

---

[3]   This approach follows the interpretation of L. Paladin, *Corso di diritto costituzionale*, Padova, 3rd ed. (1998), p. 485.

procedure of the regional Statuti and by another, much deeper, Constitutional reform (Constitutional law no. 3 of 18 October 2001, hereinafter "Constitutional law no. 3/01"), approved by Parliament in March 2001 and conformed by popular referendum in October 2001, which has now completely changed the intergovernmental system in Italy.

II. Historical Background

The Kingdom of Italy was officially proclaimed in 1861, after the army of the Kingdom of Sardinia (really the Piedmont-based Savoia dynasty) had conquered all of central and southern Italy except for the Papal State. The new Kingdom of Italy, headed by Vittorio Emanuele II, was eager to stress its continuity with the previous Kingdom of Sardinia, and that is why the *Statuto Albertino*, the Charter granted in 1848 by Vittorio Emanuele's father, King Carlo Alberto, was retained.[4]

The *Statuto* was a typical liberal Constitution, strongly influenced by the French *Charte* granted by Louis XVIII in 1814 and thus following the British model. The document provided for the protection of life, liberty, and property as "sacred rights" and tolerated religions different from Catholicism, though Catholicism was proclaimed as the official religion. As for the structure of the State, the *Statuto* was quite ambiguous, leaving open the possibilities of a dualistic (King and Parliament) or a parliamentary form of government. It provided, pursuant to art. 67, that ministers were responsible government officials, without specifying whether their accountability was to the King or the Parliament. After a decade of uncertainty, the classic parliamentary form of government came to be considered prevailing form around 1870, and it performed reasonably well until fascism introduced the dictatorship during the 1920s. The right to vote, which was initially restricted on the basis of wealth as determined by real property holdings, was only extended to universal male suffrage in 1912 (law no. 665 of 1912).

When fascism broke down in July of 1943 and Mussolini was arrested, the *Statuto* was reapplied, and a new government under Pietro Badoglio, who was appointed by the King, was formed. From a constitutional point of view, the King acted legitimately, since the *Statuto*, still in force, empowered him to dismiss the Prime Minister. But since the Parliament was still strongly associated with the fascist party, it was dissolved by a *decreto legge* and new elections were called. Most scholars consider this to have been unconstitutional. Thereafter, the Badoglio

---

[4] *See* D. Sorace, "Introduction to Administrative Law," chapter 6, part I, this volume; *see also* A. Padoa-Schioppa, "Short Sketch of Legal History," chapter 1, part V, this volume.

government continued to issue *decreti legge* without any check or activity by the Parliament. The situation changed dramatically on 8 September 1943, when the King signed an armistice with the Allied forces. Thereafter, the Third Reich deemed Italy an occupied territory and proclaimed the *Repubblica di Salò*, a Mussolini-led government based in Northern Italy and backed by the German army, as opposed to the Kingdom of Italy, which was then based in southern Italy, but was moving northwards with the Allied army.

On 25 June 1944, *decreto legge* no. 151 was enacted by the government, calling for the election of a Constitutional Assembly with the power to approve a new Constitution and to decide whether the monarchy should be abolished. Subsequently, on 16 March 1946, a new *decreto legge* stated that the choice between a Monarchy and a Republic was to be made by a referendum which was called for on the following 2 June. *Decreto legge* no. 151 of 1944 is considered a "bridge" between the *Statuto* and Italy's new Constitution, which was approved on 22 December 1947 (and enacted on 1 January 1948), by the Constitutional Assembly elected on 2 June 1946, the same day in which the referendum abolished the Monarchy.

The new Constitution explicitly spelled out the parliamentary form of government, stating that "[t]he Government must enjoy the confidence of both Chambers" (art. 94). It introduced three new institutions in the structure of the State: Regions, the Constitutional Court, and the Referendum. The Constitution's Bill of Rights maintained all the classical freedoms, but weakened the constitutional protection of property and freedom of contract in order to promote welfare rights like health, education, and social assistance.

After the first general elections of 18 April 1948, when the social-communist alliance was defeated by the coalition led by the political party known as the Christian Democrats, the new Italian Parliament was seated and the Constitution was fully applied. (Notably, the Constitutional Court entered into force in 1957, the Referendum in 1970, and the Regional system only in 1977.)

III. Constitutional Rights and Duties

This section of the Constitution follows the classical divide between liberty and welfare rights, though upon deeper analysis this division emerges as deceptively complex. The classical example of this difficult divide is provided by freedom of the press. Is freedom of the press merely a liberty right that provides everyone the right to publish what he or she wishes, or it is also cognizable as a welfare right that binds the State to offer everyone the opportunity to publish his or her thoughts for free?

In this section it will not be possible to examine the Declarations of Rights to which Italy is bound on the basis of international law, such as the UN Declaration of 1948 and the European Convention of Human Rights of 1950. It should, however, be mentioned that the Charter of Fundamental Rights for the European Union, drafted on 29 September 2000 and proclaimed in December 2000 at the Nice Conference, could have a great influence on the decisions of the European Court of Justice and probably also on the National Constitutional Courts, even if not formally inserted into the text of the European Treaties. The Charter devotes special attention to social rights and economic liberties, while confirming the protection of standard civil liberties, often using the same wording as the European Convention on Human Rights.

Three important questions must be answered before we analyze individual rights. First, who is entitled to constitutional rights? Article 2 provides that "[t]he Republic recognizes and guarantees the inviolable rights of man, both as an individual and as a member of the social groups in which one's personality finds expression." It is thus clear that not only the individual, but also the "social group" is entitled to constitutional rights, according to the Italian Constitution. The typical example of such a social group is the family, which is defined in art. 29 as a "natural association founded on marriage," but local governments (art. 5), linguistic minorities (art. 6), the Catholic Church and the other Churches (arts. 7 and 8), trade unions (art. 39), and political parties (art. 49) are all mentioned as well. Constitutional rights do not only involve a question between the individual and the State. There is also an intermediate tier (the social group) through which the individual realizes his or her constitutionally protected liberty.

When the Constitution deals with individuals, a distinction must first be made between citizens and non-citizens: some rights are given to all persons, while others are accorded only to citizens. The wording of art. 2 suggests that the State must provide a minimal level of rights to everyone, citizen or non-citizen. Other rights – namely, political rights and some welfare rights – are limited to citizens. (Thus, for example, health and education are given to all, but social assistance only to citizens.) In order to recognize Italian citizenship, law no. 91 of 1992 applies the so-called *ius sanguinis* (requirement that a person must be the son or daughter of an Italian citizen), but the *ius soli* (requiring regular residence in Italy for five or ten years) can also be relied upon.

Secondly, it is important to understand who is bound by rights afforded under the Constitution. Is it only the State (in the broad sense of all the public bodies), or does this responsibility also extend to private corporations, where such corporations represent the so-called *poteri privati* or "private powers" (*e.g.*, large corporations, political parties, Churches, and so on)?[5] The matter is highly controversial, but, as with freedom of speech, the Constitutional Court has held that no entity, public or private, shall abridge an individual's constitutional rights (decision no. 122 of 1970). From this perspective, social groups mentioned in art. 2 as possible beneficiaries of constitutional rights can also be perceived as potentially threatening to a person's individual rights, and these groups are thus also bound by them.

Thirdly, one has to deal with the problem of the interpretation of constitutional rights: can they be expanded by the Constitutional Court, or is it necessary to adhere to the original meaning of the constitutional wording? In strict legal terms, the question is whether the "inviolable rights of man" mentioned in art. 2 are only those analytically described and protected in the subsequent articles of Part 1 of the Constitution, or whether art. 2 is an "open formula," allowing for the "discovery" of new fundamental rights by the Constitutional Court through a sort of evolutionary process, and assuming that the rights provided for in the Constitution are only those which were felt to be fundamental in 1948.

In its first phase, the Constitutional Court followed an interpretation based on the notion of "original intent" (such was the decision no. 29 of 1962): an extensive construction of constitutional rights was adopted only when strictly necessary and stemming from the text. The case of the right to life, not mentioned in the Constitution but presupposed by all other rights (decision no. 26 of 1979), and the case of sexual identity (decision no. 98 of 1979) provide two examples. But by the early 1970s, the Constitutional Court had recognized a new right, the right to privacy (decision no. 38 of 1973). Even though it did so through the application of the European Convention of Human Rights, this nevertheless constituted an initial step towards an "open" interpretation of art. 2 protecting the "inviolable rights of man," which has led, among other things, to the recognition of a right to housing (decision no. 404 of 1988).

A. Civil Rights (Negative Rights)

Civil rights are also referred to as *diritti negativi*, or "negative rights," because they prohibit the State from regulating or intervening in certain areas of private life. These negative rights are listed in arts. 13 to 28 and are consistent with the tradition of western liberal democracies dating back at least to the French Declaration of Rights of 1789.

Space limitations prevent examination of each constitutionally protected freedom

---

[5] *See* G. Lombardi, *Potere privato e diritti fondamentali*, Torino (1967).

in detail. The personal liberty afforded by art. 13 and the liberty of personal domicile stated in art. 14 require a deep analysis of the system of criminal procedure, recently reformed at a constitutional level with the amendment of art. 111 (enacted by constitutional law no. 2 of 23 November 1999). They have to be read in connection with arts. 25 and 27, which provide for procedural guarantees in criminal juris-diction, as well as the general rules on judicial procedure set forth in art. 24. Articles 17 and 18, dealing with the right of assembly and freedom of association, are connected with those rights of social groups mentioned earlier, and, in particular, with the constitutional regulation of trade unions (art. 39) and political parties (art. 49). Because freedom of religion (arts. 19–20) and speech (art. 21) are commonly considered the core liberty rights in a liberal democracy, they deserve a slightly more thorough analysis.

1. Freedom of Religion

Freedom of religion, which is considered the root of all modern liberties and democracies, is a particularly hot issue in Italy due to Italy's deep link with the Catholic Church. This link is based not only on the cultural and religious history of the Italian Peninsula but also on Italy's 1929 Lateran Treaty with the Holy See. Article 19 provides that "[a]ll shall be entitled to profess their religious beliefs freely in any form, individually or in association with others, to promote them, and to celebrate their rites in public or in private, provided that they are not offensive to public morality." This language represents a significant shift towards a secular state when compared with art. 1 of the *Statuto Albertino*, which provided that "[t]he Catholic, Apostolic, Roman Religion is the only Religion of the State. Other religions presently existing are tolerated according to the Law."

Freedom of Religion is protected in all its facets – the right to promote it, the right to change it, and the right not to be participate in religious activities at all. On this last point the Constitutional Court struck down clauses in the Codes of Criminal and Civil Procedure requiring witnesses to swear "before God" before testifying in court (decision no. 117 of 1979).

Article 20, which protects religious associations, is a specification of art. 18, but its wording is constructed only in a negative sense: the religious nature of an association cannot be considered a valid reason for burdening it with any kind of negative provision. The Constitution lacks an explicit provision forbidding any "establishment" of religion, meaning any positive provision *in favor* of a religious association. This is probably due to a need to maintain harmony with arts. 7 and 8 of the Constitution, which allow the State to regulate its relationship with the Catholic Church (art. 7) and with other religions (art. 8) on the basis of special agreements, thus leaving open the possibility of more favorable treatment for religious associations that have signed those agreements.

The interpretation of art. 20 noted above, read together with the wording of art. 33 para. 2 ("The Republic shall lay down general rules for education and shall establish public schools of all kinds and grades. Public and private bodies shall be entitled to establish schools and educational institutions *without financial burdens on the State*") (emphasis added) is at the core of one of the most striking debates presently dividing constitutional lawyers and political parties over freedom of religion in Italy. The question posed is whether or how private schools will be financed (where "private" means not established by the State or any other public body). Because private schools are in large measure Catholic, their public financing is commonly perceived as the funding of Catholic schools. The special language of art. 33 para. 3, "without financial burdens for the State," has been interpreted in various ways. It has been construed by the mainstream of constitutional lawyers to mean that the State cannot spend money to finance private schools. It has also been construed to mean that the State cannot be forced to do so, but can if it wishes.

A similar hotly debated problem deals with the teaching of Catholicism in State-run schools. Law no. 121 of 1985, which changed a previous law dating back to 1929, provides for the teaching of "religious culture" in State-run schools, on the grounds that the Catholic religion is an important part of Italian culture. But students who do not wish to attend religious culture classes (or parents of students who are minors) can avoid them by signing a declaration at the beginning of the school year.

A problem lying at the border between freedom of religion and freedom of speech which has recently come before the Constitutional Court is the question of the crime of speech that offends the Catholic religion, a crime set forth in the Italian Criminal Code. Pursuant to decisions 440 of 1995 and 329 of 1997, the Constitutional Court declared that this crime extends to speech offending every religion, not only Catholicism. It is left to the legislature to define what "religion" is.

2. Freedom of Speech

Article 21 protects the freedom of expression of everyone's thoughts, by any means of communication. It also provides that freedom of the press can be limited only by subsequent seizure, and not by prior restraints like authorization or censorship. These limitations may be imposed only by judicial order and only in cases expressly provided for by the law regulating the press or for offense to public morality.

The jurisprudence of the Constitutional Court has expanded the substantial limitations of freedom of the press based on the principle of balancing constitutional rights. If a law in conflict with the principle of freedom of the press is rooted in another constitutional value and the balance weighs in favor of the latter, that law can be upheld, notwithstanding the limitation imposed on the press. The most common countervailing constitutional value is that of a person's reputation and privacy. Rules set forth by the Italian Supreme Court (*Corte di Cassazione*, decision no. 5259 of 1984) provide that a defamatory statement published in the press is legitimate only if (1) the fact reported is true (and not merely likely to be true), (2) the fact is correctly described, and (3) there is a social interest in knowing the fact (*e.g.*, the defamed person is a "public figure").

The real problem with art. 21 is that it is already obsolete in at least two respects. First, it does not mention radio or television (even though in 1948 radio was widely used in Italy). After an uncertain constitutional case law, the issue is now regulated by law no. 223 of 1990 (substantially modified by law no. 206 of 1993, and by the decision no. 420 of 1994 of the Constitutional Court), which allows national broadcasting only under State concession. Such concession cannot be granted if the petitioner can control, in connection with the ownership of newspapers, more than 25 percent of the news market. This law also provides for special authority created to avoid trusts and monopolies in the field of information.

The second aspect of art. 21's obsolescence is demonstrated by law 223/90 itself. The present Constitution still treats freedom of the press as an individual right requiring protection from State interference. It is more correctly thought of as a "private power" which has to be limited by the State in order to protect citizens' freedom.[6] That is precisely what law 223/90 aims to do. The citizen has to be protected not only against the State's interference through the production of news information, but also against the news's power over the citizen. For this purpose, the State must regulate and limit what was once called "Freedom of Speech."

B. Welfare Rights ("Positive Rights")

The constitutional foundation of social rights can be traced to art. 3 para. 2, which states that "[i]t is the duty of the Republic to remove all economic and social obstacles which, by limiting the freedom and equality of citizens, prevent the full development of the individual and the participation of all workers in the political, economic, and social organization of the country." Welfare rights are thus considered a necessary instrument for the implementation of civil rights. The Republic must remove economic and social obstacles that may prevent citizens from fully enjoying civil rights like liberty and equality and, in particular, the right to participate in those social organizations which are so crucial in the Italian Constitution's idea of what "rights" are.

---

[6] *See* A. Di Giovine, *I confini della libertà di manifestazione del pensiero*, Milano (1988).

Following a tradition that dates back to the 1919 Weimar Constitution and to the 1946 Preamble to the French Constitution, the main welfare rights granted by the Italian Constitution are health (art. 32), education (art. 34), and social assistance (art. 38). These are all "expensive rights," in the sense that in order to be granted, they require the appropriation of funds from the State budget.

Health is defined as a fundamental right to be granted to anyone who cannot afford to pay for it. Law no. 833 of 1978 created the National Health Service, providing health assistance to all persons, notwithstanding their wealth. Judicial interpretation of art. 32 expanded it by awarding damages to a person for the violation of his constitutional rights to health, even if actual damage was not proved.[7]

Education must be given to everyone for at least eight years. It is compulsory and free. But the Constitutional Court has declined to broadly interpret art. 34, holding that books and transport are not affected by art. 34 and therefore that the State is not obliged to provide them to everyone for free (decision no. 7 of 1967).

Social assistance is twofold: it consists of social security payments to people who are unable to work or who, for some reason, cannot make a living on their own; it also consists of mandatory insurance for workers in order to pay for their retirement pensions, accidents, healthcare, and so on. The Constitutional Court, while acknowledging statutory discretion of the law in defining the level of social assistance, has stated that a minimum level of assistance must be granted by the State (decision no. 80 of 1971).

The cost of social rights is embedded in these same articles of the Constitution. Article 41 recognizes the freedom of contract, but it also says that such contracts cannot be executed against the common good. Article 42 recognizes private property, but no longer considers it a fundamental right. On the contrary, private property can be limited in consideration of its "social function." Article 43 allows the State to expropriate private enterprises "of primary common interest that concern essential public services or energy sources, or act as monopolies." Private property and freedom of enterprise are thus subordinated to the social interest, an interest mainly represented by the granting of social rights.

C. Constitutional Duties

The main duties provided for in the Italian Constitution are (1) the duty to participate in public expenditures through the payment of taxes (art. 53); (2) the duty to be faithful to the Republic (art. 54); and (3) the "sacred" duty to defend the Republic. This last has until quite recently included compulsory military service for men

---

[7] Cass., decision no. 796 of 1973; Corte cost., decision no. 88 of 1979.

(art. 52), which was abolished with law no. 331 of 2000, introducing volunteer army model. The possibility of performing alternative social service constituting a significant contribution to the country's welfare was introduced under law no. 772 of 1972.

Taxes have to be paid by everyone (not only by citizens) in relation to each person's economic capacity. The fiscal system is presently divided on a progressive basis with five tax rates, ranging from 18.5% to 45.5%. The Constitutional Court usually recognizes a presumption of constitutionality for tax laws but will strike down those laws that are patently contrary to art. 53. A law may be deemed patently contrary when it imposes unjust fiscal discrimination between different categories of taxpayers.[8] Only recently has the Constitutional Court recognized – though not in crystal-clear terms – a sort of principle of "confidence" in tax legislation, according to which new tax legislation must be foreseeable, so that the tax code does not unfairly blind-side persons who decide to invest their money in certain sectors of the economy that suddenly become subject to special tax treatment.[9] Local taxes are also permitted, at the regional level, and to some extent at the municipal level.

IV. The Parliamentary Form of Government in Italy

As noted above, Italy is run by a parliamentary form of government. In its classic definition, that is a form of government in which the Executive branch needs the vote of confidence of Parliament in order to take power, as opposed to the presidential form of government, in which the Executive, like the Legislative branch, is directly elected by the people.

Among the parliamentary form of government, Italy was traditionally said to follow the "consociative" model, as opposed to the Westminster model, due mainly to its multi-party political system and its proportional electoral laws. This situation is now changing under the pressure of a new majoritarian electoral law (1993) and, more generally, as a consequence of a deep crisis of Italian politics which has led Italy from the First to the Second Republic (to adopt French terminology used in

---

[8] *See* R. Lupi, *Corso di diritto tributario*, Milano, Giuffrè, 5th ed. (1998), p. 18.

[9] *See* Decision no. 315 of 1994, which upheld an *ex post facto* tax on takings compensation because it was widely advertised by the press before its enactment, and *contra*, decision no. 111 of 1998, which struck down a law regulating the Tax Court and imposing short terms for petitioners without prior notice.

the Italian media).[10]

A. The Formation of Government: The Vote of Confidence

Article 92 para. 2 of the Constitution states that "[t]he President of the Republic appoints the President of the Council and, on his advice, the ministers," while art. 94 para. 1 states that "[t]he Government must enjoy the confidence of both Chambers." That article goes on to say that within ten days of its appointment, the Government shall appear before each Chamber to obtain its vote of confidence, and that any single Chamber can approve a no-confidence vote. Article 88 gives the President of the Republic the power to dissolve the Chambers, though it does not provide a clear indication of when and why he can do so.

Notwithstanding the relatively general language used by the Constitution to describe judicial powers, the Constitutional Court has never been asked to intervene to interpret it. The procedure of the formation of government has thus remained a field modeled mainly by political actors, primarily political parties. As a result, it has undergone significant changes since the beginning of the 1990s, when the new electoral law reshaped the party system.

When a government resigns, the President of the Republic must find a candidate for *Presidente del Consiglio*, or "Council President," who is likely to win a confidence vote in both the House of Deputies and the Senate. In order to do so, he begins the so-called *consultazioni* by meeting with all the leaders of political parties represented in Parliament as well as other people influencing Italian political life (trade union leaders, speakers of the two Chambers, former Presidents of the Republic, and so on). The power of the President is increased if he has a wider range of possible choices. Since the first general elections under the new Constitution (held in April 1948), the President of the Republic has always played an important role in the choice of Council President.[11] Coalition governments have always been the rule; even when only one party has governed, it has never enjoyed a parliamentary majority, so it has always needed to seek the backing of other parties in Parliament, thus leaving the President of the Republic with the power to choose which coalition to try first. Of course, the power of the President of the Republic has not

---

[10] Literature in English about the crisis of Italian political system is not difficult to find: *See, inter alia*, S. Z. Koff & S. P. Koff, *Italy, from the first to the second republic*, London and New York, Routledge (2000); S. Gundle & S. Parker (eds.), *The New Italian Republic*, London and New York, Routledge (1996); C. Mershon & G. Pasquino (eds.), *Italian Politics: Ending the First Republic*, Boulder, Westview (1995).

[11] *See id.*, S. Z. Koff & S. P. Koff, p. 140.

always remained the same over the last 50 years. Rather, it has depended on different political situations (higher or lower levels of coherence among coalition partners) and on the President's willingness to intervene. But it has reached certain peaks, sometimes even imposing minority governments.[12]

This role of the President of the Republic has decreased to some extent since 1994, when the new majoritarian electoral law of 1993 was first applied. That law did not reduce the number of political parties, but it forced them to declare the coalition *before* the election, with the result that the voter knew who would be the Council President if a certain coalition were to win. That is what happened in the cases of Silvio Berlusconi, leader of the political party *Forza Italia* after the 1994 elections, Romano Prodi, then leader of *l'Ulivo*, after the 1996 elections, and Mr. Berlusconi a second time, after the elections of 2001.

The President of the Republic, in contrast, retains his power when a government crisis occurs because a party of the original coalition has stepped down. In such cases, the President of the Republic is again in a situation similar to that which existed prior to the new electoral law, because the President has to nominate a new Council President without clear direction from the electorate. Thus, he is required to either attempt to form a new coalition, or to decide that a new coalition cannot be achieved, and dissolve Parliament. President Scalfaro did just that in 1995, when he appointed Lamberto Dini as Council President following the crisis of the Berlusconi government caused by the withdrawal of the *Lega Lombarda* from the coalition. President Scalfaro dissolved Parliament again in 1996, and a third time in 1998 when he appointed Mr. D'Alema after the crisis in Mr. Prodi's government caused by the exit of *Rifondazione Comunista*, the new communist party headed by Mr. Bertinotti. Current President Ciampi found himself in this situation when he appointed Mr. Giuliano Amato as Council President in 2000, since Mr. D'Alema resigned after his party's loss in the regional elections of May 2000.

B. Political Parties, Electoral Laws and Public Financing of Political Activity

Political parties, which are so central to running the Italian government like modern democratic States (so-called *Parteienstaat*), are usually not given much space in modern Constitutions. The Italian Constitution only regulates them in art. 49. Article 49 of the Italian Constitution is located in Part 1, Title IV (on political rights). The same ambiguity (or obsolescence) concerning freedom of speech also exists in art. 49, because what should be perceived as a power (the political party) is instead

---

[12] *See* K. Strom, *Minority Governments and Majority Rule*, Cambridge (1990) p. 132-188.

constitutionally protected as a liberty right. Article 49 states, in fact, that "all citizens shall have the right to associate freely in political parties in order to contribute by democratic means to the determination of national policy." However, it is silent about the role of political parties in the formation of government and in the electoral procedure.[13]

The relationship between political parties and electoral procedure is ambiguous. Political scientists often stress the reciprocal influence of the electoral process on political parties: majoritarian election yields a two-party system, while proportional election produces a multi-party system. On the other hand, a two-party political system is more likely to prefer a majoritarian electoral law, while single parties in a multi-party system find the proportional electoral law more suitable.[14]

In Italy, the gridlock of a multi-party system would never have approved a majoritarian electoral law because that would have meant self-destruction was solved only by external intervention. A referendum was called on 9 June 1991 on the initiative of two different groups, one headed by a Christian Democrat back-bencher named Mario Segni, and another by a leading Administrative Law professor and former Socialist minister, named Severo Gianini. These groups were substantially isolated in the political world and backed by the so-called "civil society." The referendum was approved and, while the consequence was limited in legal terms to the abolition of the multiple-choice preference vote, it was politically devastating because it showed that the people could actively intervene and express their distrust of the political system as a whole.

The referendum of 1991 did not significantly modify the Italian electoral law based on the proportional system, but its political consequences, coupled with other factors,[15] produced an upheaval in the 1992 general elections.[16] A new referendum called on 18 April 1993, which proposed changing the current electoral law into a quasi-majoritarian system via the elimination of single articles or portions of articles, was overwhelmingly approved. On the basis of the referendum results,

---

[13] On the contrary, one notes that art. 21 of the German *Grundgesetz* (1949) on political parties is inserted not in the section related to fundamental rights, but in the section on the organization of the form of government.

[14] M. Duverger, *L'influence des systèmes électoraux sur la vie politique*, Paris, A. Colin (1950); G. Sartori, *Comparative Constitutional Engineering*, MacMillan, 1994.

[15] More generally, for the causes of Italian crisis from 1992 onwards, *see* Ginzborg, "Explaining Italy's Crisis," in S. Gundle & S. Parker, *supra* note 10.

[16] *See* S. Parker, "Electoral Reforms and Political Change in Italy, 1991-1994," in S. Gundle & S. Parker, *supra* note 10, pp. 40, 42.

Parliament was forced to approve two new electoral laws: law no. 276 of 1993 for the Senate and law no. 277 of 1993 for the Chamber of Representatives.

The new electoral law for the Chamber provides for a mechanism by which 75 percent of the Representatives are elected in single member districts and 25 percent are elected with proportional representation, but only political partiesd with more than 4 percent of the vote at the national level can win seats. Each voter has two votes, which can be split, one for the proportional representation constituency and the other for one's electoral district. For the election of the Senate, the same proportion between the majoritarian and representative systems is retained (75 to 25), but every voter has only one vote, which can thus be used only in favor of one party. Another difference between Chamber and Senate electoral laws is that in the Senate, there is no minimum percentage of votes required in order to garner seats in the proportional part of the election.

The new electoral laws of 1993 have been applied three times – once in the 1994 election (won by Mr. Berlusconi's center-right coalition), a second time in 1996 (won by Mr. Prodi's center-left coalition), and lastly in 2001 (when Mr. Berlusconi won again). But they have only partially attained the scope for which they were approved. The Italian political system has not shifted to a two-party model. On the contrary, the number of political parties has increased. But it has, in effect, moved toward bipolarization through the creation of two coalitions, each of them headed by a recognized leader declared *before* the general elections, so that the direct investiture of the Council President can now be deemed a reality. Of course, one must consider that such pre-electoral coalitions are unstable and that their composition can change, with the consequence that the Government is forced to resign (as was the case for each of Mr. Berlusconi's and Mr. Prodi's Governments). Upon receipt of resignation the President of the Republic is compelled to appoint a new Council President not originally known to the electorate.

The two coalitions on the scene in the year 2001, before the political elections, were the center-right, headed by Mr. Berlusconi and formed by three parties (the new Berlusconi-centered *Forza Italia*, the post-fascist *Alleanza Nazionale*, and the Catholic CCD), and the center-left, organized around the former Communist party (now DS and PdCI) and composed of eleven other parties, including the Catholic PPI, the socialist SDI, and the Green Party. A number of other small parties (often one-man parties) are scattered along the parliamentary spectrum, further contributing to Italian political instability.

If the foregoing illustrates a classical use of the referendum as a tool in the hands of "the people" in order to impose their will on the political parties (or, at least, in order to force the parties to do *something*), a different tale of the law regarding the public financing of political activity, shows how political parties can in the end overturn the popular will expressed in the referendum. It also shows that perhaps the system of public financing of political activity is more vital to political parties than are the electoral laws themselves.

The Italian law on the public financing of political activity dates back to 1974. It provides for partial reimbursement of electoral costs to candidates and for a contribution to the regular activity of political parties. The second type of public financing (to parties for their non-electoral activities) was challenged in 1979 by referendum. It survived by strict majority, but was overwhelmingly abolished by another referendum in 1993 (the same referendum which modified the electoral system).

Law no. 515 of 1993 enacted a new general regulation of electoral campaign, modifying the rules regarding reimbursement of candidates' and parties' electoral expenses, and introducing limits on electoral spending and the use of media (the so-called *par condicio*), as well as the duty to disclose the donors' identity. With law no. 2 of 1997, the public financing of parties for non-electoral activities was practically reintroduced, disguised as the taxpayers' voluntary decision, to be expressed every year on the tax return. The Constitutional Court upheld the law, notwithstanding its infringement on the referendum's results (decision no. 9 of 1997). But the application of law 2/97 turned out to be very time-consuming (or, as one observer noted, steeply cutting party budgets); thus, law no. 146 of 1998 was enacted, whose art. 30 states that, for the year of 1998 only, a fund of 120 billion lira is to be divided among parties for their non-electoral activity, independent from the result of taxpayers' choices. Eventually, law 157/99, while regulating public financing of campaign spending anew, has extended (in art. 7) the temporary provision of law 146/98 until the year 2002. A new referendum held in May 2000 was called in order to abolish law 157/99, but the result was invalid, since less than 50 percent plus one of voters cast their ballots, hence not receiving the minimum turnout required by the Constitution.

Analysis of the behavior of political actors must take into consideration another element that is presently one of the hottest political issues in Italy: the legislative regulation of a candidate's electoral campaign financing and spending (even where that spending involves use of a candidate's own money), and regulations imposed on media (primarily television and newspapers) in order to guarantee the same amount of advertising to each candidate or party. Known as the *par condicio*, law 515/93 introduced such rules for the first time. These rules were modified by several law-decrees issued in 1995, but never approved by Parliament, and the *par condicio* was not renewed after the 1996 election.

V. Sources of Law

A. Monistic System

The Italian system of the sources of law can be traced in the Constitution only in its general design. In order to find specific rules solving the conflicts between different sources, one must look elsewhere. The Constitution describes the organization of the Republic as centered on the Parliament, which is the only body empowered to make legislation (art. 70), with the two exceptions of the Government and Regions. While it is true that the Government and the Regions would seem to be exceptions, both may still be said to act under the "supervision" of the Parliament. Statutory law in a civil law system is the master of the sources of law which might be seen as a political decision rooted in the Constitution. But the actual functioning of a system of sources of law requires a precise set of rules about how to solve conflicts between different sources; such a set of rules cannot be found in its entirety in the Constitution.

The simpler model of the "three" Italian sources of law follows a hierarchical pattern: the Constitution, followed by the national statute, and finally the national administrative regulations. Thus, when a law is in conflict with the Constitution, it is invalid. A regulation in conflict with a law is similarly invalid. The invalidity, however, operates differently in the two cases. In the case of an unconstitutional law, it is the Constitution itself that affords the Constitutional Court the power to declare that it "ceases to have effect" (art. 136), while for an illegal government administrative regulation, the Constitution is silent, and a determination of the rule's validity is found in the machinery of the Judicial control over Administrative Activity.[17]

From a procedural point of view, the Constitution can be amended only by the procedure provided for in art. 138: a double vote by the two chambers, and an absolute (50 percent plus 1) majority required for the second vote, with the possibility that the members of the Chamber could call a popular referendum on the amendment if it has not been approved by a two-thirds majority in the second vote. A special procedure for an organic amendment to the Constitution was introduced by Constitutional law no. 1 of 1997.[18]

The procedure for the approval of a national statute is set forth in arts. 70 to 74. A certain number of citizens (50,000 electors) can propose a law, but only in practice

---

[17] *See* D. Sorace, "Administrative Law," chapter 6, this volume.

[18] *See* part VII, *infra*.

the Government and, to a lesser extent, single Representatives or Senators have the chance to have their proposals approved. Internal Chamber or Senate Committees are widely used for the discussion and approval of bills, while the Italian Constitution does not provide for bicameral commissions in order to eliminate differences between the two Chambers. Once approved by the two Chambers, each by a simple (50% plus one vote) majority, a law still has to be promulgated by the President of the Republic, whose refusal must be accompanied by a reasonable explanation and may in any case be overturned by a second approval of both Chambers, again with a simple majority. The promulgated law is ultimately published in the *Gazzetta Ufficiale* and enters into force 30 days after publication.

When one deals with the Government's acts, the "tree" of Italian sources of law has to be broadened. The Government can, in fact, issue both acts located at the same hierarchical level of the statute and acts under that level. The latter category is that of administrative regulations, issued by the Government following the procedure set forth in law no. 400 of 1988, art. 17 (the Constitution only says that they are issued by the President of the Republic pursuant to art. 87 para. 5). Administrative regulations are always subject to the rule of law, except for the controversial case of the so-called delegated regulations designed in order to foster deregulation. The first category is that of *decreti legislativi* (art. 76) and *decreti legge* (art. 77). Both have the same force as parliamentary law, but the Constitution provides that they need prior (*decreti legislativi*) or subsequent (*decreti legge*) approval by Parliament in order to be enacted or keep their force. Thus, in both cases the principle of the sovereignty of Parliament is preserved.

Decreti legislativi are delegated legislation used in technically complex fields (*e.g.* taxation, or procedural codes) where a sophisticated system of coordination is needed: the Parliament enacts a delegating law setting the basic principles and the time required, and the Government issues the actual delegated decree. *Decreti legge* may be issued by the Government only in "exceptional cases of necessity and urgency" and they have to be immediately transmitted to Parliament, which can approve them in 60 days; otherwise, they "lose effect as of the date of issue."

The hierarchical criterion cannot be applied, obviously, if a conflict arises between two sources of law belonging to the same category (*e.g.* two laws, or a law and a *decreto legge*, or two administrative regulations, and so on). In this case, the interpreter has to apply the rule of *lex posterior priori derogat*. That is, the subsequent source of law modifies the preceding source if they both occupy the same hierarchical position. The new source of law can only set dispositions for the future, unless it is explicitly retroactive, but *ex post facto* laws are forbidden in criminal law (art. 25 Const.) and limited in tax law (argued *ex* art. 53 Const.). They are permitted in all other cases.

The chronological criterion is not applied when a conflict arises between two sources of law with the same hierarchical position but within different jurisdictional ambits. In this situation, the competence criterion is employed. The most important case is that of regional concurrent legislation, which are enacted by regions only in specific matters (listed in art. 117, para. 2). They are, however, subject to the Constitution and to general principles set forth by national laws. But national laws cannot regulate the fields reserved to the regional concurrent legislation by art. 117, para. 2 in detail. If a conflict arises, the interpreter has to determine whether it concerns a matter covered by art. 117, para. 2, in which case the regional law prevails (if it does not attempt to set general principles). If art. 117 does not apply, the regional law is unconstitutional (the approval procedure of regional laws will be discussed in part VI D, "The Regions," *infra*).

B. The Breach of Monism: The Increasing Role of the Executive Branch and the European Sources of Law

The system of the sources of law rooted in the Italian Constitution, as thus far described, is typically positivistic and it pretends to be complete. Every legal controversy must be resolved by the direct or indirect will of Parliament, and this resolution must cover every possible conflict between sources. In this sense, officially it is hermeneutically closed. But in reality, the sovereignty of Parliament has been undermined in at least two significant respects.

The first is the increasing role of government legislative activity. *Decreti legislativi* and especially *decreti legge* were originally intended as legislative tools to be used in exceptional circumstances. Notwithstanding this original constitutional intent, *decreti legge* quickly became a common legislative tool used by government to ensure that its bills would be quickly discussed by the two Houses of Parliament. When they were not discussed in time, or even when they were rejected, the government would issue a new *decreto legge* with the same content, so that the constitutional limit of sixty days for *decreti legge* was regularly violated in practice. In fact, when the trick was used continuously, the government could renew the *decreti legge* every sixty days for long periods – even years – thereby avoiding parliamentary oversight and thus practically acting as a legislator.[19]

The Constitutional Court finally declared this situation unconstitutional in 1996

---

[19] In 1993, 259 *decreti legge* were issued by the government, and in 1994 the number rose to 336, while in 1993 only 177 laws were approved, and in 1994 only 163; *see* L. Paladin, *Le fonti del diritto italiano*, Il Mulino, Bologna (1996), pp. 245-46. Examples of this practice in relation to takings of private property are discussed in chapter 11, this volume.

(decision no. 360 of 1996), thus drastically reducing the number of *decreti legge*. But since a quasi-legislative activity by the Executive seems unavoidable (it is a general modern tendency), from 1996 onward the Italian Government has been finally accorded an impressive degree of legislative power. To cite one example, the entire reform of the administrative system (the so-called *riforma Bassanini*) was enacted through *decreti legislativi*, as was a complete renovation of the taxation system.

It is evident that this shift of legislative power from the Legislative to the Executive significantly alters the original constitutional design, since the Government not only executes the will of Parliament, but increasingly takes the initiative, leaving to Parliament a role of subsequent check over the final product. Of course, one has to consider that the Government represents the majority of Parliament; but the classical constitutional framework elaborated in 1948 reserved every decision to Parliament in order to give the opposition a chance to influence legislative outcomes. To the extent decisions are made by the Government, however, the opposition is unable to participate in the process.

The second aspect of the Parliament's undermined sovereignty may be traced to the introduction of sources of law produced neither by the Italian Parliament, nor by the government, but instead by the organs of the European Community to the Italian legal system.[20] Italy's participation in the EEC, and the signature of all other treaties, up to the Treaties of Maastricht and Amsterdam, has been constitutionally justified by the Constitutional Court (decisions no. 14 of 1964 and no. 183 of 1974) with art. 11, which says that Italy "shall agree, on conditions of equality with other states, to such limitations of sovereignty as may be necessary to allow for a legal system that will ensure peace and justice between nations." Article 11 was originally approved in order to let Italy participate in NATO, but its meaning was extended so that the Italian Constitution has not been amended, as occurred in other European countries, to constitutionalize the participation in the EEC, the EC, and most recently the EU.

The EC Council of Ministers can issue directives and regulations. Directives need to be implemented in every single legal system. In Italy, in each year since 1990, a special law (the so-called *legge comunitaria*) is approved which confers upon the Government the power to issue *decreti legislativi* in order to have EC directives executed: directives are thus transformed into pieces of Italian legislation. Regulations, on the other hand, are immediately applicable in every member State

---

[20] On this point, *See* L. Antoniolli-Deflorian's contribution to this volume, "Italy and the European Union," chapter 4, this volume.

and every judge has to apply them, even if they are in conflict with national laws (Constitutional Court decision no. 170 of 1984). These regulations have an intermediate position in the hierarchical scale of Italian sources of law, standing between the Constitution and the national law. They cannot modify the Constitution, but they always preempt the national law.

VI. Checks and Balances on Parliamentary Government

The sovereignty of Parliament is severely challenged by the European sources of law, but it is also limited by internal counter-powers, explicitly provided for in the Constitution which can interfere with parliamentary (and governmental) sources of law. Some of them have already been discussed above in a different light. I will now describe them more carefully, and assess their various counterbalancing roles.

A. The Judiciary

The Italian judiciary follows the French model: judges are recruited by competitive examination on a technical basis and not appointed by the Executive, as in the Anglo-American model. They are career civil servants. Their autonomy from the Executive is guaranteed by the constitutional declaration that they "shall be subject only to the law" (art. 101 para. 2) and by a special body, the Superior Council of the Judiciary (arts. 104-107). The Council is presided over by the President of the Republic and its composition is two-thirds judges, elected by judges, and one-third experts, appointed by Parliament. The Superior Council shall have "the sole right to appoint, assign, move and promote members of the judiciary, and to take disciplinary action against them, in accordance with procedures laid down by the laws on the organization of the judiciary" (art. 105).

The Italian Constitution guarantees the principle of the "sole judiciary": "[n]o extraordinary or special judge shall be established" (art. 102.2). But it also recognizes the distinction between ordinary judges (civil and criminal) and administrative judges, who deal with litigation where public administration is involved.[21]

The constitutional rules on the independence of the Judiciary have probably contributed to what has been labeled the "legal revolution"[22] of *mani pulite* ("clean hands"), which was one of the main factors in the Italian crisis of 1992-94. The

---

[21] On this point, *see* D. Sorace, "Administrative Law," chapter 6, this volume.

[22] D. Nelken, "A Legal Revolution? The Judges and Tangentopoli," in S. Gundle & S. Parker (eds.), *supra* note 10, p. 191.

prosecutor's office in Milan began an investigation on kickbacks in a home for the elderly in early 1992; this investigation quickly mushroomed and came to involve the illegal financing of almost all Italian political parties. This was probably one of the reasons for a massive turnover in the 1994 elections that swept away most Italian political parties. It has been noted that in the regional elections of 1995, not one single party was on the ballot that was in the previous regional election of 1990. The Milan prosecutor's office was accused of fostering political goals through its judicial activity, and this critique was extended to the Judiciary as a whole. In reaction, some amendments to the Code of Criminal Procedure were proposed in order to reduce the investigative power of the prosecutor's office, and eventually, in November 1999, an amendment to art. 111 was approved. (*See* E. Grande, "Criminal Justice: The Resistance of a Mentality," chapter 8, this volume.)

B. The Referendum

The referendum was introduced in the Constitution by art. 75, but it was not implemented until law no. 352 was enacted in 1970. In order for a referendum to be called, a particular procedure must be followed. The procedure is described partly in art. 75, partly in law 352/70, and partly in the jurisprudence of the Constitutional Court. The process is initiated by at least five Regional Councils, or 500,000 voters, who can approve a proposal seeking the total or partial repeal of a law or of a government act with the force of law. The proposal is reviewed by the Supreme Court (*Corte di Cassazione*) for its procedural legitimacy, and then sent to the Constitutional Court, which is in charge of verifying whether or not the referendum abides by the terms of art. 75's prohibition of referendums on "tax or budget laws, amnesties or pardons, or laws authorizing the ratification of international treaties." Once the proposed referendum is declared constitutional, it is set forth as a decree of the President of the Republic.

In order for the referendum to be valid, at least 50 percent of the voters plus one must cast their ballot. In order for the law to be repealed, the majority of voters must vote for the proposal of repeal. If the votes against it prevail, a new referendum against the same law cannot be proposed for at least five years.

The Constitutional Court has broadened its power, stating that the limits set in art. 75 have to be considered only as a minimum, to be increased by the Court itself every time a proposed referendum turns out to be contrary to the Constitution for other reasons (decision no. 16 of 1978). The Court has thus declared the unconstitutionality of proposed referendums that were deemed ambiguous, stating that they forced the voters to decide the repeal of a complex law – or even an entire code – with a single yes-or-no vote, when the voters might perhaps have preferred to repeal it in part and retain part of it. In addition, the Constitutional Court decided not to allow proposed referendums which, if approved, would have created a legislative vacuum in vital sectors of democratic life (*e.g.* it is not possible to request repeal of the entire electoral law by referendum). On the other hand, the Court has allowed referendums that introduced new pieces of legislation, thus violating the repealing-only nature of the referendum of art. 75. Such is the case for referendums on the electoral system, and in particular of the 1993 referendum, which was formally consistent with art. 75 because it only asked for the repeal of different parts of the law (often single words), but was practically intended to construct a new electoral system, as in fact it did.[23]

Over the past thirty years, the role of the referendum has significantly changed in Italian political life. Most importantly, the number of proposed referendums has drastically jumped, from the first and only referendum (on divorce) held in 1974 to the twenty-one proposed in 2000 (of which only seven were deemed legitimate by the Constitutional Court). But the referendum's meaning has also undergone significant modifications. It was intended to let "the people" spontaneously express their will on matters of crucial importance for defining their shared values (for example, divorce or abortion), but it has been subsequently used by parties as just another tool in the Italian political game. In 1992 and 1993 the referendum system took on a new role as a real counter power to political parties and the Parliament and appeared to be an alternative approach to reforming the otherwise blocked Italian institutional system. This new role of the referendum is probably inconsistent with the original intent of the Constitution, because to some extent it changes the form of government itself by reducing the centrality of Parliament as a legislative organ. According to some constitutional lawyers, for this reason it is a potentially dangerous alteration of the original constitutional design.

The danger seems to be decreasing on its own, given that all seven referendums held on May 2000 were considered invalid for lack of *quorum* (less than 50 percent plus one voter cast their ballot), thus giving the impression that the Italian people were beginning to be fed up with the multitude of referendums.

C. The Constitutional Court

Unlike the *Statuto Albertino*, the Constitution of 1948 is a "rigid" Constitution. As such, it provided for a Constitutional Court with the power of judicial review of legislation (arts. 134-137), following the Austrian model of constitutional

---

[23] *See*, in particular, decision no. 5 of 1999.

adjudication reserved to a special judge, as opposed to the American model, in which the power to interpret the Constitution is diffused throughout the judicial system. The Court only began its work in 1956 because it had to wait for the passage of regulations governing procedure, and to grant judicial independence to judges, as provided for by art. 137, Constitutional laws no. 1 of 1948 and no. 1 of 1953, and by national law no. 87 of 1953.

The Constitutional Court is composed of fifteen judges who are appointed to nine-year terms that are not subject to renewal. Five are law professors or lawyers with twenty years or more of experience who are elected by Parliament, five are appointed by the President of the Republic, and five are judges elected by judges. Besides judicial review and control over referendums, the Constitutional Court has the power to decide on conflicts arising over the allocation of powers between branches of government within the State, between the State and the Regions, between Regions, as well as on accusations raised against the President of the Republic.

The Constitutional Court can pass judgment on the constitutionality of national laws, regional laws, and government acts having the force of law. It cannot pass judgment on administrative regulations, whose constitutional legitimacy is left to ordinary and administrative judges. Cases can be brought up to the Constitutional Court in two ways. The first and most common is called *ricorso in via incidentale*. When a case is discussed in a Court, the parties or the judge can raise the question of the constitutionality of a law that must be applied in the case. If the judge decides the question is relevant to the case and has good grounds, he or she must send the question to the Constitutional Court and at the same time suspend the proceedings until the Court has decided that preliminary question. The Constitutional Court can reject or sustain the question. In the latter case, the law is declared unconstitutional and can no longer be applied. The second mode is called *ricorso in via principale*. Here the Constitutional Court can be used by either the national Government, when it wants to challenge the constitutionality of a regional law before it enters into force (*see* part VI D, "The Regions," *infra*), or by the Region, when it wishes to maintain that a national law infringes upon its jurisdiction.

It is not easy to assess the counter-power role of the Constitutional Court because, like every other Constitutional Court, it cannot avoid having both a technical and a political nature. Judicial review of legislation may strike down laws of Parliament in violation of the Constitution, and it is thus intended to be a limit on Parliament's sovereignty. But the Italian Constitutional Court's most "political" decisions are those on the constitutionality of referendums,[24] in which it can be – and often is –

---

[24] *See* G. Zagrebelsky, "*La Giurisdizione costituzionale*," in Amato & Barbera (eds.), *Manuale di diritto pubblico*, 5th ed., Milano (1997), p. 513.

accused of acting in favor of, not against, the Legislative and Executive power if it does not approve a high number of referendums, thus avoiding the possibility of popular repeal of Parliamentary laws. In its judicial review, the Constitutional Court can also be very respectful of the Legislative power, as in the field of taxation, while in other cases the Constitutional Court has actually acted as a real anti-majoritarian power, especially in relation to welfare benefits, issuing decisions which practically condemned the State to pay enormous amounts of money in pensions and other welfare benefits increases (*e.g.* decision no. 240 of 1994). Decisions of the Constitutional Court have force of law and are binding on all other courts of law. The Court's opinions are officially published. Opinions are always rendered *per curiam* and dissenting opinions are not permitted.

D. The Regions

Italy was deemed to be (at least until October 2001, when the Court reform was approved by popular referendum) a "regional" State. It is not a unitary State like France, nor is it a federal State, like the United States or Germany. It was something in the middle, not unlike Spain. The Italian *Regioni* have a constitutionally recognized status, but do not play a role in the national political process, even when amendment of the Constitution is at stake.

The Italian regional system has undergone a complete upheaval with the Constitutional law no. 1/99 (about the regional Statuto and about the regional electoral system) and then, even more deeply, with the Constitutional law no. 3/01 (about the legislative, administrative and tax power of the Regioni).

We will try to describe the past and present system, in order to show the most significant changes even if the new system has not yet become "law in action" and it is therefore very difficult to assess it properly.

Part 2, Title V of the Constitution regulates Regions. There are twenty Regions, of which five are "special" and fifteen are regular. All of them have a regional council, elected by the people, a regional government (called the *Giunta*), and a regional President who, following constitutional law no. 1/99, is directly elected by the people.

The regular Regions have their own *Statuto* (a frame of government for the region), approved by the national Parliament but proposed by the regional Assembly, which regulates its internal organization. Constitutional law no. 1/99 has changed art. 123 of the Constitution such that the *Statuto* must now be approved only by the regional Council, and the national Government may challenge it before the Constitutional Court within thirty days of its approval. Article 117 of the Constitution listed the seventeen different fields in which regular Regions had legislative authority; these were, however, always "within the limits of fundamental principles" set forth in national laws. A regional law was approved by the regional Council and then sent for approval to the national Government. The national Government could either approve it, say nothing for thirty days (which was deemed an approval), or reject it, in which case the law went back to the regional Council. If it was approved by an absolute majority again, the Government could only challenge it before the Constitutional Court (*see* part VI C, "The Constitutional Court," *supra*). As for the administrative authority, art. 118 stated that ordinary Regions had executive authority in the same fields in which they had legislative functions, but the State could, by law, delegate to Regions other administrative functions – which it had done recently in a massive way (*see* part VII, *infra*).

Constitutional law no. 3/01 has now changed art. 117, introducing the rule of residual power to the Regions: it now lists the seventeen fields in which the State has exclusive legislative authority and another list of eighteen fields in which the State and Regions have concurrent authority. Any other field is subject to exclusive legislative power of Regions.

It has been noted that the Italian "concurrent legislation" is completely different from that of art. 72 and 74 of the German Constitution: in Italy the Regions have concurrent legislation in the sense that they can legislate, but subject to the "fundamental principles" set by State law in the field; in Germany, the Länder can legislate in the fields listed by art. 74 of the Constitution only as far as the Bund decides not to intervene itself (i.e. subsidiarity principle "à l'allemande"). The last paragraph of the new art. 117 gives to Regions also the power to sign agreements with States, in the fields where they have legislative authority and in the cases and following the procedures set by a national law.

Constitutional law no. 3/01 has also changed the procedure for approval of regional laws, eliminating any prior control by the national Government: they are now voted by the regional Council and enter into force after publication on the regional Bulletin. The national Government, if it wishes, can challenge the regional law with the Constitutional Court, not later than sixty days after publication; similarly, the Region can challenge the national law with the Constitutional Court, not later than sixty days after the publication. The control of the national Government over Regions is now performed through the mechanism of "substitution": the new art. 120 allows the national Government to substitute Regions, exercising directly their power, if they fail to perform their fundamental tasks, thus creating a situation of grave national danger.

As for the administrative authority, the new art. 118 introduces the principle of subsidiarity, stating that all administrative authority is vested in Municipalities, unless it comes out that it is necessary to give it to Regions or to the State. It remains uncertain who, and under which rules, will decide if it is necessary to transfer the power to higher tiers of government other than Municipalities.

As for taxing power, the new art. 119 states that local governments (not only Regions, but also Municipalities, Provinces and Metropolitan Cities) should pay for all their activities only with their own taxes, even if special funds are established for poorer local governments.

The Constitutional Law no. 3/01 has not changed the legal regime of the five special Regions, which do not have a common regulation in the Constitution, because art. 116 states that each of them has a special *Statuto*, approved with the procedure of art. 138 (the same required for amending the Constitution). The legislative and administrative authority of a special Region are set forth in its *Statuto*, which has constitutional force. Therefore, every special region has a different amount of legislative and administrative authority, according to its *Statuto*. But, as a practical matter, there is no great difference between the five *Statuti*.

In order to comprehend the role of Regions, it is important to understand the political system, which is the same at the regional and national levels. The typical *cursus honorum* of a politician has its first stage at the local (regional or municipal) level, followed by a promotion to the national level. This is why a political analysis of Italian regionalism leads one to conclude that, however the constitutional system may have provided for formal devolution of power, relevant political decisions are still made in Rome and then transmitted to the local offices of political parties, from which they are proposed and approved in the regional Assembly or in the regional Government. This explains why Regions have thus far not played a significant role as counter-power to the national Parliament and Government. In fact, they have often been a kind of local replay of the national political scene, up to the point that the regional government coalition has often followed the same pattern as the national coalition, and has been changed when the national coalition has changed.

The situation is now changing both from the political and from the legal point of view. After the shock that struck the party system over the period of 1992-94, new parties organized on a strong local basis (for example, the xenophobic *Lega Lombarda*, rooted in the northern part of Italy)[25] have emerged, and old parties have been reshaped, giving space to local sections. At the same time, the regional electoral law, which was completely based on proportional representation, has been changed with law no. 49 of 1995 into a partially majoritarian law (for 20 percent of

---

[25] *See* I. Diamanti, "The Northern League," in S. Gundler & S. Parker (eds.), *supra* note 10, p. 113.

the seats), which strengthens the position of the President of the regional Government (the *Giunta*). Constitutional law no. 1 of 22 November 1999 changed the Constitution, stating that every Region can have its own electoral law – until now, the regional electoral law has been a national law – and, unless otherwise provided in the *Statuto*, the President of the Region is directly elected by the people. The new majoritarian electoral law, which was applied in the regional elections held in May 2000, has further strengthened the position of the President of the Region, thus giving him the possibility to claim a certain amount of autonomy from the national parties. The process of "political regionalization" could be significantly strengthened also by the consequences of Constitutional law no. 3/01, which has impressively increased the legislative, administrative and tax power of the Regions, thus giving to the Presidents of Regions a good chance to test their political autonomy.

VII. Recent Developments: The *Commissione Bicamerale per le Riforme Istituzionale* and its Aftermath

Since 1948, the Italian Constitution has undergone several minor changes. Three Parliamentary Commissions have been convened (in 1983-85, 1992-94, and 1997-98) in order to draft a major revision of the Constitution, but none of them achieved its goal. It is particularly interesting to our project to highlight the works of the last bicameral commission, also known as the *Commissione D'Alema*, after its president, Massimo D'Alema.

The *Commissione D'Alema*, composed of thirty-five senators and thirty-five representatives, was created by Constitutional law no. 1 of 1997, and was charged with amending Part 2 of the Constitution through a procedure different from that of art. 138, intended to guarantee a unitary design of amendments and a quicker result at the same time. At the end of the procedure, a referendum was required in order for citizens to approve or reject all the proposed amendments. The Commission adopted a text in June 1997, then forwarded it to Parliament, which discussed it and sent it back to the Commission with suggestions. The Commission approved a new text, after consideration of Parliament's suggestions, in November 1997. This text was due to be approved by a double vote (twice in each Chamber, separated by an interim period of three months) in Parliament and then submitted to a popular referendum. But the political agreement between the leftist majority of Mr. D'Alema and the rightist opposition of Mr. Berlusconi, upon which the Commission proposal was based, eventually collapsed and Parliament did not even reach discussion of the proposal.

It is nevertheless worthwhile highlighting some relevant points of the new Part 2 of the Constitution as proposed by the Bicameral Commission in November 1997, for two main reasons. First, it proposes a would-be Part 2 of the Constitution upon which a large majority of the political forces did eventually agree, even if they did not proceed with it due to a subsequent breach of the agreement. In other words, since the D'Alema Commission was not only a Commission for study, but actually voted – several times – on its project, it shows us what a possible reform of the organization of the Republic might look like. Secondly, after the political failure of the Bicameral Commission, the amendment process of the Constitution was not blocked. On the contrary, some important reforms were enacted (especially those fostering federalism) which were originally agreed upon in the project of the Commission.

The Bicameral Commission proposal would have transformed Italy into a federal State, granting regions a stronger constitutional status, with self-approved statutes, an autonomous taxing power, the power to appoint a quota of constitutional judges, and a residual legislative power on all matters not reserved to the national State. As regards the form of government, the Bicameral Commission proposed the popular election of the President of the Republic, and the appointment of the Prime Minister by the President of the Republic. It was a French-style system, with a strong President of the Republic (so long as he enjoyed a parliamentary majority), and power shared by the President of the Republic and the Prime Minister (the so-called French *cohabitation*) if the Parliament's majority party was not that of the President. The bicameral system was transformed into one in which the House of Deputies was the only "political" House, while the Senate became a "guarantee chamber," with the power to appoint investigation commissions, to consent to government appointments (or to appoint directly when it is the case), and to legislate (with the representatives) only on certain matters, among which would have been the status of Regions. Finally, regarding the Judiciary, it was proposed that the single judge principle be reinforced, raising the status of administrative judges to the same level as ordinary judges and dividing their jurisdiction only based on the subject matter of the case, and no longer on the *diritto soggettivo*/*interesse legittimo* divide.[26] As for criminal procedure, the Bicameral Commission proposed constitutionalizing the due process principle and creating a distinction between the careers of the judge and of the prosecutors (which are now interchangeable in Italy).

The failure of the Bicameral Commission did not signify that all of its proposals were failures.

---

[26] *See* D. Sorace, "Administative Law," chapter 6, this volume.

On the contrary, some of the projects relating to the Judiciary and, above all, to Federalism, were subsequently fostered by constitutional laws approved with the normal procedure of art. 138, as well as, where possible, by ordinary laws.

As for the Judiciary, the amendment of art. 111, approved with Constitutional law no. 2/99 (see part VI A) introduced into the Constitution the principle of due process, with particular reference to criminal procedure, while ordinary Law 205/00 gave to the exclusive jurisdiction of the Administrative judge, without any distinction between *interesso legittimo* and *diritto soggettivo*, significant areas of administrative law like public procurements, public utilities and zoning.

As for Federalism, the project of the Commissione Bicamerale was in great part realized in two steps: Constitutional law no. 1/00 modified the regional electoral system and the regional *Statuti*, while Constitutional law no. 3/01 modified the other parts of title V of the Constitution (as described in part VI D). If one compares the final draft of the Commissione Bicamerale (dated November 1997) with the present title V of the Italian Constitution, it is possible to notice the similarity of the underlying design of federal State, of the constitutional architecture, even if a lot of changements have been made.

VIII. Conclusion

It is quite difficult to draw any certain conclusions regarding the present situation in Italian constitutional law, since almost all the principal sectors are undergoing major changes. But we can identify at least three fields in which more profound and structural modifications will take place.

If one focuses on fundamental rights, great uncertainty arises as to the role that the Charter of Fundamental Rights for the European Union will play, and in particular the future result of the interplay between the European Court of Justice and the national Constitutional Courts in defining and protecting fundamental rights. Secondly, if one looks at the form of government and the party system, after almost seven years and three general elections with a (three-quarters) majoritarian electoral law, it is not yet clear if Italy is heading towards a two-party system, or if the multi-party system still applies. Thirdly, with respect to the structure of the State, after the constitutional reforms of November 1999, and of October 2001, the Regions are now changing shape, almost moving towards the role of member States.

The first and the third phenomena are apparently contradictory: the tendency toward harmonization of fundamental rights is coupled with a strong form of regionalization, shifting towards federalism.

This can be perhaps considered the most difficult challenge presently faced by the Italian constitutional system (along with other European States): keeping, and even expanding, a common core of fundamental rights to be shared in the European context, and at the same time reforming the local government in order to apply the subsidiarity principle and therefore shift the governing power – and the political accountability – closer to people.

IX. Bibliography

The text of the Italian Constitution, translated into English and continuously brought up-to-date by Prof. Carlo Fusaro of the University of Florence, can be found at the internet site: http://www.uni-wuerzburg.de/law/it; decisions of the Constitutional Court are published in Italian at the site: http://www.giurcost.org. Other information relative to constitutional research may by obtained by consulting "How to Find the Law," chapter 18 of this volume. It is not easy to find works in English about Italian constitutional rights and duties. One of the most interesting issues – freedom of the press through television and radio – is dealt with, alongside the French and British situation, in Rachael Craufurd Smith, *Broadcasting Law and Fundamental Rights*, Oxford, Clarendon Press; New York, Oxford University Press (1997).

The Italian form of government has often been studied by English-speaking scholars, especially after the crisis of 1992-94. *See* J. Newell, *Parties and Democracy in Italy*, Ashgate, (2000); S. Z. Koff & S. P. Koff, *Italy, from the first to the second republic*, London and New York, Routledge (2000); S. Gundle & S. Parker (eds.), *The New Italian Republic*, London and New York, Routledge (1996); C. Mershon & G. Pasquino (eds.), *Italian Politics: Ending the First Republic*, Boulder, Westview (1995); G. Pasquino & P. McCarty, *The end of post-war politics in Italy: the landmark 1992 elections*, Boulder, Westview press (1993). For information about the Italian political system before the 1991-94 crisis, *see* G. Pasquino, "Party Government in Italy: Achievements and Prospects," in R. S. Katz (ed.), *The Future of Party Government, Vol. 2, Party Governments: European and American Experiences*, Walter de Gruyer, Berlin, New York (1987), p. 202. Political data about Italian elections and government composition and formation are published yearly in the *Political Data Yearbook* issue of the *European Journal of Political Research*, commented upon by P. Ignazi. The sources of law are extensively dealt with in Thomas Glyn Watkin, *The Italian Legal Tradition*, Ashgate, Dartmouth (1997). The referendums are studied in Michael Gallagher & Pier Vincenzo Uleri, *The Referendum Experience in Europe*, Basingstoke, MacMillan (1996). The Italian Constitutional Court, apart from the classic studies of Mauro Cappelletti & John Clarke Adams, *Judicial Review of Legislation: European Antecedents and Adaptations*, Cambridge, The Harvard Law Review Association (1966), has been recently studied by Mary Volcansek, *Constitutional Politics in Italy: The Constitutional Court*, New York, St. Martin's (1999). The Italian regional system is briefly described in Daniel J. Elazar, *Federal Systems of the World: A Handbook of Federal, Confederal and Autonomy Arrangements*, Harlow, Longman (1991), while the Italian local government system is described in Robert D. Putnam, *Making Democracy Work, Civic Tradition in Modern Italy*, Princeton (1993).

The works of the Bicameral Commission can be found in Italian on the web at: http://www. camera.it/_ bicamerali/ nochiosco.asp?pagina=/_dati/leg13/lavori/ rifcost/home.htm

Italy and the European Union

Luisa Antoniolli Deflorian [1]

I. Introduction

Italy has participated in the process of European integration from the start, being one of the founding member States of all three European Communities (ECSC, EEC, Euratom). It has also co-operated from the start in the difficult process that has led to the establishment of the internal market through the Single European Act, the creation of the European Union through the Maastricht Treaty, and its streamlining by the Amsterdam and the Nice Treaties.[2]

In spite of this long-lasting loyalty, the relationship between the Italian legal system and the Community legal order has been complex and often controversial. It could hardly have been otherwise, since Community law has progressively absorbed wide areas and competencies that were traditionally considered to be part of the core of national sovereignty. This process has required wide-ranging and complex institutional and legal modifications by all the member States. In fact, the European Union is considered by economists, political scientists, and

---

[1] Associate Professor of Private Comparative Law, University of Trento.

[2] From a technical point of view, the European Union (EU) is the wider "umbrella" organization which comprises the three European Communities (the European Economic Community, now the European Community (EC); the European Coal and Steal Community (ECSC), and the European Atomic Energy Community (Euratom)), plus the so-called "intergovernmental pillars," which are a hybrid between Community and international law (common foreign and security policy; cooperation in the field of justice and domestic affairs), and whose content and procedures have been introduced by the Maastricht Treaty and subsequently reformed by the Amsterdam Treaty (which has transformed the pillar on justice and domestic affairs into a new one on police and judicial cooperation in criminal matters). By far, the largest legal impact on national legal orders derives from EC law, and therefore in this chapter we will simply refer to Community law or EC law.

Jeffrey S. Lena and Ugo Mattei (eds.), *Introduction to Italian Law*, 63-98

lawyers to be one of the most effective and successful patterns of regional integration, building a unique model that is distant both from traditional international organizations and federal States.

In this chapter, I try to analyze the effects that the interaction with the Community and European Union has had on the Italian system, organizing the data according to two factors: the temporal dimension, and the vertical and horizontal dimensions. The first relates to the fact that the Community's legal system has undergone profound modifications in its institutional setting and even more in the ever-increasing range of substantive areas it undertakes to cover. This broadening of institutional and substantive power has had a deep impact upon Italy's internal legal system. The second group of effects involves the interaction of two distinct dynamics, one between the Community and Italy as a whole, and the other between the central and local components of the Italian national legal system.[3] This dimension, which I call the "vertical-horizontal" dimension, is particularly important because the integrating (and sometimes disintegrating) effects of EC law are the result of the interaction of a plurality of legal formants (statutes, case law) and actors (Community institutions, national Government, Regions, courts) that work according to different but related rules, and in pursuit of a variety of interests.

II. The Relationship Between the Community and the Italian Legal Order

International agreements are generally introduced into the Italian legal system by an incorporation order (*ordine di esecuzione*). The constitutional basis for this measure is provided by art. 10 of the Italian Constitution, which states that "Italy's legal system conforms with the generally recognized principles of international law." This provision is generally taken to imply that general principles and customs of international law are automatically valid in the Italian legal system, but that treaties require an incorporation order which must take the appropriate form (*i.e.* constitutional act, ordinary statute, or regulation) in order to introduce the changes required to become internal law. After this execution order, the rules of international origin become part of the national legal system and they are treated as national rules. This mechanism reflects the prevalence in Italy of the so-called "dual model,"

---

[3] The mechanisms of interaction within the national level are termed "horizontal" in order to contrast them with the trans-national "vertical" relationship of the EC with the member States; nevertheless, strictly speaking they are also vertical, since the various national levels often work according to a hierarchical relationship.

according to which international law can become part of the national legal system only if it is absorbed through a national legal instrument.[4]

The dual theory has had important consequences for the relationship between the European Union and the Italian legal system, particularly because the Italian legislator has determined that the form of the incorporation orders which adopt Community treaties shall be *legge ordinaria* (ordinary statutes), which is a sub-constitutional source of law.[5] This reliance on ordinary statutes as the mechanism for incorporation of Community rules has proved to be a less than suitable solution, because it has rendered difficult the reconciliation of the status of Community-derived laws, which take the statutory form but at the same time must prevail over all conflicting internal rules. A more systematic approach might have been to amend the Constitution, or to ratify European treaties through special constitutional acts, as this would have avoided a number of practical difficulties in the application of Community law within Italy. The competent Parliamentary commissions, along with many scholars, suggested during the ratification of the Maastricht Treaty that a new "European clause," explicitly acknowledging the participation of Italy in the European Union, be inserted in the Constitution, particularly in view of the widespread consequences of the new Treaty for national sovereignty. Despite its merits, this effort was ultimately unsuccessful. In fact, Italy is now practically alone in its failure to accord an explicit constitutional status for the European Union:

---

[4] Legal scholars have proposed different theories. According to some, "generally recognized principles of international law" also include the principle *pacta sunt servanda*. According to this theory, treaties would become part of the national legal order automatically, without the necessity of further action, and would have constitutional status. Others argue that art. 10 Const. does imply a legal obligation to transpose treaties into the national legal system, but this does not happen automatically; it requires appropriate legal action. Attractive as these theories may seem from a logical and practical point of view, they have never been accepted by lawmakers or by the judiciary. *See* M. Cartabia, J.H.H. Weiler, *L'Italia in Europa*, Bologna, 2000, ch. 5 (pp. 129-138).

[5] In particular, the Treaty on the European Coal and Steel Community, signed in Paris in 1951, was ratified by l. 25-6-1952, no. 766 (Suppl. Ord. GU 12-7-1952, no. 160); the Treaties on the European Economic Community and the European Atomic Energy Community, signed in Rome in 1957, were ratified by l. 14-10-1957, no. 1203 (Suppl. Ord. GU, 23-12-1957, no. 317); the European Single Act, signed in Luxembourg in 1986 (OJ L 169 of 29-06-1987) was ratified by l. 23-12-1986, no. 909 (Suppl. Ord. GU 29-12-1986, no. 300); the Treaty on the European Union, signed in Maastricht in 1992 (OJ C 191 29-07-1992) was ratified on l. 3-11-1992, no. 454 (Suppl. Ord. GU, 24-11-1992, no. 277); the amendment to the Treaty on the European Union, signed in Amsterdam in 1997 and entered into force on 1 May 1999, was ratified by l. 16-6-1998, no. 209 (Suppl. Ord. GU 6-7-1998, no. 155). The amendment to the treaty on the Eurpean Union, signed at Nice on 26 Feb. 2001 has not yet been ratified.

most member States eventually amended their constitutions to take into account the peculiarities of Community law with respect to international law.

Still, this must be our point of departure in describing the history of the evolution of the Italian legal system. Its main consequences have been that Community rules, promulgated both as Treaties and as secondary EC law, could not conflict with rules that had a superior status in the hierarchy of the sources of law. Secondly, according to the maxim *lex posterior derogat priori*, internally generated rules contained in statutes that were passed after adoption of an EC rule prevailed over the previously adopted EC rules. This was, of course, totally unacceptable from a Community point of view, since it would have impaired the uniformity of EC law application. Therefore, a solution had to be elaborated which would ensure that EC law would prevail over conflicting internal provisions. The legal basis for a solution was found in art. 11 of the Italian Constitution, which provides that "Italy … agrees, on conditions of equality with other states, to such limitation of sovereignty as may be necessary for a system calculated to ensure peace and justice between Nations; it promotes and encourages international organizations having such ends in view." This provision had originally been inserted in the Constitution in order to permit Italy to become a member of the UN, and the limitations of sovereignty were understood in the classical sense of limiting Italy's powers in its international relations with other States. Despite the limited original intent of the language, it was felt that this rule could be expanded to cover participation to the European Communities as well, and this position was finally accepted by the judiciary.

III. The Application of EC Law in National Legal Systems

The most significant element in the evolution of the relations between the Community and national legal systems, consisting of a sharp break from traditional patterns of international law, is the increased participation of individuals, who can act in various ways in order to protect their Community rights both at the Community and national levels. In this way they have enhanced their position as Community subjects, through the working of the so-called "iron triangle" composed of Community citizens, the European Commission, and the European Court of Justice, which ensures the widest application and effectiveness of Community law. In this process, the preliminary reference procedure, established by art. 177 EC (now art. 234),[6] has proven to be of paramount importance. From a quantitative point of

---

[6] Article 177 (now art. 234) EC: "Where any such question is raised in a case pending before

view, this kind of judicial action covers approximately half of the judgments of the Court of Justice, whose number has steadily increased. Moreover, this instrument has had important substantive effects, marking the cooperation between the Court of Justice and national courts (which operate as decentralized Community courts in applying Community rules), crucial in establishing a common legal culture.

Preliminary rulings have been the main source of general principles that have shaped the legal system created by the Treaties and updated it to new European needs. Among the fundamental ones, the following must be mentioned: the definition of the Community as a *sui generis* international legal system, distinct but coordinated with the systems of member States, which have given up part of their national sovereignty;[7] the supremacy of Community law over contrasting national rules;[8] the creation of a judge-made "Bill of Rights" for the protection of fundamental human rights;[9] the enlargement of direct applicability of Community rules from the self-executing provisions of the Treaties[10] to the unconditional and precise rules of directives that are not implemented correctly or in a timely manner;[11] the extension of the national bodies bound to apply Community rules from the legislative to the judicial[12] and administrative organs.[13] In short, the Court of Justice has defined some of the basic characteristics of the Community legal system (aims, limits, and relations with the national systems), deriving them through an innovative synthesis leading to the creation of a peculiar form of "Constitution" for the EC system,[14] guaranteeing both its validity and uniformity of application.

The phenomenon of the failure of States to comply with and adapt to Community law has always been one of the major problems of the Community system. This

---

a court or tribunal of a Member State against whose decisions there is no judicial remedy under national law, that court or tribunal shall bring the matter before the Court of Justice."

[7] *Van Gend en Loos*, C-26/62 [1963] *ECR* 1.

[8] *Costa v. ENEL*, C-6/64 [1964] *ECR* 585.

[9] *See, e.g., Nold v. Commission*, C-4/73, [1974] *ECR* 491.

[10] *Van Gend en Loos, supra* note 7; *Costa v. ENEL, supra* note 8; *Rewe*, C-120/78 [1979] *ECR* 649.

[11] *Costanzo*, C-103/88 [1989] *ECR* 1839; *Marleasing*, C-106/89 [1990] *ECR* I-4135.

[12] *Simmenthal*, C-35/76 [1976] *ECR* 1871; *Factortame*, C-221/89 [1991] *ECR* I-3905; *Francovich*, C-6, 9/90 [1991] *ECR* I-5357.

[13] *See Costanzo, supra* note 11.

[14] *See* opinion 1/91 [1991] *ECR* I-6079. For a challenging study of the role of case law in the Community context, *see* A. Stone Sweet, *Governing with Judges – Constitutional Politics in Europe*, Oxford, 2000.

problem has been solved through several institutional arrangements. Through its decisions, the Court of Justice has progressively enlarged the effectiveness of Community rules, simultaneously guaranteeing judicial protection of individual rights. Already by the 1960s, the Court had recognized that certain Treaty rules not only bind the States, but also confer individual rights that are self-executing upon citizens of the member States. That is to say, these rights can be invoked in national courts, as occurred in the leading cases *Van Gend en Loos* of 1963[15] and *Costa v. ENEL* of 1964.[16] In the following decade, the notion of direct effect was gradually extended to rules contained in unimplemented EC directives that are precise and unconditional (*i.e.*, rules that do not require any specification or further elaboration through internal measures).[17] Adoption of this rule avoids the risk that the failure of a member State to implement an EC directive could impair individual rights afforded by the directive. This development has unquestionably solved a wide range of problems, but any rule insufficiently defined or unconditional – as is often the case with EC directives setting general aims – is not self-executing and therefore does not become part of the national legal order until it is formally transposed.

The Court of Justice has therefore created new rules to cope with these problems. The most relevant one is the imposition of tort liability on States that infringe upon fundamental Community obligations. This is an indirect way of protecting individual rights, but it can be very effective since the financial burden imposed can be extremely heavy. The Court started by acknowledging that failure by a State to conform to a judgment declaring an infringement[18] could give rise to individual tort action against the State according to national rules.[19] It then extended the rule in the *Russo* decision, according to which if a damage stems from a State's violation of a

---

[15] *See supra* note 7.

[16] *See supra* note 8.

[17] *Van Duyn*, C-41/74 [1974] *ECR* 1337; *Ratti*, C-148/78 [1979] *ECR* 1629; *Becker*, C-8/81 [1982] *ECR* 53; *Costanzo, supra* note 11; *Marleasing*, C-106/89 [1990] *ECR* I-4135 (duty to interpret internal rules so as to conform as much as possible to rules contained in unimplemented directives).

[18] Article 169 (now art. 226) EC: "If the Commission considers that a Member State has failed to fulfil an obligation under this Treaty, it shall deliver a reasoned opinion on the matter after giving the State concerned the opportunity to submit its observations … If the State concerned does not comply with the opinion within the period laid down by the Commission, the latter may bring the matter before the Court of Justice."

[19] *See* decision 17-6-1987, C-154/85 [1987] *ECR* 2717; *see also* decision 20-2-1986, C-309/84 [1986] *ECR* 599; decision 7-2-1973, C-39/72 [1973] 101 (all these decisions concerned cases of infringements by Italy).

Community rule, it can give rise to tort liability in the national legal system;[20] in this way State liability also covered infringements that were not declared by a decision of the Court of Justice. Some flaws remained, stemming from the fact that the rules governing this kind of liability were national, and that the application of Community law therefore lacked homogeneity. The leading case *Francovich*, decided in 1990,[21] created common requirements for the rise of State's liability, leaving only the procedural aspects of the claim to national rules.[22] The conditions for State liability have been further specified in later cases, such as *Brasserie du Pêcheur*,[23] *Dillenkofer*,[24] and *Hedley Lomas*,[25] according to which liability depends on the degree of discretion left to the national lawmakers and the clarity or ambiguity of the Community rule that has been breached. Thus, if the State has manifestly and greatly disregarded the limits of its discretion, thereby causing a sufficiently serious breach of clear Community rules, it is liable for damages suffered by individuals as a consequence of its act or omission.[26]

In spite of the far-reaching evolution of the doctrine of direct effect, there is still one area of rights that remains unprotected in case of non-implementation or mis-implementation of directives. The case law of the European Court has concentrated its efforts on the field of "vertical effects," *i.e.*, effects that stemmed from relations between public entities and private parties. The concept of public bodies has been interpreted in an extremely broad way, so as to encompass not only public powers that are entrusted with institutional functions, but also every body structurally connected to a public interest (*e.g.* public corporations). Nevertheless "horizontal"

---

[20] *Russo v. AIMA*, C-60/75 [1976] *ECR* 45.

[21] *See supra* note 12.

[22] These rules stem from previous case law of the European Court, which has progressively enhanced the judicial protection of individual Community rights, and has culminated in the *Factortame* decision (*supra* note 11), in which the Court stated that in order to effectively protect Community rights, national judges may have to devise new remedies (in this case, the European Court required that interim relief be extended also to proceedings against the Crown, although this was not possible under English common law rules).

[23] *Brasserie du Pêcheur/Factortame III*, C-46,48/93 [1996] *ECR* I-1029.

[24] *Dillenkofer*, C-178, 179/94, C-188, 189, 190/94 [1996] *ECR* I-4845.

[25] *Hedley Lomas*, C-5/94 [1996] *ECR* I-2553.

[26] The implication of this doctrine has been that in a few cases, like *Denkavit* (C-283, 291, 292/94 [1996] *ECR* I-5063) and *British Telecom* (C-392/93 [1996] *ECR* I-1631), liability for mis-implementation has been denied because the Community rules were not sufficiently clear and precise and their interpretation was made in good faith.

relations – *i.e.*, those between private parties – are not covered. In the 1994 *Faccini Dori* [27] case, the Court stated that direct effect cannot be pleaded in these cases; if Community rights cannot be protected through an interpretation of internal rules compatible with Community law, the only remedy is to ask for damages from the State, according to the *Francovich* ruling. The doctrine was reaffirmed two years later in *El Corte Ingles*, [28] and is currently considered settled law. This flaw is particularly serious, because Community law increasingly interferes with private law matters (such as consumer contracts, labor relations, and product liability, to mention just a few), and the lack of protection of individual rights in private legal relationships has severe negative consequences. In spite of widespread criticism, it seems unlikely that the European Court of Justice will change this doctrine in the near future. [29]

IV. The Case Law of the Italian Constitutional Court

Italian case law has also progressively ensured and enlarged the application of Community law, although the evolution has not been synchronous with the European Court of Justice. In the beginning, the main task of the Italian Constitutional Court was to justify the limitations to national sovereignty deriving from the participation in the European Community, [30] through an extensive interpretation of Const. arts. 10 and 11. [31] It then worked on the definition of the relationship between the Italian and the Community systems, coming close to the construction of separate but coordinated systems given by the European Court of Justice. [32] A period of serious

---

[27] *Faccini Dori*, C-91/92 [1994] *ECR* I-3325.

[28] *El Corte Ingles*, C-192/94 [1996] *ECR* I-1281.

[29] In some recent cases, the Court has come to a sort of "incidental horizontal direct effect," *i.e.*, to an interpretation of the provisions of unimplemented directives that directly affect rights stemming from private relations; *see CIA Security International*, C-194/94 [1996] *ECR* I-2201; *Ruiz Bernàldez*, C-129/94 [1996] *ECR* I-1829; *Panagis Pafitis*, C-441/93 [1996] *ECR* I-1347; *Unilever Italia*, C--443/98 [2000] *ECR* I-7535. This case law points to a blurring of the distinction between "vertical" and "horizontal" direct effects, and to a complex interaction with the principle of interpretation. *See*. P. Craig, G. de Burca, *EU Law – Text, Cases and Materials*, Oxford, 1998, pp. 206-211.

[30] Judicial review is regulated in the Italian legal system by art. 134 Const.: "The Constitutional Court decides: on controversies concerning the constitutional legitimacy of laws and acts having the force of law, emanating from central and regional government ..."

[31] *See* decision 14/1964; decision 98/1965; decision 183/1973.

[32] *See* decision 183/1973; decision 232/75.

clash came when the Constitutional Court stated that, in cases of contrast between Community and internal statutory rules, Italian judges were compelled to ask the Constitutional Court for judicial review according to internal standards.[33] This clash became manifest in 1978 with the *Simmenthal* decision,[34] in which the European Court stated that member States have an obligation to protect Community rights, and this implies that national judges must apply Community rules having a direct effect, even when this involves a conflict with, and non-application of, internal rules which would otherwise have been the law of the case. A solution was found only in 1984 with the Constitutional Court decision in *Granital*,[35] where it was finally settled that Italian judges can autonomously refuse to apply internal rules that conflict with EC law, without seeking judicial review by the Constitutional Court.[36] At the same time, the Constitutional Court has enlarged the areas of Community rules having direct effect, moving from regulations[37] to unimplemented directives[38] and to decisions by the Court of Justice.[39] A parallel extension has involved the typology of national bodies that are responsible for ensuring the correct application of Community law, from the legislative bodies to judicial and executive ones.[40]

The evolution in case law concerning the relationship between Community and national law that we have just sketched has been complex and far from coherent. Basically, we can distinguish two periods: the first one, beginning in the mid-1960s, expresses the idea of dualism held by the Italian Constitutional Court, and marks a sharp contrast with the contemporary case law of the European Court of Justice; the second, commencing in 1984 and continuing to the present day, moves closer to the idea of a "coordinated system" which is totally different from the relationship between internal law and traditional international law. We will briefly review the most important decisions in order to highlight the major changes that have taken place.

---

[33] *See* decision 98/1975; decision 183/1973; decision 232/1975; decision 205/1976.

[34] *Simmenthal*, C-70/77 [1978] *ECR* 1453.

[35] *Granital*, 170/1984.

[36] *See* decision 113/1985, *BECA v. Presidente del Consiglio*, in *Foro it.* I, 1985, 1600-1604.

[37] Decision 183/1973; decision 232/1975; decision 205/1976; decision 170/1984.

[38] Decision 168/1991.

[39] Decision 113/1985 (direct effect of rules deriving from ECJ decisions on preliminary rulings ex art. 177 EC), decision 389/1989 (direct effect of all rules contained in ECJ decisions).

[40] Decision 232/1975; decision 205/1976; decision 170/1984; decision 389/1989.

A. The Supremacy of Community Law

In the first important decision, *Costa v. ENEL*,[41] which gave rise to one of the leading cases of the Court of Justice,[42] the Constitutional Court had to consider the validity of an Italian statute which nationalized electricity. The plaintiff maintained that this statute was contrary to several provisions of the EEC Treaty, and this indirectly implied its contrast with art. 11 Const., which implemented the EEC Treaty in the national legal system. The court held that the statutes ratifying the Community treaties did not have constitutional value, and therefore a subsequent statute could derogate them. This contrast only implies the liability of the Italian State at the international level, but it does not touch upon the internal system. The decision reflects the dualistic theory of relations between international and national law, and the corresponding idea that there is no intermingling between Italian and Community sources of law: the latter only becoming part of Italian law if they are incorporated through national provisions, as are other sources of international law. This result was heavily criticized, and set off an enduring conflict on the point with the Court of Justice, which rendered an entirely different decision on the same case, in which the principle of supremacy was established for the first time.[43]

Shortly thereafter, another case[44] raised the question of the constitutionality of ECSC provisions giving the power to the European Court of Justice to impose fines according to Const. arts. 25 and 102, which provide that Italian citizens have the right to have their cases tried by the natural judge established by the law, banning the establishment of special courts. The Constitutional Court rejected the claim, holding that the Community legal system is totally independent from the Italian system, and that it could not, therefore, be evaluated according to internal constitutional standards. Only in an *obiter dictum* did the court briefly state that the

---

[41] *Costa v. Società ENEL, Edison Volta*, 7-3-1964, no. 14, in *Foro it.* I, 1964, 465; *Giur. cost.*, 1964, I, 129.

[42] *See supra* note 8.

[43] *Costa v. ENEL, supra* note 8: "the law stemming from the Treaty, an independent source of law, could not, because of its special and original nature, be overridden by domestic legal provisions, however framed, without being deprived of its character as Community law and without the legal basis of the Community itself being called into question. The transfer by the states from their domestic legal system to the Community legal system of the rights and obligations arising under the Treaty carries with it a permanent limitation of their sovereign rights, against which a subsequent unilateral act incompatible with the concept of the Community cannot prevail."

[44] Decision 27-12-1965, no. 98, in *Foro it.*, I, 1966, 9 (note by Catalano); *Giur. cost.*, 1965, I, 1322.

European Court of Justice works in accordance with the guiding principles of the Italian legal system, implying the compatibility of the two systems. In this way, the problem of coordinating the relations of Community to internal law in a logically correct and practically efficient way was merely avoided by an *escamotage*, which exposed a flaw in the logical construction offered by the Constitutional Court.

After a few years of silence, this issue was raised again in *Frontini*.[45] The case concerned the compatibility of art. 189 EC, listing the types of legal acts in the Community sphere, with art. 70 Const., which provides that the legislative function is exercised by Parliament. This time the Court did not rely upon the argument of the separation of the two legal systems, but adopted the wide interpretation of the "limitation of sovereignty" clause of art. 11 Const. According to this approach, Community treaties become part of the Italian legal system not only through the ratification statutes, but also through the constitutional coverage of art. 11.

Commencing with *Frontini*, the construction of Community law as incorporated into the Italian legal system through the limitation of sovereignty provided for by art. 11 has remained unchallenged.[46] In this way, the Treaties acquire constitutional status, and therefore prevail over conflicting national statutory provisions enacted both previous and subsequent to the Treaties.

This solution constituted a significant improvement over the approach exemplified by *Costa*, but in fact it had a corollary which had lasting negative effects: by being incorporated into the Italian legal system through a specific norm of the Constitution, Community provisions could prevail over conflicting national statutory rules only through judicial review by the Constitutional Court itself. Notwithstanding the fact that this task was specifically entrusted by the Treaties to the European Court of Justice, this meant a duplication of control by the Constitutional Court in order to ensure a uniform interpretation and application of Community law. Below the surface of a strictly technical problem lurked a clash of power: which of the two courts should control the compatibility of the national legal system with Community law? Obviously, the Italian Constitutional Court (like its German counterpart, the *Bundesverfassungsgericht*) was reluctant to give up its powers of control over the national legal system. On the other hand, it was clear from the start that any choice which did not honor the primacy and direct effect of Community law as well as the consequent entrusting of its control to the European Court of

---

[45] *Frontini c. Amministrazione delle Finanze*, 27-12-1973, no. 183, in *Foro it.*, I, 1974, 314 (note by Monaco); *RDI*, 1973, 130 (note by Mengozzi); *Giur. cost.*, 1973, 1, 2401.

[46] The same interpretation was used in order to give a constitutional basis to other international organizations, such as GATT and NATO.

Justice would have severely undermined the coherence, uniformity, and validity of this legal system. This was made clear in the landmark case of *Simmenthal*.

This doctrine was applied again in the *ICIC* case in 1975.[47] There, the Constitutional Court held that Italian judges could not refrain from applying national rules that conflicted with previously enacted EC rules. These rules, therefore, either had to be repealed by Parliament or declared unconstitutional by the Constitutional Court itself. Moreover, the Constitutional Court in that case also held that Community regulations cannot be reproduced in internal acts, even if their content is identical, unless they require an internal measure in order to be directly applicable. This was necessary because an internal act reproducing the regulation delays its entry into force, which according to art. 189 EC is directly applicable in all member States, and it furthermore obliterates the jurisdiction of the European Court of Justice to interpret it and adjudicate its validity, as established by art. 177 (now 234) EC.

There was a shift in the case law of the Constitutional Court[48] in 1977, when it held for the first time that if a conflict arose between a Community provision and a previously enacted internal rule, the judge could decide not to apply it without asking for judicial review to the Constitutional Court, because Community law had implicitly repealed it.

B. The Limit of Human Rights and Fundamental Constitutional Values

In *Frontini*, the Constitutional Court also considered another fundamental question: could the constitutional provisions that affirm fundamental legal principles and basic guarantees of human rights be overridden by Community rules, or did they amount to a minimum core that prevailed in any case? According to the Court, this core of fundamental principles (the so-called *controlimiti*) could not be violated, and it was the Court's task to ensure that it was protected from any infringement, both internal and external.[49] Nevertheless, the Court also stated that the problem seemed to be merely theoretical, because it deemed it extremely unlikely that Community law would touch on social and political questions. Time has shown that this forecast was incorrect and that, in fact, Community law increasingly impinges upon significant social and political aspects of the internal life of Italy that used to

---

[47] *Industrie Chimiche Italia Centrale (ICIC) v. Ministero del commercio con l'estero*, 30-10-1975, no. 232, in *Foro it.*, I, 1975, 2661.

[48] *Unil.it. v. Amministrazione delle finanze*, 29-12-1977, no. 163, in *RDI*, 1978, 337.

[49] In fact, the Constitutional Court has considered these limits to apply to constitutional amendments in general.

be considered the province of internal legal sovereignty. Nevertheless, the rule remains valid:[50] the Constitutional Court reserves the power to guarantee the protection of fundamental principles and human rights against possible infringements by Community law, although such control is considered exceptional.[51] Originally, according to the Constitutional Court, the power of judicial review was limited to incorporation orders, and the Court could not review individual Community provisions directly applicable in the national legal system because judicial review concerns national statutory rules, not Community measures. If the Constitutional Court were actually to find some contrast between Community rules and national constitutional fundamental principles, the consequences would be extremely serious, possibly involving Italy's opting out of the EC. This hardly seems a practicable solution in the EU context, which has a much higher level of irreversibility than other international organizations.[52] In fact, the Constitutional Court overruled this doctrine in 1989,[53] when it decided that it can verify the compatibility of every rule contained in the EU Treaties, as interpreted and applied by EU institutions, with the Italian constitutional order through judicial review based on the execution order. According to this doctrine, if the Constitutional Court finds that a Community rule

---

[50] *See Granital*, 8-6-1984, no. 170, in *Foro it.* I, 1984, 2062 (note by Tizzano).; case 21-4-1989, no. 232, *infra* note 53.

[51] *Cf.* the position of the German Constitutional court, which in the *Solange I* decision of 1986 stated that it would refrain from the internal judicial review of Community law as long as the latter respected fundamental rights as defined in the Basic Law (*Grundgesetz*). The competence of the *Bundesverfassungsgericht* to guarantee fundamental rights has been reaffirmed in the important so-called "*Maasticht Urteil*" of 1993, where it upheld the compatibility of the new Treaty with the *Grundgesetz*.

[52] After the "clashes" between the Court of Justice and national constitutional courts in the 1970s, the problem seemed to be merely theoretical. On the contrary, recent litigation decided by the European Court and the German *Bundesverfassungsgericht* concerning the protection of fundamental rights of national exporters (the so-called "banana litigation") has shown that there is an actual possibility of clash between national and Community fundamental rights; *see* Craig, De Burca, *EU Law: Text, Cases and Materials*, 2nd ed. (1998), pp. 275-76.

[53] *Fragd v. Amministrazione delle finanze*, 21-4-1989, no. 232, in *Giur. cost.*, 1989, I, 1001; *Foro it.*, 1990, I, 1855 (note by Daniele); the Constitutional Court has considered the compatibility with art. 24 Cost., providing the right to judicial protection, of art. 177 (now art. 234) EC on preliminary rulings, in its aspects concerning the temporal effects of judgments on the validity of Community Acts; it finally decided that the issue was not relevant in the case at hand, and that in any case, Court of Justice case law was not yet settled on the point. *See also Zandonà c. Inps*, 18-12-1995, no. 509, in *Foro it.* I, 1996, 784 (note by Barone).

clashes with fundamental rights, it merely avoids its application, without touching upon the whole Community legal system.

C. Direct Effect of Community Law

A complete *revirement* from the previous case law of the Constitutional Court on the issue of the relationship between Community and Italian law, implying a close approximation of the position taken by the European Court of Justice, came several years later with the *Granital* decision.[54] According to *Granital*, through art. 11 Const. and the statutes ratifying the Community Treaties, the Community legal system has gained control over some sectors of national sovereignty that have been assigned to it, according to a functional division of competencies. It follows that Italian courts need not refer a case to the Constitutional Court if they find a contrast between Italian and Community rules; instead, they must enforce the prevailing EC provisions. Judges may also exercise this rule without referring the case to the European Court of Justice, unless a problem of interpretation or validity of a Community rule arises.

Although the practical results of this decision correspond to the ones foreseen by the European Court, there remain some relevant differences in the theoretical framework underpinning them. The Court of Justice adheres to the monist theory, according to which Community law becomes part of the national legal system and enjoys primacy over it, preventing the coming into force of conflicting internal rules, no matter what their status in the internal system of sources of law may be. This marks a difference from the Italian Constitutional Court which, faithful to the dualist idea, considers the Community legal system as autonomous and separate, although coordinated with the Italian one. Community rules are directly applicable by the Italian judges, but in this case they act in a "Community capacity." This implies that contrasting internal rules remain part of the national legal system, but do not apply where Community law prevails. This ambiguity in the construction of the relationship between the Community and the Italian legal systems is still present today, even though its practical consequences have increasingly lost significance.

The scope of directly applicable Community law was gradually enlarged beyond regulations and directly applicable Treaty rules. In 1985, the Constitutional Court stated that decisions on preliminary rulings by the European Court of Justice prevail

---

[54] *Granital v. Amministrazione delle finanze*, 8-6-1984, no. 170, in *Foro it.*, IV, 1984, 2062 (note by Tizzano). The case concerned a statutory rule that refrained the State from asking for reimbursement from exporters which were afforded by a Community rule.

over conflicting internal statutory rules.[55] A further step came in 1989 with the widening of the direct applicability of rules contained in decisions of the Court of Justice other than preliminary rulings.[56] The Constitutional Court also specified that the duty to enforce directly applicable Community rules over contrasting internal rules concerns not only the judiciary, but all public bodies entrusted with the application of the laws, particularly the administrative entities.

In 1991, the Constitutional Court adhered to the doctrine of direct effect of rules of unimplemented directives,[57] whereby if States fail to implement Community directives properly or in a timely manner, their citizens can still rely on their provisions and request protection of the rights granted by them, provided that they are sufficiently specified in the directive. It must be noted that the Italian legal system has also adapted to the European case law in the field of horizontal direct effect: although many lower court judges have protected Community rights derived from unimplemented directives in actions between private parties, the Italian Supreme Court (*Corte di Cassazione*) has continued to adhere to the doctrine announced in *Faccini Dori*, and has held that direct effect for unimplemented directive rules can only be invoked against public bodies.[58]

Even if Community rules do not become part of the national legal systems of the member States, the Constitutional Court could still intervene if it believes that the national rule clashes with Community law. For example, if a national statutory provision contradicts a fundamental principle of EC law, this amounts to an indirect

---

[55] *Beca v. Ministero delle finanze*, 23-4-1985, no. 113, in *Giur. cost.*, 1985, I, 694; *Riv. dir. agr.*, 1987, II, 330.

[56] *Provincia di Bolzano v. Presidente del Consiglio dei ministri*, 4-11-1989, no. 389, in *Riv. it. dir. pubbl. com.*, 1991, 1065; *Giur. cost.* 1989, I, 1757. The case originated from a claim of the autonomous province of Bolzano that a governmental decree concerning the access of European citizens to public funding for housing infringed on its powers. The Court rejected this argument, considering that the decree merely recalled obligations derived from the provisions of the EC Treaty concerning freedom of establishment, and therefore did not impose any new obligation on the Province.

[57] *Giampaolo v. Ufficio del registro di Ancona*, 18-4-1991, no. 168, in *Giust. cost.* 1991, I, 1409; *Foro amm.*, 1992, 1837; *Foro it.* I, 1992, 660 (note by Daniele).

[58] *See* Cass., I sez. civ., 21-7-1981, no. 4686, *Smithett v. Terruzzi*, in *Mass. Foro it.*, 1981; Cass., II sez. civ., 27-6-1994, 27-2-1995, no. 2275, *Recreb v. Capillo*, in *Giur. it.*, 1996, 1, I, 100 (note by Scannicchio); Cass., I sez. civ., 19-1-1995, 15-5-1995, no. 5289, *Recreb v. Rosto Cappadonna*, in *Guida al dir.*, 17-6-1995, 46; Cass., sez. lav., 1995, no. 1271, in *Giur. it.*, 1996, I, 1, 110 (note by Jannarelli); Cass. sez. lav., 20-11-1997, no. 11571, *Forin c. TI UNO s.n.c.*, in *Riv. it. dir. pubbl. com.*, 1998, 1391 (note by Faro). For a different position *see* Cass., 3-2-1995, no. 1271, in *Nuova giur. civ.*, 1995, 837 (note by Calò).

violation of art. 11 Const., and can therefore be held unconstitutional.[59]

This case was also important because it declared, although in *obiter*, that the Constitutional Court can decide to refer a case for a preliminary ruling to the Court of Justice. Once more, this was not only technically important (since it ensured a higher degree of certainty and uniformity of the law), but it also signaled the development of an attitude of mutual trust between the two judicial bodies. It must nevertheless be noted that in a later decree (*ordinanza*) of 1995,[60] the Court has overruled this decision, stating that it is not to be considered as a court for the application of art. 177 (now art. 234) EC, since its competence concerns judicial review, as distinct from all other Italian courts. This argument raises some doubts, since the determination of which bodies constitute a court according to art. 177 (now 234) EC is an issue which must ultimately be determined by the Court of Justice and not by national courts, not even Constitutional Courts. This doctrine might therefore spur contrasting decisions in the future.

D. Regional Statutes and Community Law

The foregoing discussion has focused on conflicts between Italian national statutes and EC rules. But Italy is also divided into regions that have the power to pass statutes relating to regional matters. Thus, the question arises: what happens when a regional statute generated within the Italian legal system conflicts with a Community law, and what guarantees the timely and effective application of Community law in the Italian legal system?

In 1994, the Italian government took a case[61] before the Constitutional Court because it considered that a regional statute was contrary to Community law.[62] The Region took the position that even if such a conflict existed it could not be cured

---

[59] *Pulos*, 23-12-1986, no. 286, in *Giur. cost.*, 1986, I, 2309. *See also Toso v. Regione Friuli-Venezia Giulia*, 3-6-1998, no. 196, in *Riv. it dir. pubbl. com.*, 1998, 1061, in which the court deemed constitutional a regional statute that bans the transportation of waste from other regions for disposal, because it corresponds to the aim of environmental protection mandated both by Italian and Community law.

[60] Soc. *Messaggero v. Ufficio registro Padova*, 29-12-1995, no. 536, in *Foro it.*, I, 1996, 783 (note by Barone); *Riv. it. dir. pubbl. com.*, 1996, 777.

[61] *Presidente del Consiglio v. Regione Umbria*, 7-10-1994, no. 384, in *Foro amm.*, 1996, 377 (note by Caranta); *Giur. cost.* 1994, I, 3449.

[62] According to art. 127 Const., "The Government of the Republic, when it considers that a law approved by the Regional Council exceeds the competence of the Region or conflicts with the interest of the Nation or with those of other Regions, returns it to the Regional Council

by constitutional judicial review, since Community rules would prevail in any case. The Court rejected this argument, stating that the function of judicial review in such a case is to avoid the coming into force of the regional statute, thereby preventing the conflict with Community law and guaranteeing legal certainty.

In a subsequent case, the Constitutional Court had to decide again whether some regional rules were in contrast with Community law.[63] Once again, the Court underscored the fact that even if it were true that EC rules would prevail against incompatible internal rules without the necessity of a constitutional judgment, this situation was unsatisfactory because it created uncertainty as to which rule applied and did not guarantee the correct fulfillment of Community obligations.[64] The novelty of this case is that the Court extended this rule to national statutes as well, although only in *obiter*. In this way the role of judicial review was significantly extended, because even though it is not a prerequisite for the applicability of Community law, it can be invoked every time a contrast between a Community rule and a national statutory provision (both regional and national) can be established.[65] It is not clear, though, whether regions must wait for a decision by the Constitutional Court, or whether they can simply apply Community rules having direct effect

---

within the period established for approval. When the Regional Council approves it again by an absolute majority of its members, the Government of the Republic may, within fifteen days of communication of the fact, submit the question of its legitimacy to the Constitutional Court ..."

[63] *Commissario di Stato per la Regione Sicilia c. Regione Sicilia*, 30-3-1995, no. 94, in *Giur. It.*, 1996, I, 73; *Giur. cost.*, 1995, 789.

[64] The argument of the Constitutional Court is similar to that employed by the European Court of Justice in *Commission v. Italian Republic*, C-168/85,[1986] *ECR* 2945: in an action brought by the Commission against Italy concerning some Italian statutory provisions that limited the rights of Community citizens to exercise certain professions (journalists, tour guides, and pharmacists), Italy maintained that since Community law prevailed against any contrasting internal rule, there was no need to amend or repeal them, being sufficient to circulate administrative directions recalling Community obligations. The Court of Justice forcefully dismissed this claim, stating that "the rights of individuals to rely on directly applicable provisions of the treaty before national courts is only a minimum guarantee and is not sufficient in itself to ensure the full and complete implementation of the Treaty" [because] "this creates an ambiguous state of affairs by keeping the persons concerned in a state of uncertainty as to the possibility of relying on Community law." The consequence is that "maintaining such a provision in force therefore amounts to a failure by the State in question to comply with its obligations under the treaty" (no. 11).

[65] The Court has relied on this rule in a later decision, *Regione Sicilia v. Presidente del Consiglio*, 28-12-1995, no. 520, in *Giur It.*, 1997, I, 269.

while disregarding contrasting national statutory provisions.

Summing up this case law, we can say the Italian Constitutional Court has followed a complex pattern in order to coordinate Community law with the national legal system and guarantee the highest degree of implementation to the former. This process has been strongly propelled by the action of lower court judges, who have been very active in promoting the application of Community law through internal judicial review and requesting preliminary rulings by the Court of Justice.

V. The Implementation of Community Law in the Italian Legal System

In contrast to the stance of the Italian judiciary, which has gradually but steadily moved towards acceptance of Community law, the legislative and executive powers have always openly proclaimed complete support for it. The actual application has nevertheless been far from either complete or flawless. In fact, their stance has been schizophrenic because the proclaimed approval has often clashed with the practical failure to duly implement EC law. These difficulties have derived both from a lack of awareness of the peculiarities and needs of Community law and from internal complexities in the lawmaking machinery.[66] Many measures of Community law require some implementing intervention of the member States in order to become applicable in their legal systems; directives are a particularly significant example, but other acts require national action as well. Community law does not impose any procedure, leaving it to member States to develop their own processes, according to the characteristics of their legal systems.

Italy's compliance with Community obligations has been characterized by persistent and widespread delay.[67] This delay, which was often condemned by the Court of Justice in enforcement actions (art. 169, now 226 EC), was remedied by throwing together all of the unimplemented Community measures in huge and

---

[66] A comprehensive reform of the organization of Government in 1988 has also touched upon the issue of implementation of Community obligations by entrusting specific powers to the Council of Ministers and its President, and by creating a special ministry for the coordination of Community policies (*Ministro senza portafoglio per il coordinamento delle politiche comunitarie*); act 23-8-1988, no. 400, GU 12-9-1988, no. 214, S.O, arts. 2(3)(h), 5(3), 9. The coordinating role of the President of the Council of Ministers has been strengthened by legislative decree 30-7-1999, no. 303, in Suppl. Ord. GU 1-9-1999, no. 205.

[67] In 1992, 78 directives were unimplemented.

heterogeneous omnibus statutes.[68] In order to achieve these results, Parliament has made wide use of delegated powers to the Government, through which it has enacted numerous measures necessary to adapt the national legal system to Community obligations.[69] The problem with this method has been that it was often implemented when Italy was already failing to fulfil its duties, and the tasks at hand were often so numerous and diverse that Parliament could hardly set meaningful guidelines for the exercise of these powers. In order to remedy these drawbacks, Parliament passed the *La Pergola* statute in 1989.[70] This act compels Parliament to enact a Community Act (*legge comunitaria*) each year, through which Italy fulfils all of its pending Community obligations (transposition of directives, specification of regulations, and application of judgments by the Court of Justice).

The implementation of Community law can take different forms. First, it can be accomplished directly by the Community Act, though this option is not frequently employed. Secondly, the Community Act can provide that matters that were previously regulated by statutory provisions, but are not constitutionally required to be regulated by statute (which are commonly referred to as subjects outside the *riserva di legge*, *i.e.*, not covered by a saving clause), will be disciplined through regulations. This option, which is called *delegificazione*, has the advantage of permitting swifter action by assigning the task of fixing guidelines and criteria to Parliament.[71] Thirdly, Community obligations can be implemented through regulations in all subjects that are not covered by a saving clause, as is frequently the case. Finally, the most common procedure is to give delegated powers to the Government, controlled by the principles and criteria fixed by Parliament.[72]

---

[68] For example, act 42/87 implemented 97 directives and act 183/87 100.

[69] Statutory decrees (*decreti legislativi*) are regulated by art. 76 Const.: "The exercise of legislative functions may not be delegated to the Government save by the laying down of principles and criteria and only for a limited period of time and for defined objects"; art. 77 Const.: "The Government may not, unless properly delegated by the Chambers, issue decrees having the value of ordinary laws ..." Some of the most important of such delegating acts in Community matters are: l. 14-10-1957, no. 1203; l. 13-7-1965, no. 871; l. 13-10-1969, no. 740; l. 9-2-1982, no. 42; l. 16-4-1987, no. 183.

[70] Act 9-3-1989, no. 86 (*Norme generali sulla partecipazione dell'Italia al processo normativo comunitario e sulle procedure di esecuzione degli obblighi comunitari*), in GU 10-3-1989, no. 58.

[71] This mechanism was previously established by act 16-4-1987, no. 183, Suppl. Ord. GU 13-5-1987, no. 109, which has also established a rotation fund (*Fondo di rotazione*) in order to guarantee a proper use of the funding coming from Community institutions.

[72] According to art. 76 of the Constitution, delegated legislation must confirm to the directing principles and criteria established by Parliament in the delegating act (*see supra* note 69). In

According to a 1999 statute, responsibility for Italy's participation in the European Union and the process of European integration is given to the President of the Council of Ministers (who acts through a special Department in the Council of Ministers' Presidency[73]), while decisions of the main lines of action in EU matters are entrusted to the Council of Ministers. The powers of the Prime Minister are generally delegated to the Minister coordinating Community matters (*ministro competente per il coordinamento delle politiche comunitarie*). The Community Act for 1995-1997, enacted in April 1998,[74] increases the Prime Minister's powers. He or she has the task of transmitting the measures enacted by the European Community to Parliament and checking the conformity of the Italian legal system and of governmental policies with them; every year the Minister must present the bill for the Community Act to Parliament before the end of January, and must also identify each directive for which transposition deadlines have expired and which is not inserted in the bill, with a statement of reasons therefore.[75] This trend has been confirmed by the Community Act for 1998, enacted in February 1999, which empowers the Government to establish special criminal and administrative sanctions

---

the case of the implementation of EC law, these criteria must be found in the EC rules themselves, as well as in the delegating Community Act and in the national legislation relevant for the area of law affected. This has been recently confirmed by the Constitutional Court, which has determined that both Community and national criteria and principles must be taken into consideration and coordinated: *see Predieri v. Banca d'Italia*, 4-3-1999, no. 49, in *Riv. it. dir. pubbl. com.*, 1999, 909; *Foro it.*, 2000, I, 29; decision 10-11-1999, no. 425 (direct action by the Region of Emilia-Romagna), in *Gazzetta giur.*, 1999, 46, 58; decision 27-11-1998, no. 83, in *Foro it.*, 1999, I, 32; *Riv. it. dir. pubbl. com*, 1999, 251 (concerning the constitutional admissibility of a statute that gave the Ministry of University and scientific research the power to fix a *numerus clausus* for university admissions; the Court decided that the question was irrelevant, since the *numerus clausus* was mandated in some faculties by Community directives harmonizing rules concerning certain diplomas and professions).

[73] Legislative decree 30-7-1999, no. 303, in Suppl. Ord. GU 1-9-1999, no. 205. The main powers of the President of the Council of Ministers concern the relations with EU institutions, the coordination of governmental action both in the elaboration of EC measures and in their implementation, and the relationship between the Government and Parliament.

[74] Act 24-4-1998, no. 128, in Suppl. Ord. GU 7-5-1998, no. 88/L.

[75] In its yearly report to Parliament, the Government must provide information on the conformity of the Italian legal system with Community law, and give notice of any infringement action concerning Italy.

for infringement of Community obligations.[76]

The introduction of Community Acts has significantly improved the record of Italy's compliance with Community obligations in recent years.[77] Nevertheless, drawbacks and defects exist: bringing all Community measures together is sometimes a hindrance because modifications of the complex ones delays implementation of the simpler ones. Besides, the delegation of implementing powers to the Government is often so broad and general that its actions can hardly be said to be effectively constrained by Parliamentary criteria, and this implies a shift of power in the constitutional balance.

VI. The Role of the Italian Parliament

The gradual enlargement of the areas influenced by Community law has increased the role of Government in areas that were traditionally entrusted to Parliament. This process is particularly relevant because its effects combine with two other phenomena: the first is a general trend in Western countries, particularly evident in Italy, to shift powers from democratic assemblies to executive bodies – either governmental or independent agencies – in order to cope with numerous problems of an increasingly technical character. Secondly, the Community legal process is characterized by a strong prevalence of executive bodies: the Commission, which enjoys a monopoly over legislative initiative, is composed of independent members selected by the national governments.[78] The Council is composed of ministerial

---

[76] Act 5-2-1999, no. 25, in Suppl. Ord. GU 12-2-1999, no. 35. Article 7 of the Act empowers the government to coordinate and collect the rules implementing Community Acts through the enactment of "*testi unici,*" *i.e.* consolidating statutes (taking the form of *decreti legislativi*). Similar rules also appear in the Community Act for 1999 (act no. 522 of 1999) and 2000 (act no. 422 of 2000).

[77] *See* the Community Acts for 1990 (29-12-1990, no. 428), 1991 (19-2-1992, no. 142), 1993 (22-2-1994, no. 146), 1994 (6-2-1996, no. 52); 1995-1997 (24-4-1998, no. 128); 1998 (5-2-1999, no. 25); 1999 (21-12-1999, no. 526); 2000 (29-12-2000, no. 422). As can be seen from the dates, a Community Act was not passed by Parliament every year due to delay.

[78] Under the new art. 214(2) EU (previously art. 158 EU), introduced by the Amsterdam Treaty, the Governments of the member States nominate the person they intend to appoint as President of the Commission by common accord, and this nomination must be approved by the European Parliament. The Governments of member States then nominate, together with the nominee for President, the persons selected as Commissioners, and all of them are subject to approval by the European Parliament. The procedure will be changed, granting greater power to the President of the Commission in the selection of the commissioners, if the amendments to the EC treaty voted by the European Council of Nice (*see infra* note 81) enter in force (see art. 214 (2)).

representatives of national governments. Although recent amendments to the Treaties (the European Single Act, Maastricht Treaty, Amsterdam Treaty and the Nice Treaty) have increased the role of the European Parliament in the lawmaking process through the introduction of new procedures (cooperation and co-decision[79]), it is nevertheless true that executive bodies remain dominant. The interaction of these factors is summed up by a term now widespread in the European debate: "democratic deficit." The expression, reflecting the changes that have taken place in the last two decades, implies the need for new instruments that guarantee that the integration process will not be a bureaucratic enterprise, but will be guided by and be accountable to bodies representing the peoples of Europe.

The Italian legal system is still far from having found a comprehensive solution to the problem of democratic control, but there are some signs of change. Just before the 1989 election for the European Parliament, the Italian Parliament passed a Constitutional Act announcing a referendum which concerned the empowerment of the new European Parliament to transform the European Community into a European Union by means of a Constitution creating a European Government accountable to it.[80] The vote produced an overwhelming majority of 88 percent in favor of this proposal, demonstrating once again the fundamental acceptance of the European Union ideal by Italian citizens. But, except for a generic reinforcement of the integration process, nothing came of it, either on the Italian or on the Community side.[81]

In the past few years, Italian politicians and scholars have forcefully debated the possibility and the direction of a comprehensive constitutional reform of the Italian system. A special parliamentary commission (*Commissione bicamerale per le riforme costituzionali*) was established in 1997 and entrusted with the task of

---

[79] Article 251 EC (formerly art. 189b) (co-decision) and art. 252 EC (formerly art. 189c) (cooperation).

[80] Act 3-4-1989, no. 2, in GU 6-4-1989. The referendum posed difficult legal problems because the Italian Constitution does not provide for advisory or directing referenda (*referenda consultivi o di indirizzo*), but only for abrogating ones (*see* art. 75 Const.). Since nothing came out of the vote, the problem remained moot.

[81] This situation has not been fundamentally altered by the decisions taken at the European Council of Nice, held on 7-9 December 2000, at which the governments of the member States voted a charter of fundamental rights for the EU and several important reforms to the institutional machinery of the EU (weighing of votes in the Council, majority decisions, structure and powers of the Commission, etc.). These reforms must now be approved by all member States according to their internal procedures, as all amendments to the European Treaties.

elaborating a complete scheme for reform.[82] Among the many issues that were dealt with in the commission's final November 1997 report was the participation of Italy in the European Communities and the European Union (arts. 114-116). The report amended the text of art. 11 Const. to provide for an explicit constitutional basis for the European unification process, such that Italy can participate on an equal basis with all other member States[83] – provided that the basic principles and fundamental human rights which are part of the Italian constitutional order are respected, together with the principle of subsidiarity and the democratic character of the institutions of the European Union. The report also created a special lawmaking procedure for the incorporation of the European Treaties into the Italian legal system, in order to strengthen democratic control.[84] This aim was also pursued by increasing Parliament's role in the definition of European policies and in the appointment of Italian representatives to the EU institutions. Finally, the new institutional architecture also enhanced the cooperation of Regions, both in the formation and application of Community law. After fierce political battles among the left and right-wing parties, the whole proposal for revision was finally dropped, and the destiny of constitutional reform in Italy in the near future remains unclear, although it is likely that further action will depart from the Commission's report.

Currently, several statutory rules have reinforced the system for keeping Parliament informed regarding governmental activity in EC matters. Every year, the Ministry for Community matters presents a report concerning Italy's participation in the European integration process, which is then discussed in both Chambers.[85]

At a lower level (though one that has significant practical effects), the Italian Parliament's role in the Community lawmaking process has been enhanced by modifying the rules of procedure of both the Chamber of Deputies (in 1990 and 1996) and the Senate (in 1988). Through these changes, the Commissions competent for EU matters (the *Commissione politiche dell'Unione Europea* in the Chamber of Deputies and the *Giunta per gli affari delle Comunità europee* in the Senate),

---

[82] Constitutional act 1997, no. 1, in GU 28-1-1997, no. 22.

[83] The original text of art. 11 Const. refers to the reciprocity of obligations among States, not to equality.

[84] The act should be passed by an absolute majority of the members of each chamber. If one third of the members of each chamber, or 800,000 citizens, or five regional assemblies, should make a request within three months of the passing of the act, it should be submitted to a popular referendum, which would succeed if it received a majority of votes.

[85] The yearly report on EC matters was first established by the *La Pergola* Act (act. no. 86 of 1989, art. 7) and subsequently reformed by act no. 128 of 1998, act no. 25 of 1999, art. 10, and act no. 526 of 1999.

which mirror the political composition of Parliament, have acquired important new powers for receiving information from the Government, submitting proposals and opinions to it, and controlling its action. In addition, according to act no. 183 of 1987, as amended by act no. 128 of 1998,[86] all Community proposals for regulations, directives, and recommendations must be communicated to Parliament, in order to facilitate its tasks of proposal and oversight.

Although technically effective, these mechanisms have not significantly increased the input of Parliament in the Community lawmaking process.[87] In fact, some scholars think that while, until the 1980s the "invisibility" of Parliament in European issues was due to the lack of legal instruments, today its marginal role can mainly be attributed to its inability to make sound use of the legal instruments at its disposal, as well as to a lack of a "European consciousness" among Italian parliamentarians.[88]

VII. The Role of Regions

The Italian Constitution of 1948 created a State structure divided among the State, Regions, Provinces and *Comuni* (municipalities), and now, as of March 2001, Metropolitan Towns. According to art. 115 Const., "[t]he Regions are constituted as autonomous territorial units with their own powers and functions according to the principles established by the Constitution."[89] Article 117 Const. then enumerated the subjects in which Regions can legislate, provided that such legislation did not conflict with the interests of the nation and of other Regions. These competencies were wide-ranging and included health care, vocational training, town planning, tourism, local transport, agriculture, and artisanship. More extensive powers were given to five Regions that have social and historical peculiarities, and therefore enjoy broader autonomy (the so-called autonomous Regions).[90]

---

[86] *See* also Community Act for 2000, art. 6; for Regional Acts, *see infra*.

[87] A report of 1991 following a Senate enquiry on the issue of Italian participation in the creation and implementation of Community law has underlined the scant role of Parliament.

[88] M. Cartabia, *"L'ordinamento italiano e la comunità europea,"* in B. Beutler, R. Bieber, J. Pipkorn, J. Streil, J.H.H. Weiler, *L'Unione europea – Istituzioni, ordinamento e politiche,* Bologna, 1998, 121.

[89] In the first part of the Constitution, devoted to basic principles, art. 5 states: "The Republic, which is one and indivisible, recognizes and promotes local autonomy; it applies the fullest measure of administrative decentralization in services dependent on the State and adjusts the principles and methods of its legislation to the requirements of autonomy and decentralization."

[90] According to art. 116 Const., particular forms and conditions of autonomy, in accordance

These constitutional provisions have long remained a dead letter, and a comprehensive shift of competencies to the Regions took place only in the late 1970s.[91]

In March 2001, Parliament passed a constitutional reform concerning the powers of regions, which was subsequently approved by popular referendum in October 2001. After this reform (to which the current conservative Government has been opposed), the State has exclusive powers in a limited number of fields, concurrent powers with the regions in some others, while regions have residual powers in all other areas.

Many of the competencies that are now vested in the Regions are relevant to Community law, and it is therefore necessary to define the respective spheres of action of the Community, the State, and the Regions. This issue has two dimensions: the first concerns regional intervention in the creation of Community rules that affect their powers. The second, which has been given greater attention by the lawmaker, deals with the problem of implementation at the national level through the Regions. Although the Constitution vests extensive powers in the Regions, the State has historically been reluctant to recognize them. Formally, this choice was due to the fact that at the Community level, as in other international organizations, the responsibility for the fulfillment of obligations is reserved to the State,[92] and as a consequence of its liability for any failure by the sub-State levels, it retained firm control over their actions. This, however, does not fully explain the reluctance and delay, since history shows that the holding of those powers by the State has not overcome the fundamental problem of failed implementation of Community obligations, and most of all it does not justify the lack of instruments for ensuring the participation of Regions in the elaboration of Community rules relevant to them. In fact, it is only by giving them a proper role at the adoption stage that correct implementation can follow.

---

with special statutes adopted by constitutional law, are attributed to Sicily, Sardinia, Trentino-Alto Adige, Friuli-Venetia Julia and the Valle d'Aosta. The autonomous Provinces of Trento and Bolzano enjoy wide competencies similar to those of the other special Regions.

[91] DPR (Decree of the President of the Republic) 24-7-1977, no. 616, in Suppl. Ord. GU 29-8-1977, no. 234, which has carried out the delegation of art. 1 of Act 22-07-1975, no. 382 (*Norme sull'ordinamento regionale e sulla organizzazione della pubblica amministrazione*), in GU 20-8-1975, no. 220.

[92] *See* Constitutional Court, 24-7-1972, no. 142, in *Giur. cost.*, 1972, I, 1432; *Presidente del Consiglio v. Provincia autonoma di Bolzano*, 18-10-1996, no. 343, in *Regioni*, 1997, 189 (note by Camerlengo); *Presidente del Consiglio v. Provincia autonoma di Bolzano*, 23-12-1997, no. 428, in *Riv. it. dir. pubbl. com.*, 1998, 241; *Foro it.*, 1998, I, 706.

A. The Role of Regions in the Implementing Process

With the new Constitutional reform, Regions have a general power to implement EU acts and international agreements in their fields of competence, though the State retains the power to intervene following inaction by the regions. Still, in order to understand the developments that have taken place, we must look at the previous phases of legal development in this area. According to art. 6 of the DPR 616/1977, Regions have administrative powers for the application of Community law in the field of jurisdiction granted to them;[93] they can directly apply Community regulations, whereas for the transposition of directives they must follow the principles established by a corresponding State act. If Regions fail to take action, the State act is applicable. If this failure involves the breach of Community obligations, the Government can act in the place of the Region through the so-called *intervento sostitutivo* ("substituting intervention"). The Constitutional Court has ruled several times on this issue. In 1979 it held that the division of powers between State and Regions in the sphere of Community obligations, as outlined in the relevant statutory provisions, is coherent with the constitutional structure;[94] in 1987[95] it further stated that the State can act whenever this is required to ensure the timely and correct implementation of Community obligations, as well as the preservation of unitary State interests. The interpretation was very extensive, and has frequently justified interventions by the State so detailed as to leave to the Regions virtually no room for action.[96]

---

[93] The first devolution of powers to the Regions was made in 1975 in the field of agriculture: act 9-5-1975, no. 153, in GU 26-5-1975, no. 137; act 22-7-1975, no. 382, in GU 20-8-1975, no. 220.

[94] *Regione Friuli-Venezia Giulia v. Presidente del Consiglio*, 26-7-1979, no. 86, in *Giur. cost.* 1979, I, 646. Some of the Regions had made a claim of unconstitutionality of DPR 616/1977, because by reserving to the State the power to set framework rules, it permitted its interference with regional powers, and also because the act did not provide for any mechanism with which to remedy possible State inaction.

[95] *Provincia autonoma di Trento v. Presidente del Consiglio*, 30-9-1987, no. 304, in *Giur. cost.* 1987, I, 2484.

[96] Autonomous Regions have similar limits on concurrent powers; where they are vested with exclusive powers, they must only comply with fundamental principles, but not with the special guidelines fixed by the State for the implementation of Community rules. The *La Pergola* Act of 1989 widened the room for action for exclusive powers: according to art. 9, these Regions can immediately transpose EC directives, without having to wait for State intervention, and when this latter occurs, they only have to conform to it as required by constitutional principles. The Constitutional Court has intervened on this provision, and it again has

The mechanism was first modified by act no. 183 of 1987[97] and was further refined by the *La Pergola* Act of 1989, which empowered Regions in fields of shared competencies to apply directives after the coming into force of the first Community Act following their notification. This meant that if the State did not act in a timely fashion, Regions could transpose EC directives autonomously to remedy the inaction. Conversely, the State retained the power to intervene if Regions failed to do so, and this double mechanism ensured the widest degree of compliance with Community obligations.[98]

The Constitutional Court intervened on this issue in an important 1996 decision in which it confirmed that Italy's participation in the process of European integration must be coordinated with its fundamental constitutional structure, of which regional autonomy is a founding element.[99] According to this scheme, Regions retain primary competence in matters that are reserved to them by the Constitution, and the State can only intervene in order to supplement or substitute them when the correct implementation of Community obligations is at risk. This would imply that the Constitutional Court must ensure the respect of regional competencies not only by the State, but also by the European institutions, which can directly interfere with the internal divisions of national legal systems.[100] Nevertheless, in this decision

---

interpreted the power of State intervention broadly. *See Provincia autonoma di Bolzano v. Presidente del Consiglio*, 16-7-1991, no. 349, in *Giur. cost.*, 1991, I, 2787; *see also Provincia autonoma di Trento v. Presidente del Consiglio*, 17-7-1998, no. 273, in *Riv. it. dir. pubbl. com.*, 1998, 1067.

[97] Act 16-4-1987, no. 183 (*Coordinamento delle politiche riguardanti l'appartenenza dell'Italia alle Comunità europee ed adeguamento dell'ordinamento interno agli atti normativi comunitari*), Suppl. Ord. GU, 13-5-1987, no. 109.

[98] The intervention by the Government, which must first receive the opinion of the competent Parliamentary commissions and of the Region involved, must fix a deadline for the Region to fulfil its obligations; the Government intervene only after there is no action by the region when the deadline is up.

[99] *Provincia autonoma di Trento v. Presidente del Consiglio*, 24-4-1996, no. 126, in *Giur. cost.*, 1996, 1062 (note by Anzon); *Riv. it. dir. pubbl. com.* 1996, 1250 (note by Marzanati). *See also Regione Veneto v. Presidente del Consiglio*, 11-12-1998, no. 398, in *Foro it.*, I, 5, where a series of national rules concerning the allotment to the Regions of milk production quotas mandated by EC law were considered unconstitutional because the Regions had not been consulted.

[100] *See e.g.* the Integrated Mediterranean Programmes and the mechanism of structural funds introduced by the European Single Act which instituted a partnership among European Regions, avoiding the State level. More frequently, though, Community action entrusts specific tasks to the States.

the Court explicitly stated that Community law can depart from the national constitutional framework, as long as it does not infringe upon fundamental constitutional principles.[101] It has reaffirmed this doctrine in a decision of 1997,[102] stating that if a modification of the constitutional division of competencies between State and Region is produced by a Community measure, this is not subject to judicial review by the Italian Constitutional Court. This development could prove dangerous for the preservation of regional powers, since Regions do not participate fully in the lawmaking process on European issues either at the Community or at the national level; besides, they do not have direct access to Community judicial protection (*i.e.* they cannot go to the European Court of Justice to have their competencies protected),[103] so the only instrument left is the Constitutional Court, which may intervene in order to guarantee the constitutional division of powers. The abandonment of this control is a serious threat to the State-Regional balance, particularly because there is no clear-cut delimitation of the Community's sphere of intervention.

This system has been amended by the Community Act for the years 1995-1997, enacted in April 1998,[104] which abolishes the requirement of a previous national Community Act in order to transpose EC directives where they have concurring powers (art. 9) for all Regions, both ordinary and autonomous. Regions can therefore take action independently from the State, and acquire a wider ambit of discretion.[105]

---

[101] As in all previous case law on point, the judgment did not define the content of these principles.

[102] *Regione Umbria v. Presidente del Consiglio*, 11-4-1997, no. 93, in *Riv. it. dir. pubbl. com.*, 1997, 718 (note by Marzanati). The case concerned a Community programme for employment and training which created a partnership between the Commission and the State, obliterating the constitutional competencies of the Regions in this fields.

[103] The final report of the Parliamentary Commission for the Constitutional Reform of 1997 contains a rule that empowers Regions to challenge the legitimacy of Community measures that infringe upon their competencies through the action of Government.

[104] Act 24-4-1998, no. 128, in Suppl. Ord. GU 7-5-1998, no. 88/L.

[105] Regional acts must contain the title and number of the directive they transpose, and Regions must give notice of them to the Government. *See* art 2-bis of act no. 86 of 1983, as amended by art. 6 of community act for 2000 (act 29-12-2000, no. 422 in Suppl. Ord. GU 20-1-2000, no. 16). On the other hand, the Government can determine the guiding principles that cannot be derogated by regional acts and prevail against contrasting regional rules. It can also enact detailed rules transposing EC measures in fields reserved to the Regions, but these remain in force only as long as Regions do not pass regional statutes on the same issue: *see* Constitutional Court, decision 10-11-1999, no. 425, in *Gazzetta giur.*, 1999, 46, 58, according to which if Government implements EC rules in fields pertaining to the Regions (in the case rules for the protection of the natural environment), the latter can regain their competence by passing

Some important changes involving the substantial devolution of power from the State to the Regions have been achieved through ordinary legislation. In 1997, the so-called *Bassanini* Act[106] revolutionized the previously existent division of administrative powers between the State, the Regions, and local governmental entities (*enti locali*), devolving the majority of competencies to the lower levels, and retaining for the Government the crucial task of co-ordination and supervision. Administrative functions and tasks are vested in *comuni* (townships), *province* (provinces), and mountain communities (*comunità montane*), reserving to the Regions only those tasks that require unitary activity (art. 3). This model transposes the principle of subsidiarity (according to which decisions must be made as close as possible to the communities that they regulate) to the national level. The content of this important act was then specified by several governmental decrees. Although a complete analysis of this new system is beyond the scope of this chapter, we can mention a few rules that concern the issues with which we have been dealing. A decree of August 1997[107] has significantly expanded the tasks of the Permanent Conference for the Relations between State and Regions (*Conferenza permanente per i rapporti tra lo Stato e le Regioni*).[108] This consultative body lacks legislative power, but ensures the distribution of proper information to the Regions, and functions as the core institution for the coordination between governing levels, not only for Community matters, but also respecting all those competencies devolved to sub-State levels. Another decree of March 1998, devolving administrative functions to the Regions and lower bodies,[109] explicitly defines the coordinating role of the State in relations with the European Union; this also implies the task of ensuring the enforcement of Community obligations and a unitary representation at the international level (art. 2). The result of the wide devolution is that Regions and lower levels acquire broad powers, but the State retains an important coordinating and directing power (*potere di indirizzo e coordinamento*) (art. 4), as

---

regional measures which prevail over the national ones (although they must comply with the guiding principles).

[106] Act 15-3-1997, no. 59, Suppl. Ord. GU 17-3-1997, no. 63.

[107] Legislative decree 28-8-1997, no. 281, in Suppl. Ord. 21-4-1998, no. 92.

[108] The Conference was established in 1988 by act 2-8-1988, no. 400, Suppl. Ord. GU 12-09-1988, no. 214.

[109] Legislative decree 31-3-1998, no. 112 (*conferimento di funzioni e compiti amministrativi dello Stato alle regioni ed agli enti locali, in attuazione del Capo I della legge 15 marzo 1997, no. 59*).

well as an extensive power of substitution (*poteri sostitutivi*)[110] where the nominally competent bodies have failed to implement Community obligations, or when the national interest may be damaged (art. 5).

This devolutionary model is also adopted by the Constitutional reform of March 2001, which assigns the administrative function to municipalities, except where, for unitary reasons they are assigned to the Region or the State. Regulatory functions belong to the State only where it enjoys exclusive power. In all other areas, they belong to the Regions.

B. The Role of Regions in the Elaboration of Community Law

The situation regarding the role of Regions in the elaboration of Community rules is still far from satisfactory, although some improvements have been made in recent years.

At the Community level, the Maastricht Treaty has introduced a new body into the legal process called the Committee of the Regions.[111] This body represents regional and local entities at the European level in order to include their voices in Community decisions concerning them. It must be consulted by the Commission and the Council when the Treaty so specifies, and it may be consulted, even directly by Parliament, in any instance deemed necessary. Every State can appoint a certain number of members based on its size (although formal appointment is made by the Council), and it can decide which of its internal subdivisions are to be represented. This reflects the differing patterns of organization of member States, but it produces the negative result of a highly heterogeneous composition, which can sometimes hinder the Council's performance.

Another relevant feature is the principle of subsidiarity, which has been inserted as one of the central features of the new European system created by the Maastricht Treaty and consolidated by the Amsterdam Treaty. According to the subsidiarity principle, political and economic decisions must be made as close as possible to the people,[112] pointing not only to the strengthening of the lower levels of govern-

---

[110] Although substituting powers were already present in the Italian legal system, art. 5 enlarges and modifies them as a necessary counterbalance to the significant increase of competencies of the lower levels.

[111] Article 263 EC (formerly art. 198A-C).

[112] Article 2 EC (formerly art. B): "The objectives of the Union shall be achieved ... respecting the principle of subsidiarity"; art. 5 EC (formerly art. 3B): "In areas which do not fall within its exclusive competence, the Community shall take action, in accordance with the principle of subsidiarity, only if and insofar as the objectives of the proposed action cannot be sufficiently

ment in the relationship between the European Union and the member States, but within the national legal systems as well. In fact, the special Parliamentary Commission established in 1997 for the comprehensive constitutional reform of the Italian legal system placed among its central issues the decentralization of the State in favor of the lower levels, either through a truly federal structure or through a far-reaching devolution. This has been partially accomplished by the Constitutional Reform of March 2001, which has significantly strengthened the legislative powers of Regions, and the administrative powers of all subnational levels, according to the subsidiarity model.

In the Italian legal system, any contact between the Regions and Community institutions was initially filtered through the intervention of the national ministries, whose action was to be coordinated by the Foreign Office, following the traditional model of international law.[113] Community proposals for legislation initially had to be communicated to the Regions in the fields in which they had enumerated powers.[114] A significant change came with the *La Pergola* Act of 1989, according to which matters of interest to the Regions must be discussed in the Permanent Conference for the Relations between State and Regions. According to the 1989 statute, the President of the Council of Ministers had to convene the conference every six months in order to discuss Community matters relevant to regional competencies (art. 10). The Community Act for the years 1995-1997 enacted in April 1998 modified the procedure, extending the power to convene the Community session of the State-Regions Conference to the Regions as well, and explicitly entrusting to them the power to give their opinions on the Bill for the Community Act (art. 10). The same act provides that regions can send proposals to the Government in their fields of competence, in order to influence the content of national regulations implementing Community acts. Finally, the Community act of 2000 compels the Government to transmit to Parliament and the Regions all projects related to EC and EU acts. In this way Regions can also intervene proactively, without having to wait for governmental input.

The 1998 Act also modifies a rule concerning the composition of the Italian permanent delegation (*rappresentanza permanente*) at the European Union, and adds one more member appointed by the Conference of the Regional Presi-

---

achieved by the Member States and can therefore, by reason of the scale or effects of the proposed action, be better achieved by the Community."

[113] Decree of the President of the Council of Ministries, 11-3-1980.

[114] Act 16-4-1987, no. 183, *supra* note 97.

dents.[115] Furthermore, the Minister of Foreign Affairs, in giving directions to the permanent delegation at the EU, is bound to take into consideration the topics that the State-Regions Conference has pointed out as particularly relevant to regional interests.

Finally, Regions can set up offices for relations (*uffici di collegamento*) with European institutions, either separately or along with other Regions or European bodies, in order to favor trans-border cooperation and international agreements.[116] This new rule marks a break with the old idea[117] that Regions could not manage relations with foreign entities by themselves, since this amounted to international activity reserved exclusively to the State.[118] According to the new version of art. 117 Const., following the March 2001 Constitutional reform, regions can make agreements with foreign States or with subnational entities of foreign States. Thus, the rule acknowledges that Regions may play an active and significant role in the process of European integration.

VIII. Concluding Remarks

Following the two dimensions of development outlined above – time and the vertical-horizontal dimension – we can now suggest a few conclusions.

The first period – roughly the 1960s through the 1970s – was marked by a search for a solid foundation upon which to ground Italy's participation in the European process of integration and the subsequent devolution of powers. This process was led by the Constitutional Court which, in spite of the weakness stemming from the transposition of the Treaties through ordinary statutes, managed to find a suitable constitutional basis through a broad interpretation of Article 11 of the Italian Constitution. The succeeding phase centered on the definition of the

---

[115] The rule was part of the Community Act for 1994, passed in 1996 (Act 6-2-1996, no. 52, art. 58 (2)); it added some regional representatives to the *rappresentanza permanente* at the EU.

[116] *See* act no. 128 of 1999, art. 13, c. I.

[117] DPR 31-3-1994. According to the decree, Regions can have direct relations with Community institutions and bodies for information and preparatory activities. This implies, for the first time, a differentiation of the legal regime between Community matters and other international relationship.

[118] *See* Constitutional Court decision 9-4-1963, no. 49; *Presidente del Consiglio v. Regione Puglia*, 22-5-1987, no. 179, in *Foro it.*, 1989, I, 2121; *Presidente del Consiglio v. Provincia autonoma di Bolzano*, 23-12-1997, no. 428 in *Riv. it. dir. pubbl. com.*, 1998, 241 *Foro it.*, 1998, I, 706.

respective spheres of competence of Community and internal law, streamlining the inevitable areas of interaction. After a period of divergence from the Court of Justice, the Constitutional Court acknowledged the primacy of Community law, eliminating the requirement of judicial review, and entrusting all judges (and later all public entities) with the task of guaranteeing the application of Community law in place of conflicting internal rules. The last area of intervention, which was developed simultaneously by the Italian and the European judges, was the enlargement of the body of Community rules having direct effect, which has entailed the strengthening of the role of individuals, who can ask for the protection of their rights at both levels, indirectly favoring a broad and uniform application of Community law. This change has been driven forcefully by lower court judges, who have made extensive use of both judicial review and preliminary reference procedures.

The role of the Italian Parliament displays some ambiguity because, although it has always demonstrated a very favorable stance toward the European integrating process, its performance both in the definition of Community policies and in their implementation in the national legal system has often been unsatisfactory. The problem of the ascending phase (*i.e.* the formulation of policies at the Community level) has been tackled by increasing the flow of information from the Government (which is the leading internal actor in the Community), to Parliament, and by entrusting the competent Parliamentary commissions with greater powers of proposal and control over governmental action. In spite of their technical accomplishments, these institutional devices do not seem to have a significant practical impact. The descending phase, *i.e.* the implementation of Community measures in the national legal system, has been characterized in its first decades by sporadic and unsystematic intervention. The frequent failure of implementation has led to the creation of new mechanisms in the late 1980s, the most relevant being the Parliament's obligation to pass a yearly Community Act implementing all pending Community measures and obligations. This new framework has proved rather successful, but it entails a significant shift of power from Parliament to the executive branch, since in most cases the former only establishes guidelines, while actual implementation is left to delegated legislation and regulations.

The Italian Constitutional structure is based on a division of competencies between the State and lower levels, of which Regions are the most important. This division of powers, which has been marked by a gradual increase of regional tasks from the internal point of view, has been significantly affected by Community law, which often intervenes in areas that fall within areas of local competence (agriculture, environmental protection, tourism, vocation training, etc.). The process of integration has pushed in an opposite direction with respect to the internal one;

the State which is the only subject responsible for the performance of obligations at the Community level has tended to centralize the management of all Community issues. In the 1980s and 1990s, several statutes have been passed to guarantee regional competence both in the ascending and descending phases. While the role of Regions in defining Community policies remains marginal (due in part to their lack of institutional representation in the EC), some significant progress has been made on the issue of the implementation of Community measures.

The integration of the Community and the Italian legal systems is a dynamic process, and it is difficult to foresee its evolving patterns. Evolution will depend upon different political, economic and social variables. Yet there is one element that will surely be central in future developments: at both Community and national levels, the deepening integration has resulted in a gradual yet significant concentration of powers in bodies lacking direct democratic legitimacy (such as the Commission and Council of Ministers at the Community level, and Government, local administrations, and agencies at the State level). No redefinition of the European institutional framework has counterbalanced the loss of power by national Parliaments. In this sense, the increased role of the European Parliament, although positive, is only a partial solution. What we need is a new model of interaction between the EU, the member States, and their internal subdivisions capable of organizing a system of relations that has moved a long way from the original system. The core of this development could probably be centered around the principle of subsidiarity, with its flexible division of competencies among all institutional levels.

IX. Bibliography

G. Benacchio, *Diritto privato della Comunità europea – Fonti, modelli, regole*, Padova (1998).

M. Cartabia, *Principi inviolabili e integrazione europea*, Milano (1995).

M. Cartabia, "*L'ordinamento italiano e la comunità europea*," in B. Beutler, R. Bieber, J. Pipkorn, J. Streil, J.H.H. Weiler, *L'Unione europea – Istituzioni, ordinamento e politiche*, Bologna (1998), 111.

M. Cartabia, J.H.H. Weiler, *L'Italia in Europa – Profili istituzionali e costituzionali*, Bologna (2000).

P. Craig, G. de Burca, *EU Law – Text, Cases and Materials*, 2nd ed., Oxford (1998).

F. Donati, *Diritto comunitario e sindacato di costituzionalità*, Milano (1995).

G. Falcon (ed.), *Lo Stato autonomista*, Bologna (1998).

G. Gaja, "New Developments in a Continuing Story. the Relationship between EEC Law and Italian Law," in *CMLRev* (1990), 83.

A. La Pergola, P. Del Duca, *Community Law, International Law and the Italian Constitution*, in *AmJIntL* (1985) 598.

F. Musio, *Comunità europea, Stato e Regione*, Milano (1994).

P. Perlingeri, *Diritto comunitario e legalità costituzionale. Per un sistema italo-comunitario delle fonti*, Napoli (1992).

R. Petriccione, "Italy: Supremacy of Community Law over National Law," *ELRev* (1986), 320.

H.G. Schermers, D. Waelbroek, *Judicial Protection in the European Communities*, 5th ed., Deventer (1992).

A. Stone Sweet, *Governing with Judges: Constitutional Politics in Europe*, Oxford (2000).

G. Tesauro, "*Procedura di adeguamento al diritto comunitario: problemi antichi e nuovi propositi*," in *Riv. it. dir. pubbl. com.* (1992), 385.

A. Tizzano, "*L'articolazione del diritto comunitario e di quello interno*," in *Riv. dir. eur.* (1994), 651.

CHAPTER FIVE

Machinery of Justice

Vincenzo Varano [1]

I. Introduction

The structure of the administration of justice in Italy is rather typical of the civil law approach. With regard to the organization of courts, like most civil law countries, Italy is characterized by a plurality of court hierarchies, as opposed to common law countries, in which Court organization is based on the principle of a single court hierarchy. In Italy, one finds the ordinary courts on one side dealing with civil and criminal matters, and the administrative courts on the other side dealing generally with public law disputes. We shall limit our description of the machinery of justice in Italy to these two sets of courts, which are undoubtedly its most important components. However, the reader should be aware that besides the Constitutional Court, which is dealt with extensively in other chapters of this book, there are several other courts dealing with special subjects.[2] The other feature which

---

[1] Professor of Comparative Law, University of Florence. This chapter is updated to 31 May 2001.

[2] Among the various special courts, three are particularly worthy of mention. First, there are the juvenile courts (*tribunali per i minorenni*) attached to each court of appeal; these courts have broad civil and criminal jurisdiction whenever minors are involved. The *tribunali per i minorenni* adjudicate as a mixed bench of professional judges and two social workers – one male, one female. The *tribunali per i minorenni* are regulated by royal decree no. 1404 of 20 July 1934, as amended. Secondly, cases involving public water rights are heard by regional tribunals of public waters (*tribunali regionali delle acque pubbliche*) which are attached to some courts of appeal and adjudicate in panels of three judges, one of whom is an expert. The superior tribunal of public waters (*tribunale superiore delle acque pubbliche*) is the appellate tribunal. This tribunal sits in Rome, is chaired by a high ranking judge of the *Corte di Cassazione* (Supreme Court) and is composed of five ordinary judges, four administrative judges, and three experts. Cases are heard by panels of five or seven judges depending on the circumstances. These tribunals are regulated by arts. 138-210 of royal decree no. 1775

Jeffrey S. Lena and Ugo Mattei (eds.), *Introduction to Italian Law*, 99-124
©2002 Kluwer Law International. Printed in the Netherlands.

Italy shares with other civil law countries is that the core of its judiciary is made up of career judges.

This traditional picture, which has remained practically unaltered in its basic features since the political unification of Italy in 1861, underwent profound changes in the late 1980s and 1990s due to a number of reforms, some of which are still underway. Some of the reforms deal with procedure. Foremost among them is the new Code of Criminal Procedure, enacted by legislative decree no. 447 of 22 September 1988 and effective since 24 October 1989. It replaced the previous 1930 Code based on a judge-dominated trial with a more adversarial procedure, but on the whole it cannot be said that the reform has been entirely successful, given that the Code has been repeatedly modified by numerous decisions of the Constitutional Court and amending statutes. Also very important is law no. 353 of 26 November 1990, effective since 1 May 1995, which enacted "emergency measures for civil procedure." Other reforms, which are of more immediate concern here, deal with the administration of justice, and are mainly the result of the bankruptcy of the system of civil and criminal justice in Italy, which is plagued by intolerable delays and which results in a real denial of justice.[3] The reforms do not change the basic features of the administration of justice sketched above – a plurality of court hierarchies and career judiciary remain fixed features of the Italian system. But the reforms are a significant contribution to a comprehensive project of renewal

---

of 11 December 1933. Thirdly, mention should be made of the tax courts (*commissioni tributarie*), which are very important and sit as first instance provincial courts and appellate regional courts, presided over by ordinary or administrative judges, and composed of people who have an adequate legal or economic qualification. The most important reform introduced by legislative decree nos. 545 and 546 of 31 December 1992, is that appeals from the decisions of the regional tax courts are taken to the Supreme Court on the grounds indicated by art. 360 para. 1 CPC.

[3] For some statistical data, *see* II. E. *infra*. The level of delay reached in Italy has given rise to many complaints to the European Court of Human Rights for violation of art. 6 para. 1 of the European Convention for the Protection of Human Rights and Fundamental Freedoms, according to which "in the determination of his civil rights and obligations or of any criminal charge against him, everyone is entitled to a fair and public hearing *within a reasonable time* ..." [italics added]. As to the cases decided by the Strasbourg Court against Italy, *see*, *e.g.*, *Capuano v. Italy* (1991), 13 *EHRR* 271; *Santilli v. Italy* (1992), 14 *EHRR* 421; *Massa v. Italy* (1994), 18 *EHRR* 266; *Paccione v. Italy* (1995), 20 *EHRR* 396. The *Consiglio Superiore della Magistratura*, *i.e.* the governing body of the judiciary (*see* III B *infra*), has recently published a volume on the problem of delay: *La durata ragionevole del processo* (2000). The principle of "reasonable delay" is now expressly mentioned in art. 111, para 2 of the Constitution as an essential component of the guarantee of due process of law (*giusto processo*) introduced by Constitutional law no. 2 of 23 November 1999.

of antiquated machinery. On the one hand, the reforms emphasize the role and the contribution of a non-professional judiciary. I refer to the new justices of the peace (*giudici di pace, see* part II A, below), with jurisdiction over minor civil and criminal cases; and to the so-called *sezioni stralcio* (*see* part II B, below), which are special temporary divisions of the "*tribunali*," introduced to deal with the civil proceedings pending on April 30, 1995, and which are chaired by professional judges but staffed by honorary judges appointed from among lawyers, notaries, and law professors. On the other hand, the reforms rationalize the administration of justice in the first instance by merging the "*preture*" and the "*tribunali*" into one court of first instance of general civil and criminal jurisdiction. The "*tribunale*," normally sits as a single-judge court, with only the most serious civil and criminal cases being reserved to a three-judge panel. Last but not least, the selection process of ordinary judges has also been recently reformed.

II. Organization of Ordinary Courts

Following the reforms which have been enacted in the last few years, and those to which we referred in the preceding paragraph, the system of civil courts in Italy is presently based on the following pattern: the justices of the peace are at the bottom of the hierarchy; the *tribunale* is the court of first instance of general jurisdiction; the appeals court ("*corte d'appello*") is the court of appeal at the intermediate level; and finally, the Italian Supreme Court (*Corte di Cassazione*) is the court of last resort for non-constitutional controversies. The criminal justice system follows the same pattern. The justices of the peace will begin to exercise their criminal jurisdiction on January 2, 2002, according to law no. 163 of 3 May 2001.[4]

A. The Justices of the Peace

Law no. 374 of 21 November 1991 replaces the old *conciliatori* with 4,700 justices of the peace (art. 3), distributed over 828 offices. According to some commentators, the new justices of the peace have succeeded in relieving the ordinary courts of first instance of about one fourth of their present workload.[5]

The new justice of the peace is an honorary, rather than a career judge, appointed by the *Consiglio Superiore della Magistratura* (Superior Council of the Judiciary,

---

[4] On the criminal jurisdiction of the justices of the peace, *see* Tonini, *Manuale di procedura penale* 3rd ed. (2001, forthcoming), ch. III.

[5] *See* Proto Pisani, *Lezioni di diritto processuale civile* 3rd ed. (1999), p. 17.

discussed below at III B) for a term of four years, renewable only once. He or she is a law graduate, at least thirty years old, and receives compensation based upon the amount of work done. The position is not compatible with any private or public employment; justices of the peace who are practicing attorneys cannot appear before the office at which they must discharge their judicial functions. All this suggests a conception of the office as a full-time job, radically different from the *conciliatore*, a lay judge whose office was without pay.

The civil jurisdiction of the justice of the peace extends to controversies over movables up to five million lire (roughly US$ 2,500), as well as controversies for the recovery of damages arising from the circulation of motor vehicles and motor boats up to the amount of thirty million lire (roughly US$ 15,000). The justice of the peace also has an interesting subject-matter jurisdiction over neighborhood-related controversies (including cases of nuisance), not to mention a broad extra-judicial conciliatory function which, however, based on the experience of the *conciliatore*, may very well turn out to be a failure.[6] The criminal jurisdiction of justices of the peace extends to minor offenses, where the sentence does not provide for imprisonment.[7]

The procedure before the justices of the peace is not as informal as many would have expected, and as had been recommended. Especially as far as the proof-taking activity is concerned (which remains modeled on that before the higher courts), it is bound to be long, non-concentrated, formalistic, and inefficient. It is probably also for this reason that the parties are required to be assisted by a lawyer if the amount at stake exceeds the relatively paltry sum of one million lire (roughly US$ 500).[8]

The judgments of the justices of the peace may be appealed to the *tribunali*.[9] Nonetheless, art. 339 of the Code of Civil Procedure (CPC) establishes that there

---

[6] The jurisdiction of the justice of the peace is spelled out in art. 7 of the Code of Civil Procedure, as reformed by art. 17 of law no. 374 of 1991. As to the extra-judicial conciliatory function of the justices of the peace, *see* art. 322 of the CPC, as reformed by art. 31 of the law no. 374. For doubts on the effectiveness of the latter provision, *see* Comoglio, Ferri & Taruffo, *Lezioni sul processo civile*, 2nd ed. (1998), p. 142.

[7] *See* Tonini, *supra* note 3.

[8] *See* art. 82 para. 1 of the CPC, as amended by art. 20 of law no. 374 of 1991. Para. 2 of the same art. 82 provides that the justices of the peace may allow the party to appear in person beyond the limits indicated in para. 1, in consideration of the nature of the case and the amount at stake.

[9] *See* art. 9 of the legislative decree no. 51 of 19 February 1998, instituting single-judge courts in first instance.

is no right of appeal against a justice of the peace's equitable decisions (*i.e.*, decisions where the amount at stake is not higher than two million lire – art. 113 CPC). These can only be attacked before the Supreme Court (*see* art. 360 para. 1 CPC).

Although it may still be too early to assess the success of the reform introducing the justice of the peace for civil cases, the overall impression is positive, and it has been confirmed authoritatively by the General Prosecutors attached to the Supreme Court in their Reports on the Administration of Justice for the last three years. As a matter of fact, the workload is so substantial that there are signs of a troublesome growth of backlog and delay.[10]

B. The *Giudice Unico di Primo Grado* (The Merger of *Preture* and *Tribunali* and the Institution of Single-Judge Courts)

As already anticipated, legislative decree no. 51 of 19 February 1998, pursuant to enabling law no. 254 of 16 July 1997,[11] finally introduced the single-judge court of first instance – a long-advocated reform whose purpose is to favor a more rational distribution of judicial resources by merging the offices of the *pretori* and the *tribunali*. Also conducive to the reform of 1998 is the fact that the 1990 reform, besides increasing the civil jurisdiction of the *pretori* to controversies up to fifty million lire (roughly US$ 25,000), leaving untouched the cases where they had unlimited subject matter jurisdiction,[12] had set the principle that the *tribunale* sits normally as a single-judge court in civil matters, subject to a limited number of

---

[10] *See, e.g.*, the last report by the General Prosecutor Francesco Favara, *Relazione sull' Amministrazione della Giustizia nell'Anno 2000* (Rome, 12 January 2001), p. 50. For some statistical data, *see* II E, *infra*. The same report, however, underscores that, though the new honorary magistracy can boast good productivity, the workload is increasing, and is bound to increase even more as of 2 January 2002, when the justices of the peace will begin to hear criminal cases also. It is worrisome that the average duration of civil proceedings has already moved upwards from 241 days in the year 1999 to 269 days in the year 2000. The Report of Judge Favara can be viewed at http://www.giustizia.it/studierapporti/ag2001/cass2001index. htm.

[11] On 15 July 1996, the Superior Council of the Judiciary published its annual Report to Parliament on the state of the administration of justice, advocating this reform; *see Giudice unico di primo grado e revisione della geografia giudiziaria* (1996). The Government approved an analogous reform proposal and submitted it to Parliament, which quickly enacted the law.

[12] *See* art. 8 of the CPC, as reformed by art. 3 of law no. 353 of 1990.

exceptions, concerning cases considered to be more complex.[13] The reform became effective on 2 June 1999 as far as civil cases are concerned, while decree law no. 145 of 24 May 1999 had delayed the coming into effect of the reform with respect to criminal cases until 2 January 2000. In order to have a full understanding of its impact, it may be useful to offer to the reader a very concise summary of the jurisdiction of the old *pretori* and *tribunali*.

The *pretori*, who have always sat as single judges, had criminal jurisdiction over certain minor crimes (art. 7 of the Code of Criminal Procedure, CCrPr), and a wide civil jurisdiction over cases up to fifty million lire (insofar as they did not fall within the subject matter jurisdiction of the justices of the peace), and over certain other matters specifically indicated by law (art. 8 CPC). Particularly important areas of jurisdiction had been vested, in recent years, in the *pretori*, especially in the fields of the protection of workers' rights in connection with their trade union affiliations (law no. 300 of 20 May 1970, especially arts. 18 and 28) and individual labor and welfare benefits disputes (arts. 409-447 CPC as modified by the law no. 533 of 11 August 1973). The offices of the *pretori* (called *preture*) had been reorganized by law no. 30 of 1 February 1989, so that on the eve of the 1998 reform there were 165 of them.

The *tribunali*, of which there were 164, were the courts of first instance of general jurisdiction over civil (art. 9 CPC) and criminal (art. 6 CCrPr) cases, and had appellate jurisdiction against the judgments of the justices of the peace and the *pretori* in civil cases (art. 341 CPC). In both capacities, the *tribunali* used to sit as three-judge panels; after the reform of 1990, they sit as single judges when deciding most civil cases in the first instance.

The first important idea of the 1998 reform was to create a single professional court of first instance by abolishing the offices of the *pretori* and the prosecutors' offices attached to them, and transferring their jurisdiction and functions respectively to the *tribunali* and the related prosecutors' offices (arts. 1 and 2 of legislative decree no. 51 of 1998). Consequently, the *tribunale* became the court of first instance of general jurisdiction over criminal, civil, labor, and social security matters, and at the same time the court before which appeals are brought from the civil decisions of the justices of the peace (art. 9 of legislative decree no. 51 of 1998).

---

[13] *See* art. 48 of royal decree no. 12 of 30 January 1941, as reformed by art. 88 of law no. 353 of 1990. On the aspiration to generalize single-judge courts in the first instance, *see* Denti, *"Giudice onorario e giudice monocratico nella riforma della giustizia civile,"* 33 *Rivista di Diritto Processuale* 609 (1978), 622-30; Cappelletti, *Giustizia e società* (1972), pp. 119-20.

Since the 1998 reform took effect, Italy has had 164 *tribunali* and 218 branch sections, replacing an equal number of *preture* and old branch sections. This guarantees that the *tribunali* extend throughout Italy, and that they are as close to the citizens as the old *preture*.

Secondly, the reform of 1998 extends the idea that the first instance court sits, as a rule, as a single-judge court for criminal proceedings (art. 14).[14] Articles 56 and 169 of the 1998 legislative decree amended the Codes of Civil and Criminal Procedure, and indicate the cases in which the *tribunale* is required to sit in panels of three judges. In general, it can be said that jurisdiction is vested in the three-judge panel when the questions involved are more serious or technically complicated. The reader should also bear in mind that in criminal matters, there is a special section of the *tribunale*, the so-called *corte d'assise*, which hears the most serious cases (*e.g.* crimes leading to a sentence of life imprisonment; *see* art. 5 CCrPr). This Court has been left untouched by the reform. The *corte d'assise* sits with two ordinary judges (one of whom has the status of a court of appeals judge and presides over it) and six laymen acting as popular judges. Contrary to what happens in a common law jurisdiction when cases are heard by a judge and a jury, judges and laymen decide together on the facts as well as the law. A majority vote convicts, and a tied vote acquits.

Concerning the new *tribunali*, mention should also be made of arts. 8 and 21 of legislative decree no. 51 of 1998, which institute, although on a temporary basis (art. 245), the honorary judges of the *tribunali* and the honorary prosecutors attached to them. The rules governing their appointment, their terms of office, their duties and rights, and the professional incompatibility rules they are subject to are analytically spelled out and are largely modeled on the rules established by law no. 374 of 1991 for the justices of the peace. Article 10 of the decree provides that the honorary judges can hear cases when ordinary judges are missing or unavailable. Furthermore, the same provision, together with art. 23 of the decree, provides that certain cases cannot be dealt with by honorary judges and prosecutors. These include cases concerning provisional or possessory remedies, or cases which may lead to a sentence of over four years of imprisonment.

Another reform, which has particular bearing on the administration of civil justice by the *tribunali*, was introduced by law no. 276 of 22 July 1997. This statute must

---

[14] It is fair to say that the reform has not been well received as far as criminal cases are concerned. Criticisms are mainly directed toward the seriousness of the sentence – up to ten years' imprisonment – which the single-judge court is empowered to impose. *See, e.g.*, Tonini, *Manuale di procedura penale* 2nd ed. (2000), pp. 75-77.

be seen in connection with the above-mentioned law no. 353 of 26 November 1990, enacting "emergency measures for civil procedure," pursuant to which the proceedings pending on the effective date were to be decided according to the old procedural rules. The law eventually went into effect on 30 April 1995, on which date a record of almost three million proceedings were pending, compared with the 1,700,000 pending at the end of 1989. Such a backlog could have nullified any beneficial effect of the procedural reform at its very outset. Law no. 276 of 1997 aims at solving this problem by instituting special divisions in each *tribunale* to deal exclusively with the backlog. The peculiar feature of the *sezioni stralcio* is that they are chaired by a professional judge and staffed with honorary judges (called *giudici onorari aggregati*) selected for a five-year term from among retired judges, law professors, attorneys (provided they practice in another district), and notaries. It is assumed that these special divisions, which began to function on 11 November 1998 and which decide cases as a single-judge court, should dispose of the backlog in five years, after which they are to be dissolved.[15]

C. The Intermediate Appellate Courts

There are twenty-six courts of appeal in Italy. Each of them has jurisdiction over a district which generally corresponds to a region of the country. However, there are regions in which there is no court of appeal (such as Valle d'Aosta, which falls within the district of the court of appeal of Turin in Piedmont), and others in which there are several districts (Lombardy, Puglia, Calabria, and Campania have two court-of-appeal districts, while Sicily has four).

The courts of appeal sit in three-judge panels, according to law no. 532 of 8 August 1977. Until then, panels had been composed of five judges. The courts of appeal decide over appeals against civil and criminal judgments rendered by the *tribunali* in their capacity of courts of first instance (art. 341 CPC; art. 596 CCrPr).[16] Labor proceedings, which are now brought before the *tribunali* in the first instance, are reviewed on appeal by special divisions instituted in each court of appeal

---

[15] According to the General Prosecutor attached to the Court of Cassation, in his Report quoted *supra*, note 10, at p. 49, the success of the special divisions is uneven throughout Italy, due especially to the difficulty of recruiting enough honorary judges. Law no. 276 of 1997 provided for the appointment of 1,000 judges; the divisions began to operate with roughly only 300 judges. Another 400 were appointed in the year 2000.

[16] Prior to the reform introducing the single-judge court of first instance, appeals against criminal judgments of the *pretori* were also brought before the courts of appeal.

(art. 38 of legislative decree no. 51 of 1998).

The right of appeal has no constitutional basis in the Italian legal system, though it is so deeply rooted in tradition as to be considered, as in other civil law countries, a part of the fundamental guarantee of a fair hearing in both civil and criminal cases.[17] As a rule, appeal involves a full review of the whole case and is not limited to questions of law.

With particular reference to civil appeals, mention must be made of the trend, inaugurated by law no. 533 of 11 August 1973, concerned with individual labor disputes, and culminating in the general reform brought about by law no. 353 of 1990, regarding the limitation of the scope of appeal and the revaluation of first instance proceedings. Article 345 CPC, as amended by law no. 353 of 1990, confirms that new claims cannot be introduced on appeal – and if introduced, they must be dismissed by the court on its own motion, unless they are limited to interests, rents, profits, and the like, which mature after the rendering of the judgment below (along with the recovery of damages consequent to it). However, contrary to the previous system, new defenses and new evidence cannot be introduced, with a few minor exceptions. New defenses can be employed if they could also be raised *ex officio* – such as in the lack of jurisdiction of the ordinary courts on the case (art. 37 para. 1 CPC) or the nullity of a contract (art. 1421 CPC). In turn, new evidence can be introduced, if either the court considers it indispensable to deciding the case, or if the party shows that he could not introduce it through no fault of his own. Article 282 CPC as amended provides, by extending the principle accepted for the first time by law no. 533 of 1973, that the first instance decision is now immediately enforceable, subject to the possibility for the court of appeal, upon request of the interested party, to suspend the enforcement for serious reasons. In time, the two reforms should reduce that peculiar phenomenon of the Italian system of civil procedure which has been defined as a "devaluation of proceedings of the first instance and a glorification of attacks."[18]

With particular regard to criminal appellate proceedings, which in general follow the same pattern as civil appellate proceedings, it is interesting to note that when the appeal is made by the accused only, the appellate court cannot impose a more

---

[17] The guarantee of a double degree of jurisdiction was introduced by art. 131 of the Project of Constitutional Revision of the *Commissione Bicamerale per le Riforme Costituzionali*, published in November 1997, which, however, did not have any legislative sequel. On the works of the *Commissione, see* Caretti (ed.), *La riforma della Costituzione nel progetto della bicamerale* (1998); and Costanzo *et al.*, *La Commissione bicamerale per le riforme costituzionali* (1998).

[18] Cappelletti, *supra* note 13, at 116-17.

severe penalty (art. 597 para. 3 CCrPr). Also noteworthy is that appeals from the *corti d'assise*[19] go to a special criminal court, called *corte d'assise d'appello*, composed of two professional judges, a judge of the court of appeals, six lay judges, and a judge having the status of judge of the Supreme Court, who presides over it.

D. The Italian Supreme Court (*Corte di Cassazione*)

The Supreme Court, which sits in Rome, is the highest court in civil and criminal matters, and reviews only errors of law (art. 360 CPC; art. 606 CCrPr). Only appellate judgments can be reviewed by the Supreme Court, or judgments which may not be appealed either by law (such as judgments based on equity; *see* art. 339 CPC; for criminal cases, *see* art. 593 CCrPr) or by agreement of the parties (art. 360 para. 2 CPC; for criminal cases, *see* art. 569 CCrPr).

The function of the Supreme Court is not only that of reviewing appellate or non-appealable judgments. According to art. 65 of the royal decree of 30 January 1941, which is the basic law on court organization, the Court, "as the supreme court of justice, ... assures the exact observance and the uniform interpretation of the law, the unity of national law ..."

The Supreme Court is divided into three civil and six criminal divisions, each sitting with five members (seven prior to the law no. 532 of 8 August 1977, art. 3). A labor division was introduced by the law no. 533 of 8 August 1977. Following the legislative decree no. 545 of 31 December 1992, effective from April 1996, the first civil division of the Court was vested with jurisdiction over appeals from the decisions of the regional tax courts (*commissioni tributarie regionali*).[20] To give the reader an idea of the workload caused by this extension of jurisdiction, 4,210 such appeals were pending on 30 November 1998, 3,172 of which were filed during 1998.[21]

In certain cases, especially when there is a conflict between different divisions of the court, or in civil cases when the case involves a question of particular importance, the decision is rendered by a plenary session (*sezioni unite*), sitting as a nine-judge panel (fifteen prior to law no. 532 of 8 August 1977; arts. 374 and 376 CPC; art. 618 CCrPr).

---

[19] *See* part II B, *supra.*

[20] *See supra* note 2.

[21] For these data, *see* A. La Torre, "*Relazione sull'amministrazione della giustizia nell'anno 1998*" (Rome, 9 January 1999), at p. 5. They have not been updated in the latest "*Relazione*" by Judge Favara, *supra* note 10.

Unlike appeal, review by the Supreme Court has a constitutional basis in art. 111 para. 2 Const., according to which "recourse shall always be allowed to the *Corte di Cassazione*, on the ground of violation of law, against judgments as well as rulings affecting personal liberty, whether pronounced by courts of ordinary or of special jurisdiction." This does not mean, however, that review does not suffer from anachronisms. First of all, this provision has been interpreted extensively by the Court itself, which has held that not only formal judgments, but also other rulings (*ordinanze, decreti*) that have a decisive effect and are capable of attaining a *res judicata* effect are included in the guarantee.[22] Secondly, the grounds for review of judgments specified by art. 360 CPC, or by art. 606 CCrPr exceed the constitutional requirement that provides review of judgments on account of violation of law, and some of them have actually opened the door to review of questions of fact. The classic example is given by art. 360, no. 5 CPC, which allows recourse for omissions, or for insufficient or contradictory reasons for the decision of an essential point of the controversy, which has been raised by the parties, or which *could have been* raised by the court below on its own motion. Clearly, this wording, which was introduced in the Code by law no. 581 of 14 July 1950, reflects the aspiration of some scholars, and above all of practicing lawyers to transform review into a third instance.[23] In fact, this clause, abused by practicing lawyers, authorizes the court to review findings of fact in the attacked judgment when the explanation given for them has been omitted, or is insufficient or contradictory. Article 360, no. 5 clearly paves the way for the Court to review the evidence, both from the point of view of violation of the rules governing its relevance and admissibility, and from that of its evaluation.[24] Even if the Court has shown that it is prepared to quash the attacked judgment only when the inadequacy and logical inconsistency

---

[22] This is the interpretation inaugurated by the Court in its judgment no. 2593 of 30 July 1953, 78 *Foro it.* I, 1240 (1953).

[23] The original wording of art. 360, no. 5 of the CPC only allowed omission of explanation as a ground for review; *see* Cappelletti & Perillo, *Civil Procedure in Italy* (1965), p. 276, fn. 150. The Code of Criminal Procedure contains provisions to the same effect (*see, e.g.,* art. 606 para. 1e), which also allows control over the explanation given by the lower court. *See* Tonini, *supra* note 14, at pp. 623-26. In addition, one must consider that the presumption of innocence operates in the Italian legal system until a final decision has been rendered (art. 27 para. 2 Const.), which in most cases means a judgment by the Supreme Court. This provides another incentive to recourse due to the possibility of benefiting from the statute of limitations, or from an amnesty.

[24] For further discussion, *see* Proto Pisani, *supra* note 5, at 557-61; *see also* Comoglio, Ferri & Taruffo, *supra* note 6, at 842.

of the reasons is so serious as to amount to a clear injustice of the decision, art. 360, no. 5 is much criticized today as being at least in part responsible for the heavy workload of the Supreme Court.[25]

The Italian Supreme Court is based on the French model introduced after the Revolution of 1789. This means that it either affirms the judgment from below, which then becomes final, or quashes it. In the latter case, the Court cannot normally render a judgment of its own, but must remand the case for a new decision to a different court, on the same level as the court that rendered the judgment that has been quashed.[26]

The guarantee of art. 111 Const. – a peculiar feature of the Italian legal system – and its expansive interpretation, as well as some of the grounds for review indicated by the procedural codes, have flooded the Court with several thousand applications every year, and resulted in a dramatic rise in the average duration of the proceedings before the Court. However, the introduction of such filters as the American *certiorari* or the British *leave to apply* would not only require a substantial departure from our legal tradition, but perhaps a constitutional amendment as well. This does not seem foreseeable, at least in the near future.[27]

As to the style and authority of appellate judgments, and in particular those of Supreme Court judgments, first they must state, as in any other judicial ruling, the

---

[25] *See*, generally, Comoglio, Ferri & Taruffo, *supra* note 6, at 841*ff*. For some statistical data concerning the workload of the Supreme Court, *see* part II E, *infra*.

[26] A recent innovation concerns art. 384 CPC as amended by law no. 353 of 1990, according to which the Court, when it reverses the judgment for violation or misapplication of rules of law (*i.e.*, the ground provided for by art. 360 para. 3 of the same Code), can decide the case without remanding it to the lower court, if no other findings of fact are deemed to be necessary. A more recent reform, which expands the jurisdiction of the Supreme Court to decide in chambers, has been brought about by law no. 89 of 24 March 2001, modifying art. 375 of the CPC.

[27] The debate on the *Corte di Cassazione* and its reform, so as to allow it to better perform the function spelled out in art. 65 of the law on judicial organization, has been extremely lively in the last decade or so; *see*, *e.g.*, the contributions collected in *Per la Corte di Cassazione*, 112 *Foro it.* V, 205 (1987); *La Cassazione civile*, 113 *Foro it.* V, 1 (1988); *La Cassazione penale: problemi di funzionamento e di ruolo*, *id.* at 441 *ff. See also* Denti, "*Commento all'art. 111*," in *Commentario alla Costituzione* a cura di G. Branca, *La magistratura*, IV, arts. 111-113 (1987), at 1; Mannuzzu & Sestini (eds.), *Il giudizio di Cassazione nel sistema delle impugnazioni* (1992). An interesting proposal was included in art. 131 of the Project of the *Commissione Bicamerale per le Riforme Costituzionali*, *supra* note 17, which would have left to the legislature the right to indicate the grounds for review and, consequently, to limit review by the Supreme Court, even radically.

reasons for the decision, as prescribed by art. 111 para. 1 Const.[28] Secondly, and contrary to the practice in common law countries, separate opinions – whether dissenting or concurring – are not announced. In other words, appellate decisions appear as unanimous and anonymous decisions of the Court.[29] Thirdly, decisions, even if issued by the plenary session of the Supreme Court, do not bind lower courts, as would be the case in a common law jurisdiction, although they do enjoy a strong persuasive authority. As a matter of fact, previous decisions, especially if consistently sanctioned by the Supreme Court, will usually be followed by the Supreme Court itself. Departure from them, even if legitimate in theory and correct in practice, must be carefully explained.[30]

E. Workload and Delay

Certain available statistics produce a more complete view of the excessive duration of civil and criminal proceedings which has often been referred to, and complained about, as an intolerable feature of the administration of justice in Italy, especially for the poorer and weaker sections of the community.

Unless otherwise indicated, the statistics relate to the year 1999, and are the

---

[28] On the guarantee of a reasoned decision, which "represents the ultimate development of a principle which has been solemnly affirmed by the French revolution ... and insures a basic tool for review of judicial action by appellate courts," *see* Cappelletti & Vigoriti, "Fundamental Guarantees of the Litigants in Civil Proceedings. Italy," in Cappelletti & Tallon (eds.), *Fundamental Guarantees of the Parties in Civil Litigation* (1973), pp. 556-57; Taruffo, *La motivazione della sentenza civile* (1975), pp. 319-470.

[29] For criticisms, and suggestions of abolition of the secrecy of judicial decisions, *see* Denti, "*Per il ritorno al voto di scissura nelle decisioni giudiziarie,*" in Mortati (ed.), *Le opinioni dissenzienti dei giudici costituzionali ed internazionali* (1964), p. 1; Cappelletti, Merryman & Perillo, *The Italian Legal System* (1967), pp. 129-30, fn. 80, and accompanying text; Anzon (ed.), *L'opinione dissenziente* (1995) (this volume collects the contributions to a seminar organized by the Italian Constitutional Court in November 1993). The Project of constitutional revision drafted by the *Commissione Bicamerale per le Riforme Costituzionali, supra* note 17, art. 136 para. 1, provided that the decisions of the Constitutional Court could be accompanied by dissenting opinions.

[30] On the role of precedents in the Italian legal system, *see* Cappelletti, Merryman & Perillo, *supra* note 29, at 270-74. For a wider perspective on the real role of precedents in the Civil Law world, *see* Cappelletti, "The Doctrine of Stare Decisis and the Civil Law: A Fundamental Difference – or no Difference at All?" in Bernstein, Drobnig & Koetz (eds.), *Festschrift für Konrad Zweigert* (1981), p. 381.

latest available on the website of the Italian Ministry of Justice.[31]

As for civil justice, the number of actions instituted in first instance before all courts in 1999 was 1,536,233, as opposed to the 1,451,833 actions instituted in 1998. 1,480,147 cases were disposed of in the same period. At the end of 1999, a total of 3,575,000 cases were pending before the courts of first instance. This figure shows a slight increase as compared to the previous year's total of 3,200,000 cases. Appellate courts had a backlog of 76,000 cases and the Supreme Court had 49,984 cases.

The figures for the year 1999 indicate that an average of 269 days were needed to dispose of a case before the justices of the peace, and 824 before the *preture*. Cases before the *tribunali* as courts of first instance required 1,343 days; cases before the courts of appeal required 952 days, while proceedings before the Supreme Court took as long as 829 days. Therefore, it can be safely said that an average of roughly ten years is needed for the final determination of a civil dispute through first instance, appeal, and Supreme Court.

As for criminal proceedings, as of 30 June 1999, there was a total of 5,913,557 cases pending in all judicial organs of the country, including both adjudicatory bodies and prosecutorial offices where criminal complaints are filed. As to the number of criminal actions instituted between 1 July 1998 and 30 June 1999, there were 8,895,840; in the same period 8,579,147 criminal actions were disposed of. As to the average duration of criminal proceedings in their trial stage, the figures are as follows: 443 days in the *tribunali*, 370 days in the *corti d'assise*, 601 days in the courts of appeal, and 245 days in the *corti d'assise di appello*. As for the Supreme Court, 51,133 new recourses were filed between 1 July 1999 and 30 June 2000; 51,334 were disposed of, and 23,501 were pending on June 30, 2000, with an average duration of 167 days.[32]

This data, which indicates a worsening situation throughout the years, explain why delay is the most frequent ground for the growing number of applications to the European Court of Human Rights, where decisions against Italy for the violation of the right to a reasonable duration of proceedings, provided for by article 6 of the European Convention, are now countless. "Every day," according to Judge Margherita Cassano of the Superior Council of the Judiciary, "at least four to five decisions are delivered against Italy."[33]

---

[31] http://www.giustizia.it/misc/mgweb2bis.htm

[32] Favara, *supra* note 9, at pp. 59-60.

[33] Cassano, Introduction, in CSM, *supra* note 10, at p. 13. Law no. 89 of 24 March 2001 provides for a fair recovery ("*equa riparazione*") for damages suffered as a consequence of the violation

III. Ordinary Judges and Prosecutors: Selection and Tenure

A. Selection of Judges and Prosecutors

There are presently roughly 8,000 ordinary judges in Italy, over 5,000 of whom are assigned to the administration of criminal justice.[34] This number includes the public prosecutors (*pubblici ministeri*), who are part of the judicial organization according to the Italian Constitution. The prosecutors, who have the duty of prosecution in criminal proceedings (art. 112 Const.), are grouped into prosecutorial offices which are attached to every court level. There is a *Procura della Repubblica* attached to each *tribunale*, a *Procura Generale della Repubblica* attached to each court of appeal, and a *Procura Generale della Repubblica* attached to the Supreme Court. There is no career separation between judges and prosecutors; actually, it is not totally uncommon for a judge to move from judicial to prosecutorial duties and vice versa.

As mentioned at the beginning of this chapter, one of the features which Italy shares with the rest of the civil law world is that ordinary judges are career judges. Access to the judiciary is open to law graduates who must pass a difficult, highly competitive national examination. Successful candidates then must go through a period of apprenticeship as *uditori giudiziari* which, in theory, lasts two years. Afterwards, they become full judges and advance in their career as judges and/or prosecutors, substantially on the basis of seniority. The Constitution assures ordinary judges very strong guarantees of independence (*see* arts. 101-110 Const.).

It is worth examining the various relevant points in greater detail:

1. Article 106 para. 1 Const. affirms the traditional rule that judges are appointed by competition – a rule which is designed to assure that the selection is based only on the ascertainment of technical skills and is immune from political considerations.

The Constitution itself provides for a couple of exceptions. First, art. 106 para. 2 Const. states that honorary judges may be appointed, or even elected, to discharge the functions of single-judge courts, and this has been the case for the justices of the peace and the *sezioni stralcio*, both mentioned above.[35] Article 106 para. 3 Const.

---

by the state of the right "to a fair and public hearing *within a reasonable time*" guaranteed by art. 6.1 of the European Convention.

[34] For these figures, *see* Proto Pisani, *supra* note 5, at 17-19. The number of judges has been increased by 1,000 following the enactment of law no. 48 of 13 February 2001.

[35] *See* parts II A and II B, *supra* (last full paragraph), respectively.

provides, in turn, that for outstanding merit, law professors and attorneys with at least 15 years of experience may be appointed as judges of the Supreme Court – a method of appointment which also existed prior to the enactment of the Constitution (although it had been resorted to very rarely). The provision of art. 106 para. 3 Const. also remained a dead letter for fifty years, until it was implemented by law no. 303 of 5 August 1998. Since then, a handful of such appointments have been made.

The competition to become a judge is based on a national examination held in Rome, normally held once a year, for a number of vacancies which fluctuates between two and three hundred positions annually. It is administered by a Commission appointed by the *Consiglio Superiore della Magistratura* – the governing body of the judiciary, which is discussed below, and composed largely of judges. The examination is very difficult and is largely theoretical. It consists of three written essays on private, criminal, and administrative law. Candidates who have successfully passed the essay portion are then expected to take oral examinations in those subjects as well as a number of other subjects. This method of judicial selection, which dates from the end of the nineteenth century, has been severely criticized, and is presently undergoing a process of reform. The main criticism is that the field, and thus the exam, is overcrowded, due to the enduring prestige of the judicial career (a record number of more than 7,000 candidates participated in the 1994 examination),[36] that it takes too long for an examination to be completed (possibly more than two years),[37] and that it is not well-suited to the selection of the best possible candidates.

Recently, law no. 127 of 15 May 1997, art. 17, paras. 113 and 114, as implemented by legislative decree no. 398 of 17 November 1997 (as amended by art. 17 of law no. 48 of 13 February 2001), has laid down the foundations for a radical reform of the methods of judicial selection. First, a computerized multiple-choice pre-selection procedure has been introduced, which will admit a number of candidates no higher than five times the number of positions to be filled to the actual examination. This is clearly an important measure, though it is intended merely to rationalize the existing selection procedure, rather than to assure a better preparation for prospective judges. This is the purpose of the second and more important reform, introduced by the above-mentioned statutes, which have instituted post-graduate schools where law graduates will receive theoretical and practical training for two years before

---

[36] *See* Giunta, *Il concorso per uditore giudiziario: l'esperienza di un commissario*, 122 *Foro It.* V, 255 (1997), at 256.

[37] *Id.* at 258.

they can take the exam to become judges. The law makes attendance at the school compulsory for judicial candidates who will have enrolled as first-year law students, beginning with the 1999-2000 school year. The other important feature of the newly instituted schools is that they are to be open to potential attorneys and notaries as well, so that, hopefully, it will be possible to recover some sense of unity within the Italian legal profession, whose members – attorneys, judges, and notaries – have been traditionally accustomed to thinking of themselves as belonging to separate professions.[38]

2. The candidate who passes the examination is appointed *uditore giudiziario* and is assigned to a court of first instance or to a prosecutorial office to begin a period of apprenticeship which in theory lasts two years. In practice, after six months, the *uditori giudiziari* may perform judicial functions, so that all available energy can be directed to the tremendous workload and reducing the backlog of the Italian administration of justice.

Following a number of statutes enacted between 1966 and 1979, advancement in the career is based largely on seniority. Promotion is granted unless there are reasons to refuse or postpone it. Thus, the *uditore giudiziario* is eligible for promotion to the status and salary of judge of *tribunale* two years after the appointment; as a judge of *tribunale*, he or she may be appointed to serve as judge in a *tribunale* or as a prosecutor attached to a *tribunale*. After eleven years in this position, the judge may apply to the position of appellate court judge; after seven additional years, the appellate court judge may apply for the position of judge in the Supreme Court. After eight years in the latter position, the judge may aspire to become the head of a higher judicial office.

Two remarks should be made respecting the career of judges. First, promotion to a higher position means that the judge is entitled but not obliged to perform the higher level functions. According to the Constitution, judges may not be removed, and cannot be transferred to other offices or functions without their consent (art. 107 Const.). Therefore, a judge may have the status and the salary of an appellate court judge, but may prefer to continue and serve as a judge of the *tribunale*, and is indeed allowed to do so. As has been rightly pointed out, "[t]here are in all some eight thousand magistrates in Italy and, given a retirement age of seventy, hundreds have the status of office superior while a couple of thousand enjoy the status of judges of *Cassazione*."[39]

---

[38] *See* Merryman, *The Civil Law Tradition*, 2nd ed. (1985), p. 102, and in general the whole of chapter 14 of this volume.

[39] *See* Watkin, *The Italian Legal Tradition* (1997), p. 117.

Secondly, promotions based on seniority certainly foster the internal independence of judges, who until the mid-1960s depended for their career on senior judges (who were essentially expected to evaluate their written judicial opinions). On the other hand, it is unanimously acknowledged that the present system of negative selection is unsatisfactory. In fact, it is quite uncommon for a judge not to be promoted, or to be dismissed from office for inability prior to the age of mandatory retirement.[40]

B. The Independence of Judges and Prosecutors

The Constitution guarantees the independence of the judiciary as a whole – which is defined, pursuant to the idea of separation of powers, as "an autonomous order independent of any other power" (art. 104 para. 1 Const.) – as well as the independence of individual judges. The Constitution subjects the judges "only to the law" (art. 101 para. 2 Const.), and prohibits the appointment of extraordinary or special judges (art. 102 para. 1 Const.); it establishes, as we have seen, that judges will be appointed by competition (art. 106 para. 1 Const.); it requires that they shall be differentiated only by the diversity of their functions (art. 107 para. 4 Const.); and it states that they shall not be removed without their consent either from office (art. 107 para. 1 Const.) or from the functions they exercise (art. 107 para. 2 Const.). The bulwark of judicial independence, well beyond the proclamations which can be contained in a written text, is the *Consiglio Superiore della Magistratura* (CSM), which is the governing body of the judiciary.

The CSM was established by the Constitution of 1948, art. 104, but it only began to function ten years later, after the enactment of the implementing statute (law no. 195 of 25 March 1958). The CSM is chaired, at least formally, by the President of the Republic. It is composed of two other *ex officio* members, the President of the Supreme Court, the General Prosecutor attached to that Court, and thirty elective members. Twenty of them are from the *Magistratura* (*i.e.*, judges and prosecutors), elected from their own ranks to serve on the CSM, while the remainder are attorneys of at least fifteen years' experience or law professors, elected by the two Houses of Parliament in joint session. A vice-president, who in practice functions as the president, is elected from among the lay members of the whole CSM. The elective members sit on the *Consiglio* for a non-renewable four-year term. Due to the fact that the magistrates prevail over the lay members, the CSM clearly has the authority to represent the judicial power. On the other hand,

---

[40] *See* Pizzorusso, *L'organizzazione della giustizia in Italia*, 2nd ed. (1990) pp. 203, 208.

participation in the CSM by the head of state and by lay members elected by Parliament serves as a link between the judicial power and the other powers of the state.

Judges are appointed, promoted, disciplined and, in general, supervised by the CSM. This assures that they are independent from outside pressures. In particular, disciplinary action can be initiated either by the Ministry of Justice (actually *only* by it, according to art. 107 para. 3 Const.) or by the General Prosecutor attached to the Supreme Court (according to art. 14 of law no. 195 of 24 March 1958), and it can lead to sanctions such as removal from office or transfer to other offices or functions. Jurisdiction over disciplinary action is vested in a special section of the CSM and, on appeal therefrom, in the plenary civil session of the Supreme Court.

According to art. 107 para. 4 Const., public prosecutors enjoy the guarantees established for them by the rules governing the judicial organization. Notwithstanding this wording, which might allude to a lesser degree of independence for prosecutors as opposed to judges, they have come to enjoy substantially the same guarantees as the other judges. Since law no. 511 of 31 May 1946, public prosecutors no longer work under the direction of the Ministry of Justice, but rather under its supervision. This means that there is no longer any hierarchical subordination of the various prosecutorial offices from the Ministry or from a higher office subordinated to the Ministry. Today, the prosecutorial functions are exercised by a number of separate offices independent from each other and from any other authorities. Within the offices, however, the structure is still hierarchical, though art. 53 of the new Code of Criminal Procedure provides that the prosecutor conducts the trial with "full autonomy."

In any event, prosecutors are subject to the CSM, and therefore they have come to achieve very much the same amount of independence as any other judge. This has been demonstrated especially in the last decade or so by a number of prosecutorial offices and prosecutors who have launched a massive attack against organized crime and its political connections, and against political corruption. Some of them, like Giovanni Falcone and Paolo Borsellino, have paid with their lives for their battles against the Mafia. Others, among whom the most famous is Antonio Di Pietro, have become "folk heroes"[41] for pursuing their war on corruption (known as the *mani pulite*, or "clean hands," operation). This movement has practically effected the removal from the political scene of an entire political ruling class, but has also, and not unexpectedly, caused a strong reaction against an allegedly excessive, uncontrolled, and unaccountable prosecutorial power. Its outcome,

---

[41] I borrow this expression from Watkin, *supra* note 39, at 119.

however, is still uncertain, though it is well known that the center-right coalition, which won the general elections on 13 May 2001, has marked the "problem of justice" as a priority on its agenda.

IV. The Administrative Courts

Chapter 6 of this book deals with the machinery of judicial control of administrative action and the criteria of its distribution between the ordinary courts, which have jurisdiction over violations of "subjective rights" by the administration, and the administrative courts, which have jurisdiction over violations of "legitimate interests" by the administration. In that chapter, the origins of this dichotomy are also discussed, along with the difficult borderline problems which, in an increasing number of cases, have led the legislator to vest jurisdiction exclusively in the administrative courts. Here, we will deal briefly with the organs of administrative justice, *i.e.*, the *Consiglio di Stato* (Council of State) and the *Tribunali amministrativi regionali* (hereinafter TAR, *i.e.*, regional administrative tribunals, instituted in 1971).[42] Both of them have constitutional dignity because a number of articles of the Constitution expressly recognize the *Consiglio di Stato* and the TAR, while a transitional provision annexed to the Constitution, art. VI, imposes a duty upon the legislature to review all special courts with the exception of the Council of State, the Court of Accounts,[43] and the military tribunals.

As noted in chapter 6, the origins of the Council of State are French, and it was that model which was first instituted in 1805 in the Kingdom of Italy and in 1806 in the Kingdom of Naples. In 1831, a *Consiglio di Stato* was introduced in the Kingdom of Sardinia which is the immediate ancestor of the present institution. The main function of all these antecedents to the Council of State was advisory. It

---

[42] Until then, cases against local administrative organs were decided by judicial divisions of the *giunte provinciali amministrative* (provincial administrative committees), and subject to appeal to the Council of State. The composition of the *Giunte* was such that their independence could be seriously questioned. In fact, they were declared unconstitutional by judgment no. 30 of the Constitutional Court of 22 March 1967, 90 *Foro it.* I, 681 (1967).

[43] The *Corte dei Conti* (Court of Accounts), which has supervisory and advisory as well as judicial functions, is concerned with the handling of public money. It has jurisdiction over cases against public officials involving their management of public funds. Six of its eight divisions are concerned with pension claims. Appeals may be taken to the plenary session of the court, while issues of jurisdiction may be taken to the Supreme Court, pursuant to art. 111 para. 3 Const. *See* generally, Correale, "*Corte dei Conti*," in *Digesto delle Discipline Pubblicistiche*, IV (1989), p. 215.

was only in 1859, by royal decree no. 3708 of 8 November, that the Sardinian Council began to take on judicial functions. These were strengthened in the post-unitarian *Consiglio di Stato* by law no. 5982 of 31 March 1889, which instituted an *ad hoc* section IV for administrative justice.

Currently, the Council of State continues to be both an advisory and a judicial body, sanctioned by art. 100 para. 1 Const., which states that "the Council of State acts as a legal-administrative body concerned with safeguarding justice in the administration." There are now two more judicial sections of the Council in addition to section IV: section V, instituted by law no. 62 of 7 March 1907, and section VI, created by law no. 6421 of 5 May 1948. Sections I, II, and III are advisory. Law no. 1034 of 6 December 1971, implementing art. 125 para. 2 Const., introduced a network of regional administrative tribunals. Since then, the Council of State has exclusively been an appellate court, while administrative justice in the first instance is handled by the TAR. The judicial functions of both courts are dealt with by art. 103 para. 1 Const., stating that "[t]he Council of State and the other organs of administrative justice have jurisdiction to protect legitimate interests and, in particular matters indicated by law, subjective rights against the public administration." According to art. 111 para. 8 Const., decisions of the Council of State can be attacked before the Supreme Court only on grounds of jurisdiction (*e.g.* when a certain matter, not vested exclusively in the administrative courts, involves a "subjective right" or a "legitimate interest").

Each judicial section of the Council is composed of two presidents and at least twelve judges (called *consiglieri di stato*, or "councillors of state"), and decides together with one of the presidents and four councillors. A plenary session may be convened in order to solve conflicts among the sections or answer questions of particular interest. It is normally chaired by the President of the Council, and is composed of twelve councillors, four from each section. The councillors attached to the Council as judges number 72, while there are 15 councillors with the status of presidents.

The TARs sit in each Region's capital, although sections of them may sit in other cities in a given Region. Each TAR has a president, assisted by a varying number of other judges. The personnel of the TARs consists of 310 judges and 22 presidents. They adjudicate in three-judge panels.

The governing body of the administrative judiciary that oversees its operation, as well as the career and independence of the judges, is the so-called *Consiglio di Presidenza*. It is chaired by the President of the Council of State, who is assisted by the two senior presidents of the section, ten judges elected from among the councillors of state, and the judges of the TARs, of which there are six.

Access to the administrative judiciary is characterized by the fact that it is not open to law graduates, as is the case with the ordinary judiciary, but rather is restricted to persons who have gained experience in other careers. In fact, 50 percent of the councillors of state are appointed from the ranks of the judges of the TARs with at least twelve years of service, upon recommendation of the *Consiglio di Presidenza*. One quarter of them are appointed by the government, upon the advice of the *Consiglio di Presidenza*, from among certain categories (law professors, attorneys with at least 15 years' experience, ordinary judges, and high-ranking civil servants). The remainder are appointed on the basis of a competitive examination open to members of other careers, including ordinary judges with at least four years' service. In turn, access to the TARs requires passing a competitive examination open to civil servants, attorneys, and ordinary judges.

As to the independence of administrative judges, article 100 para. 3 Const. requires that they shall be assured independence from government. Law no. 186 of 27 April 1982 attempted to achieve this goal, but the administrative judges still seem to enjoy less independence than the ordinary judges, or at least they seem to be much too close to the government.

A look at some statistical data shows that the Italian system of administrative justice suffers from the same troubles which plague civil and criminal justice systems. It should suffice to mention here that the average duration of proceedings before the TARs has increased steadily from 1,347 days in 1977 to 4,274 days (11.7 years!) in 1997, that an average of 989 days is needed to dispose of a case before the Council of State, and that 818,744 cases were pending before the TARs at the end of 1997.[44] With respect to administrative justice, the Bicameral Commission made some interesting proposals. I refer in particular to the fact that the *Consiglio di Stato* remained only as an advisory body, while the adjudicatory function in administrative matters is entrusted to a distinct Court for Administrative Justice. The Court, together with the regional tribunals of the first instance, was expected to adjudicate "homogeneous subjects indicated by law concerning the exercise of public powers." This move seemingly does away with the distinction between rights and legitimate interests, and all the consequent problems of demarcation. There is a wide consensus on this point among commentators.[45] Last but not least, the administrative judges appeared to gain in terms of independence: together with

---

[44] For these data, and some interesting reflections thereon, *see* Il Sole-24 Ore del Lunedi, 22 February 1999, p. 23.

[45] *See* Sorace, *Diritto delle amministrazioni pubbliche. Una introduzione* (2000), at pp. 394-97; Proto Pisani, "*Intervento breve per il superamento della giurisdizione amministrativa,*" 46 *Rivista di diritto civile* 775 (2000).

the ordinary judges and the public prosecutors, they were to constitute an autonomous order, independent from any power; as the ordinary judges, they were subject only to the law. Finally, the project introduced a Superior Council of the administrative judiciary, the governing body of administrative judges, and the watchdog of their independence, modeled on the governing body of ordinary judges and prosecutors.

V. Concluding Remarks

In Italy today, the most serious problem in the administration of both civil and criminal justice is delay. The data suggest an intolerable situation. This is so much the case that art. 111 of the Constitution has been amended by law no. 2 of 23 November 1999 in order to include the guarantee of "due process of law" (*giusto processo*), and to proclaim the principle of no reasonable delay as a principle that contributes to its existence. On the other hand, nothing practical has been done to ameliorate the situation for decades, although some of Italy's best scholars have denounced this state of affairs for years, and warned that the system is bound to deteriorate.[46] Some steps toward a solution, however, seem to have been taken in the last few years.

Measures aimed at speeding up and re-evaluating first instance civil proceedings have been enacted, but they do not seem to have been particularly successful. However, this is not the place to deal with those measures.[47]

As to the administration of justice, in the last few years a number of important reforms have been enacted – often in the face of opposition and criticism – which indicate that the attitude of governments towards the crisis of civil and criminal justice is ebbing. As mentioned, justices of the peace have been introduced and seem to work satisfactorily;[48] it is to be hoped that they can begin to function as criminal judges without further delay, that their offices will be properly staffed, and that selection procedures will continue to improve so as to assure a highly qualified lay bench. The merger of *preture* and *tribunali* and the generalization of single-judge courts of first instance is a reform long overdue[49] that rationalize the

---

[46] *See* Cappelletti, *Procédure orale et procédure écrite* (1971), pp. 65-66.

[47] *See* chapter 7, this volume. *See also*, Varano, "Civil Procedure Reform in Italy," 45 *AmJCompL* 657 (1997).

[48] *See* part II A, *supra*.

[49] *See* Denti, *supra* note 13, esp. at 622 *ff.*, where the author, one of the leading Italian proceduralists, reports that attempts to introduce single-judge courts date back to 1912, while other projects were drafted in 1920, 1937, and 1939.

distribution of judicial manpower over the territory on the one hand, and reduce the luxury of having a panel on the other. The *pretore*, whose jurisdiction has been steadily increased since 1973, has demonstrated that single-judge courts can work very well in our legal system, as they do in many others, and that panels, if needed, can be reserved to adjudicate particularly important matters.

It is also noteworthy that legislators have turned their attention to the crucial question of judge selection. The system which had been in force for a century or so was no longer suited to recruit the best possible magistrates, but simply decimated thousands of candidates through an examination very much left to chance in order to fill two or three hundred vacancies per year, a goal that has occasionally not even been reached. The new post-graduate schools, which should be functioning by 2000, are intended to *form* new magistrates, as well as new attorneys and notaries, rather than merely training candidates to survive the selection procedure.

The other issue concerning the administration of justice that has been the subject of a very hot and ongoing political debate in the last few years regards the status of the judge, and, more particularly, the independence and accountability of public prosecutors. It is fair to say that much of the discussion about the reform of the Constitution of 1948, which led to the appointment of a Bicameral Commission for Constitutional Reforms,[50] originated in the *questione giustizia*, that is, the "problem of justice." In the end, the proposals of the Commission did not find their way through parliament, so that the Constitution has remained unaltered, with the exception of art. 111, which has been amended to explicitly include the principle of due process (*giusto processo*).

There are certainly problems concerning the excessive activism of a few magistrates, especially prosecutors; there are also problems concerning the accountability of magistrates, given that they are still practically immune from civil liability and the mechanisms intended to subject them to disciplinary responsibility do not seem to work effectively.[51] There are certainly problems with the article of the Constitution

---

[50] The Commission, which has been quoted several times over the course of this chapter, was set up following the enactment of constitutional law no. 1 of 24 January 1997, which authorized parliament to derogate from the procedure for constitutional amendment provided for by art. 138 Const., in order to reform the whole of Part 2 of the Constitution. The proposals of the Commission, especially those concerned with the administration of justice, have raised negative comments by some authoritative scholars. *See, e.g.*, Pizzorusso, *La costituzione ferita* (1999), and the short comments by another leading constitutionalist, the late Paolo Barile, in his Introduction to the book edited by Caretti, *supra* note 17, at xiv-xvi.

[51] *See* my heading *"Responsabilità del magistrato,"* in *Digesto delle Discipline Privatistiche,* Sezione civile, vol. XVII (1998), p. 111.

establishing that the public prosecutor is under a duty to prosecute in criminal proceedings (art. 112 Const.). The problem at hand is to at least reduce the degree of discretion which the prosecutors are inevitably forced to exercise in view of the workload of every prosecutorial office.[52] The objective should be to render the duty to prosecute effective, so as to assure the principle of equality of the citizens before the criminal law.

It is to be expected that the Government that was formed after the general elections of 13 May 2001, and is now led by Mr. Berlusconi, the founder of the conservative party *Forza Italia*, will pursue its long-advocated reform proposals. At the time of writing, it is too early to predict the lines of the reform process. However, it is not difficult to imagine that the center-right coalition will place particular emphasis on the separation of the careers of judges and prosecutors, on the subjection of prosecutorial discretion to guidelines indicated every year by parliament, and on the status, independence, and accountability of judges and prosecutors. Besides reforms dictated by differences in the conception and philosophy of justice in a modern democracy, it is to be expected that the new Government will also pursue goals of efficiency and effectiveness through structural and procedural reforms.

VI. Bibliography

Chapters on the administration of justice are contained in the major introductions to the Italian legal system published in English. I refer in particular to M. Cappelletti, J. Merryman & Perillo, *The Italian Legal System* (1967); G. Certoma, *The Italian Legal System* (1985); and T. Watkin, *The Italian Legal Tradition* (1997). M. Cappelletti & Perillo, *Civil Procedure in Italy* (1965) place special emphasis on civil justice.

Among the many publications in Italian, I refer the reader to A. Pizzorusso, *L'organizzazione della giustizia in Italia*, 3rd ed. (1990), which is the most complete treatise on the ordinary judiciary. The treatises on civil procedure, criminal procedure, and administrative justice normally dedicate one or more chapters to the organization of the courts and the judges. *See, e.g.*, L.P. Comoglio, C. Ferri &

---

[52] That the prosecutors also have to exercise some discretion in legal systems where they are not supposed to enjoy any discretion, or, in any event, discretion comparable to their common law counterparts, was underlined in a seminal article by Goldstein & Marcus, "The Myth of Judicial Supervision in Three 'Inquisitorial' Systems: France, Italy and Germany," 87 *Yale LJ* 240 (1977).

M. Taruffo, *Lezioni sul processo civile*, 2nd ed. (1998); P. Tonini, *Manuale di Procedura penale*, 2nd ed. (2000; the 3rd edition will be published in the course of the year 2001); Nigro, *Giustizia amministrativa*, 4th ed. (1994), Cardi, (ed.).

Administrative Law

Domenico Sorace [1]

I. Introduction

This chapter outlines the basic systems and functions of administrative law in Italy with attention to its historical development, the relationship between ordinary and administrative court jurisdictions, and recent modifications in the area of administrative law.

Some preliminary remarks will facilitate the reader's understanding of the subject.

To begin with, notwithstanding the large number of statutes dealing with administrative matters, the general principles that govern them are mainly a product of a long and well-established tradition of judge-made law and of legislative self-restraint. As will be seen later, the most important general statutes governing judicial review date back to the first decades after the establishment of the Italian State in 1861. However, the first organic statute containing general rules, mainly procedural in nature, on administrative action was enacted only in 1990.

The case law in this area has some features that will not be at all familiar to common lawyers. First, it is not produced by common law courts but mainly by a separate judicial hierarchy of administrative courts. Moreover, given that any aggrieved subject is entitled to bring a complaint up to the highest courts without any leave, and given the lack of a rule of *stare decisis*, there are a tremendous number of judgments from which it is almost impossible to single out real leading cases. Thus, legal scholarship plays an important role in identifying leading cases.

Therefore, one must acknowledge the key function of case law and yet also keep in mind the civil law context in which those cases are decided.

It is worth bearing in mind that both scholarly and judicial approaches to administrative law problems are mainly formalistic. A primary reason for this, as will be

---

[1]   Professor of Administrative Law, University of Florence.

Jeffrey S. Lena and Ugo Mattei (eds.), *Introduction to Italian Law*, 125-158
©2002 Kluwer Law International. Printed in the Netherlands.

seen, is the central position that the highly formal distinction between "subjective rights" (*diritti soggettivi*) and "legitimate interests" (*interessi legittimi*) plays, or at least has played, in administrative law until very recently.

Finally, it is worth noting the copious and widespread reforms of administrative law that are now being undertaken. This is also because, to an ever increasing degree, Italian bureaucracy (like those of the other member states of the European Union) is working, as a sort of indirect administration, on behalf of the European Union.

This reality renders the current administrative law as a kind of transitional law.

II. Some Features of the Italian Administrative State

A. Historical Background

The following can be recognized as the earmarks of the historical development of Italian state administration.

First, it should be stressed that the Italian state administration originates from the bureaucracies of the Piedmont kings restored to their thrones after Napoleon's defeat. In fact, until 1948, the Italian Constitution was Piedmont's *Statuto*, which was not enacted through popular representation, but was rather granted, *octroyée*, by King Carlo Alberto in 1848 and preserved by the new Italian State.

The *Statuto* provided for a parliament with legislative powers, bicameral in form, and featured an elected chamber of deputies. Through the Parliament, the bourgeoisie increasingly acquired real power during this early period, so that the exercise of the bureaucratic authoritative powers had to be authorized by statutes; in this sense it can be said that the rule of law was thereby established.

However, given the origin of this Constitution, the king, and not the representatives of the people, could be seen as the real source of power. This is particularly the case with respect to discretionary administrative power,[2] which could not be viewed as delegated by the legislature, much less the people.

On the other hand, franchise and eligibility were severely restricted, principally on the basis of a citizen's wealth. Both voters and eligible citizens were very few until 1911, when all male citizens gained the right to vote; female citizens had to wait until 1947 to acquire the same rights. Of course, even universal male suffrage had significant effects on the real distribution of power among the state organs, increasing the role of the parliament. But first the problems of the First World War

---

[2] Article 5 of the *Statuto* provided that "The King alone is the holder of the executive power."

and then the coming of fascism[3] prevented the development of truly democratic ideologies. However, it may also be said that in the Republican era and after the enactment of the new Constitution in 1948 (which provides in its first article that "the sovereignty is vested in the people"), the idea that administrative power could stem only from the legislature hardly expanded. Indeed it is fair to say that some authoritarian views about public administration have not yet been completely eradicated.

It should also be kept in mind that in 1865, four years after the proclamation of the Kingdom of Italy, when the organization of the new State was to be determined, the proposal to choose a quasi-federal form (grounded in the Regions) was defeated. The new State was therefore modeled on the centralist French pattern, with a weak local government. Only the Constitution of 1948 provided that regional governments with legislative powers should be created. But it was necessary to wait until 1972 before the "regionalization" began – and only began – to be put into effect.

As for individual rights, only the Constitution of 1948 enacted a real Bill of Rights (*see* Const. art. 3 para. 1 and arts.13 to 24). Besides civil and political freedoms and rights, the new Charter also asserts the so-called social rights, including the right to education (art. 34), health (art. 32), and welfare and social security (art. 38), and it also recognizes the right to work (art. 4). Furthermore, "it shall be the task of the Republic to remove obstacles of an economic or social nature which, by restricting in practice the freedom and equality of citizens, prevent the full development of the human personality and the effective participation of all workers in the political, economic, and social organization of the country" (art. 3 para. 2).[4]

The Constitution also recognizes the freedom of trade and industry (art. 41 para. 1), but allows extensive State intervention in the area of the economy when justified by social goals (arts. 41-47).

With regard to the latter, from the 1930s until very recently, regulatory intervention steadily grew; public enterprise also grew until very recently in the last century. Through the latter, public utilities industries were managed, according to the notion – also quite developed in France – that the modern State must be legitimated through the production of both social (*i.e.* education, health, welfare) and economic (*i.e.* utilities) services for the citizens. Yet banks, insurance companies,

---

[3] During the fascist era (1923-1943), the freedom to vote was greatly hampered and, in the end, the Italian Parliament based upon universal suffrage was abolished entirely.

[4] This, and the following translations of Constitutional articles, are adapted from the translations appearing in Appendix A of M. Cappelletti, J.H. Merryman, & J.M. Perillo, *The Italian Legal System – An Introduction*, Stanford University Press, Stanford (1967), and in Blaustein & Flanz, *Constitutions of the Countries of the World*, Oceana, Dobbs Ferry, New York, 1971.

and factories producing all manner of things were also included, particularly when private enterprises began to fall apart after the world crisis of 1929.

B. At the Threshold of the 1990s

As a consequence of this historical experience, the following may be delineated as the main features of the Italian administrative state at the threshold of the last decade of the twentieth century.

Even with the establishment of regional governments and the devolution of some administrative tasks and powers from the central government to the regional governments in 1972 and 1977, public administration remained highly centralized. Notwithstanding the acknowledgment of the legality principle and the great number of laws enacted by parliament, public administration was still frequently thought of as endowed with some inherent enforcement powers over the citizens, and therefore not in need of any legislative delegation of powers.

Despite its identity as the administration of a democratic state, its decision-making process was frequently insulated from both the participation of the citizenry at large, as well as from those individually affected, to whom the right to be heard upon an issue of personal importance was granted only in particular cases (such as the issue of sanctions or the repeal of a permit). Neither citizens at large nor individuals affected had rights of access to administrative records, except after having demanded judicial review of a particular decision.

A large number of private activities needed to be authorized before they could be commenced, which meant that the authorizations could be denied and the activities could therefore be forbidden. The alleged aim of this previously required mass of permits was to ensure that these activities were not directed against the "public interest." That meant, for instance, that they should not disturb the peace or that they should meet sanitary, safety and environmental requirements, or that they had to adhere a plan of orderly town expansion.

In particular, almost all economic activities required authorization to be performed, from taxi driving or retail trading in the smallest shops to conducting banking activities. In this case the aim, more or less openly declared, was to restrict economic competition. In fact, any legislation similar to the Sherman Act in the United States was lacking.

Abiding by the numerous regulatory requirements imposed upon them, the citizens were also burdened by a lot of time-wasting red tape. All regulatory tasks, in any field and for whatever purpose, were carried out by offices of ministries and other public agencies in which tasks and duties of the politicians and the professionals were confusingly mixed. And entities similar to the Independent Regulatory

Authorities were nearly unknown at the time.[5] A very large number of persons worked in the public service sector, and their labor rights and duties were all grounded in public law.

Along with the regulatory functions, a number of entrepreneurial tasks were also performed by the State. As mentioned above, the State managed the major public utilities industries: *e.g.*, postal services and telecommunications, railroads, electric power, and gas. To this end, public organizational forms were used; earlier they were particular branches of the state enjoying some degree of autonomy (*aziende autonome*), and later they were public commercial bodies with legal personality, acting like private bodies (*enti pubblici economici*). Similar kinds of activities, from waste services to local transportation, were also managed by local authorities through similar organizational forms.

While other kinds of economic activities, such as banking and insurance services, were carried out in organizationally similar ways, in several other public undertakings (ranging from the production of candy to cars) the private joint stock company form was usually utilized. These were only formally private companies, since their shares were held by the State,[6] so that in 1956,[7] a Ministry was set up with jurisdiction over the policies to be carried on by the State as a shareholder (*Ministero per le partecipazioni statali*).

Finally, it is worth noting that, even if Italy was one of the founding States of the European Economic Community, the "Europeanization" of its administrative law was not yet significant, both because implementation of the European Directives was ordinarily delayed (if not avoided entirely), and because the actions taken by the European institutions until that time had not yet had upsetting effects on Italian public administration.

C. Recent Developments

Some major administrative reforms have taken place (or have at least been planned) in the 1990s with respect to various matters, including the reorganization of central, regional, and local governments, agency access to records, participation in and

---

[5] Only the *Banca d'Italia* could be perhaps ascribed to this organizational pattern. The *Commissione nazionale per le società e la borsa – CONSOB*, when established in 1974, was not independent at all.

[6] Directly or through public holdings, like the *Istituto per la ricostruzione industriale – IRI* and the *Ente nazionale per gli idrocarburi – ENI*.

[7] *See* law no. 1589 of 22 December 1956.

simplification of administrative procedures, and the new economic regulations. These reforms are linked with the liberalization and privatization of public enterprises.

1. The Reformation of Central, Regional, and Local Governments

It is worth quickly mentioning the reforms of central, regional and local governments.

In 1990,[8] a new organic legislation was passed regarding the reciprocal tasks and jurisdictions of the municipalities (*comuni*) and counties (*province*), which together form the first two tiers of the local government.[9] More recently, the executive has been empowered by the legislature[10] to devolve new powers to the regional and local governments, so that almost all administrative functions will be performed by local governments. This process is still ongoing.[11]

Some new rules concerning internal management also deserve mention.[7] First, an effort has been made to clearly establish the division of the reciprocal tasks and duties of politicians and professionals. To the former is given the power to determine policies and issue directives, instructions, and regulations, and to the latter is reserved the authority to issue all kinds of orders,[13] together with all managerial jobs. Secondly, the labor relations of the employees, from the lowest clerks to the top managers, will no longer be a public law matter (therefore, the labor controversies no longer fall under the jurisdiction of the administrative courts), except for the competitive procedures needed, as a rule, for the hiring of personnel.

---

[8] *See* law no. 142 of 8 June, now consolidated, together with others subsequent statutes, in the Local Government Code: "*Testo Unico delle leggi sull'ordinamento locale*," Legislative Decree (*Decreto Legislativo*) no. 267 of 18 August 2000.

[9] However, within the municipalities (except the smallest) there are a kind of borough councils, named *consigli di quartiere* or *consigli di circoscrizione*.

[10] Law no. 59 of 15 March 1997.

[11] *See* Legislative Decree no. 112 of 31 March 1998.

[12] This matter is dealt with by Legislative Decree no. 29 of 3 February 1993, which implements the delegation given by law no. 421 of 23 October 1992. The Decree is now consolidated, together with several subsequent amending laws, in Legislative Decree no. 165 of 30 March 2001.

[13] In the meaning of the definition given by APA, 5 USC, ch. 5, para. 551.

2. Access to Agencies' Records

New regulations have been enacted regarding access to agency records. Before this reform, all administrative acts of central, regional, and local governments (and also of some agencies endowed with similar powers) having regulatory power (such as the *regolamenti*) had to be published, just like laws, before becoming effective,[14] even when they had only organizational content. The publication may take place in different official journals such as the *Gazzetta Ufficiale*[15] for State acts, the *Bollettino Ufficiale* for regional acts, or in reserved places open to the public such as the *Albo* for municipalities.

By contrast, an order had to be noticed to the addressees, but it was not clear whether this kind of act could or could not be examined by other persons. Also in doubt was the existence of a right of access to the records of the procedure, even if the person seeking them was the party directly affected by the final administrative decision. Given this ambiguous law, the officers usually invoked their claimed duty to keep official secrets and denied everyone access to official records.[16]

Following the reform pursuant to statute no. 241/1990, public agencies must now publish guidelines, instructions, programs, and every kind of act which contains general provisions concerning the organizations, tasks, objectives, or procedures of a public agency, or which state the construction of legal rules or give directions for the implementation of them (art. 26 para. 1).

Moreover, according to the new law, whoever is interested in examining the administrative documents to protect a legal interest has a right of access to them (art. 22 para. 1). Any graphic, photographic, film-based, electromagnetic, or other type of representation of the contents of acts made by the administrative agencies (or in any case employed in the course of administrative actions) is regarded as an administrative document (art. 22 para. 2). Notably, the statute makes clear that the records concerned are those kept by any kind of state agency, public corporation, or private corporation as well, when such a private corporation operates public utilities or other public services through a franchising agreement.

The right of access to the records is recognized in order to guarantee the transparency of administrative actions and promote their unbiased making (art. 22, para. 1).

---

[14] *See* art. 10 Civil Code *Disposizioni sulla legge in generale.*

[15] *See* law no. 839 of 11 December 1984 and Decree of the President of the Republic (DPR) no. 1092 of 28 December 1985.

[16] The law on the office secrets, as modified by art. 28 of law no. 241 of 7 August 1991, now makes clear that there is no duty of secrecy in cases in which a right of access can be claimed.

This right is not given to "busybodies," since a "legal interest" must be shown in order to have access to the records. However, given the purposes stated in the statute, it can be maintained that this interest must be construed more broadly and vaguely than that required for judicial standing in a particular matter.

The right to access is not provided for all kinds of records. The exceptions are in part similar to those stated in the United States Administrative Procedure Act (APA) paragraph 552. They concern, first of all, records affected by state secrecy, according to the relevant statute,[17] or by other legal duties of secrecy or non-disclosure. Moreover, access is precluded in cases provided for by regulations made by agencies according to the general rules and requirements set forth in a national executive order implementing the statute. Information is safeguarded with respect to national security and defense, foreign relations, currency policies, the preservation of law and order, the prevention and repression of crime, and the privacy of third parties (comprised of individuals, groups, and corporations). However, access to some of these records may nevertheless be obtained in cases where the knowledge is needed by the applicants for purposes of judicial defense of their legal interests (art. 24, paras. 2 and 4), except that, when privacy about health or sexual behavior is at stake, the access is allowed only for purpose of defense of "a right of equal dignity to that of the interested people."[18]

In addition, access to certain records can be delayed (but not prohibited) where the information, if disseminated, would prevent or seriously hamper administrative actions. This is always deemed to be the case with regard to documents pertaining to procedures aimed at making legal rules or general regulations, as well as plan or program decisions not yet concluded (art. 24 para. 6).

An application for access has to be addressed to the agency which made the document or which holds it permanently. The records can be freely inspected. To obtain copies, the requesting party must pay the costs of duplication and certain fees (art. 25, paras. 1 and 2).

The law provides that denials, delays, and other limitations to access must be explained. Any application to which a reply is not made within 30 days is deemed refused (art. 25, paras. 3 and 4). If the right to access is denied, or if there is a failure by the administrative agency to reach a conclusion in the time prescribed, the applicant can complain before the regional administrative court (*Tribunale Amministrativo Regionale* – TAR), which must decide the question, *in camera*,

---

[17] Law no. 801 of 23 August 1988.

[18] *See* art. 22, para 4, of law no. 675 of 31 December 1996.

within thirty days and is empowered to order the agency to produce any improperly withheld records (art. 25, paras. 5 and 6).

3. Participation in the Administrative Procedure and Agreements

The Italian Constitution does not contain any "due process" clause. According to case law, however, some sanctions could not be imposed without first allowing the interested party to express his or her view. In any case, most scholars have advocated a general legislative regulation of administrative procedure over the years.

Law no. 241/1990 contains this advocated regulation. This law is really just a kind of minimal regulation without the detailed requirements of the APA, but it applies without the need of any external reference.

The agencies are obliged to inform the interested parties of the beginning of a procedure. With the exception of cases in which very rapid administrative action is required, notice of the start of a procedure must always be given to the interested parties who are the objects of an administrative decision and to the parties who are obliged to take part in the procedure. Others who might suffer detrimental effects from the decision must also be informed if they are either identified or are easily identifiable. However, in any case, the agency is free to take provisional measures before having given the notice due (art. 7).

The interested persons are to be informed of the subject matter of the procedure, the agency which has jurisdiction over the matter, the department, the officer personally in charge of the procedure, and finally the place where the records can be located and examined (art. 8 para. 2). The communication is to be given by personal notice or, when this is not possible or would entail too heavy a burden on the administrative agency (in case, for example, a large number of interested persons), by suitable advertisement (art. 8, paras. 1 and 3).

The general duty to inform is not provided for with respect to the procedures aimed at issuing legal rules or general regulations and plans or program decisions, nor does it apply to taxation procedures. To these only the particular norms, if any, apply, provided for by the statutes and procedures that regulate these matters (art. 13). All those to whom notice of the start of the procedure has to be given may take part in the procedure. That means that they may inspect the relevant records (with the exceptions mentioned above) and submit documents and written arguments (art. 10). Aside from these subjects, any subject bearer of private or public interests, or bearers of diffuse interests who have formed into associations, may take part in the procedure, with the same powers (arts. 9 and 10).

An interesting feature of this law is the attempt to give a public law regulation to the well-known practice of informal and hidden agreements between the agencies and the individuals, giving them legal effect when they comply with procedural requirements. To this end, the new law provides that whoever takes part in a procedure may also submit proposals to reach an agreement on the discretionary content of the decision to be made by the agency. The agency can sign the proposed agreements for public interest purposes and without prejudicing the interests of any third party's interest. The principles of the law of contracts apply to these agreements when they are compatible with the public interest, except in cases when different legal provisions exist. But the agency has the power to withdraw if new reasons implicating the public interest arise. In this case, however, an indemnification is to be paid that takes into account possible damages to the counterpart (art. 11, paras. 1, 2, and 4).

4. The Simplification of Agency Procedures

The reform of procedural law brought about by statute no. 241/1990 may perhaps be viewed as "customer oriented," not so much because of the opportunity given to the interested parties to have a say in the procedure, but rather because of the attention focussed on protecting citizens against bureaucratic vexation. The law makes an attempt both to alleviate their bureaucratic burdens and to set out the bases for the recognition of new kinds of rights against the agencies.

As for the former, its target is called the "simplification" of procedures. The reform presents two main novelties in this regard. As mentioned above, one frequently needs some sort of previous authorization (or license, permit, approval, or other similar agency consent) to begin a private activity. According to law no. 241/1990,[19] normally it is now only necessary to give prior notice to the competent agency,[20] asserting the conformity of the planned action to the conditions provided by the law,[21] together with a self-certification of the results of the needed tests or examinations, if any. The onus is on the agency to check all the circumstances and, if necessary, to enjoin the applicant, and within a 60-day mandatory period, to cease any operation, and to undo the effects of the illegal operations.

The new procedure cannot apply when there are a fixed number of authorizations that can be granted. Nor does it apply when the issue depends on the evaluation of circumstances which entails the exercise of some discretion, even if such discretion only regards the choice of the technical rules according to which the tests or

---

[19] Article 19, as amended by art. 2 para. 10, law no. 537 of 24 December 1993.

[20] Except for the planning permits and some authorization aimed at the protection of the environment, landscape, or historical buildings.

[21] The false declaration of circumstances is considered a crime and prevents any advantageous effect for the applicant. *See* art. 21.

examinations suited to the case are to be carried out (what Italian administrative lawyers call "technical discretion"). Central Executive regulations list the acts of this sort.[22]

On the other hand, a different Executive regulation[23] lists the cases in which an application for authorizations, licenses, and the like are deemed as granted if the agency does not refuse it within sixty days. Here, the agency's silence functions as an agreement (called "assent-silence") whereas before, in principle, the agency's inactivity was deemed a disagreement ("refusal-silence"). However, if the authorization deemed as given by silence turns out to be illegal, it can be annulled by the agency itself, but only if this is required by the public interest.

Furthermore, law no. 241/1990 opens the way to legislation aimed at avoiding overly complicated and time-wasting procedures. In its first article (para. 2), the law states as a general rule that departments and agencies cannot increase the number steps required for the conclusion of a procedure, except when extraordinary and well-founded needs arise in the proof-taking stage.

It is then established (art. 2, paras. 2, 3, and 4) that every department and agency must fix deadlines (to be published) for the conclusion of their procedures. For those cases in which they must receive official advice from an external advisory organ before making the final decision, the agency, after the expiration date, can decide without waiting any longer.[24] Moreover, subsequent laws have revised long lists of procedures with the goal of eliminating non-essential steps, and it has recently been decided that a list of procedures must be "simplified" annually.[25] Similarly, when several agencies take part in a procedure and the agency wishes to shorten its length, the agency responsible for the final decision can, instead of waiting for the assent of each, call all of them to a meeting (*conferenza di servizi*) in which all must decide together.[26]

Among these simplification measures, it is worth stressing the importance of certain laws and regulations. On the one hand, they provide that citizens cannot be asked to give evidence of facts, personal status, or titles the evidence for which can

---

[22] *See* Table A attached to DPR no. 411 of 9 May 1994.

[23] *See* art. 20 law no. 241/1990 and Table C attached to DPR no. 300 of 26 April 1992, as amended by the *Allegato* 2, attached to DPR no. 407 of 9 May 1994.

[24] *See also* art. 17 for the cases in which an expert evaluation is needed.

[25] *See* art. 20 para. 1 of law no. 59 of 15 March 1997 and the first yearly law no. 50 of 8 March 1999.

[26] Article 14, as subsequently amended, also establishes the rules for the functioning of the meeting.

be drawn from records held by any public agency.[27] On the other hand, when citizens are required to provide documentation of such facts as age or place of birth they are allowed to execute declarations on their own behalf on these matters and other matters relating to personal data.[28]

Finally, it is worth mentioning another novelty pertaining to an agency's management field that tries to make these reforms more effective. It is provided that for each procedure an officer must be named who is personally in charge of the procedure (the *responsabile del procedimento*) and whose name, as noted above, has to be made known to the interested parties at the beginning of the procedure. This officer has the task of carrying out the proof-taking stage of the procedure with maximum promptness. He must also assist the interested persons by, for example, indicating any problems or faults with their applications that they need to address in order for the application to be successful.[29]

5. Privatization and the Regulatory Independent Authorities

The recent major developments, largely resulting from the impact of European Community law, concern economic regulations and public enterprises. The acceleration of the European integration process brought about by the 1986 Single European Act[30] and by the 1992 Treaty on European Union[31] compelled a revision of the attitude of the Italian State towards the economy.

Law no. 287 of 10 October 1990 contains rules similar to those of arts. 81 and 82 of the EC Treaty that prohibit agreements between competitors and the activities that constrain competition, or the abuse of a dominant position in the market, even when the European rules do not apply.[32] The enforcement of these rules is the burden of the Authority for the Defense of Competition and the Market (*Autorità per la garanzia della concorrenza e del mercato*), an independent regulatory commission (antitrust authority) whose members are appointed by agreement of

---

[27] *See* art. 18 of law no. 241/1990. It is a duty of the officer responsible for the procedure to collect these records.

[28] *See* art. 47 *ff*, of the DPR no. 445 of 28 December 2000, code of the administrative documentation.

[29] *See* arts. 5 and 6 of law 241/1990.

[30] The Single European Act stated the end of 1992 as the deadline for the completion of the European Internal Market.

[31] Commonly referred to as the "Maastricht Treaty."

[32] That is, when they do not affect the trade between Member States of the EC, but only the Italian market.

the speakers of the House of Deputies and the Senate. This new agency joins the Commission for the Regulation of the Stock Exchange (*Commissione nazionale per le società e la borsa – CONSOB*), set up in 1974 and updated in 1985,[33] whose jurisdiction[34] was widened to nearly all kinds of financial markets in the last decade.[35]

Moreover, in the 1990s, a decision was reached to sell most public enterprises in order to both obtain liquidity (or at least to alleviate the losses suffered by some of these entities) and to eliminate some open or hidden public monopolies. The first move to this end was the transformation of public enterprises in the form of public corporations into joint stock corporations (making it possible to sell shares in the companies),[36] and the abolition of the Ministry of the State shareholdings (*Ministero delle partecipazioni statali*).[37] The subsequent steps, for those enterprises producing common goods, ought to take the form of sales of the shares on the market,[38] where the competition is to be protected by the new independent antitrust authority.

For public utilities, the aim could not simply consist of their sale to private entrepreneurs, because public monopolistic ownership is aimed at satisfying the needs of public interest, which could not be fulfilled through the market. Moreover, the EC Treaty states that "undertakings[39] entrusted with the operation of services of general economic interest … shall be subject to the rules contained in this Treaty, in particular to the rules on competition, insofar as the application of such rules does not obstruct the performance, in law or in fact, of the particular tasks assigned to them."[40] Therefore, it was decided that shares could not be sold in these kinds of enterprises before independent agencies with the power to fix tariffs and control

---

[33] *See* Law Decree no. 95 of 8 April 1974, converted into law no. 216 of 6 June 1974 and updated by law no. 281 of 7 June 1985.

[34] Sometimes exercised jointly with the Italian Central Bank (*Banca d'Italia*).

[35] *See*, for the latest legislation, the Legislative Decree no. 58 of 24 February 1998.

[36] Which was allowed or directly decided upon by the Executive, for public banks, public holdings, and other public entities. *See* law no. 218 of 30 July 1990, and Legislative Decree no. 356 of 20 November 1990, and Law Decree no. 333 of 11 July 1992, converted into law no. 359 of 8 August 1992.

[37] *See* Law Decree no. 118 of 23 April 1993, converted into law no. 202 of 23 June 1993.

[38] The sales are still going on: until now, the amount of money obtained is over US$ 15 billion.

[39] Which the EC Treaty does not ask to be necessarily privately owned; *see* art. 86 para. 1 and art. 295.

[40] Article 86 para. 2 of the EC Treaty.

the quality of services were set up.[41] Accordingly, until now, these questions have been settled by two other independent authorities, one with jurisdiction over the electric power and gas industries, and the other with jurisdiction over the telecommunications industry.[42] Meanwhile, some European Directives have been enacted to harmonize the partial liberalization in these fields,[43] and their implementation is imminent.

III. The Machinery of the Judicial Control of Administrative Action

A. French Origins

Unlike England, Italy belongs to that group of European countries in which, after the Middle Ages, the idea of administration was sharply separated from the idea of judicial jurisdiction, to the point where even the name of the administrative authority (which is called "competence" and never "jurisdiction") and the administrative decision (which is called "administrative measure" and, more generally, "administrative act," and never "adjudication") lost any resemblance to those of judicial authority and decision. (For purposes of this chapter, an "administrative act" may be defined as a decision concluding an administrative procedure.)

With particular regard to the French experience, it is important to note that, during the *ancien régime*, the administrative bureaucracies of the kings experienced increasing growth separate from the judiciary.[44] And, at a certain point, it was no longer necessary to have the legality of their authoritarian measures (by which we mean acts impinging upon the freedom and property of individuals) ascertained by the judiciary before being enforced against the addressees.[45]

It is unclear when exactly the last novelty in this area occurred. However, it is certain that after the long struggle against parliament initiated during the first half

---

[41] *See* art. 1*bis* of Law Decree no. 332 of 31 May 1994, converted into law no. 474 of 30 July 1994.

[42] *See* law no. 481 of 14 November 1995, and no. 249 of 31 July 1997.

[43] To which must be added the postal services.

[44] L. Mannori, "*Diritto amministrativo dal Medioevo al XIX secolo*," in *Digesto – delle discipline pubblicistiche*, vol. V, UTET, Torino (1990), p. 172 *ff.*

[45] *Id.* at p. 179, fn. 43.

of the seventeenth century,[46] the result was fully achieved during the French Revolution,[47] or at least after 1799,[48] when Napoleon established the *Conseil d' État* (which may be viewed as the heir of the *Conseil privé* of the king of the *Ancien Régime*)[49] as the prominent advisory body on administrative, legislative, and contentious affairs regarding the central government.

Subsequently, a citizen could sue the government before a court solely to obtain compensation for expropriation, damages, or breach of contract, but only provided that no specific public interest was at stake. By contrast, a complaint against the order to do or not do something, or against the refusal of a license, could be made only through an administrative appeal (usually a hierarchical appeal), which was decided by the government, very frequently on the advice of the *Conseil d' État*. This sort of administrative self-made justice, labeled as the system of the "*contentieux administrative*" or "administrative justice," was later, following the fortunes of Napoleon, exported to other European countries, including the old Italian States.[50]

The reason given for establishing this kind of system was to guarantee that administrative discretion was not hindered by undue court intervention; this brought the principle of the separation of government powers into effect.[51] But it is

---

[46] *See* the prohibition against the Parliaments (which were the judiciary) to *prendre connaissance des affaires d´état et d´administration*, settled by the Saint Germain Edict in 1641.

[47] *See* Law 16/24-8-1790, art. 13, "*Les juges ne pourron troubler, de quelque manière que ce soit, les opération des corps adminstratifs ni citer devant eux les administrateurs à raison de leurs fonctions.*" This prohibition would be confirmed in 1794: "*Défenses itératives son faites aux tribunaux de connaître des actes d'administration, de quelqu' espèce qu' ils soient, aux peines de droit.*"

[48] By the Constitution of 22 *frimaire a. VIII* (13 December 1799). In the same VIII year (17 February 1800) the *Conseils de Prefecture* were established in the Provinces.

[49] The whole organization of the *Conseil du Roi* of Louis XIV can be seen in P. Fanachi, *La justice administrative*, 3rd ed., Paris (1992), p. 7, fn. 1. A *Conseil d'Etat* which gathered the Ministries of the King together was reestablished by a Law of 27 April – 25 May, 1791.

[50] The competence of the French Council of State expanded to Piedmont in 1800, to Parma in 1802, to Liguria in 1805, to Tuscany in 1808, and to Latium and Umbria in 1809. When the formally independent Napoleonic Reign of Italy was founded, which included all of Northern Italy, something similar to the French Council of State had been established there in 1805. A Council of State was established in 1805 in the Reign of Naples, as well. *See* V. Wright, "*Conseil d'Etat e Consiglio di Stato: le radici storiche della loro diversità,*" in Y. Meny (ed.), *Il Consiglio di Stato in Francia e in Italia*, Bologna (1995), p. 31.

[51] In fact, the first words of the above-mentioned Law of 1790 (*see supra* note 47) were: "*Les fonctions judiciaires sont distinctes et demeureront toujours séparées des fonctions administratifs.*"

indisputable that, at the same time, the public administration could be seen as freed, unlike the common people, from the obligation to respect the ordinary law. This was the well-known criticism leveled against the *Droit Administrative* by A.V. Dicey in the wake of A. de Tocqueville's first remarks.[52]

However, one cannot underestimate the fact that decisions by the government playing a quasi-judicial role usually had to be taken on the advice of the *Conseil d'État*. The government always conformed to this advice (even if, theoretically, such conformity was unnecessary), so that it can be said that the decisions came substantially from the *Conseil d'État*. In fact, perhaps because it could act as an hierarchical superior,[53] the latter was able to develop a range of specific legal principles to confine the exercise of discretionary powers (*contentieux d'excés de pouvoir*). Through such powers, the rule of law was, after all, imposed with perhaps more efficacy than was attained by the English Courts, for instance (as Dicey himself appears to have partially acknowledged).[54]

Also, since 1872 the *Conseil d'État* was given the formal authority to directly decide appeals. This new authority was in addition to its continuing duties to advise on administrative and legislative affairs of the government. In any case, it was already understood at this time as performing a judicial task, and was actually regarded as a judge, or as just one of the so-called administrative jurisdictions that were established in the second half of the nineteenth century in other continental European States as well (as, for instance, in some German States)[55] where they were not, however, also advisory bodies of the government on administrative affairs.

---

[52] *See* the passages of A. de Tocqueville, *Democracy in America*, quoted by A.V. Dicey, *Introduction to the Study of the Law of the Constitution*, 8th ed. (1914), repr., Indianapolis (1982), p. 233.

[53] *See* Yves Gaudemet, "*Pouvoir discretionnaire de l'administration moderne*," Landesbericht Franckreich, in M. Bullinger (ed.), *Verwaltungsermessen in modernen Staat*, Baden Baden (1986), p. 113 *ff*.

[54] *See* "Rule of Law compared with *Droit Administratif*," in *Introduction to the Study of the Law of the Constituition, supra* note 52, at 213 *ff*.

[55] *See* Walter Leisner, "Legal protection against the State in the Federal Republic of Germany," in Aldo Piras (ed.), *Administrative Law – The problem of Justice*, vol. III, Milano 1997, p. 149 *ff*.

B. Italian History

Coming now to the particular history of Italian administrative law,[56] it is important to note that the Italian State was the result of the unification of several pre-existing States in Italy. The steps prior to the unification were the annexations of the other States by Piedmont, followed by the proclamation of the Kingdom of Italy in 1861, and the enactment of the so-called Unification Laws of 1865, which replaced the different statutes in force in the pre-unification States.

Many of these States – above all the Kingdom of Piedmont, to which the Kingdom of Italy was first heir – had been influenced by the French administrative reforms brought by Napoleon and his armies. After the "restoration" that followed the fall of Napoleon, the old monarchies maintained or re-established French-style institutions, which included the previously discussed system of administrative justice. For instance, a Council of State had been established in Piedmont in 1831, along with similar institutions in other States.

However, having to decide on the new national system for protecting individuals against the government administration, the new Italian parliament decided to depart from the administrative justice system and try to build a new system by enacting law no. 2248 of 20 March 1865. This statute (Appendix E of which is still in force) gave on the one hand (*per* art. 2) ordinary courts the competence to protect the "civil or political rights" of the citizens (by and large respecting franchise and eligibility, personal and contract freedoms, and property). On the other hand, hierarchical appeals[57] could be brought against the administrative acts concerning affairs which involved legitimate interests other than "civil or political rights" (art. 3). Furthermore, *per* Appendix D, citizens who exhausted their hierarchical appeals were allowed to bring an "extraordinary" appeal to the king, who had to decide, as a rule, in conformity with the advice of the Council of State.[58]

In order to comply with the principle of the division of powers, the annulment of unlawful administrative acts was precluded to the ordinary courts, which having ascertained violations of the rights protected, could only make a judgment against the administrative agencies for damages, but could not in any case annul the administrative measure inducing the act.

---

[56] *See* M. Nigro, *Giustizia amministrativa*, 5th ed. (E. Cardi, A. Nigro eds.), Bologna (1994), pp.51-87; A. Travi, *Lezioni di giustizia amministrativa*, 4th ed., Torino (2000), pp. 15-30.

[57] Which were to be decided after having heard the opinions of advisory bodies (art. 3).

[58] The Piedmont Council of State was preserved: its members were named, and could be recalled by the king on the proposal of the Minister of Home Affairs.

Finally, the Council of State was made judge of the complaints of the public administration about alleged infringements of the boundaries of their jurisdictions by the courts. However, the Italian Supreme Court (*Corte di Cassazione*) replaced it in this role of "judge of conflicts," sitting in joined divisions (*Sezioni Unite*), constituting the highest tier of the system of the ordinary courts of justice.[59]

In spite of a number of scholarly analyses of this legislation,[60] it is not yet clear whether the legislative intent was to enhance the guarantees of citizens or to limit them. In any case, the courts – and, above all, first the Council of State and then the Italian Supreme Court in their role as "judge of conflicts" – narrowly construed the ambit of jurisdiction over "civil and political rights." As a result (according to the allegations of opponents to this law), a number of legitimate interests lost the protection previously received through the system of administrative justice.

Therefore, some bills were proposed on the matter, and in 1898 a statute was passed[61] creating a new 4th section (*IV sezione*) of the Council of State, before which an administrative act could be challenged if it impinged upon the interest of an individual or a juridical person, in order to have it quashed on the grounds that it was unlawful "for incompetence for excess of power or for violation of law." However, the Council of State in this case had power of annulment over acts, but not the power of condemnation for damages. It could not collect evidence through examination of witnesses or by expert reports. Even though the statute did not define the new division of the Council of State as a judicial organ, the view of it as such came to prevail soon afterwards.

It can be said that since that time Italy has had two separate judicial hierarchies, one composed of ordinary courts and another composed of administrative courts. As a result, there were two venues for citizens to obtain judicial protection against administrative agencies. They had to complain before the ordinary courts for infringement of "subjective rights" and before the administrative courts when "legitimate interests" were at stake. And, as we have seen, there were also two different kinds of judicial protection in the two different cases. On the one hand, when "subjective rights" were at stake, the ordinary courts could only give

---

[59] In fact, in the first period, before there was only one Supreme Court, the task was entrusted to the *Corte di Cassazione* of Rome: Act no. 3761 of 31 March 1977.

[60] *See* Aldo Piras, "Trends of administrative law," in Aldo Piras (ed.), *supra* note 55, at 237 *ff*, fn. 7.

[61] Law no. 5992 of 31 March 1898. Another Act of the same year established in every Province the *Giunte Provinciali Amministrative*, to which law no. 6837 of 1 May 1890 gave first instance jurisdiction over local government administrative acts.

judgments for damages against the administrative agencies, but they could not annul the administrative measures. On the other hand, when the litigation concerned "legitimate interests," the administrative courts, which had limited proof-taking powers, could only annul administrative acts, and could not give judgments for damages.

Until very recently, the system did not undergo any substantial reform.

It is worth recalling that two more jurisdictional divisions of the Council of State (the 5th[62] and 6th[63] sections) and the Regional Administrative Courts (TAR) with general jurisdiction in the first instance had also been established. Also worthy of mention is one provision of a law passed in 1923 for the extension of the competence of administrative courts to complaints involving subjective rights, including public employment litigation. This "exclusive jurisdiction" has been extended over the years and, as we will see, it is the basis of a recent major reform.

Finally, it may be recalled that the system of administrative courts also includes the Court of Accounts (*Corte dei Conti*).[66]

Without lingering to discuss its historical origins (which are similar to those of the Council of State), we will note that the responsibility of this court is to check the legality of the acts of government, perform crucial auditing tasks,[67] and carry out the task of prosecuting public officials and employees who damage the State or other public bodies (so-called administrative liability).[68]

C. The Constitution

The Constitution of 1948 itself confirms the typical features of the system. It guarantees, always and to all people, the judicial protection of both subjective rights and legitimate interests (arts. 24 para. 1 and 113 para. 1) and, in any case, full judicial protection against all administrative acts (art. 113 para. 2).

---

[62] Law no. 62 of 7 March 1907.

[63] Law Decree no. 642 of 5 May 1948.

[64] Law no. 1034 of 6 December 1971.

[65] Law no. 2840 of 30 December 1923.

[66] The *Corte dei Conti* of the Italian Reign was instituted by law no. 800 of 14 August 1862.

[67] Roughly comparable with the functions of the US General Accounting Office.

[68] *See* arts. 81, 82, and 83, Royal Decree no. 2440 of 18 November 1923, and arts. 18 and 19 DPR no. 3 of 10 January 1957. The damages can also come from having held the agencies liable for damages to third parties.

First, it preserves both the ordinary and the administrative courts. But, with regard to the latter, it adds to the already existent "organs of administrative justice" (art. 103 para. 1) (*i.e.* the Council of State and the Court of Accounts) "organs of administrative justice" to be established in the Regions (art. 125 para. 2). Secondly, it preserves the role of the Council of State as the main legal and administrative advisory body to the government administration (art. 100 para. 1).[69] Thirdly, it divides judicial jurisdiction between ordinary and administrative courts, as a rule, on the grounds of the subjective position (either "subjective rights" or "legitimate interests") whose infringement is alleged by the citizen. However, the Constitution allows the legislator to give the administrative courts jurisdiction over litigation of subjective rights (art. 103 para. 1) in particular matters and, on the other hand, to authorize, in certain cases, the annulment of administrative acts by the ordinary courts (*see* art. 113 para. 3, for implication). Fourthly, it maintains the Court of Accounts both as an organ with competence over the preventive control of the legality of government acts and subsequent control of the management of the budget (art. 100 para. 2), and as a judicial organ with jurisdiction over matters of public accounts and such other questions as are specified by law (art. 103 para. 2). Finally, the Constitution states that the law ensures the independence of the judges of special courts (art. 108 para. 2), among which are included the administrative courts.

D. At the Beginning of the 21st Century

1. Judicial Review and Administrative Discretionary Powers

The judicial review of administrative acts is the main task of what is called administrative justice; the other is formed by the administrative appeals, the importance of which is far less relevant in practice. The greater importance of judicial review now results also from the above-mentioned constitutional rules. It is important to note that the combination of constitutional and legislative provisions and judge-made law brings to an end the principle that the whole of administrative action is subject to judicial review.

The class of political or governmental acts, which are in principle not reviewable, as opposed to administrative acts, has been increasingly narrowed by judge-made law. Exempted from judicial review are only the acts issued by the Executive concerning relationships with foreign countries or the definition of the main lines of a policy (*e.g.*, the establishment of criteria and plans to distribute special strategic

---

[69] According to which the tasks of the Council of State include safeguarding justice within the public administration.

funds) or certain top-level fiduciary appointments (*e.g.*, the appointment of the presidents of some public agencies).

It must also be borne in mind that the review of regulations enacted by the central and local governments, which have a legislative, even if secondary, character, falls under the jurisdiction of the administrative courts (whereas it is within the exclusive jurisdiction of the Constitutional Court to review the constitutionality of State and regional laws, as well as other acts having the same force, such as *decreti legislativi* and *decreti legge, see supra*, chapter 3, p. 52).

However, it is still a commonly held belief that the constitutional rule of judicial review of administrative actions has to be reconciled with the separation of powers principle. Therefore, whereas no problem arises when the action is completely bound by law, this reconciliation is problematic when the law grants discretionary powers to the administrative agencies.

On the other hand, in some cases it could prove a somewhat difficult task to establish whether or not an agency has such discretion; and yet the distinction is highly important in the Italian system, where, as described below, such a distinction could still be central in many cases to overcoming the difficulty of drawing the line between the jurisdictions of ordinary and administrative courts.

According to the current doctrine, both the principles of reviewability and separation of powers mentioned above are met when review by the courts is confined to reviewing the legality, and not the merits, of the administrative action. Yet when an administrative act is attacked on the grounds of a so-called excess of power – a subject addressed below – the borderline between legality and merits becomes blurred.

As for the distinction between discretionary and non-discretionary administrative actions, according to the prevailing view, an agency has administrative discretionary powers when different interests, whether public or private, have to be taken into account and balanced. In this view, a discretionary decision, even if it can be viewed as always intended to enhance the public interest, actually must reconcile different interests if possible, or to choose among them.

However, under certain factual circumstances, an agency is often bound to issue only a certain act. But the existence of such circumstances can be disputable, as when, for example, its proof depends on divergent scientific or technical opinions. Suppose, for instance, that an agency for environmental protection must order a mill to cease its activity because waste water flowing from the mill into a river contains some kind of toxic substance. Suppose also that there are several technical methods of testing the toxicity and quantity of the substances, which produce differing results. In this case, it is unclear whether the courts can condemn the agency's choice or must defer to it (apart from a review on questions of legality, such as reasonableness, or consistency of the decision-making process, both discussed below). According to the case law, the second solution must be followed on the ground that in this case, as maintained by some legal scholars, the agencies enjoy a "technical discretion" (as contrasted with the "administrative discretion," which could after all be political in nature).

2. Rights, Legitimate Interests, and Standing

As we have seen above, the Constitution states that judicial protection against administrative acts must always be accorded – as an absolute right, not submitted to any previous screening or leave, and exempt from any ousting whatsoever – before the ordinary or administrative courts. Again, the Constitution assigns the general protection of legitimate interests to the jurisdiction of the *Consiglio di Stato* and of the other administrative courts of first instance. This excludes particular subject matters, where the laws may give administrative courts exclusive jurisdiction (*giurisdizione esclusiva*).[70] It is irrelevant in these cases if the issue involves rights or legitimate interests.

As a rule, jurisdiction belongs to the ordinary courts if the issue concerns "subjective rights" (*diritti soggettivi*) and to the administrative courts if the issue concerns "legitimate interests" (*interessi legittimi*). The kind of entitlement, the protection of which is sought before the judge, sets forth the criterion for the distribution of jurisdiction between the two kinds of court.

Given these circumstances, when the subject matter does not fall within the exclusive jurisdiction of the administrative courts, the crucial question faced by anyone seeking judicial protection is how to distinguish "subjective rights" from "legitimate interests" and the latter from other legally irrelevant interests which (even if they possibly constitute matter for the political process) fall outside any jurisdiction. However, the boundary between the second and third categories can be uncertain (take, for example, certain diffuse interests), and the issue can emerge as not easily distinguishable from that of standing (see below).

Roughly speaking, and without specific reference to the public administration, we can say, using a hypothetical subject, that:

  a) Ms. White has a "right" when another person or all persons, according to the law, ought to behave in a specified way that would satisfy a specific interest held by Ms. White. In this case, Ms. White may demand the full and specific satisfaction of her specific interest before a court.

---

[70] However, we will see below that the exclusive jurisdiction of the administrative courts has been expanded recently to include very broad and important new fields.

Some examples of this include the legal obligation not to disturb Ms. White in the enjoyment of her property, or the contractual obligation of giving something or paying an amount of money to Ms. White.

b) By contrast, when Ms. White claims to have a specific interest (which is lawful and distinguishable from that of the general public) and another person does not have a corresponding specific obligation to satisfy that interest, but has the power to choose among a number of courses of action, just one of which would satisfy the interest of Ms. White, a "legitimate interest" arises if he who has the power to choose has the duty to comply with certain legal standards in making the decision (so that the latter is, for instance, not only lawful but also reasonable, unbiased, or at least not capricious, etc.). In this case, Ms. White may demand that a court check the compliance with these legal standards (and to set aside the decision if the standards are not complied with).

For example: a local authority may have the power to decide to give (or not to give) Ms. White the taxi-driver's license that she requires. Or the administrative authority in certain circumstances may also decide (or not) to expropriate Ms. White's land, which might be needed to widen a town square. In these cases, Ms. White has a merely "legitimate interest," not a "right" to acquire this privilege, or better this "new property"[71] (in the first case), or to preserve the property (in the second case).

c) Finally, there is neither a "subjective right" nor a "legitimate interest" if the law may be construed as neither imposing an obligation of behaving in the specific way which meets Ms. White's interests nor as establishing some legal standards to be followed when it is to make a decision that can interfere with these interests.

To conclude, from a legal relation with any other natural or legal person there may originate, in the abstract, either a right or a legitimate interest. However, the latter may be more easily and normally found when there is a relation with public agencies, due to the principles that govern their activity and, more specifically, their discretionary decisions, according to the rule of law.

Therefore, in administrative law relations, a simple way of describing the difference between subjective rights and legitimate interests is to say that:

a) a person is entitled to a "legitimate interest" if the administrative agency has a discretionary power (subject to legal standards) to decide if his or her specific interest should or should not be satisfied;

---

[71] *See* C. A. Reich, "The New Property," 72 *Yale LJ* 733 (1964).

b) a person has a "subjective right" when the law does not accord any power of choice to the agency, but directly establishes the conditions under which his or her specific interest must be satisfied by the administration.

However, according to the traditional doctrine[72] still followed by the courts, we should also speak of legitimate interest (and not of right) when an agency is legally bound to behave in a way that actually satisfies the interest of a person, provided that this obligation of the agency has to be construed as aimed to the satisfaction not of the individual interest, but of the public interest, so that the satisfaction of the individual interest should be seen as a mere consequence of the satisfaction of the public interest.

Nevertheless, it is easy to see that when no "right" (in the above-described strict sense) is at stake, it can be uncertain if an interest must be seen as a "legitimate interest" or merely as an interest without any judicial protection. To be "legitimate," an interest needs to be protected by law, which means that it must be within the zone of interests to the protection of which a statute or other source of law is designed.

From the American point of view, legitimate interests can sometimes be compared to "privileges," and sometimes the distinction between "legitimate interests" and mere interests may be seen as an issue of standing. By contrast, from the Italian point of view, the problem of standing is now[73] seen as a different issue. The applicant must show both that he or she is the bearer of the "legitimate interest" at stake and that the remedy sought could be truly useful in redressing the allegedly unlawful infringement of his or her interest. This should help avoid public actions (*azioni popolari*) that are merely aimed at preserving the lawfulness of official actions, which are allowed by some statutes only in very few cases.

Moreover, the interests that can be given judicial protection must belong to a "person" (either a natural or a legal person).[74] Therefore, establishing it may be

---

[72] Even if it is now suffering criticism by some scholars as a doctrine whose results are not as certain as they should be in order to operate as a criterion for distributing the jurisdiction. In any case, to return to a problem noted above, following this approach, even when it is denied that the judges must defer to the agencies about their technical choices or, in other words, that the agencies have a "technical discretion," the jurisdiction would still belong to the administrative courts.

[73] Actually, according to ancient doctrines, the "legitimate interest" was in fact substantially the equivalent of standing.

[74] *See* art. 26 of Royal Decree no. 1054 of 26 June 1924, and art. 2 of law no. 1034 of 6 December 1971.

problematic if and when judicial redress can be sought for unlawful infringement of diffuse interests. Some statutes provide that certain private associations may always bring an action before the courts to review administrative actions in order to protect environmental or consumer interests.[75]

3. Tasks, Powers and Procedures of the Ordinary Courts and the Administrative Courts

It is worth pointing out that the protection given by the two different judicial hierarchies against the unlawful behavior of administrative agencies differs, not only with respect to the different kinds of entitlements for which the protection is sought, but also with regard to the tasks, powers, and procedures of each hierarchy.

Things now seem to be undergoing substantial change, both because of the widening of the exclusive jurisdiction of the administrative courts and the narrowing of the differences between the powers of the two types of jurisdictions. However, the dual system has been preserved.

a. Tasks

The traditional task of the ordinary civil courts was to protect subjective rights (as distinct from the protection of personal freedom that is mostly the business of the criminal courts), as contrasted with legitimate interests. Thus, their jurisdiction traditionally covers (and is confined to) controversies over rights against public administration. However, since, as we shall see, not all kinds of ordinary judgments are admitted where an administrative agency is a defendant, it was mainly up to the ordinary courts to adjudicate complaints grounded on contract or tort law.

On the other hand, there are now a great number of controversies over rights that fall within the exclusive jurisdiction of the administrative courts.

As for contract-related litigation, even though the agreements regarding the discretionary content of an administrative decision are governed in principle by ordinary contract law,[76] these controversies fall within the exclusive jurisdiction of the administrative courts.

As for torts litigation, it should first be noted that in principle, the general tort law applies. And yet, according to long-established case law, compensation could not be awarded for alleged damages claimed on the grounds of the infringement

---

[75] *See* art. 18 of law no. 349 of 8 July 1989, and art. 3 of law no. 281 of 30 July 1998.

[76] Part II B 3, *supra*.

not of a "right" but of a "legitimate interest."[77] Indeed, these precedents have been overruled by a recent judgment of the Unified Sections of the Italian Supreme Court (no. 500/1999),[78] which asserts that an individual can claim before an ordinary court the right to be indemnified for an illegal infringement, not only of a subjective right, but also of a legitimate interest. (Losses due to a discretionary decision taken by an administrative agency, even if unlawful, are not recoverable damages when even a lawful decision could not have satisfied the interested parties). However, as we shall soon see, the more recent law reforms thwarted this expansion of the tasks of ordinary civil courts.

The original task of the administrative courts was the judicial review of administrative action, and thus the protection of legitimate interests. Judicial review is aimed at ensuring the legality of the administrative decision – that is, the compliance with a set of special rules, consisting of explicit or implicit principles of law rooted in the Constitution and regarded as stemming from the legality principle, most of which are the standards usually gathered under the traditional heading of manifold significance, "excess of power."

Technically speaking, judicial review constitutes a check on the administrative acts aimed at determining whether the acts are flawed by an irregularity under one of the three headings described since 1889 by the laws regulating the administrative courts as "incompetence," "excess of power," and "violation of law."

To be brief, an act is said to be flawed by "incompetence" when its author lacked the authority to issue it. This may occur either because the act was issued after the expiration of a mandatory time limit, or the author acted outside of his geographical jurisdiction, or the officer not have jurisdiction over the subject matter to which the act refers.

"Excess of power" is a very far-reaching heading, since it encompasses both what the French call *détournement de pouvoir*, or diversion of power, and certain hypotheses embraced by the English doctrine of *ultra vires*.

Agencies have the primary duty to pursue the aims established in the statutes empowering them or those established by other government policy directions, such as government guidelines or programs (provided that they are not contrary to law),

---

[77] Indeed, some damages caused by administrative decisions infringing upon legitimate interests were usually compensated. For instance, the Italian courts maintained that when a building permit or a commercial license, lawfully granted, was unlawfully repealed or unrenewed, the damages issuing therefrom should be indemnified (even though following the long process explained in note 85, *infra*).

[78] Of 22 July (*Comune di Fiesole v. Vitali*). See *Foro italiano*, 1999, I, 2487. *See also* Appellate Court of Florence Case no. 1055 of 28 May 2001.

which are usually deemed to be in the public interest. An administrative act is seen as flawed by diversion of power when it is turned to an improper purpose, *i.e.* towards a goal (a private or public interest) different from the peculiar public interest upon which the power to act was given by the law (*e.g.*, when a prohibition to cut some stunted trees is issued on the grounds of a power granted in order to protect the landscape, whereas the real aim was to prevent building in an overly-crowded urban zone).

As for the other flaws, suffice it to note that administrative acts must, above all, be "reasonable," which means not arbitrary or capricious, nor grounded on irrelevant considerations, nor inconsistent with their premises or with other administrative decisions, nor grounded on errors of fact, and so on.

Under the influence of the case law of the European Community Court of Justice, the reasonableness of an administrative measure is also going to be tested frequently on the grounds of its "proportionality." This concept, which comes from German case law, has a substantive meaning long-recognized in Italian administrative law: the measure must be suitable and necessary for the achievement of its objective and may not, in any case, impose on the concerned individual a greater burden than that strictly needed to satisfy the public interest at stake.

The decision must be also impartial. That is to say, it must be free of bias and must also take into account all the relevant interests, whether public or private, that emerge over the course of the procedure.

Finally, a "violation of law" can be alleged when a primary or secondary piece of legislation, including European regulations, is infringed upon. For instance, on these grounds, the compliance of a decision-making process is tested against the due process rules established by law no. 241/1990, but compliance with other rules of the same law (for example, the rules on access to administrative records)[79] is also checked.

Moreover, according to the so-called principle of "typicality" of administrative measures (regarded as a corollary to the principle of legality), an administrative act impinging upon a subject's liberties or rights would be considered flawed if it is not of a kind specifically provided for by law.

Until very recently, judicial review was the only task of administrative courts. However, just before judgment no. 500/1999, mentioned above, Legislative Decree no. 80/1998[80] provided that they can also adjudicate damages in subject matters

---

[79]   *See* part I A 2, *Access to the Agencies' Records, supra.*

[80]   *See* arts. 33-35 of Legislative Decree no. 80 of 31 March 1998 on delegation by law no. 59 of 15 March 1997, c. 4, g.

falling within their exclusive jurisdiction. At the same time, decree no. 80 added many broad new subjects[81] (even though they are not always clearly defined) to this jurisdiction, so that now it encompasses the larger portion of litigation of the public administrations, ranging, for instance, from land and urban planning, access to public records, or agreements on the content of administrative decisions to public utilities, public procurements, or independent authorities acts.[82]

On the other hand, just after judgment no. 500, a new law (no. 205/2000)[83] stated that the administrative courts can also adjudicate damages whenever they have jurisdiction, not just when they have exclusive jurisdiction.

b. Final and Provisional Judgments

According to the law of 1865,[84] the ordinary courts can neither annul, suspend, nor modify an administrative act, but can only set it aside if they conclude that it is contrary to the law. According to case law, the courts have no power to order an administrative agency to undertake a specific administrative act, whereas they can order the agency to pay a sum of money. They can also declare the right of the plaintiff, in the very limited circumstances in which a declaratory judgment is allowed. In fact, until judgment no. 500/1999 of the Unified Sections of the Italian Supreme Court, in order for an ordinary court to hold an administrative agency liable for damages caused by an administrative act, the act had first to be quashed by an administrative court.[85] Now, an ordinary court can award damages without

---

[81] It remains to be seen what results will proceed from the Constitutional challenge to this law already pending, because it is doubtful that such an extension of the exclusive jurisdiction is Constitutional without amending the Constitution, which allows this kind of jurisdiction of the administrative courts only in "particular matters" (art. 103).

[82] Before Legislative Decree no. 80/1998, the main subject matter falling within the exclusive jurisdiction of the administrative courts was public employment. Since 1 July 1998, the jurisdiction over public employment litigation has been up to the ordinary courts.

[83] Law no. 2005 of 21 July 2000 whose art. 7, modified art. 35 para, 4 of Legislative Decree no. 80/98.

[84] *See* part II B, *supra.*

[85] Therefore, the allegedly harmed person first had to appear as a plaintiff before a TAR; then likely had to appear as a defendant, or as a plaintiff again, before the *Consiglio di Stato*; then, had to go before an ordinary judiciary office of the first instance, as a plaintiff; then likely had to present the case either as a defendant or as a plaintiff before the Court of Appeal, which could again review the merits of the case; and then needed to appear before the Italian Supreme Court for questions of law. Later, possibly, he or she would have been required to bring a new action to cause the final judgment to be enforced. Statistics suggest the entire proceeding could take more than twenty years.

any previous judgment of the administrative court, but the prohibition of the annulment, suspension and modification of administrative acts remains in force (grounded, as noted above, in a now anachronistic idea of the separation of powers).

Both the administrative agency[86] and the officer who personally caused the damages can be sued. Usually, the agency is sued. In this case, if the agency must pay damages, the Public Prosecutor of the Court of Accounts[87] can bring the officer before this Court to recover the damages paid by the agency or at least an equitable sum of money, taking into account the seriousness of his or her violations of duty, if any.

The ordinary courts may also adjudicate questions of contracts for public works or procurements. However, the selection of the counterpart and the awarding of the contract are thought of as administrative acts; as we have seen above, the administrative courts enjoy exclusive jurisdiction in this matter, and therefore also adjudicate the question of damages.

The action before an administrative court must take the form of an appeal against an "administrative act" in order to be quashed. The administrative act is thought of as absolutely necessary for the commencement of such an action, to the point that, to challenge the failure to act by an administrative agency, the aggrieved party must attempt to impugn the silence of the agency.

According to case law, annulment prohibits the agency from renewing the quashed act (unless it has been amended according to the judgment), and requires the agency to arrive at a new decision on the unsuccessful original application for the act. This new decision must conform to the points of law on which the judgment is grounded (*e.g.*, if the refusal of a building permit is annulled, the application shall be newly considered in compliance with the directions which may be elicited from the judgment). This effect of the judgment, called "conformative" effect by scholars, is in some ways greater than that of *res judicata* because it is tied to the *ratio decidendi* itself, and not solely with to final orders and decisions of the judgment.

As we have seen, whereas traditionally the administrative courts could not enter judgments against an administrative agency to pay money (except in a limited number of cases), they now have the power to adjudicate damages against the public administration whenever they have jurisdiction, whether or not such jurisdiction is exclusive.

---

[86] Because the agents of the administration, according to the so-called "organic doctrine," can be thought of as organs of the State without personal relevance.

[87] *See* part II B, *supra*.

The administrative courts can also issue a specific provisional remedy: they may order a stay of execution of challenged acts in order to suspend their legal effects and enforcement. The stay is granted when the judges are persuaded, after a *prima facie* examination, that doubts about the legality of the act under attack appear grounded and that, without the stay, the plaintiff (which can be a private party, but can also be another agency) will suffer serious and irreparable prejudice before the final judgment is entered. Quite often the administrative courts also compare and balance the feared prejudice alleged by the plaintiff with the urgency of acting in view of the public interest.

As can be seen, this provisional remedy is negative in nature. Thus, it can be useful when the plaintiff's attack is aimed at preventing the agency from enacting a measure contrary to his or her interests (*e.g.*, an expropriation). But it is not useful when the plaintiff seeks an administrative act (*e.g.*, a license) because the stay of execution of an act's refusal would not result in any case in the issuance of the act sought. Indeed, the case law has extended the reach of the stay in some cases, furnishing it with it positive effects as well (*e.g.*, the stay of the refusal of the renewal of a license for a shop has been construed as a stay of the effects of the expiration of the license to be renewed).

In any case, these restrictions of provisional remedies hampered effective judicial protection, and was considered inadmissible by commentators. Law no. 205/2000 removes these restrictions, and the administrative courts now also have the power to grant any provisional remedy which they determine appropriate to the case.

c. Enforcement of Judgments

We can also note remarkable differences between the enforcement of judgments of the ordinary and the administrative courts, flowing from the different constraints affecting their powers that we have discussed.

The judgments of the ordinary courts that only declare the unlawfulness of an act give rise to the agencies' duty to act according to the statements of law embodied in the judgment. This general (but essentially vague) obligation may be enforced by means of an action for compliance (*giudizio di ottemperanza*), which is a special action before the administrative courts aimed at compelling the agencies to render a new decision according to the law embodied in the judgment of a court.

The enforcement of the judgment against an administrative agency to pay a sum of money is in principle analogous to that which follows the end of a private lawsuit. However, not all property belonging to the public administrations can be seized, and one frequently has to bring the action for compliance before the administrative courts in order to obtain payment.

The judgments rendered by the administrative courts are self-executing and do not require any enforcement concerning the annulment of an administrative act. However, we have seen that after the quashing of the challenged act, the agency has the duty to issue a new act abiding by the "conformative content" of the judgment – that is to say, by the directions which can be drawn by the judgment regarding the renewal of the act that has been quashed. In cases in which the agency infringes upon these duties, taking a new measure in contrast with the judgment and therefore one considered invalid, the administrative court may be asked, via an action for compliance, to enforce its own judgment with regard to its conformative effect. Such a measure prevents an endless chain of appeals against subsequent acts of the administration. In such cases, the procedure for compliance before the administrative court (the same court that rendered the judgment) may end with issuance of an order that substitutes the due decision (which can occur only when no discretion is left to the administration), or committing to issue the due decision to a commissioner of justice appointed to the case (*commissario ad acta*).

d. Time Limits

The time limits applicable to actions before the administrative courts differ from those for the ordinary courts. Five-year limitation terms usually apply for complaints falling within the jurisdiction of the ordinary courts (those concerning "rights"). By contrast, an administrative act must be challenged before the administrative courts within 60 days of the date on which the party has knowledge thereof (knowledge that does not necessarily result from notification). This is a mandatory term, even though the judge retains the traditional power, exercised with strict self-restraint, to toll the prescription for excusable delay.

e. Evidence

There is no limitation on admissible evidence within the general system of evidence employed by the ordinary courts; thus, they can even consider and ascertain facts outside of the record. By contrast, the process before the administrative courts was once characterized by a strong limitation on evidence relied upon: they could not admit nor use testimony or expert witnesses, so that the review was made almost exclusively on the record. Now, law no. 205/2000 removes these restrictions, according them the power to admit expert witnesses and, in cases of exclusive jurisdiction, testimonial evidence as well.

E. The Main Faults of the System

This machinery for protecting citizens from unlawful actions by the public administration has some serious flaws.

1. Conflicts of Jurisdiction

Since ordinary courts and administrative courts constitute two separate judicial hierarchies, a court that adjudicates conflicts of jurisdiction is needed for the system to work. This role is performed by the *Sezioni Unite* of the Italian Supreme Court, whose decisions mostly turn on whether the issue before a particular court concerns rights or legitimate interests.

Indeed, in every country in which there are both ordinary and administrative courts (or, as in England, where particular procedures exist which apply to the judicial review of administrative actions), a single criterion for distinguishing between the different judicial authorities is needed, and some problems arise when such a criterion comes into operation. Let us take as an example the distinction between what is and is not a government service,[88] or that between private law rights and public law rights,[89] or between private law and public law.[90]

The task of the Italian conflicts court was at one time thought of as very difficult because, as noted above, drawing the distinction between the two kinds of entitlements can prove highly problematic. Following recent reforms, the job of the United Sections of the Italian Supreme Court should become easier because in many fields of litigation it is no longer necessary to distinguish between rights and legitimate interests. There are, however, still fields in which the old distinction is needed, and whether the controversy falls within the exclusive jurisdiction of the administrative courts can still sometimes be disputed. Now the expansion of the exclusive jurisdiction of the administrative courts in new matters, reduces problems of distinction between subjective rights and legitimate interests on the one hand, though on the other hand it spurs new doubts since the boundaries of these new fields are sometimes indistinct. Because the possible need for a conflict judgment – which, according to past experience, can also be abused just to waste time – is a serious burden for anyone seeking justice, and because law no. 205/2000 assimilated the authorities of the ordinary and administrative courts much more than in the past, some commentators hold the view that the separation between the two tiers of courts should be abolished, providing for some divisions of ordinary courts

---

[88] A criterion applying in France.

[89] A criterion applying in Germany.

[90] A criterion applying in England.

staffed with specialized judges.[91] Such a measure would also eliminate the anomaly common to France and Italy of the Council of State, which simultaneously acts as judge and advisor to the public administration.

2. The Inflation of Judicial Remedies

The output of the Italian system of protection against wrongful administrative actions is an apparent inflation of judicial claims. This may be explained as follows.

First, insufficient attention has been given to the hearings of interested persons before administrative decisions are rendered.[92] It is not yet clear whether the general right to a written opinion given by the above-mentioned law no. 241/1990 on the administrative procedure will help in avoiding litigation.

Secondly, since the regional administrative courts were set up, it has no longer been necessary that hierarchical administrative appeals be exhausted before an issue is taken to the administrative court.[93] On the other hand, people do not like these now optional remedies, because they are usually adjudicated by the same authority that rendered the decision appealed (*ricorsi in opposizione*), or by a hierarchically superior authority (*ricorsi gerarchici*), both of which are seen as biased by those who are convinced that the agencies will always have the last laugh.

Finally, there is a shortage of alternative, non-judicial channels through which one can seek redress either instead of or before resorting to the courts. There are very few organs composed of independent lawyers and other experts similar to the English Administrative Tribunals, to which people can address their problems without excessive formalism.

Where such tribunals operate, as in the field of social security, a very large percentage of controversies are settled without the need to file complaints with the courts. In addition, for controversies that pertain to public works, a recent law

---

[91] Another proposal is to preserve the administrative courts, but redefine their judicial authority on new grounds abolishing a conflicts court (along the lines of the German model). Moreover, the administrative courts would have to be deprived of any advisory competence. All these sorts of reforms would require constitutional amendments. Therefore, they became topical when Parliament set up a special Bicameral charged with proposing extensive constitutional reform (*Commissione Bicamerale per le Riforme Costituzionali*). Indeed, the Committee made proposals similar to those of the second kind (that can be seen in *Diritto Pubblico*, 1997, no. 3). However, the special constitutional reform procedure has been interrupted. *See* chapter 3, *supra*.

[92] However, in this direction, the new independent authorities have taken some meaningful steps.

[93] *See* DPR no. 1199 of 24 November 1971.

provides for a procedure aimed at reaching an agreement before the lawsuit is filed and allows the parties to present themselves before a special organ for arbitration (*camera arbitrale*) when they do not reach an agreement.[94]

IV. Selected Bibliography

E. Casetta, *Manuale di diritto amministrativo*, 2nd ed., Giuffrè, Milano (2000).

S. Cassese, *Le basi del diritto amministrativo*, 6th ed., Garzanti, Milano (1995).

M. S. Giannini, *Diritto Amministrativo*, 2 vols., 3rd ed., Giuffrè, Milano (1993).

Mario Nigro, *Giustizia Amministrativa*, 5th ed., Il Mulino, Bologna (2000). E. Cardi and A. Nigro (eds.).

L. Mannori, B. Sordi, *Storia del diritto amministrativo*, Laterza, Bari (2001).

L. Mazzarolli *et al.* (eds.), *Diritto Amministrativo*, 2 vols., 2nd ed., Monduzzi, Bologna (1998).

A. Romano, *Commentario breve alle leggi sulla giustizia amministrativa*, CEDAM, Padova (1992).

D. Sorace *et al.* (eds.), *Materiali del diritto amministrativo*, CEDAM, Padova (2000).

D. Sorace, *Diritto delle amministrazioni pubbliche. Una introduzione*, Il Mulino, Bologna (2000).

A. Travi, *Lezioni di giustizia amministrativa*, 4th ed., Giappichelli, Torino (1998).

P. Virga, *Diritto Amministrativo*, Giuffrè, Milano,vol. 1, *I principi*, 5th ed., (1999); vol. 2, *Atti e ricorsi*, 5th ed. (1999); vol. 3, *Amministrazione locale*, 3rd ed. (1998); vol. 4, *Attività e prestazioni*, 2nd ed. (1996).

---

[94] *See* art. 32 of law no. 109 of 11 February 1994, as modified by art. 10 of law no. 415 of 18 November 1998.

Civil Procedure and the Path of a Civil Case

Michele Taruffo [1]

I. Preliminary Problems

The Italian John Doe who needs the support of a court in order to obtain the fulfillment of a right or of a legally protected interest is in a very unfortunate situation. First of all, he has to find a lawyer who agrees to represent him; secondly, he will need to have the money to pay the lawyer he wishes to hire. The two, of course, are intimately related. To find a lawyer is usually not difficult at all. Italy has about 100,000 practicing lawyers now, one of the highest rates *per capita* in Europe. On the other hand, fees are not extremely high when compared with the money at stake in the case, except in small claims and in other cases where the amounts in controversy are relatively minor. Moreover, John Doe may rely on the fundamental rule governing attorney fees and costs in Italy, according to which "the loser pays all" and the winner will be compensated for all the costs he has been required to incur. If our hypothetical client's claim is well-founded, he has a high probability of winning his case and his party-opponent will be compelled to pay for everything. But this does not solve the problem entirely. In Italy, contingent fees are forbidden by the law and lawyers will not bear the costs of a case by themselves without being paid for their work throughout the entire proceedings. Therefore, our John Doe will be required to pay in advance, and in the course of the process, all the money necessary to cover the costs of the case and at least a part of the attorney's fees, until the moment when the judgment allocates all these costs according to the "loser pays all" rule. This would not be a great problem if the time required to achieve the judgment were short. On the contrary, however, the length of civil proceedings in Italy is, in most cases, excessive. An average case may require three or four years to proceed through the court of first instance. But eight

---

[1]   Professor of Civil Procedure, University of Pavia.

Jeffrey S. Lena and Ugo Mattei (eds.), *Introduction to Italian Law*, 159-180
©2002 Kluwer Law International. Printed in the Netherlands.

or ten years, especially in complex cases, is not uncommon. This means that our John Doe must be able to bear all these costs for several years, until his case comes to a conclusion in the court of first instance.

Delays in civil justice have other negative consequences as well. Their main effect is that, unless a preliminary order is obtained (*see infra* part II), John Doe will be obliged to wait a long time before actually obtaining a judgment that acknowledges his right and provides for the protection and fulfillment of that right. In some cases this may not be a problem, but in most cases the old maxim "justice delayed, justice denied" is a faithful picture of Italian reality.

II. Strategic Choices

Let us imagine, however, that all these preliminary obstacles are overcome, and that our John Doe decides that his case deserves to be filed. The following step is to decide *how* to proceed. This is the moment at which several important choices have to be made by his lawyer.

Such choices concern four main problems: (i) jurisdiction; (ii) the types of proceedings; (iii) whether to file the case in court or to use some kind of alternative dispute resolution (ADR); and (iv) whether to move for preliminary injunctions and orders.

Jurisdiction is the threshold problem, and essentially concerns the fundamental distinction existing in Italy between the ordinary civil jurisdiction and the special administrative jurisdiction. If John Doe's legal situation may be defined as a "right" in the proper sense of the word, then his case can be filed in an ordinary civil court of first instance (assuming that Italian courts have jurisdiction over the case, according to the ordinary rules of venue). But if the controversy involves what is considered to be no more than a "legitimate interest" that John Doe has on the basis of his relationship with any body, branch, or agency of the state of local administration, then his case has to be filed before a special Administrative Regional Tribunal (TAR) in the first instance. Making such a distinction may be very difficult in specific cases, since the criteria used to define and distinguish "rights" and "legitimate interests" are often vague and uncertain. The reason for this is that such criteria refer to the relationship between the regulatory power of the administration and John Doe's legal situation, so that in many cases a "right" becomes a "legitimate interest" when the administration is vested with a prevailing power to regulate the situation.

A mistake in defining the "nature" of the legal situation involved may have significant negative effects, such as having to recommence the matter as a new case in a different court. This assumes, of course, that refiling under the applicable statute of limitations is still possible after having lost one's case in the "wrong" jurisdiction.

The second question involves the type of proceedings. If John Doe's legal situation is a "right," then the "ordinary" jurisdiction applies, and the consequent problem which flows from that conclusion is to choose the procedure most appropriate to the specific case. This problem arises because in the Italian procedural system a variety of proceedings exist. Aside from the "ordinary" proceedings, considered a kind of general model, there are several "special" proceedings that are used when the case deals with particular matters. The most important examples of special proceedings concern labor disputes and landlord-tenant cases. In such matters, the law takes into consideration the peculiar need for a speedy resolution of disputes. Accordingly, streamlined procedural rules apply, with the aim of a quicker and more effective disposition of cases. Therefore, an important preliminary decision is whether the particular case falls into one of the legally recognized categories covered by these special regulations, and hence whether the procedure employed to dispose of the case will be abbreviated and relatively tolerable compared with the more lengthy "ordinary" cases.

Other special procedures are used in areas such as divorce or bankruptcy because of the special nature of the subject matters involved. On the other hand, there are no special proceedings for commercial cases, which are tried and decided by ordinary civil courts according to the common procedural rules (with limited special provisions concerning some types of evidence).

An important type of "special" proceeding is a peculiar form of summary judgment that is frequently used for the collection of debts called the *procedimento di ingiunzione*. This procedure is available to the creditor with written proof of his or her right to a monetary payment or to the delivery of movable goods. In such cases, the creditor may obtain from the court a decree *inaudita altera parte* (*i.e.* without hearing from the debtor) with an order of payment issued to the debtor. This may occur even within a few hours, and the order may be made immediately enforceable. If the debtor thinks that it has been wrongly issued, the order may be attacked in subsequent proceedings. These special proceedings are very useful because of their summary nature, and their rapidity and effectiveness. However, they may be used only for the protection of the creditor in legal relationships that are based on written documents and have a determined content.

The third question faced by the attorney and client when filing a claim is whether he should go to court at all. In fact, in the Italian system, there are some Alternative Dispute Resolution devices that may be used in order to avoid resort to proceedings in court. The main ADR devices available are conciliation and arbitration.

Conciliation includes a group of procedures aimed at inducing the parties to settle their dispute. Conciliation may take place privately, but the law also provides several forms of "institutional" conciliation. Important examples exist in the area of labor disputes, where conciliation proceedings are provided both by collective agreements and by the law: special mediation committees exist for labor disputes and the Code of Civil Procedure regulates the legal effects of the settlements achieved before such committees. Parties are often obliged to attempt to settle their dispute before filing a complaint in court.

Arbitration is the main means of "private justice" in the civil domain. The parties may choose to employ arbitrators both in advance (*i.e.* when they make a contract), with reference to the disputes possibly arising from the contract, through the so-called *clausola compromissoria*, and when the dispute has already arisen, by a special agreement called the *compromesso*. In any case, a set of rules exists in the Italian Code of Civil Procedure providing for the choice of arbitrators, the fundamental principles governing the arbitration proceedings, and the form, effects, and recognition of arbitration awards. Several types of arbitration are permitted, according to the choice of the parties. They may choose an arbitration that will follow the procedural rules stated in the code (*arbitrato rituale*) or an arbitration that is managed by the arbitrators (*arbitrato irrituale*). The parties may also choose whether to bind the arbitrators to decide according to the law or to let them decide the case according to equitable standards.

The main advantages of arbitration are usually that the proceedings are quicker, and the parties may choose the arbitrators and stipulate the rules governing the proceedings. The main disadvantage is that arbitration is normally much more expensive than court proceedings. Therefore, a rational choice in favor of arbitration should take into consideration whether higher costs would be worth a more rapid resolution of the dispute.

If the option of arbitration is not chosen and the claim is filed in court, the attorney and client must decide whether to apply for a preliminary injunction or an order aimed at maintaining the *status quo*, or at realizing some sort of temporary protection until a final judgment is entered. The Italian system includes a variety of specific provisional orders (the most important is the attachment of real property or other assets), but a preliminary injunction may be obtained (*ex parte*, if necessary) in any case in which a claim is apparently well-founded (*fumus boni juris*) and the period of time needed to obtain a final judgment would cause an irreparable damage to the party (*periculum in mora*). Under such circumstances, the court may grant an order providing the remedies needed to prevent such a danger until the final judgment is issued. The Italian Code of Civil Procedure regulates this matter in detail, specifying the rights of the parties, the powers of the court, the form and content of the orders, and the remedies available to the parties. A 1990 reform introduced a new and complex regulation of preliminary injunctions, providing litigants with the possibility of having the order reconsidered and withdrawn by the same judge that delivered it when the situation has changed, as well as the right to file an appeal against the order to a higher court. This regulation includes a more sophisticated set of rules about preliminary injunctions, but one of its consequences is that the case is quite often actually tried in the proceedings concerning the injunction, rather than in the trial proceedings. A negative effect of this is that the procedure aimed at obtaining the preliminary injunction may become very long and complex.

III. The Structure of the Ordinary Proceedings

Having examined in brief the various threshold options available to the client, we turn now to the structure of the so-called ordinary proceedings. The ordinary proceedings commence when a complaint is filed by the *attore*, or plaintiff. The *convenuto*, or defendant, is supposed to answer (*see infra* part IV), and the process will usually end with a final judgment (*see infra* part VI). Between these two extremes of the complaint/answer and the final judgment, proceedings with a rather peculiar structure exist.

The most important feature of these proceedings is that they are not centered on a "trial" phase or on a single "trial hearing." Correspondingly, there is no "pre-trial" phase in the Anglo-American sense. The basic structure of the proceedings derives from their being organized "by installments," *i.e.* from the fact that they are composed of several hearings before the judge, the number of which is not determined in advance by law. Such hearings may be more or less numerous depending on the complexity of the case, and particularly on how many items of evidence must be presented. The hearings are fixed by the judge, but there is no necessary continuity in their sequence; not infrequently a delay of several months or even of one or two years may occur between hearings, depending on the docket of the judge.

There is, however, some order to the activities that occur over the course of the proceedings. At the first hearing, the judge checks whether all the conditions required by the law for the valid commencement of the case (such as jurisdiction, venue, proper parties, service, etc.) are present. If not, the judge will issue whatever orders are necessary to remedy the defects. If these preliminary conditions are met, a subsequent hearing is set that is devoted to the "preparation" of the case and to the attempt to settle the dispute. The preparation of the case includes a personal examination of the parties carried out by the judge, essentially with the aim of clarifying the facts in dispute, and an opportunity for the parties to clarify or modify their claims and defenses and, to a limited extent, to introduce new claims and defenses (with this aim, a delay may be granted to the parties and a further hearing may be fixed). In this same hearing, the judge invites the parties to consider the possibility of a settlement. If a settlement is reached (which occurs infrequently), the case is resolved and a record of the settlement is drafted. This record is enforceable, as if it were a judgment. If the case is not settled, a third or fourth hearing will then be devoted to the offer of further evidence by the parties and the decision of the judge concerning the relevancy and admissibility of the evidence offered. This group of hearings is used for the preparation of the case and often requires from six to twelve months, but in very busy courts it may even require a couple of years. With this, however, only the first phase of the proceedings has been accomplished.

If the defendant does not appear, and if the judge finds from the record that a complaint has been properly served upon him or her, the judge states that the proceedings will continue in defendant's default (*contumacia*). It must be stressed, however, that in Italy "default" does not have the same meaning that it has in Anglo-American systems. Under Italian rules, in fact, the proceedings will continue according to the ordinary rules, and the party will not automatically "lose." In fact, the only difference between a case defaulted and one not defaulted is that the defaulting party is not able to defend his or her case or to offer evidence. On the other hand, the defaulting party may decide at any moment to appear in order to defend the case, with the only limitation that he or she is not allowed to do things that are already barred at the moment when he or she appears. Thus, the loss of rights is limited. What is important to note is that the court will continue to inquire into the merits of the case presented by the plaintiff and will not decide in favor of the plaintiff merely because the defendant has defaulted. Rather, it will decide the case on its merits after having established the relevant facts according to the evidence available, and after due consideration of the law of the case.

It is worth emphasizing that the Italian procedural system does not have tools at its disposal similar to American discovery procedures. The parties have an obligation of reciprocal disclosure of relevant documents, but such an obligation may not be complied with and there are no special sanctions for non-compliance. If a relevant document is in the possession of the adverse party or of a non-party, and it is not produced voluntarily, the party interested in using the document to prove a fact may apply for a court order roughly corresponding to the American *subpoena duces tecum*. This order may be issued, however, only under very strict conditions (*e.g.* actual "necessity" of the document to prove a material fact, precise identification of the document and of the person in possession of it, and overcoming the protections afforded by privilege rules, etc.). If the order is not complied with, however, nearly irrelevant sanctions are applied, and therefore, where the document is damaging to the party holding it, there is little incentive to hand it over.

All other items of evidence must be identified and discovered by the lawyers, usually *before* starting the case and mainly on the basis of information supplied by the clients. In a sense, finding the available evidence is the most important way to decide *whether* it is worth filing the case, and to estimate the probability of prevailing if the case is commenced. Actually, facts should be stated and evidence offered in the first pleadings (*see infra* part IV). In order to do so, the plaintiff's lawyer must discover the available evidence *before* writing the complaint, and the defendant's lawyer has to do the same before writing the answer. In the course of the proceedings, further evidence may be discovered by the lawyers, but such discovery usually happens *outside of* the proceedings themselves. Therefore, this evidence has to be presented in court, provided it is still possible (that is, if the terms for the presentation of evidence have not yet expired). As a result of these rules, the preparation of a case should begin long before drafting the first pleadings: the case may be started only when it has already been prepared, at least in its most important factual and legal features.

When the subject matter of the case is defined, and the evidence has been admitted, one or more hearings will be devoted to the presentation of evidence (*see infra* part V). If the case is complex and the evidence includes several witnesses, the hearings may be numerous. Several months, or even years, may be required, again depending upon the judge's docket.

A further important characteristic of civil proceedings in Italy concerns the allocation of procedural powers between the parties and the judge. American lawyers are inclined to believe that Italian civil procedure (as well as the procedure in other civil law systems) is basically *inquisitorial*, especially when compared with the adversarial Anglo-American procedures. However, if one looks at the actual structure of the Italian civil process, this simplistic distinction turns out to be false, or least more apparent than real. While it is true that some rules of the Italian Code of Civil Procedure vest the judge with several powers concerning the direction and the management of cases, one must consider that in practice these powers are used very lightly, since the prevailing attitude of judges is to not interfere with the management of the case, leaving that task to the parties. Secondly, these powers are roughly equivalent to the managerial powers of an American judge, and in many cases the Italian judge is, in fact, more passive than his or her American counterpart. Therefore, the commonplace caricature of the Italian civil judge as active and inquisitorial in the management of cases actually proves quite inaccurate. On the contrary, the prevailing model of the Italian judge is that of one overburdened by his or her caseload, who does not actively manage the proceedings, and who largely relies on the parties for the actual development of the case.

Such is not the case, however, in some special proceedings. The main example of this divergence from the norm concerns labor disputes. A 1973 reform aimed at reducing delays and improving the efficiency of procedures in labor matters. In order to do so, a different model of proceedings was adopted, centered on the possibility of only one initial pleading for each party, on short terms, and on a concentrated, compressed, or condensed oral hearing before the judge. In this type of hearing, all elements (examination of the parties, attempt to settle the dispute, admission and presentation of evidence, and judgment) are meant to be carried forth without interruption or delay. Although such a model is rarely enforced in its pure form, significant improvements have been achieved by the use of this procedural model in comparison with ordinary civil proceedings. Labor cases actually proceed much more quickly than ordinary cases, and a judgment is frequently delivered in roughly one year, or even some months from the date of the case's beginning. In labor disputes, the management of the case is mainly in the hands of the judge, which greatly increases the efficiency of the disposition of cases.

IV. Pleadings

The plaintiff commences civil proceedings by filing a complaint and having it served upon the defendant in the manner specified by law. The complaint must identify the *judge*, the *parties*, and the *claim* that is submitted to the court. The hearing at which the parties should appear before the judge must also be indicated. The *statement of claim* is aimed at defining the nature of the claim that the plaintiff has filed in the clearest and most complete way. Correspondingly, a detailed and possibly complete *statement of the facts* at issue is required, together with the legal arguments supporting the claim. The complaint must include the offer of evidence, oral and written, and the request for relief addressed to the judge (in effect, what judgment the judge is being requested to deliver). An especially important provision concerns the requirement of an analytical and complete statement of the legally relevant facts. It is usually said that the rationale for such a requirement is the need to have the claim clearly and completely identified by the plaintiff from the outset of the case in order to avoid uncertainties, prevent wasting time, and allow a quick assessment by the judge of the logical relevancy of evidence. Speaking in American terms, the Italian system is one based upon *fact pleading*, rather than bare *notice pleading*, although the intent and effect of the fact-based pleading is clearly to inform the defendant that there has been a claim filed against him or her. Therefore, it is assumed that by reading the complaint, the defendant will receive complete and detailed information not only about the subject matter of the claim, but also about the specific facts at issue, the legal arguments proposed, and the evidence offered by the plaintiff.

Within a period of time fixed by the law (twenty days before the hearing indicated by the plaintiff for the first appearance of the parties in court), the defendant may file the *answer*. The answer is a written pleading that is roughly symmetrical to the plaintiff's complaint, since it contains all of the defendant's defenses. Different defense strategies are available. Defendants may limit themselves to a *denial* of the plaintiff's statements of fact and/or of law, but can also propose affirmative defenses by stating new facts that may block or eliminate the legal effects of the material facts stated by the plaintiff. In such cases, these facts should be completely and analytically stated (another feature of the fact-pleading system), since defendants are also required to establish their own versions of the case, in adequate terms, in the first pleading. Defendants will also develop legal arguments and offer any relevant evidence which may support their versions of the facts of the case. If the defendant has a right that can be asserted against the plaintiff, then a counterclaim shall be filed in the same pleading. The counterclaim shall also include a complete statement of the relevant facts, and an offer of evidence supporting such facts.

Theoretically the initial pleadings of the parties, taken together, should provide the judge and the parties with a complete statement of the case, including opposing versions of the factual and legal issues. In some simple cases, this may in fact occur. But things are often much more complicated.

On the one hand, it may be that the plaintiff has affirmative counter-defenses that may be opposed to the defendant's defenses or counterclaims. The law, therefore, allows the plaintiff to file such defenses later on, at one of the hearings during the preparatory phase. On the other hand, the law allows a sort of fragmentation of the defendant's defenses, insofar as they may be filed at a later part of this phase (*i.e.* the defendant may appear and file a counterclaim but postpone the defenses to a later moment). Moreover, the law allows both parties to make amendments to their first pleadings at the second hearing before the judge. At the same hearing, both parties are allowed to adjust or change their claims and defenses, and even to file new claims under certain conditions determined by the law. Finally, both parties are allowed to allege new circumstantial facts and to offer new evidence at a later hearing (it may be the third or the fourth one, and may take place several months or even more than one year after the filing of the complaint). All of this happens very frequently. It is clear, therefore, that the first pleadings are just the beginning of a complex and long phase of the proceedings, which is devoted just to achieving a reliable and reasonably complete definition of the legal and factual issues representing the actual "content" of the case as it is viewed by both parties.

In fact, only at the end of this phase will the court and the parties be fully aware of the real nature of the case.

If one considers that the preparation of the case may require several months (or even a couple of years, in the worst case), and that many months or even some years may be necessary for the presentation of evidence (*see infra* part V), it is clear that first instance proceedings going from the complaint to the judgment may frequently be a very long, burdensome, and complex enterprise. It is also clear that this situation does not foster an effective administration of justice and an adequate protection of the parties' rights and interests. In order to reduce to some extent the awful consequences of such a system recent reforms – in 1973 for labor disputes, and in 1990 in general – introduced various kinds of provisional remedies. One primary example of these reforms is the court's obtaining power to issue orders in the course of ordinary proceedings in a sort of anticipation of certain possible contents of the final judgment. The aim of these orders is to allow the parties to receive some protection of their rights or interests, although with provisional and incon- clusive effects, without waiting until the final decision is delivered. These orders may be issued, on a party's motion, under the following circumstances: (i) when a party has written proof of a right concerning the payment of a precise sum of money or the delivery of determined movable goods; (ii) when the adverse party does not deny the other party's right to receive a specific sum of money; (iii) in limited cases, when a party proves a right to receive a partial payment; and (iv) after the presentation of evidence, again, when a party has the right to receive a sum of money or the delivery of certain goods. In most cases, these orders are immediately enforceable, so that the interested party rapidly achieves some concrete effects. At any rate, the function of these orders is to anticipate some parts of the final judgment, which will actually lay out the final statement of the parties' rights.

V. Evidence

As we have seen, the relevant evidence must be offered *by the parties* in their pleadings, or at the initial hearings before the judge. In fact, the Italian procedural system is based mainly on the principle of the party-presentation of evidence. One needs to say "mainly" because some types of evidence can be ordered by the court on its own motion: expert evidence, some types of sworn statements, the inspection of places or persons, and the request of information from governmental bodies. However, these *ex officio* powers of the court have limited importance in the general context of the presentation of evidence. From this point of view, the Italian system belies its "inquisitorial" reputation.

The general principle concerning the admission of evidence is that evidence is admitted by the judge when it is *relevant* and *legally admissible*. Relevancy depends upon the logical connection of the single item of evidence with the facts of the case. Evidence directly concerning a material fact is obviously relevant. Evidence concerning a circumstantial fact is also relevant, when this fact is logically relevant, *i.e.* when it may serve as a premise for a logical inference producing conclusions about a material fact. As we have seen above, the "fact-pleading" system is aimed at allowing the judge to properly assess the relevance of the evidence offered by the parties.

The legal admissibility of evidence is determined by various rules limiting or excluding some types of evidence under special circumstances recognized by law. The most important exclusionary rules deal with cases in which the only evidence admitted consists of *written documents*. In this realm, the Italian system follows the traditional French model, according to which several types of contracts can be proved only by means of written evidence, with oral (and particularly testimonial) evidence excluded. In some cases, this results from the fact that a written form is required as a condition for the validity of the contract and, correspondingly, for its proof as well. In other cases, the exclusion is based on the assumption of the relatively lower reliability of testimonial evidence. There are additional specific rules of exclusion. For instance, non-parties who might possibly intervene in the case are not allowed to testify. Moreover, parties cannot be heard as witnesses, although they can make probative statements in the form of either confessions or oaths. On the other hand, there is nothing similar to the American hearsay rule, since secondhand testimony is ordinarily admitted (although the court may order the examination of the "firsthand" witness, when possible, and the probative weight of hearsay evidence should be cautiously assessed).

Another important group of rules excluding evidence is aimed at the protection of several types of secrets. These rules are the Italian equivalent of Anglo-American rules concerning privileges. They relate to facts covered by professional secrets (such as in attorney-client, doctor-patient, and penitent-priest relationships), those concerning husband-wife privacy, and those covered by State or Government secrets.

Another important issue is that of the admissibility of items of evidence that are not explicitly considered by the law (so-called *atypical evidence*). The largely prevailing opinion is that every kind of evidence that is not expressly excluded by the law is admissible when relevant, and that the same is also true of atypical evidence. However, it is usually stressed that courts should be very careful in assessing the probative value of such evidence, since it is usually created outside of the judicial context, absent from any control or guarantee of reliability.

On the basis of standards of relevancy and admissibility, the court makes a selection from the evidence offered by the parties and determines what evidence will actually be presented. The order admitting or excluding the various items of evidence is issued by the court at the end of the phase devoted to the preparation of the case. After this stage, the parties may no longer file new claims or defenses or offer new evidence (although a widely held view admits that the parties should be allowed to exhibit documents at any moment).

Then a further phase of the proceedings begins, which is devoted to the presentation of evidence. As noted above, evidence is not presented in a trial-type concentrated hearing. Several hearings may be necessary when many items of oral evidence have to be presented, and there may be long intervals between the several hearings devoted to this, depending on the judge's discretion. In complex cases, many hearings may be required. This means that years may even be required for the presentation of evidence (when, for instance, a busy or lazy judge fixes one hearing per year, or even less, for the same case).

The presentation of oral evidence is made according to the *court prosecution principle*. A witness is examined by the judge rather than by the parties' lawyers. The witness swears to tell the truth; perjury is punished by the criminal law. The judge examines the witness by asking questions concerning the facts of the case, sometimes allowing the witness to speak freely about his or her knowledge of the facts. The examination is made on the basis of the statements of fact made by the parties in their pleadings. The judge may ask the witness further questions aimed at clarifying the facts in issue, but even when this occurs, the examination is far from being an inquisitorial search of truth carried on by the judge. Lawyers for the parties may suggest further questions to the judge that are designed to clarify the witness's testimony, but, unlike in the Anglo-American system, they cannot ask any questions of the witnesses directly.

A written record of the presentation of evidence is drawn up by the clerk of the court at the judge's direction. It is important to stress that this record is not made *verbatim*; rather the judge dictates a reconstruction of the witness's answers in summary form. The witness signs the record and thereby becomes the author of the written statements, but the record is not a perfect and analytical reproduction of what was actually said by the witness. The parties may ask to insert specific statements into the record and the judge may authorize such insertions.

The law provides for a specific regulation of certain kinds of evidence (so-called *typical evidence*) dealing with the admissibility of such evidence, and with the means that should be used to present it and, in some cases, to check its reliability. The typology distinguishes *oral, written, expert,* and *circumstantial* evidence.

Oral evidence includes three main items. Testimony may be given by any non-party who knows anything relevant to the facts in issue. From the Anglo-American perspective, it is no doubt remarkable that the parties and third parties *cannot* testify as witnesses; even potential third parties are not competent to testify. The parties can be – or according to the law, *should* be, but sometimes this does not actually occur – examined by the judge in an informal way and without swearing to tell the truth (the so-called *interrogatorio libero*), but this is not testimony in the proper sense. This kind of examination is aimed only at clarifying the subject matter of the case, and possibly at inducing the parties to settle their dispute.

A *civil confession* may be made by a party who admits that a fact contrary to his or her interest is true. Such a statement may be either spontaneous (and thus it may be made in court or out of court), or provoked by questions asked by the judge on the basis of a specific motion made by the opposing party. A denial of an unfavorable fact has no probative value. The admission of the truth of such a fact is a *legal proof*, which means that such a statement is binding both upon the court and the parties. In a word, the judgment shall be based upon such a statement, without any discretionary assessment by the court.

Another legal proof is the *civil oath*. The civil oath may take three different forms: first, it may be initiated by a party challenging the other party to swear the truth of a favorable material fact (the so-called *giuramento decisorio*), under threat of religious and moral sanctions, and criminal sanctions in the case of perjury; secondly, it may be initiated by the court when there is some evidence of a fact but the court thinks that it should be supported by a sworn statement (the so-called *giuramento suppletorio*); and thirdly, it may be initiated by the court simply in order to determine the value of something (the so-called *giuramento estimatorio*). In any case, if the oath is taken, its outcome is strictly binding for both the judge and the parties. Therefore, it directly determines the final decision.

Written or *documentary evidence* may consist of any written document bearing any statement that may be relevant to prove a fact at issue. There are, however, two particularly important kinds of documents. One is the *public deed* that is drawn up by a public notary. This document is used to prove the most important transactions, and in some cases, it is required by the law. The public deed has a legal probative value; it is a *legal proof*. This means that its content is binding upon the court and the parties, unless its authenticity is contested (the authenticity of a public deed can be contested only by a special device called the *querela di falso*; a court will then decide whether or not the public deed is authentic). The other important type of documentary evidence includes any written statement that is signed by its author (the so-called *scrittura privata*). The probative value of such a document is established by the court by discretionary evaluation. However, the connection between the statement and the signature of its assumed author is fixed with binding effects when the authenticity of the signature is stated by a public notary, when it is not denied by the opposing party, or when it has been checked by the means provided by the law (the so-called *verificazione*). However, any kind of written document may be used by the parties and by the court when it is relevant to the proof of a fact at issue. The problem with these *atypical* documents is how to assess their probative value, taking into account the necessity of checking their origin and their authenticity. Special types of written documents, such as copies, photocopies, telegrams, telexes, and so on, are also regulated by the law. Other special types of documents are not written, but they are nevertheless considered as "documents," although a peculiar use of the word is assumed. Such "documents" include pictures, films, tapes, records, videotapes, and any other kind of *reproduction*. Such reproductions are presumed to give a faithful representation of the facts concerned, unless the opposing party denies that the reproduction corresponds to the facts. Where there is no opposition, the court is free to use the reproduced document as evidence of the facts, or not. Special problems, not yet adequately dealt with by the law, arise in the domain of so-called "computer evidence."

Expert evidence is used when the court decides that special technical or scientific knowledge is needed in order to decide a case. The court decides this issue on its own motion; a party may make suggestions, but the court is free to determine whether to appoint an expert or not. When the court so decides, an expert is appointed by the court; in this case the court will usually (but not necessarily) choose the expert from a list. Experts must be neutral and impartial with reference to the parties and the subject matter of the case. If their position is such that their neutrality and impartiality are not ensured, they must withdraw or may be challenged. The expert becomes an officer of the court. He or she is not a witness, is in no way linked to a party, and is assumed to provide the court with independent technical and scientific knowledge. On acceptance by the expert, the court states the issues that he or she must solve. The expert can obtain everything needed in order to answer the questions asked by the court by hearing from people who know the facts, and conducting tests, experiments, inspections, and so on.

Within the time limit fixed by the court, the expert will submit a written report describing his or her activities and giving the answers to the issues stated by the court. If necessary, the expert can be examined by the court in order to clarify the report, but oral examination is not the usual method of obtaining the expert's answers. If the court is satisfied with the expert's report, it will be used as a basis for the final decision. However, the court is not bound by the expert's opinion; it is free to decide the case differently. As is commonly said, the judge is the *peritus peritorum*. Accordingly, the judge will check whether it is worth following the expert's opinion. If not, the court should explain why the expert opinion has not been accepted.

When the court appoints an expert, the parties may appoint their own experts. These experts aid the parties in defending themselves in connection with the activity of the court's expert. They are allowed to participate in this activity, to raise questions and to make remarks. However, the parties' experts are not considered a source of evidence. They are the technical *longa manus* of the parties, and therefore they are neither neutral nor impartial. Correspondingly, they cannot provide the court with reliable independent knowledge.

Circumstantial evidence essentially consists of the inferences that the court may draw from any fact or circumstance that is known or proved, when such a fact or circumstance may be assumed as a premise supporting conclusions that deal with the existence or nonexistence of a material fact. The court may draw such inferences by relying mainly upon the common sense and background knowledge typical of the average person in the place and at the time of the decision. These inferences (the so-called *praesumptiones hominis*) may produce a reasonable proof of a fact when they are precise, clear, and tend towards the same conclusion. However, the use of circumstantial evidence is typically in the hands of the court, which determines the possible factual inferences and controls their consistency and rational reliability.

VI. The Judgment

When all the evidence has been presented, the proceedings reach their final phase, which is aimed at decision-making. Before that, the parties' lawyers have the opportunity to sum up their own versions of the main legal and factual points of the case. Each of them submits a brief (called the *comparsa conclusionale*) restating their position in its final terms, drawing the conclusions that may be derived from the evidence presented and from all the things that happened in the course of the process. Such briefs are exchanged between the parties and presented to the court. Then each party has the opportunity to file a further short brief (called the *note di replica*) in order to reply to some points raised by the concluding brief of the other party. These two briefs are the final pleadings of the case. On very rare occasions, an oral discussion may be held in court. In contrast with the above procedure, some special proceedings, such as labor proceedings, do not employ such final written pleadings. Instead, the conclusions of both parties are stated orally in court by lawyers.

The next step is the making of the final decision by the court. The final judgment is usually rendered in written form and delivered to the clerk's office. In some cases, as in labor proceedings, the judge will state the final outcome of the decision orally, at a hearing, and deposit the written judgment later on.

A typical decision deals with all the relevant issues of fact and of law that were raised by the parties. With regard to the issues of fact, the judge decides whether the material facts alleged may be considered true, on the basis of the proof presented. As a rule, judges are free to assess the probative value of such proofs according to their own discretionary evaluation, but in some cases (*see* part V, *supra*) there are still rules of *legal proof* determining the value of some evidence with binding effects for the parties and for the court. A fact is "true" when the statement concerning this fact is confirmed by a reasonably sufficient amount of evidence. When there is not sufficient proof of the facts in issue, a decision will be made according to the principle of the *burden of proof*. According to this principle, the plaintiff will lose when the fact upon which the claim is grounded is not proved, and the defendant will lose when the fact grounding his or her defenses has not been proved. It is worth stressing that in the Italian procedural system, there is nothing similar to the American *burden of producing evidence*. Each party has a strong interest in producing all evidence that is available in order to maximize the chances of victory, but the proceedings will continue in any case until the final judgment is delivered, and the court will take into account any relevant item of evidence, independent of its origin. The Italian burden of proof enters into play only at the end of the proceedings, when a decision has to be made and some or all the material facts have not been proved. It is an *objective* and *pre-determined* standard of decision: the court has no discretion in allocating the burden of proof between the parties. However, the basic rule may be inverted or modified by the law by means of the so-called *presunzioni legali*, or legal presumptions. A legal presumption may come into play when the legislator wishes to favor a given party (for instance, an employee or the injured person), or when the proof of a given fact would be too difficult or impossible to achieve by ordinary means.

While deciding issues of law, the court has the power to determine the correct legal qualification (the so-called *nomen juris*) of the facts of the case, referring them to the legal rules that seem adequate. This means that the court is not bound by the legal qualifications proposed by the parties, although the court may adopt the legal version of the case proposed by one of them. It is up to the court to select the proper rule governing the case, to interpret this rule, and to apply it to the facts drawing the conclusions derived from the law-fact relationship.

The final judgment is delivered, as we have already stated, in written form. In addition to a description of the identity of the parties and the court, the final judgment includes a narrative section summing up the most important events that occurred in the course of the proceedings, the final *dictum* determining the court's answer to the claims and defenses submitted by the parties (the *dispositivo*), and an opinion containing the arguments that the court has developed in support of the solutions reached regarding all the legal and factual issues of the case. This is the *motivazione* – that is, the justification of the decision adopted by the court. As a rule, the justificatory opinion should be complete, reasonable, coherent, and consistent. This is important because the opinion should not only express the reasons why the decision should be generally accepted as reasonably well-founded, but it should also be the basis for the appeals that may be filed by the parties, and for the review that should be made by the appellate court.

Once delivered in its proper form, the judgment is immediately enforceable, although the losing party has the right to file an appeal (*see infra* part VII). In 1990, an important change occurred in the Italian system with regard to the enforceability of judgments delivered by first instance courts. The traditional principle held that only a final judgment having all the effects of *res judicata* was enforceable; before this, judgments were made enforceable only under specific conditions and by a special order of the court. However, the need for judgments to yield concrete effects as soon as possible pushed the legislator to introduce a different system. All first instance judgments are now enforceable *per se*, but the aggrieved party may ask the appellate judge for a stay of execution if there are good reasons to do so in that specific situation.

If none of the parties file an appeal against the judgment (*see infra* part VII), the judgment becomes *res judicata* on the case. No further ordinary appeals are admitted, and therefore the judgment is final. The substantive *res judicata* effects deal with the stability of the decision. The content of the judgment concerning the claims becomes unalterable and binding for the parties and their privies, as well as for any further judge that may have to deal with the same matter.

VII. Appeals

Within time limits fixed by law, the losing party may file an appeal against the first instance judgment. Such an appeal will usually be tried and decided by an intermediate appellate court. The appeal is of right. That is, no leave is required and there are no conditions or limits (except in the case of very small claims, *i.e.* for judgments delivered by a justice of the peace for an amount up to one million lire). The claim may deal with any feature of the first instance judgment that may make the decision "unjust": for instance, the appeal may be grounded on errors of fact concerning the evaluation of proofs, on errors of law concerning the choice, interpretation, and application of the governing rule, or on both types of errors. On the other hand, the appellate court may revise any aspect of the appealed judgment. If the appeal is found to be well-founded, the appellate court makes a new decision on the merits of the case, by reconsidering both facts and law. This decision will take the place of the first instance decision. There is no trial *de novo* in the first instance court (except for a few cases in which the first instance judgment is found to be invalid for specific procedural reasons). Although the appellate court may take into consideration any kind of factual and legal error, the admissibility of fresh evidence in the appellate proceedings is limited to the items of evidence that could possibly lead the court to reverse the decision of the lower court. No other new evidence is admitted. Therefore, the appellate court will make a new judgment on the facts, but rely mainly on the same evidence that was presented in the first instance proceedings. This is the outcome of a recent change in Italian civil procedure – the traditional system used to admit fresh evidence before the appellate court, allowing this court to make a completely new decision on the facts of the case. The rule was changed in 1990 with the aim of accelerating appellate proceedings, but also of deterring people from filing appeals in the hope of attaining a new judgment on a different evidentiary basis. For the same reasons, new claims and new defenses are not admitted in appellate proceedings.

The judgment delivered by the intermediate appellate court is final and enforceable. However, a further appeal may be filed in the Italian Supreme Court (*Corte di Cassazione*, the court of last resort) for civil disputes in the Italian system. It is worth stressing that the appeal to the Supreme Court is granted not only by the ordinary rules of the Code of Civil Procedure, but also by art. 111 para. 7 of the Italian Constitution. Along the same lines as the traditional French model that inspired the Italian system, the Supreme Court is only a court "of legitimacy." That is to say, the main role of this court is to check whether the lower court interpreted and correctly and validly applied substantive and procedural legal rules. The basic function of the court is, in fact, to ensure the legality and legitimacy of the legal system as a whole, and also to help to achieve an adequate degree of uniformity in the interpretation and application of the law. Therefore, an appeal to the Supreme Court may be grounded only upon errors of law. Such errors may concern the violation of both procedural and substantive rules. Besides, a very peculiar ground of appeal to the Supreme Court deals with the opinion supporting the decision of the lower court: if the justificatory opinion does not exist, or if it is not sufficient or contradictory, an appeal may be filed to the Supreme Court. In accordance with the role of the Supreme Court, no evidence is admitted (though no new evidence is actually needed) in proceedings before the Court.

When the Supreme Court finds that the appeal is well-grounded, it quashes the judgment and sends the case back to a lower court (usually another intermediate appellate court) for a new judgment. The Supreme Court states the legal rule that the lower court is required to follow when making its new decision on the case. No fresh evidence is admitted in these further proceedings. Therefore, the new judgment is based upon the legal principle stated by the Supreme Court, and possibly upon a new consideration of the facts and evidence that was presented in the earlier phases of the proceedings. However, in accordance with a recent reform, there are some cases in which the Supreme Court may make a decision on the merits of the whole case, including the facts. This may happen when the Court quashes the judgment of the lower court, but finds that a new judgment on the merits may be delivered without any reconsideration of the facts at issue. Then the Supreme Court may "take the facts as they were established" by the lower court and deliver a new final judgment on the merits of the case directly.

Two other devices of attack against a judgment must be considered. First, a non-party who is affected by a judgment delivered between the proper parties, because of a substantive connection among legal situations, may challenge that judgment in order not to be "touched" by its effects (this device is called the *opposizione di terzo*), since a judgment may only be effective between the subjects that were the proper parties in the proceedings.

Also, if a final judgment (even if it is already *res judicata*) conflicts with another judgment *res judicata*, if it is considered the effect of a fraud by either one of the parties or the judge; or if it is found that the judgment is based on a clear mistake or on evidence that is discovered to be false; or if new relevant evidence is found after the end of the proceedings, such a judgment may be challenged by means of a specific device called *revocazione*.

VIII. Enforcement

Once our Italian John Doe has survived all the delays, complexities, and traps of the proceedings described so far, and he finally obtains an enforceable judgment, his problems are not over. On the contrary, if, as often occurs, the judgment includes the condemnation of the debtor enjoining him or her to pay a sum of money or to do some specified thing, and the debtor does not comply voluntarily, a new problem arises (although this is not the case with declaratory or constitutive judgments, which are considered to be self-executing). Theoretically, judgment-holders are entitled to have their expectations quickly fulfilled by means of enforcement devices aimed at satisfying their rights as they have been established by the court. In practice, however, enforcement proceedings are cumbersome, long, and highly ineffective. Procedures are complex and outdated, and there are no efficient indirect compulsory measures. Rather, one often finds no way to overcome the debtor's obduracy. Consequently, in many cases John Doe's legal rights are doomed to remain in-effective, since the system does not provide for adequate remedies. At most, the creditor will obtain an award of damages for the wrong inflicted by the defaulting judgment-obligee.

There are various kinds of enforcement proceedings, but the choice is not left to the judgment-holder. Such proceedings are not interchangeable. Each of them is conceived in order to fit the specific kind of obligation the debtor is expected to discharge. Therefore, if the judgment-holder initiates the wrong proceeding, it will be nullified and no purpose will be achieved.

When the judgment includes the order to pay a given sum of money, and the debtor does not pay, the enforcement machinery is based upon the transformation of the debtor's property or assets into money, in order to fulfill the creditor's right to get this money. This is a very complex procedure in which several stages may be distinguished: (i) the attachment or seizure of the debtor's goods; (ii) the sale of these goods by public auction; and (iii) payment to the creditor of the sum of money he or she has the right to receive. Each of these phases may be very complex because of the formal details provided by old and ineffective regulations. Some years may be necessary to reach the final moment when the creditor receives his money. Moreover, the proceedings are very expensive and the debtor's goods may be insufficient to satisfy the judgment. The result is that in many cases the sale of the goods is just enough to pay the lawyers' fees and the costs of the procedure. In such cases, our poor John Doe will have waited for some years to get nothing or, at best, just a small percentage of what is owed.

Other complexities may arise to waste time. For instance, other creditors may intervene in the enforcement proceedings begun by John Doe and, in such cases, the sum obtained by the sale of the debtor's good may be shared among several creditors. Moreover, at the same time, the debtor has a number of opportunities to slow down the enforcement proceedings or even to block them for years. Objections may be raised against virtually any act of the procedure, provoking answers from the other parties and a decision by the court. This may occur dozens of times in the course of proceedings. Thus, the creditor has to overcome a long series of obstacles in order to arrive at a conclusion that in many cases is more theoretical than effective.

Things are a little simpler when the problem is that of obtaining the delivery of specified assets or property. In such cases, the judge and the court officers do what is needed to make the delivery concretely possible, against the debtor's will if necessary. However, many of the hurdles the debtor may erect in order to postpone or block the enforcement may also take place in these proceedings.

Things are even worse when we come to the problem of enforcing a court order enjoining the judgment-obligee to do, or refrain from doing, something. In this domain, the judgment can be effectively enforced only when the "doing" consists of producing something material and the "not doing" consists of destroying something material that was illegally produced (a building, for instance), provided the nature of the thing is such that another person (different from the debtor) may perform the "doing" or the "undoing." Under such conditions, the judge may order that a third person does what is necessary to fulfill the obligation, and the original debtor will be charged with the costs of all of this. However, these proceedings may also be long and cumbersome. But the real problem arises when a non-monetary remedy is awarded by the court, and nobody else may take the place of the original debtor. Cases of this kind are increasingly common in the areas of labor disputes, consumer protection, discrimination by gender or race, environmental control, and so forth. Here, the core of the problem is that, except in very rare and peculiar specific cases (in the domain of patents and trademarks, and in some cases that of labor disputes), the Italian system of enforcement does not include efficient devices of coercive indirect pressure on the debtor's will, such as the contempt of court, the French *astreintes*, or the German *Zwangstrafen*. Correspondingly, most of the non-monetary orders issued by courts are not enforced because the traditional enforcement devices do not apply, and there are no effective sanctions for noncompliance to be used as means of coercion upon the debtor in order to induce her compliance with the judgment.

To sum up: if John Doe obtains a monetary judgment, he has some hope of achieving the fulfillment of his right, although long and expensive procedures are required, with the risk of obtaining only partial, or no, satisfaction in the end. But if John Doe receives a non-monetary remedy, the hope of having it complied with is illusory, unless he relies on the goodwill of the judgment-obligee. In other words, very frequently, enforcement procedures, if available, take the creditor nowhere slowly, and there are frequently cases in which there is no means of getting there at all.

Brief Bibliography

A. Attardi, *Diritto processuale civile*, Padova (1999).

L.P. Comoglio, C. Ferri, M. Taruffo, *lezione sul processo civile*, 2nd ed., Bologna (1998).

C. Consolo, *Spiegazioni di diritto processuale civile*, Bologna (2000).

E.T. Liebman, *Manuale di diritto processuale civile*, Milano (1992).

F.P. Luiso, *Diritto processuale civile*, Milano (2000).

C. Mandrioli, *Diritto processuale civile*, Torino (2000).

G.A. Monteleone, *Diritto processuale civile*, Padova (2000).

L. Montesano, G. Arieta, *Diritto processuale civile*, Torino (2000).

C.A. Nicoletti, *Profili Istituzionali del processo esecutivo*, Milano (2001).

E. Redenti, M. Vellani, *Diritto processuale civile*, Milano (2000).

S. Satta, C. Punzi, *Diritto processuale civile*, Padova (2000).

G. Tarzia, *Lineamenti del nuovo processo di cognizione*, Milano (1996).

G. Verde, *Profili del processo civile, Processo di cognizione*, Napoli (2000).

Criminal Justice: The Resistance of a Mentality

Elisabetta Grande [1]

I. Introduction

The Italian criminal justice system has been profoundly affected by the recent reform of criminal procedure. The ambitious attempt to shift from a centuries-old non-adversarial procedure to an adversarial mode modeled upon practices in the United States has made the Italian experiment quite interesting from the perspective of law reform: perhaps for the first time in the modern period, the Italian legal system is the subject of international academic debate.

This chapter will focus on Italian procedural law, the reception of some significant elements of the adversarial system, and the evaluation of transplants from the common law. The second and third parts will briefly deal with the Italian criminal procedure as it existed before 1988, and with the reasons that led to the adoption of a new Code. In reforming Italian criminal procedure, codifiers had two goals. First, they aimed at reconstructing Italian criminal procedure along adversarial lines. Secondly, they meant to provide Italian criminal justice with new, efficient procedures to cope with its judicial overload problem. Part IV addresses the question of how successfully the first goal has been accomplished. To this extent, I will summarize the new Italian criminal proceedings, focusing on the resistance of the traditional institutional background on the new "adversary" Code of Criminal Procedure.[2] Part IV A deals with the preliminary investigation. It shows the impact

---

[1] Professor of Comparative Law, Eastern Piedmont University School of Law, Alessandria, Italy. This is a revised version of "Italian Criminal Justice: Borrowing and Resistance," first published in 48 *Am J Comp L* 227 (2000).

[2] "... [T]he meaning and the impact of procedural regulation turn on external conditions – most directly on the institutional context in which justice is administered in a particular country. If imported rules are combined with native ones in disregard of this context, unintended

Jeffrey S. Lena and Ugo Mattei (eds.), *Introduction to Italian Law*, 181-216
©2002 Kluwer Law International. Printed in the Netherlands.

of the traditional prosecutor's role and of the principle of compulsory prosecution on the attempt to follow the adversary system in making the prosecutor a party. Part IV B deals with the preliminary hearing and part IV C deals with the trial. The Italian trial can be seen as a unitary trial from two perspectives. A single body of adjudicators – consisting of professional judges, who sit together with lay assessors in the most serious cases – passes on issues of law as well as fact. Thus, no distinction between judge and jury as two adjudicating bodies can be made. Moreover, the same unitary adjudicating body determines both guilt and sentence. As a result, the trial does not have to be bifurcated into a first hearing devoted solely to the issue of guilt, and a subsequent second hearing dealing with the sentence.[3] In this section, I will focus on the practical results of combining the juryless Italian system with the imported adversarial rules of evidence. As the triers of fact, Italian judges feel a sense of personal responsibility for aiming at a just and accurate result. Thus, in a short period of time, they have been able to recapture authority over the fact-finding process, and have regained the possibility of knowing and evaluating as much evidence as that which was gathered at the preliminary investigation. Part V addresses the issue of how successfully the Italian reformers' second goal has been accomplished. A brief description of Italian special procedures aiming at the system's efficiency will show how difficult it is to reconcile the Italian distrust of a party-controlled system and the Italian prosecutor's bureaucratic career system with the need to expedite Italian criminal justice. Finally, part VI briefly addresses the most recent developments in Italian criminal procedure in order to discern their underlying rationale.

On the whole, the resistance of a different institutional context coupled with a "civil law" mentality severely undermined the Italian attempt to borrow the American adversary model.

---

consequences are likely to follow in living law," points out Professor Damaska in "The Uncertain Fate of Evidentiary Transplants: Anglo-American and Continental Experiments," 45 *Am J Comp L* 839 (1997).

[3] On the advantages and disadvantages of the American jury trial compared to the European mixed court, *see* Langbein, "Mixed Court and Jury Court: could the Continental Alternative fill the American Need?" *American Bar Foundation Research Journal* 195 (1981).

II. From the "Rocco" Code of 1930 to the New Code of 1988

On 24 October 1988, a new Code of Criminal Procedure was enacted by the Italian Parliament and became effective the following year. Prior to the enactment of the new Code, Italian criminal procedure was a dual procedure in which the first phase was framed according to an inquisitorial model and the second phase had a more accusatorial orientation (in the sense that it tried to comply with the principle that the evidence be taken in the presence of the defense, who is entitled to offer counter-proof and counter-arguments – *principio del contraddittorio*). The first phase was conducted either by a public prosecutor,[4] in an *istruzione sommaria* (summary investigation), or by an examining judge, called the "instruction judge," in an *istruzione formale* (formal investigation). In either case, the public official was committed to a non-partisan investigation during which he or she assembled the evidence both for and against the accused. The procedure was written and largely secret, even though, after some important Constitutional Court decisions handed down between 1965 and 1972, the defendant was allowed to participate in some pre-trial activities.

The second phase was conducted in front of the trial judge and was theoretically characterized by the principles of orality, publicity, temporal concentration of the trial, and by the defendant's right to oppose evidence offered against him. The evidence gathered during the pre-trial inquiry was supposed to be controlled by an impartial and active trial judge in the presence of the defendant, who was entitled to offer counter-proof and counter-arguments. In practice, this rarely occurred. Indeed, the trial judge at the time of the trial was already aware of the results of the preliminary inquiry, as the evidence and testimony thereby collected – and reduced to a written summary – were placed in the official file of the case and submitted before the start of the trial. The trial judge, in the capacity of a trier of fact, was then able to evaluate the evidence in advance – and was therefore in a position to be prejudiced by it.

Many scholars hold the view that the trial court's review of the pre-trial material inevitably affected the court's final decision and encouraged – consciously or unconsciously – the trial judge to accept the approach taken by the public official during the pre-trial phase. On the other hand, the orality principle and the right of the accused to confront the witnesses and evidence offered against him or her seemed to be seriously affected by the formal reception of written summaries of

---

[4]   I translate the term *pubblico ministero* here as "public prosecutor": the differences between the American public prosecutor and the Italian *pubblico ministero* are explored *infra*.

the evidence gathered in the earlier phase. The doctrine of refreshing witnesses' memories or that of highlighting inconsistencies with their prior declarations provided one of the avenues through which all their previous statements could be read at trial and considered as substantive evidence in court. Moreover, even if witnesses were not present in court, their previous statements could be taken into consideration as substantive evidence by the adjudicator. Thus, the trial tended to amount to little more than a mere repetition and confirmation of what had taken place in the earlier phase, and conviction of the accused could be based upon evidence collected secretly – though in a non-partisan manner – in the pre-trial inquiry.

The more sophisticated Italian public opinion was profoundly dissatisfied with a machinery of justice that was, on the one hand, perceived as unable to fully protect the defendant's right to a fair trial and, on the other hand, as excruciatingly slow (Italian governments were repeatedly condemned by the European Court of Human Rights for the excessive delay of their criminal justice procedure – a delay that routinely amounted to an astonishing ten years or longer. See the comments in chapter 5 in this regard.). This ultimately led the Italian Parliament to approve a new Code of Criminal Procedure restructured along adversarial lines. The new Code would be a "party-controlled fact-finding" model – to borrow Professor Damaska's expression[5] – in which the evidence would be presented at trial in a partisan manner and the adjudicator would perform a relatively passive role (*secundum alligata et probata a partibus iudex iudicare debet*, art. 190 of the Code of Criminal Procedure – hereinafter CCrPr – no. 1); a model in which the adjudicator would have no prior knowledge of the case and the defendant would enjoy the right to be confronted with all the opposing evidence, and in which witnesses' prior inconsistent statements collected and reduced to a written form during the pre-trial investigation could be used at trial for impeachment purposes only. According to the intent of the reformers, these were in principle the basic features of the new Italian system of criminal procedure.

The break with the inquisitorial continental tradition seemed to be plain, and the Italian criminal procedure appeared to be the first civil law system effectuating a transplant of the common law adversary model. Yet more than ten years after the new Code's enactment, it can be argued that the impression was a false one: the transplant was in reality not of the intact adversary model, but rather the transplant of some of its features which, removed from their original context, accomplished

---

[5] M. Damaska, *The Faces of Justice and State Authority, A Comparative Approach to the Legal Process*, New Haven (1986); M. Damaska, *Evidence Law Adrift*, New Haven (1997).

little more than to create another type of non-adversary model – a model which does not appear to protect the rights of the defendant any more than the previous one did.

III. Why Consider the Adversary Model?

Why did the Italian system look to, and seek to import, the adversary model? As in the case of any other legal transplants, no matter how successful, two reasons have been identified. A transplant may occur either as a matter of imposition or as a matter of prestige.[6] The Italian imitation of the adversary model of criminal procedure is an example of the latter case. But what, exactly, is the meaning of "prestige"?

Since the end of World War II, American culture in general, and American legal culture in particular, has acquired a position of worldwide leadership. The reception of American law abroad has even been compared to the dissemination of Roman law throughout Europe during the *ius commune* period.[7] To what may we ascribe this great success?

First, the prestige of the American legal model has been associated with the strength of the United States' political and economic structure, but also with certain characteristics of its legal scholarship. Legal scholarship, being the least inherently parochial of the legal formants, and therefore the most apt to diffuse legal ideas abroad,[8] has been identified as the most important vehicle for the circulation of legal culture, provided that two requirements are met. It needs to be simultaneously meta-positivistic and perceived by foreign scholars as leading within its own borders. Since 1930, these requirements appear to have been met by American legal scholarship. As a consequence of its prestige, American legal scholarship was able to export such general ideas as legal realism or law and economics, methodologies for understanding the law as a phenomenon of social organization.[9]

---

[6]   R. Sacco, *Introduzione al diritto comparato*, Torino (1992), 147*ff*.

[7]   Wiegand, "Reception of American Law in Europe," 39 *Am J Comp L* 229 (1991).

[8]   *See* Sacco, "Legal Formants: A Dynamic Approach to Comparative Law," 37 *Am J Comp L* 1 (1991) and P.G. Monateri "'Legal Doctine' as a Source of Law. A Transnational Factor and a Historical Paradox," in *Italian National Reports to the XII International Congress of Comparative Law*, Sydney (1986).

[9]   Mattei, *Why the Wind Changed: Intellectual Leadership in Western Law*, 42 *Am J Comp L* 195 (1994).

Another clue to understanding why a particular model becomes prestigious is related to its underlying ideology and its capacity to protect individuals against abuses of power. From this perspective, the circulation of the nineteenth-century French codes, more than the diffusion of their rules, proved to be a diffusion of the protection of the individual rights ideal that they represented. Analogously, the imitation of the adversary system seems to be strongly connected with its ideological underpinnings. Being associated with Lockean liberal values, distrust of the State, restraint of State power, and freedom from the State's intrusion into private lives,[10] adversary criminal procedure symbolizes the procedural model that would appear to best safeguard the individual against State abuses.[11] Twentieth-century world history confirms this impression.

Given the prestige enjoyed by the American legal system in general and by American criminal procedure in particular, it is not surprising that the Italian legislator, seeking a way to "open up" its criminal justice system in order to reflect its status as a modern democratic society,[12] looked at the United States for its inspiration. What is surprising is that it has been thought possible to import the adversary model by importing only some of its features and transplanting these features into a non-adversary institutional context. The result, as I will try to show, is that the transplant ended up constituting little more than an "acoustic" imitation,[13] in which the mixture of the new "adversarial" elements with the old non-adversarial ones produced effects diametrically opposed to those expected: today's Italian legal system affords the defendant less protection against abuses of power than were enjoyed prior to the introduction of common law adversarial elements.

---

[10] On the connection between choices of procedural arrangements and broad ideological orientations, *see* Damaska, "Evidentiary Barriers to Conviction and Two Models of Criminal Procedure: A Comparative Study," 121 *UPaLRev* 506, 565 (1973). On the rise of the adversary criminal procedure in the Anglo-American system, *see* Langbein, "The Criminal Trial before the Lawyers," 45 *UChiLRev* 263 (1978) and *id.*, "Historical Foundations of the Law of Evidence: A View from the Ryder Sources," 96 *ColumLRev* 1168 (1996).

[11] The link between the adversary system and an ideology that fears State power has been extensively explored by Damaska in "Structures of Authority and Comparative Criminal Procedure," 84 *Yale LJ* 480, 532-39 (1975)

[12] *See* Pizzi and Marafioti, "The New Italian Code of Criminal Procedure: The Difficulties of Building an Adversary Trial System on a Civil Law Foundation," 17 *Yale J Int'l Law*, 1, 6 (1992).

[13] To borrow Professor Schlesinger's expression. *See* R. Schlesinger, H. Baade, P. Herzog, E. Wise, *Comparative Law*, New York (1998), 481.

IV. Adversarial and Non-Adversarial Features of the New Italian Criminal Procedure System

The new Code divides ordinary criminal proceedings into three phases: (1) the preliminary investigation, (2) the preliminary hearing, and (3) the trial.[14]

A. The Preliminary Investigation (*Le Indagini Preliminari*)

1. General Outline

Under Italian law, everyone has the right, but not the duty, to report an offense to the police or the public prosecutor. Reporting a crime is compulsory only for certain serious offenses against the State. While the Italian system does not provide for, and does not permit, private criminal prosecution, some offenses cannot be prosecuted without a victim's complaint.

Whenever the police or the public prosecutor receives notice of a crime, or collects information about a crime on its own initiative, a formal investigation is instituted by the prosecutor.[15]

Upon learning of the *notitia criminis*, the public prosecutor must record the event in the crime register. From the moment of registration, the prosecutor is required to complete the investigation within six months, unless an extension of time from the judge in charge of the preliminary investigation is applied for and received (the so-called *gip*, for *giudice per le indagini preliminari*). Such an extension may be granted for up to 18 months or, in exceptional cases, two years (arts. 405-7 CCrPr). Any evidence obtained after expiration of the time limit cannot be used by the public prosecutor.

In sharp contrast with what occurred under the former Code, the new Code provided for a clear-cut separation between the investigative and judicial functions during the preliminary phase. Before 1999, the investigative function was exclusively assigned to the public prosecutor, while the judicial function is carried out by the *gip*.

---

[14] What I call here the "ordinary" Italian criminal proceedings are those conducted in first instance before a panel made of a plurality of judges. The *decreto legislativo* no. 51 of 19 February 1998, which abolished the feature of the "*pretore*" (a single-judge court in charge of less serious crimes) and extended the single-judge court jurisdiction, provided (in its final version of 16 December 1999, on which *see* the part VI, *infra*) such a single-judge court with a slightly different procedure.

[15] The police are at the prosecutor's disposition (art. 109 Const.) and can rarely act on their own in the investigation of a crime.

Deprived of any investigative powers (but *see* now the amendments provided by law no. 479/99, discussed *infra*, part VI) the *gip* supervises the activities of the investigating authorities, making sure that the rights of those under investigation are respected. For example, any restraints on personal freedom requested by the prosecutor and any activities such as wire-taps or other interceptions that impinge upon an individual's right of privacy require the authorization of the *gip*, following a hearing.

Another important task performed by the *gip* is presiding over the *incidente probatorio* (a mechanism for preservation of evidence). At any time before trial, the prosecutor or person under investigation may request that the *gip* receives evidence which can be used at the trial itself. This occurs when there is reason to believe that the evidence may not be available during the trial or would cause the trial to be suspended for too long. During such a special hearing the same rules as those for receiving evidence at trial will be followed and the evidence, thus "frozen," will be included in the file the trial judge receives at the beginning of the trial.

The prosecutor's task is that of gathering the evidence[16] in order to decide whether or not to prosecute the offense. Since the Italian Constitution mandates compulsory prosecution (art. 112), the prosecutor can ask the *gip* for a judgment of dismissal only if he or she deems that his case is too weak to lead to a conviction at trial. ("The prosecutor presents a request of dismissal to the judge of preliminary investigation when the evidence gathered by the preliminary investigation is insufficient to uphold the charge," art. 125, provisions for the implementation of the Code of Criminal Procedure.) The *gip* reviews the prosecutor's decision to dismiss the case, and if she disagrees with the prosecutor she can order the prosecutor – sometimes upon the victim's request – to conduct further investigation, or (in sharp contrast with the Anglo-American system) can mandate the bringing of a formal charge against the suspect (art. 409 CCrPr, no. 5). A judgment of dismissal does not prevent a later reopening of the case if new evidence emerges: the *gip* can then allow the case to be reopened upon the prosecutor's request.

If, upon completion of the preliminary investigation, the prosecutor believes he has collected enough evidence to sustain a conviction at trial, he will make a formal request that the person under investigation be committed for trial. At this moment, under Italian law (art. 405 CCrPr) the person under investigation formally becomes

---

[16] Under Italian law the sources of information are transformed into proper evidence only through their production in court (or at the *incidente probatorio*). However, for the sake of simplicity, I will use the term "evidence" as applying both to the information gathered during the pre-trial phase and that produced at the proof-taking phase.

a "defendant" (*imputato*).[17]

The decision of whether or not to refer the case for trial will be made by the judge of the preliminary hearing. Prior to rendering this decision, a full evidentiary disclosure takes place, and the defendant and his or her counsel acquire a right to inspect the case file (art. 419 CCrPr, no. 2).

This briefly outlines the preliminary stage. Yet in order to grasp the scope of the changes that the new Code brought about in the Italian system, it is important to outline a few more aspects of the preliminary investigation phase which demonstrates the system in action.

2. The Italian Prosecutor as a Fourth Power?

a. The Italian Prosecutor as a Party to the Proceedings

It is important to clarify what kind of investigation the prosecutor must carry out and particularly how partisan his investigation can be.

Under the previous Code – as is true for all inquisitorial, as well as "mixed" (inquisitorial and accusatorial) models[18] – the "instructor judge"[19] and the prosecutor, when charged with the collection of evidence, had to conduct the preliminary inquiry in an impartial way. This means that they had to gather not only the inculpatory, but also the exculpatory evidence, so that the trial judge, in receiving the file of the case before the trial, could familiarize him or herself with all the evidence previously assembled. The "official controlled system" – to utilize borrowing's terminology – meant that, since the fact-finding process was in official and impartial hands, the evidence had to be officially and impartially collected.[20]

By contrast, the new Code configures the prosecutor as a party to the proceedings and deprives him of the judicial powers he previously enjoyed at the preliminary inquiry. The prosecutor is no longer required to pursue the search for truth in his investigation. Moreover, in presenting the evidence in court he is expected to be

---

[17] However, for the sake of simplicity I will sometimes use the term "defendant" as applied both to a person under investigation and one who is formally considered a "defendant."

[18] Damaska, "Evidentiary Barriers," *supra* note 10, 559.

[19] *See supra*, para. 1.

[20] According to the "family" model, as opposed to the "battle" model, as described by J. Griffiths, "Ideology in Criminal Procedure or a Third 'Model' of the Criminal Process," 79 *Yale LJ* 359 (1970); or to the very similar "parental" model as opposed to "arm's length" system of criminal justice, as depicted by K. Lewellyn, *Jurisprudence* 439, 444-50 (1962), on which *see* Damaska comments, in "Evidentiary Barriers," *supra* note 10, 571.

partisan (art. 190 CCrPr). According to the most authoritative Italian scholarship,[21] that means that the Italian prosecutor is now no longer in charge of collecting evidence on behalf of the person under investigation.

To be sure, art. 358 CCrPr states that "[t]he prosecutor completes every activity necessary under art. 326 CCrPr and also assesses the facts and circumstances favoring the person under investigation." Yet, as read together with art. 326 CCrPr, art. 358 CCrPr has been interpreted as requiring the prosecutor to collect the evidence in favor of the suspect only for the very limited purpose of deciding whether to prosecute or not. In other words, in deciding whether the evidence collected is sufficient to obtain a conviction at trial, the prosecutor shall not disregard the evidence favoring the person under investigation, because, as Cordero says, "[i]f the prosecutor disregards [evidence favorable to the suspect], looking just in one direction, he risks a failure at trial or even before, at the preliminary hearing; that the prosecutor must also consider the suspect's side is a matter of elementary caution, it is not a matter of inquisitorial opportunity."[22] The prosecutor, having determined that his case is strong enough to go forward to trial, is consequently under no obligation to look for exculpatory evidence.

In making the prosecutor a straight "accuser," *i.e.* a party to the proceedings who collects the evidence in the pursuit in his own prosecutorial interest, the 1988 Code seemed to have answered the call of scholars who thought that in the old system the prosecutor, often depicted as an "organ of justice," was a hybrid institutional actor.[23] The Italian prosecutor, indeed, was severely criticized for being, in Calamandrei's words, both an accuser with no passion and a judge with no neutrality.

The partisan collection and presentation of evidence that is envisaged in principle by the new Code makes the Italian system adopt, in appearance, an adversarial approach toward truth-finding. According to this approach, the search for truth in the criminal process is not officially pursued; the truth instead stems from two (or more, as is the case in the Italian system) partisan accounts before an essentially passive adjudicator – provided, of course, that equal chances are granted to the parties.[24] As we shall see, this is not in fact the case in Italy today.

---

[21] G. Lozzi, *Lezioni di Procedura Penale*, Torino (1997), 90*ff*.; F. Cordero, *Procedura Penale*, 4th ed., Milano (1998), *passim*, but particularly 742*ff*.

[22] F. Cordero, *supra* note 21, 742.

[23] However, according to the new Code, the prosecutor is still allowed to ask for the defendant's acquittal in court and to appeal a conviction in the defendant's interest.

[24] On justice as synonymous with fairness, *see* J. Rawls, *A Theory of Justice*, Milano (1980).

b. The Italian Prosecutor's Recruitment System

In order to ascertain the true nature of the Italian reception of the adversarial approach, one also needs to verify who the Italian prosecutor is. The Italian prosecutor is a full-fledged member of the judicial body (with all the expectations of neutrality that, in the Italian public eye, comes with this designation). Like any other member of the judiciary, the prosecutor is appointed after a national competition, usually just after law school graduation, in accordance with the rules of the judicial system (art. 101 Const.). Prosecutors, preliminary investigation judges, preliminary hearing judges, and trial judges all belong to the same professional group, within which they may, upon request, move from one position to another with no substantial restrictions. They all follow the same professional and age-based bureaucratic career; they all enjoy the same economic treatment; they are all members of the same professional associations, which are very strong and effective in protecting and promoting collective interests. Prosecutors, preliminary investigation judges, preliminary hearing judges, and trial judges, moreover, all elect their representative together at the CSM (*Consiglio Superiore della Magistratura*, the self-governing body that takes care of any matter concerning the status of the judiciary); and of course they share the sense of being members of the same professional group, and thereby have developed a strong feeling of solidarity towards one another.

Given such a close relationship, can the defendant really be conceived of as benefiting from a level playing field with the Italian prosecutor, in a situation in which the trier of the fact is one of the prosecutor's "colleagues"?[25]

The lack of separation between adjudicating and prosecuting members of the judiciary – consistent with the previous officially controlled system, in which all officials were in charge of discovering the truth and, consequently, of collecting

---

[25] The strong solidarity between adjudicating and prosecuting members of the judiciary becomes manifest if one looks at the high percentage of acceptances granted by the *gip* and the *gup* (*i.e. giudice dell'udienza preliminare*, or judge of the preliminary hearing) to the prosecution's requests, concerning pre-trial detentions, telephone tappings, interceptions, or committals for trial. *See* Di Federico, "*I diritti della difesa: la drammatica testimonianza degli avvocati penalisti e le difficili prospettive di riforma,*" in G. Di Federico, D. Giori *et al., Codice di procedura penale e diritti della difesa*, Working papers IRSIG-CNR, no. 7 (1996). Moreover this explains why pre-trial detention in Italy has proved to be a useful weapon to make the defendant confess and cooperate in determining accomplices' responsibilities. Pressure, such as the threat of a lengthy pre-trial detention, can be successfully applied by the prosecutor interrogating the accused, with no substantial fear of a *gip*'s denial of his request.

and introducing evidence both for and against the accused – *denies* defendants a fair trial under the new system for collecting and presenting evidence.

c. Preliminary Investigation's Probative Value and Parties' Power Disparity

The next question to be addressed here is how extensively the prosecutor's preliminary investigation activities can be introduced in court for substantive evidentiary purposes.

It seems to be the philosophy of an adversary system that the truth stems from the dialectic between equal parties. Accordingly, if the parties are not granted even chances in presenting their side of the story, a neutral and passive decision-maker will not be able to ascertain the truth. Therefore, adversarial fairness underlies the truth-discovery process. Because the power of the parties at the preliminary investigation is entirely unbalanced, any use in court of parties' pre-trial activities for substantive evidentiary purposes will reproduce that power disparity at trial, thereby once again granting the prosecutor a strong advantage over the defendant, which in turn negatively interferes with the search for the truth.

Consistent with its underlying adversarial approach, the 1988 Code strictly limited the number of situations in which pre-trial activities could have substantive probative value at trial. The new Code of Criminal Procedure required that in principle, the evidence be produced in court, the elements collected by the prosecutor during the partisan preliminary investigation no longer have evidentiary value at trial, and the prosecution dossier no longer be available for use in court. Only a few activities performed during the preliminary investigation phase were made exceptions to this rule and given value as substantive evidence in court.[26]

Yet, after certain Constitutional Court decisions[27] and legislative reforms took

---

[26] Beside the case of the *incidente probatorio* (where the evidence is taken according with the rules applied at trial), art. 500 CCrPr allowed the introduction of previous out-of-court declarations of witnesses for impeachment purposes only, except if collected by the police or the prosecutor at the moment of search or at the exact time and place of the commission of the crime: in that case, prior inconsistent statements could have substantive probative value. Article 503 CCrPr allowed the introduction of the defendant's and other parties' prior inconsistent statements as substantive evidence when provided to the prosecutor in the presence of the defense counsel; art. 511 CCrPr allowed the introduction *ex officio* of the records of investigative acts contained in the file for the judge (art. 431 CCrPr); art. 512 CCrPr allowed the introduction, as substantive evidence, of records of the prosecutor's investigative acts that subsequently turned out to be impossible to repeat.

[27] Judgment no. 254/1992, related to art. 513 CCrPr, broadened the possibility of introducing accomplices' out-of-court statements in court as substantive evidence, whether or not the accomplice shows up or refuses to answer in court (*see also* note 30 *infra*); judgment no. 255/

place in 1992,[28] the exception turned out to be the rule, so that the probative value of the preliminary investigation activities at trial has become extremely widespread today. The result was that, according to the new rules, a defendant's conviction could now be based not only upon secretly gathered evidence – as was the case under the old system – but also upon evidence collected in a partisan manner.[29]

Article 500 CCrPr as amended by the legislators in 1992 (act no. 306) exemplifies the matter. According to the 1988/89 rule, art. 500 CCrPr allowed out-of-court witness declarations contained in the prosecution dossier were to be produced in court for impeachment purposes only, except if collected by the police or the prosecutor during a search or at the exact time and place of the commission of the crime. In such a case, prior inconsistent statements could have substantive probative value as well.

In 1992, the Italian Constitutional Court held art. 500 CCrPr partially unconstitutional, because of the irrational disparity between the situations considered. Demonstrating the resistance of the civil law's mentality – that it does not connect the fairness of the trial with the truth-discovery process – the court made clear its distaste for excluding probative evidence, maintaining that in order to discover the truth, trial judges, as the triers of fact, need to be able to evaluate and take into account as much of the information they happen to learn about during the trial as possible.[30] Thus, the great difficulties encountered by Italian legal culture in accepting the 1988 Code's adversarial approach toward truth-finding resulted in an unfair extension of the written materials a court may consider at trial.

According to the 1992 version of art. 500 CCrPr, as amended in response to the Constitutional Court's decision, any prior statement of a witness contained in the prosecutor's dossier could be produced at trial upon each party's request and, if inconsistent with the declaration in open court, these had the value of substantive evidence. This was so – and this was particularly crucial – even when in court the witness refused or failed to answer, in full or in part, questions related to previously stated facts. To make the rule more acceptable, art. 500 CCrPr, in its new language,

---

1992, related to art. 500 CCrPr (*see infra* in text); judgment no. 24/1992, related to art. 195 CCrPr, no. 4 (that the provision that police officers may not recount in court the content of witness statements is unconstitutional).

[28] Particularly *decreto legge* no. 306 of 8 June 1992 amending, *inter alia*, arts. 500 CCrPr, 503 CCrPr, 512 CCrPr, and 512*bis* CCrPr.

[29] Unless the prosecutor feels a personal responsibility for aiming at just results, thus practically acting as an impartial official in the preliminary investigation and consequently frustrating the adversarial aims of the Italian reform. *See infra*, law of 16 December 1999, mentioned in part VI.

assigned a reduced probative value to out-of-court declarations, which in fact needed to be corroborated in order to prove the fact(s) stated conclusively. However, out-of-court statements enjoyed full probative value if it became clear that the witness had been the object of violence, threat, or other undue influence which might have made him or her reluctant to testify truthfully at trial.

To relate a sense of the advantages that the new provision gave to police and prosecutors over defendants until a very recent statute was enacted on 16 November 2000, one may point to the unequal opportunities enjoyed by the parties trying to collect an out-of-court statement during the preliminary investigation. While prosecutors could compel any potential informant to make a declaration by placing an informant under threat of prosecution for refusing to answer or for giving false information,[31] suspects and their counsel were not even entitled to obtain an affidavit in the same situation. In cases in which defense counsel was able to convince potential witnesses in their favor to speak, they could (since 1995) ask the *gip* to include the statement in the prosecutor's investigative file (or, after the enactment of law 479/1999, could ask the prosecutor – at the end of his investigation – to include it in his file: art. 415*bis* CCrPr). But of course, a different probative weight was to be attached in court to a statement that, if false, would have led to imposition of criminal liability (the one borne before the prosecutor) as compared to a declaration, the falsity of which had no legal consequences (*i.e.* the one borne before the suspect's counsel).[32]

---

[30] The concept that trial judges, in order to ascertain the truth, need to be able to know and take into account as much evidence as possible was also expressed by the Italian Constitutional Court in a previous judgment (254/1992) related to art. 513, no. 2 (in its original formulation). In its holding, the Court ruled as unconstitutional the prohibition to introduce an accomplice's out-of-court declaration at trial when the accomplice, being tried in separate proceedings, invokes his privilege against self-incrimination at the accused's trial (according to art. 513, no. 2, first draft). It is worth pointing out that the US Supreme Court was recently confronted with the same issue and took the opposite view. In *Lilly v. Virginia*, 527 US, 144 L.Ed. 2d 117, 119 SCt (1999), the Court ruled that the accused's rights under the confrontation clause of Federal Constitution's Sixth Amendment were violated by the introduction at trial (in which the accomplice was invoking the privilege against self-incrimination) of an accomplice's confession that incriminated the accused for murder.

[31] *Ex* art. 371*bis* Italian CCrPr, a provision enacted in 1992.

[32] To cope with these inequalities, the law of 16 November 2000 attached criminal liability to the making of a false statement in front of the suspect's counsel. The same statute also made it possible for the counsel of the suspect to ask the prosecutor to obtain a declaration from the potential informant for him or her, under the threat of prosecution for refusing to answer.

Moreover, in order to effectively search for exculpatory evidence, suspects need to enjoy personal freedom. Yet keeping them in pre-trial detention is extremely common in practice, and the prosecution's decision on the matter routinely receives judicial approval.

In addition to the above-mentioned prosecutorial powers, it is worth noting that the prosecutor, but not the suspect or his counsel, can – in the cases and forms provided by the law – make inspections, searches, or seizures, or can intercept conversations and communications. The prosecutor can even oblige the suspect whose counsel has been given timely notice of an interrogation to submit to that interrogation. Though suspects will be informed of their right not to answer, refusal to answer will be documented in written form and included in the investigative file, with the consequence that the suspect, suffering no adverse legal consequence for lying, usually feels a psychological pressure to speak. Formally, no unfavorable inferences – except possibly as far as sentencing is concerned[33] – can be drawn in court from the suspect's silence, yet the preliminary interrogation record can be produced at trial upon a party's request, and the defendant's pre-trial statements can be given full probative value, whether he or she takes the stand or not.[34]

d. The Italian Prosecutor and the Myth of the Compulsory Prosecution Principle

One more feature of the function of the Italian public prosecutor needs to be outlined here. Despite the abstract constitutional provision that mandates compulsory prosecution, Italian prosecutors actually enjoy substantial discretion in deciding whether or not to prosecute a suspect. Indeed, to mandate compulsory prosecution does not alter the daily reality of their job, which prevents them from taking into equal consideration and prosecuting the large variety of crimes that come to their attention. Hence, in Italy, as everywhere, selection among those crimes reported is inevitable.[35]

---

[33] On this matter, *see* F. Cordero, *supra* note 21, 248.

[34] According to art. 503 CCrPr, if the defendant takes the stand; according to art. 513 CCrPr, if he decides not to.

[35] Informal surveys suggest that 90 percent of reported crimes are not prosecuted. On prosecutorial discretion in Italy, *see*, Di Federico, *"Obbligatorieta' dell'azione penale, coordinamento delle attivita' del pubblico ministero e loro rispondenza alle aspettative della comunità,"* in A. Gaito (ed.), *Accusa penale e ruolo del pubblico ministero*, Napoli (1991), 170-208; *idem*, in J. De Figueiredo Dias, G. Di Federico, R. Ottenhof, J.F. Renucci, L.C. Henry, M. Shikita, *The Role of the Public Prosecutor in Criminal Justice according to the Different Constitutional Systems*, Working Papers IRSIG-CNR, Special Issue, Bologna (1996).

The notion of compulsory prosecution has nevertheless found its way into the 1948 Italian Constitution. Its rationale has been the same fostering of prosecutorial impartiality that has justified its introduction into the German system. According to this theory, the lack of discretion on the side of the prosecutor would avoid the future unfair treatment of crimes perpetrated by the political regime. Moreover, the theoretical absence of prosecutorial discretion justified, in turn, the further Italian constitutional choice of making the prosecutor's office entirely independent from the politically responsible Ministry of Justice. Compulsory prosecution, combined with the prosecutor's independence, seemed to the Italian framers to be the best way to pursue equality before the law. Unfortunately, because of the lack of realistic assumptions behind the compulsory prosecution principle, Italian prosecutors' independence from political power resulted in a total lack of accountability for their *de facto* choices, related either to the criteria for setting priorities adopted in prosecuting reported crimes, or to the amount of energy and resources to be spent on each individual case. Henceforth, Italian prosecutors enjoy unfettered freedom in deciding where to concentrate their activities – and therefore, whether or not to prosecute a case. But in terms of equality before the law, this had results that were diametrically opposed to what had been envisaged by the constitutional framers. Disregarded cases are resolved by dismissal, expiration of the limitation period, or by periodic mercy measures.

On the whole, it is no wonder that Italian legal scholars refer to the Italian prosecutor as the "fourth power," next to the legislative, executive, and judicial powers.[36]

B. The Preliminary Hearing (*L'udienza preliminare*)

If, upon completion of the preliminary investigation, the prosecutor determines that he has collected enough evidence to sustain a conviction at trial, he will make a request to refer the case for trial. The decision will be made by a judge – the *giudice dell'udienza preliminare* or *gup* – in a hearing held in camera, called an *udienza preliminare*, or "preliminary hearing."[37] Unlike its American counterpart,

---

[36] Nobili, "*Un quarto potere?*," in M. Tirelli (ed.), *Recenti orientamenti in tema di pubblico ministero ed esercizio dell'azione penale*, Milano (1998), 29-43.

[37] According to art. 34 CCrPr, no. 2*bis*, as amended by *decreto legislativo* no. 51 of 19 February 1998 (which came into force only very recently – in June 1999 – and after an harsh political debate) the same judge who presided over the preliminary investigation phase (*gip*) can no longer be in charge of the preliminary hearing phase (*gup*).

the Italian preliminary hearing is essentially based on the documents contained in the prosecutor's investigative file, which the *gup* will receive together with the request for committal to trial and which the defendant and his counsel have the right to inspect before the preliminary hearing.

The hearing is necessarily held in the presence of the parties, and a debate between the parties takes place. The prosecutor will summarize the results of his investigation and will summarily indicate the elements collected against the accused that justify his request to refer the case for trial. The defendant, working from the investigation file and the documents that the judge can admit at the outset of the hearing, has the opportunity to argue against setting the case for trial. The defendant can also ask to be submitted to an interrogation process to be conducted according to the examination rules applied in court. In such a case, the interrogation will have full probative value when produced at trial (art. 514 CCrPr). At the end of the hearing, the judge determines whether or not the matter should be set for trial, or whether further information needs to be gathered before making a decision. In determining that the matter should be set for trial, the judge will commit the case to trial by means of an unreviewable decree; in deciding not to send the case to trial, an order of dismissal subject to appeal is issued. Dismissing a case does not foreclose the matter being reopened should new evidence arise (arts. 434*ff* CCrPr).

If the judge deems that further information must be acquired before reaching a decision, he or she before the enactment of the law 479/1999 (see *infra* part VI) would have informed the parties of which matters still needed to be addressed. Originally envisaged as not being an "instructor judge"[38] and as having no *ex officio* evidence-gathering power, until January 2000 the judge of the preliminary hearing could only receive the additional evidence deemed clearly conclusive to decide for either a committal order or a dismissal order. Today however, the *gip* enjoys an extensive power of inquiry to gather the information he deems necessary in order to dismiss the case.[39] Except for the documents (which will be included in the file for the trial judge), all the evidence so produced will be included in the prosecutor's file.

The preliminary hearing has three aims. The first is to select the cases to be sent to trial, in order to restrict the workload of trial judges, thus increasing the efficiency of the machinery of justice. According to leading Italian scholarship,[40] particularly

---

[38] *See supra* para. 1

[39] *See infra*, part VI.

[40] Lozzi, *supra* note 21, 338*ff*. In this sense, *see* now art. 23, no. 3, law no. 479 of 16 December 1999.

after art. 425 CCrPr was amended in 1993, the judge of the preliminary hearing, in deciding whether to commit the case to trial, is supposed to apply the same standard as the prosecutor asking for a dismissal at the end of the preliminary investigation. In other words, in order to work as an effective gatekeeper of cases to be sent to trial, the preliminary hearing should prevent cases in which the judge deems the evidence collected to be insufficient to sustain a conviction in court from going to trial.

The second function assigned to the preliminary hearing is to allow defendants to adduce any exculpatory evidence they have collected in order to stop the case from moving forward to trial. If, indeed, only the prosecution were permitted to produce the evidence gathered during the investigation, defendants would be unfairly deprived[41] of the right to demonstrate that there is no need to go to trial. Having the chance to avoid trial is in fact crucial to the innocent defendant, who will be affected by an unnecessary trial not only in his economic capacity, but also in his professional and personal ones.

Finally, the preliminary hearing is aimed at allowing alternatives to trial procedure: namely the "sentencing by parties' request" and the "summary proceedings," which I will address later. It is worth noting here that, in contrast with the traditional American system, sentence bargaining occurs in light of full discovery. This allows the defendant to thoroughly evaluate the advantages of accepting the bargain and prevents the prosecution from bluffing as well as the employment of overcharging strategies.

C. The Trial (*Il Dibattimento*)

1. Outline

Whenever the judge at the preliminary hearing grants the prosecutor's request to refer the case for trial, a file for the trial judge is created in addition to the prosecutor's file. The prosecutor's file (or full "dossier"), containing the evidence accumulated during the pre-trial investigation, is in fact no longer available to the trial judge.

In sharp contrast with the previous model, the new Code envisaged a trial in which, in principle, adjudicators, like their common law counterparts, approach the case as a *tabula rasa*, *i.e.* without familiarity with sources of information gathered by the prosecutor during the pre-trial stages of the criminal process. In

---

[41] Except if the eventuality of an *incidente probatorio* took place.

[42] On this point, *see* Damaska's considerations in "Evidentiary Barriers," *supra* note 10, 517 and 544.

order to keep the prosecution's dossier from unduly influencing the presiding judge's mind, the principle of "immediacy"[42] is implemented and all evidence is required to be produced to the trial judge in its original form; only through their production in court are sources of information transformed into proper evidence. The principle of immediacy encompasses the notion that the judge who receives the evidence in court shall be the same judge who decides the case upon its merits. Two other notions necessarily follow from the immediacy principle. The first is that of orality, according to which no prior out-of-court statements should be read out in court for evidentiary purposes (though a few exceptions were originally present in the Code, and many more have been subsequently introduced). The second is that of the temporal concentration of the proceedings, also known as the concentrated day-in-court trial principle. (Article 477 CCrPr states that if it is *absolutely impossible* to end the trial in one day, it must be continued the following day.)

Thus, art. 431 CCrPr limits the file sent to the trial judge to the charging documents, the physical evidence connected with the crime, the record of evidence gathered using the *incidente probatorio*, the defendant's prior criminal record, documents concerning the civil claims, and the record of evidence gathered by the prosecutor or the police, whenever it is impossible to acquire it again. The rest of the evidence must be presented at the trial by the parties.

Unlike the former criminal procedure model, in which the entire proof-taking process was officially conducted and the fact-finding process was officially controlled (since the evidence was assembled by judges and other impartial officials, and produced in court by the trial judge), the new Code, in principle, took the opposite approach, envisaging a system of adjudication in which the evidence is essentially presented by the parties.

Accordingly, in sharp contrast to a system in which the presiding judge used to first interrogate the defendant and the other private parties, and then, *ex officio*, examine witnesses by exclusively questioning them, introduce documents, examine expert witnesses and finally admit and examine the evidence presented by the parties,[43] the Italian Code of Criminal Procedure now provides that "evidence is received upon the party's request" (art. 190, CCrPr, no. 1). Thus, each party presents their own case, calls witnesses, and examines them. In order to exclude the possibility of surprise evidence, seven days before the trial begins the parties must draft and submit to the court a list with the names of the witnesses, experts and technical

---

[43] However, in this last case the evidence examined was also considered as being the judge's, "or, rather, the court's evidence," to use Damaska's words, in "Evidentiary Barriers," *supra* note 10, 525.

counsel they wish to examine in court, as well as indicate the subject matter of the examination.

The trial begins with the discussion of any preliminary matters, such as venue or claims of procedural error. Then the prosecutor, like his American counterpart, delivers an opening statement. The prosecutor's statement is followed by the opening statements of the "private parties," *i.e.* plaintiffs asking for damages and parties "civilly accountable for the fines." The party injured by the criminal act can intervene in the criminal action and become a co-plaintiff together with the public prosecutor.[44] Thereafter, the accused makes an opening statement. Each side then indicates the facts to be proved and the evidence they intend to introduce. The prosecutor presents evidence first, after which it is other party's turn to produce evidence. As there is no *prima facie* case to be proven by the prosecution (due to the absence of a bifurcated trial, in which the jury is the ultimate trier of facts), this order of evidence production may be subject to derogation by agreement of the parties.

Unlike the previous Code, the defendant can today decide not to take the stand.[45] While this decision not to take the stand cannot be used to draw any unfavorable inference against him or her, in case the accused decides otherwise, anything they say or *do not say* can be used against the accused. Yet, as was the case before 1989, and unlike in the common law system, the defendant is not put under oath, so that no prosecution for perjury could be sustained if the falsity of his "testimony" is established at trial. Unlike in the common law system, moreover, defendants are given the opportunity to issue spontaneous statements whenever they deem it necessary.

The parties pose questions to witnesses, technical consultants, and private parties through direct, cross, and re-direct examination. Answers to leading questions are not admissible during direct examination, but they are admissible during cross-examination.[46] Character evidence related to the defendant as well as the victim of the crime is prohibited, unless necessary as a proof of *modus operandi* (art. 194 CCrPr). Hearsay testimony is prohibited, unless parties consent to it.

---

[44] For details on the *partie civile*'s participation in the Continental criminal trial, *see* R. Schlesinger, *et al.*, *Comparative Law*, note 13 *supra*, 532*ff.*

[45] For the implications of such an approach in terms of a diminished psychological pressure to speak, *see* Damaska, "Evidentiary Barriers," *supra* note 10, 527, comparing the interrogation process of the non-adversarial continental model to the defendant consenting examination in the common law adversary system.

[46] Though questions and answers in the examinations should be specific, in the Italian system there is little preparation of witnesses outside of court (*see* the recent law of 16 November 2000). As a consequence, narrative answers are less dangerous to truth-finding than in a system like the American one, where lawyers typically "prepare," or "coach," witnesses.

The Italian trial is not entirely party-controlled. It involves four departures from a purely adversarial approach to fact-finding. First, if parties consent to the admission of hearsay, the trial judge may require original proof (*i.e.* non-hearsay evidence), according to art. 195 CCrPr, no. 3. Secondly, the presiding judge is allowed not only to question witnesses at the conclusion of the examination (as in the US system), but also to indicate new issues to the parties that need to be addressed during the examination. Thirdly, expert witnesses, always officially appointed, unlike in the US system, may be examined *ex officio* in court (art. 224 CCrPr, no. 1, but also arts. 468 CCrPr, no. 5 and 501 CCrPr, no. 2). Moreover – and this has proven to be a very influential provision in a legal system rooted in the continental tradition – art. 507 CCrPr provides that, after all the evidence has been produced in court, whenever absolutely necessary, the trial judge is subsidiarily authorized to examine proof *sua sponte*. The presiding judge will then examine the witnesses and decide afterwards who among the parties will pose questions first (usually it is the party that appears to be favored by the witness's statements). Originally envisaged by the legislators as a strict exception ("whenever *absolutely* necessary") to the principle of partisan presentation of evidence, art. 507 CCrPr has subsequently been broadly construed by the continental-law-trained Italian courts,[47] who have essentially thrown open a half-closed door.

The central role presently assigned to the trial judge in the fact-finding process has been severely criticized by scholars, who fear that judicial activism can affect adjudicator neutrality.[48] If the structure of the proceedings is envisaged as a dispute between two parties, where each of them bears the burden of proving the facts stated in court, any official adducing of evidence will indeed inevitably help one of the two sides.

On the other hand, judicial activism in producing evidence has been considered (hypocritically, in my view[49]) a necessary consequence of the constitutionally

---

[47] *See* the 1992 Italian Supreme Court decision – upheld in 1993 by the Italian Constitutional Court (judgment no. 111/1993). These decisions express the view that the necessity is "*absolute,*" according to art. 507 CCrPr, not only when the trial judge needs to clarify matters that emerged from the partisan presentation of evidence, but also any time the partisan-presented evidence is deemed to be insufficient to determine guilt. The Italian trial judge has consequently been allocated the responsibility for *ex officio* subsidiarily collecting and producing all evidence the parties refrain from presenting.

[48] Lozzi, *supra* note 21, 429.

[49] I have already tried to explain how fictitious the principle of compulsory prosecution is; thus, I do not see why the system should care about its implementation in court, if it practically does not care about its implementation at pre-trial stages.

mandated compulsory prosecution principle. If the prosecutor is required to prosecute by law, the argument goes, the prosecution cannot be dropped in court simply as a result of prosecutorial inaction. From this point of view, the subsidiary judicial powers, in presenting evidence, are aimed at preventing the violation of the principle.[50]

More than on the grounds of implementation of compulsory prosecution, the presence of the article in the Code can perhaps be explained by the forcible hostility that the continental system maintains towards a purely party-controlled fact-finding process, in which the fission into two distinct cases eliminates the possibility of investigating other possibilities. A model in which, as Damaska puts it, "[a]s in a car driving at night, two narrow beams continue to illuminate the world presented to the adjudicator from the beginning until the end of trial"[51] and in which, by consequence, all information that does not clearly aid one of the parties is filtered out, has been rejected in Italy since 1989. The codifier probably had in mind limited judicial activism, designed solely to remedy the ills of a selectively partisan system of presenting evidence. Yet the Italian courts' inquisitorial attitude toward an officially dominated search for truth effectively turned the provision into an avenue for extensive judicial inquiry.[52] A similarly broad construction of art. 603 CCrPr, moreover, allows substantial judicial activism to be practiced today, even at the appellate court level.

When all evidence has been submitted – including the readings of the documents and records that may be read aloud in court – the public prosecutor and the counsel of the private parties set forth their closing arguments. Unlike in many American jurisdictions, the defense is always allowed to make the final statement in an Italian trial.

After the hearing of evidence and arguments at trial, the court makes a decision both on guilt and sentencing matters, and must give written reasons for its findings.

2. The Admissibility of Evidence

The partisan presentation of evidence model, adopted in principle by the new Italian Code, also raised the issue of admissibility of evidence presented by the parties, which for the most part had been previously disregarded. Under the previous Code, when the trial judge introduced evidence *ex officio*, the moment at which the judge

---

[50] *See* Constitutional Court, judgment no. 111/1993 and Cordero, *supra* note 21 at 847.

[51] M. Damaska, *Evidence Law Adrift*, *supra* note 5 at 92.

[52] On the judiciary's extensive use of investigative powers in Italian trials and on the consequent practical distortion of other provisions, *see* Lozzi, *supra* note 21 at 429.

decided what evidence would be examined at trial was rarely separated from the proof-taking moment. The new system has made the admission of evidence stage of the proceedings a formal and very crucial one.

Yet while importing part of the American law of evidence and its exclusionary rules (the rules against introduction of hearsay and, to some extent, character evidence, the prohibition against leading questions on direct examination, testimonial privileges, and illegally obtained interceptions, etc.), the Italian system differs significantly from the common law model in two respects. First, exclusionary rules are not aimed at insulating the trier of fact from the impact of the inadmissible evidence. As already pointed out, the Italian tribunal is made up of professional judges who in the most serious cases sit together with lay members of the panel. Therefore, the bifurcated trial common to the Anglo-American setting, in which the judge handles questions of law – including the admissibility of evidence – and the lay jury handles questions of fact, does not exist in the Italian model. Rather, the same people decide the question of admissibility and the ultimate issue of guilt. Thus, the function of the exclusionary rules in Italy is obviously not to insulate the trier of fact from the impact of inadmissible evidence. Instead, their function is to prevent the trier of fact from taking the evidence into consideration to determine the defendant's guilt or innocence. Because the Italian trial judge, unlike the American jury, must give written reasons for a finding of guilt or innocence, violation of an exclusionary rule is supposed to be redressed at the appellate level. Yet it is, of course, far from certain that excluding evidence is the same thing as forgetting evidence, so that the Italian exclusionary rules system cannot provide "the institutional black velvet on which the jewels of the common law's exclusionary doctrine can display their full potential and allure."[53]

The second considerable difference between the Italian model and the American model concerning the rules of exclusion is that in the Italian system, as distinguished from its common law counterpart, the parties do not have control over the application of the rules of evidence. In the Italian system, the principle of partisan presentation of evidence does not involve the judge ruling, in the manner of a neutral umpire, that the parties abide by the rules regulating evidence production only upon the objection of the side adversely affected. Rather, in the Italian criminal trial, the parties cannot allow the evidence rules to be modified by a failure of a party to make a relevant objection, nor can the parties stipulate variations to the rules.

---

[53] M. Damaska, *Evidence Law Adrift, supra* note 5, 52; *see also* Roger Park's book review of Damaska's work. "An Outsider's View of Common Law Evidence," 96 *Michigan LRev* 1486, 1489 (1998).

Violation of the rules of evidence can in fact always be officially raised, at any stage or level of the proceedings (art. 191 CCrPr, no. 2).

In the Italian system, as in the common law model, exclusionary rules are, to borrow Damaska's important distinction, either "intrinsic" (rules designed to improve fact-finding accuracy) or "extrinsic" (rules governed by considerations extraneous to truth-finding).

Among the rules that exclude evidence due to the belief that it may impede the pursuit of the truth, the hearsay prohibition ensures that the affected party is able to cross-examine the otherwise out-of-court declarant, on the assumption that a statement can be deemed sufficiently trustworthy to be admitted into evidence only if properly challenged by an able cross-examination.[54] Anonymous documents, testimony based on word of mouth shared by the community, character evidence, and co-defendant testimony[55] are deemed untrustworthy, and are therefore excluded.

Extrinsic exclusionary rules that make evidence inadmissable in court for reasons extraneous to truth-finding considerations, and which are often at odds with such considerations, are also present in the Italian system.[56] Many testimonial privileges belong to this category, as well as rules excluding documents illegally seized at the counsel for the defendant's premises, or rules excluding illegally performed interceptions of otherwise private communications. Yet the great bulk of the American exclusionary rules in the search and seizure area, together with the doctrine known as the "fruit of the poisonous tree," has been rejected in the Italian model. Evidence obtained by way of an illegal search or as a by-product of an illegal interception (for example, the *corpus delicti*, discovered through abusive telephone tapping) is consequently admissible in the Italian court.

Finally, a third kind of exclusionary rule, sharing both kinds of characteristics, can be seen at work in the Italian trial. Rules excluding evidence obtained in a way likely to modify the declarant's self-determination (via lie detectors, narco-analysis, and so forth) are prime examples. Unless inadmissible or clearly superfluous, the Italian trial judge is compelled to admit all evidence presented by the parties (art. 190 CCrPr, no. 1).

---

[54] For a critical perspective on hearsay rule foundations in the US system, *see* Van Kessel, "Hearsay Hazards in the American Criminal Trial: An Adversary-Oriented Approach," 49 *Hastings LJ* 469 (1998).

[55] A co-defendant consequently cannot be put under oath.

[56] On the commitment to other values – such as privacy, individual dignity, and similar values – evinced by all the procedural systems as alongside of, but more often competing with, the desire to discover the truth in the criminal process, *see* Jescheck, "Principles of German Criminal Procedure in Comparison with American Law," 56 *VaLRev* 239, 240*ff.* (1970).

3. Some Concluding Remarks

If we adopt as the definition of an adversary system "a system of adjudication in which procedural action is controlled by the parties and the adjudicator remains essentially passive,"[57] the above sketch may lead one to seriously doubt that Italian criminal procedure may be defined as such.

Official contributions to the introduction of evidence, official application of evidence rules, and the defendant's acquittal *ex officio* whenever the judge finds the accused innocent (whether or not the parties arrived at a bargained-for conviction and sentence) (art. 129 CCrPr), show in fact how strong judicial control over the process is in the Italian system. Moreover, an adversarial structure for the proceedings is seriously affected by the presence of more than two parties, as is the case in the Italian criminal trial, in which a private party pursuing civil remedies can participate (albeit for the limited purpose of pursuing his civil interests).[58] And pleadings and stipulations that are essential to an adversarial structure[59] can play only a very marginal role in the Italian criminal procedure (*see* part IV, *infra*).

Even if bifurcation into two adjudicating bodies (the first one accountable for determining facts and the second one for applying the law, as in the judge-jury system) is not a necessary feature of the adversary system, its absence from the Italian model has greatly enhanced the official control over the proceedings. When judges become directly accountable for guilt determination, their sense of "personal responsibility for the accuracy of fact-finding cannot but induce them to become involved in proof-taking activity more than they do in jury trials."[60] To this extent, the lack of a bifurcated adjudicating body, coupled with a long civilian tradition of non-adversary proceedings, is the reason, in my view, for the extensive judicial activism of Italian courts. Italian judges, unlike their American counterparts,[61] feel personal responsibility to achieve an accurate and just result; therefore, they want

---

[57] *See* Damaska, *Evidence Law Adrift, supra* note 5 at 74.

[58] Nor can dispute resolution be seriously considered as the goal of all procedure in Italy, unlike – according to some common law scholars – in the common law system. *See*, for instance, Goldstein, "The State and the Accused: Balance of Advantage in Criminal Procedure," 69 *Yale LJ* 1149 (1960) and, more recently, M. Damaska, *Evidence Law Adrift, supra* note 5,113*ff*.

[59] On the matter *see* Damaska, "Evidentiary Barriers," *supra* note 10 at 563 and 582 and *idem, Evidence Law Adrift, ibid.*

[60] M. Damaska, *Evidence Law Adrift, supra* note 5 at 135, quoting J. Jackson and S. Doran's work, *Judge without Jury: Diplock Trials in the Adversary System*, Oxford (1995).

[61] On this point *see* Van Kessel, "Adversary Excesses in the American Criminal Trial," 67 *Notre Dame LRev* 403, 527 (1992). *See* moreover the same article for a general and extensive overview of the differences between Anglo-American and continental criminal procedures.

authority over the fact-finding process. Moreover, the Italian judges' sense of responsibility is at the same time enhanced and justified by the duty to give written reasons for their findings. Accordingly, unaccustomed to a passive role, Italian judges broadly interpreted art. 507 CCrPr in order to repossess their traditional role in the fact-finding process. Besides, the Italian Constitutional Court – demonstrating the civil law tradition's distaste for excluding probative evidence from the determination of guilt by the trial judge[62] – ruled as unconstitutional provisions such as art. 500 CCrPr and art. 513 CCrPr (as amended in 1997),[63] which had prevented the trial judge from treating the out-of-court statements of witnesses or co-defendants, which the defendant cannot confront at trial, as substantive evidence.

Thus, the traditional, official-dominated search-for-truth approach gradually prevailed over an adversarial approach toward truth-finding, and judges' cognitive needs regained predominance over the fairness of the trial. Yet, unlike under the

---

[62] "If a matter important to their cognitive need has not been illuminated can [the judges in a bench trial] – as fact-finder now – be faulted for seeking illumination on their own initiative? *Si iudicas, cognosce,*" Damaska reminds us, *ibid.* If judges know, they also want to be able to take into consideration the main part of what they know, as long as written reasons for their fact-finding will theoretically provide a basis for a review of it.

[63] After a Constitutional Court decision in 1992 (judgment no. 254), art. 513 CCrPr provided for the substantive probative value in court of out-of-court declarations of co-defendants who decided not to take the stand (or who were not present at the trial) and of out-of-court declarations of accomplices, tried in different proceedings, that (legitimately) refused to answer in court or were impossible to take to trial. Reasons similar to that which underlie the so-called *Bruton*'s rule in the US system or which more recently rendered the US Supreme Court ruling on the admission into evidence of the non-testifying accomplice's incriminating confession unconstitutional (*Lilly v.Virginia, supra* note 30), led the Italian Parliament to amend art. 513 CCrPr in 1997, to preserve the defendant's right to be confronted in court with the accomplice's inculpatory declaration. Article 513 CCrPr, after 7 August 1997 (statute no. 267), provided thereafter that the co-defendant's (or the accomplice's, when tried in different proceedings) out-of-court declarations could not be taken into consideration for evidentiary purposes by the court, as far as the defendants' criminal liability was concerned, except upon the parties' consent. Yet in 1998 (judgment no. 361 of 26 October 1998), the Italian Constitutional Court held the new art. 513 CCrPr unconstitutional, because of the pro-bative evidence dispersion that it encompassed. On very recently the Italian Parliament reacted against the Constitutional Court's judgment, amending the Constitution in order to introduce a new constitutional principle granting the defendant a fair trial (on which see part VI, *infra*). Thus, the struggle between the Italian Parliament and the Italian Constitutional Court over art. 513 CCrPr became the symbol of the struggle between the attempt to introduce an adversary model, on the one hand, and the resistance of a non-adversary tradition on the other.

previous model, Italian official truth discovery is in the new system hampered by the principle (though often derogated) of the partisan presentation of evidence. Trial judges, indeed, know only what the parties allow them to be aware of in the prosecution's dossier. The result seems to produce the worst of both worlds, and recently induced the Italian Parliament to react against the previously described trend of the Italian judiciary to satisfy its cognitive needs at the expense of due process guarantees (*see infra*, part VI).

If, moreover, the fact of relative judicial passivity in the common law, which symbolized the defendant's protection against official abuses of power, was the very feature of the adversary system that made it so ideologically appealing to transplant to Italy, the failure of the transplant becomes even more apparent.

V. Special Procedures and the System's Efficiency

A. General Outline

In addition to the goal of reconstructing Italian criminal procedure along adversarial lines, Italian codifiers also aimed at "providing the Italian criminal justice system with new, efficient procedures to combat its perennial backlog."[64] Yet more than a decade after the new Code's enactment, this second task seems not to have been fully achieved either.

It is well known how the Anglo-American system handles the problem of judicial overload. First, prosecutorial discretion openly grants the prosecutor the power not to prosecute cases that are deemed unworthy of prosecution. Consequently, some cases are simply dismissed, while others are diverted to alternatives to trial – *e.g.* treatment, vocational training, or mediation. Secondly, prosecutorial discretion legitimizes and encourages plea bargaining, so that purportedly, between 90 and 95 percent of all criminal prosecutions in the US are disposed of in this way. Plea bargains are often criticized for the implicit coercion they place on defendants, for the sentencing disparity they produce between defendants accepting a bargain and defendants facing a trial, and for leading to convictions without sufficient procedural safeguards. Yet plea bargaining, consistent with a conflict-resolving vision of criminal procedure, represents the trade-off between efficiency and justice, where the full protection of a trial can only be granted to a small percentage of the totality

---

[64] *See* Pizzi and Marafioti, "New Italian Code," *supra* note 12 at 17. *See*, moreover, this same article for details on the special Italian procedures.

of the cases (supposedly the most serious ones).[65]

By contrast, the Italian system formally mandates compulsory prosecution.[66] Accordingly, plea bargaining cannot involve the charge, but only the sentence. Formal pleadings and stipulations, moreover, are very much extraneous to the continental mentality, which – irrespective of any attempt to transplant an adversary model – hardly accepts that judges play no role in the search for truth[67] and that parties shape the criminal outcome.

Consequently, in order to cope with the judicial backlog, Italy's new Code had to take a more moderate and many-sided approach than that taken by the common law system. Thus, a variety of special procedures have been envisaged to achieve efficiency. They can be classified according to the stage of the criminal proceedings that they aim to eliminate in order to expedite the case. First, procedures exist which permit the system to avoid the preliminary hearing and set the matter for immediate trial, on the grounds that the strength of the evidence against the defendant warrants such an approach. These are the *giudizio direttissimo* and the *giudizio immediato* procedures, which encompass situations in which the evidence of the defendant's criminal responsibility is very strong. Secondly, there are procedures that allow the system to avoid trial and that were consequently designed to become the primary solution to solving the Italian judicial overload problem. These are the *applicazione della pena su richiesta delle parti* or "sentencing by parties' request," the *giudizio abbreviato* or "summary proceedings," and the *procedimento per decreto penale* or "proceedings by penal decree."

The second kind of simplified procedure provides the defendant with an incentive in the form of a significant sentencing reduction in exchange for waiving his right to trial. All three procedures involve decisions based only, or primarily, upon the investigative file records, which acquire a full probative value for this purpose.

---

[65] Even if efficiency is often pursued at justice's expense, it is nevertheless impossible to achieve justice in a system that is inefficient. In an inefficient system plagued by backlog, indeed, how many innocent people would be kept in pre-trial detention and for how long, and how many guilty people would escape punishment because the limitation period had expired? On plea bargaining from a critical and comparative point of view, *see* Langbein, "Land Without Plea Bargaining: How the Germans Do It," 78 *MichLRev* 204 (1978) advocating an eradication of plea bargaining by importing the European mixed court. For a reply *see:* Herrmann, "Bargaining Justice. A Bargain for German Criminal Justice," 53 *UPittLRev* 755 (1992) and Dubber, "American Plea Bargains, German Lay Judges, and the Crisis of Criminal Procedure," 49 *StanLRev* 547 (1997).

[66] But *see supra*, part IV A.

[67] Even in this case, lack of bifurcation represents fertile soil for the burgeoning of a civilian mentality of resistance.

B. The "Sentencing by Parties' Request" (*L'Applicazione Della Pena su Richiesta Delle Parti*)

Formally enjoying no discretion in whether or not to bring charges, the Italian prosecutor is only allowed to enter stipulations regarding the sentence to be imposed, and can do so only within boundaries that are quite strict. The "sentencing by parties' request" procedure, indeed, shows how weak the prosecutorial bargaining power is and how great is the system's reluctance to allow the parties to shape the outcome of criminal proceedings. According to art. 444 CCrPr, at the preliminary hearing, until the moment at which the parties' closing arguments have been formulated, the defendant and the prosecutor can request that the judge apply a negotiated reduced sentence, *so long as* the final sentence does not exceed two years' imprisonment (including a reduction of up to one third of the normal sentence). Still, the judge cannot accept the stipulation if he or she finds that the defendant is not guilty, and in this case he must acquit. The precise scope of this judicial check is quite controversial, but according to many Italian scholars, it permits an extensive review of the merits of the case. To this extent, the judge would be bound to acquit not only when the defendant is obviously innocent, but also whenever the judge is not positively convinced of the defendant's guilt.[68] Since the parties cannot stipulate as to the nature of the crime charged, the judge who receives a request for imposition of a negotiated sentence will review the legal qualification of the facts charged against the defendant; he or she will also review the application of the aggravating and mitigating circumstances. On finding an error, the judge must refuse the bargained agreement, and the ordinary proceedings will take place instead. The Italian system's distrust of the contest structure for the criminal process (in which the parties are substantially in control) has become particularly clear after a decision of the Italian Constitutional Court made in 1990.[69] According to this decision, the judge can finally refuse to accept the stipulation on finding that the negotiated sentence is inappropriate to the crime committed (*see now also* art. 444 as amended by law no. 479/1999).

---

[68] *See* Cordero, *supra* note 21 at 931; Lozzi, *supra* note 21 at 383*ff*. If broadly construed, the factual basis review provision of art. 444 CCrPr, no. 2 would possibly frustrate the prosecutor's desire to use this kind of special procedure. The Italian Supreme Court, however, has until now refused to extensively review the merits of the case, when asked to apply a bargained sentence (*see* first panel, judgment of 19 February 1990, *Cass. pen.*, II, 44*ff*, 1990; plenary session, judgment of 8 May 1996, De Leo; plenary session, judgment of 26 February 1997 Bahrouni; plenary session, judgment of 20 June 1997, Lisuzzo; plenary session, judgments of 28 May 1997 and 25 March 1998).

C. The "Proceeding by Penal Decree" (*Il Procedimento per Decreto Penale*)

The "proceeding by penal decree" is available for a very limited number of minor crimes, for which the prosecutor believes that a fine would constitute a sufficient punishment. In such cases, the prosecutor can ask the judge[70] to issue a decree of conviction against the defendant. In order to avoid a defendant's demand for a "sentencing by parties' request" or for a "summary proceedings," the new Code allows the prosecutor to ask the judge to impose a sentence that can be reduced by up to one-half (whereas the maximum reduction in cases of a "summary proceedings" or of a "sentencing by parties' request" is up to one third). If the judge deems the request acceptable and shall not pronounce a decision of acquittal, he or she will then issue the decree, which the defendant can oppose within fifteen days, demanding either a trial or some different special procedure. If the request is deemed unacceptable, the judge will return the file to the prosecutor for prosecution of the case.

D. The "Summary Proceeding" (*Il Giudizio Abbreviato*)

Finally, the procedure known as *giudizio abbreviato* is available for all crimes. It is a quasi-trial procedure, wherein the defendant asks the judge of the preliminary hearing for a decision on the merits of the case, based primarily upon the investigative file records. In return for sparing the state a full trial, the defendant, if found guilty, will enjoy a reduction by one third of the sentence that the judge would otherwise have imposed. In order to institute a "summary proceeding," until very recently (*see infra*, part VI) the prosecutor had to give his consent and the judge of the preliminary hearing had to deem the case appropriate to be resolved in such a manner on the basis of the investigative file.

Unlike at the preliminary hearing, until law no. 479/1999 was enacted (*see infra*, part VI) at the *giudizio abbreviato* the parties could not ask for additional evidence to be produced. This aspect of the procedure, which was challenged unsuccessfully before the Constitutional Court,[71] while requiring an accurate investigation and a straightforward case, bore considerable responsibility for the less-than-satisfactory

---

[69] Judgment no. 313 of 3 July 1990, Corte Cost., 35 *Giur. Cost.* 1981 (1990), involving art. 27 para. 3 Const.

[70] Article 34 CCrPr, no. 2*bis* – as amended by the *decreto legislativo* no. 51 of 19 February 1998 – prohibits the same judge who presided over the preliminary investigation phase to also preside over the procedure by penal decree.

[71] Judgment no. 92, 1992, 37 *Giur. Cost.* 904 (1992).

performance of the "summary proceedings" as an effective mode of coping with judicial backlog. On the one hand, without being able to adduce all the additional evidence related to the mitigating circumstances that could lower the base sentence, it was indeed unlikely that the defendant would have requested a *giudizio abbreviato*. On the other hand, the prosecutor – although required to give reasons for his refusal to consent to a "summary proceeding" (so that if after the trial the reasons were deemed insufficient, the judge could give the defendant the same one-third reduction as would have been received after a *giudizio abbreviato*)[72] – would legitimately prevent the selection of the "summary proceeding" just by refraining from performing a complete investigation.

Moreover, in light of the judge's sentencing discretion, the defendant can never be sure that the promised reduction will in fact be given. This continues to discourage defendants from choosing the "summary proceeding."

E. Some Concluding Remarks

On the whole, one may note how difficult it is to reconcile the ideal of an efficient judicial system with the continental ideal of justice, which hands the truth-finding role over to the judge and requires proper and uniform sentencing of convicted defendants. The civil law's inherent distrust of any formal plea bargaining and negotiation between the parties, which are apt to prevent the judge from performing fact-finding and sentencing functions, runs counter to the quick disposition of criminal cases. Moreover, attenuated forms of negotiation between the parties, while negating the continental ideal of justice,[73] do not result in a significant diversion of cases from full trial.

One more consideration needs to be added here. As has been correctly pointed out,[74] the main challenge for the Italian system's achievement of efficiency by way of its special procedures is that of making the Italian prosecutor feel a stronger sense of personal responsibility for the outcome of the criminal process. The problem is that, no matter how many acquittals or convictions he secures, no matter how much he may waste the system's resources, no matter how many cases in his docket fail to find a quick solution, or find none at all, the Italian prosecutor will nevertheless

---

[72] Judgment no. 81 of 15 February 1991.

[73] Thus making, for instance, Italian scholars advocate for extensive judicial review of the merits of the case in the "sentencing by parties' request." *See supra* note 68.

[74] *See* Pizzi and Marafioti, "New Italian Code," *supra* note 12, particularly the paragraph IV C: *The Achilles' Heel of the Italian System: The Pubblico Ministero*, p. 29*ff*.

advance in his bureaucratic career and enjoy an increase in salary. Given these institutional realities, the system is unlikely to receive serious cooperation from the institutionally un-pressured Italian prosecutor in the effective resolution of criminal cases.

In sum, special procedures do not provide the system with an effective way to expedite Italian criminal justice. This is a particularly crucial problem in light of the increased length of the new Italian trial, which the new adversarial rules of evidence have produced.[75]

VI. Recent Developments

Very recently two major normative changes took place in Italian criminal procedure signalling movement in opposite directions. First, the Italian Parliament approved

---

[75] It is worth pointing out that in addition to prosecutorial discretion, the efficiency of the Anglo-American machinery of justice is also achieved by way of devices that do not impinge on a defendant's procedural guarantees: namely, through the double jeopardy prohibition, according to which a verdict of acquittal is final (with the only exception to the principle recognized in the English system, where from the magistrates' court, by way of case stated, the prosecutor can appeal on a question of law to the Divisional Court of the Queen's Bench Division against a defendant's acquittal), and also through the exclusion from the criminal process of third parties claiming civil damages.

For reasons once more strongly linked to a different legal tradition, the Italian system does not make use of the same devices. In Italy, apart from few limited exceptions, all parties may appeal the trial court's decision, no matter whether the decision was one of acquittal or of conviction, as the double jeopardy principle has a totally different meaning in Italy than it does in the common law. In the common law world, the double jeopardy prohibition in fact prevents the prosecutor from appealing against a verdict of acquittal, whereas in the Italian system, and throughout the civil law, the *ne bis in idem* principle works only against the reopening of a case that has been finally decided, the court having issued a decision no longer subject to revision. Moreover, in the Italian system, an acquittal decision can even be appealed by the defendant asking for a stronger acquittal (except, however, where the acquittal stems from a "summary proceedings"), due to the fact that the Italian system provides for more than one type of acquittal (*see* art. 530 CCrPr). Although representing a source of inefficiency, the right of appeal against any decision is justified by the need to review the criteria adopted by the fact or truth-finder in the search for historical verity.

On the other hand, although no longer a "forced twinship" (*see*, Gambaro, *Azione civile e processo penale- Appunti di diritto comparato* in *Responsabilita' civile e previdenza* (1977), 386, approaching the issue from a comparative perspective) as it was before 1989, the connection between the criminal prosecution and the civil suit is still very close in the Italian system, and of course the participation of more than two parties at the trial surely does not quicken the proceedings.

the amendment of art. 111 of the Italian Constitution. Winning a battle in the war for the fairness of the trial, the Italian Parliament reacted against the Constitutional Court's holding on art. 513 CCrPr of October 1998. On 23 November 1999, the Italian legislature added the following sentences to art. 111 of the Italian Constitution:

"The judicial function is carried on according to the due process of law. Every trial should be carried on giving the parties the right to offer counter-proof and counter-arguments against unfavorable evidence (*nel contraddittorio tra le parti*), on equal standing before an impartial judge. The law guarantees the reasonable length of the trial. In the criminal trial, the law guarantees that the accused be privately informed as soon as possible of the nature of and the reasons for the allegations against him; that the accused has enough time and viable conditions to prepare his defense; that the accused has the possibility to examine, or to have examined, the witnesses against him, as well as to have favorable witnesses summoned for examination at trial on equal standing with the prosecution; that the accused has the opportunity to examine any other evidence in his favor; that the accused be assisted by a translator in the event that he does not understand or speak the language used in the trial. The criminal trial is organized around the principle that the evidence is taken in the presence of the parties, who are entitled to offer counter-proof and counter-arguments against opposing evidence (*principio del contraddittorio nella formazione della prova*). The accused cannot be found guilty upon the declaration of anyone who willingly avoided being examined by the accused or by his lawyer.

The law shall determine the cases in which the evidence is not taken according to the aforementioned principle (*principio del contraddittorio nella formazione della prova*) by reasons of the accused's consent, an objective impossibility, or a proven unlawful conduct."

Complying with that part of the new art. 111 of the Italian Constitution relating to the right of confrontation of opposing witnesses, law no. 63 of 1 March 2001 provided new rules for witnesses and accomplices examinations. Law no. 63/2001 reinstated art. 513 CCrPr as it was before the Italian Constitutional Court's judgment of 1999 (no. 361, on which *see supra* note 63). It also restored the original rule that out-of-court declarations are in principle to be used for impeachment purposes only, unless otherwise agreed upon by the parties, or unless it becomes clear that the witness has been the object of violence, threat or monetary persuasion which might have made him or her reluctant to testify, or truthfully testify, at trial (art. 500 CCrP, revised).

Moreover, law no. 63/2001 provided for an obligation to take the stand and to testify under oath for a particular class of certain individuals who are being prosecuted in related proceedings, whenever their out-of-court declarations incriminated the defendant (arts. 12, 64, 197, 197*bis*, 210 CCrPr).

The analogies between the Fifth and Sixth Amendments of the US Constitution and the new art. 111 of the Italian Constitution are self-evident. Indeed, the rights to a speedy trial, to receiving notice of the nature and cause of the accusation, to the confrontation of opposing witnesses, and to the compulsory process for obtaining favorable witnesses are now embodied in the Italian Constitution as well. Nevertheless, as I have argued in this chapter, once more the real meaning and impact of this most recent borrowing will depend upon the intensity of the resistance that it will encounter. This very same consideration can surely be extended to law no. 63/ 2001 whose effectiveness relies as usual upon the judiciary itself.

Secondly, the law instituting the single-judge court in criminal matters was finally brought into effect at the beginning of the year 2000. Law no. 479 of 16 December 1999 provided the single-judge court with jurisdiction for crimes the punishment for which the law imposes a sentence of up to ten years' imprisonment, and for drug-producing and trafficking offenses, no matter how heavy the sentence that can be imposed.

Moreover, law no. 479/1999 amended many provisions of the Italian Code of Criminal Procedure, significantly modifying the criminal proceedings thus far described as ordinary proceedings. In contrast with the previous rules, since 2 January 2000, the judge of the preliminary hearing has an extensive power of inquiry. According to the new arts. 421*bis* and 422 CCrPr, at the end of the hearing the judge, if he does not determine to either send the matter for trial or dismiss it (*see* part III B, *supra*), can either ask the prosecutor to complete his investigation or introduce *sua sponte* the evidence he deems conclusive to decide for a dismissal order. In examining witnesses, technical consultants, and accomplices he produced at the hearing, the judge will exclusively question them: the defense and the prosecution can pose their questions only through the judge. According to the new art. 441 CCrPr, the extensive power to introduce *ex officio* any new evidence he deems necessary to decide the case is now given to the judge of the preliminary hearing when a "summary proceeding" (*giudizio abbreviato*) is instituted as well. In such a case, the described rules governing the official introduction of the evidence at the preliminary hearing will govern the (officially conducted) proof-taking process at the "summary proceeding." The "summary proceeding" is today instituted merely upon a defense demand, which – in order to cope with criticism and the problems highlighted *supra* in part V D – can include, as a condition, the request that more evidence be acquired during the proceedings.

Moreover, rendering the configuration of the prosecutor as a "straight accuser" meaningless to some extent, law no. 479/1999 provides that at the end of the preliminary investigation (and, in any case, after six – or in some special cases twelve – months have elapsed since it started) the suspect can ask the prosecutor to gather new exculpatory evidence. If the prosecutor accepts, he has 30 days to complete the additional investigation activities (art. 415*bis* CCrPr).

The new strong judicial activism at the preliminary hearing and during the "summary proceedings," together with the weakening of the prosecutor's role as a party to the proceedings that this second reform brought to the system, appear totally consistent with the trend depicted in this chapter, and are to be considered as a new step back to a "civilian" past.

VII. Conclusion

The powerful Italian continental legal tradition, supported by an institutional structure that has not been modified by the new Code, has rendered the Italian transplant of the American adversary system generally unsuccessful. Whereas certain elements of the American system have been formally imported, a combination of institutional resistance, remnants of old procedural forms, and a series of decisions by the Italian Constitutional Court and *Corte di Cassazione* (the Supreme Court) have rendered the shift to an adversarial process more apparent than real. In the end, the 1989 Italian Code of Criminal Procedure, when applied as "law in action," has retained a very strong civilian flavor that will very possibly survive the challenge recently brought against some of its aspects by the Italian Parliament.

Brief Bibliography

M. Chiavario, *Procedura Penale: Un codice tra "storia" e cronaca*, Turin (1996).

V. Perchinunno (ed.), *Percorsi di procedura penale: dal garantismo inquisitorio a un accusatorio non garantito*, Milan (1996).

D. Siracusano, *Diritto Processuale Penale*, Milan (1996).

A. Nappi, *Guida al codice di procedura penale*, Milan (1997).

P. Ferrua, *Studi sul Processo penale*, 3rd ed., *Declino del conradditorio e garantismo reattivo*, Turin (1997).

M. Nobili, *Scenari e trasformazioni del processo penale*, Padua (1998).

M. Pisani, *Italian Style: figure e forme del nuovo processo penale*, Padua (1998).

A. Dalia & M. Ferraioli, *Manuale di diritto processuale penale*, Padua (1999).

G. Lozzi, *Lezioni di Procedura Penale*, Turin (2000).

F. Cordero, *Procedura Penale*, Milan (2000).

E. Amodio & N. Galantini, *Giudice Unico e Garanzie Difensive*, Milan (2000).

CHAPTER NINE

Tort Law

Mauro Bussani, Barbara Pozzo, & Angelo Venchiarutti [1]

I. Tort Law in the Civil Code

A. Introduction

Faced with the traditional problem of distinguishing recoverable from non-recoverable losses, the Italian Civil Code adopts a general rule in art. 2043. It states that "[a]ny fraudulent, malicious, or negligent act that causes an unjustified injury to others obliges the person who has committed the act to pay damages."[2]

Though the general discipline of tort law is covered by a set of provisions (arts. 2043-59) under the same Civil Code chapter entitled "Unlawful Events," art. 2043 outlines a general feature that should be stressed because it must always be present in order for an action in tort to be successful; it refers to the element of "unjustified injury." This element has been a crux in the debate over the role and aims of Italian tort law.

B. The Unjustified Injury

Unjustified injury was introduced by the legislator when drafting the Civil Code in 1942, and interpreting this novelty soon became the cause of considerable argument.

---

[1]   Mauro Bussani, Professor of Comparative Law, University of Trieste; Angelo Venchiarutti, Associate Professor of Comparative Law, University of Trieste; Barbara Pozzo, Professor of Comparative Law, University of Como. Jointly written by Professors Bussani and Venchiarutti, with Professor Pozzo contributing part I H.

[2]   *The Italian Civil Code and Complementary Legislation*, trans. by M. Beltramo, G.E. Longo, & J.H. Merryman, Oceana, New York (1991).

Jeffrey S. Lena and Ugo Mattei (eds.), *Introduction to Italian Law*, 217-246
©2002 Kluwer Law International. Printed in the Netherlands.

Until recently, the standard doctrine stated that an injury was unjustified whenever an absolute right of the victim, such as ownership or other property rights,[3] liberty, life, physical integrity, or reputation, was infringed upon. Only in such cases could the tort-feasor be required to pay damages. Otherwise the victim could not recover. This rule, however, has never been applied with respect to intentional torts, because the interpreters have always recognized intentional harm as an unjustified injury entitling the injured party to recovery.[4]

From a comparative perspective, the standard approach to the problem of the recoverability of damages was therefore still embedded in the matrix of the Western legal tradition of tort, where the pattern of typical, or "nominate," torts has historically resided at the very core of Roman, German, and common law civil liability systems.[5]

The debate became particularly heated in the early 1960s, when the increase in cases in which damages could be claimed and the growing attention to the rights of the victims made clear the inadequacy of the traditional equation between unjustified injury and the violation of an absolute right.

Today, even if differences of opinion persist,[6] prevailing scholarship would appear to interpret art. 2043 CC as a general clause designed to outline a system of atypical, or "innominate," torts. This view is supported by those favoring a particularly broad interpretation of "unjustified injury," going so far as to include all violations of situations and interests regarded as legally relevant (or, as some prefer, those requiring protection through a comparison with the principles of the legal system).[7]

---

[3] For an overview of this notion, *see* R. Sacco, R. Caterina, "*Il possesso*," 2nd ed., in L. Mengoni (ed.), *Tratt. dir. civ. e comm. Cicu-Messineo*, Milan (2000); as to the related tort law rules, *see* C. Tenella Sillani, *Il risarcimento del danno da lesione del possesso*, Milan (1989).

[4] P. Cendon, *Il dolo nella responsabilità extracontrattuale*, Turin (1976); L. Gaudino, "*Il dolo*." in *La responsabilità civile. 1988-1996*, in G. Alpa & M. Bessone (eds.), *Bigiavi's Treatise*, I, Turin (1997), p. 21*ff*.

[5] *See* R. Sacco, "Legal Formants: A Dynamic Approach to Comparative Law (II)," 39 *Am J Comp L* 343 (1991), 358*ff*. With regard to the French gap between the broadly stated Code provisions and the narrower operative rules implemented by scholars and judges over the history, *see* P.G. Monateri, *La Sineddoche*, Milan (1984).

[6] For a critical review of current opinions, *see* P.G. Monateri, "*La responsabilità civile*," in R. Sacco (ed.), *Trattato di diritto civile*, Turin (1998), p. 195*ff*.

[7] P. Schlesinger, "*L'ingiustizia del danno nell'illecito civile*," in *Jus* (1960), 342; F.D. Busnelli, *La lesione del credito da parte di terzi*, Milan (1964), p. 67; S. Rodotà, *Il problema della responsabilità civile*, Milan (1964), p. 139; P. Trimarchi, "*Illecito*," in *Enc. dir.*, XX, Milan (1970), p. 97; G. Tucci, *Il danno ingiusto*, Naples (1970), p. 20*ff*; F. Galgano, "*Le mobili frontiere del danno ingiusto*," in *Contr. e impr.* (1985), p. 7; C. Salvi, "*Responsabilità*

Viewed through the case law, the history over recent decades appears more straightforward, characterized as it is by a progressive extension of the range of interests protected.

This trend has proceeded formally by various technical means. On the one hand, to overcome the threshold of absolute rights, the notion of "unjustified injury" has been enlarged to include the impairment of obligations, the infringement of legal expectations, and recently also the infringement of so-called *legitimate interests*.[8] On the other hand, in formally respecting earlier precedents, case law has frequently broadened the definition of rights to include situations that had been previously overlooked such as, for example, the "integrity of one's assets."[9]

C. Fault and Strict Liability: A False Opposition

The Italian Civil Code makes use of an articulated system in order to identify cases in which unjustified injury gives rise to an obligation to pay damages. Malicious or negligent behavior of the wrongdoer is required by art. 2043 of the Civil Code as a general condition of liability,[10] but a wide array of cases basing liability on

---

extracontrattuale (dir. vig.)," in *Enc. dir.*, XXXIX, Milan (1988), p. 1212; M. Franzoni, "*Dei fatti illeciti*," in F. Galgano (ed.), *Comm. cod. civ. Scialoja-Branca*, Bologna-Roma (1993), p. 80; G. Alpa, M. Bessone, & V. Zeno-Zenovich, "*I fatti illeciti*," in P. Rescigno (ed.), *Tratt. dir. priv.*, Turin (1995), p. 129*ff*; G. Visintini, *Trattato breve della responsabilità civile*, 2nd ed., Padua (1999), p. 359*ff*; G. Alpa, *Tratt. dir. civ.*, IV, *La responsabilità civile*, Milano (1999), p. 357*ff*. However, several scholars, for various reasons, have denied that art. 2043 is a general clause, claiming that there is no principle of innominate torts in our legal system. *See* C. Castronovo, *La nuova responsabilità civile. Regola e metafora*, Milan (1997), p. 14*ff*, 39*ff*.

[8] This is the cause of action brought before administrative courts when a citizen claims to have a personal and direct interest in the activity of a public body in pursuance of its statutory powers. Details on the notion are in V. Denti, "Civil and Administrative Procedure," in *Italian National Reports to the XIIth International Congress of Comparative Law. Montreal 1990*, Milan (1990), pp. 193, 195*ff*. Overruling a long list of contrary precedents, the recoverability of losses stemming from the infringement of an *interesse legittimo* has been allowed by Cass., 26 March 1999, no. 500, *Risp. civ. prev.*, (1999) 981. *See also* Sorace, chapter 6, this volume.

[9] *See* Cass. 4 May 1982, no. 2765, in *Giust. civ.*, 1982, I, 1745, note Di Majo, in *Giust. civ.*, 1982, I, 3103 (m), note De Cupis; Cass. 19 December 1985, no. 6506, in *Foro it.*, 1986, I, 383; Cass. 25 July 1986, no. 4755, in *Nuova giur. civ. comm.*, 1987, I, 386 m. *See also* Cass. 13 January 1993, no. 343, in *Resp. civ. e prev.* 1993, 808.

[10] Both misfeasance and nonfeasance are taken into account. The traditional view, still accepted in case law, according to which liability is the exception and occurs only following the breach of a pre-existing obligation to act, is set against the view stressing the general nature of liability due to omission; *see* G. Alpa, *Il problema dell'atipicità dell'illecito*, Naples (1979), p. 127*ff*; G. Alpa, *Responsabiltà civile e danno*, Bologna (1991), p. 257*ff*.

very different criteria co-exists with those informing the first provision under heading IX of Book 4 of the Civil Code.

Among the rules stated in the Code, one finds the discipline of liability for injury caused either by things (art. 2051 CC) or by animals the defendant uses or controls (arts. 2052 and 2053 CC). Furthermore, according to the Code, one is liable for damage caused while engaging in a dangerous activity (art. 2050 CC), and for damage caused by a vehicle in motion (art. 2054 CC). Liability also extends to the acts committed by others in cases where there is some special relationship between the parties: persons charged with the custody of a person lacking capacity (art. 2047 CC), parents, tutors, guardians, apprentice-masters with regard to minors (art. 2048 CC), and employers (art. 2049 CC). In all other cases, excepting the latter, the Code allows the defendant to invoke certain defenses. These are differently worded in the Code, but roughly consist of proving the impossibility of preventing the harm's occurrence.

It is this variety of causes of action, together with the articulated molding of them through case law which makes it unproductive to approach Italian tort law in terms of conflict between the principles of fault and strict liability.[11] Indeed, the most advanced line of scholarship acknowledges that the various situations in which liability is possible, as defined in written law and understood by case law, end up as arrayed along a single broad, graduated scale, rather than clustered around two opposing poles. Along this graduated scale, the role of the defendant's conduct is assessed as a factor affecting the imposition of liability, moving from cases in which the proof of actual intent is required toward those cases involving so-called "absolute liability."[12]

D. Mental Capacity

As far as fault liability is concerned, the law expressly requires that the defendant's mental capacity be shown not to have been impaired at the time the act was

---

[11] The survey of the debate in C. Salvi, "*La responsabilità civile*," in G. Iudica & P. Zatti (eds.), *Tratt. dir. Priv.*, Milan (1998), p. 33*ff*; *see* further remarks in P. Cendon, "*Il dolo nella responsabilità extracontrattuale*," *op. cit.*, p. 194*ff*; M. Bussani, *La colpa soggettiva*, Padua (1991), p. 76*ff*.

[12] *See, e.g.* arts. 965 and 978 of the Maritime and Air Navigation Code; art. 15, 31.12.1962, no. 1860, on nuclear accidents; and art. 5, law no. 23 of 25 January 1983, on damage caused by objects from space.

committed (art. 2046 CC).[13] This is a matter purely of mental capacity, and not of "legal" capacity: its determination does not presume or require that the defendant has reached any pre-determined age. In fact, and in contrast to the Criminal Code, the Civil Code does not list the natural or legal factors that exclude the capacity of the tort-feasor. Rather, it is up to the judge to assess mental capacity according to all the circumstances surrounding the individual case. Mental capacity may be found lacking owing to youth, hypnotic states, influence of alcohol or drugs, mental illness, or other disability. If the state of incapacity derives from a fault of the wrongdoer, then the wrongdoer remains responsible for his or her actions; otherwise the victim can sue the wrongdoer's supervisors (if any), who are held accountable under a strict liability rule (art. 2047 para. 1 CC).

As a supplementary measure, the Code empowers the judge, should the plaintiff for some reason not obtain compensation from someone else, to oblige the wrongdoer lacking capacity to make an "equitable indemnity." The payment and quantification of this indemnity depend in concrete terms upon the results of a comparative assessment of the financial status of the parties (art. 2047 para. 2 CC).[14]

E. Defenses

Tort liability can be obviated by the existence of appropriate circumstances justifying the otherwise tortious act. This subject has been developed mainly through the criminal courts (*see* Criminal Code arts. 50-54), and even today, scholarship and case law supplement the concise rules of the Civil Code with references to provisions derived from criminal law.

Defenses set forth in the Civil Code are those of self-defense and defense of necessity. Reasonable defense of one's physical integrity or property negates liability

---

[13] From the comparative point of view, *see* M. Bussani, "*Responsabilité des sujets atteints de troubles mentaux en Italie et en Common Law*," in F. Chabas (ed.), *Gazette du Palais, numéro spécial: Responsabilité civile*, nos. 45-46 (1997), p. 11*ff.* On the broader issue related to the role of disabilities as a factor affecting tort liability, *see* M. Bussani, "*Faiblesse oblige*," in *Scritti in onore di Rodolfo Sacco*, I, Milan (1994), p. 69*ff*; Id., "*Perfiles comparativos sobre la responsabilidad civil: La culpa al servicio de los débiles*," in J.F. Palomino Manchego & R. Velasquez Ramirez (eds.), *Modernas tendencias del derecho en America Latina. Actas de la I Convención Latinoamericana de Derecho*, Lima, Perú (1997), p. 393*ff.*

[14] *See* C. Salvi, *supra* note 11, at 107; A. Venchiarutti, "*L'imputabilità del fatto dannoso e la responsabilità del sorvegliante per il fatto dell'incapace*," in *La responsabilità civile, 1988-1996*, in G. Alpa & M. Bessone, *supra* note 4, at p. 115*ff.*

in tort law. Case law takes into consideration both art. 2044 of the Civil Code and art. 52 of the Criminal Code. Thus, there will not be any protection at law for the plaintiff if the defendant can demonstrate that (i) the injury was caused in defense of her own (or another's) right against a real danger brought about by an unlawful act of the plaintiff, and (ii) that the legitimate reaction was proportionate to the level of aggression.

When necessity is invoked, the defendant must have caused harm to the plaintiff in the attempt to protect his or her own, or another's, physical integrity from a serious and actual danger; unlike the case of self-defense, the harm inflicted upon the plaintiff in this case is not provoked by any actual or threatened illegal wrong of the plaintiff. Article 2045 CC reproduces the text of art. 54 para. 1 of the Criminal Code almost in its entirety. However, in criminal law, the existence of a state of necessity renders the defendant not punishable; on the contrary, balancing the interests in conflict lead the civil law to view the condition as a mitigating factor in assessing the liability of the defendant who acts out of necessity (as long as the reaction is proportionate to the danger: art. 54 para. 1, Criminal Code).[16] Consequently, the defendant is bound to indemnify rather than compensate if this seems equitable to the judge.[17]

Defenses not set forth in the Civil Code are partly framed according to provisions of criminal law. So, just as under art. 50 of the Criminal Code, there are occasions in which harm may be inflicted upon a person who will have no remedy in tort, because he or she consented to commission of the act that caused harm. The effect of such consent or assent is commonly expressed in the maxim "*volenti non fit injuria*."[18] Similarly, the reference to art. 51 of the Criminal Code allows tort scholars and judges to remove any obligation to compensate so long as the injury caused to

---

[15] It is also necessary to consider criminal case law, since rulings on this subject in the civil courts are extremely rare; *see* G. Visintini, *supra* note 7, at 514*ff*; *see also* A. Venchiarutti, "*La legittima difesa*," in P. Cendon (ed.), *La responsabilità civile. Saggi critici e rassegne di giurisprudenza*, Milan (1988), p. 473*ff*.

[16] On the legal nature of the "necessitated" act, *see* P.G. Monateri, *supra* note 6, at p. 240*ff*.

[17] In cases in which the danger is caused by a third party, the Italian Supreme Court has established that the lawsuit against the third party (for damages) and against the "necessitated" wrongdoer (for the indemnity) should be alternately available (Cass. 8 November 1978, no. 4047; Cass. 21 June 1972, no. 2025), unless the injury is entirely attributable to the third party; *see* P.G. Monateri, *supra* note 6, at 253*ff*.

[18] The Copyright law explicitly refers to the consent of the injured party as a defense (art. 96 para. 1) Law 22 April 1971, n. 633.

third parties is the inevitable and proportionate result of the exercise of that right by its holder.

F. Causation

In order for a victim to recover losses, the defendant must be shown to have caused the injury. From a practical point of view this involves distinguishing, among all the possible factors, those that might have influenced the action from those that actually influenced the action *and* are legally relevant.[19]

Article 2043 CC does not provide the necessary logical and analytical tools to carry out this operation, and it is frequently claimed that the main points of reference – arts. 2056 and 1223 of the Civil Code and arts. 40 and 41 of the Criminal Code – appear to be designed largely so as to refer the problem back to the interpreter.[20] In an attempt to find the solution most suitable to the variety of possible situations, both the case law and scholars either refer to a multitude of rules,[21] or rely, as discussed below, upon the causal link concept as a tool to discriminate between recoverable and non-recoverable losses.

1. Comparative Negligence and Joint Liability

There are some cases in which the same damage is caused by independent and separate wrongful acts. Upon finding of the defendant's liability, it still remains to be determined whether there are contributory causes that may reduce liability. The issue is usually represented as twofold. The first concerns the victim's behavior, while the second concerns the finding of a joint and several liability.

In line with the underlying social policy goal of fostering bilateral deterrence,[22] art. 1227 para. 1 CC, applicable to tort law matters, through art. 2056 CC, includes

---

[19] P. Forchielli, *Il rapporto di causalità nel diritto civile*, Padua (1960), p. 9; F. Realmonte, *Il problema del rapporto di causalità nel risarcimento del danno*, Milan (1967), p. 33; P. Trimarchi, *Causalità e danno*, Milan (1967), p. 5.

[20] *See* F. Antolisei, *Il rapporto di causalità nel diritto penale*, Padua (1934), p. 161; *see also* P. Forchielli, *id.*, at 23, 36, 315; F. Realmonte, *id.*, at 123, 156, 172; R. Sconamiglio, *"Responsabilità civile,"* in *Noviss. Dig. it.*, XV, Turin (1968), p. 650; P. Trimarchi, *id.*, at 19; A. De Cupis, *Il dann. Teoria generale della responsabilità civile*, 3rd ed., Milan (1979), p. 225; *see also* S. Patti, *"Danno patrimoniale,"* in *Digesto IV, Disc. priv. Sez. civ.*, V, Turin (1989), p. 45.

[21] P. Trimarchi, *id.*, at 53.

[22] P.G. Monateri, *supra* note 6, at p. 28*ff*, 287*ff*.

a comparative negligence rule providing that if negligence on the part of the plaintiff has contributed to the injury, then compensation is reduced or rejected.[23]

Joint and several liability is a more complex subject, handled by art. 2055 CC. The topic is usually approached by taking the viability of two opposing principles into consideration: that of the normal irrelevance of contributory causes – except for the victim's comparative negligence – and that of their general relevance, in view of a reduction of damages to be paid by the wrongdoer (barring joint and several liability as set out in art. 2055 para. 1). This rule is designed to provide the victim broader guarantees of recovery.

Thus, it is worth examining briefly the two possible situations that may actually occur: concurrence with the defendant's liability (i) for a wrongful act by a third party, and (ii) for a chance event (*e.g.*, an "Act of God").

---

[23] In point of fact, the two criteria do not necessarily match. *See* F. Cafaggi, *Profili di relazionalità della colpa*, Padua (1996). This rule, however, is not applied as against a tortfeasor acting intentionally, and the law rejecting provocation of the victim as a factor determining the latter's contributory negligence is adduced in support (Cass. 14.4.1988, no. 2956; Cass. pen. 19 April 1982, in *Rep. Foro it.*, 1983, *Danni civili*, no. 99; Cass. 25 November 1975, no. 3941, in *Giur. it.*, 1976, I, 1, 1922). The discussion thus far refers to the initial tort. Once this has occurred, not only is the injured party obliged not to aggravate the consequences, but compensation is not due for any further injury which the victim should have avoided by means of reasonable behavior (art. 1227 para. 2 CC and art. 2056 para. 1 CC). The injured party's obligation to ensure that further losses do not occur does not include the need to carry out acts which might be particularly burdensome, expensive, or hazardous in relation to the injury to be avoided (Cass. 20 November 1991, no. 12439; Cass. 29 April 1982, no. 2651; Cass. 3 April 1979, no. 1898; Cass. 8 July 1978, no. 3423). In cases of personal injury, the victim should seek medical attention, but is not required to undergo a surgical operation which might be dangerous or of uncertain outcome (Cass. 17 January 1979, no. 118, in *Resp. civ. prev.*, 1960, 298). Expenses incurred by the injured party to mitigate losses or prevent their aggravation are included in the compensation payable. In regard to both cases considered until now, the Code employs the term, "negligent act" of the victim. Since ordinary reasonable care may be expected only of people in full command of their faculties, the prevailing view used to be that the victim's mental incapacity would eliminate the possibility of contributory negligence. However, the most recent scholarship and case law do recognize that acts by an incapable victim may lead to a reduction in compensation (Cass. 24 February 1983, no. 1442; Cass. 15 May 1978, no. 2380; Cass. S.U. 17 February 1974, no. 351, in *Foro it.*, 1964, I, 752). Finally, it should be pointed out that the provision concerning the victim's contributory negligence is also to be applied when the fault attaches to the victim's legal representative, or his or her employee (arts. 2049 and 1228 CC). *See* A. Venchiarutti, *supra* note 14.

a. The Wrongful Act by a Third Party

In connection with the first possibility, the provisions set forth in art. 2055 CC (providing for the case in which more than one person is liable) envisage joint and several liability, and vest the action in contribution against each of the other liable persons in the party paying damages.[24] The uniqueness of the harm is an essential premise in order for the regulation to be applicable. In other words, with regard to art. 2055 CC, concerted action is not necessary, whereas the uniqueness of the act causing injury is. This explains why the provision is equally applied to cases in which defendants are liable according to a strict liability rule and those in which they are liable according to a negligence rule.[25]

Paragraph 2 of art. 2055 CC regulates the apportionment of liability between the defendants "according to the degree of fault and the seriousness of the ensuing consequences." In point of fact, the two criteria do not necessarily match, so that when a small degree of fault coincides with extremely serious consequences (or *vice versa*), the judge has to balance one against the other.[26]

In cases in which the defendants are liable under different strict liability rules, the problem of apportioning liability is more complex. As a matter of principle, the solution is not univocal, but is differentiated in light of the function to be attributed to each liability rule, and on the basis of the comparative weight of the criteria that can be inferred from para. 2 of art. 2055 regarding the different causal links producing the harm.[27]

b. A Chance Event

Still to be considered is the possibility that the causation of the harm stems, aside from the defendant's liability, from a chance event not attributable to a third party. According to the traditional point of view, when such a natural cause concurs with that determining the defendant's liability, the problem is to ascertain whether the former interrupted the causal link between the defendant's liability and the harmful event. There would thus be no possible determination other than complete liability

---

[24] By contrast, in cases of so-called environmental damage, Law 18 para. 7, act no. 349 of 8 July 1986, establishes that "[i]n cases of contribution to the same damage, each person is liable according to his own individual responsibility." *See infra* Part I H, "Liability for Environmental Harm."

[25] C. Salvi, *supra* note 11, at p. 1254*ff*.

[26] P. Cendon, *supra* note 4, at p. 90*ff*.

[27] C. Salvi, *supra* note 11, at p. 1255.

or total absence of liability.[28] Some have raised the objection that this conclusion is based on a presumed principle of the irrelevance of contributory causes, which appears to lack any grounding in positive law. It has been argued, indeed, that from arts. 1227 para. 1, and 2055 para. 2, one could derive the opposite principle, according to which the contributing "natural cause" would determine the reduction of damages to be paid in proportion to the degree of the defendant's fault and the seriousness of the ensuing consequences – just as provided for by the above-mentioned rules set forth in the Code.[29]

However, choosing between a principle of the general irrelevance of contributory causes, and the opposite position, in which partial causality gives rise to partial liability, does not seem amenable to a "logical" solution.[30] Therefore, case law approaches the issue pragmatically: either the chance (non-human) event is *per se* sufficient to have caused the harm (and therefore eliminates any liability), or it is irrelevant and becomes absorbed by and part of defendant's liability.[31]

G. Non-Material Damages

Recovery for pain and suffering is allowed by the Italian tort system only under exceptional circumstances. Article 2059 CC states that these kinds of damages "shall be awarded only in cases provided by the law," by far the most important of which is art. 185 of the Criminal Code, which bases claims for pain and suffering on a breach of criminal law.[32]

The idea of non-material damage carries with it a negative and residual connota-

---

[28] For all, *see* P. Forchielli, *supra* note 19, at p. 97.

[29] *See* F.D. Busnelli, *L'obbligazione soggettivamente complessa*, Milan (1974), p. 137*ff.*

[30] In fact, a quantitative equivalence between partial causality and partial liability does not always hold, since liability is not always based directly on causality. Although this position does avoid the defendant's total liability for an injury caused only in part by him, it is also true that this outcome may appear unequitable to the victim, who was not involved in causing the injury at all. For an overview of the debate, *see* C. Salvi, *supra* note 11, at p. 1255.

[31] *See* Cass. 8 March 1963, no. 568, in *Giust. civ.*, 1964, I, 205; Cass. 11 August 1966, no. 2126, in *Giust. civ.*, 1966, I, 2109; Cass. 25 October 1974, no. 3133, in *Giust. civ.*, 1974, I, 489; Cass. 1 February 1991, no. 981, in *Nuova giur. civ. comm.*, 1991, I, 797. For a survey of the articulation of legal reasoning veiled by this apparently clear-cut attitude, *see* P.G. Monateri, *supra* note 6, at p. 168*ff.*

[32] *See* M. Franzoni, *supra* note 7, at 1179; *see also* C. Salvi, *supra* note 11, at 48. *See also* arts. 9 and 29 para. 9, of law no. 675 of 31 December 1996, regarding the unlawful collection and processing of personal data.

tion, which can really only be determined based upon an analysis of the case in which compensation is actually awarded. Indeed, the restricted nature of situations in which the law, through art. 2059 CC, allows for the payment of non-material damages has led to a strong tendency in case law, and in scholarship as well, to put forward different interpretations of the Code provision. Most of them are variously aimed at molding its applicability and, in this regard, one of the most important devices exploited by the civil courts to bypass the art. 2059 bottleneck lies in expanding the legal borders of the area within which it is possible to qualify the case as a crime.[33]

H. Liability Rules in the Environmental Harm Context

Until 1986, Italian law relied upon traditional Civil Code provisions to assess damages for environmental harm. Since then, three major attempts to deal with controversies that arise from pollution can be traced.

Previously, judges used to rely upon art. 2050 CC, which establishes the liability rule arising out the exercise of dangerous activities: "Whoever causes injury to another in the performance of an activity dangerous by its nature or by reason of the instrumentalities employed, is liable for damages, unless he proves that he has taken all suitable measures to avoid the injury." Given the problem of demonstrating "that all suitable measures were taken," Italian courts responded to the demands for a principle of strict liability by drawing on their broad procedural arsenal: by applying the doctrine of *res ipsa loquitur*, by shifting the burden of proof, and by developing various legal fictions which integrated the element of negligence.[34]

On the other hand, in cases in which the polluting activity involved damages to persons, case law also used to rely on art. 2043 CC, together with art. 32 of the Italian Constitution, which recognizes a fundamental right to health.

Finally, art. 844 CC provides that if the polluter is not conducting a "dangerous activity" in the sense of art. 2050 CC, and if damages relate only to proprietary interests, but if the victim is a neighbor of the polluter, the damaged party may also sue pursuant to art. 844 CC without the necessity of proving fault, provided that the polluting effects exceed normal tolerability.

---

[33] For the current debate, *see* P.G. Monateri, *supra* note 6, at p. 295*ff*; P. Ziviz, *La tutela risarcitoria della persona. Danno morale e danno esistenziale*, Milan (1999).

[34] Generally, on legal fictions, *see* L.L. Fuller, *Legal Fictions*, Stanford (1967), and F. Geny, *Science et Technique en Droit Privé Positif*, III, Paris (1921), p. 360*ff. See also* A. Gambaro, *"Finzione giuridica nel diritto positivo,"* in *Digesto delle Discipline privatistiche*, in *Sez. Civ.* vol. VIII, 4th ed., Turin (1992), 342*ff*; F. Galgano, *"La commedia della responsabilità civile,"* in *Riv. Critica di Diritto Privato* (1987), p. 191; M. Franzoni, *"Danno da cose in custodia nei supermercati e obiter dicta della giurisprudenza,"* in *Contratto e Impresa* (1987), at 47.

Article 844 CC, which was inspired by German doctrine and by para. 906 BGB,[35] states that "The owner of land cannot prevent the emission of smoke, heat, fumes, noises, vibrations or similar propagation from the land of a neighbor unless they exceed normal tolerability, with regard to the condition of the sites. In applying this rule the court shall reconcile the requirements of production with rights of ownership. It can also take account of the priority of given use."

Lacking a basis in the Civil Code that clarified the matter, the Italian case law could not develop a unitary system regarding the problem of strict liability, and therefore had to rely upon rather unrefined legal techniques.

The uneasiness of Italian interpreters with respect to this issue has cultural roots.[36] To rely upon various legal fictions, hoping to find negligence even where there was none, might have effected justice in solitary cases, but it has not helped to unravel this tangled theoretical skein.

1. The New Italian Statute of 1986

a. The Liability Rule

In 1986, the Italian Parliament enacted a new statute concerning civil liability for environmental damages.[37] With respect to the tort-feasors's conduct, art. 18 of this statute provides that there must be "fraudulent or faulty acts in violation of statutory provisions or of measures adopted according to the law."[38] Thus, as is apparent from the face of the statute, the Italian legislator did not want to follow the approaches adopted in other legal systems, nor the suggestions derived from economic analysis, nor from the Italian scholars who favored the introduction of a

---

[35] *See* A. Gambaro, *"Il diritto di proprietà,"* in *Trattato di Diritto Civile e Commerciale Cicu-Messineo-Mengoni,* Milano (1995), p. 496*ff*; G. Visintini, *"Le immissioni nel quadro dei conflitti di vicinato, II, L'esperienza italiana,"* in *Riv. dir.civ.,* (1975), I, p. 29*ff*; C. Salvi, *Le immissioni industriali, rapporti di vicinato e tutela dell'ambiente,* Milano (1979), p. 147*ff*; A. Procida Mirabelli di Lauro, *Immissioni e "rapporto proprietario,"* Napoli (1984) in English language, U. Mattei, *Basic Principles of Property Law,* Westport Ct. Greenwood (2000), p. 97*ff*.

[36] C. Castronovo, *supra* note 7 at 9.

[37] Law no. 349 of 8 July 1986 – *Istituzione del Ministero dell'ambiente e norme in materia di danno ambientale.* On the practical application in the last decade, *see* B. Pozzo, *Danno ambientale,* Milan (1998), which also refers to the several original solutions developed by the case law.

[38] The Italian version of art. 18 Law 349/86 speaks about intentional or negligent acts in violation of dispositions of law or provisions based upon a law.

strict liability rule.[39]

For reasons relating to the genesis of the rule, the Italian approach tends to follow criminal law schemes and, in fact, recalls Penal Code art. 42 in defining the faulty act as that deriving from "non-observance of the laws, rules, ordinances or disciplines."[40]

Its debt to the criminal law is also suggested by the criteria according to which the Italian judge must assess and quantify environmental damages (according to art. 18, no. 6 of the same statute). Among these criteria, we find the "gravity of individual fault," with a clear reference to Penal Code art. 133, which disciplines the valuation of the gravity of the offence for the purpose of determining the penalty to be imposed.[41]

Fault is also required by art. 18 as an instrument for distributing the compensatory obligation among tortfeasors who have contributed to the damage (art.18, no. 7), notwithstanding the rule of joint liability (*in solido*) established by art. 2055 CC.[42]

The formulation of the Law, though authoritatively defended, is unsatisfying in some respects.[43] The Italian solution engenders remarkable incoherence at an internal level and diverges from the trend followed by most legislators in the West.

With regard to internal incoherence, it is worth noting that Italy is a signatory of the 1961 Brussels Convention on civil liability for damages caused by hydrocarbon pollution, a Convention which imposes strict liability rule for damages caused to

---

[39] *See, e.g.*, P. Trimarchi, "*Responsabilità civile per danno all'ambiente: prime riflessioni*," in *Amm. re* (1987), p. 189; E. Briganti, "*Considerazioni in tema di danno ambientale e responsabilità oggettiva*," in *Rass. Dir. Civ.* (1987), p. 289; A. Gambaro, "*Il danno ecologico nella recente elaborazione legislativa letta alla luce del diritto comparato*," in *Studi parl. pol. cost.*, n.71-(1) trim. (1986), p. 73; A. Costanzo & C. Verardi, "*La responsabilità per danno ambientale*," in *Riv. trimestrale di diritto e procedura civile* (1988), 691.

[40] R. Bajno, "*Profili penalistici nella legge istitutiva del Ministero dell'Ambiente*," in *Studi parlamentari e di politica costituzionale*, anno 19, no. 71, (1), 1986, p. 209*ff*.

[41] *See* S. Patti, "*La valutazione del danno ambientale*," in *Riv. di diritto civile* (1992), p. 447 and, above all, p. 460*ff*.

[42] Article. 2055 CC states: "Liability *in solido* – If the act causing damage can be attributed to more than one person, all are liable *in solido* for the damages ... The person who has compensated for the damage has recourse against each of the others in proportion to the degree of fault of each and to the consequences arising therefrom ... In case of doubt, the degree of fault attributable to each is presumed to be equal." *See supra*, p. 250*ff*.

[43] The critiques to the formulation of art. 18 law 349/86 are numerous. *See, e.g.*, L. Bibgliazzi Geri, "*Quale futuro per l'art. 18 Legge 8 lugli 1986, no. 349?*," in *Riv. crit. dir. priv.*, (1987), p. 685; P. Cendon & P. Ziviz, "*L'art. 18 della legge n. 349/86 nel sistema di responsabilità civile*," in *Riv. crit. dir. priv.*, anno V (1987), p. 521.

sea waters and the environment.[44] The 1982 Law on the Sea introduces the same principle of strict liability.[45] Thus, two different civil liability rules concerning water pollution currently exist in Italy: a fault liability rule for internal waters and a strict liability rule for sea waters. This situation inevitably generates disconcerting consequences.[46]

b. Problems of Proof

We should also note that one powerful legal argument in favor of strict liability is that the fault system seems rather inappropriate in the field of environmental law, as it imposes a sort of *probatio diabolica*, which has the fault or the malice of the polluter as its object.

However, the burden of proof is linked neither with the fault system nor with the strict liability system. Rather, it is linked with the rules of concrete decisions in the case law. Indeed, the fault principle is logically consistent with the criterion of *res ipsa loquitur*.

This occurs because the notion of fault refers back to the notion of negligence, and negligence implies a violation of the standard of care deemed appropriate. This standard of care is a psychologically conditioned attitude commonly shared in a certain period of time. When a mentality is inclined toward the benefit of security, this means that a judge will be inclined to find negligence in everything that went wrong. For this reason, the criterion *res ipsa loquitur* can be explicit or implicit, but the result is the same. On the one hand, the fault principle gives way to judgments that are not so different from those generated by strict liability; on the other hand, it is not true that the victim will be required to demonstrate his or her case by an extremely high burden of proof. Indeed, when *res ipsa loquitur* works, the burden of proof is limited to showing that the victim has been victimized.

c. Access to Information

This does not mean that obtaining information of an extremely technical character is particularly difficult in environmental matters alone. As one might imagine, this kind of information is generally not freely accessible to the public and obtaining it can represent a relatively high hurdle in any case. In this regard, we must consider the fact that, in cases of alteration of the environment, the damage can be revealed

---

[44] Convention of 29 November 1961, introduced in Italy by law no. 185 of 6 April 1977.

[45] Law 979 of 1982, art. 21.

[46] *See* P. Trimarchi, *supra* note 19, at p. 1193.

only a long time after the beginning of the tortfeasor's action, and can often result from the interaction of many elements.

With regard to this subject, we must recall how the victim's difficulty in receiving adequate information has been taken into consideration by several national legislators, and even by the European Community, which has drafted a special directive on the matter.[47]

The intricacy of concrete cases makes it difficult to prove the existence of fault in each case. As a consequence, most foreign legislators have rejected fault-based criteria for assessing liability, because it could leave a fraction of the environmental damage as an external cost borne by the tortfeasor, and this would be in contrast with the objective of full internalization of environmental costs. Opting for a regime based on fault is certainly one of the most evident shortcomings of the Italian statutes.

d. Restoration and Damages

Article 18 provides that, whenever materially feasible, restoration in kind is the preferred option.[48] The polluter should restore the environment to its state prior to the occurrence of damage. The court will award damages only in cases in which this is not possible.

It is necessary to underscore that neither the Italian legislator nor Italian administrative bodies have ever articulated the criteria that should be applied by the courts to assess environmental damages, as occurred in the United States with the Assessment of Damages for Natural Resource Injuries regulations.[49] The absence of such criteria leaves judges with the difficult task of working without guidelines. The 1986 statute only establishes that where damages cannot be easily quantified, courts should develop an equitable appraisal in which different variables indicated by the Act itself should be taken into account – *i.e.* the degree of fault, the cost of

---

[47] On the content of this directive, *see* G. Morandi, "*Informazione ambientale e accesso ai documenti amministrativi*," in *Riv. Giur. Amb.* (1992), p. 805; *see also* H. Blumberg, "*Die Umwelt-Informations-Richtlinie der EG und ihre Umsetzung in das deutsche Recht*," in *NuR*, (1992), p. 8; A. Scherzberg, "*Der freie Zugang zu Informationen über die Umwelt – Rechtsfragen der Richtlinie 90/313*," in *UPR*, (1992), p. 48.

[48] Article 18 para. 8: "The judge in the decision shall provide, whenever possible, for the restoration of the place [damaged] at the cost of the responsible party."

[49] *Regulations for the assessment of Damages for Natural Resource Injuries* were published by the Department of the Interior at 43 CFR para. 11.10-11.93 (1987).

restoration, and the profit unduly gained by the polluter as a consequence of the wrongful act.[50]

e. The Problem of Standing

Private citizens may not claim damages for environmental harm in Italy. Even if they can still sue on the grounds of tortious liability when their individual rights are affected, art. 18 of law no. 349/1986 establishes that only the State, the "municipality," or the "Region" in whose territory damage has occurred may make a claim for "environmental damages."

The State, like any bureaucracy, is not always faced with adequate incentives to act promptly. The Italian statute of 1986 does not introduce any serious incentives to ensure that the State or local authorities properly carry the act out. The Italian civil procedure system does not recognize citizen suits as in the United States, where citizen suit provisions were introduced in nearly every major federal environmental statute because Congress tacitly recognized that the executive branch often lacks either the resources or the will to prosecute polluters.[51]

In Italy, environmental associations may only bring "notice" to the public authorities that damage to the environment has occurred; they do not have standing to bring suit themselves, or to bring suit on behalf of the State.

f. Some Final Remarks

After ten years on the books, Italian statute no. 349/86 has revealed its shortcomings. Courts have tried to develop new solutions on the legislative basis of art. 18, often with unpredictable results.[52] For this reason, it is interesting to investigate how the landscape may change if new regulations are adopted at the European Level and become law in Italy.[53]

---

[50] Article 18 para. 6: "The judge, when a precise quantification of damages is not possible, shall determine according to equity, taking into consideration, however the gravity of individual negligence, the costs necessary for restoration, and profit made by the transgressor [tortfeasor] as a consequence of his behavior harmful to the environment."

[51] For the United States experience, *see* Tolbert, "The Public as a Plaintiff: Public Nuisance and Federal Citizen Suits in The Exxon-Valdez Litigation," 14 *Harv Env L Rev* 511 (1990).

[52] *See, e.g.*, a recent case-annotation: B. Pozzo, "*La retroattività della responsabilità civile per danno ambientale. alla ricerca delle ragioni di un obiter della Cassazione*," in *Foro it.*, (1998), I, 1143.

[53] The reference is to the Green Paper of 1993 and to the recent White Paper of 2000 of the European Commission. *See* on this matter B. Pozzo, "*Verso una responsabilità civile per danni all'ambiente in Europa: il nuovo Libro Bianco della Commissione delle Comunità Europee*," in *Rivista Giuridica dell'Ambiente*, (2000), p. 623. An English version of the

II. Legal Remedies

A. Monetary and Non-Monetary Remedies

Harm sustained by the victim is translated into monetary terms through equivalent compensation. Because monetary compensation is a surrogate for the harm, injured parties are not obliged to accept redress of this kind: they can demand that the situation that would have existed had the offending action not been committed be restored at the expense of the party responsible (*restitutio in integrum*, restoration of the harmed party to *status quo ante*) under art. 2058 CC.

Very often this specific redress is not materially or juridically possible, and even when it is, it is not sufficient to eliminate harmful effects that have already occurred. Furthermore, recourse to restoration in kind, as an alternative to equivalent compensation, is unavailable whenever it is determined to be overly burdensome for the defendant (art. 2058 para. 2, CC), owing either to the cost, or to the objective difficulties the defendant would face in fulfilling the duty.[54] This is why monetary damages is the form of redress most widely applied in Italy.

B. Injunctive Relief

It is a sound principle of economics that it is better to prevent than to cure. The law, too, sometimes provides immediate measures designed to prevent harm or its aggravation. Aside from exceptional situations (*e.g.* when an individual is legally entitled to use force in self-defense, *per* art. 2044 CC), private law provides the injured party with injunctive relief through a judicial action aimed at preventing the harmful event altogether, or its continuation or repetition.

In truth, with regard to the area of civil liability, the action is expressly permitted only in special situations.[55] Thus, it is still controversial whether this remedy is to

---

same article will appear at *Global Jurist*, www.bepress.com/GJ.

[54] As to the so-called environmental damage and the restoration of the site measure that can be ordered by the judge, *see* art. 18, par. 6, law no. 349 of 8 July 1986, in this chapter, Part I H.

[55] In particular, in case of others' unlawful use of a name or pseudonym (arts. 7, 8, and 9 CC), or of the illegal display or publication of a picture (art. 10 CC); in view of a protection against unfair competition (art. 2599 CC) or the unlawful collection and processing of personal data (art. 29, law no. 675 of 31 December 1996; against infringements of copyright (art. 156 copyright law), patent rights (arts. 83, 85, and 86 R.D. no. 1127 of 29 June 1939), trademark rights (arts. 63 and 66 R.D. no. 929 of 29 June 1942), or against those acts that could be drawn near to the notion of nuisance (arts. 844, 949, 1170*ff* CC).

be qualified as exceptional or not – even though one should consider that there is another preventive (and provisional) remedy available in situations where there are good grounds to fear that a right is threatened, *ex* art. 700 CC.[56]

For the injunctive remedy to be successful, the law generally requires that a tort has already been committed, and that its continuation or repetition is feared (arts. 7 and 2599 CC). In certain situations, evidence of preliminary actions in preparation for the commission of the tort suffices (*e.g.*, art. 157 copyright law). In order to avoid simple suspicion leading to unacceptable interference with personal freedom and legal activities, the judge is required to find that the fear is reasonable.

Redress for a feared injury is sometimes accomplished through a declaratory judgment. With regard to situations in which the tort consists of the spreading of false information, this form of redress may well serve the purpose. In any case, declaring that a given behavior is unlawful has a *per se* intimidating effect; and this effect is likely to be particularly powerful in cases in which the court also orders the payment of damages in advance (art. 86 para. 1, patent law).[57]

C. Limitation Period

With respect to the action for damages, art. 2947 CC provides for a five-year limitation period shorter than the ordinary ten-year term set forth in art. 2946 CC.

This short-term period is applied to actions designed to achieve compensation (either equivalent or by specific redress), not to other actions of a different nature that might arise from an unlawful act.

More specifically, art. 2947 CC examines three distinct possibilities: actions for damages in general, damages arising from a traffic accident, or damages from a crime.

The limitation period commences on the day on which the right can be exercised. Article 2947 para. 1 CC establishes that the right to compensation can be exercised

---

[56] A. Frignani, *L'injuction nella common law e l'inibitoria nel diritto italiano*, Milan (1974); U. Mattei, *Tutela inibitoria e tutela risarcitoria*, Milan (1987).

[57] In some cases the law authorizes more energetic anticipatory measures, designed to prevent commission of a tort. Thus, copyright law prohibits the unlawful representation or execution of a work (art. 157), ordering the destruction of illegally reproduced or distributed specimens or copies of the work, and of the equipment used in the reproduction or distribution (arts. 158, 159, 160). Similarly, the destruction of not only the objects produced, imported, or sold in breach of another's patent, but also of the specific means employed in producing them, may be ordered, just as it may be ordered that they become the property of the patent's holder (arts. 85 and 86 R.D. no. 1127/1930); similar measures are laid down by trademark law (art. 66 R.D. 929/1942).

from the day when the act occurred. However, recent case law has come to define this point as the moment when all the aspects of the act causing injury are known. This pro-victim interpretation has far-reaching consequences because the operational rules end up overturning the outlines of the Code and ignoring the intention of the legislator to strictly limit the time-frame within which compensatory action can take place.[58]

Section 2 of art. 2947 CC establishes a special rule. In case of compensation for damages resulting from traffic accidents, the prescription term is set at two years from the event's occurrence. If the tort qualifies as a crime, there are two further possibilities. Either the limitation period set by the criminal law is longer, and the same period is applied in the civil action (art. 2947 para. 3);[59] or the criminal law prescription term is shorter than the civil prescription, in which case the prevailing view is that the civil period remains unaffected.[60]

D. Tort and Contract: Concurrence of Actions

The mere non-performance of a contractual obligation does not amount to an unjustified injury. But when there is a breach not only of the rights based in contract but also of the rights that a person has independent of the existence of the contract itself, the doctrine of concurrent causes of action controls the relationship between tort and contractual claims.

Both contract and tort law may be invoked by the injured party in combination any time the same action simultaneously affects the holder's rights in both spheres (quite distinct from the previous existence of a legal relationship with the defendant), and from rights derived from contract or some pre-existing *vinculum iuris*.[61]

Most, if not all, cases concern infringements of absolute rights and, more precisely, injury to persons occurring during the fulfillment of a transport contract, or medical treatment, to which the breach of contract qualified as deliberate or resulting in a crime should be added. However, there has been a good deal of criticism aimed at the inconsistency of such a rule, which restricts concurrence of

---

[58] *See* P.G. Monateri, *supra* note 6, at 373*ff.*

[59] This decision is based on the need to avoid the duration of the criminal proceedings being prejudicial to the exercise of the civil action: *see* R. Roselli & P. Vitucci, "*La prescizione e la decadenza*," in Rescigno (ed.), *Trattato di diritto privato*, 20, II, Turin (1985), p. 454*ff.*

[60] P.G. Monateri, *supra* note 6, at p. 385*ff.*

[61] On the subject, *see* P.G. Monateri, *Cumulo di responsabilità contrattuale e extracontrattuale*, Padua (1989).

actions to injuries of an absolute right, when such injuries are no longer considered necessary for tort law to be applied.[62]

III. Issues and Formants

A. The Scholars' Leadership

In Italy, the lack of a detailed set of Code provisions along with the variety of possible conflicts largely leave it up to the interpreters to give substance and concrete meaning to broad and ambivalent formulae. Italian scholars have gradually become aware of this essential task. Since the 1960s, increasingly close attention has been paid to the growing economic and social impact of both lawfully and unlawfully produced accidents,[63] since it has become clear that tort law functions as a form of social engineering in the hands of the interpreters, and that legal policies are crucial in carrying out the adjudication process.[64]

Thus, it is not surprising that the field of tort law has seen the most interesting case law developments in the past few years, forecast and driven by an increasingly active scholarship. Scholars dealing with civil liability have advanced, with judicial approval, new approaches that have profoundly altered the rules governing the subject.

---

[62] *See id.* As to the territory recently conquered by the doctrine of concurrence of actions with regard to the liability for false information, *see* F.D. Busnelli, in Ch. von Bar (ed.), *Deliktsrecht in Europa*, Cologne etc. (1993), p. 42*ff.*

[63] *See* the analyses by Trimarchi on risk and causation (P. Trimarchi, *supra* note 19).

[64] From a cultural perspective, the strength of Italian comparative law scholarship and the subsequent spread of interest in other systems of civil liability has contributed to the introduction of new forms of analysis in Italy. It is usual to associate the introduction of methods from the economic analysis of law with the translation by A. De Vita, V. Varano & V. Vigoriti of Calabresi's book, *The Costs of Accidents. A Legal and Economic Analysis* (*Costo degli incidenti e responsabilità civile. Analisi economica e giuridica*, Milano (1975)). *See*, more recently, P.G. Monateri, *supra* note 6, at 1*ff*; G. Alpa *et al.* (eds.), *Analisi economica del diritto privato*, Milan (1998); R. Cooter, U. Mattei, P.G. Monateri, R. Pardolesi, & T. Ulen, *Il mercato delle regole*, Bologna (1999); U. Mattei, *Comparative Law and Economics*, Ann Arbor (1997). Throughout the 1980s, the subject of civil liability was at the center of critiques and debates, involving the most illustrious scholars of private law. The huge literary production of G. Alpa and M. Bessone finally made the literature on this subject take off. Other works of general interest include contributions by C. Castronovo, P. Cendon, F. Galgano, M. Libertini, C. Salvi, G. Visintini, and others.

As an example of these advances, we may cite the doctrine[65] that formed the basis of the *revirement* of the Italian Supreme Court in 1971 (regarding the compensation due under art. 2043 CC for the loss suffered by a creditor as a result of the wrongful act of a third party), which overcame the equation between unjustified injury and violation of an absolute right.[66]

The development of personal injury law is also emblematic of these changes. A prestigious line of scholarship ended up imposing an entirely new orientation on the Italian Supreme Court. The question arose out of the difficulties with the traditional system of compensation for damage to the psychological or physical well-being of a person, on account of the restrictions of art. 2059 CC. These only guaranteed compensation for material damage, as applied to medical expenses and loss of earnings suffered by the victim. The inadequacy of the compensatory mechanism available for the protection of such an important asset led scholars, and then judges, to create an entirely new category of injury termed "biological damage," as a recoverable loss stemming from any injury to health.[67]

Over the years the notion of biological damage evolved so as to currently include

---

[65] This refers in particular to F.D. Busnelli, *supra* note 7, which forecasts the judicial *revirement* by Cass. sez. un. 26 January 1971, no. 174.

[66] In this case, a soccer club brought its claim under art. 2043 against a third party who had caused the death by negligence of one of its best players, Meroni. The soccer team sued for damages alleging an economic loss. The Court held in *Meroni (Torino Calcio S.p.a. v. Romero*, Cass. civ., S.U., 26 January 1971, n.174, in *Giur. it.*, 1971, I,1, 681 note Visintini; in *Foro it.*, 1971, I, 342, note Busnelli) that the creditor can recover damages for the pecuniary losses suffered from an injury to his debtor. Though the creditor had only a relative right derived from the contract with the player, and no kind of absolute right against the third parties, nevertheless, the Italian Supreme Court stated that, in principle, he was entitled to recover damages. It was clear with this decision that the old doctrine had collapsed. This "Meroni" doctrine is now used not only when an employee is wounded or killed in an accident, but even when the recovery for a loss representing an infringement to the "integrity of one's own assets is at stake." *See* P.G. Monateri, "Economic Losses in Italy," in S. Banakas (ed.), *Civil Liability for Pure Economic Loss*, I, London (1996), 197*ff*; G. Ponzanelli, "The Compensation for Pure Economic Loss in Italian Law," in *Italian National Reports to the XVth International Congress of Comparative Law (Bristol 1998)*, Milan (1998), p. 178*ff*.

[67] The bibliography on this subject is extensive: *see, e.g.*, G. Alpa, *Il danno biologico*, 2nd ed., Padua (1993); M. Bargagna & F.D. Busnelli (ed.), *La valutazione del danno alla salute*, 3rd ed., Padua (1995); M. Franzoni, *Il danno alla persona*, Milan (1995); C. Castronovo, *Danno biologico. Un itinerario di diritto giurisprudenziale*, Milan (1998); P.G. Monateri & M. Bona, *Il danno alla persona*, Padua (1998).

any change for the worse suffered by the victim with regard to "all the activities, situations and relationships in which a person is involved during his life."[68]

B. The Autonomous Paths of Case Law

In other situations, case law, rather than being driven by the contributions of tort law scholarship, has followed a more independent course. Its trends have always been characterized by an expansion of compensation to interests not included within the traditional pattern.[69] For example, courts have proceeded to gradually remove the obstructions to compensation for losses stemming from the impairment of obligations due to the unlawful conduct of third parties. Emblematic cases in this field concern the extension of tort liability for the dissemination of false

---

[68] Corte cost. 18 July 1991, no. 356, in *Foro it.*, 1991, I, 2967, notes De Marzo, and D. Poletti; in *Quadr.*, 1992, p. 149, note E. Navarretta. The creation of a novel category of "existential damage" has been proposed in response to the need to provide more complete compensation for any event impairing the person's well-being. P. Ziviz, "*Alla scoperta del danno esistenziale*," in *Contr. impresa* (1994), p. 864*ff.* Today, most courts calculate payment for biological damage by means of tables giving a monetary value to a certain percentage of invalidity (the value being determined on the basis of an average of the sums paid in previous legal cases). *See* P.G. Monateri, *supra* note 6, at p. 302*ff.*

[69] Another field traditionally worked out by case law is that of professional liability. Up to a certain extent, the introduction in the Civil Code of a rule such as art. 2236 ("if the professional services involve the solution of technical problems of particular difficulty, the person who renders such services in not liable for damages, expect in cases of fraud, malice, or gross negligence") has proven to be troublesome for case law. Courts, however, have ended up establishing that the provision concerns only the services involving special professional skill; *see* Corte cost. 28 November 1973, no. 166, in *Foro it.*, 974, I, 19, and subsequently Cass. 21 December 1978, no. 6141, in *Giur. it.*, (1979), I, 1, 953 (as to the broader issue regarding the role of subjective superior skills and features as factors affecting tort liability, *see*, from the comparative law perspective, M. Bussani, *supra* note 11, at pp. 17, 43, 75, 215*ff*). Besides, when events occur within the normal course of the exercise of one's profession, the courts, with increasing frequency, have recourse to the *res ipsa loquitur* rule. On this subject, the bibliography is almost endless; *see, e.g.*, G. Cattaneo, *La responsabilità del professionista*, Milan (1958); and, more recently, for a critical analysis of case law and doctrine trends, G. Visintini, *I fatti illeciti. II. L'imputabilità e la colpa in rapporto agli altri criteri di imputazione della responsabilità*, 2nd ed., Padua (1998), p. 183*ff*; G. Alpa, M. Bessone, & V. Zeno-Zencovich, *supra* note 7, at 84*ff*; F. Cafaggi, "*Responsabilità del professionista*," in *Dig. IV, Disc. priv., Sez. civ.*, XVII (1998), p. 137*ff.*

information,[70] as well as for the double sale of real estate.[71]

Equally important is the line of decisions handed down by judges regarding the protection of one's private sphere from intrusion and interference by others. The Italian legal system does not include a general protection of the right to privacy, except for the reference to the right to the confidentiality of private life in the European Convention of Human Rights, 4 November 1950, incorporated into Italian law by law no. 848 of 4 August 1955, and the tort liability arising from unlawful collection and processing of personal data set forth by law no. 675 of 31 December 1996.[72] Nevertheless, other special provisions, scattered among different statutes, protect specific aspects of confidentiality. The right to one's own image is protected by art. 10 CC; the inviolability of one's address (personal as well as professional) and the secrecy of correspondence are principles laid down in the Italian Constitution (arts. 14 and 15), and the breach of these rules can amount to a criminal offense (arts. 614 and 616, Criminal Code).

Faced with the fragmentation of written law, case law has been able to go beyond the specific nature of each single provision, granting the right to privacy a general legal protection comparable to that afforded for absolute rights.[73]

Though it has been granted great breadth of application, this protection has been subjected by courts themselves to firmly established limitations. All of these limitations are subject to the usual balance between the comparative weight of conflicting interests. Freedom of the press and of speech, as well as didactic, cultural, artistic, and scientific interests, represent some of these limitations. Another is a person's fame, or involvement with acts or events of public interest or occurring in public (art. 97 para. 1, copyright law). However, it should be added that even when private matters are allowed into the public domain, the case law recognizes the

---

[70] *See* references in F.D. Busnelli, *"Itinerari europei nella 'terra di nessuno tra contratto e fatto illecito': la responsabilità per informazioni inesatte,"* in *Contr. Impr* (1991), 539*ff*.

[71] In this case, the buyer's liability (when registering first after buying second) see Chap. 12, p. 333*ff* is recognized according to tort law, so long as the defendant's malice or bad faith is demonstrated: Cass. 22 November 1984, no. 6006, in *Mass Foro. It.*, (1984); Cass. 8 January 1982, no. 76, in *Foro it.*, (1982), I, 393 note R. Pardolesi, in *Resp. civ. prev.* 1982, p. 174 note Benacchio; *see* references in M. Costanza, *"Doppia vendita immobiliare e responsabilità del secondo acquirente,"* in *Riv. Dir. civ.*, (1983), I, p. 520*ff*; in general on this point, *see* G. Ponzanelli, *"Il tort of interference nei rapporti contrattuali: le esperienze nord-americana e italiana a confronto,"* in *Quadr.*, (1989), p. 69*ff*.

[72] *See* E. Giannantonio, M. Losano, & V. Zeno Zencovich, *La tutela dei dati personali. Commentario alla l. 675/1996*, Padua (1997).

[73] For references, *see* G. Visintini, *supra* note 7, at p. 398*ff*.

need to protect the person's identity, in the sense of not ascribing to them facts, ideas, events, or professions of faith that would place them in a false light in the eyes of the public.[74]

C. Special Statutes

Notwithstanding the leadership vested in scholars and judges, other legal formants have contributed to the development of Italian tort law. These factors – European Community Law, social and political pressure, and the effects of a repealing referendum – have led to the adoption of a series of legislative provisions concerning civil liability over the past few years.[75] It is worth considering them briefly, even though this new legislation has not left any considerable mark on the case law.[76]

---

[74] A. Gambaro, *"Falsa luce agli occhi del pubblico,"* in *Riv. Dir. civ.*, I (1981), p. 84*ff*; *Id.*, *"Ancora in tema di falsa luce agli occhi del pubblico,"* in *Quadr.* (1988), p. 301*ff*. Though the protection of the individual's privacy is given due recognition, the problem regarding forms of compensation for those suffering harm to their private lives remains to be solved. Beyond ordering the discontinuation of the action causing injury, and its correction through the press, the redress available in our system is not altogether satisfactory. The difficulties derive from the nature of the injury. Often, this is mainly of a moral kind (such as annoyance or irritation caused by an intrusion which one has had to suffer). The inevitable publicity following the publishing of the judge's ruling in one or more newspapers (art. 120 CC) can itself excite further morbid curiosity, instead of helping to provide redress. The most serious obstacle to ensuring redress for prejudices of this kind are the limits placed on pain and suffering damages (art. 2059 CC). At the same time, the application of deterrent measures (encouraged by some scholars) comes up against our system's marked lack of enthusiasm for granting punitive damages and *astreintes* measures. For the debate on this matter, *see* P. Cendon, *"Le misure compulsorie a carattere pecuniario,"* in *Contr. impr.* (1988), p. 65*ff*; P. Gallo, *Le Pene private e responsabilità civile*, Milan (1996).

[75] Various forms of compulsory insurance have been introduced over the years by the Italian legislature. Among the most important, *see* law no. 990 of 24 December 1969, regarding motor vehicles; law no. 1860 of 31 December 1962, regarding pacific utilization of nuclear energy; DPR no. 136 of 31 March 1975, regarding auditors' liability; art. 1015 Maritime and Air Navigation Code and law no. 274 of 7 July 1988, regarding air transportation; law no. 226 of 11 August 1991, regarding members of non-profit organizations; legislative decree no. 111 of 17 March 1995, regarding tour operators. More generally, on the impact of insurance upon tort law issues, *see* A. Procida Mirabelli di Lauro, *Dalla responsabilità civile alla sicurezza sociale. A proposito dei diversi sistemi di imputazione dei danni da circolazione di veicoli*, Naples (1993); A.D. Candian, *Responsabilità civile e assicurazione*, Milan (1993); M. Franzoni, *Il terzo danneggiato nell'assicurazione della responsabilità civile*, Padua (1986).

[76] *See* G. Ponzanelli, *La responsabilità civile. Profili di diritto comparato*, Bologna (1992), p. 288*ff*.

Let us first examine products liability.[77] Italy employs a strict liability regime for damages resulting from defective products that was introduced by presidential decree no. 224 of 24 May 1988, in observance of EEC directive 85/374.[78] This was in keeping with previous legislation, such as law no. 713 of 11 October 1986, enforcing the EEC directive of 27 July 1986, regarding the convergence of member States' legislation on cosmetic products. Liability is "strict" in that it does not depend on fault but with the existence of a defect, and the demonstration of a causal link between the defect and the damage. In this regard, the principles expressed in the directive did not introduce any real changes, as compared with the rulings made on the basis of the more general provisions of the Civil Code in the relatively rare cases previously brought before Italian courts.[79]

Decree no. 224/88 provides a compromise solution to the problem of the conflict between the need to contain enterprise liability and the requirement to protect consumers. Indeed, the liability of manufacturers is contained within limits (described variously, according to the type of defect causing the damage) appropriate to reducing the compensation risk. Moreover, according to art. 6e of presidential decree no. 224/88, following art. 7e of the directive, the producer can avoid liability by proving that at the time the product was placed on the market, the defect could not have been recognized, owing to the prevailing state of scientific and technical knowledge.

Unlike products liability regulation, liability for environmental damage, introduced by art. 18 of law no. 349 of 1986 (addressed *supra* at I H) and judges' liability regime (modified by law no. 117 of 1988, ensuing a repealing referendum) seem to be united in their chief function of deterrence.

With respect to the act on judges' liability,[80] when one of the nominate torts

---

[77] On the subject, *see, e.g.*, U. Carnevali, *La responsabilità del produttore*, Milan (1974); G. Alpa, *Responsabilità dell'impresa e tutela del consumatore*, Milan (1975); C. Castronovo, *Problema e sistema del danno da prodotti*, Milan (1979); and on the presidential decree no. 224/1988, G. Alpa, M., Bin, & P. Cendon (eds.), *La responsabilità del produttore*, Padua (1989); R. Pardolesi & G. Ponzanelli, *"La responsabilità per danno da prodotti difettosi (commentario DPR 24.5.1988, no. 224),"* in *Nuove leggi civ. comm.* (1989), 497*ff*.

[78] *See*, more recently, the act on general product safety (legislative decree no 155 of 17 March 1995), with which the Italian legislator has implemented in Italy the ECC directive 92/59 of 29 June 1992 – these rules, however, are not concerned with civil liability issues.

[79] In Italy, the leading case in this field – the *Saiwa* case – dates back to 1964; *see* Cass. 25 May 1964, no. 1270, in *Foro it.*, 1965, 2098.

[80] *See* M. Graziadei & U. Mattei, "Judicial Responsibility in Italy," 38 *Am J Comp L* (1990), 103*ff*.

falling under the statute can be shown to have been committed, the victim can bring the tort lawsuit not against the judge, but against the State. The latter, in turn, has a right of recourse against the magistrate for a sum not exceeding one-third of the judge's annual income. The *numerus clausus* of the situations in which a tort action can be brought against the State, along with the victim's need to prove maliciousness or gross negligence on the judge's part, clearly illustrate the preventive and punitive rather than compensatory function performed in this field by the rules of civil liability.

IV. Conclusion

A. Summary

As we stated at the beginning of this chapter, the Italian legislator does not expressly require the violation of a right in order to impose liability, but does allow for the characterization of damage as "unjustified" (*ex* art. 2043 CC). By failing to clarify this idea of "injustice," he grants the judge true discretionary power. The Italian judge, in turn, usually exploits this power in accordance with input and developments issuing from both established scholarship and previous case law.

From the 1960s onward, an extensive effort by scholars and judges made it possible to enlarge the scope of tort law.[81] These endeavors led, with the exception of the broadening of strict liability protection, to a rejection of the old interpretation of "unjustified injury" as referring solely to the violation of a victim's absolute right, to give various "protected interests" a right to recover.

Thus, in spite of the extensive and long-standing debate over the *danno ingiusto*, current operative rules do not differ very much from the ones adopted in systems (such as those of Spain, Belgium, and France) in which the general clause on tort liability is the same as in Italian law (art. 1151 of the 1865 Civil Code) operative prior to the 1942 codification.

---

[81] *See, e.g.*, R. Sacco, "*L'ingiustizia di cui all'art. 2043 CC*," in *Foro pad.*, (1960), I, 1420; P. Schlesinger, "*La ingiustizia del danno nell'illecito civile*," in *Jus*, (1960), 336; P. Trimarchi, *Rischio e responsabilità oggettiva*, Milan (1961); *id., Causalità e danno*, Milan, (1967); F.D. Busnelli, *La lesione del credito da parte di terzi*, Milan (1964); S. Rodotà, *Il problema della responsabilità civile*, Milan (1964).

B. Watertight Compartments

What has not changed over the decades is the deeply rooted mentality of tort law jurists – an attitude shared, incidentally, by most of the civil and common lawyers[82] – that contributes to keep widespread Italian labels and formulas removed from the "real life" of tort law.[83]

What we are referring to here is the traditional and still prevalent mode of conceiving of the elements of the cause of action – or to be more precise, the tendency of judges and scholars to represent the various parts of the tort liability as completely separate from one another, each to be considered as an independent variable in its turn. According to this approach, each element plays its own distinct role in constructing the facts and orienting the solution.

This approach does not simply pursue aims of a descriptive nature, because it has the effect of justifying the need to perform analytical verifications – in both legal writings and case law regarding the causation link, standard of conduct, damages, defenses, and so forth. All these inquiries end up being presented as if they were not interrelated.

It is a short step from such treatment to the definition of the plaintiff's right to claim as dependent on the mere existence of either an infringement of a protected interest or a breach of a duty – a definition conceiving of all the other elements of tort liability as self-contained, and devoid of any mutual interference. Thus, no importance should be attributed, for example, to the subjective characteristics of the wrongdoer with regard to establishing the existence and the extent of the duty. Similarly, the kind of interest at stake, whether protected or not, has no bearing on determining the standard of conduct required of the defendant, or on ascertaining the causal link, and so forth.

In spite of its pleasing simplicity, such an approach inadequately describes the reality of tort law. In fact, if we adopt this perspective, it immediately becomes difficult to explain the familiar phenomenon of the recurrence of decisions (and theoretical outcomes) in which the variation of one of the elements emerging from the comparison between the "classical" scheme and the actual situation is balanced by the different role awarded, in the concrete case, to one of the other elements of the cause of action.

A simple example may render our critique more precise: it becomes difficult to understand why the fact that a causal link that is indirect, or that a right infringed

---

[82] For some examples, *see* P. Cendon, *supra* note 4, at p. 203*ff*, 353*ff*; M. Bussani, *supra* note 11, at 76*ff*, 99*ff*.

[83] *See* the remarks of R. Sacco, *supra* note 5, at p. 358*ff*, 369.

upon was not absolute (consider, *e.g.*, intentional torts or liability for false information), are circumstances of no import in exempting a defendant from liability.

Similarly, it is clear why, in order to make the given defendant liable, it is sometimes not even sufficient to show that he has infringed upon an absolute right of the victim, or that there is an immediate and direct causal link, as well as a violation of the ordinary standard of conduct (the "double sale" of real estate cases are an example). Our point is that very often in situations like these, only the consideration of "other factors" is able to determine whether or not to shift the loss to the defendant. These factors can emerge, for example, through the consideration of the ways in which the given defendant could, under those circumstances, have avoided incurring that special degree of fault necessary in order to trigger the tort liability, or utilized the information available to him regarding the probable course of events stemming from his or her behavior,[84] and so forth.[85]

The mere acknowledgement that relationships exist between the various elements of the cause of action allows us to reach a preliminary conclusion in such cases. No interpretation can be taken seriously which views tort liability as a system of independent modules, and attributes the same, unvarying role to each element, a role never affected by the specific circumstances of the case.[86] The interactions

---

[84] *See* G. Gorla, "*Sulla cosiddetta causalità giuridica: 'fatto dannoso' e 'conseguenze,'*" in *Riv. dir. comm.*, I (1951), 410*ff*; P. Cendon, *supra* note 4, at 203*ff*, 353*ff*; M. Bussani, *supra* note 10, at 76*ff*, 99*ff*.

[85] *See also*, in Western literature, G. Durry, "*Obs.*," in *Rev. trim. dir. civ.* (1975), 310*f*; J.J. Honorat, *L'idée d'acceptation des risques dans la responsabilité civile*, Paris (1969), *passim*, esp. 28*ff*, 89, 230; G. Viney & P. Jourdain, *Les conditions de la responsabilité*, 2nd ed., Paris (1998), p. 491*ff*; J.G. Fleming, *The Law of Torts*, 7th ed., Sydney (1987), pp. 69*ff*, 265*ff*; P. Cane, *Atiyah's Accidents, Compensation and the Law*, 5th ed., London (1993), pp. 5, 95; H.R.W. Hart & A. Honoré, *Causation in the Law*, 2nd ed., Oxford (1985), pp. 40*f*, 77, 149*ff*, 482*ff*.

[86] *See, e.g.*, J.S. Colyer, *A Modern View of the Law of Torts* (1966), p. 30 ("some interests are protected against certain types of conduct, others against other types of conduct"); H.T. Terry, "Proximate Consequences in the Law of Torts," 28 *Harvard LRev* (1914), 10, 15 f., 26*f*; D. Payne, "Foresight and Remoteness in Negligence," 25 *ModLRev* 16pp. (1962); W.L. Prosser & W.P. Keeton, *On Torts*, 5th ed., St. Paul (1984), pp. 205*ff*, 296*ff*; E. Deutsch, *Fahrlässigkeit und erforderliche Sorgfalt*, Köln (1963), pp. 62*ff*, 157*ff*, 171; J. Delyannis, *La notion d'acte illicite considéré en sa qualité d'élément de la faute délictuelle*, Paris (1952), p. 119: "*la diligence requise à l'égard des biens garantis est beaucoup plus grande que celle requise à l'égard des intérêts purement économiques ou moraux des autres*"; C. Aubry & C.F. Rau, *Cours de droit civil français*, 6th ed., par P. Esmein, Paris (1956), (English trans., St. Paul (1969)), para. 444*bis*, 445: "certain interests are not protected, either because they are counterbalanced by interests judged to be more important for society, such as the case of

between fault and duty, or between the forseeability factor and the establishment of a causal link, or between causation and the nature of the violated interest, show how a distinction between the structural elements of the cause of action is possible only on the basis of the real autonomy each of these elements possesses under the given circumstances.

It is only by adopting this approach that we can understand that both the role and the content of any element of the cause of action may be bound to change depending on the specific circumstances and the requirements of the specific type of liability in question.

With this in mind, one comes to understand why an infringement of the absolute right *par excellence* needs to be carried out by a malicious defendant in order for the latter to be liable; or why the notion of causation can be expanded or contracted according to the sort of interest infringed upon in a particular case; or why any kind of loss – even a pure economic one – can be restored if it is the result of the defendant's intentional conduct; or why a loss related to the exploitation of bad advice or false representation can be shifted to the defendant only if the latter (under identical factual circumstances) could have foreseen that the given third party would rely on his or her statements.

C. Interpretive Fate

Awareness of the cultural attitudes of judges and scholars helps us to understand the nature of debate over new tort-related issues, and what technical tools are likely to be exploited in implementing the decision-makers' point of view.

It is well known that the real, general problem tort law must face involves establishing technically and socially acceptable limits to shifting the losses suffered by the victim to the actor. It is also true that whenever there is no agreement about this shift between the person who suffers the loss and the would-be defendant, it is up to tort law to provide the solution. Therefore, the task of deciding whether or not to award compensation to the victim falls upon the institutional interpreter of law, the judge.

The judge, however, has his own legal culture: he has admired or criticized the judicial precedents, has learned the opinions of the legal authorities he encountered in law school, and possesses both an attitude of self-restraint and a reservoir of

---

damage caused by lawful competition, or because they cannot be fully safeguarded, and because anyone suffering an injury to them has the advantage of being able to inflict the same inconvenience upon others, as in the case of reasonable disturbances of neighborhood."

legal reactions and answers that stem from the legal culture and tradition of the country in which he lives.[87]

It is certain that the usually loose-fitting provisions of tort law offer the judge little assistance in coming to a decision. Hence, the decisions end up being grounded in the interpretive culture of the decision-maker, and the interpretative fate of tort law, more so than other fields of private law, comes to rest upon the policy considerations which inevitably frame outcomes according to social and economic needs.

---

[87] From the comparative law and economics point of view, *see* M. Bussani & U. Mattei, "Making the Other Path Efficient. Economic Analysis and Tort Law in Less Developed Countries," in E. Buscaglia, W. Ratliff & R. Cooter (eds.), *The Law and Economics of Development*, Greenwich, Ct.-London, U.K. (1997), p. 149*ff.*

Contract Law

Alberto M. Musy & Alberto Monti[1]

I. Sources and Structure of Italian Contract Law

A. Sources

In the Italian legal system, the main sources of the law of contracts are the legislative provisions comprised in the Civil Code of 1942 and in various statutory laws enacted to regulate individual contracts or specific aspects thereof. Customs and equitable principles in general are residual sources, pursuant to arts. 1374 and 1340 of the Civil Code (hereinafter CC).[2] Judicial decisions, in turn, play a primary role in the process of implementing legislative rules. The rationalization of the system as a whole, as well as the most relevant efforts toward the innovation and modernization of the law of contracts, however, spring from the works of legal scholars.

1. The Constitution, the Civil Code, and other Statutory Sources

The principle of freedom of contract is not positively recognized as a general principle by the Italian Constitution of 1948. Some scholars hold that the freedom

---

[1] Alberto M. Musy, Associate Professor of Comparative Law, University of Novara; Alberto Monti, University of Milan and ICER (International Centre for Economic Research). Alberto M. Musy contributed parts II C, III and IV A to this work; Alberto Monti contributed parts I, II A-B, IV B and V.

[2] Article 1374 CC – Integration of contract: "A contract binds the parties not only as to what it expressly provides, but also to all the consequences deriving from it by the law or, in its absence, according to usage and equity." Article 1340 CC – Customary terms: "Customary terms are deemed to be included in the contract, unless it appears that they were not intended by the parties."

Jeffrey S. Lena and Ugo Mattei (eds.), *Introduction to Italian Law*, 247-282
©2002 Kluwer Law International. Printed in the Netherlands.

of contract principle is embodied in art. 2, while others refer to arts. 41 and 42 of the Constitution.[3]

On the one hand, any restriction of the freedom of contract is regarded as the restriction of private enterprise. On the other hand, constitutional norms, and the values protected thereby, work to limit the private autonomy to contract.

The Civil Code of 1942 is the basic source of the law of contracts. The rules on contracts are mainly included in Titles II and III of Book 4 on "Obligations," but other provisions are located elsewhere. For example, the rules on gifts, which are considered a type of contract,[4] are contained in Book 3 on "Succession."

During the last four decades, moreover, many statutes on contracts have been enacted, more commonly due to the growing pressure of EEC rules and directives. Some of them have been recently integrated in the text of the Civil Code, such as law no. 52 of 2 February 1996 on unfair terms in consumer contracts[5] that added arts. 1469*bis* to *sexies*. Others simply stand separately as special statutes designed to handle specific contracts or peculiar aspects thereof.[6]

2. Judicial Decisions and Scholarly Writings

Courts play a fundamental role in the dynamics of Italian contract law because they are called upon to implement general legislative rules and to apply equitable principles on a case-by-case basis. One example is the analysis of the duty to act and perform the contract in accordance with good faith and fair dealing set forth by arts. 1175 and 1375 CC.[7]

---

[3] *See* Gambaro, "Freedom of Contract and Constitutional Law in Italy," in Rabello & Sarcevic (eds.), *Freedom of Contract and Constitutional Law*, Sacher Institute, Jerusalem (1998), pp. 169-80.

Articles 2, 41 and 42 Const. grant protection respectively to the fundamental human rights, the freedom of private enterprise, and the right to private property. The freedom of contract can logically be considered as the instrument that sustains private enterprise. *See*, in more detail, M. Comba "Constitutional Law," chapter 3, this volume.

[4] Article 769 CC – Definition: "A gift is a contract by which, in the spirit of liberality, one party enriches the other, disposing of one of his rights in the other's favor or undertaking an obligation toward him."

[5] Enacted pursuant to the EEC Directive 93/13.

[6] *See*, law no. 392 of 27 July 1978 on urban leases, law no. 1 of 2 January 1991 on securities sales, and law no. 990 of 24 December 1969 on mandatory insurance for motor vehicles.

[7] Article 1175 CC – Fair behavior: "The debtor and the creditor shall behave according to rules of fairness." art. 1375 CC – Performance according to good faith: "The contract shall be performed according to good faith."

With respect to general clauses, Italian case law has never managed to give truly satisfactory results. The importance of judicial decision-making emerged when new types of contracts entered the Italian legal and business panorama and courts were called upon to legitimate them.[8] Moreover, courts have to deal with many disputed issues left unresolved at a normative level, such as the relevance of the requisite of *causa*[9] or the applicability of the doctrine of supervening excessive hardship in case of depreciation of the counter-performance.[10] Academics and legal scholars are in turn relied upon to elaborate and provide the judiciary with those conceptual tools needed to resolve such controversial issues, aiming to rationalize the law of contracts, in view of the progressive integration of European private law.[11]

B. The Conceptual Structure of Italian Contract Law: General Rules, Nominate Contracts, and Atypical Agreements

The conceptual approach to the law of contract is reflected by the peculiar structure of the Civil Code treating this matter. In addition to a first general section on "typical" contracts,[12] which contains rules on requirements, interpretation, effects, discharge, rescission, assignment, and validity of a contract, there is another section on individual contracts,[13] comprising specific rules and exceptions for the so-called "nominate" or "typical" contracts.[14]

---

[8]   *See infra* next paragraph.

[9]   *See infra*, part II A.

[10] *See infra*, part IV B 2.

[11] *See, e.g.*, the *Principles of European Contract Law* set forth by the Lando Commission under the auspices of the EU, or the UNIDROIT Principles of International Commercial Contracts; *see also* the comparative law project carried on by the University of Trento (Italy), entitled *The Common Core of European Private Law*. Cambridge University Press has published the first two volumes.

[12] Title II of Book 4 on "Obligations," arts. 1321 to 1469.

[13] Title III of Book 4 on "Obligations," arts. 1470 to 1986.

[14] There are more than thirty nominate contracts or "legal types": sale; exchange; contract for sale or return; supply contracts; lease of property; contract for work or services; carriage contracts; mandate; agency; brokerage; deposit; contractual sequestration; loan for use; loan of fungibles; current account; banking contracts; perpetual annuity; life annuity; insurance; gambling and wagering; suretyship; mandate to grant credit; antichresis; compromise; and assignment for benefit of creditors. *See* G. De Nova, *Il Tipo Contrattuale*, Padua, Cedam (1974).

The general section applies to nominate contracts so long as it does not conflict with specific rules set forth for the individual contract at issue. Private parties can freely determine the contents of the contract within the limits imposed by the law.

Moreover, pursuant to art. 1322 para. 2 CC the parties can also make contracts that are not of the types specifically regulated in the Code provided that they are directed to the realization of interests worthy of protection according to the legal order. The courts must determine that such contracts are worthy. When a certain form of agreement is widely accepted within the international legal community,[15] therefore, Italian courts always consider it enforceable.[16]

These "innominate," "atypical," agreements are subject to the general rules on contracts contained in Title II of Book 4. The general tendency, however, is to treat innominate contracts in a manner similar to the closest "legal type," in order to apply the discipline of the specific nominate contract. Only when the court for some reason does not want to apply a special provision to the contract at stake will the agreement be simply treated as atypical.[17] An example is given by the so-called "contract of assistance," by which one party, in exchange for either real property or an amount of money, undertakes the obligation to assist the other party, providing them with food, company, and care for the rest of his or her life. In order to exclude the application of art. 1878 CC,[18] which rules out the remedy of dissolution for non-performance for "life annuities" (a legal type), the Italian Supreme Court[19] recently held that the "contract of assistance" is an atypical and innominate one, therefore subject to the general rules on dissolution (arts. 1453ff CC).[20] There also exist other types of contract that may be considered mixed contracts and socially typical contracts. The former have the characteristics of two or more nominate

---

[15] As in the case of leasing, factoring, franchising, performance bond, etc.

[16] *See* Galgano, "La giurisprudenza nella società post-industriale," in *Contratto & Impresa* (1989), no. 2, p. 357.

[17] *See* Sacco, "*Autonomia contrattuale e tipi*," in *Riv. trim. dir. e proc. civ.* (1966), 788ff and De Nova, *supra*, note 14.

[18] Article 1878 CC – Non-payment of due installments: "In case of non-payment of due installments of annuities, the creditor of the annuity, even if he is a party to the contract, cannot demand dissolution of the contract, but can cause the sequestration and sale of his debtor's property for the purpose of investing out the proceeds of the sale a sum sufficient to assure payment of the annuity."

[19] *See* Cass. Civ., sez. I, 9 October 1996, no. 8825, in *Foro it.* I (1997), 2227.

[20] *See* A. Monti, "*Sull' atipicità del contratto di assistenza*," in *Foro it.* I (1997), 2227 for further references.

contracts, resulting in a combination thereof, and therefore differing from each legal type. The latter are atypical contracts that have become common in commercial practice. These contracts, for leasing, factoring, project financing, franchising, and engineering, are nowadays considered socially typical and courts treat them as specific types with their own peculiar set of rules.[21]

II. Formation

A. The Enforceability of a Promise

In the Italian legal system, not every promise[22] is deemed enforceable. Gino Gorla's[23] fundamental comparative work on this topic focused on those other elements required for a promise to be legally binding. Despite the language of art. 1321

---

[21] *See* M. Dogliotti & A. Figone (ed.), *Giurisprudenza del contratto – Parte I*, Giuffrè, Milan (1998), p. 473*ff.*

[22] In this section, we analyze a set of problems concerning the enforceability of a promise, trying to go beyond the dogmatic continental opposition between contract and promise and assuming that the promise itself has not been refused by the promisee. *See* J. Gordley, *Enforceability of promises in European Law*, in M. Bussani and U. Mattei (Gen. ed.), *The Common Core of European Private Law Project*, Cambridge, Cambridge University Press, 2001. Article 1987 CC states that a unilateral promise is not binding except in specific cases permitted by the law. The unenforceability of unilateral promises would not in any case be due to the fact that they have not been accepted by the promisee, but will depend on a case-by-case determination of the lack of adequate *vestimenta*. Therefore, we will point out the need of express or formal acceptance by the promisee only in those cases in which it has a practical relevance.

In Italian contract law, a related set of problems regards the controversial nature of promises disciplined by art. 1333 CC, by which the promisor alone undertakes obligations. These promises do not need express acceptance to be legally binding but can be timely refused by the promisee (art. 1333 CC – Contract binding on offeror only: "An offer for the purpose of forming a contract that creates obligations only for the offeror is irrevocable as soon as it comes to the knowledge of the party to whom it is directed. The offeree can reject the offer within the time required by the nature of the transaction or by usage. In the absence of such rejection the contract is concluded.").

[23] *See* G. Gorla, *Il contratto. Problemi fondamentali trattati con il metodo comparativo e casistico*, vols. 1 & 2, Giuffrè, Milan (1955); *Id.*, *Le contrat dans le droit continental et en particulier dans le droit français et italien*, Turin (1958) (lit.); *id.*, "*Causa, consideration e forma nell'atto d'alienazione inter vivos*," in *Riv. dir. com.* (1952), 173; *id.*, "*Promesse 'condizionate' ad una prestazione*," in *Riv. dir. com.*, I (1968), 431.

CC,[24] the mere agreement (*nudum pactum*) of the parties is not itself enforceable;[25] other requirements are necessary (*vestimenta*).[26]

In particular, art. 1325 CC states that every contract must have a *causa*. The scope and definition of this requirement has historically been rather controversial.[27] It does not seem appropriate here to report all the conflicting theories as well as their complex implications; suffice it to say that the concept of *causa* has been described from both subjective and objective perspectives.[28] The former interpretation referred to the aim pursued by the party in undertaking the obligation, while the latter identified the *causa* with the typical social and economic function of the contract,[29] entrusting to the State extensive control over atypical private

---

[24] Article 1321 CC – Notion: "A contract is the agreement of two or more parties to establish, regulate or extinguish a patrimonial legal relationship among themselves."

[25] *See* Gorla, *Il potere della volontà nella promessa come negozio giuridico*, and *supra* note 23, at 42*ff*; A. D'Angelo, *Promessa e ragioni del vincolo*, Giappichelli, Turin (1992); G. Sbisà, *La promessa al pubblico*, Milan (1974), p. 47*ff*; R. Sacco, "*Il Contratto*," in *Trattato di dir. civ. Vassalli*, Turin (1975), 6*ff*, points out the conceptual flaws in the Civil Code definition of the term contract and – analyzing the rule of art. 1333 para. 2 CC – shows how the agreement, in the sense of "meeting of offer and acceptance," may not itself be a requisite for the existence of a contract; *see also* Gorla, *Il dogma del "consenso" o "accordo" e la formazione del contratto di madato gratuito nel diritto continentale*; Franco Carresi, "*Contratti e atti unilaterali*," in *Studi in memoria di Vassalli* (1960); id., "*Il contratto con obbligazioni del solo proponente*," in *Riv. dir. civ.* I (1974), 393.

[26] For an historical analysis of the theory of *vestimenta*, *see*, most recently, Birocchi, *Causa e categoria generale del contratto*, Giappichelli, Turin (1997).

[27] *See*, generally, Giorgianni, entry "*Causa (diritto privato)*," in *Enc. Dir.*, Giuffrè, Milan (1960); Betti, "*Teoria generale del negozio giuridico*," in *Trattato di dir. civ. Vassalli*, Utet, Turin (1955); on the equivocal use of the term: G. Gorla, *Il contratto*, *supra* note 23, at 161-162, 262*ff*; R. Sacco, *supra* note 25, at 8*ff*, 621*ff*; G. Alpa, "*L'uso giurisprudenziale della causa del contratto*," in *Nuova giur. civ. comm.* II (1995), 1; G. Alpa & M. Bessone (eds.), *Causa e consideration*, *Quaderni di diritto comparato*, Padua (1984); A. Gambaro, "*Sintesi inconclusiva in tema di causa e contratto*," in L. Vacca (ed.), *Causa e contratto nella prospettiva storico-comparatistica*, Giappichelli, Turin (1997), p. 551*ff*.

[28] *See* Mirabelli, "*Causa subiettiva e causa obiettiva*," in *Riv. trim. dir. proc. civ.* (1951), 323. *See also*, *infra*, part III C.

[29] Betti, "*Teoria generale del negozio giuridico*," in *Trattato di dir. civ. Vassalli*, Utet, Turin (1955); but, *see also* R. Sacco, *supra* note 25, at 577*ff*; Gorla, *Il contratto*, *supra* note 23, at 199*ff*.

This is the concept of *causa* generally declared by Italian case law even in those situations where the concepts of cause *suffisante* or *raisonnable et juste* (*see infra*, note 32) are effectively used by judges to reach the decision.

agreements.[30]

For our purposes, however, a third approach to the problem of *causa* seems the most profitable. This approach refers to the *"causa di giustificazione,"*[31] *i.e.*, the reason that justifies the promise and the obligation. This is characterized by the concepts of *cause suffisante, raisonnable et juste* introduced by Gorla to describe some of the *vestimenta* required by Italian contract law – even if these *vestimenta* are not clearly stated in the Civil Code or held by case law to be enforce promises.[32] Whenever these requisites are lacking, the promise is not enforceable unless it is made according to the formality of the *contratto di donazione* (gift), which is therefore considered by many scholars as another *vestimentum*.[33]

The aim of these requirements, which flesh out the mere agreement of the parties, is basically to establish with certainty the intention of the promisor to be legally

---

[30] Let us recall here the notion of typical and atypical contracts (nominate and innominate contracts). "Nominate contracts are those commonplace contracts which are dealt with specifically by the law, which gives them a distinctive name and lays down a special set of rules which, in case of conflict, prevail over the general law of contract ... Innominate contracts are those which are not specifically regulated by law." Criscuoli & Pugsley, *Italian Contract Law*, Jovene, Naples (1991), p. 19. *See also* De Nova, *Il tipo contrattuale, supra*, note 14.

[31] *See* G. Castiglia, *"Promesse unilaterali atipiche,"* in *Riv. dir. comm.* I (1983), 327, at 332*ff*; *see also* Deiana, *"Alcuni chiarimenti sulla causa del negozio e dell'obbligazione,"* in *Riv. dir. civ.* I (1938), 1*ff*; 105*ff*.

On the distinction between *causa dell'attribuzione* (*causa dandi*) and *causa di giustificazione* (*causa retinendi*), *see* B. Kupisch, *"Arricchimento nel diritto romano, medioevale e moderno,"* in *Disc. Priv.*, sez. civ. I, Digesto IV ed., Utet, Turin (1987), 423.

[32] Gino Gorla makes a distinction between the obligations to give and all other types of obligations. As for the promises to give something, their enforceability is subject to the requirement of the *cause suffisante* (an objectively valid reason to undertake an obligation), or to the fact that the promise is made formally, while the promise to perform an act is binding whenever there is a *cause juste et raisonnable*, which is a lighter requirement involving an evaluation of conflicting interests of the promisor to withdraw the promise and of the promisee to enforce it. *See* Gorla, *Il contratto, supra* note 23 (affirming that a gratuitous promise to do something can never be classified as a donation); Torrente, *"La donazione,"* in *Trattato dir. civ.* Cicu-Messineo, Giuffrè, Milan (1956); Cass. civ., 5 May 1956, no. 1427, in *Giust. civ.* I (1956), 1247; but, *see also*, the partial revision made by Gorla in *Le contrat dans le droit continental et en particulier dans le droit français et italien, supra* note 23, at 56*ff*; 65*ff*; contra Biondi, *"Le Donazioni,"* in *Tratt. dir. civ. Vassalli*, vol. XII, tomo IV, Utet, Turin (1961). The point is quite controversial among scholars.

[33] *See* R. Sacco, *supra* note 25, at 588; but, *see also*, contra, Gazzoni, *Manuale di Diritto Privato*, 7th ed., *Edizioni Scientifiche Italiane* (1998), Cap. XLIV.12.

bound by his promise, to assure the certainty and stability of some types of legal relationship, to protect the promisor from ill-considered acts (in particular with respect to the obligation to give), and to enforce promises as justice requires.

Thus, the analysis focuses again on all those factual, legal, and social circumstances which justify the enforcement of a promise.

The most important case in which a promise is considered binding under Italian contract law is the typical economic exchange. This means that a promise is enforceable whenever it is part of an exchange of an economic nature, such that a counter-promise, or a reciprocal performance, can be identified ("*contratto di scambio*" – *causa onerosa*). This typical economic exchange structure shows the clear intention of the promisor to be legally bound and justifies the enforcement of the promise according to the other reasons stated above. Therefore, when the parties face reciprocal legal detriment, corresponding to reciprocal economic interests,[34] the *causa* requirement is fully satisfied and there is no enforceability problem related to the absence of *causa*.[35]

The matter is more doubtful whenever this structure is abandoned and only one party faces an immediate legal detriment by promising without receiving a reciprocal counter-promise or performance by the promisee. The possibility that only one party undertakes an obligation in a contractual relationship, however, is explicitly provided for by art. 1333 CC and the opportunity to conclude atypical contracts is granted to private parties by art. 1322 para. 2 CC.

At this level, the requisites (*vestimenta*) of *cause suffisante* for the obligations to give and *cause raisonnable et juste* for the obligations to perform an act, become an important tool for discriminating between enforceable and non-enforceable promises. It has been said that civil law is traditionally quite suspicious of atypical private agreements,[36] and generally of all those relationships in which only one party undertakes obligations, as shown by the rule of art. 1987 CC concerning

---

[34] *See* A. D'Angelo, *supra* note 25.

[35] For general references, *see* R. Sacco, *supra* note 25, at 582*ff.* The contract must be lawful according to arts. 1343, 1346, and 1418 CC to be enforceable. A contract is unlawful whenever it contrasts with mandatory rules, public policy (*ordine pubblico*), and good morals (*buon costume*); *see infra* part III C. In the Civil Code, a plurality of rules is devoted to moderate the full enforceability of lawful contractual agreements in some special cases (*see, e.g.* arts. 1447-48 CC and 1467-68 CC, not to mention the special treatment of consumer contracts or labor contracts). *See*, in more detail, *infra* parts III and IV.

[36] *See* Gorla, *Il contratto*, *supra* note 23; *see also*, *supra*, note 32.

unilateral promises.[37] The enforceability of such promises is therefore subject to a strict case-by-case analysis.

Thus, a promise could be considered legally binding whenever the promisor sought an economic advantage by making it, even if the promise had no direct or apparent counterpart similar to the typical economic exchange (only in this narrow sense, the promise is said to be gratuitous – *"promessa gratuita ma interessata"*). Modern Italian case law has recently reached this result with respect to the obligation to perform an act.[38]

As mentioned above, according to some scholars, the formality of the contract of donation (gift) – a notarized act in the presence of two witnesses – could itself be considered another *vestimentum* of the promise to give. When there is no exchange and the promisor seeks no economic advantage, but merely desires to enrich the promisee spontaneously (*animus donandi*), assuming an obligation to give toward him or her, Italian contract law refers to the *contratto di donazione* (gift) disciplined by arts. 769-809 CC. The general rule for this type states that this promise has to be made formally by public act, according to art. 782 CC and the notarial law, and has to be accepted by the promisee.[39]

Some scholars say that in practice, the formalities of the contract of donation could grant protection to a full variety of gratuitous promises to give, in which the aim pursued by the promisor is unrelated to the spontaneous enrichment of the promisee (*i.e.* promises to give motivated by a past moral obligation or by another *causa* which is not *suffisante*).[40] Moreover, a variety of promises are considered enforceable because they are legally or socially typical and they refer to a previous legal agreement or relationship (promises *solvendi causa* and *cavendi causa*,

---

[37] For the limited practical effects of art. 1987 CC on the system and its relationship with art. 1333 CC, *see, e.g.*, C.A. Graziani, *"Le promesse unilaterali,"* in *Tratt. di dir. priv. Rescigno*, 9, Utet, Turin (1982); G. Sbisà, *supra* note 25, at 40*ff*; A. D'Angelo, *supra* note 25, at 421*ff*; P. Spada, *"Cautio quae indiscrete loquitur: lineamenti funzionali e strutturali della promessa di pagamento,"* in *Riv. dir. civ.* I (1978), 673, at 754.

[38] *See, e.g.*, Cass. Civ., sez. II, 14 November 1994, no. 9562, in *Giurisprudenza Italiana* (hereinafter *GI*), I (1995), 1, 1920; Cass. Civ., sez. II, 15 July 1993, no. 7844, in *GI* I (1995), 734; Checchini, *"L'interesse a donare,"* in *Riv. dir. civ.* I (1976), 254, at 274; R. Sacco, *supra* note 25, at 583*ff*; G. Gorla, *supra* note 23, at 177*ff*; Gazzoni, *supra* note 33; A. Gianola, *"Verso il riconoscimento della promessa atipica, informale, gratuita ma interessata,"* in *GI* I (1995), 1921.

[39] For specifications and exceptions to this rule, *see* Gazzoni, *supra* note 33.

[40] *See* R. Sacco, *supra* note 25, at 588; in a sense, these promises would be enforced because of the formality even if lacking a *causa*. *See, supra*, note 32 and accompanying text.

promises to pay someone else's debt).

As regards promises *cavendi causa* developed in commercial practice, from a causal perspective the agreement known as *Garantievertrag*[41] is remarkable for its practical consequences. A special typical case of enforceable unilateral promise is disciplined by the Civil Code. This is the public promise which, according to art. 1989 CC, is binding mainly because it has been made to the public at large.[42]

Apart from these cases, however, the legal consequences of informal, atypical promises based on the non-economic interests of the promisor (or, more generally, based on an interest which does not constitute a *cause suffisante or raisonnable et juste*) are doubtful and controversial, especially when such promises induced a reasonable detrimental reliance of, or damage to, the promisee. Here begins the fog that closes in upon the border of the promise between tort and contract and obscures whether the promisor could be held liable by the terms of the contract, or whether the breach sounds in tort.[43]

We conclude this brief overview on enforceability of promises by pointing out that art. 1988 CC (promise of payment and the acknowledgement of debt)[44] has no substantial value and does not stand against the general principle that an informal promise lacking *causa* is unenforceable. The rule of article 1988 CC, in fact, merely has the procedural effect of reversing the burden of proving the source of the obligation, which is presumed.[45] There must be an underlying civil obligation to pay which is presumed according to the rule of art. 1988 CC, but the promise itself is not an independent source of obligation.[46]

---

[41] *See* Portale, *"Fideiussione e Garantievertrag nella prassi bancaria,"* in Portale (ed.), *Le operazioni bancarie*, II, Giuffrè, Milan (1978), 1056; P. Spada, *supra* note 37, at 741; M. Viale, *"Le garanzie bancarie,"* in *Trattato di diritto commerciale e di diritto pubblico dell'economia diretto da Galgano*, XVIII, Cedam, Padua (1994); G. Meo, *"Fideiussioni bancarie e garanzie a prima richiesta: le tutele cautelari,"* in *Banca borsa e titoli di credito* I (1995), p. 443.

[42] *See* G. Sbisà, *La promessa al pubblico*, Milano (1974); C. Falqui Massida, *"Le promesse unilaterali,"* in *Giur. sist. civ. e comm. diretta da W. Bigiavi*, Utet, Turin (1968).

[43] *See* G. Marini, *Promessa ed affidamento nel diritto dei contratti*, Jovene, Naples (1995), p. 303; A. Gianola, *supra* note 38, at 1924; Cass. civ., 22 January 1976, no. 185, in *Foro it.* (1976), I, 618.

[44] Article 1988 CC: "A promise to pay or the acknowledgement of a debt exonerates the promisee from the burden of proving the underlying obligation. Such obligation is presumed, subject to contrary evidence."

[45] *See* Cass. civ., sez. III, 18 July 1997, no. 6642 (Cigiemme Spa c. Media Trade Srl).

[46] *See*, most recently, Cass. civ., sez. III, 17 March 1993, no. 3173, in *GI* I (1994), 1, 1398.

The practical consequences of such a procedural abstraction could be very important, especially in those cases in which the promise to pay or the acknowledgement of a debt does not refer explicitly to any particular source of obligation. In this event promisors face a *probatio diabolica* because they bear the burden of proving the non-existence of any relationship that may justify the payment promised or the debt acknowledged.

B. Offer and Acceptance

1. The Consent of the Parties

Almost every legal system recognizes the general principle that a contract originates from the agreement of two or more parties and that it is substantially the expression of the consent of those parties to the promises made.[47] Article 1321 CC, in fact, states that a contract is the agreement of two or more parties to establish, regulate, or extinguish an economic[48] legal relationship among themselves.

The validity of this concept is undercut by art. 1333 CC, according to which an offer for the purpose of forming a contract that creates obligations for the offeror becomes binding if it is not timely rejected by the offeree. But in the absence of such rejection, the contract is concluded without the need of any acceptance.[49] The matter is still much debated among scholars.[50] The acceptance of an offer is nevertheless considered by the Civil Code as the standard form for the conclusion of a contract. This peculiar view is common to many systems belonging to the Western legal tradition.[51]

---

[47] *See* Kötz & Flessner, *European Contract Law -Vol. 1: Formation Validity and Content of Contracts; Contract and Third Parties* by Hein Kötz, translated from the German by Tony Weir, Oxford Clarendon Press (1997), p. 16*ff. See also* Monateri & Sacco, "*Contratto in Diritto Comparato*," in *Digesto*, 4th ed., Utet, Turin, p. 138.

[48] A legal relation is considered patrimonial if it has recognizable economic value.

[49] *See* R. Sacco, *supra* note 25; *id.*, "*Contratto e negozio a formazione unilaterale*," in *Studi in onore di P. Greco*, II, Milan (1965); F. Carresi, "*Contratti e atti unilaterali*," in *Studi in memoria di Vassalli* (1960); *id.*, "*Il contratto con obbligazioni del solo proponente*," in *Riv. dir. civ.* I (1974), 393; *id.*, "*Il contratto*," in *Trattato di dir. civile Cicu-Messineo*, Giuffrè, Milan (1987).

[50] *See* E. Roppo, *Contratto*, in *Digesto*, 4th ed., Utet, Turin (1987), p. 105; *see also* C. Massimo Bianca, *Diritto civile*, III, *Il contratto*, Giuffrè, Milan (1984); Bigliazzi, Geri, Breccia, Busnelli, & Natoli (eds.), *Diritto civile*, III, *Obbligazioni e contratti*, Utet, Turin (1989); Ravazzoni, *La formazione del contratto*, Milan (1966).

[51] *See* K. Zweigert & H. Kötz, *Introduction to Comparative Law*, 3rd rev. ed., translated from the German by Tony Weir, Oxford Clarendon Press (1998), p. 356*ff*.

2. Binding Force of the Offer

The first problem that arises concerns the binding force of an offer. While in common law systems the dominant rule is that an offer can always be revoked pursuant to the doctrine of consideration,[52] the Italian Civil Code regulates different situations in which the offer is deemed to be irrevocable or the revocation gives rise to liability.

Pursuant to article 1329 CC, if the offeror has bound himself to keep the offer open for a certain time, the revocation is without effect. Case law holds that the statement of a certain time limit for the validity of a revocable offer *ex* art. 1326 CC[53] is considered different from the statement of a period of irrevocability of the offer *ex* art. 1329 CC[54] If no period of irrevocability is specified, according to art. 1328 CC, the offer can be withdrawn at any time before the contract is concluded. If the accepting party has begun performance in good faith before having received notice of revocation, the offeror is bound to indemnify him for the expenses and losses suffered in beginning performance of the contract.[55]

Revocation of an offer to the public has to be made in the same or equivalent form as the offer.[56]

The Italian system, therefore, takes its stand halfway between the common law (full revocability) and the strict German approach to the binding force of an offer, thus placing it right alongside the French judicial approach to the matter.[57]

3. Acceptance and Conclusion of the Contract

Pursuant to article 1326 CC, a contract is formed at the moment the person who made the offer gains knowledge of the other party's acceptance. The acceptance

---

[52] Fuller & Eisenberg, *Basic Contract Law*, 7th ed., West Group (2001); J. Beatson (ed.), *Anson's Law of Contract*, 28th ed., Oxford Clarendon Press (1998).

[53] Article 1326 CC – Formation of Contract: "A contract is formed at the moment when he who made the offer has knowledge of the acceptance of the other party. The acceptance must reach the offeror within the time set by him or within that ordinarily necessary according to the nature of the transaction or usage. The offeror can treat late acceptance as effective, provided that he immediately so informs the other party. When the offeror requires a specific form of acceptance, the acceptance is ineffective if given in a different form. An acceptance that does not conform to the offer is equivalent to a new offer."

[54] *See* Cass. Civ., 11 January 1990 no. 41, in *Corriere giur.* (1990), 842.

[55] Article 1328 CC.

[56] Article 1336 CC.

[57] *See* K. Zweigert & H. Kötz, *supra* note 51, at 361.

may be revoked, but revocation must come to the knowledge of the offeror before acceptance. This general statement must be read together with the presumption of knowledge set forth in art. 1335 CC, according to which an offer, acceptance, and their revocation, and any other declaration directed to a given person, are deemed to be known at the moment they reach the address of the person to whom they are directed. For the rebuttal of this presumption, the addressee must prove that, without his fault, it was impossible for him to have received notice. The general rules set forth in articles 1326-1335 CC[58] therefore contrasts the Anglo-Saxon "mailbox rule" on contract formation.[59]

When, however, at the request of the offeror, or by the nature of the transaction or according to custom, the performance is to take place without a prior reply, the contract is concluded when performance begins.[60] According to some scholars, "offers calling for an act" – well-known in common law systems – fall into this latter conceptual category.[61]

In any event, the simple standard form of offer and acceptance is not necessarily the only, or even the typical, way in which a contract is concluded in commercial practice. Think of a sale of land in which the document is drafted by a notary[62] and signed simultaneously by both parties.[63] A more interesting example is presented by the complex negotiations among entrepreneurs, which entail various proposals, counter-offers, letters of intent, and memoranda before a binding and enforceable agreement is definitively reached. It is usually from such complex transactions that the problem of pre-contractual liability springs.

---

[58] Which is identical to the German rule in art. 130 BGB.

[59] *See* Monateri & Sacco, *supra* note 47, at 142.

[60] Article 1327 CC.

[61] *See, e.g.,* Gorla, *Promesse 'condizionate' ad una prestazione, supra* note 23; G. Sbisà, *La promessa al pubblico,* Milan (1974); G. Castiglia, *"Promesse unilaterali atipiche,"* in *Riv. dir. comm.* I (1983), 327, at 378. *Contra, see* Sacco, *supra* note 25, at 32*ff;* C.A. Graziani, *"Le promesse unilaterali,"* in *Tratt. di dir. priv. Rescigno,* 9, Utet, Turin (1982), 661; P. Spada, *"Cautio quae indiscrete loquitur: lineamenti funzionali e strutturali della promessa di pagamento,"* in *Riv. dir. civ.* I (1978), 673, at 742, footnote 173.

[62] The figure of the notary in Italian law, and the civil law generally, is quite different from its common law counterpart. It is more than a merely ministerial profession and in fact involves drafting contracts, counseling parties in economic transactions, and approving and certifying official State acts.

[63] The example is in Kötz & Flessner, *supra* note 47, at 17.

C. Liability and Preliminary Negotiations

Preliminary negotiations may be defined as including any communication prior to the time of acceptance.[64] The Italian Civil Code of 1942, which was drafted with paragraph 242 of the German BGB in mind, highlights the importance of "good faith" in contractual relationships throughout several articles: "Contract must be interpreted following good faith" (art. 1366); "Contract must be executed in good faith" (art. 1375); "Debtor and creditor must behave following the rules of good faith and fair dealing" (art. 1175); and finally the parties "must behave in good faith during the pre-contractual bargaining and contract drafting" (art. 1337).

1. Pre-Contractual Liability[65]

During preliminary negotiations in the bargaining process, parties are under the obligation of good faith and fair dealing. The cause of action is in tort.[66]

2. Foundation of Pre-Contractual Liability

Parties enter into a bargaining process under the principle of freedom of contract. Contract law after the 1942 Code has rejected the concept that an actual, subjective meeting of minds is necessary to form a contract and operates on a theory that protects the parties' reasonable expectations in relying on promises and communications.[67] Fair dealing obligations are also designed to enforce a standard of conduct in preliminary negotiations.

The current approach of the Italian courts is to consider pre-contractual liability

---

[64] Cass. 30 August 1995, no. 9157; Cass. 11 May 1990, no. 4051, *CG*, 1990, 832.

[65] G. Alpa, "Italian report to the XIIIth Congress International Academy of Comparative Law," in *Pre-contractual liability*, Kluwer (1991), p. 165.

[66] Sacco, in Sacco and De Nova (eds.), *Il contratto*, I, Turin (1993), p. 255; Cass. 4 October 1948, no. 1667, in *GI* (1949), I,1, 29; and other nine decisions up to Cass. 11 May 1990, no. 4051, in *Foro it.* (1991), I, 184; the opposite solution, similar to that of the German tradition, has been followed in Italy by Mengoni in *Riv. dir. comm.* II (1956), 365.

[67] Allara, *Teoria generale del contratto*, 2nd ed. (1955), p. 148*ff*; Martorano, *La tutela del compratore per vizi della cosa* (1959), p. 217; Pietrobon, *Errore, volontà e affidamento* (1990), no. 29*ff*; for the Italian case law, *see* Cass. 9 February 1952, no. 316, *GI* (1952), 1, 162; Cass. 20 May 1954, no. 1623, *GI*, I (1954), 1, 700; Cass. 22 May 1958, no. 1721; Cass. 9 October 1963, no. 2684 *Foro it.* (1963), I, 2088, and *Rivista di Diritto Commerciale* (hereinafter *RDCo*), II (1963), 468; Cass. 20 September 1978, no. 4240. Some authors, though, consider the rule to be still relied upon in the Italian courts.

an appropriate cause of action, especially in situations involving knowledge of contract invalidity and unjustified breakdown of negotiations.

3. Knowledge of Contract Invalidity

Article 1338 CC states, "[h]e, who knows or must know there is ground for contract invalidity and did not disclose it to the counterpart, has to pay the damages suffered by the other which relied, without fault, on the validity of the contract." The actor is protected by law only if he or she relied on the validity of the contract "without any fault;" generally the party that has ignored the rules respecting the formalities of the transaction is considered to be at fault.[68]

4. Unjustified Breakdown of Negotiations

Whenever the parties reach a stage during the bargaining process when one of them is induced to rely on the conclusion of the contract, the party who decides to abandon the negotiations without a valid justification is liable for damages. This is a classic situation in which article 1337 CC is applied,[69] and is the only common and frequent use that courts make of this article.

The withdrawal from negotiations, indeed, gives rise to liability only when it is unjustified. A better offer coming from a third party, or any other circumstances making the deal less favorable, may be considered a valid justification for withdrawal.[70]

5. "Culpa in Contrahendo": When a Valid Contract Has Been Concluded

Italian law frames this question as a "violation of the duty to disclose information." Some recent statutes have specified which kinds of information a bank must provide to the client (law no. 154 of 17 February 1992) and what information must be provided to investors by stock brokers (law no. 1 of 2 January 1991). Besides the special cases ruled by the statutes, it is possible to apply either art. 1439 CC on fraud or art. 1337 CC on pre-contractual liability. The article on fraud states that a contract is voidable when it has been entered into through trickery (frauds or

---

[68] Cass. 10 May 1950, no. 1205, in *Foro it.* (1950), I, 1307; Cass., 27 May 1960, no. 1358, in *Foro it.* (1960), I, 1508; Cass., 27 June 1972, no. 2199; Cass., 11 July 1972, no. 2325.

[69] Cass. 7 May 1952, no. 1279, in *Foro it.* (1952), I, 1638 and many similar decisions up to Cass. 5 March 1992, no. 2704, in *GI* I (1993), 1, 1560.

[70] App. Venezia, 6 July 1955, abridged in *Giust.civ., Mass. App. Venezia* (1955), 97; App. Roma, 20 May 1955, abridged in *Giur. civ., Mass. App. Roma* (1955), 72.

raggiri). "Failure to act" was once not considered a fraud, while today the old approach has become controversial.[71] According to court decisions, however, the party's behavior must in any event be intentional in order to be relevant.[72]

6. Duty to Inform

Whenever a party knows (or has reason to know) that the other party is lacking essential information about the transaction that could foreseeably cause damage, that party is under a duty to properly represent the situation, and possibly disclose the information.

Though widely supported by scholars, this doctrine is narrowly applied by courts. Italian scholars,[73] like the French, set the violations of the duty to inform within the doctrine of the lack of consent and link them to art. 1439 CC, which provides that the contract is void "when the deception employed by one of the contracting parties was such that, without it, the other contracting party would not have entered into the contract." The text is similar to French Civil Code art. 1116.[74]

The duty to disclose information has been broadened over time. Until recently, the legal sources were the Code articles which provide for invalidity of contracts vitiated by mistake, fraud or duress (arts. 1427-40) and the articles ordering the rescission of contracts made under the threat of danger or need (art. 1447*ff*) or in a state of diminished responsibility (art. 428).

During the last decade, unfair surprise, subliminal advertisement, the exploitation

---

[71] The following decisions are favorable to the relevance of a fraud by omission: Cass. 7 July 1976, no. 2528; Cass. 24 July 1976, no. 2961; Cass. 12 January 1991, no. 257; Cass. 14 October 1991, no. 10779, in *GI* I (1993), 1, 190; while the opposite has been held by Cass.18 January 1979, no. 363; Cass. 21 October 1981, no. 5503; Cass. 18 October 1991, no. 11038.

[72] Cass. 23 July 1960, no. 2119; Cass. Lav., 4. July 1981, n.4383, in *Giust. civ.* (1981), I, 2515.

[73] Liability arising from a non-disclosure is always dealt with along with pre-contractual good faith obligations. The most recent and relevant works on this topic are by D. Caruso, *La culpa in contrahendo.L'esperienza statunitense e quella italiana*, Milan (1993); Grisi, *L'obbligo precontrattuale di informazione*, Naples (1990); Nanni, *La buona fede contrattuale*, Padua (1988), pp. 1-143; Benatti, "*Culpa in contrahendo*," in *Contratto e Impresa* (1987), p. 287*ff*; Benatti, *La responsabilità precontrattuale*, Milan (1963); Cuffaro, *voce "Responsabilità precontrattuale*," in *Enciclopedia del diritto*, XXXIX, Milan (1988), p. 1265*ff*; Chiola, *voce "Informazione*," in *Enciclopedia giuridica Treccani;* Ferrarini, "*Investment banking, prospetti falsi e culpa in contrahendo*," in *Giur. comm.* II (1988), 585. Despite the large number of scholarly articles that take this position, it remains largely unreflected in the case law.

[74] R. Sacco & G. De Nova, "*Il Contratto*," in *Trattato di Diritto Civile*, directed by Rodolfo Sacco, Turin (1993), vol. I, 310.

of monopolistic as well of other dominant positions by one of the parties, as well as the problem of asymmetrical information, were regulated by new legislation, mostly flowing from European Community directives.[75] The most remarkable example of this trend is represented by the evolution of the doctrine of *culpa in contrahendo*. Article 1337 of the Civil Code prohibits bad faith during pre-contractual bargaining. That section which provides that the parties shall conduct themselves in good faith during preliminary negotiations, was created in order to implement the doctrine of *culpa in contrahendo*[76] after the influence of Von Jhering's legal thought on the Code drafters.[77] Article 1337 can be considered as a tool to implement a duty to disclose during negotiations, if it is conceived as a "general clause," which therefore stands on its own and implements an equitable principle without referring to any specific positive rule.[78] The EU-derived regulations now offer a model for the kind of fairness in negotiations that the legislator decided to rely upon.

Silence itself does not constitute fraud,[79] unless there has been a fraudulent concealment of true facts, or an explicit duty to speak enforced by the law has been violated.[80] Pursuant to article 1337 CC, the Code imposes a duty to bargain in good faith. This provision might be read in order to oblige the parties to inform each other when they discover the other party's mistake.

---

[75] *See* Gambaro, entry *"Codice Civile,"* in *Digesto* IV, Turin (1988), on the relationship between the importance of the Civil Code and the business transactions. The Civil Code rules are no longer able to regulate the world economy. A worldwide market is now taking over the internal one, the exchange of goods between individuals has been substituted by the trade between economic groups, or between these groups and the individuals, provoking a huge change in the contractual relationships.

[76] *See* the role of the *culpa in contrahendo* in Italy and in the United States in the excellent work of D. Caruso, *supra* note 73.

[77] Sacco & De Nova, *supra* note 74, at 356; Sacco foresaw a development of art. 1337's use as a contract liability threshold rule, in order to assure appropriate protection through the comparative evaluation of the parties' behavior, considering that the prevention of injustice in the contract is in the prevention of bad faith conducts.

[78] Rodota, *Il tempo delle clausole generali*, Riv. Crit. Dir. Priv. (1987), p. 709, and Di Majo, *Clausole generali e diritto delle obbligazioni*, Riv. Crit. Dir. Priv. (1984), p. 539, *contra* Castronovo, *L'avventura delle clausole generali*, Riv. Crit. Dir. Priv. (1986), p. 24.

[79] This statement could be found in a decision of the Trib. Verona, 18 November 1946, in *Foro pad.* (1947), p. 199. The sale of a truck, without disclosing that it belonged to the State, was considered fraudulent and voided.

[80] The Civil Code contains an explicit duty to disclose in arts. 1892-93 concerning insurance contracts.

Recent statutes regulating door-to-door contracts[81] and securities sales,[82] as well as *glasnost* in the financial services sector,[83] all deal with a new and broader concept of good faith and fair dealing which addresses those situations in which the parties do not have equal bargaining power. Other recent statutes require third parties to disclose all relevant information in order to help ensure that the contracting parties are more knowledgeable as they make their decisions to enter into a contract.[84]

The duty of corporations to have their balance sheets certified and published,[85] the mandatory publication of towns' zoning plans, the expiration date on pharmaceutical products and packed food, the duty to issue a truthful *prospectus* of the companies' assets[86] and the ban on deceptive advertising[87] are only a few examples of a growing phenomenon.

On the one hand, the principle of "transparency" is clearly emerging and we may foresee the rapid extension of its use outside of the specific contexts in which it was originally introduced.[88] On the other hand, we are gradually abandoning, at least in scholarship and legislation, the so-called "will principle," and heading instead toward solutions similar to the German law on *überraschende Klauseln*, and the American doctrines of *reasonable expectation* and *unconscionability*.[89]

---

[81] Law no. 216 of 7 June 1974, *decreto legislativo* no. 95 of 8 April 1974, modified by the EEC directive 89/298, enacted by the *decreto legislativo* no. 74 of 25 January 1992, law no. 428 of 29 December 1990.

[82] Law no. 1 of 2 January 1991, in *GU* no. 3 of 4 January 1991.

[83] Law no. 154 of 17 February 1992.

[84] G. Alpa, "*La 'trasparenza' del contratto nei settori bancario, finanziario e assicurativo,*" in *GI* IV (1992), 409, and De Nova, "*Informazione e contratto: il regolamento contrattuale,*" in *Riv. trim. dir. civ.* (1993), 705.

[85] DPR no. 136 of 31 March 1975.

[86] EEC directive 80/310, law no. 281 of 4 June 1985 and law no. 428 of 29 December 1990.

[87] *Decreto legislativo* no. 74 of 25 January 1992.

[88] The "transparency" principle is visible in all Italian legislation of European derivation (*see* all the previously cited statutes). It could be divided into a "direct principle" and an "indirect principle." The first appears when the information is given straight from the bargaining party together with the contract text, the title, or the good, through informative notes, annexes, prospect tables, or advertising messages; the second appears when the information is in the hands of a third party, who has the duty to disclose it in a truthful way. Such is the case for accountants, banks, or finance brokers. Consumer protection and favoring the lay person are linked to the transparency principle.

[89] The contract is increasingly becoming a frame in which the will of the parties is of decreasing importance.

7. Damages

Reliance damages (*interesse negativo*) are recoverable in cases of unjustified withdrawal.[90] For instance, all expenses incurred by a prospective landlord in order to restructure a rental space to fit the requirements of a prospective lessee must be refunded when the negotiation has been interrupted without a well-founded reason.[91] In such cases, the amount of damages can never exceed the value of the prospective contract.[92]

III. Conditions of Substantive Validity

A. Capacity of the Parties

The capacity to have rights enjoyed by all persons[93] must be distinguished from the capacity to enter into legal transactions. Any person who has not been formally declared incapable of entering into legal transactions by the law may enter into a contract. In the Civil Code, scattered articles on legal capacity may be found in the sections on "Obligations"[94] and "Persons and Family."[95]

The fundamental principle regarding these matters is that legal transactions involving a person lacking capacity must be concluded by a statutory guardian who acts in the name and on behalf of one deemed incapable. The agent's consent may be given *ex post*. The guardian is generally under court supervision, and specific court permits are required for important transactions.[96]

Italian law treats persons who are wholly lacking capacity and persons partially lacking capacity to enter into legal transactions differently.[97] Article 414 CC states that a person under a permanent incapacity must be declared incapable. A legal

---

[90] Cass. 12 February 1982, no. 855; Cass. 25 January 1988, no. 582.

[91] Trib. Roma, 25 September 1973, in *Temi Romana* (1974), 89.

[92] R. Sacco & G. De Nova, *supra* note 74, vol. II, at 568 and 575*ff*.

[93] Article 3 of the Italian Constitution (1948).

[94] Articles 1190-91 CC and arts. 1425-26 CC.

[95] Book I, Title XII, arts. 414-32 CC.

[96] Article 374 CC.

[97] Those wholly lacking capacity include minors (*see infra*) and persons placed under conservatorship. Those partially lacking capacity include minors who obtained the *emancipatio* and the *inabilitati* pursuant to art. 415 CC. The former always need a representative, while the latter may act under the guidance of a guardian.

transaction or a contract is voidable when it has been entered into by a person legally determined to lack capacity.[98] Persons *momentarily* under incapacity may render a transaction void only if they prove the existence of incapacity at the time of the transaction. Such annulment claims are subject to a five-year limitation.[99]

1. Minors

A minor is a person who has not reached the age of eighteen. Married minors can obtain the *emancipatio* by filing a request with the court. If the minor is declared emancipated by the court, he or she may then act independently from a guardian, but only with respect to those issues that do not exceed ordinary management. In cases of decisions exceeding the ordinary course of business,[100] the statutory guardian must counsel the minor under court supervision.[101]

A payment to a minor is not valid if the debtor does not prove that it has been made to the minor's benefit.[102] The due payment made by the minor cannot be revoked because of incapacity.[103]

The mere statement by a minor that he or she is of age does not bar a claim for contractual annulment. On the contrary, fraudulent behavior by minors in order to misrepresent their age renders the contract fully valid and enforceable.[104]

2. Insanity

As mentioned above, a legal transaction or contract is void when entered into by a person lacking capacity. An insane person placed by judicial act under full court-supervised conservatorship does not require any further evidence of his or her incapacity and, even when acting in a lucid period, all transactions into which he or she has entered are voidable. Criminals subject to sentences of a certain degree of severity are placed under conservatorship. The Civil Code also affords a status of minor incapacity for those considered prodigals, spendthrifts, or "mental defectives" (a distasteful term). The law treats such persons as *inabilitati*, and may

---

[98] Article 1425 CC.

[99] Article 428 CC.

[100] Decisions concerning real property provide an example.

[101] Article 394 CC.

[102] Article 1190 CC.

[103] Article 1191 CC.

[104] Article 1426 CC.

place them under the supervision of a guardian. Under article 415 CC blind persons, deaf-mutes from birth, drunkards, and drug addicts are afforded the same protection.

B. Absence of Consent

Article 1427 CC declares that the contract might be annulled if consent was given only by error, or was extorted by duress, or obtained by deceit.

1. Mistake

The rules in the Italian Civil Code (artt.1427-33) have been influenced by Austrian, Swiss and French law.[105] The Italian Civil Code provides that a contracting party whose consent was given by mistake can demand annulment of the contract (art. 1427) when the mistake is essential and recognizable by the other contracting party at the time of the contract's making (art. 1428).[106]

The Code contains a long list of cases in which the mistake could be considered essential, (art. 1429 CC) and it requires that the parties should have been able to recognize the mistake by exercising reasonable and proper care.[107] The difference in the level of sophistication of the parties' (art. 1431 CC) can be a sufficient ground for the court to assert that the mistake was recognizable.[108]

---

[105] K. Zweigert & H. Kötz, *supra* note 51, at 419. U. Mattei, *"Errore e raggiro nei Contratti in diritto comparato,"* in *Digesto Discepline Privatistiche Civile*, Torino, Utet, 1990.

[106] The Civil Code deals with mistake in the following articles: 1428 CC – Relevance of mistake: "Mistake is cause of annulment of a contract when it is essential (1429) and recognizable (1431) by the other contracting party"; 1429 CC – Essential mistake: "Mistake is essential: 1) when it concerns the nature or the object of contract; 2) when it concerns the identity of the object of the performance or a quality of said object which, according to common understanding or under the circumstances, should be considered determinative of consent; 3) when it concerns the identity or personal qualities of the other contracting party, so long as the one or the others were determinative of consent; 4) when the mistake was one of law and was the only or the principal reason for entering into the contract"; 1431 CC – Recognizable Mistake: "A mistake is considered recognizable when, with respect to the content, the circumstances of the contract, or the quality of the contacting parties, it would have been detected by a person of normal diligence."

[107] Cass. 16 May 1960, no. 1177, *GI*, I, 1, 112 noted by G. Amorth.

[108] Pietrobon, *supra* note 67, at 220*ff*.

a. Mistake as to the Essential Substance

Another way to annul a contract of sale is to demonstrate that the goods contracted for are completely different from those received. This is a claim for lack of quality (sale of *aliud pro alio*) in the object, pursuant to art. 1497 CC. Whenever the thing sold lacks the qualities promised or those essential for its intended use, the buyer is entitled to obtain dissolution of the contract according to the general provisions on dissolution for non-performance (art. 1453*ff*), provided that the defect in quality exceeds the limits of tolerance established by usage. However, the right to obtain dissolution is subject to the rules on forfeiture (arts. 2964*ff* and 1495 para.1 CC) and prescription (arts. 2946*ff* and 1495 para.3 CC) stated in art. 1495 CC.[109]

The defendant will likely raise the argument that the goods are within tolerable limits of quality. This is a situation in which the facts at issue are more relevant than the applicable law.[110] In *Automega s.p.a. v. Pezzillo*, the Tribunale, the Court of Appeals of Palermo, and finally the Italian Supreme Court[111] held that the sale of a "Mercedes Benz 190 full optioned" was vitiated by a lack of quality due to the fact that the air conditioner was not an original Mercedes option but had been installed separately in Palermo.[112]

b. Mistake as to the Person

Mistake as to the person is a ground of annulment only in contracts where the identity of the contracting party is a fundamental ground of consent.[113] Examples are the so-called "utmost good faith contracts," in which the relationships between parties has a strong trustee nature (*i.e.* insurance, labor, and partnership).

---

[109] Cass. 1981, no. 247; Cass. 1969, no. 3695; Cass. 1967, no. 2488; Rubino, *"Compravendita,"* in *Trattato Cicu e Messineo*; Bianca, *supra* note 50, at 589.

[110] Cass. 1995, no. 3550; Cass. 1977, no. 4923.

[111] Trib. Palermo, 7 October 1989; A. Palermo, 7 June 1991; Cass. 25 March 1995, no. 3550.

[112] Before the 1942 Code, the Italian courts considered the sale of a painting as a risk contract: "… one who has sold an ancient painting, ignoring its artistic value, cannot, once discovered, plead to annul the sale for factual mistake" or "once sold an ancient painting without a warranty about the value … there is no fraud by the vendor, nor substantial mistake that could annul the sale" (A. Firenze 15 March 1910 *Filangeri*, 1910, 459). The approach did not change after the new Code, but few cases have recently arisen. An Italian court, indeed, used both the former doctrine of risk contract (*contratto aleatorio*) and the new doctrine of essential mistake on quality (art. 1429 no. 2 CC) in the case of a Carraccio painting sold for a few liras by an antique store (A. Roma 23 November 1948 *RDCo* II (1949), 192 note by Sacco.

[113] Article 1429 para. 3 CC.

2. Fraud (Deceit)

Article 1439 of the Civil Code declares that fraud is a cause for annulment of the contract when the deception carried on by one of the contracting parties was such that without it, the other contracting party would not have entered into the contract. If the deception was committed by a third party, the contract is voidable if said deception was known to the party who benefited from it. If the deception was not such as to compel consent, the contract is valid, even though without the deception it would have included different terms. However, the contracting party in bad faith is liable for damages.[114]

A deception that arises from innocent misrepresentation is not fraud, nor is the exaggerated praise of one's own ware (*dolus bonus*). Italian courts face some difficulties in according the annulment of a contract for non-disclosure amounting to misrepresentation.[115] In *Manifatture Spugne v. Intermarittima*, for example, the Supreme Court said that in order to decide whether fraud had occurred, the silence or concealment by one party must be construed taking into consideration the subjective conditions of the other party.[116] Many authors think that a misrepresentation amounting to deceit could be found in fraud perpetrated through the failure to do something (*dolo negativo*).

As noted, silence by itself does not amount to fraud, unless an express duty to speak has been violated.[117] In order to consider a legal duty to speak violated, the plaintiff must convince the court that art. 1337 CC imposes a general duty to speak during negotiations. *Banca Manusardi* is the only case in which a court has accepted such legal reasoning; there, the court concluded that a bank that failed to disclose information concerning the economic situation of a company whose stocks it wanted to sell was liable for violation of art. 1337 CC. The decisions of the Court of Appeals of Milan have a strong influence all over Italy. However, the issue in that case was peculiar since the liability of a professional institution toward consumers in the sale of securities.[118]

---

[114] Article 1440 CC.

[115] The criminal law courts, indeed, are using it; moreover the civil *dolo* and the criminal *truffa* are to be constituted by the same factual situation; *see* Cass. 1986, no. 7322.

[116] Cass. 12 January 1991, no. 257.

[117] *See supra* part II C 6, "Duty to inform."

[118] App. Milan, 2 February 1990, in *GI* I (1992), 2, 49, note by M. Arietti.

3. Duress

Civil Code art. 1434 states that duress is ground for annulment even if it has been committed by a third party. There is no definition of duress in the Code, but it is fair to say that it consists of physical or moral restraint upon the will of a person, which induces him or her to give consent. The nature of the duress must be such as to induce a sane person to fear that an unjust wrong will be done to him or to his goods.[119]

4. Laesio

The Code describes two totally different kinds of action under the heading *"recissione del contratto"* (contract recission). Article 1437 CC refers to maritime salvage (art. 7 law no. 938 of 14 June 1925) and covers contracts that has been signed under dangerous circumstances. The party in danger may subsequently rescind the contract, but the judge may grant an equitable compensation to the rescuer.

Article 1448 CC rules the general action of *laesio* or undue harm. In the Code, the action is subjectively rather than objectively grounded and is therefore difficult to prove. In order to rescind a contract for undue harm, the following conditions must be met: (i) one party is in a situation of need, (ii) the other is exploiting the situation, and (iii) the party in need is prejudiced by loss or a pecuniary disadvantage of more than a half of the value that is the subject matter of the contract. According to the Italian Supreme Court, all of these conditions must be jointly met.[120]

Most Italian authors are convinced that an objective value should be attributed to the *laesio*.[121] The extremely difficult evidentiary regime makes this action unappealing as an effective contractual remedy.

5. "Presupposizione" (Contractual Basic Assumption)

Another doctrine that leads to the annulment of the contract is the doctrine of "basic contractual assumption."[122] When parties reach an agreement on an implied

---

[119] Article 1435 CC.

[120] Cass. no. 2071, 1978; Cass. no. 5040, 1978; Cass. no. 5535, 1981; Cass. no. 6732, 1982; Cass. no. 7709, 1987).

[121] R. Sacco & G. De Nova, *supra* note 74, vol. I, at 477; Gazzoni, *Trattato di diritto privato*, Padua (1995), p. 456.

[122] The doctrine of *presupposizione* has a German origin; Windscheid was considering a factual situation in which the reason for the contract was so important that it became its real cause,

basic assumption which is left indefinite there is a strong possibility that the missing term may be inferred by the court from attendant circumstances.[123] Italian courts often find *presupposizione* in the sale of land contracts[124] and in relational contracts. The courts have considered art. 1467 CC on contracts for mutual counter-performance as an explicit adoption of the *presupposizione* principle by the legislature.[125]

According to the Tribunal of Milan in *Banca Manusardi*, the *presupposizione* and essential mistake are two different aspects of the same factual situation. The principle of good faith (*buona fede*, *ex* arts. 1337 and 1375 CC) adds new strength to arguments in favor of the use of the *presupposizione* theory as a practical criterion for contract interpretation.[126]

---

and the reason becomes "*Voraussetzung,*" Örtmann, *Die Geschäftsgrundlage. Ein neuer Rechtsbegriff* (1921), and Larenz, *Geschäftsgrundlage und Vertragserfüllung* (1963), modified the doctrine considering the concept of contract ground: if the contract ground is substantially modified, the contract itself will not be enforceable. The English coronation cases, such as *Krell v. Henry*, (1903) 2 K.B. 740, offer a factual example of a situation in which the *Geschäftsgrundlage* could have been invoked. *See* A. Pontani, *La presupposizione nella sua evoluzione, con particolare riferimento all'errore ed alla causa, Quadrimestre* (1991), p. 833.

[123] Cass. 17 September 1970, no. 1512, *Foro. it.* (1971), I, 3028; Cass. 7 April 1971, no. 1025 *Foro it.* (1971), I, 2574; Cass. 22 September 1981, no. 5168, *Foro it.* (1982), I, 104; Cass. 31 October 1989, no. 4554, *Riv. di Diritto Civile* (hereinafter *RDC*) (1990), II, 350; Cass. 11 August 1990, no. 8200; Cass. 3 December 1991, no. 12921, *GI* (1992), I, 1, 2210 noted by ODDI: the latter is a case of a stock purchase subsequently annulled when the only immovable good in the company asset was under an Action to Obtain Revocation (art. 2901 CC); Cass. 1995, no. 1040; Cass. 1995, no. 8689: the sale of company shares under the implied term that the company owns a boat as its single estate.

[124] Cass. 1983 no. 6933, Cass. 1984, no. 5512.

[125] Cass. 1995, no. 1040; Cass. 31 October 1989, no. 4554, *RDC* (1990), II, 350; Cass. 1986, no. 20. Article 1467 CC – Contract for Mutual Counter-performances: "In contracts for continuous or periodic performance or for deferred performance, if extraordinary and unforeseeable events make the performance of one of the parties excessively onerous, the party who owes such performance can demand dissolution of the contract, with the effects set forth in art. 1458. Dissolution cannot be demanded if the supervening onerousness is part of the normal risk of the contract. A party against whom dissolution is demanded can avoid it by offering to modify equitably the conditions of the contract."

[126] Trib. Milano, 11 October 1948, in *Diritto del Lavoro* (hereinafter *DL*) (1949), II, 17, where the mistake concerned the essential quality of the counterpart, but the judges used the *presupposizione* doctrine instead of the essential mistake rule; this favors a broad interpretation of the *presupposizione* Cass. 3 October 1972, no. 2828.

If the *presupposizione* is read as a new kind of mistake[127] the remedy is annulment (art.1441 CC).[128]

C. Other Conditions of Validity

As already noted, art. 1325 CC mentions *causa* as the second contractual requirement. Article 1343 CC, moreover, provides that *causa* is illicit when it proves contrary to mandatory rules, public policy, *ordine publicco* or good morals.

A contractual obligation is valid only if it has a legal *causa*. The Code drafters adopted an objective theory of *causa* as the economic and social function of the contract. The presence of a cause does not signify the existence of a bargain. Though it functionally overlaps the common law doctrine of consideration, the doctrine of cause should not be viewed as a version of consideration, but as one of the distinguishing marks of the French Civil Code influence on Italian law.[129]

Article 1343 CC, by calling on the broad concept of mandatory rules, public policy, and good morals, offers the judge a powerful tool to test the compatibility of the contractual situation with the fundamental values of the legal order.[130]

1. Mandatory Rules

The mandatory nature of a private law rule is, due to public interest, protected by the rule itself. The case law does not consider mandatory private dispositions when their violation is not directly sanctioned by invalidity.[131] Tax regulations do not have a direct effect on contractual *causa*.[132] The violation of a criminal rule does not immediately imply the invalidity of the contract – rather, the contract is void when it requires one of the parties to commit a crime.[133] But in those situations in which the criminal rule violated does not protect public interest, the contract may

---

[127] *See* note following Pietrobon, *supra* note 67, at 357, and Bianca, *Diritto Civile*, 3, *Il Contratto* (1987), p. 610, it is possible to create a new hypothesis of essential mistake independently from those stated in art. 1429 CC. *See*, Sacco, *supra* note 25, at 389.

[128] The difference between the annulment and voiding of an agreement, which has recently bee the subject of scholarly controversy, depends how the judge interprets the circumstances.

[129] *See* G. Gorla, *Il Contratto*, *supra* note 23, for further information.

[130] Cass. no. 4700 (1988).

[131] Cass. no. 6601 (1982).

[132] Cass. no. 4024 (1981); Cass. no. 5571 (1981).

[133] Cass. no. 1728 (1977).

stand.[134] The great number of criminal regulations produced by the Italian legislature suggests the usefulness of this approach.

2. Illegality and Public Policy

The basic idea in this area of contract law is that private individuals cannot disregard public policy through their private obligations and contracts.[135] The Constitution of 1948 is the basic source of legal principles and values characterizing the Italian legal system. Economic and public policy comprises a large amount of recent mandatory legislation on consumer contracts, rent restrictions, insurance, labor law, and many other fields.

A contract in which a worker sold his position of employment to another worker, for example, has been held contrary to public policy.[136] Contracts by which the employer collects money in exchange for providing employment are illicit.[137] It is contrary to public policy to pay the other party in a civil trial to proceed in a certain manner during litigation.[138] It is also contrary to public policy to buy political and electoral consent during an election.[139]

D. The Consequences of Absence of Consent or Lack of Substantive Quality

1. Defect of Consent

A contract vitiated by mistake, fraud or duress can be annulled. However, the party who suffered the fraud, the mistake or the duress bears the burden to enforce the right to annulment against the other party. When the fraud generates an essential mistake, the plaintiff may be better off by seeking annulment for mistake (*azione di annullamento*) rather than for fraud because the objective evidence of the mistake is easier to reach than the mental evidence of the fraud.[140]

The action for fraud (arts. 1441-46 CC) and the action brought for lack of quality or warranty against defects (*azione redibitoria* – arts. 1490 and 1495 CC) are

---

[134] Cass. no. 6601 (1982).

[135] Cass. no. 4769 (1989); Cass. no. 8 (1990); Cass. no. 3181 (1990).

[136] Cass. no. 2859 (1974).

[137] App. Napoli, 2 February 1967, *Giust. Civ.* (1967), I, 1359.

[138] Trib. Genova, 17September 1984, *NGCC* (1985), I, 65.

[139] Cass. no. 1574 (1971).

[140] Bianca, *Il Contratto, supra* note 127.

independent from one another, though both legal theories can be considered concurrently in the same factual situation.[141]

The real differences between the two actions are based on evidentiary grounds and on the limitation on actions. Only those persons whose interest is protected by the provision grounding invalidity can seek annulment of the contract. The claim is barred by prescription after five years. Whenever the lack of validity depends on a defect of consent, the period of the claim's validity begins on the day upon which the fraud or mistake was discovered. The defendant in an action for performance of the contract can plead invalidity even if the claim for annulment has already been barred by prescription.

A contract lacking one of its essential elements (consent, licit cause, object) is void under Italian law. The parties thereto, as well as all other interested persons can always oppose the party who wants to enforce the contract by affirming its nullity. Moreover, if the contract is void the action to obtain a declaration of nullity can be brought by anyone, provided that they have an interest in the matter, and the court may declare a contract void *ex officio*, while resolving a controversy or dispute arising from it. By contrast, in cases of *annullabilità* (that is, merely voidable and not void) the only party entitled to seek annulment is the one whose protection has formed the basis of legal invalidity. The claim is barred by prescription after five years. While the person who could have claimed the annulment may validate a voidable contract pursuant to art. 1444 CC, a void contract can never be validated by anyone, and the claim to obtain a declaration of nullity is barred by prescription after 20 years.

2. Lack of Substantive Quality

In an *azione redibitoria*, the buyer is entitled to the action for lack of quality or to a breach of warranty against defects. The warranty is forfeited if he or she fails to notify the seller of the defects within eight days from the date of discovery, unless a different time limit is established by the parties or by the law.[142] Such notification is not necessary if the seller has disclosed the existence of the defects. The claim is barred one year from delivery; but the buyer who sued for performance of the contract can always plead the breach of warranty, provided that he or she had notified the seller of the product's defect within eight days of its discovery and within one year of the product's delivery.

---

[141] Cass. no. 1573 (1968).

[142] In the independent contract for building construction, the terms are longer as provided by arts. 1667-68 CC.

The plaintiff in such an action could also possibly claim the dissolution of contract for non-performance (*azione di risoluzione per inadempimento*) in all cases in which the contractual promise made by the defendant was materially and legally possible (art. 1453 CC). In such a case, damages will be measured by taking into consideration both the loss suffered by the creditor and the lost profits, insofar as they are the direct and immediate consequence of non-performance.[143]

IV. Termination

A. Performance and Breach

1. Characteristics of Performance

The purpose of the contract is performance of the parties, and full performance is its natural conclusion: it is what the parties have in mind when they enter into the agreement. In this sense, performance means the exact fulfillment of the promises made. The Italian phraseology *esatto adempimento* (exact performance) refers precisely to this concept.[144]

Articles 1176 to 1200 of Title I, Book 4 on Obligations of the Italian Civil Code lay down the default rules that regulate exact performance. Other provisions on performance can be found in Titles II and III of the same Book 4. Scattered examples include art. 1375 CC (imposing a duty to perform the contract in good faith), arts. 1477 and 1510 CC (regulating in detail the phase of delivery in a contract of sale), and art. 1710 CC (setting forth rules on performance of the contract of mandate (*mandato*)).

As regards the conduct of the parties in the course of performance, art. 1176 CC sets forth two different levels of care and diligence. The first is the so-called "*bonus paterfamilias* standard of care." This is the general standard of care, which is based upon the idealized reasonable man. The second standard is higher and it refers to the obligations undertaken by persons acting in their professional capacity (lawyers, accountants, doctors, consultants, etc.). This standard requires a higher level of care proportionate to the special knowledge of professionals and to the nature of the activity as well as its social implications.

---

[143] Bianca, *supra* note 140, at 628-29.

[144] Mengoni, "*Responsabilità contrattuale (diritto vigente)*," in *Enc. dir.*, XXXIX, Milan (1988), p. 1072; Bessone, *Adempimento e rischio contrattuale*, Milan (1969), p. 121*ff*; Alpa, *I contratti in generale. Introduzione alla nuova giurisprudenza*, Turin (1990).

The parties to a contract, moreover, must behave according to the fundamental rules of fairness, pursuant to art. 1175 CC. And, according to art. 1375 CC, they must comply with the duty of good faith in performance.[145] The violation of the good faith principle during negotiations does not amount to a breach of contract and it does not offer grounds for dissolution pursuant to art. 1453 CC. Instead, bad faith conduct gives rise to a claim for pre-contractual liability under the rules of arts. 1337, 1338 and 1427 CC.[146]

As a general rule, in contracts providing for mutual counter-performance, when one of the parties fails to perform his obligations properly, he is considered in breach, and the other party can choose to demand either exact performance or termination. The non-breaching party is also entitled to recover compensation for damages suffered as a consequence of the breach (arts. 1453 and 1223 CC).[147]

2. Dissolution for Breach

Breach of contract opens up to the non-defaulting party a choice between (i) a claim to obtain performance, and (ii) a claim to dissolve and terminate the contract.

Termination can be demanded even when an action has been brought to demand performance. But performance can no longer be demanded after an action for termination has been brought (art. 1453 para. 2 CC).[148] This prohibition to switch

---

[145] The Italian Supreme Court recently reaffirmed the importance, at an operational level, of the general principle of good faith in contract performance. *See* Cass. Civ., sez. I, 20 April 1994, no. 3775 (Comune di Fiuggi v. Ente Fiuggi s.p.a.), in *GI* I (1995), 1, 852 e in *Foro it.* (1995), I, 1296. As for scholarly writings on this topic *see*, *i.e.*, L. Bigliazzi Geri, *Buona Fede nel diritto civile*, in *Digesto* IV ed., Disc. Priv., Sez. Civ., II, Turin (1988), 154; *id.*, "*La buona fede nel diritto privato (spunti ricostruttivi),*" in *Il principio di buona fede – Quaderni della Scuola Superiore di studi universitari e di perfezionamento*, vol. III, Giuffrè, Milan (1987), p. 51*ff*; S. Rodotà, "*Appunti sul principio di buona fede,*" in *Foro pad.* (1964), I, 1284*ff*; Bianca, "*La nozione di buona fede quale regola di comportamento contrattuale,*" in *Riv. dir. civ.* (1983), I, 205*ff*; U. Natoli, *L'attuazione del rapporto obbligatorio*, t. 1, Milan (1974); Nanni, *La buona fede contrattuale*, Padua (1988); A. Monti, "Learned Hand Formula *e Buona Fede nell'Esecuzione del Contratto. Analisi Economica e Comparata,*" in *Riv. Critica del Diritto Privato* (1998) no. 1-2, 125.

[146] Cass. 19 November 1994, no. 9802, *Rass. Locaz. e condominio* (1995), 65, note by Guida.

[147] Monateri, *La responsabilità contrattuale e precontrattuale*, Turin (1997); G. De Nova, *Recesso e risoluzione nei contratti*, Milan (1994); Palmieri, *La responsabilità contrattuale*, Milan (1994); Giardina, *Responsabilità contrattuale e responsabilità extracontrattuale – Significato attuale di una distinzione tradizionale*, Milan (1993).

[148] Cass. 2 March 1996 no. 1636, *GC* (1996), I, 1963; in the *ius variandi* Cass. 27 November 1996 no. 10506; Cass. 27 March 1996 no. 2715; Cass. 17 April 1996 no. 3623; Cass. 22

from a claim for termination to a claim for performance is not, however, an absolute and immutable principle of the Italian law of contract. In fact, The Italian Supreme Court recently held that a claim for performance of a contract is permissible following the rejection of the claim for its termination, or after such claim was time-barred.[149]

The party in breach, in any event, can no longer perform his obligation at will after the claim for termination has been filed (art. 1453 para. 3 CC).[150] The other party can serve written notice on the defaulting party to perform within an appropriate time, declaring that unless performance takes place within such time the contract shall be deemed dissolved (art. 1454 CC).[151] The time period cannot be less than 15 days unless the parties have agreed otherwise or a shorter period appears justified by the nature of the contract or by usage. If the time elapses without performance, the contract is dissolved by operation of law.[152]

A contract cannot be dissolved if the non-performance of one of the parties is of slight importance with respect to the interest of the other (art. 1455 CC). The court evaluates such importance on a case-by-case basis. The determination of the criteria is difficult, and rather controversial among scholars.[153] The contracting parties can

---

December 1995 no. 12092; Cass. 19 December 1995 no. 12943; Cass. 24 May 1993 no. 5838, *GI* (1994), I, 1, 1376; Cass. 27 March 1996 no. 2715; Cass. 22 July 1993 no. 8192; Cass. 2 June 1992 no. 6701.

[149] Cass. 11 May 1996 no. 4444, *Corr. Giur.* (1996), 898 noted by Carnevali, *GI* I (1997), 1, 1121, note by Casola, *Contratti* (1997), 121, note by Zappata, *Nuova Giur. Civ.* (1997), I, 742, no. Cubeddu; Cass. 9 February 1995 no. 1457, *GI* (1996), I, 1, 1150 noted by Lascialfari.

[150] Cass. 14 February 1994 no. 1460, *GI* (1995), I, 1, 1379 note by Vitiello; Trib. Bari, 7 October 1994, *Giur. Pugliese* (1995), 13.; Cass. S.U. 10 April 1995 no. 4126, *GC* (1995), I, 2394; *Corr. Giur.* (1995), 557 note by Carbone.

[151] Cass. 27 January 1996 no. 639, *Vita not.* (1996), 853; Cass. 29 January 1996 no. 908; Cass. 8 April 1997 no. 3446.

[152] Spirito, *Diffida ad adempiere e risoluzione del contratto, Corr. Giur.* (1994), 838 commenting on Cass. 4 May 1994 no. 4275.

[153] The Italian literature on the issue is immense; recent contributions include: Monateri, *La responsabilità contrattuale e precontrattuale*, Turin (1997); G. De Nova, *Recesso e risoluzione nei contratti*, Milan (1994); Sacco & De Nova, *supra* note 66, vol. II, at 599; De Lorenzi, *Inadempimento doloso*, Dig. IV, IX, Turin (1993), p. 360; De Nova, *Risoluzione dei contratti di fornitura dei sistemi informatici*, commenting on Trib. Torino, 13 March 1993 *Contratti*, b 1993, 440.

The case law is a fundamental ground for evaluating the standard set by the courts in evaluating the importance of the non performance: Cass. 14 February 1994 no. 1460, *GI*

expressly agree that the contract will be dissolved if a specified obligation is not performed in the designated manner.[154] In this case, dissolution takes place *ex lege* by a simple declaration of the non-defaulting party when the breach occurs (art. 1456 CC).[155]

If the time set for performance by one of the parties is expressly considered as essential to the interest of the other, the latter must notify the former within three days (unless there is an agreement or usage to the contrary) should they intend to demand performance of the obligation notwithstanding the expiration of the time. In the absence of such a notice, the contract is deemed dissolved by operation of law, even if dissolution was not expressly agreed upon (art. 1457 CC).[156]

Dissolution of a contract for non-performance has retroactive effect as between the parties, except in the case of contracts for continuous or periodic performance (with respect to which the dissolution's effect does not extend to performance already rendered) (art. 1467 CC). Dissolution, even if expressly agreed upon (art. 1456 CC), does not prejudice rights acquired by third parties, except for the effects of transcription (art. 2652 para. 1 CC) of the claim for dissolution (art. 1458 CC).[157]

Non-performance by one of the parties in multilateral contracts does not cause dissolution of the contract with respect to the others, unless the non-performance of such party must be considered essential to them under the circumstances (arts. 1446, 1459 and 1466 CC).[158]

(1995), I, 1, 1379; Cass. 16 February 1994 no. 1507, *FI* (1995), I, 3548; Cass. 7 June 1993 no. 6367, *GI* (1994), I, 1, 1209; Pret. Torino, 5 April 1994, *Giur. Piemontese* (1995), 126.

[154] Amadio, *La condizione d'inadempimento*, Padua (1996); Barone, Chirico, Cirillo & Di Meo, *La clausola risolutiva espressa. Rassegna di giurisprudenza 1942-1992*, Padua (1993).

[155] Cass. 17 May 1995 no. 5436, *GI* (1996), I, 1, 367; Cass. 26 March 1997 no. 2674.; Trib. Cagliari, 28 February 1995 *Riv. giur. Sarda* (1996), 405; Cass. 18 June 1997 no. 5455.

[156] Cass. 24 February 1993 no. 2263, *FI* (1993), I, 3447; Trib. Piacenza 2 May 1994, *Arch. civ.* (1995), 406; App. Perugia 22 January 1993, *Rass. giur. umbra* (1993), 257 and recently Cass. 27 February 1996 no. 1537; Cass. 3 March 1997 no. 1851.

[157] Di Majo, *Risoluzione del contratto ed effetti restitutori: debito di valore o debito di valuta?*, commenting on Cass. S.U. 4 December 1992 no. 12942 *Corr. giur.* (1993), 322; *id.*, "*Restituzioni e responsabilità nelle obbligazioni e nei contratti*," in *Riv. crit. dir. priv.* (1994), 291. Cass. 24 February 1995 no. 2135, *GI* (1995), I, 1, 1632; Cass. 16 February 1994 no. 2456, *GI* (1994), I, 1, 680; Trib. Potenza 20 June 1991, *Merito* 1993, 364; Trib. Cagliari 29 April 1991, *Riv. giur. Sarda* (1993), 29; App. Milano 4 March 1994 *Società e dir.* (1994), 508.

[158] App. Roma 15 July 1997 no. 2413; Pret. Forlì 31 May 1993, *GC* (1994), I, 815 noted by Cali.

B. The Effect of Supervening Events

1. Supervening Impossibility

According to art. 1463 CC, in contracts providing for mutual counter-performance, the party released for supervening impossibility (art. 1256 CC) cannot demand performance by the other party, and is bound to restore that which was already received in accordance with the rules concerning restitution of payments not due (art. 2033 CC).[159]

When one party's performance has become impossible only in part, the other party enjoys a corresponding right of reduction in the performance due. The party suffering the original breach can also withdraw from the contract if he or she lacks an appreciable interest in partial performance (art. 1464 CC).[160] In contracts which transfer ownership of a specified thing, or constitute or transfer property rights (art. 1376 CC), destruction of the thing by a cause not imputable to the transferor does not release the transferee from performance of his obligations, even if the thing was not delivered to him or her (art. 1465 CC).[161] The same provision applies if the translative or constitutive effect is deferred until the expiration of a time limit. Whenever the object of the transfer is a thing specified only as to kind (art. 1178 CC), and the transferor has completed delivery or the thing has been identified (art. 1378 CC), the transferee remains bound by the obligation of counter-performance.[162] In all cases, the transferee is released from his or her obligation if the transfer was subject to a condition precedent and impossibility intervened before fulfillment of the condition (art. 1465 para. 3 CC).

In multilateral contracts, impossibility of performance by one of the parties does not cause dissolution of the contract with regard to the others, unless the

---

[159] Inzitari, *Inesigibilità della prestazione, impossibilità della prestazione per l'embargo contro l'Iraq*, *NGCC* (1995), II, 48; Stella, *Impossibilità della prestazione per fatto imputabile al creditore*, Milan (1995), p. 352. Cass. 9 November 1994 no. 9304; Cass. 28 January 1995 no. 1037; Cass. 28 August 1993 no. 9125, *FI* (1995), I, 1601 noted by Cosentino; Cass. 14 February 1996 no. 1104; Trib. Napoli, 25 February 1993 Riv. dir.comm. (1994), II, 545 noted by De Michel; Cass. 13 July 1996 no. 6354; App. Roma 10 June 1997 no. 2007; Cass. 10 April 1995 no. 4119; Cass. 20 March 1997 no. 2487.

[160] Cass. 29 April 1993 no. 5066, *NGCC* (1994), I, 489 noted by De Poli; Cass. 12 February 1993 no. 1782; Cass. 14 March 1997 no. 2274.

[161] Lopez De Gonzalo, *Consegna e trasferimento del rischio nella vendita marittima*, Dir.maritt. (1994), 105; Cass. 15 November 1995 no. 11834, *Società* (1996), 771.

[162] Trib. Cagliari 15 March 1993, BBTC (1994), II, 442.

performance that became impossible is essential under the circumstances (art. 1466 CC).[163]

2. Supervening Excessive Hardship

A more interesting supervening circumstance is hardship. Since the enactment of the Civil Code of 1942, the Italian legal system has allowed the discharge of contractual obligations for supervening excessive hardship.[164] In theory, this doctrine may be considered analogous to the American doctrine of commercial impracticability, illustrated by para. 2-615 of the Uniform Commercial Code, and to the concept of hardship set forth in art. 6.2.2. of the UNIDROIT *Principles of International Commercial Contracts.*[165]

In fact, according to art. 1467 CC, in contracts for continuous or periodic performance or for deferred performance, if extraordinary and unforeseeable events make the performance excessively onerous for one of the parties, the party who owes such performance can demand dissolution of the contract. In the case of contracts for continuous or periodic performance, the effect of dissolution does not extend to performance already rendered.[166] Dissolution cannot be obtained if the supervening hardship was taken into account by the parties as part of the normal risk of the contract – that is to say, if the contract allocated the risk of the event's occurrance to the promisor.[167]

Despite similarities in the formulation of the theory, the impact of the doctrine of excessive hardship in Italy has a much greater relevance at an operational level than does commercial impracticability in the American law of contracts. Courts in

---

[163] App. Roma 15 July 1997 no. 2413.

[164] *See* Terranova, *L'eccessiva onerosità sopravvenuta nei contratti*, Milan (1996); G. Accardo, "*L'istituto della risoluzione per eccessiva onerosità sopravvenuta della prestazione nei più recenti orientamenti giurisprudenziali,*" in *NGCC* (1996), II, 1; E. Gabrielli, *La risoluzione del contratto per eccessiva onerosità*, in *Contratto e impresa* (1995), no. 3, 921.

[165] *See* J.M. Perillo, "Hardship and Its Impact on Contractual Obligations: A Comparative Analysis," *Centro Studi e Ricerche di Diritto Comparato e Straniero, 'Saggi, Conferenze e Seminari'* series, no. 20, Rome (1996); M.C.A. Prado, "*La theorie du hardship dans le principes de l'Unidroit relatifs aux contrats du commerce international,*" in *Diritto del commercio internazionale* (1997), no. 11-2, 323.

[166] Costanza, *Minimo garantito o rinuncia alla revisione prezzi?*, commenting on Cass. 29 January 1993, no. 948; Terranova, *L'eccessiva onerosità sopravvenuta nei contratti*, Milan (1996); Breccia, *Le obbligazioni*, Milan (1991), p. 743.

[167] *See* P. Gallo, *La gestione delle sopravvenienze contrattuali*, Milan (1992).

our system are more inclined to allow dissolution or modification of the contract. The case law approach to this doctrine identifies the *ratio* for adaptation or dissolution in the fact that the supervening circumstances altered the original economic allocation of reciprocal benefits in the contract.[168] A strong depreciation of the counter-performance is also considered by case law, and by the majority of scholars, as a ground for dissolution due to excessive hardship because the focus of the analysis is placed on equilibrium between performances.

As a consequence, a party can avoid dissolution by offering to equitably modify the contract terms.[169] Moreover, if the contract is one in which only one of the parties has undertaken obligations, that party can demand a reduction in performance or a modification of the mode of performance sufficient to restore an equitable basis to the contract (art. 1468 CC).[170] However, there is no reported case law applying the doctrine of supervening excessive hardship to this latter scenario.

Of course, the doctrine of supervening excessive hardship does not apply to contracts that are aleatory by nature or by intention of the parties (art. 1469 CC).[171] Contracts in which risk is the essential element and the economic advantage of one of the parties is radically uncertain are considered aleatory.[172] Nominate contracts that are aleatory by nature include, for example, insurance, annuity, and gambling contracts.

---

[168] *See* Cass. 9 January 1980 no. 166; Cass. 31 October 1989 no. 4554; Cass. 21 February 1994 no. 1649.

[169] Cass. 13 June 1997 no. 5349; Cass. 30 January 1995 no. 1090; Cass. 5 January 1995 no. 191, *FP* (1995), fasc.2, I, 11; Cass. 13 February 1995 no. 1559, *FI* (1995), I, 2897; Cass. 28 January 1995 no. 1027, *FI* (1995), I, 2898

[170] Cass. 13 January 1995 no. 369; App. Milano 4 March 1994, in *Dir. Ind.* (1995), 33 noted by Leone.

[171] Cass. 19 February 1997 no. 1516; Cass. 26 January 1993 no. 948, *Contratti* (1993), 532; Trib. Torino 15 October 1996, in *GC* (1997), I, 1409 noted by Cervini, *Risoluzione per eccessiva onerosità sopravvenuta nei mutui di valuta*; id., *Mutui di valuta e rischi di cambio per realità e presupposizione*, *GC* (1996), II, 327. Trib. Pescara, 24 January 1997, in *GC* (1997), I, 1093 with case note by F. Di Marzio, *Eccessiva onerosità sopravvenuta nei contratti di mutuo indicizzati all'ECU*.

[172] *See ex multis* Cass. 26 January 1993 no. 948.

V. Conclusions

We have attempted to sketch current trends in Italian contract law from a comparative perspective.[173]

The principle of freedom of contract, the sanctity of the will of the parties, and the immovability of the binding force of contractual obligations are presently undergoing thorough review and revision. The status of the contracting parties has recently gained in importance (thus, for example, the rules applicable to commercial contracts between traders are significantly different from those applicable to contracts involving consumers). As well, adjudication based on the principles of contractual justice and of equality in exchange have increasing importance. General clauses, such as *good faith* and *fair dealing*, more frequently govern the conduct of the parties during negotiations as well as the conclusion and performance of the agreement. Changed or supervening circumstances that alter the original value of the economic transaction pursued have acquired growing relevance in the European law of contracts; renegotiation of the contractual terms seems to be the preferred remedy. New and innovative forms of agreement, created and shaped by the international commercial praxis, are gradually "codified" and accepted by legislators and judges who recognize their validity and importance in the global market economy. As regards the critical phase of contractual dispute resolution, alternative methods such as mediation, arbitration, and supervised renegotiations (collectively known as "ADR") enjoy a growing role.

The trends in Italian contract law appear to be similar to the major legal systems belonging to the Western legal tradition. They have clearly emerged in recent EU legislation, as well as in the harmonization and unification projects of both the European,[174] and the international[175] law of contracts.

---

[173] *See*, generally, Alpa, "*Nuove frontiere del diritto contrattuale,*" preface to *Contratti in Generale, Aggiornamento 1991-1998*, vol. I, coll. *Giur. Sist. Dir. Civ. e Comm.* Founded by W. Bigiavi, Utet, Turin (1999).

[174] *See Principles of European Contract Law (PECL)* and the project of a European Contract Code.

[175] *See* the *UNIDROIT Principles of International Commercial Contracts.*

Property Law

Antonio Gambaro & Ugo Mattei [1]

This chapter will introduce the Italian law of property to the Anglophone reader and explain some basic technical concepts that are peculiar to the Italian civil law tradition.[2] After a short discussion of terminology, the chapter dwells on two basic issues. First, the relationship between the property owner and the state with respect to regulation and expropriation. This area may be termed "constitutional property." Secondly we examine the relationship between the owner and other private individuals as regards some aspects of property use and ownership transfer, as traditionally handled in the third book of the Civil Code.

I. The Terminology of the Italian Law of Property

The English expression "ownership of property" may be technically translated into Italian as "*proprietà dei beni*," which in non-technical English is "property in goods." In the following pages we will try to use a language as familiar as possible to English-speaking readers. Property will therefore refer to the possible objects of the right of ownership.[3]

---

[1]   Antonio Gambaro, Professor of Comparative Law, University of Milano; Ugo Mattei, Professor of Civil Law, University of Torino. We would like to acknowledge Andrea Pradi, Filippo Sartori, and Filippo Ruffato for assistance in the preparation of this chapter.

[2]   For a recent general introduction in English, which contains additional details on Italian law, *see* U. Mattei, *Basic Principles of Property Law. A Comparative Legal and Economic Introduction*, Greenwood Press, Westport, Ct. (2000).

[3]   This terminology is also used by M. Beltramo, G.E. Longo, & J.H. Merryman, *The Italian Civil Code*, Oceana, Dobbs Ferry, N.Y. (1969). All the articles of the Civil Code quoted in the footnotes of this review are from that translation. A new edition of this translation was published in 1990.

Jeffrey S. Lena and Ugo Mattei (eds.), *Introduction to Italian Law*, 283-316
©2002 Kluwer Law International. Printed in the Netherlands.

Italian law offers a broad definition of what property is in this sense. According to art. 810 of the Civil Code, property consists of anything that may be the object of rights.[4] Legal scholars focus on economic value in order to explain this vague provision of the Code. Everybody agrees that public policy or different provisions of law may prevent certain things of economic value from being classified as property. Human body parts provide an example.[5]

The 20 articles of the Code beginning with art. 810 CC are devoted to a detailed description of different kinds of property: land, immovables, chattels, energy, fruits, property of the State, Church property, and so forth. These detailed provisions have the ultimate effect of preventing scholars and courts from extending the concept of property to things that are not described in these sections of the Code.

In Italian, the word "*proprietà*" technically means the right of ownership. Apart from the idea of equitable interests and of different types of estates in land, the English word "ownership" is most similar to our word "*proprietà*," which roughly means ownership in fee simple absolute.[6] Of course, Italian law does not ignore ownership that is less than absolute. The Code recognizes a number of forms of less than absolute ownership, which are referred to as the so-called limited real rights (*diritti reali*). These rights are described in arts. 952 to 1099 CC. Other articles deal with multiple ownership and condominium. Nonetheless, references in the Code and in other sources to "*la proprietà*" can nearly always be understood to refer to absolute ownership.

Italian law and lawyers traditionally take a unitary approach to ownership. Unlike their common law colleagues, they do not differentiate in theory between land (and other immovables) and chattels. Both of these very different kinds of property are approached within the single framework of ownership, the definition of which, as usual rather empty, is contained in art. 832 CC.[7]

It is worth mentioning that many Italian scholars proudly emphasize what they regard as a fundamental paradigm shift from the old Code: instead of defining the

---

[4] In the translation cited above: "Things that can form the subject matter of rights are property."

[5] Article 5 CC is used for this purpose: "Acts of disposition of one's body. Acts of disposition of one's body which cause a permanent impairment of one's physical integrity or are otherwise contrary to law, public policy or morals are forbidden." This is probably the most important inalienability rule of Italian law.

[6] *See* A. Gambaro, "*La proprietà in diritto comparato*," in *Digesto disc. priv.*, Utet, Turin (1997).

[7] Article 832 CC: "Content of the right. The owner has the right to enjoy and dispose of things fully and exclusively, within the limits and with the observance of the duties established by the legal order."

right of ownership, the "new" 1942 Code defines the rights of the owner.[8] This is considered a clear break with the natural law tradition enshrined in the Napoleonic Code. But in reality, the unitary tradition inherited from the Napoleonic Code and from the natural law lives on, and a gap exists between the law in the books and the law in action.

At the level of broad definitions, what is said about ownership is intended to be valid both as to movables and immovables.[9] But in the law as it is applied, the very substantial social and economic differences between land and chattels has largely superceded the unitary approach. Land law in Italy is based on very different sources. As far as transfer and protection of property are concerned, one must look to the Civil Code and its subsequent elaboration by case law. And special legislation on the use of property outside the Code must also be consulted.

The division between the two types of sources is not merely a matter of location within the sources of law. Civil Code rules are framed in a civil law tradition that has its roots in Roman law and in the *jus commune*. Special legislation is distinctly detached from this tradition, being connected instead to administrative law and welfare state legislation. The distinction between transfer and protection on the one hand and concrete use on the other is not clear cut, and makes no claim whatsoever to being complete or exhaustive.

The use of real estate falls under the provisions of two types of special legislation: one concerning land planning and development and another concerning the relations between landlords and tenants. The law referring to land planning and development is moreover usually subdivided into town-planning law in its strict sense; law for the protection of the landscape; and law for the protection of the environment. The sources of the different regimes related to land-planning and development are, in turn, varied. According to arts. 117 and 118 Const., town planning is entrusted to the Regions within the framework of statutes. Italian law not only recognizes the difference between land law and the law of movable property, but also provides that very different legal regimes, usually located outside of the Civil Code, govern such diverse economic issues as urban planning, rural development, protection of environmental and artistic resources, and protection of small stock owners, all of

---

[8] *See* M. Costantino, "*I beni,*" in *Trattato di diritto civile diretto da P. Rescigno,* 7th vol., Giuffrè, Milan (1982). There is a large bibliography on this impressive achievement of the so-called neo-systematic Italian school of thought. Deeply involved in searching the roots of this change of paradigm is S. Rodotà, *Il terribile diritto,* 2nd ed., Il Mulino, Bologna (1991).

[9] *See* S. Ferreri, *Le azioni ripersecutorie in diritto comparato,* Giuffrè, Milan (1988), p. 1*ff.*

[10] S. Pugliatti, *La proprietà nel nuovo diritto,* Giuffrè, Milan (1964), p. 145.

which are deeply connected with the law of property. A seminal work by Professor Salvatore Pugliatti during the 1950s challenged the unitary framework of ownership by significantly using the plural form "*le proprietà*" ("ownership*s*") to indicate different kinds of ownership.[10] In the following discussion, we will distinguish the rules on movable property from those on immovable property.

As elsewhere in the world, Italian lawyers distinguish between ownership and possession (*possesso*). But this worldwide pattern does not express itself uniformly. In Italy, possession is defined by art. 1140 CC as the power to exercise that dgree of control over property that is commensurate with ownership.[11] Scholars who have been deeply dissatisfied with the Code's definition have tried to ameliorate the situation by introducing the old Roman law idea of possession as *animus possidendi* plus *corpus possessionis*, or by introducing the misleading idea that possession is a mere condition of fact while ownership is a matter of law.[12]

On the other hand, the best recent scholarship attempts to persuade Italian lawyers that possession is a legal institution as much as ownership and the concept of *de facto* power is a poor analytical tool unless legal protection of that power is taken into account.[13] Indeed, the owner who is also a possessor will generally find the remedies for protection of his possession more significant than those to which he is specifically entitled. Consequently, to not consider possession while studying ownership becomes a sterile analytical effort in which, unfortunately, many Italian scholars have long been engaged. Further rules, inspired by a variety of social problems, are devoted to good-faith and bad-faith possession. These differences are justified by the assumption that the former deserves broader legal protection.

Article 1140 CC introduces another notion indispensable to an understanding of Italian property law. Possession may be exercised either directly or through another person. In the latter case, the relationship between this other individual and the property is known as *detenzione*, or "detention." English speakers might recognize this as "custody."[14] Under Italian law, custody over property is held by whoever receives it from someone else and acknowledges that his title is ancillary. In Roman law terminology, this individual is said to have *corpus possessionis* but

---

[11] Article 1140 CC: "Possession. Possession is the power over a thing that is manifested by an activity corresponding to the exercise of ownership or other real rights …"

[12] *See* A. Trabucchi, *Istituzioni di diritto civile*, 28th ed., Cedam, Padua (1986), p. 433*ff.*

[13] R. Sacco and R. Caterina, *Il possesso*, Giuffrè, Milan (2000).

[14] Article 1140 CC: "… One can possess directly or by means of another person, who has custody of the thing." See, for a comparative discussion, J. Gordley and U. Mattei, "Protecting Possession," 44 *Am J Comp L* 293 (1996).

not *animus possidendi*. He does not behave as an owner with regard to that particular property over which he has physical control. One example of custody is illustrated by the relationship between my car and the mechanic who is fixing it. The holder of custody does not enjoy direct remedies to protect the property. He needs to be protected by either the owner or the possessor.

Interestingly, according to a long tradition in Italian law the relationship between landlord and tenant is part of the law of contracts, not property.[15] The tenant is considered as having custody. Nonetheless, we find an article of the Code that "exceptionally" extends direct remedies to the tenant against third parties.[16] If we move outside the Code we find that regulations of the relations between landlord and tenant frequently offer such strong protection to the latter that he could well be considered a quasi-owner in some respects. Thus, labeling the tenant's relationship to his home as one of "custody" is certainly inadequate.[17]

The legislation addressing housing issues, in concert with the various regulations regarding agricultural property, has resulted in such a significant solidification and expansion of the rights of residential tenants with respect to landlords as to have created something resembling a new type of proprietary relationship between the parties.[18] The existence of these new property rights not only creates a crisis in the distinction between real rights and creditors rights, but also introduces a *tertium genus* different from the property law of both movables and immovables, which reintroduced the notion that ultimately led to the elaboration of the *chattel real*.[19]

---

[15] For a comparative analysis, *see* A. De Vita, *Il rapporto di locazione abitativa tra teoria e prassi*, Giuffrè, Milan (1985).

[16] Article 1585 CC: "Warranty of peaceful enjoyment. The lessor is bound to warrant the lessee against disturbances which diminish the use or enjoyment of the thing, caused by third persons claiming rights in it. The lessor is not bound to warrant against disturbances which diminish the use or enjoyment of the thing caused by third persons who do not claim rights, but the lessee has the power to bring action against them in his own name."

[17] Act no. 392 of 17 July 1978. A thorough article-by-article commentary may be found in *Le Nuove Leggi Civili Commentate* (1980).

[18] U. Mattei, *La proprietà immobiliare*, 2nd ed., Giappichelli, Turin (1995), p. 20.

[19] For an analysis of the crisis in the taxonomic distinction between real rights and creditor's rights, *see* A. Guarneri, *Diritti reali e diritti di credito: valore attuale di una distinzione*, Milan (1979).

II. Constitutional Protection of Private Property

The economic relations section of the Italian Constitution dedicates three articles to private property. Article 42, the most important, states: "Property is either public or private. Economic assets may belong to the State, to institutions, or to private persons. / Private property is recognized and guaranteed by the law, which determines the manner of its acquisition and enjoyment and its limits, in order to assure its social function and render it accessible to all. / Private property, in such cases as are prescribed by law and with provisions for compensation, may be expropriated for reasons of general public interest. The rules and limitations of inheritance and testamentary succession, and the rights of the State in respect of estates of deceased persons, shall be established by law."

Article 43 states: "For purposes of public advantage, the law may reserve from the outset or may transfer, by means of expropriation with compensation, to the States or to public bodies or to communities of workers or users, certain enterprises or categories of enterprises that are connected with essential public services or sources of energy, or that are in a position of monopoly, and which are of outstanding public interest."

Article 44 states: "For the purpose of achieving the proper cultivation of the soil and of establishing fair social relations, the law will impose obligations and restrictions upon private property in land, will fix limits to its extension, according to regions and agricultural zones; will promote and enforce the reclamation of waste land, the transformation of vast estates, and the reconstituting of productive units; and will assist small and medium-sized properties. / The law will make special provisions in favor of mountainous areas."[20]

Like all constitutional legislatures, the Italian Constitutional Assembly tackled the problem of property as a political and social problem, and adopted the language proper to such a viewpoint. Italian legal scholarship, however, had for the most part tackled the problem of property from the perspective of its exact definition[21] and had turned to the language of German pandectist dogmatics for answers.[22]

---

[20] All translations into English of the Italian Constitution published in this chapter are taken from M. Cappelletti, J.H. Merryman, & J.M. Perillo, *The Italian Legal System*, Stanford University Press, Stanford (1967).

[21] *See* S. Romano, "*Sulla nozione di proprietà*," in *Rivista trimestrale di Diritto e Procedura Civile* XIV (1960), p. 337*ff.*

[22] *See* V. Scialoja, *Teoria della proprietà nel diritto romano*, Rome (1928); *see also* M. Allara, *Le nozioni fondamentali del diritto civile*, Giappichelli, Turin (1955), p. 527; C. Maiorca,

Since there was little communication between the two modes of reasoning, the result has been that from the 1948 enactment of the Constitution until 1960, private law scholars substantially ignored the text. By contrast, from 1960 until the present they have worked on re-defining arguments about private property while adhering closely to the Constitutional text.[23] Particular attention has been devoted to rendering the social function clause of art. 42 meaningful,[24] but the many years of effort have proven insufficient.[25]

The only result has been that certain regulations restricting the powers of the owner were acceptable even without compensation because the Constitution provides that property must have a social function.[26] However, very similar provisions have also been adopted in other countries whose constitutions ignore the clause relating to the social function of property.

In general, we may think that modern countries should adopt laws that foster town planning, protect the environment, protect properties of cultural worth, that impose fair relationships between landlords and tenants, and so on. Where mention of the social function of property exists in the Constitution, it may be said that the

---

"*Diritto di proprietà e diritti del proprietario*," in *Studi senesi in memoria di Ottorino Vannini*, Giuffrè, Milan (1957), p. 480. See the recent discussion in P. Gross, *Scienza Giuridica Italiana. Un profilo storico*, Giuffrè, Milan (2001).

[23] *See* S. Rodotà, "*Note critiche in tema di proprietà*," in *Rivista Trimestrale di Diritto e Procedura Civile* XIV (1960), p. 1252; P. Perlingieri, *Introduzione alla problematica della proprietà*, Jovene, Naples (1971); F. Santoro Passarelli, "*Proprietà privata e costituzione*," in *Rivista Trimestrale di Diritto e Procedura Civile* XXVI (1972), p. 953; A. Jannelli, *La proprietà costituzionale*, ESI, Naples (1980); C. Mazzù, *Proprietà e società pluralistica*, Giuffrè, Milan (1984); V. Scalisi, "*Proprietà e governo democratico dell' economia*," in *Rivista di Diritto Civile* XXXI (1985), I, p. 221; C. Salvi, "*Modelli di proprietà e principi costituzionali*," in *Rivista Critica del Diritto Privato* IV (1986), p. 317.

[24] *See* P. Rescigno, "*Per uno studio sulla proprietà*," in *Rivista di Diritto Civile* XVIII (1972), 1, p. 1; U. Natoli, *La proprietà*, 2nd ed., Giuffrè, Milan (1980); S. Rodotà, *supra* note 8.

[25] *See* U. Breccia, "*I quarant' anni del libro terzo del codice civile*," in *Rivista Critica del Diritto Privato* I (1983), p. 337; S. Rodotà, "*Intorno alla proprietà. Ricerche, ipotesi, problemi dal dopoguerra ad oggi*," in *Rivista Critica del Diritto* Privato VI (1988), p. 223; A. Gambaro, *La proprietà*, Giuffrè, Milan (1990), p. 85*ff.* U. Mattei, *La Proprietà*, Utet, Turin (2001).

[26] *See* A. Predieri, *Urbanistica, tutela del paesaggio, espropriazione*, Giuffrè, Milan (1969); L. Barsotti & F. Spantigati, *Potere di piano e proprietà*, Einaudi, Turin (1971); but *see also* L. Mengoni, "*Proprietà e libertà*," in *Rivista Critica del Diritto Privato* VI (1988), p. 427; L. Paladin, "*Il diritto e la funzione della proprietà fondiaria nell' Italia di oggi: le premesse costituzionali*," in *Quadrimestre* V (1988), p. 9.

law implements the Constitution. When a constitutional text does not deal with this social function, lawyers are forced to renounce such a statement, but the statute or regulation will be adopted anyway.[27]

The Constitution clearly reserves the subject of limits to property rights to legislative action (*riserva di legge*). Only State legislation can impose limits on property rights aimed at shaping them according to a social function. Even though such a notion is interpreted elastically in order to allow property to be shaped by means of administrative acts, case law remains absolutely excluded as a source of law in this field. The judge does not directly implement the social function of property. Indeed, neither ordinary judges nor the Constitutional Court have ever made any use of the social function of property beyond that of a purely rhetorical and aesthetic nature in connection with conclusions already reached.[28]

In Italy, as elsewhere, the problem of property in the Constitution is that of the limitations on the guarantees that the Constitution assigns to private property. This problem has been tackled by the Italian Constitutional Court from the perspective of the need to specify the measures that have the character of expropriation (*espropriazione*, *i.e.* "takings" – the compulsory purchase by the State of land or other immovables) and to calculate the amount of just compensation. Until now, only sub-section 3 of art. 42 has received attention from Italian constitutional case law, and the problem of the constitutional guarantees of property seems to be absorbed by that of expropriation.[29]

The Italian system adopts a centralized model of judicial review.[30] Only the Constitutional Court can strike down a statute as unconstitutional. The Court can

---

[27] *See* A. Gambaro & R. Pardolesi, "*L'influenza dei valori costituzionali sul diritto civile italiano*," in A. Pizzorusso & V. Varano (eds.), *L'influenza dei valori costituzionali sui sistemi giuridici contemporanei*, vol. I, Giuffrè, Milan (1985), p. 5; A. Gambaro, "*Il diritto di proprietà*," in *Trattato di diritto civile e commerciale Cicu/Messineo*, Giuffrè, Milan (1995), p. 21*ff*; U. Mattei, "*Proprietà*," in *Digesto disc. priv.*, Utet, Turin (1997), p. 441*ff*; P. Perlingeri, *Il diritto civile nella legalità costituzionale*, 2nd ed., Naples (1994); P. Barcellona, "*Proprietà (tutela costituzionale)*," in *Digesto disc. priv.*, Utet, Turin (1997); C. Salvi, "*Il contenuto del diritto di proprietà*," in *Il Codice Civile Commentario*, Giuffrè, Milan (1994), p. 3*ff*; G. Zagrabelsky, *Il diritto mite*, Utet, Turin (1992).

[28] A. Gambaro, "*Il diritto di proprietà*," *supra* note 27, at 99; U. Mattei, *supra* note 18, at 14*ff*.

[29] *See* the conflicting views of A.M. Sandulli, "*Profili costituzionali della proprietà privata*," in *Rivista Trimestrale di Diritto e Procedura Civile* XXVI (1972), p. 465, and M.S. Giannini, "*Basi costituzionali della proprietà privata*," in *Politica del Diritto* II (1971), p. 443.

[30] *See* M. Cappelletti, *Judicial Review in the Contemporary World*, Bobbs-Merril, Indianapolis (1971). *See also* V. Varano, "Organization of Justice," chapter 5, this volume.

be invested with such power only in the course of a judicial proceeding in which a party challenges a statute as unconstitutional and the judge believes that applying such a statute may be relevant to the decision. The Italian Constitutional Court was instituted in 1956, several years after the coming into force of the Constitution in 1948, and that in its first few years of existence it employed considerable self-restraint in declaring statutes unconstitutional.

Such an initial attitude of judicial self-restraint was particularly evident with respect to compensation for expropriation. As is clear from the text, the Italian Constitution does not link compensation for expropriation to the market value of the property, nor does it demand that compensation be paid in advance. The legislation on the subject has invented an astonishing variety of new formulas capable of setting parameters for compensation. Briefly, the trend that emerged in the period prior to the enactment of the Constitution was to finance a portion of the programs for public works and public social assistance by maintaining very a low compensation for expropriation.[31] The fact that every public works program in Italy is established by statute has engendered a mass of specific legislation controlling the amount and manner of calculating compensation according to the purpose of each individual statute. This mass of specific legislation has been submitted to review by the Constitutional Court.

Initially, the generally restrained attitude adopted by the Constitutional Court led it to determine that the word "compensation" in article 42 para. 3 could only mean the maximum contribution and restoration that, in the light of public interest, the public administration could guarantee to the private interest, in the framework of a complex comparative evaluation of interests that only the legislature can perform.[32]

Once the court became aware that this approach was mistaken because it ignored a rule written in the Constitution (as well as forgetting the historical roots of expropriation by rendering it indistinguishable from requisition), the Court changed direction, though without candidly acknowledging that it had done so.

Commencing with decisions no. 67 of 1959 and no. 6 of 1960,[33] the Court actually

---

[31] *See* D. Sorace, *Espropriazione della proprietà e misura dell' indennizzo*, Giuffrè, Milan (1974); G. Rolla, *Il privato e l' espropriazione*, Giuffrè, Milan (1980).

[32] Const. Court, 25 May 1957, no. 61, in *Giurisprudenza Italiana* CXI (1957), I, column 1098; Const. Court, 24 March 1958, no. 60, in *Giurisprudenza Italiana* CXIII (1959), I, 1, column 8; Const. Court, 18 January 1958, no. 3, in *Giurisprudenza Costituzionale* 111 (1958), p. 10

[33] Const. Court, 29 December 1959, no. 67, in *Giurisprudenza Italiana* CXIV (1960), I, column 373; Const. Court, 18 June 1963, no. 91, in *Il Foro Italiano* LXXXVI (1963), I, 1, column

began to exercise its power of judicial review by declaring unconstitutional some specific statutory rules regulating the amount of compensation, thereby repudiating the idea that such a calculation should be the fruit of a complex balancing of interests that only the legislature perform. The overruling was deftly cast as an attempt to treat it as an interpretation or closer investigation of the previous orientation. Consequently, it decided that the legislature should always remain vested with the power to determine the method for calculating all expropriation compensation. According to this approach, while the Constitution establishes no detailed parameters of compensation, it does guarantee that compensation will be "serious."[34]

The question of what constitutes "serious compensation" has dominated the law in this area for years, thus evincing the need to strike a balance between the need to expropriate property and the duty of the State towards the property owner. Unfortunately, the Court did not indicate either a definite rule or even the general patterns of reference. Until now, no substituting criterion has been found, and the Court has not been able to provide any unitary rationale with regard to the individual provisions submitted for its review.[35]

The perplexity of the judge becomes the scholar's opportunity, and comments and interpretations have flourished. But even scholarship has not been unanimous in providing adequate solutions. Thirty years of debate were required to clarify positions, and today it is plain that the only difficulty to be resolved is the treatment of profit from development. Market value is generally acknowledged as the proper criterion for just compensation for the expropriation of agricultural lands, buildings, and the like.[36]

The problem of compensation for expropriation is linked to the need for the equality of citizens *vis-à-vis* the state. Unfortunately, the legislator's discretionary power tends to frustrate citizens in an unconstitutional way, particularly after the introduction of general criteria that clearly break with the idea of compensation at market value.[37] (Meanwhile a vacuous mass of constitutional and ordinary case

---

1090; Const. Court, 9 April 1965, no. 22, in *Il Foro Italiano* LXXXVIII (1965), 1, column 585.

[34] *See* Const. Court, June 1963, no. 91, *supra* note 33.

[35] *See* A. Gambaro, *La proprietà, supra* note 25, at 125*ff.* U. Mattei, *La Proprietà, supra* note 25.

[36] This is obviously to be understood as compensation calculated more or less at current values, *see* D. Sorace, *"Gli indennizzi espropriativi nella costituzione fra tutela dell'affidamento, esigenze risarcitorie e problemi della rendita urbana,"* in *Riv. Critica del Diritto Privato* VII (1989), pp. 405-95.

[37] *See* art. 5*bis* law 8; 1992 no. 359 (40 percent below the market value).

law and contingent legislative interventions have piled up relating to the problem of the amount of compensation that would be senseless to describe here.)

Until recent developments, the predominant pattern formulated a standoff between the legislator, defender of the needs of redistribution (or perhaps only those of the government) and the Constitutional Court, supporter of property rights. However, the Constitutional Court ultimately shifted towards the legislator's position as expressed in art. 5*bis* of law 359/1992 concerning urgent provisions to restructure public finance.[38] Although the new principles contained in this article were only temporarily in force, questions immediately arose regarding their constitutionality.[39]

By means of this new rule, the legislator attempted to further reduce the cost of compensation. The legislator referred to the criteria introduced by law no. 2892/1885 (already interpreted as providing for costs substantially lower than market value) and reduced them by an additional 40 percent. The owner could, however, voluntarily sell to avoid this further reduction. In practice, the compensation was reduced by approximately 65 percent with respect to the market value.

The reaction of the Court was unanticipated. In decision no. 283/1993, the Court held that an indemnity ranging between 30 and 35 percent of the market value (disregarding the further 20 percent taxation value introduced by subsequent finance law), represented a sufficient and fair reimbursement, considering the nation's economic condition, as the "maximum contribution and reparation that, within the general interest, the government can guarantee to the private interest."[40]

The compensation obtained under the system set forth in art. 5*bis* can be defined in numerous ways, but is certainly inadequate given the major reductions in the market values of property mandated by the law.[41]

The judgment of the Court has nevertheless been confirmed by two subsequent decisions declaring that the compensation fixed by the Region of Sicily and the Autonomous Province of Bolzano (as a sort of flat-rate reduction of the market value of approximately 25 percent) are unconstitutional, since they introduced

---

[38] *See* M. Atelli, "*Lo Stato di diritto e occupazione appropriativa: storie di un rapporto difficile,*" in *Rivista critica di diritto privato* (1998), p. 225.

[39] *See* M.T. Bocchetti, "*La nuova disciplina dell' indennità di esproprio per le aree edificabili,*" in *Nuove Leggi Civ.* (1992).

[40] *See* A. Di Maio, "*Ascesa e declino dell' indennità di esproprio,*" in *Corriere Giuridico* (1993), p. 922.

[41] *See* F. Caringella & G. De Marzo, *Indennità di esproprio ed occupazione appropriativa nel panorama normativo – giurisprudenziale*, Milan (1997).

criteria that are much more burdensome for the public administration and deviate from the principle introduced by art. 5*bis* by not compelling the owner to contribute to Italy's economic growth.

Actually, the problem facing the legislator remains that of the relationship between expropriation law and town planning statutes, but there are few signs of a political awareness of this subject. One of the reasons that the legislator finds it difficult to tackle the problem of the relation between expropriation and town planning statutes is that we continue to face the effects of the judgment contained in Constitutional Court decision no. 55 of 1968,[42] which declared unconstitutional zoning provisions absolutely banning building on urban land for an undetermined period and without compensation. It was through this decision that the "expropriation issue" first made its appearance as a constitutional problem.[43]

In the Italian tradition, following the French model, the problem of the difference between the use of "police power" and that of "eminent domain" did not exist, since the clear separation between them was assured by a formal criterion. If the State took possession of private property, authoritatively transferring the right of ownership from the current owner to itself or to someone else, then it was considered an expropriation. However, if the property remained with the owner, then it could not be considered an expropriation, but merely the exercise of police power. This solution was consistent with the civil law idea of property – for which such a right is unitary – and with the concept, also clearly of French origin, that the content of the right of property is defined by both law and regulation. In this concept, the residual powers of the owner are not taken into account in defining the existence of a property right. For this reason, a single property could remain entirely devoid of any possibility of profitable utilization, without being considered as having been subject to expropriation.

Naturally, this State-linked concept of private property cannot survive in a legal system with a rigid Constitution, a power of judicial review, and a clause in the Constitution expressing a guarantee for private property.

---

[42] Const. Court, 29 May 1969, no. 55, published in *Il Foro Italiano* XIC (1968), I, column 1361; *Giustizia Civile* XIV (1968), III, p. 137; *Il Foro Amministrativo* XLIV (1968), I, 1, p. 282; *Rivista Giuridica dell'Edilizia* XI (1968), p. 408; *Giurisprudenza Italiana* CXXIII (1969), 1, I, column 7.

[43] *See* the comments of A. Testa, "*Incostituzionalità dei vincoli inseriti nel piano regolatore,*" in *Foro Amministrativo* XLIV (1968), II, p. 115; A. Agro, "*Orientamenti costituzionali sui limiti alla proprietà privata: a proposito delta senterza no. 55 della Corte costituzionale,*" in *Giurisprudenza Italiana* CXXIII (1969), I, 1, column 7; M. Bon Valsassina, "*Vincoli espropriativi e diritto all' indennnizzo,*" in *Giurisprudenza Costituzionale* XIII (1968), p. 846.

The problem of expropriation made its first appearance in connection with military servitudes. In accordance with tradition, the imposition of easements which, for example, allowed the passage of military vehicles on private land and forbade the owner to modify the land in any way that could hinder their passage, did not involve compensation. Legally, however, such policies were properly treated as a question of servitudes, which are recognized in the Italian system as limited property rights. Therefore, the Constitutional Court had no choice when it decided[44] that such impositions were unconstitutional unless accompanied by compensation. If the Court had decided that the imposition of servitudes did not imply compensation, it would also have had to decide that the removal of a limited real right (which is what an easement is – but also usufruct, or emphyteusis) does not constitute expropriation. That would be absurd. Indeed, there is general agreement that the constitutional guarantee of property provided for by art. 42 Const. refers not only to property in a narrow sense, but logically extends to all limited property rights.[45] However, once it was established that the imposition of administrative restraints completely analogous with servitudes may constitute a form of expropriation, it was difficult to deny that other forms of administrative restraints imposed on privately owned lands could also constitute expropriation.

In decision no. 55 of 1968, the Constitutional Court therefore decided that art. 42 of the Town Planning Act, allowing the imposition of absolute bans of building for an undetermined period on lands that otherwise would have been suitable for building (labeled as "area restraints," or *vincoli di zona*), constitutes a form of expropriation. This important decision of the Constitutional Court has, however, not had practical effects. Since the Court established that only restraints in the form of an absolute building ban for an undetermined period were a kind of expropriation, the legislator intervened to declare that all building bans provided for in general land-use plans had to be viewed as valid for only five years.[46] At the end of this period, the legislator established that restraints which were about to elapse

---

[44] Const. Court, 20 January 1966, no. 6, in *Il Foro Italiano* LXXXIX (1966), I, column 203; *Giustizia Civile* XII (1966), III, p. 73; *Giurisprudenza Italiana* CXX (I966), I, 1, column 700; *Foro Amministrativo* XLII (1966), I, 1, p. 61; *Giurisprudenza Costituzionale* XI (1966), p. 72.

[45] *See* comments in V. Andrioli, *"Sulla sentenza intepretativa di accoglimento della Corte costituzionale in tema di servitù militari,"* in *Il Foro Italiano* LXXXIX (1966), I, column 203; F. Lubrano, *"Alcune osservazioni sui limiti delle questioni di legittimità costituzionale,"* in *Giurisprudenza Costituzionale* XI (1966), p. 76; A. Gambaro, *"'Jus aedificandi' e nozione civilistica della proprietà,* Giuffrè, Milan (1975).

[46] Act no. 1187 of 19 November 1968.

must be viewed as extendible for another two years.[47] Once the two years were over, a statute could be issued to provide a further one-year extension.[48] After that year, an extension of six months was provided for.[49]

The Constitutional Court declared all these further extensions unconstitutional,[50] without provoking reaction from the legislator. By then it was understood that where the legislator expressly provides for the possibility of imposing restraints with the character of an expropriation, it runs the risk of seeing this provision invalidated by the Constitutional Court. Whereas if the legislator relies on the default response of the system the same result will be achieved without running any such risk. In fact, administrative court case law holds that five-year restraints, once elapsed, can be reinstated by adopting an area provision exactly like the preceding one.[51] If the municipality does not do this, the administrative case law provides that the area that was submitted to restraints must be considered not as free of them, but rather as devoid of town planning prescriptions. As a general rule, in areas without town planning prescriptions, the suitability for building is limited to the irrelevant amount of 0.03 m^3 per m^2.[52] In this, Italian administrative case law has acted as a good guardian of the original French model, according to which a property of immovables unshaped by regulations are inconceivable.

For its part, the case law of the ordinary courts continues to adhere to the principle that, when faced with authoritative interventions by the public administration, legitimate interests (rights adjudicated by the administrative courts) exist, but individual subjective rights do not, and that any eventual harm through illegal administrative action never leads to compensation for damages. Changes in the administrative law, discussed in chapter 6 by Professor Sorace, are too recent to be treated here.

---

[47] Act no. 756 of 30 November 1973.

[48] Act no. 696 of 22 December 1975.

[49] Act no. 10 of 28 January 1977.

[50] Const. Court, 12 May 1982, no. 92, in *Il Foro Italiano* CV (1982), 1, column 2116; *Giustizia Civile* XXVM (1982), I, p. 1683; *Giurisprudenza Italiana* CXXXIV (1982), I, 1, column 1302; *Rivista Giuridica dell'Edilizia* XXV (1982), I, p. 421; *Giurisprudenza Costituzionale* XXVII (1982), 1, p. 942.

[51] *Tribunale Amministrativo Regionale della Lombardia*, 27 February 1987, no. 19, in *Rivista Giuridica dell'Edilizia* XXX (1987), I, p. 667; *Tribunale Amministrativo Regionale della Lombardia*, 3 May 1988, no. 154, in *Rivista Giuridica dell'Edilizia* XXXI (1988), I, p. 636.

[52] *Consiglio di Stato, Adunanza Plenaria – i.e.* a special panel of the Italian Administrative Supreme Court – 2 April 1984, no. 7, in 11 *Foro Italiano* CVII (1984), 111, column 229.

The principle that "The King can do no wrong" still applies to Italian public administration as it operates through administrative actions.[53] When, however, the issue of the lack of adequate protection for private property – faced with the immunity enjoyed by the public administration with regard to land planning and development – was brought before the Constitutional Court, it was not able to get beyond the impasse in which the strategy of the legislator had confined the promising decision no. 55 of 1968. Faced with this obstacle, the Court[54] simply surrendered. Such surrender is reflected in the fact that there is no relevant statutory provision that can be declared unconstitutional, since the lack of protection of private property against the public administration is entirely attributable to both administrative and ordinary case law. In conclusion, the problem of expropriation, though it continues to exist, lies dormant in Italian law.

Nevertheless, scholars faced with the challenges arising from the decisions of the Constitutional Court, have been anything but silent. In fact, it is worth clarifying that case law – constitutional, administrative, and ordinary – has occasionally done nothing other than actually adopt one or another legal view worked out in the relevant scholarship.

The doctrines, upheld in the first decisions of the Constitutional Court, holding that compensation for expropriation must correspond to the maximum contribution that the State can afford to provide to private individuals who have suffered it have been proposed by an influential work of scholarship by Motzo and Piras.[55] These scholars also suggested that to quantify this amount the public authority should consider the total expenses necessary for the realization of the project of public interest. This work echoes, in its turn, some approaches articulated by German scholars during the Weimar Republic, which were of substantial academic interest to the later Italian scholars.

The doctrine according to which expropriation includes every limitation of the right of ownership that is based on a single administrative act, and which removes property rights over and above their minimum content as conceived of in every historical period, was formulated at the end of a long period of intellectual anguish

---

[53] *Corte di Cassazione, Sezioni Unite* – *i.e.* a special panel of the Italian Supreme Court – 21 January 1988, no. 433, in *Rivista Giuridica dell'Edilizia* XXXI (1988), I, p. 565; *Caff., Sez. Un.*, December 1987, no. 9096, in *Nuova Giurisprudenza Civile Commentata* IV (1988), 1, p. 555.

[54] Compare Const. Court, 25 March 1980, no. 35, in *Giustizia Civile* XXVI (1980), I, p. 993.

[55] *See* G. Motzo & A. Piras, "*Espropriazione e 'pubblica utilità'*," in *Giurisprudenza Costituzionale* IV (1959), p. 153.

by another influential scholar,[56] who happened also to be the Chief Justice at the time decision no. 55 of 1968 was issued.

Administrative case law merely follows its own legal tradition, formed prior to the enactment of the Constitution (in other words, it considers the constitutional language in this regard to be an unimportant mishap), but justifies retaining its own direction by relying on doctrines formulated by other legal scholars that nullify the constitutional guarantee of private property.

According to this approach, the lack of a notion of private property in the Constitution forces us to draw this notion from the positive rules defining property rights. Consequently, every time the legislator regulates property rights, it reshapes them. The constitutional guarantee of property therefore only refers to situations legally shaped as such by the legislator, with the ultimate consequence that it becomes logically absurd to imagine a "framing statute" that contrasts with the constitutional guarantee of private property.[57]

This explanation is not considered very reliable by scholars today, since every constitutional guarantee is clearly either made a function of a parameter outside the ordinary law, or is superfluous.[58] In fact, the Constitutional Assembly adopted art. 42 because it felt obliged to follow a long historical tradition, according to which every constitutional document must contain a certain guarantee for private property against its requisition by public authorities. Actually, such guarantees have never been lacking, even in the constitutional documents of socialist states.

However, the ability to develop the very existence of a constitutional guarantee of private property to a minimally consistent degree depends on a complex of factors that are beyond the reach of any constitutional document. Prior to the 1948 Constitution, private property in the Italian system was in a rather weak position *vis-à-vis* the power of public administration. There were few effective remedies that the individual owner could rely on to challenge public administration plans. However, the administration was so respectful of private property that such remedies, though scarce, could be said to be substantially guaranteed.

In the current system, in which the traditional respect of the public administration

---

[56] *See* A.M. Sandulli, *"Natura ed effetti dell' imposizione di vincoli paesaggistici,"* in *Atti del convegno di studi giuridici sulla tutela del paesaggio Sanremo 8-10 dicembre 1961,* Giuffrè, Milan (1963).

[57] *See* M.S. Giannini, *supra* note 29.

[58] *See* M. Luciani, *"Vecchi e nuovi principi in materia di espropriazione e indennizzo,"* in *Giurisprudenza Costituzionale* XXV (1980), 1, p. 40; *see also* S. Mangiameli, *La proprietà privata nella costituzione,* Giuffrè, Milan (1986).

for private property rights has for the most part been lost, the guarantee of property can only result from the reasonableness and control exercised by independent judges. In its concrete solutions, the case law of the Constitutional Court is not far from such an approach. Indeed, the Court has constantly maintained that restraints imposed for landscape protection or historical or artistic reasons do not constitute expropriation, and they can therefore be imposed without being accompanied by compensation, even though they may be so severe as to divest the property of any economic value.[59] The Court has maintained that even though it has been incapable of producing concrete effects through its own solutions restraints of a town planning nature can also have the character of an expropriation when the owner formally remains the holder of the property right.[60]

The difference between the two types of restraint lies in the fact that restraints imposed to preserve a certain landscape – or things of a historical or artistic value – have to be imposed on certain properties and not on others, whereas restraints of a town planning nature are *per se* necessary, but it is not always necessary to impose them on certain pieces of land and not on others which are contiguous. In other words, in the first case, there is a necessary connection between the realization of the public program and the restraint, which deprives the public administration of all discretion in the singling out of the properties to be restrained. Consequently, the sacrifice imposed on the private individual is directly justified by the primary public purpose. In the second case, such a necessary connection is broken by the administrative discretion which singles out the owners to be sacrificed, therefore requiring further justification for the imposition of individual restraints. Very often, however, the decisions of the zoning decision-maker seem constrained by the techniques of sound town planning. In such cases, the problem of rational justification of the sacrifice imposed on the private individual is quickly resolved. The problem of the constitutional guarantee of private property arises again, however, as a of due process guarantee every time the public administration imposes restraints on private individuals when incapable of supplying a specific justification for their imposition beyond that of the "desirability of differentiated urban planning."[61]

---

[59] Const. Court, 29 May 1968, no. 56, in *Il Foro Italiano* XIC (1968), 1, column 1361; *Giustizia Civile* XIV (1968), III, p. 137; *Rivista Giuridica dell'Edilizia* XI (1968), p. 1784; *Giurisprudenza Italiana* CXXIII (1969), I, 1, column 4.

[60] Const. Court, May 1968, no. 55, *supra* note 59.

[61] *See* G. Lombardi, "*Espropiazione dei suoli urbani e criterio del* due process of law," in *Giurisprudenza Costituzionale* XXV (1980), 1, p. 481.

The indication supplied by the Constitutional Court is to be understood in the sense that this generic justification is less than what the constitutional guarantee of private property demands.

III. Transfer of Ownership

We will now examine the transfer of ownership from one party to another. There are various ways to categorize such transfers. The broad division in the common law tradition is that between voluntary and involuntary transfers. The former are more important in a modern legal system, since they include the major commercial transactions that concern property: sale, mortgage and, in common law, leases.[62] In Italian law, as in the civil law tradition generally, the landlord who leases to a tenant does not transfer ownership to him. This is due to the absence of the concept of non-freehold estates, according to which a lease constitutes a voluntary transfer of ownership just as much as an outright sale of the land does.

In the following pages we will make use of the distinction between voluntary and involuntary transfers of ownership, but we will utilize it in conjunction with the fundamental distinction between transfers *inter vivos* and transfers *mortis causa*. Since in Italy, the latter type of transfer is not part of the law of property, but belongs to a completely different branch of the law, we will mention it only briefly.[63]

A. Transfer of Ownership at Death

Voluntary transfers at death take place by will.[64] For a will to be valid, certain formal requirements must be met. "Holographic wills" must be handwritten and signed by the testator. Even when there are clear risks of forgery, the holographic will is presumed valid unless the contrary is proved by a special judicial procedure known as *querela di falso*. Two other types of wills are recognized by Italian law. In both of them, the notary, a special and important figure in Italian Law of the civil law,[65] plays a fundamental role. In the first case, known as a secret will, the

---

[62] *See*, for a common lawyer's approach, J.E. Cribbet & C.W. Johnson, *Principles of the Law of Property*, 3rd ed. (1989), p. 142*ff*.

[63] *See* U. Mattei, *La proprietà immobiliare*, *supra* note 18, at 89-90.

[64] For a bibliography and a basic treatment, *see* A. Trabucchi, *supra* note 12, para. 1, at p. 825*ff*; further details on succession in chapter 16, this volume.

[65] On this figure in the civil law tradition, *see* R.B. Schlesinger *et al.*, *Comparative Law*, 5th ed., Foundation Press, Mineola, N.Y. (1988), pp. 18-20.

notary acts as a mere depository of the will, which has been drafted by the testator. In the other case, the so-called "public will," the notary plays an active role: the testator dictates his will to the notary before two witnesses, and the notary may advise the testator on the making of the will.

The freedom to make a will is not unrestricted. The power of the deceased to choose an heir cannot impair the rights of a number of immediate relatives to inherit. They receive a portion of the deceased's property, despite the will. If the will has abridged this portion, it is void. The value of the property transferred by will is reduced until the legal limit is respected. It is important to mention, however, that these immediate relatives are not entitled to the ownership of any particular property. They receive a part of the value of the global estate.

Another kind of involuntary transfer of ownership *mortis causa*, this time familiar to common law, is intestate succession. In Italian law, relatives are ranked in series of categories according to closeness of kinship. The existence of relatives belonging to one of them excludes all those ranked in a lower position.[66] Thus, the claim of a descendant prevails over claims of collaterals or ascendants.

B. Involuntary Transfer of Ownership *Inter Vivos*

Many changes of ownership take place against the express desires of the owner. Judgments may be obtained which are liens against the property, giving rise to execution and forced sale. The rules governing such involuntary transfers of ownership are not considered part of the law of property in Italian law; nor are the rules related to involuntary bankruptcy proceedings that may force debtors to strip themselves of their assets.

Nonetheless, some other involuntary transfers of ownership are a classic part of Italian property law – the statutes of limitations contained in the Civil Code which may cause adverse possession by a rival claimant to ripen into a new title; the variety of doctrines related to accession and confusion; the legal provisions concerning rivers that change course, taking land from one riparian owner and giving it to another; the good faith purchase of chattel from a non-owner who transfers title to the purchaser for value; and many others. Apart from the last-mentioned case, all these involuntary transfers of ownership are known in Italian

---

[66] For a comparative analysis, *see* U. Mattei, *"La successione contro la volontà del testatore. Radici profane di una contrapposizione sacra fra common law e sistemi romanisti,"* in *Studi Sacco* (1996).

legal terminology as original acquisitions of ownership,[67] as opposed to derivative acquisitions of ownership, such as those resulting from transfers by sale or by gift, which form part of the law of contracts.[68]

Any chattel which is not owned by any person may be acquired through possession. This is true both of property which never had an owner (*res nullius*) and of property that has been abandoned by its owner (*res derelictae*). This sort of acquisition of ownership used to be extended to wild animals, which could be possessed by hunters. A special statute aimed at protecting wild animals[69] has now classified them as owned by the State. As a consequence, a successful hunter without a regular State license may be prosecuted for theft.[70] Immovables may not be occupied. Immovables without an owner are automatically owned by the State.

When lost property is found, the finder may become the owner provided that he or she follows an administrative procedure and waits for one year in which the owner does not come forth. If the owner appears, the finder is entitled to compensation of up to 10 percent of the value of the found object. This involuntary transfer of ownership is known as "invention," from the Latin word for "to find."

Italian legal thought classifies a variety of different situations under the term *accessione*. Accession is commonly classified in three categories: movable to immovable; immovable to immovable; and movable to movable.[71] All of these have different names in the Code, and the name *accessioni* is used there only for the first of them.

It is a well-known maxim of Roman law folklore that the right of ownership over land is extended *usque ad sidera et usque ad inferos*, that is, from the sky to the center of the earth. The principles of accession are commonly said to come from an idea of absolute ownership that resists fragmentation: everything that happens to be on someone's land becomes his property. The reality is of course much more complex. First of all, Italian law provides a major exception to the rule

---

[67] Indeed, this kind of acquisition of ownership is the only one which is expressly part of the chapters related to the law of property. *See* the leading hornbooks, A.Trabucchi, *supra* note 12, at 446*ff*; P. Trimarchi, *Istituzioni di diritto privato*, 7th ed., Giuffrè, Milan (1986), p. 551*ff*.

[68] *See* U. Mattei, *La proprietà immobiliare*, *supra* note 18, at 91; A. Gambaro, *Il diritto di proprietà*, *supra* note 27, at 681.

[69] Act no. 968 of 27 February 1977.

[70] P. Cendon, *Proprietà, riserva e occupozione*, ESI, Naples (1977).

[71] A. Trabucchi, *supra* note 12, at 451.

superficies solo caedit, in recognizing the right of *superficie* among the strictly limited number of "limited real rights." This real right, unknown to the Napoleonic Code and first introduced into modern civil law by the Belgian scholar Laurent, provides for a true ownership of buildings separated from the ownership of land that belongs to a different owner.[72] Secondly, there are a variety of rules in the Civil Code that allow the owner of property which has accidentally ended up on someone else's land to set foot onto the land in order to rescue the property.[73] Finally, another important exception to the accession rules is codified in art. 938 CC,[74] which provides for ownership of land occupied in good faith during construction of a building on the adjoining land.

As a matter of principle, it may be said that the owner of a piece of land becomes, if he wishes, the owner of buildings, trees, and everything else which happens to be on the land.[75] The general principles of unjust enrichment will nonetheless compel the good faith occupier to pay compensation to the former owner. If the landowner does not want to acquire the ownership of the property, however, he may make use of the usual remedies to protect his land, with the limits stated in some details in the Code to protect good faith.

Article 938 CC deserves particular attention due to its originality and importance. In Italian legal terminology this doctrine is known as "inverted accession."[76] Some

---

[72] Article 952 CC: "Const. of the right of *superficie*. The owner can constitute the right to erect and maintain a structure above the soil in favor of others, who acquire ownership of it. He can likewise transfer ownership of an existing structure, separately from ownership of the soil."

[73] Article 843 CC: "… The owner must also permit entry by one who wishes to recover something of his that is there by accident or an animal that has escaped there from custody. The owner can prevent the entry by delivering the thing or the animal."

[74] Article 938 CC: "Occupation of portion of adjoining land. If a portion of the adjoining land is occupied in good faith in the construction of a building, and the owner of that land does not object within three months from the day on which the construction began, the Court taking account of the circumstances, can attribute the ownership of the building and the occupied soil to the builder. The builder is required to pay the owner of the soil double the value of the area occupied, as well as compensation for damage." *See* A. Gambaro, *Il diritto di proprietà*, *supra* note 27, at 758-59.

[75] Article 934 CC: "Works performed upon or under soil. Any planting, structure, or works existing upon or under the soil belong to the owner of the soil except as provided by arts. 935, 937 and 938, and unless it appears otherwise by the source of the right or by law."

[76] *See* F. De Martino, *Della proprietà*, in *Commentario del codice civile a cura* di A. Scialoja e G. Branca, 4th ed., Zanichelli, Bologna (1976), p. 511.

scholars have proposed calling it "lateral accession," an expression with greater analytical power.[77] If the owner of land erects even a small part of a building on a neighbor's land, the doctrine of accession would compel him either to lose the property or to remove the building. Considerations of equity and efficiency have suggested an important exception to this principle, to be applied when the building has been built in good faith. Judicial discretion is granted to decide whether to transfer the ownership of the piece of land to the builder, provided that no objection has been made by the land owner within three months from the beginning of the construction, and that the intrusion is partial (*i.e.* only involves part of the building). The builder will not, however, obtain the ownership for free. If he wishes to enjoy this transfer of ownership, he must pay double the market value of the land, plus damages to the former land owner. This important provision of the Code has nevertheless been restrictively applied.[78]

The category of "immovable to immovable" accession includes the transfers of ownership between riparian owners. They are distinguished according to whether they occur incrementally or suddenly. Only in the latter case, provided that the detached piece of land is recognizable, can the former owner receive compensation, which is limited to the equivalent of the increased value of the new owner's riparian property.

The last category includes cases in which two chattels inseparably merge (*e.g.*, fusion of two metals). If there is no great difference in value, the new property will be jointly owned. Otherwise, the accession principle requires the owner of the more valuable portion to acquire the less valuable portion.

Finally, when someone builds something with someone else's property (*e.g.*, Joe builds a sculpture with Bill's metal) the conflict is constructed as between ownership and labor. That person whose contribution is higher in value prevails. Compensation is then due for the value of the property or labor that is lower in value.

A deep-rooted principle of Romanist law of property is that there is no statute of limitations for ownership. Nonetheless, an involuntary transfer of ownership can occur by adverse possession. Both ownership and limited real rights may be acquired by *usucapione*. The requisites are possession (not acquired with violence or fraud)

---

[77] G. Branca, "*Sconfinamento e buona fede*," in *Il Foro Italiano* XCI (1968), I, column 60; A. Pozzi, "*Spunti critici in tema di accessione invertita*," in *Il Foro Italiano* VIIIC (1975), I, column 2479.

[78] *See* A. Gambaro, *Il diritto di proprietà, supra* note 27, at 779*ff*; U. Mattei, *La proprietà immobiliare, supra* note 18, at 33; U. Mattei, *La Proprietà, supra* note 25.

and time. The requirements of time are different for immovables and movables, and may be greatly reduced if possession is in good faith and has been acquired in a manner which would have sufficed to transfer the title to the possessor if the transferor had been the owner (*e.g.*, as in a contract of sale of land with someone who appeared to be the owner but was not). Article 1158 CC states a prescription period of 20 years for immovables. This is reduced to ten years by art. 1159 CC in cases of good faith possession. Article 1161 CC provides for similar lapses of time for movables as well. There must not exist a good title of acquisition, otherwise art. 1153 CC, discussed *infra*, is applied.

Article 1153 CC contains the very important doctrine taken from the Napoleonic Code making possession title, in the sense just explained, together with good faith sufficient ingredients to acquire value ownership of chattels.[79]

This provision, which leaves the former owner protected only by a liability rule against the seller of his property, is the equivalent of the common law open market rule. It is, however, much broader than its common law equivalent, and must be kept in mind when analyzing what is commonly said about voluntary transfers of ownership. It is, moreover, a clear refutation of the "unitary approach" in the law of property.[80]

C. Voluntary Transfer of Ownership *Inter Vivos*

The whole subject of voluntary transfers of ownership, or, in Italian legal terminology, "derivative" acquisitions of ownership, is not usually discussed in property law treatises. Most of it is divided among the chapters related to succession, donations, or contracts. In chapters on property law, one finds, at most, the broad and deeply misleading general principle that ownership is transferred through consent. The number of exceptions to the consent rule is so huge, as we will see, that its validity even as a general principle is questionable.[81]

---

[79] Article 1153 CC: "Effects of acquisition of possession. He to whom movable property is conveyed by one who is not the owner acquires ownership of it through possession, provided that he be in good faith at the moment of consignment and there be an instrument or transaction capable of transferring ownership." Discussion in English in U. Mattei, *Basic Principles*, *supra* note 2.

[80] *See* the classic book on this point, L. Mengoni, *Gli acquisti "a non domino,"* Giuffrè, Milan (1958); A. Gambaro, *Il diritto di proprietà*, *supra* note 27, at 692*ff*; R. Sacco, *La buona fede nella teoria dei fatti giuridici di diritto privato*, Utet, Turin (1949).

[81] A. Gambaro, "*Le transfert de la propriété par acte entre vifs dans le systeme italien*," in *Italian National Reports. X Congress International Academy of Comparative Law*, Giuffrè, Milan (1978).

Voluntary transfers of ownership *inter vivos* may occur by gift or by sale. Although both gifts and sales are considered contracts in Italian law, very different principles and rules apply in the two cases. Gifts are divided into two categories according to their value.[82] If a gift is of small value, ownership is transferred by delivery. If the value is substantial, the completion of a formal procedure before a notary and two witnesses is necessary to transfer ownership. In the case of gifts, therefore, the difference in the method of transfer is not based on the movable or immovable nature of property.

In either case, a formality (whether delivery or notarial act) is required for the gift's validity. A promise to make a gift is not binding in Italian law. This is an important exception to the broad rule that agreement is both necessary and sufficient to form a contract.

Sale is defined in Italian law as a contract by which a party obliges itself to transfer ownership of property for a sum of money.[83] Where the parties agree to transfer property ownership in exchange for the ownership of other property, we are not dealing with a sale but with a different sort of contract known as *permuta*. However, with regard to the transfer of ownership, the principles and rules are much the same.[84] In Italy, as in France, ownership is said to be transferred by agreement. In the case of fungible property (for example, a pound of flour), ownership (and risk) is transferred at the moment of its separation from the undifferentiated mass.

Although many doubts have been raised about identifying the notion of contract with that of agreement,[85] the former is considered sufficient to transfer ownership in Italian law (in Italian legal terminology, the contract has "real effects"). Delivery or formal procedures are not required. Italian legal scholars are careful to state, in light of this broad rule, that this is true only between the parties to the transaction. Other principles, particularly those concerning reliance, apply to third parties.

Ownership, however, is defined as a real right that, by its very essence, is to be

---

[82] *See*, for a bibliography and a concise discussion, A. Trabucchi, *Istituzioni, supra* note 12, at 915.

[83] Article 1470 CC: "Notion. Sale is the contract having as its object the transfer of the ownership of a thing or the transfer of other rights in exchange for a price." For a concise treatment and an updated bibliography, *see* A. Trabucchi, *Istituzioni, supra* note 12, at 737*ff*.

[84] Article 1555 CC: "Application of provisions governing sale. The provisions governing sale apply to an exchange in those cases in which they are compatible."

[85] For a profound discussion of the entire Italian law of contracts, *see* R. Sacco, *Il contratto*, UTET, Turin (1975); *see also* the discussion of contracts in chapter 10, this volume.

respected by the entire world. What is transferred by consent, therefore, is less than full ownership. We may safely state that from the complex bundle of legal rights and obligations which constitute a property right, only a part is transferred by contractual agreement. A much more complex legal transaction is necessary to transfer all of them.[86]

Without delving into details we may nevertheless distinguish our analysis of chattels from that of immovables. With respect to the former, we have already noted the broadest exception to the principle of transfer by consent. Since the good-faith purchaser for value from the non-owner prevails over the true owner if he or she has possession of the movable, we may state that delivery is usually necessary to transfer complete ownership of chattels. A number of rules concerning such important topics as the law of restitution, remedies to recover possession, or natural obligations show that delivery plays a much broader role in Italian law than is commonly believed.[87]

Certain movables receive the same legal treatment as immovable property in Italy. These are the so-called registered movables, of which cars and boats are the most important. Consent is not sufficient to transfer ownership of immovables. The proper completion of a written form is necessary. In order to register the contract, a notarial formality is unavoidable as a practical matter (art. 2657 CC). What renders the law in action here different from theoretical statements is not delivery, as in the case of chattels, but recordation in the land register.

The Italian Civil Code has in fact enacted a system similar to the US "race notice statute."[88] If John sells land (or a car) first to Sam and then to Bill, then according to general principles, Sam becomes the owner, as Bill could not acquire title land that was no longer owned by John. However, if Bill is the first to register his contract in good faith, he becomes the owner even against Sam. This is a huge exception to the rule that Italian scholars always cite when dealing with "derivative acquisitions of ownership," which states that one cannot transfer more rights than he actually enjoys. It should be noted in passing that any limited real right such as, for example, a servitude, although supposedly transferable by mere contract, must be registered in order to become effective.[89]

---

[86] For a comparative discussion on this point, *see* R. Sacco, "Legal Formants: A Dynamic Approach to Comparative Law," 39 *Am J Comp L* 1 (1991).

[87] *See* P.G. Monateri, *La sineddoche*, Giuffrè, Milan (1984), p. 295*ff*.

[88] *See* R.R. Powell, *Powell on Real Property*, vol. 6, para. 913, Matthew Bender, New York (1979).

[89] This topic is contained in arts. 2643*ff* CC. This is part of the sixth book of the Code devoted to "protection of rights." On the subject of transcription, the classic work is S. Pugliatti, *La trascrizione*, Giuffrè, Milan (1957).

The registration requirement makes the transfer of ownership of immovables as well as movables a much more complex situation than is commonly recognized in Italy. (In certain Italian Regions, such as Trentino-Alto Adige, the Austrian system of registration is used, under which ownership is transferred at the moment of registration.) A recent reform of the Civil Code allows for the registration of "preliminary contracts" of real estate transfer, making the whole picture even more complicated.[90]

IV. Remedies to Protect Property

The typical social situation that we will consider is that of an individual enjoying the three basic "rights" with respect to a certain property: ownership, possession, and custody. Of course different problems arise when possession, custody, and property are held by different individuals. The fact that this may occur, however, does not justify the lack of a unitary treatment of the problem of protection of property, a lack peculiar to Italian legal scholarship. Let us state as a predicate that the mere possessor, whether in good or in bad faith, enjoys very effective protection of his property. He has a peculiar economic incentive to protect it effectively because he bears the risk of being held liable to the owner for lost or damaged property. The rules as to custody, on the other hand, introduce an element of inefficiency in the protection of property. Leaving aside the peculiar landlord-tenant situation, custody separates the individual who has the direct control over property from the one who has the standing to protect it legally.

Remedies to protect property usually do not receive unitary treatment in the scholarship, despite the common social and economic rationale. This is due partly to the systematics of the Code and partly to the old Roman law tradition sharply distinguishing between ownership and possession. In the following pages, we will not follow that tradition. We will describe the different remedies through a unitary approach, dividing them according to their economic function. Those related to the recovery of a lost possession of a property will be analyzed first. Then we will deal with remedies to protect the quiet enjoyment of property rather than protect a complete seizure of it.[91]

---

[90] For an updated discussion, *see* A. Chianale, *Trascrizione del contratto preliminare e trasferimento della proprieta*, Giappichelli, Turin (1998).

[91] Two comparative studies are devoted to these two different aspects of the law of property. The first problem is closely considered by S. Ferreri, *supra* note 9, para. 1; the second by U. Mattei, *Tutela inibitoria e tutela risarcitoria*, Giuffrè, Milan (1987). Both these aspects are

A. Recovery of Possession

Let us state first that this subject is structured around an action unknown in the common law – the so-called *rei vindicatio*. Italian law considers this action as generally available for both chattels and immovables. Italian scholars do not follow their French colleagues in considering it exceptional with regard to the former, where the rule is that good faith possession equals ownership.[92]

This action is defined as real because it follows the thing. It may be taken against both the possessor and the person with custody. The owner has standing. Holders of limited real rights also enjoy a similar action to recover their (limited) possession. This action is not subject to a statute of limitations. A common lawyer may at first admire this broad and effective remedy to protect ownership. In Anglo-American law, neither chapters on real property nor those on chattels deal with such a general action. Nonetheless, this action entails a major inconvenience because it requires ownership to be proven. This proof is known as *probatio diabolica*, as to show a "derivative" title is not sufficient (*see supra*, part III B). Usually, it is considered sufficient to prove good title for the period of time necessary for usucaption, which is fairly long.[93] This is why this action overlaps with real, quasi-real, or personal actions for restitution.

If property has been seized against the will of the possessor, he or she will have an action to recover it against the perpetrator of the seizure. In this case, only proof of seizure is required. Also, the holder of custody (provided that it is not for reasons of service or hospitality) has standing.[94]

The Code describes two different actions: a broader one against violent or

---

dealt with by R. Sacco, *Il possesso*, *supra* note 13, § 1, and by A. Gambaro, *La legittimazione passiva alle azioni possessorie*, Giuffrè, Milan (1979), in the analysis of possession; A. Gambaro, *Il diritto di proprietà*, *supra* note 27, at 871*ff*; U. Mattei, *La proprietà immobiliare*, *supra* note 18, at 225*ff*.

[92] *See* S. Ferreri, *supra* note 9, at 2; A. Gambaro, *Il diritto di proprietà*, *supra* note 27, at 925*ff*; U. Mattei, *La proprietà immobiliare*, *supra* note 18, at 268*ff*.

[93] *See supra*, para. 2.

[94] Article 1168 CC: "Action for recovery of possession. One who has been violently or by stealth deprived of possession can, within a year of the loss, sue the taker for recovery of possession. / The action is also available to he who has custody of the thing, except in the case in which he has it for reason of service or hospitality. / If the taking is clandestine, the term for bringing the action runs from the day of discovery of the taking. / The restoration of possession shall be ordered by the judge, if a *prima facie* case is made, without delay." *See* J. Gordley and U. Mattei, *Protecting Passion*, *supra* note 14.

fraudulent takings, and a narrower one against non-violent seizures of immovables. There is a limitation of one year, running from the taking. This difference between the two actions has, however, been abolished by case law, which has interpreted the requirement of violence as contrary to the possessor's will.[95]

Scholars are divided as to whether this action has a tortuous nature or is to be considered real. Article 1169 CC also provides for an action against whoever is actually in possession (even if this person is not the author of the seizure), provided that they had knowledge of the taking. This provision leads us to consider this action at least as quasi-real.

If possession is lost voluntarily, but without a legal reason (*i.e.* mistaken delivery), the owner will still be able to recover it by *rei vindicatio*, but the possessor (non-owner) will not be able to use the remedies just described. The owner, on the other hand, will find it inconvenient to offer the *probatio diabolica*. Italian law therefore offers a variety of personal remedies of a contractual or quasi-contractual nature.[96]

B. Remedies for the Quiet Enjoyment of Property

A large variety of quiet enjoyment type remedies are known to Italian law. Some of them are available only to the owner. Others, also quite effective, are available to the possessor as well. Recent case law developments have extended to many other individuals a variety of remedies structurally similar to those that protect property. These developments are used as a tool. One example is art. 700 of the Code of Civil Procedure, which provides urgent effective relief against behaviors endangering legal rights. We should distinguish here the case of intrusions upon property by a single act from invasions of a continuous character. Other structural differences can be found between those remedies designed to address past wrongs and those intended to offer prospective relief.

Although Italian scholars have traditionally been less interested in analyzing concrete remedies than in discussing rights, this more abstract approach has been challenged in recent years.[97] In this section we will focus our attention on concrete remedies that may be exercised by the owner or by the possessor of property.

In order to understand the potential effectiveness of such remedies, we must first briefly consider a deep institutional divergence between Italian and common

---

[95] *See* R. Sacco, *Il possesso, supra* note 13, at 236*ff.*

[96] *See* S. Ferreri, *supra* note 9, at 9-10.

[97] Among others, a remedial approach to private law has been taken by A. Di Majo, *La tutela civile dei diritti*, Giuffrè, Milan (1987).

law approaches. Italian law does not give courts anything like a contempt power, except in a very limited sense. On the other hand, it does provide the machinery to give effect to the orders of the courts, which is something foreign to the common law tradition.[98] Let us offer an example. John obtains a judgment that Tom should remove a wall unlawfully built on his land. If Tom does not obey the order, John may obtain an order from the court to have someone do the work at Tom's expense. An article of our Code states that, whenever possible, money judgments should be avoided in favor of specific performance to return things to the *status quo ante*.[99]

The machinery to do so is provided for by duties both to do or not to do a specified thing. This system is ineffective only in those cases in which the performance can be accomplished only by a particular person. But this is very unusual in the field of property law.[100]

With respect to remedies against a continuous activity that impairs a property value, the typical remedy is by way of injunction. Nevertheless, there is no unitary chapter of Italian law devoted to injunctive relief. Judges only have authority to grant injunctive relief in particular circumstances, as provided in a limited number of articles of the Code related to specific violations. Ownership is generally protected by injunction, however, according to an action known as negatory action.[101]

The drafting of the article concerning this action is misleading, and has given rise to many problems long discussed by Italian scholars and judges. First of all, it has never been clear how this action is related to the general action for unlawful acts provided by art. 2043 CC which, as we have seen, may have a specific character.[102] Moreover, a long tradition derived from Roman law seemed to grant the negatory action only when one claimed a right to another's property, and not when he had merely intruded on it. This narrow construction, however, has been abandoned in more recent scholarship.

---

[98] For an interesting English article on this topic, *see* C. Cremonini, *An Italian Lawyer Looks at Civil Contempt. From Rome to Glastonbury*, Civil Justice Q. (1984), p. 133.

[99] Article 2058 CC: "Specific redress. The injured party can demand specific redress when this is wholly or partially possible. / The judge however can order that the redress be made only by providing an equivalent, if specific redress would prove to be excessively onerous for the debtor."

[100] Two seminal works are S. Chiarloni, *Misure coercitive e tutela dei diritti*, Giuffrè, Milan (1980); and S. Mazzamuto, *L'attuazione degli obblighi di fare*, Jovene, Naples (1978).

[101] Article 949 CC: "Negatory action. The owner can sue to have declared the non-existence of rights claimed by others in the thing, when he has reason to fear prejudice from them. / If disturbances or molestations also occur, the owner can request their cessation as well as judgment for compensation for damages."

The negatory action can today be safely described as a general injunctive, declaratory, or damage remedy, which protects the owner against all intrusions that do not amount to a seizure. Relief may be framed in one of the various ways mentioned, according to the nature of the intrusion. It can be obtained whenever the intrusion itself does not receive a particular protection by the legal system. An example of such a protected intrusion may be that of the good-faith builder on someone else's land, which may be protected by arts. 936-38 CC, or that of the hunter trespassing on non-fenced land, excused by art. 842 CC.[103]

The broad power of injunctive relief given to the judge in order to protect the right of ownership has led some scholars to exploit it to achieve environmental protection.[104] An attempt has been made to build up a system of decentralized environmental protection based on a rational mixture of property rules and liability rules, along the lines suggested by Calabresi and Melamed.[105] This attempt enjoys very strong textual support from art. 844 CC, which is enacted on the famous theory of balancing interests advanced by the German scholar Rudolph Jehring. This provision authorizes reasonable nuisances deriving from "smoke, heat, fumes, noises, vibrations, or similar propagation from the land of a neighbor" while forbidding unreasonable ones. Reasonableness is to be decided "with regard to the condition of the sites." The second section of the article states that "[i]n applying this rule the Court shall reconcile the needs of industrial productivity with the conflicting property rights." Courts should also take account of "the priority of a given use." According to this article, then, there are three categories of nuisance. Case law and legal scholarship have provided different remedies for the different situations. Reasonable nuisances are allowed and the owner has no remedy against them. Unreasonable nuisances are usually prohibited by means of an injunction. If, however, they come from a productive activity, after a balancing test very similar to the one associated in America with *Boomer v. Atlantic Cement Co.*, the court

---

[102] U. Mattei, *Tutela, supra* note 91, at 281*ff*, devotes substantial attention to the analysis of this relationship.

[103] On the former example, U. Mattei, *Tutela, supra* note 91, at 314*ff*. On the latter, compare P. Rescigno, *Per uno studio, supra* note 24, at para. 2.

[104] *See* S. Patti, *La tutela civile dell'ambiente*, Cedam, Padua (1979).

[105] *See* U. Mattei, "*I modelli nella tutela dell'ambiente*," in *Rivista di Diritto Civile* XXXI (1985), II, p. 390; F. Nappi, *Le regale proprietarie e la teoria delle immissioni*, ESI, Naples (1985); U. Mattei, "*Diritto e rimedio nell'esperienza italiana ed in quella statunitense: un primo approccio*," in *Quadrimestre* (1987), p. 341*ff*.

may allow the nuisance provided that compensation is paid to the owner.[106] Scholars are divided on practically every issue, from the nature of compensation, to its amount, and the requisites for obtaining it. It is, however, clear that by compelling the polluting activity either to stop or to internalize its costs, we have what is potentially a very effective tool of decentralized control over pollution.

However, some scholars dislike the idea that standing for decentralized decision-making in environmental matters should be linked to ownership.[107] They have therefore tried, with some success, to link it to the right of personal health. The ultimate result of this generous idea, however, has been to loosen the liability rule and revert to the extremes: injunction versus no remedy at all. A recent enactment, moreover, has moved the matter of environmental protection outside the ordinary courts. (*See* the discussion in chapter 9 of this volume.) The important principle of decentralized decision-making contained in art. 844 CC therefore seems to be wasted. The public law mentality which characterizes much of the civil law tradition in matters of public policy has prevailed again.[108] Two other actions may be found among the remedies to protect ownership in the Italian Civil Code: the action for settlement of boundaries (art. 950) and the action for placement of boundary markers (art. 951). These provisions, devoid of theoretical interest, still have some importance in the everyday practice of the law.

Very important provisions are found, on the other hand, in arts. 1171, 1172 and 1173 CC. These actions are given to both the owner and the possessor and provide a quite efficient remedy to protect property. It is important to focus our attention here, again, on the very high status of possession in Italian law. The good-faith possessor is protected not only against everybody else but also against the true owner. A variety of rules entitle him to the products of property that bears fruit to a compensation for improvements to the property (art. 1148 CC: Acquisition of fruits; art. 1149 CC: Reimbursements of costs of production and collection of fruits; art. 1150 CC: Repairs, improvements and additions; art. 1151 CC: Payment of indemnities; art. 1152 CC: Retention in favor of possessor in good faith), and in many instances the owner is deprived of his usual remedies (arts. 936, 937, 938 CC).

---

[106] A comparative discussion between American law under *Boomer* and Italian law under art. 844 is provided in U. Mattei, *Tutela*, *supra* note 91, at 257*ff*. More generally see U. Mattei, *Basic Principles*, *supra* note 2.

[107] *See* C. Salvi, *Le immissonii industriali*, Giuffrè, Milan (1979); A. Procida-Mirabelli Di Lauro, *Immissioni e rapporto proprietario*, ESI, Naples (1984).

[108] A. Pradi, "*Immissioni*," in *Rivista di diritto civile*, II, 1995, p. 589.

The bad-faith possessor also receives protection, albeit more limited as to the owner, but very effective as to the outside world.[109] An action enacted in broader terms than the owner's negatory action, with the huge advantage of not requiring proof of ownership, is granted without regard to bad or good faith. According to it, "[o]ne who has been disturbed in possession of an immovable, of a real right in an immovable, or of a universality of movables, can, within a year of the disturbance, sue for protection of possession." The Code of Civil Procedure provides a very effective special trial for all possessory actions.

This important opportunity for relief has led some courts to use possessory remedies to create and protect property rights in broadcasting frequencies. In the absence of regulation in this area, this form of decentralized decision-making has been one of the most interesting developments of our recent case law. It is no surprise then that the best Italian scholarship has devoted a lot of energy to understanding and potentially shaping these developments.[110] These developments, together with those based on the general urgent relief provision of our Code of Civil Procedure (which lies outside the scope of this chapter), are the best evidence that whenever the judicial process works decently, decentralized decision-making may be better than collective choices allotted to governmental agencies.

Two important and effective actions complete the arsenal of remedies to protect property. In both of these cases, injunctive relief plus damages are available: "The owner, the holder of other limited real rights, or the possessor, who has reason to fear that new work undertaken by others on his own or someone else's land can cause damage to his property, can denounce the new work to the court, provided that the work is not completed and a year has not passed since its beginning." This action is known as "denunciation of new work" (art. 1171 CC). The other action, known as "denunciation of feared damage," does not even require the undertaking of a positive action: "The owner, the holder of other limited real rights, or the possessor who has reason to fear that any building, tree or other thing threatens serious proximate damage to his property can denounce the fact to the Court and obtain, according to the circumstances, a remedy to obviate the damage."[111]

---

[109] *See* R. Sacco and R. Catarina, *Il possesso*, *supra* note 13, para. 1, at 211*ff.*

[110] *See* A. Pace, "*La radio-televisione in Italia con particolare riguardo all' emittenza private,*" in *Rivista Trimestrale di Diritto Pubblico* XXXVII (1987), pp. 615*ff.*

[111] On these actions, *see* R. Sacco and R. Catarina, *Il possesso*, *supra* note 13, at 248*ff.*

Conclusion

The foregoing discussion demonstrates that despite the unitary and traditionally civilian rhetoric of Italian Property Law, this branch of the law has developed in a highly varied fashion, following several different legislative, judicial, and scholarly contributions and approaches. The variegated texture of Italian property law today confirms Professor Salvatore Pugiatti's prescient notion, first presented in the 1950s, that there is not one concept of ownership but rather different ownerships. This approach has remained a powerful and accurate interpretive tool.

CHAPTER TWELVE

Trust Law

Michele Graziadei [1]

I. Introduction

Readers who have studied comparative law using David and Brierly's *Major Legal Systems of the World*[2] or R.B. Schlesinger's *Comparative Law*[3] will probably think that the title of this chapter is a misnomer. According to those classics, trusts are institutions of the common law world. Indeed, they are very frequently considered a distinctive feature of the common law tradition. How, then, can there be a law of trusts in a civil law jurisdiction like Italy? This chapter does not intend to challenge the classical approach, but rather suggests that the picture is more complex than one might at first imagine.[4]

The starting point of the following analysis is the entry into force in Italy of the Hague Convention of 1985 on the Law Applicable to Trusts and on their recognition on 1 January 1992.[5] The prompt ratification of the Convention in Italy may be

---

[1] Professor of Private Comparative Law, University of Western Piedmont. This is a revised version of "Trusts in Italian Law: A Matter of Property or of Obligation?," first published in *Italian National Reports to the XVth Congress of the International Academy of Comparative Law* (1998), p. 190*ff.*

[2] David & Brierly, *Major Legal Systems in the World Today: An Introduction to Comparative Study of Law*, 2nd ed. (1985).

[3] Schlesinger, *et al.*, *Comparative Law: Cases, Text, Materials*, 6th ed. (1998), p. 868*ff.*

[4] *See* Lupoi, *Trusts*, 2nd ed., Milano (2001). *See also* Mattei, *Comparative Law and Economics* (1997), p. 147*ff*; Helmholz & Zimmermann (eds.), *Itinera Fiduciae – Trust and Treuhand in Historical Perspective*, Berlin (1998); Hayton, Kortmann & Verhagen (eds.), *Principles of European Trust Law* (1999). D.M.W. Waters, *The Institution of Trust in Civil Law and Common Law*, 252 Collected Courses of The Hague Academy of International Law 1995, 112.

[5] Hereinafter, the Convention. Italy ratified the Convention with the law no. 364 of 16 October 1989, *Ratifica ed esecuzione della Convenzione sulla legge applicabile ai trusts e sul loro*

Jeffrey S. Lena and Ugo Mattei (eds.), *Introduction to Italian Law*, 317-340

explained by the conviction – widely shared by those Italian lawyers who are familiar with the law of trusts of common law jurisdictions – that trusts are "perfectly clean and moral"[6] and that they do not subvert any fundamental principle of Italian substantive law. Indeed, as this contribution will show, Italy has long had a law of trusts, if by "trusts" we mean institutions such as those described by art. 2 of the Convention. Yet Italian trusts are not as ubiquitous as their common law counterparts, nor are they rooted in the jurisdictional distinction between law and equity which marks the common law provenance of trust.[7]

This chapter examines Italian institutions that may be considered trusts for the purposes of art. 2 of the Convention, together with their main uses and their shortcomings, and the concepts involved in shaping legal discourse about them. The coverage is limited to trusts voluntarily created, with special regard to trusts in business and commercial settings (parts II to IV of this chapter). The impact of the Convention in Italy will be considered in part V, which shows that the current interpretation of the Convention in Italy allows the creation and the recognition in Italy of purely internal trusts governed by the applicable foreign law.[8] This approach follows from the principle of party autonomy in the choice of the applicable law enshrined in art. 6 of the Convention. The last part of the chapter (part VI) discusses the possibility of future legislation in the field of trusts in Italy.

---

riconoscimento adottata a L'Aja il 1° luglio 1985, Gazzetta ufficiale, 8 November 1989, no. 261, *supplemento ordinario*.

[6] Thus reported Prof. Antonio Gambaro in *Hague Conference on private international law, Proceedings of the Fifteenth Session*, II (1985), p. 288.

[7] On the necessity to rethink the present value of that distinction, *see* Rudden, "Equity as an Alibi," in Goldstein (ed.), *Equity and Contemporary Legal Developments* (1992), p. 46. For the historical background of trusts in Italian law, *see* Graziadei, "The Development of Fiducia in Italian and French Law from the 14th Century to the End of the Ancien Régime," in Helmholz & Zimmermann (eds.), *supra* note 4, at 327. This essay casts new light on the history of trusts in Italian law and highlights the existence of historical evidence (hitherto largely ignored by comparative legal historians) relevant to the study of the intellectual history of trust law across the Channel. For a topical treatment of the historical point, *see* M. Lupoi, *The Civil Law Trust*, 32 *J Trans L* 967, 973 (1999).

[8] The expression "purely internal trust" was introduced in Italy by Maurizio Lupoi to mean trusts which are placed under a foreign law providing for trusts (through the designation of the applicable law in accordance with art. 6, first paragraph, of the Convention), but which lack other connecting factors with a foreign jurisdiction.

II. What is a Trust?

What is a trust? This is a notoriously troublesome question. Luckily, it may be left for another day. Here we are concerned solely with the notion of "trust" adopted by art. 2 of the Hague Convention. This article lists the hallmarks of the institution for the purposes of that instrument.[9] All the elements referred to in art. 2 of the Convention characterize trusts governed by the law of jurisdictions belonging to the common law world, as well as a number of civil law institutions serving purposes commonly associated with express trusts in Anglophone countries.[10] Lawyers accustomed to dealing with a comprehensive law of trusts may be puzzled by the variety of these civil law institutions. Yet even in countries where a synthesis of the institution has emerged, there is an ever-increasing differentiation of trusts.[11]

III. A Survey of Trusts in Italy

A. Trusts for Non-Profit Purposes

The present survey of trusts in Italy starts with the analysis of trust relationships created to further non-profit purposes (in this regard, *see* Professor Ponzanelli's chapter 13 in this volume on non-profit organizations). In Italian law there are

---

[9] Hague Convention, *op. cit.*, art. 2: "For the purposes of this Convention the term 'trust' refers to the legal relationship created – *inter vivos* or on death – by a settlor when assets have been placed under the control of a trustee for the benefit of a beneficiary or for a specified purpose. A trust has the following characteristics:

   a) the assets constitute a separate fund and are not part of the trustee's own estate;

   b) title to the assets stands in the name of the trustee or in the name of another person on behalf of the trustee;

   c) the trustee has the power and duty, in respect of which he is accountable, to manage, employ or dispose of the assets in accordance with the terms of the trust and the special duties imposed upon him by law.

   The reservation by the settlor of certain rights and powers, and the fact that the trustee may himself have rights as a beneficiary, are not necessarily inconsistent with the existence of a trust."

[10] On the interpretation of art. 2 of the Convention, *see* below.

[11] *See, e.g.*, Langbein, "The Secret Life of the Trust: The Trust as an Instrument of Commerce," 107 *Yale LJ* 165 (1997); Moffat, "Pension Funds: A Fragmentation of Trust Law?" (1993), *MLR* 471.

some standard legal forms currently used to pursue idealistic goals without resorting to incorporation.[12] The most common of these forms are the unincorporated association (arts. 36-38 CC), the unincorporated or fiduciary foundation (cp. art. 32 CC), and the committee (arts. 39-41 CC).[13] Each of these institutions poses property-holding problems that are solved by the use of techniques redolent of trusts.[14] Unincorporated associations are created informally by contract. They need not be registered and they may pursue any legitimate goal other than the carrying on of business activities for profit, which in Italy is reserved to partnerships and companies.[15] Since these entities have no legal personality, any property acquired for the members of the association must vest in the association as represented by one or more of its members, or in one of its members acting on behalf of the association. In this case, the holder of the property is in the position of a trustee with respect to the property acquired for the association. If the contract among the original members of the association announces a purpose to the public invited to fund the association, we have a distinct legal form: the committee. Property held by the unincorporated committee resembles that of the unincorporated association. However, while the members of the unincorporated association may dissolve it and partition its assets[16] among themselves, the committee may not. Any property held directly by the committee (or on its behalf by one of its members) must be employed for the purpose announced to the public, or for like purposes if a change of circumstances makes achieving the original purpose impossible (art. 42 CC).[17] This rule, mirrored by the common law *cy près* doctrine for charitable

---

[12] For a comparative treatment, *see* Verrucoli, *Non-Profit Organisations (A Comparative Approach)* (1985).

[13] Here, I will concentrate on the basic frame provided by the Civil Code articles on associations, foundations, and committees, though several important recent laws have supplemented and modified the Civil Code to promote the growth of the non-profit sector. *See* Professor Ponzanelli's discussion of non profits in chapter 13, this volume.

[14] Gambaro, "*Il diritto di proprietà*," in *Trattato di diritto civile e commerciale già diretto da Cicu e Messineo, continuato da Mengoni*, VIII, t. 2 (1995), 600*ff.*

[15] For present purposes, I will ignore the exceptions to the rule.

[16] Note that any entity subject to the tax treatment of the "*organizzazioni non lucrative a scopo di utilità sociale*" must respect the non-distribution constraint.

[17] Cass., 12 June 1986, no. 3898, *Giur. it.* (1987), I, 1, 1015, obs. Scognamiglio, *Foro it.* (1986), I, 2126, noted by Graziadei, "*Acquisto per conto di un comitato non riconosciuto e dissociazione della proprietà*," in *Riv. dir. civ.* (1988), II 120; Cass., 23 June 1994, no. 6032, *Foro it* (1995) I, 1268, obs. V. Lenoci.

trusts,[18] applies more generally where property is transferred to a legal person for a specific purpose (art. 32 CC),[19] and is in the nature of a fiduciary foundation wherein the recipient of the property holds it as trustee for the purpose declared by the transferor.[20] The fiduciary foundation does not have legal personality. The property-holding techniques examined so far may be contrasted with *inter vivos* donations (arts. 793-794 CC) or testamentary dispositions charged with a *modus* (arts. 647-648 CC) which is imposed to advance private purposes or purposes beneficial to the community. Gifts *sub modo* do not segregate the property transferred by the donor to the donee from the rest of the donee's property.

B. Trusts in the Personal or Family Context

Common law trusts play several important functions in the personal or family context. Leaving aside questions related to the law of matrimonial property, in common law jurisdictions, trusts are employed to provide for spendthrifts and incompetents, as well as to plan the intergenerational transmission of wealth. Similar functions are fulfilled in Italy by a host of legal institutions, some of which are clearly within the scope of the notion of "trust" emerging from art. 2 of the Convention, such as the fiduciary disposition mentioned in art. 627 CC, or the *fondo patrimoniale della famiglia* (arts. 167-171 CC).

The creation of protected interests in property by way of *fideicommissum* is still possible in Italy, but solely where the instituted heir or legatee charged with the duty to preserve the property and to restore it to the ultimate beneficiaries appointed by the testator is judicially declared insane (arts. 692-699 CC).[21] Since 1975, any

---

[18] Zimmermann, "Cy-Près," in *Festgabe fuer Max Kaser* H.P. Benör *et al.*, eds., *Iuris Professio: Festgabe für Max Kaser zum 80 Geburtstag*, Wien, Böhlau (1986), p. 395*ff*, shows that the convergence owes little to chance.

[19] Since the same rule applies to funds collected by a single individual (Trib. Lucca, 4 May 1960, *Dir. eccl.* (1960), 270, obs. Scavo Lombardo), it is easy to conclude that a general principle is at work here.

[20] Galgano, "*Delle persone giuridiche*," in *Commentario al Codice Civile Scialoja-Branca* (1969), 148, 150, fn. 27, 172; *id.*, "*Delle associazioni non riconosciute e dei comitati*," in *Commentario al Codice Civile Scialoja-Branca*, 2nd ed. (1976), 290*ff*. This opinion is widely accepted. More recently, *see* Zoppini, *Le fondazioni* (1995), p. 286*ff*. (which contains a thorough review of previous literature and cases on this issue); *id.*, "*Fondazioni e trusts (spunti per un confronto)*," in Beneventi (ed.), *I trusts in Italia oggi*, with an introduction by Lupoi (1997), p. 147*ff*.

[21] On the Roman law background of the institution, *see* Johnston, *The Roman law of Trusts* (1988).

other kind of *fideicommissum* is null and void (art. 692 para. 5 CC).[22]

By contrast, according to art. 627 CC, secret and half-secret fiduciary dispositions created by testament are merely unenforceable. Such a trust is different from a *fideicommissum*, because the fiduciary heir or legatee is a *nudus minister*, who does not receive any benefit from it, unlike the heir or legatee charged with the *fideicommissum*. But nowadays this institution is almost unknown in practice.

Yet in Italy, as elsewhere, the wealthy feel the need to control the transmission of property across the generations.[23] Furthermore, no one can contemplate arts. 536-564 CC governing the *legitime* (that share of the decedent's estate, sometimes referred to as the "non-disposable share," which must pass as a matter of law to the decedent's spouse and issue) without asking how they can be reconciled with the need to avoid their disruptive effects on the management of the family business. Testamentary execution (arts. 700-712 CC) cannot be the answer to the problem. Following the French model, the Italian Civil Code limits the period during which executors can withhold possession of the property from those taking under the testament to two years from the testator's death (art. 703 para. 3 CC). Nevertheless, the skilled drafting of limited partnership contracts (currently employed like holdings) has done much to reassure Italian tycoons that they can give unity of direction to industrial enterprises and select those who will run the businesses in the future.[24] This approach to estate planning also responds to the contemporary need to anticipate the effects of succession upon death which were formerly governed by testaments.[25]

---

[22] Though *fideicommissa* created abroad produce their effects in Italy because they do not violate our *ordre public*: Cass., 15 March 1984, no. 2215, *Foro it.* (1984), I, 2253; *Giur. it.* (1984), I, 1, 1368. The case involved a *fideicommissum* governed by Austrian law producing its effects on immovable property situated in Italy.

[23] *See* VV.AA., *La trasmissione familiare della ricchezza* (1995); Iudica, "*Fondazioni, fedecommesserie, trusts e trasmissione della ricchezza familiare*," in *Scritti in onore di Rodolfo Sacco*, II (1994), p. 639.

[24] Weigmann, "*L'accomandita per azioni come cassaforte familiare*," in *Scintillae Iuris. Studi in memoria di Gino Gorla*, III (1985), p. 2519. *See* Zoppini, "*Contributo allo studio delle disposizioni testamentarie 'in forma indiretta'*," in *Rivista trimestrale di diritto e procedura civile* (1998), 1077.

[25] Palazzo, "*Attribuzioni patrimoniali tra vivi e assetti successori per la trasmissione della ricchezza familiare*," in VV.AA., *La trasmissione familiare della ricchezza*, p. 17; Langbein, "The Twentieth-Century Revolution in Family Wealth Transmission," 86 *MichLRev* 723 (1988).

Before leaving the family context, it is worth mentioning that the need to protect property from the claims of the general creditors of the spouses is usually satisfied by setting up the *fondo patrimoniale della famiglia* (arts. 167-171 CC).[26] The spouses or a third party may create the fund in question by dedicating property (immovables, registered movables, or securities which are capable of being earmarked) to the satisfaction of family needs. The act creating the fund may be unilateral.[27] Ownership of the assets included in the fund vests in the spouses, unless otherwise provided by the settlor. The fund is managed by the spouses in accordance with the rules on the administration of community property (arts. 180-185 CC) and is immune from creditor claims of that are unrelated to the needs of the family. The *fondo patrimoniale della famiglia* lasts until all the of the couple's children come of age, or the marriage is dissolved.

From a broader perspective, it is worth noting that Italian law makes it possible to create rights in favor of a person without enriching his or her creditors, even outside the framework of family law or succession law. The common instance is provided by insurance law, which is also applicable to financial products linked to life insurance contracts. Life insurance proceeds paid to a beneficiary are immune from the claims of the payee's creditors (art. 1923 para. 1 CC). The same rule applies to payments under a life annuity, if they are limited to maintenance of the annuitant (art. 1881 CC). The owner of a thing may create an inalienable right of usufruct, or a right of use which is inalienable according to the law and immune from the claims of the creditors of the holder of the limited right.[28] But while annuitants are mere creditors and will be paid *pro rata* in case of insolvency of their debtors,[29] holders of the right of usufruct or of use have real rights which cannot be seized by the creditors of the naked owner.

---

[26] *See* Lupoi, *supra* note 4, at 514*ff*; Lupoi & Arrigo, in Hayton, Kortmann & Verhagen (eds.), *supra* note 4, at 123*ff.*

[27] *See* Fusaro, "*'Affectation,' 'Destination' e vincoli di destinazione*," in *Scritti in onore di Rodolfo Sacco*, II (1994), p. 453.

[28] Inalienability of the right of use is established by art. 1024 CC. The inalienability of the usufruct can be stipulated, when it is not imposed by the law (art. 326 CC). Immunity of the right from the claims of the usuary or usufructuary follows from its inalienability.

[29] The beneficiaries of life insurance contracts are in a better position: the funds held by the insurer under those contracts cannot be reached by the insurer's creditors (law decree no. 8 of 18 January 1993, converted into law no. 68 of 19 March 1993).

C. Trusts in the Commercial or Business Sphere

Approaching the topic of trusts in the commercial or business sphere, it is important to recognize that the relevant Italian law is not wholly codified or set out in statutes.

The notion of fiduciary legal transactions (*negozio fiduciario*) remains uncodified, just like the distinction between *fiducia cum amico* and *fiducia cum creditore*, which was revived during the early decades of the twentieth century under the influence of German legal scholarship.[30] The arrangements which became known by these names were essentially: (i) an *inter vivos* transfer of property to a person bound by contract to deal with it on behalf of the transferor or for a designated third person, or (ii) an *inter vivos* transfer of property for security purposes, whereby the creditor became full owner of the property, with the promise to return it to the debtor in case of timely payment of the debt. Whereas these legal devices were molded by scholars and judges, the creation of trustee companies or partnerships (*società fiduciarie*) was expressly authorized by a royal decree in 1926 and then by law no. 1966 of 1939.[31] This statute regulated the activity of partnerships and companies "which managed assets for third parties." For many years, however, the ill-defined legislative innovation passed almost *sub silentio*. The booming stock exchange of the 1980s highlighted the potential of such partnerships and companies to carry on investment business.

At the outset of the twenty-first century, the picture has changed in many respects. First, fiduciary transactions whereby one person holds title to assets on behalf of another are now in most cases considered akin to a mandate, even where one of the parties is a *società fiduciaria*. Secondly, the growth of the financial services industry has stimulated the development of new legal forms that have taken over most of the investment business formerly carried on by trustee companies or partnerships. Thirdly, in most cases the transfer of title to movable or immovable things for security purposes is now considered contrary to the Civil Code prohibition against forfeiture clauses (*lex commissoria*). Each of these points needs to be examined in detail.

---

[30] For a concise overview *see* A. Mazzoni, "*Les opérations fiduciaires en droit italien*," in VV. AA., *Les opérations fiduciaires – Colloque de Luxembourg* (1985), p. 335.

[31] Law no. 1966 of 23 January 1939, *Disciplina delle società fiduciarie e di revisione*; D.M. 16 January 1995, *Autorizzazione all'esercizio dell'attività fiduciaria. See* now *decreto legislativo* no. 58 of 24 February 1998, *Testo unico delle disposizioni in materia di intermediazione finanziaria*, art. 199. *See also* De Angelis, "*Fiduciaria (Società),*" in *Digesto*, 4th ed., *sezione commerciale*, VI (1991), 91.

1. Fiducia *and Mandate*

The model of *inter vivos* fiduciary transfer of property labeled as *fiducia cum amico*, which Italian lawyers refined in the first decades of this century, seemed at first to bear no resemblance to any institution regulated by the Italian Civil Code of 1865. A closer look, however, discloses an interrelationship between *fiducia cum amico* and the contract of mandate regulated by the Civil Code of 1942 (arts. 1703*ff*).[32]

The Civil Code articles on mandate apply whenever one party (the *mandatario*, or agent) acts on behalf of another party (the *mandante*, or principal) in legal transactions (art. 1703 CC). According to the Civil Code, the agent may act either in the principal's name, in a representative capacity, or in his own name, without disclosing his status as agent. Yet, even when the intermediary does not communicate to the third party that he is acting in a representative capacity, movables or claims acquired by him while performing the mandate are not available to his creditors. To this effect, the contract of mandate must be proved by a document bearing a date prior to the seizure of that property or insolvency of the agent (art. 1707 CC, arts. 45 and 79 l.f.).[33] Furthermore, the principal may recover movables acquired by the agent from a third party (art. 1706 para. 1 CC) in his own name. The principal may also intervene in the relationship between the agent and a third party to enforce claims of the former against the latter (art. 1705 para. 1 CC). Immovables and registered movables acquired by the agent do not belong to the principal before they are conveyed to him voluntarily or by judicial action (art. 1706 para. 2 CC). Nevertheless, such assets cease to be available to the creditors of the agent as soon as the principal registers, in the appropriate register, the action for specific performance of the transfer (art. 2652 para. 2 CC).

The above-mentioned rules (especially those concerning movables and claims) were suited to develop a doctrine of fiduciary ownership identical to a common law conception which envisages the possibility of an agent-trustee.[34] The strict nexus between mandate and *fiducia cum amico* explains why in recent years the Italian Parliament has enacted several norms concerning fiduciary holdings, only

---

[32] P.G. Jaeger, *La separazione del patrimonio fiduciario nel fallimento* (1968), p. 386; Graziadei, "*Proprietà fiduciaria e proprietà del mandatario*," in *Quadrimestre* (1990), 1; Morello, "*Fiducia e negozio fiduciario: dalla 'riservatezza' alla 'trasparenza'*," in Beneventi (ed.), *supra* note 20, at 81*ff*.

[33] The notion of a "document having a date certain" (*atto scritto avente data certa*) is technical. The document has a date certain when it is created by a public official (as a notary), or in the cases listed in arts. 2703, 2704 CC.

[34] *See, e.g., Restatement of the Law*, Agency, Second (1958), para. 14 b.

to make sure that where – as is usually the case – the *fiduciario* is controlled by the *fiduciante*, the former is treated as an *alter ego* of the latter.[35]

This legislation is important because it suggests that the use of *fiducia cum amico* in the commercial context has been frequently motivated by a desire to hide the true owner of certain assets, rather than by the decision to look for effective asset management. The curtain has been lifted for fiscal reasons,[36] or to comply with other mandatory provisions of law requiring the disclosure of the real state of affairs, but otherwise it has been allowed to stand. Thus, quite frequently *fiducia* has been used to satisfy the requirement of a minimum of two shareholders to set up a company.[37] Fiduciary contracts have also been employed to enforce shareholders' agreements. By transferring their shares to a trusted person, or to a *società fiduciaria*, the transferors give the transferee the power to enforce their pact pursuant to the fiduciary contract, which is nothing other than a mandate.[38] However, one application of *fiducia* remains more difficult to bring within the domain of mandate. This is the so-called *fiducia statica*, triggered by the unilateral declaration of the owner of certain property who affirms that he holds the property in question for a named person.[39] This is the Italian version of the *inter vivos* unilateral declaration of trust, whereby the settlor becomes trustee of the trust property.[40] In Italian law,

---

[35] *See, e.g.*, law no. 233 of 6 August 1990, *Disciplina del sistema televisivo pubblico e privato*, art. 37; law no. 416 of 5 December 1981, *recante disciplina delle imprese editrici e provvidenze per l'editoria*, art. 1.

[36] *See* royal decree 29 March 1942, no. 239, art. 1; law no. 1745 of 29 December 1962, art. 9. Cass., 10 December 194, no. 6478, *Foro it.*, (1985) I, 2325 obs. Mazzia.

[37] *See* Scotti Camuzzi, in *Trattato delle società per azioni diretto da Colombo e Portale*, II, t. 2 (1991), 898*ff*. *Società a responsabilità limitata* can now be created by one shareholder.

[38] On the validity of these pacts with respect to listed companies, *see* now *decreto legislativo* no. 58 of 24 February 1998, *Testo unico delle disposizioni in materia di intermediazione finanziaria*, arts. 122-23. For a discussion of some examples of shareholders' agreements which involved the transfer of the shares to a *società fiduciaria*, *see* Cariello, "*Controllo congiunto*" *e accordi parasociali* (1997), pp. 45-46.

[39] *See* Cass., 21 November 1975, no. 3911, *Giur. it.* (1977), I, 1, 984 (the leading case on *fiducia statica*); Cass., 14 December 1982, no. 4438; Cass., 18 October 1991, no. 11025, *Giur. it.* (1992), I, 1, 1786, obs. Ongaro; Cass., 29 May 1993, no. 6024, *Giur. it.* (1994), I, 1, 528, obs. G. Chinè; *Foro it.* (1994), I, 2495, *Giur. comm.* (1994), II, 5, obs. F.M. Giuliani.

[40] The doctrinal category "*fiducia statica*" was introduced by Lipari, *Il negozio fiduciario* (1964), p. 153*ff*, 182, 187*ff*, 303*ff*, 390*ff*, who developed it with an eye to English law. *See also id.*, *Fiducia statica e trusts*, in Beneventi (ed.), *supra* note 20, at 66.

the beneficiary of this arrangement, who is usually entitled to the property on demand, can enforce this undertaking and obtain the transfer of the property in his name by judicial action (cp. art. 2932 CC). Yet for other purposes (*i.e.*, *vis-à-vis* the executing creditors), the beneficiary of the *fiducia statica* usually ranks as a general creditor, especially where the property in question is an immovable. Furthermore, the litigated cases show that this device has little appeal for the business lawyer: *fiducia statica* typically occurs in the personal or family context. Nevertheless, these cases are important because they demonstrate that private parties often act as though Italian law gave full effect to these declarations, even *vis-à-vis* creditors or third parties.

2. *Trusts and Financial Services*

Beginning in the 1980s, the Italian legislation on financial services has been modernized. This process was largely achieved through several statutes concerning individual portfolio management, collective investment schemes like the *fondi comuni di investimento*, and pension funds.

According to the laws regulating portfolio management for individual investors, the creditors of a firm have no recourse against the assets managed on behalf of their clients. This is so even where the firm acts in its own name, without disclosing to the other party the name of the client for whom the transaction was entered.[41]

Collective investment schemes in the form of *fondi comuni di investimento* were first introduced in Italy by a 1983 law[42] that provided the model for subsequent legislation concerning these vehicles.[43] A specialized company acts as manager of the scheme on behalf of the investors by trading securities which are held in the custody of a custodian bank. The law does not say who is the owner of the fund

---

[41] *Decreto legislativo* no. 58 of 24 February 1998, *Testo unico delle disposizioni in materia di intermediazione finanziaria, ai sensi degli articoli 8 e 21 della legge 6 febbraio 1996*, no. 52, art. 22. An English version of this text is available at: *www.consob.it/english/en_testo_unico_/ fr_decree58.htm*. Previous legislation enacted similar protection; *see*, on this point, P.G. Jaeger, "Segregation of Assets and Insolvency under Italian Law," in G. Ferrarini (ed.), *European Securities Markets* (1998), p. 105.

[42] Law no. 77 of 23 March 1983, *Istituzione e disciplina dei fondi comuni d'investimento mobiliare*.

[43] Law no. 344 of 14 August 1994, *Istituzione e disciplina dei fondi comuni d'investimento mobiliare chiusi*; law no. 86 of 25 January 1994, *Istituzione e disciplina dei fondi comuni d'investimento immobiliare*. See now *decreto legislativo* no. 58 of 24 February 1998, *Testo unico delle disposizioni in materia di intermediazione finanziaria, ai sensi degli articoli 8 e 21 della legge 6 febbraio 1996*, no. 52, arts. 34*ff*.

managed by the manager on behalf of the investors, but enacts a system whereby the creditors of the manager have no recourse to it, while the creditors of the investors may solely obtain the certificates which represent the value of their shares of the fund.[44]

Pension funds were reformed in 1993, 1995, and 1997.[45] Before these enactments, the legal form of pension funds was that of a separate fund formally vested in the entrepreneur (art. 2117 CC). Today pension funds can still take this form, but they can also be set up as incorporated associations or foundations. In any case, the assets belonging to the fund can neither be diverted from the purposes for which the fund was established nor seized by the creditors of the manager. And, like the *fondi comuni di investimento*, they must be kept in the custody of a bank.[46]

3. Conveyance of Property upon Trust as Security Device

The use of *fiducia* to create security interests in property will be briefly treated here because it does not correspond to the notion of trust emerging from the Convention, but it does invite comparison with foreign rules concerning security interests in personal or real property.[47]

The Italian Civil Code regulates in detail the pledge of movables (art. 2784-99 CC) and of accounts receivable (arts. 2800-07 CC), as well as the hypothecation of immovables and of registered movables (arts. 2808-99 CC). The creation of pledges of movables and of receivables is, however, inconvenient for commercial purposes because it requires the transfer of possession of movables to the pledgee and, with respect to accounts receivable, a disclosure to the debtor of the creation of the pledge.[48] Hypothecation regulated by the Code is also unsatisfactory when compared

---

[44] *See decreto legislativo* no. 58 of 24 February 1998, *supra* note 31, at 36.6.

[45] *Decreto legge* no. 124 of 21 April 1993, *Disciplina delle forme di previdenza complementari, a norma dell'art. 3 comma 1, lettera V della legge 23 ottobre 1992, no. 421*, as amended by law no. 335 of 8 August 1995 and by law no. 449 of 27 December 1997. For a first comment, *see* A.D. Candian, *I fondi pensione* (1998).

[46] *Decreto legge* no. 124 of 1993, art. 6.4*ter*; art. 6*bis*.

[47] For recent critical discussions of the Italian law on the topic, *see* Anelli, *I trasferimenti in funzione di garanzia* (1997); Bussani, *Il modello italiano delle garanzia reali*, *Contratto e impresa* (1997), p. 163; E. Gabrielli, *"Autonomia privata e diritto comune europeo delle garanzie mobiliari,"* in *Riv. crit. dir. priv.* 643 (1996).

[48] The situation is different if the goods or the claims against the third party are represented by a negotiable instrument. The situation is also different for paperless financial instruments, which are dematerialized pursuant to *decreto legislativo* no. 213 of 24 June 1998, in *Gazzetta.*

to the ideal type of security interest in real property. The weakness of our law on hypothecation is attributable to the accessory character of this type of security and the impossibility of creating a certificate of hypotheca (or ground debt) similar to found in German law (*BGB*, paras. 1116, 1192).[49] While courts and scholars allow the transfer for security purposes of accounts receivable (*cessione del credito a scopo di garanzia*),[50] the transfer of title to movables, immovables, or registered movables for the same reason is considered to be null and void because they are now considered contrary to the Civil Code article against forfeiture clauses annexed to pledges or hypothecs (art. 2744).[51] The rigidity of the Civil Code rules on pledge and hypothecation is criticized by the great majority of scholars, and the courts have in some respects recognized the need for a wider array of security devices.[52] Recently, the legislature has taken steps in this direction by enacting special rules concerning the taking of collateral by banks. These rules allow the creation of the

---

These are all the financial instruments traded on a regulated exchange, and the instruments of the public debt. According to art. 34 of this legislative decree, securities over these instruments are created by book entries in the archives of authorized intermediaries, which are regulated by the same text.

[49] Riesenfeld, "Security Interests in Land in Modern Civil Law," in Yiannopolous (ed.), *Civil Law in the Modern World* (1965), p. 134. Since Riesenfeld wrote, the excessive length of Italian foreclosure proceedings has worsened the position of the secured creditor. The recent reform of the proceedings available to the executing creditor to enforce judgments tries to address the problem (*see* law no. 302 of 3 August 1998, and *decreto legge* no. 328 of 21 September 1998, *riforma delle procedure esecutive*).

[50] The point is not disputed. *See, e.g.*, Cass., 6 March 1991, no. 2343, *Foro it.* (1991), I, 2088, obs. Simone; Cass., 22 September 1990, no. 9650 (previous cases do not differ). Anelli, *supra* note 47, at 189*ff*. For an overview on the assigment of receivable in Italy, *see* A. Candian, *La transmission des créances dans le monde des finances modernes, Rapports nationaux italiens au XVeme Congrès international de droit comparé* (1998), p. 380.

[51] *See* Cass., sez. un., 3 April 1989, no. 1611, *Foro it.* (1989), I, 1428, obs. Mariconda & Realmonte; *Giur. it.* (1990), I, 1, 104; Cass., sez. un., 21 April 1989, no. 1907, *Foro it.* (1990), I, 205. On the other hand, after some uncertainty, Cass., 16 October 1995, no. 10805, *Giur. it.* (1996), I, 1, 1374, obs. Cinquemani; *Foro it.* (1996), I, 3492, affirmed the validity of true sale and lease-back operations. In support of this solution, *see* Bussani, *Proprietà-garanzia e contratto. Formule e regole nel leasing finanziario* (1992, repr. 1995), pp. 147*ff*, 174*ff*.

[52] On revolving pledges, *see* E. Gabrielli, "Le garanzie rotative," in Galgano (ed.) *I contratti del commercio, dell' industria e del mercato finanziario*, I (1995), pp. 853, 859*ff*; on irrevocable mandates and powers of attorney as security devices, *see* Graziadei, "*Mandato*," in *Riv. dir. civ.* II (1997), 147, 178*ff*.

functional equivalents of floating charges (*privilegi*) over business assets in favor of banking institutions.[53]

IV. An Assessment of the Italian Law of Trusts

A. The Italian Law of Trusts: Shortcomings of Present Institutions in Light of the Realities of a Modern Law of Property

Before our treatment of the interpretation and the implementation of the Convention in Italy, there is room for a critical assessment of Italian law on trusts.

Italian law has sensible rules on dispositions in favor of unincorporated bodies or corporations. While these rules could certainly be refined, all in all they are flexible enough to ensure that purposes beneficial to the community may be pursued by such entities with the property they acquire in a fiduciary capacity. The creation of protected interests in property is not wholly unknown in Italy. At least one of the devices currently used to achieve this result (the *fondo patrimoniale della famiglia*) corresponds to the basic structure of private trusts which are set up for the same purpose in common law jurisdictions. Compared with its common law counterpart, however, the *fondo patrimoniale della famiglia* has a severe limitation: it cannot outlast the marriage of the couple involved in its administration. Compared with the law of other civil law jurisdictions, such as France or Germany, Italian law also scores fairly well where property is entrusted to an agent who acts in his own name for a competent principal. The Civil Code rules on mandate provide a convenient framework for the relationship between the parties. The agent who holds property for the principal is empowered to deal with it. Yet with the exception stated for immovables and registered movables, such property is not considered part of the personal estate for insolvency purposes, or in case of succession upon death, provided the property is kept separate from the rest of the property under his or her control, and that the mandate has a certain date prior to the seizure of the property by the executing creditor or to the bankruptcy of the agent. Needless to say, the mandate will normally be terminated by the death or bankruptcy of the principal or agent.

---

[53] *Decreto legge* no. 385 of 1 September 1993, *Testo unico delle leggi in materia bancaria e creditizia*, arts. 44, 46. For a first appraisal of this decree, *see* Veneziano, "*La garanzia sull'intero patrimonio dell'imprenditore nella nuova legge bancaria italiana al confronto con i modelli stranieri: una riforma a metà,*" in *Riv. dir. comm. int.* (1996), 947. Similar rules apply to agricultural loans, as well.

Important as they are, all the above-mentioned institutions do not fit within a constellation of rules such as that making up the general legal form labeled "trust" in common law countries. The need for such a general legal form becomes apparent, however, if we reflect on the fact that the Italian legislature has, in due course, repeatedly modified the law to introduce solutions which replicate the effects of the common law trust in one way or another. After the enactment of the Civil Code of 1942, this was done for individual portfolio management, *fondi comuni di investimento*, and pension funds. The law on *società fiduciarie* elicited this tendency at work even before 1942. Yet each time the legislature intervened, commentators were quick to argue for the necessity of a further step in the same direction. This happened again recently with respect to securing assets.[54] Italian law has been ill-equipped to deal with such operations. The impossibility of creating a thinly capitalized special purpose vehicle like the trust, whereby property is segregated in favor of the investors, was one the major obstacles hampering the recourse to such a technique in Italy.[55] This obstacle has now been removed by law no. 130 of 30 April 1999, *"disposizioni sulla cartolarizzazione dei crediti."*[56] According to the new law, asset security operations are carried on by special-purpose companies. The receivables connected to each operation are for all purposes a patrimony separate from the patrimony of the company which carries on the operation, as well as from any patrimony connected to other operations. Only the creditors of the holders of the instruments issued to finance the operation may attach it.[57]

Despite all these developments, Italy still lacks a general legal form by which property can be entrusted to an *independent* manager – either an agent of the settlor,

---

[54] See, e.g., Rucellai, *"I problemi legati allo sviluppo della securitization in Italia: prospettive di soluzione,"* in *Giur. Comm.* I (1995), 114; *id.*, *"Un progetto normativo per la cartolarizzazione dei crediti,"* in *Giur. Comm.* I (1997), 161. The example provided in the text is certainly not the only one that comes to mind. *See, e.g.*, Guaccero, *"Brevi note su un recente disegno di legge in tema di conflitto di interessi tra attività di Governo ed impresa,"* in *Giur. comm.* I (1995), 129.

[55] For an anlysis of the shortcomings of the previous regime, *see* D'Ambrosio, "Italy," in Baums & Wymeersch (eds.), *Asset-Backed Securitization in Europe* (1996), p. 133*ff.*

[56] *Gazzetta ufficiale*, 14 May 1999, no. 111. Special laws govern the securitization of assets held by public entities.

[57] Law no. 130 of 30 April 1999, art. 3.2.: *"I crediti relativi a ciascuna operazione costituiscono patrimonio separato a tutti gli effetti da quello della società e da quello relativo alle altre operazioni. Su ciascun patrimonio non sono ammesse azioni da parte di creditori diversi dai portatori dei titoli emessi per finanziare l'acquisto dei crediti stessi."*

or of the beneficiaries – charged with the duty of managing property for the beneficiaries with the effects listed in art. 11 of the Convention.

The real question, therefore, is: what obstacles keep us from broadening and refining our law of trusts in the absence of legislative initiatives? The conventional answer is that the unitary notion of ownership, which is peculiar to the civil law tradition after the enactment of the Civil Code, poses a serious obstacle to the recognition of private autonomy in the field of trusts.[58] This answer betrays a naïve approach to the law of property which fails to distinguish between traditional concepts and modern realities of ownership in civil law countries.[59] Furthermore, it demonstrates a lack of awareness of key developments in the law of trusts in the major common law jurisdictions.

Dealing first with this point, the law of express trusts in England and the US has definitely moved away from a model of trust law which fettered the trustees' power of alienation over the assets under trusteeship.[60] The contemporary law of trusts does not endanger the capital value of trust property, which is a function of the power to alienate. It is true that trust property still cannot be considered risk capital, and this is one of the reasons for a rule against perpetuities.[61] Yet even most risk-prone individuals do not want to be fully exposed to the possibility of financial

---

[58] This is a recurrent theme in civilian literature on trusts. The typical argument is encapsulated by Lipstein, "Trusts," in *International Encyclopedia of Comparative Law* III, ch. 23 Tübingen, 1994 para. 41, and it usually involves a reminder to the *numerus clausus* of real rights. Many civilians approaching trusts like examples of split or dual ownership, fail to grasp the meaning of "ownership" in the context when they assume (without more) that the English word stands for the concept associated with the notion of ownership in civil law countries. If this were not enough, all too often civilian students of the law of trusts do not realize that trusts in common law jurisdictions do work under the constraint of a *numerus clausus* of real rights (*see* in general on this point Rudden, "Economic Theory v. Property Law: The Numerus Clausus Problem," in J. Bell *et al.* ed., *Oxford Essays in Jurisprudence*, 3rd ser. (1987), p. 239).

[59] *See* Gambaro, "Trust in Continental Europe," in Rabello (ed.), *Aequitas and Equity: Equity in Civil Law and Mixed Jurisdictions* (1993) p. 776; *see also* Honoré, *Obstacles to the reception of Trust Law? The Examples of South Africa and Scotland, ibid.* p. 792. On the methodological issue, *see* Sacco, "The System of European Private Law: Premises for a European Code," in *Italian Studies in Law* (1992).

[60] *See* Rudden, *Things as Thing and Things as Wealth*, Oxford J. Leg. Studies (1994), 81; Langbein, "The Contractarian Basis of the Law of Trusts," 105 *Yale LJ* 625 (1995). The Trustee Act 2000 (England and Wales) is the latest manifestation of this trend.

[61] There are, of course, rough functional equivalents of the rule against perpetuities in Italian law, such as the rules concerning legacies and donations to unborn persons (arts. 643, 784 CC).

disaster. The history of the limited liability concept in company law should at least remind us of this basic truth. But it is not so clear why nowadays the effective management of assets should be available solely to those willing to provide risk capital. In the long run, a choice contrary to trusts whereby property entrusted to a manager becomes immediately available to his creditors has the sole effect of attracting business to highly capitalized institutions.[62] Therefore, this approach simply increases the cost of services that would be cut if thinly capitalized vehicles like trusts could compete without restrictions on the market for management services. In a global market for these services, even the strongest opponents of the choice favoring trusts may soon discover that they represent the losing side.[63]

Turning to the more familiar scenario dominated by the rhetoric of a single, compact notion of ownership, it is now clear that the ideological reasons undergirding that discourse vanished long ago. From a technical point of view, the possibility to carve a variety of different property interests out of the largest property right recognized in a given legal system is certainly a source of wealth for the holder of that right as well as for society. Yet no legal system in the world allows unlimited freedom to private actors in this sphere. The necessity to control externalities, to facilitate the marketability of titles, and to achieve a balance between the powers of successive generations of owners establishes the boundaries of private actors in shaping the institution of property. The comparison between civil law and common law experiences in this field shows that most civil law systems have stopped short of adopting rules like those for trusts which are both feasible and convenient. This is why incursions into the traditional concept of property as indivisible unit have grown in quantity and quality over the years, and scholars are now uncomfortable with it.[64] The changes in this field are so vast that they map the emergence of an alternative model of property law that will not remain recessive

---

[62] Gambaro, "Trust in Continental Europe," in Rabello (ed.), *supra* note 59, at 776.

[63] Ashall, "The Investment Services Directive: What Was the Conflict All About?" in Andenas & Kenyon-Slade (eds.), *EC Financial Market Regulation and Company Law* (1993), p. 91.

[64] This is the *leitmotiv* of a number of studies dedicated to the transfer of property. *See* Sacco, "*Le transfert de la propriété des choses mobilières déterminées par acte entre vifs en droit comparé*," in *Riv. dir. civ.* I (1979), 442 (a path-breaking contribution); *see also* Monateri, *La sineddoche – Formule e regole nel diritto delle obbligazioni e dei contratti* (1984), p. 297*ff*; Chianale, *L'obbligazione di dare e trasferimento della proprietà* (1990). For a broader perspective, *see* Guarneri, *Diritti reali e diritti di credito: valore attuale di una distinzione* (1979); Morello, *Multiproprietà e autonomia privata* (1984). *See* now on this point Gambaro, *Il diritto di proprietà*, *supra* note 14.

for much longer.[65] In this context, the concept of obligation undergoes similar transformations. Applied to describe the relation between the trustee and the beneficiary of the trust, the notion of obligation has been so twisted that it has acquired a proprietary connotation. Several pieces of this odd collection of legal rules come from the statute book itself, and they reflect an effort to overcome the difficulty of thinking of a trust in terms of ownership or obligation. Sometimes the legislature openly resorts to doctrinal labels which reveal that ownership is divorced from one of the other of its constituent parts and that the essential features of relation between the parties diverge far from the standard concept of obligation. Thus, the laws concerning *fondi comuni di investimento*, portfolio management, and pension funds state that the fund managed by the manager is a *"patrimonio separato e autonomo,"* or a *"patrimonio di destinazione autonomo e separato,"* meaning that the holder of the fund cannot be considered the full unrestricted owner thereof and that the investors do not run the risk typical of the debtor-creditor relationship.[66] At the same time, the notion of patrimony which is employed in these laws is a transparent signpost for the idea of rights over changing objects, or a fund. This is probably the key to understanding one of the most important features of contemporary trust law. In other cases, the task of finding a doctrinal pigeonhole for enacted rules deviating from the unitary model of ownership has been left entirely to interpreters, as in the case of the *fondo patrimoniale della famiglia*, or the property held by the unincorporated association, the committee, and the fiduciary foundation. Yet if we consider the plethora of devices mentioned so far without bearing in mind solely the conceptual problem they pose, we soon understand that the elementary pattern of the transactions resulting from the Civil Code or approved by various Acts of Parliament is simply that which private actors would have agreed upon if left free to bargain. To be more explicit, the legislature did not invent a new form of property holding, but rather removed obstacles to its use by private actors and signaled its existence. By signaling the existence of the standard form, the legislature lowered the transaction costs that would otherwise have been borne by

---

[65] The best Italian treatise on the law of property devotes an entire chapter to fiduciary ownership: Gambaro, *Il diritto di proprietà, supra* note 14, at 69*ff*. The leading treatise on the law of contract remarks that contrary to fiduciary operations raise problems concerning the law of property, rather than the law of contract. *See* Sacco & De Nova, *"Il contratto,"* I (1993), in *Trattato di diritto civile* diretto da Sacco, p. 667.

[66] Before the enactment of these laws, such concepts were mostly used to describe the legal position of the administrator of the insolvent's estate, or of an estate in abeyance (*haereditas iacens*), etc.

private parties to achieve the desired outcome.[67] Once more, however, there is no *a priori* answer to the question of why this important function should not also be performed by other actors on the marketplace for efficient legal institutions.

B. Evolving Tracing Remedies

The Italian experience with proprietary remedies relating to trusts shows that the competition for the development of efficient legal rules governing trusts is now a reality even at the national level. Italian law has not adopted an integrated approach to these remedies, but this is hardly surprising because there is no general legal form corresponding to the trust in Italy presently.[68] Nevertheless, the need to protect the position of beneficiaries with regard to property placed under the control of a manager is perceived in Italy as clearly as it is abroad. In recent years, new developments in the law matching more closely the operative rules that common lawyers group under the heading "tracing or following the trust property" witnessed a growing awareness of the necessity to improve the beneficiaries' protection. To illustrate one of the most interesting examples of this trend, I will briefly discuss the rules which have evolved to enhance the principal's position where property is entrusted to an agent. The Civil Code articles on mandate without representation already affirmed the principal's right to follow property entrusted to the agent into its exchange product, be it a debt or a "thing certain."[69] Until recently, however, courts and scholars alike maintained that the principal was left with a personal claim against the agent whenever the property in question was mixed with assets belonging to the agent or to other clients of the agent. Thus the principal ranked as

---

[67] On these aspects, *see* Mattei, *Comparative Law and Economics, supra* note 4, at 175-77; Graziadei, *Trust nel diritto anglo-americano*, in Digesto, 4th ed., sez. comm., XVI (1998).

[68] For a sophisticated study of the operative rules governing proprietary remedies in civil law and common law systems, *see* Ferreri, *Le azioni reipersecutorie in diritto comparato* (1988). The terminology adopted in this paragraph reflects the traditional English usage, though tracing properly considered is not a remedy, nor a cause of action, but rather the technique by which the defendant is identified as the recipient of the plaintiff's property. *See, e.g., Boscawen v. Bajwa* [1996] 1 WLR 328, at 345 (CA), per Millitt L.J.

[69] Italian Civil Code, arts. 1705.2 and 1706.2. These rules show that the protection of the principal in Italian law is not hindered by the rules that in German law are grouped under the headings "prohibition of subrogation" (*Surrogationsverbot*) and "principle of immediacy" (*Unmittelbarkeitsprinzip*). The Italian norms have their roots in the *lex mercatoria*, like some of the early English authorities on the tracing of money or property owed to (or entrusted to) factors or other agents acting for their principals.

an unsecured creditor in the crucial case in which the agent declared bankruptcy after mixing property belonging to the principal with his own or with that belonging to other clients.[70] The reaction against this interpretation mounted when this outcome was upheld in the face of law proclaiming that assets managed by investment firms were the property of the clients.[71] At this point, commentators began to criticize the traditional approach and to propose solutions more favorable to the principal.[72] The legislature took notice and amended the law on pension funds by enlarging the scope of the vindication action given to pension funds,[73] as well as the law on investment firms.[74] Eventually, the landmark decision of the Italian Supreme Court in *Garrone v. Fundus-Fiduciaria per l'investimento azionario S.P.A.* established that the assets held by the investment firm for the clients as a group belong to them if the firm becomes insolvent, despite the fact that they were not allocated to each investment contract.[75] The arguments advanced to substantiate this judgment show that the Italian Supreme Court is ready to apply this principle beyond the facts of the case.

V. The Interpretation and the Application of the Hague Convention in Italy

The Hague Convention needs to be considered here solely to discuss those perspectives on its interpretation and application that are changing the Italian legal landscape concerning trusts. I will try to summarize the ongoing debates by limiting my discussion to the main doctrinal positions that have emerged in Italy since the Convention was ratified.

---

[70] Luminoso, "*Il mandato la commissione, la spedizione,*" in *Trattato di diritto civile e commerciale diretto da Cicu e Messineo* (1984), p. 268, no. 200.

[71] T. Ferrara, *ordinanza,* 30 December 1993, *Fallimento* (1994), 628; *Banca, borsa, tit. cred.* (1995), II, 68

[72] Portale & Dolmetta, "*Deposito regolare di cose fungibili e fallimento del depositario,*" *Banca, borsa, tit. cred.,* I (1994), 842; D' Alessandro, "*Dissesto di intermediario mobiliare e tutela dei clienti,*" in *Giur. comm.* I (1997), 465.

[73] Law no. 355 of 8 August 1995, art. 6.4.

[74] *See decreto legislativo* no. 415 of 1996, art. 34.3; *decreto legislativo* no. 385 of 1993, art. 91.2 (rights of the clients over assets which are collectively held on their behalf, on a non-allocated basis).

[75] Cass., 14 October 1997, no. 10031, *Foro it.* (1998) I, 851, obs. M. Crisostomo, F. Macario; *Giur. Comm.* (1998) II, 299, obs. F. Di Majo.

The common ground among the numerous participants in these debates is that the Convention regulates the law applicable to trusts and their recognition. The riddle lurking in this platitude is the very notion of "trust" which must be the cornerstone of every analysis dedicated to the Convention.

If the word "trust" in the Convention signifies those institutions which are known in common law jurisdictions by that name, the principle of party autonomy in the choice of the applicable law (enshrined in art. 6 of the Convention) can have no application in jurisdictions where such trusts are unknown.[76] Defending this approach, the first commentators of the text stressed that the Convention was definitely not a uniform law introducing common law trusts in Italian law.[77] This interpretation was immediately challenged by a radically different approach to the questions raised by the Convention, which is now prevailing over the more restrictive reading of its text.[78] This second interpretation, advanced by Maurizio Lupoi, holds that the notion of "trust" employed by the Convention denotes several legal institutions rooted in civil law countries besides common law trusts.[79] Hence, *for the purposes of the Convention*, the distinction between trust countries and non-trust countries has little to do with certain traditional classifications of the world's legal systems, such as that confronting common law and civil law

---

[76] *See* Broggini, "*Il trust nel diritto internazionale privato italiano*," in Beneventi (ed.), *supra* note 20, at 11 and 23. Note that the Italian statute on conflict of laws (law no. 218 of 31 May 1995, *Riforma del sistema italiano di diritto internazionale privato*), art. 46.2, allows an Italian decedent who is resident in a common law country at the time of his death to set up trusts under certain conditions.

[77] *See* Gambaro, in Gambaro, Giardina & Ponzanelli, "*Convenzione relativa alla legge sui trusts ed al loro riconoscimento*," in *Le nuove leggi civili commentate* (1993), 1211, at 1216; Ponzanelli, *ibid.*, 1225*ff*. This approach needs to be qualified, however, even if one does not share the opinion that purely internal trusts can be recognized in Italy. *See* Lipstein, *supra* note 58, at para. 60. *See also* Lupoi, "*I trusts puramente 'interni'*," in Beneventi (ed.), *supra* note 20, at 39*ff*; Lipari, *Fiducia statica e trusts*, p. 73*ff*.

[78] Lupoi presented this interpretation to the public when the Convention entered into force: Lupoi, *Il trust nell'ordinamento giuridico italiano dopo la convenzione dell'Aja del 1° luglio 1985*, *Vita notarile* (1992), p. 966. For a condensed English version of Lupoi's contribution, *see id.*, "The Effects of the Hague Convention in a Civil Law Country," in Jackson & Wilde (eds.), *The Reform of Property Law* (1997), p. 222.

[79] The point should, perhaps, be considered beyond dispute. *See* Lupoi, *Trusts*, *supra* note 4, at 411*ff*, who shows that the drafters of the Convention set out to deal with common law trusts, but ended up with a description of the trusts encompassing civil law institutions as well. In the same sense, *see* Lipstein, *supra* note 58, at para. 60. But *see* Broggini, "*Il trust nel diritto internazionale privato italiano*," in Beneventi (ed.), *supra* note 20, at 20-22.

systems.[80] That division is irrelevant when establishing whether citizens or residents in civil law countries should be able to create trusts through the choice of law rules enacted by the Convention. Article 6 of the Convention does not make the freedom of choice of the applicable law dependent upon whether the settlor is a domiciliary or resident of a common law country. Indeed, art. 6 of the Convention is silent on the existence of *any* nexus with the forum country where the Convention is in force as a precondition for the validity of the choice of law exercise. In other words, the choice of a foreign law (within the limits established by art. 5) is by itself sufficient to trigger the application of the Convention. Thus, just as an English domiciliary may set up trusts governed by Jersey law on assets located in England for the benefit of English beneficiaries, so an Italian citizen can create trusts governed by English law on assets located in Italy for Italian beneficiaries. Fantastic as this may seem to some commentators, this is precisely what is presently occurring in Italy. With the assistance of a select number of Italian lawyers and notaries (in contact with foreign consultants of the relevant jurisdictions), Italian citizens and companies having their seat in Italy have executed instruments creating *inter vivos* trusts for Italian beneficiaries governed by the law of jurisdictions like England, Jersey, and Malta.[81]

The Convention does not prevent the application of the mandatory rules designated by the conflicts rules of the forum concerning the matters listed in art. 15, nor of the forum provisions of immediate application (art. 16). The provisions of the Convention may also be disregarded when manifestly incompatible with the *ordre public* (art. 18). Furthermore, the right to recover the trust assets from a third party holder remains subject to the law determined by the conflicts rules of the forum (art. 11 para. d).

Given all these concessions to the forum rules, one may wonder whether it is possible to reap any concrete advantage from the decision to set up a purely internal trust governed by a foreign law in Italy. Yet in certain cases it is crucial to have the

---

[80] Whatever the merit is of such classification today, *see* Gordley, "Common law v. Civil law – *Una distinzione che va scomparendo?*," in *Scritti in onore di Rodolfo Sacco*, I (1994), p. 559.

[81] *See* Matthews, "Italian trust for debenture holders," in *Trust Law Intern.* (1997), 20. For another recent instance of the recourse to the trust by an Italian settlor, *see* the appendix to Lèbano, "*Esperienze notarili nell'istituzione di trusts: il trust 'Mevio'*," in Beneventi (ed.), *supra* note 20, at 205, 208, reproduces the notarial act of an Italian notary setting up a purely internal trust governed by English law for the benefit of a complete incompetent. On the validity of a Trust created by an Italian testator over immovables situated in Italy, *see* T. Lucca, *Foro it.* (1998), I, 2007, obs. E. Brunetti; and *ibid.*, I, 391, obs. M. Lupoi (holding confirmed by the Florence Court of Appeals).

possibility to transfer assets to an independent trustee with the effects listed in art. 11 of the Convention. Many of the trusts that have been set up in Italy in recent years are created for parties who have conflicting interests, so that the trustee will act as an impartial stakeholder for each of them.[82] It seems unlikely that the interpretation of the Convention enhancing private autonomy in the choice of the applicable law may have disruptive effects on the texture of our law simply because it facilitates transactions like these. Nevertheless, should such disruptions occur (for reasons that are not yet clear), art. 13 of the Convention will certainly come into play. In that case, trusts, the significant elements of which (except for the choice of the applicable law, the place of administration, and the habitual residence of the trustee) are more closely connected with our forum, though governed by the law chosen by the settlor, could not be recognized in Italy.

This approach to the Convention has at least one advantage over the alternative and more restrictive interpretation mentioned above: it represents a choice for candor. By interposing foreign entities between the trustees and the assets located in our jurisdiction, or by removing assets from the forum, Italian companies and well-to-do individuals had already availed themselves of trusts for years before the ratification of the Convention. They will certainly continue to do so even though all the Italian interpreters of the Convention were opposed to the creation of purely internal trusts in Italy.[83] Admittedly, the future of this approach depends on spreading knowledge about trusts among professionals and academics.[84] Much has been done in this regard in recent years and more efforts in the same direction will certainly follow in the future. Clearly, the success of this program also depends on the availability of effective judicial proceedings for the supervision of every phase of trust administration. From this point of view, court proceedings to obtain interim protection of trust property, or to make fiduciaries account, or to approve accounts voluntarily rendered are well in place. However, in Italy trustees may not be able to obtain directions from the court. In this respect, the powers of Italian courts over the administration of property belonging to minors (cp. arts. 320-321 CC) and incompetents do not compare favorably with those of English or American Courts over the administration of trust property.[85]

---

[82]   For current developments, *see* the internet site: www.il-trust-in-italia.it.

[83]   *See* Andreoli, *Il trust nella prassi bancaria e finanziaria* (1998).

[84]   Thus addressing the preoccupation expressed by Gambaro, "Trust in Continental Europe," in Rabello (ed.), *supra* note 59, at 781.

[85]   Schlesinger *et al.*, *supra* note 3, at 783, fn. 3, make this point with regard to civil law jurisdictions in general.

VI. A Comprehensive Trust Law for Italy?

The final question is whether Italy should pass a statute introducing a general legal form that could compete with common law trusts on the same footing.[86] At the moment, the enactment of a comprehensive law on trusts is not on Parliament's agenda, despite some progress made in this direction.[87] But parliamentary restraint in this field need not be criticized. The codification of the law of trusts in jurisdictions like Louisiana and Québec shows that it takes time before the critical amount of comparative knowledge necessary to draft a trust law for a civilian jurisdiction trickles down to the lawmaking body. So far, many Italian lawyers have stopped thinking about trusts as the preserve of the international tax planner. They have come to see why trusts are, in many ways, a precious addition to the tools of the civilian lawyer. In the long run, this awareness may be, by itself, more important and more productive than any hastily drafted legislative text.

---

[86] The French experience in this field is not wholly encouraging. The first bill concerning *la fiducie* defined the institution as a contract, and distinguished among the *fiducie gestion*, the *fiducie liberalité* and the *fiducie sûreté*. The definition of the institution in terms of contract fails to clearly convey the idea that the settlor must relinquish control over the trust property unless he is prepared to be treated like a principal. Furthermore, the distinction among *fiducie gestion, fiducie liberalité* and *fiducie sureté*, the backbone of the first version of the French bill, makes some sense solely in the light of the special problems posed by the Civil Code mandatory provisions on the indefeasible shares of spouses and relatives and on the prohibition of forfeiture clauses in security transactions. On this bill, *see* Ph. Rémy, in Hayton, Kortmann & Verhagen (eds.), *supra* note 4, at 131*ff*, 145*ff*.

[87] For an initiative of more limited scope, *see* the bill presented to the House of Representatives on 4 December 1999 by M. Paissan *et al.*, "*Norme in materia di trust a favore di soggetti portatori di handicap.*"

CHAPTER THIRTEEN

Non-Profit Organizations

Giulio Ponzanelli[1]

I. Introduction

The subject of the non-profit organization has been and still is one of those most analyzed in the Italian legal scholarship of the past few years. In order to achieve a better understanding of the actual debate, it is useful to divide the history of non-profit organizations in Italy into three main periods.

II. The History of Non-Profit Organizations

A. The First Period (1865-1948)

From 1865 to 1948, non-profit organizations had almost no history at all. Under the Napoleonic model of authoritative government, characterized by a strong mistrust of private groups acting as intermediaries between government and individuals, non-profit organizations were stifled. When they existed at all, these organizations concentrated on social welfare, an activity of secondary importance in an industrializing society. This approach to the non-profit entity continued throughout the period, and was articulated in the 1942 Civil Code's first and fifth books, reserved for "collective" organizations.

The first book deals with *associazioni riconosciute* ("recognized" or incorporated associations), *associazioni non riconosciute* (unincorporated associations), *fondazioni* (foundations, also incorporated), and *comitati* (committees). The fifth book deals with *società* (partnerships and corporations) and *società cooperative* (cooperatives). While this second group is defined (under art. 2247 CC, the *società*

---

[1]   Professor of Private Comparative Law, University of Brescia.

Jeffrey S. Lena and Ugo Mattei (eds.), *Introduction to Italian Law*, 341-356
©2002 Kluwer Law International. Printed in the Netherlands.

is a contract between two or more persons who contribute goods or services for the common exercise of an economic activity with the purpose of distributing its profits; under art. 2247 CC, *cooperatives* are enterprises having a mutual purpose), partnerships and associations, by contrast, are not. In fact, the debate and uncertainty as to the purposes that associations and foundations may pursue stems from the vagueness of the law itself.

The differences between the organizations of the first and the fifth books, which are immediately apparent from reading the Code, are related to the procedure for incorporation and the liability to creditors. Whereas *società* are incorporated by law if they meet the legal requirements, as determined by a *decreto* (decree) issued by the court, associations and foundations are incorporated by a discretionary act of the President of the Republic or by act of the *Prefetto* (a local administrative authority).

Article 2 of the Italian Constitution states, however, that "[t]he Republic recognizes and guarantees the inviolable rights of man ... in the social formations where he expresses his personality." This clause of the Constitution is currently interpreted as restraining the government's power to deny the right to incorporate. Thus, the denial of the right to incorporate is in practice restricted to non-democratic organizations – *i.e.* those that do not state definite purposes in their charter and those that do not appear to possess adequate funds.

As to liability to creditors, while in unincorporated *società* all members are usually held personally liable for the acts of the society or its members, in unincorporated associations and in committees, liability is restricted to the common fund and to the individuals who have acted in the organization's name.

This brief sketch explains how non-profit organizations' economic activity has traditionally been organized under the rules of the fifth book, and how cultural, political, and charitable activities have been organized under the rules of the first book.

The result was obviously undesirable. Nineteenth-century liberalism's dislike for private non-economic organizations, viewed as potential threats to the State's authority, together with the anti-democratic nature of fascism, helps explain why the 1942 Code was adopted as it was with respect to non-profit organizations. The aim was to forbid non-profit activities from organizing under the rules of the fifth book, thereby forcing them either to incorporate (and thereby be subject to a degree of administrative control), or to operate as unincorporated associations in a condition of what amounted to a legislative void, offering few guarantees to either members or creditors.

If this historical background helps explain the existing non-profit rules, it nevertheless does not tell us whether associations and foundations must *only* be regarded as non-profit organizations, nor does it give a definition of "non-profit" (a definition which, as comparative law experience teaches us, is far from obvious). The answers given by scholars and the courts make sense if one recalls that the Code forbids the creation of atypical *società* and atypical *società cooperative* – that is, those not corresponding to the seven types explicitly set forth by the Code itself (*e.g.*, share corporations, non-share corporations, etc). The reconstruction of the purposes of associations and foundations must therefore always avoid creating an organization whose salient features are indistinguishable from those of the *società*.

B. The Second Period (1948-1984): Institutional Pluralism and Article 2 of the Italian Constitution

When the Italian Constitution was approved in 1948, the situation described above changed completely, and the Constitution's art. 2 provided formal support for intermediate groups. In this way, the institutional pluralism made possible by the new constitutional framework could – and did – promote decentralization, and encouraged the spontaneous growth of social groups. One notes the influence of Catholicism in this regard, which recalls the idea of an intermediary society, the family community, and the notion of the trade organization, which progressively leads to trade unions and political parties.[2]

It is interesting to compare the great differences between the Italian and the American constitutional systems in this regard, as well as the degree of impact that constitutional principles have had on private law in these countries. While the Italian idea of pluralism has favored typical groups of intermediate communities, the American constitution does not devote a single article to pluralism. And yet, as already mentioned, American society is certainly based on the efficient role of the non-profit sector, as Alexis de Tocqueville pointed out in some of the most beautiful pages of his famous essay, *Démocratie en Amérique*.

Having analyzed the two different systems, we can conclude that third-sector growth does not seem to depend on constitutional privileges. Notwithstanding the declamations of our Constitution, the third sector in Italy was mainly restricted to trade unions and political parties (as well as the family), which constituted new expressions of political freedom, since both of them were once banned from public life by the Fascist government.

---

[2] On art. 2 Const. and the importance of social institutions, *see* A. Barbera, in G. Branca (ed.), *Commentario alla Costituzione*, sub art. 2, Bologna-Rome (1975), p. 110*ff*; P. Rescigno, *Persona e comunità. Saggi di diritto privato*, Padua (1987); M. Nigro, "*Formazioni sociali, poteri dei privati e libertà del terzo,*" in *Pol. dir.* (1975), p. 583*ff.*

C. The Third Period (1984-2001): The Growth of New Non-Profit Organizations, the Boom of Private Associations, and the Discovery of the Legal Form of Foundations

The enactment of statutes by the Italian parliament has played the most important role in the growth of the third sector in Italy. Parliamentary statutes have both expanded the legal powers of private associations and created new kinds of non-profit groups. Law no. 52*bis* of 27 February 1985 recognized the full legal power of unincorporated organizations. This law has, in fact, modified some rules of the Italian Civil Code dealing with the transcription (*i.e.* form of taking title) of real property such that now even unincorporated organizations are allowed to become owners of real property without need of prior government authorization.[3]

The third sector has recently been greatly encouraged by law no. 364 of 16 October 1989, which implemented the Hague Convention on trusts and their recognition,[4] and by law no. 266 of 11 August 1991, on volunteerism,[5] which was followed by a detailed and rich regional legislation. The most promising areas for non-profit organization development are those sectors concerning public interests, such as the environment, hunting, and consumer protection.[6] Last but not least in promoting the growth of the third sector is law no. 381 of 1991, governing social cooperatives.

A government bill has recently been approved (law no. 383 of 7 December 2000) regarding the establishment of *associazionismo sociale*, or "social associations." These organizations are mainly devoted to accomplishing social aims.[7] In December 1998, a law was approved transforming banking foundations from public entities into private foundations (law no. 461 of 23 December 1998).[8]

There has also been a change in the policy of our legislation. Until the 1970s,

---

[3] *See Gli enti non profit*, Milan (1993), Notary Regional Committee of Lombardia, publ.

[4] For commentary on the law, *see* A. Gambaro, A. Giardina & G. Ponzanelli, *Le nuove leggi civili commentate* (1993), p. 1211*ff.*

[5] For commentary on the law, *see* L. Bruscuglia, *Le nuove leggi civili commentate* (1993), p. 775ff.

[6] *See* the exhaustive essay by G. Napolitano, "*Le associazioni private 'a rilievo pubblicistico'*," in *Riv. Crit. Dir. priv.* (1994), p. 583*ff.*

[7] It is possible to read the proposed law in *Giur. comm.* (1995), I, p. 656, with observations by Fauceglia, *Una proposta di legge sulle associazioni sociali. See*, for a first comment on law no. 383 of 7 December 2000, G. Ponzanelli, "*La nuova disciplina sull'associazionismo sociale*," in *Corriere Giuridico* (2001), 155.

the main approach chosen was to create non-profit business corporations (such as sports companies), thus altering the very nature of business corporations as are they are defined in our Civil Code. Currently there is a reversal of direction: non-profit associations are preferred to business corporations as legal forms for conducting enterprises (this is the case for banking foundations, social security services, societies devoted to art and opera, and the like). More recently, the work carried on by the so-called Zamagni Commission has resulted in a new law that recognizes different fiscal treatment for different organizations, set according to their aims.[9]

In conclusion, the debate on non-profit organizations has been greatly enriched by the introduction of many new statutes, the growth of the non-profit world, and the analysis of the North American system.

The starting point of the third period of the non-profit sector owes its origin to those scholars who adopted the analytical approaches offered by law and economics. In the light cast by this new discipline, it would appear that the success of the non-profit sector in Italy may be ascribed to the "market failure" existing in certain areas where consumers tend to repose greater faith, or to the crisis of the government welfare state.

Thus, the fiduciary function fulfilled by non-profit organizations has to be examined in the context of, and as a response to, the dysfunction of market rules. In other words, the problem lies in determining the effectiveness of the social assets of the "social services" rendered by the non-profit sector. The fiscal privileges enjoyed by these organs should offer remarkable utility to the community. In the United States, this kind of research has been conducted on hospitals run as non-profit organizations. Such research is needed in Italy as well: the so-called "perform-ance evaluation" is an efficient instrument for both obviating the establishment of organizations whose assets are insufficient for attaining their aims, and for comply-ing with the principles of a rational fiscal policy.

---

[8] *See* A. Zoppini, *"La legge sulle c.d. fondazioni bancarie,"* in *Corriere Giuridico* (1999), p. 411.

[9] *See decreto legislativo* no. 460 of 4 December 1997. The content of the law refers mainly to the new special fiscal discipline of non-profit organizations with purposes of social solidarity. Two main categories of non-profit organizations have been identified: *ente non commerciale* and *onlus.*

III. An Analysis of the New Era of Non-Profit Corporations: Comparative Aspects

The new period of non-profit organizations in Italy began some ten years ago, and the sector is now much richer than before. In this period, it has moved towards the North American model, even though the two systems remain distinct. The attribute shared by the Italian and American non-profit worlds inheres in the diversity of organizations belonging to the same non-profit sector. In the United States, non-profit organizations include associations, chambers of commerce, charities, churches, clubs, condominiums, foundations, fraternal orders, hospitals, labor unions, museums, schools and colleges, social services organizations, societies, and so on. Similarly, in Italy there still exists a great variety of organizations classified under the non-profit sector: political parties, trade unions, churches, foundations, hospitals managed by religious orders, communities caring for drug addicts, museums, volunteer groups, and the like.[10]

A. The Enlightening Example of Cultural Foundations

The cultural foundation sector presents us with important elements necessary for understanding both the growth of the non-profit organization and the differences between the American and Italian systems.

There are various explanations for the widespread use and reliance on foundations in the United States and the relative poverty of the European – and particularly Italian – experience in this regard. First, the United States and Italy are at different stages of economic growth. Simply put, America is a wealthier and more powerful country than Italy. And the United States is predominantly, and historically, Protestant, whereas Italy is predominantly and historically Catholic. Secondly, the United States has a fiscal (primarily tax) policy that favors and encourages the growth of cultural foundations. Italian fiscal policy, by contrast, has traditionally reflected a suspicion of such institutions, at least until the enactment of the new statute no. 460 of 4 December 1997. Thirdly, the United States is marked by a relatively weak system of governmental oversight. This tends to encourage the system's abuse in the United States. Italy, on the other hand, suffers from a stifling regime of governmental oversight that continues to operate as a strong deterrent to the employment of economic resources.

---

[10] A very good practical research text on non-profit organizations was conducted by the Institute for Social Research, at the Catholic University in Milan, under the supervision of G. Barbetta.

Nevertheless, things have changed in Italy over the last ten years, and two trends have emerged. First, there has been an increase in the number of foundations created in different social areas, such as art and culture. Secondly, there is an increasing interest in making donations to the juridical assets of foundations in order to promote different kinds of economic enterprises (the best known examples are bank foundations and integrating social security). Even in the area of opera, there is a proposal to introduce a separation between the theater as foundation, on the one hand, and as a stock company, dealing mainly with entrepreneurial assets, on the other.

IV. Different Kinds of Non-Profit Organizations

A. The Different Theories Proposed

The non-profit world contains different types of associations and foundations. Hence diverse theories of associations and foundations have been developed by scholars to attend to these differences.

The first type consists of associations and foundations that may pursue only non-economic activities, that is, activities that do not produce goods or services of recognized economic value. The relevant articles of the Code are therefore constructed to forbid not only the distribution of dividends to members, but also the distribution of assets among them upon dissolution, as well as any appraisal right to those members who withdraw during the life of the organization. This theory is an old one and has now been abandoned. It is indeed completely inconsistent with the modern reality of associations and foundations, which increasingly conduct economic activities – both instrumentally, as organs for fund raising on behalf of other activities (charities, for example), and as their immediate and direct object and goal (*e.g.*, performing arts non-profits, day care, hospitals, and so on).

The second type consists of associations that may pursue only altruistic objectives.[11] Even this theory has been abandoned for the same reason. It remains important, however, because this second type of non-profit organization was the first to shift the criteria for qualification from the organization's *activity* to its *purpose*.

The third type consists of associations that may pursue both economic and non-economic activities for egoistic, altruistic, or ego-altruistic purposes, as long as

---

[11] *See* Ferri, *Manuale di diritto commerciale*, 2nd ed., Turin (1960), p. 185, F. Ferrara, *Gli imprenditori e la società*, 4th ed., Milan (1962), p. 20.

they do not pursue the purposes typical of *società*.[12] This is the so-called residual theory. Its most recent development suggests[13] different applicable rules, depending on what purpose the organization pursues – that is, whether it is "ideal" or economic-egoistic. If the purpose is "ideal," *i.e.* either altruistic or egoistic, but has as its object the satisfaction of a non-economic interest, such as the promotion of some cultural benefit, then the "non-distribution constraint" is enforced. Otherwise, the theory construes the relevant articles of the Code as allowing the distribution of assets among members at dissolution as well as appraisal rights to withdrawing members, though never the distribution of dividends. The distinction between *società* and cooperatives in the latter case is further assured by requiring that the distribution of assets at dissolution be in equal parts rather than proportional to the members' contributions, and by forbidding the establishment of a proportion between members' initial and periodic contributions and the economically valuable services of the organization, to which they have a right. The acceptance of these constraints should ensure that members are not pursuing a purely economic purpose.

Associations may pursue only predominantly ideal purposes.[14] This theory, however, does not deny the right to carry on economic activities and pursue the satisfaction of the members' economic interests. Ideal, non-economically valuable interests should, however, predominate. The non-distribution constraint is consequently fully enforced.

The notion of ideal purpose and its predominance is construed quite broadly. The theory allows associations to be established for the operation of libraries, theaters, movie theaters, automobile clubs, health clubs, and entertainment clubs, on the principle that in all these cases the members' interests do not converge around the enjoyment of economically valuable services that the organization offers at a favorable cost, but rather around the advancement of culture, sport, or research (on driving safety, for example).

Foundations may be established only for activities and purposes in the public interest.[15] This theory argues in favor of the analogical application of an article on wills in the Civil Code that allows the establishment of perpetuities only in a few

---

[12] *See* Rubino, *Associazioni non riconosciute*, Milan (1952), p. 13*ff*.

[13] *See* G. Volpe Putzolu, *La tutela dell'associato in un sistema pluralistico*, Milan (1967).

[14] *See* F. Galgano, "*Delle associazioni non riconosciute e dei comitati*," in A. Scialoja & G. Branca (eds.), *Commentario al Codice Civile*, sub art. 36-42, Bologna-Rome (1967).

[15] *See* F. Galgano, "*Delle persone giuridiche, delle associazioni e delle fondazioni*," in A. Scialoja & G. Branca (eds.), *Commentario al Codice Civile*, sub arts. 11-35, Bologna-Rome (1972).

special circumstances and for the public good (art. 699). A foundation, it is argued, impairs the free circulation of goods by linking it to fixed purposes embodied in the founding charter. Therefore, it should not be allowed to satisfy private needs, even when those needs are different from the founder's, but only for the pursuit of the public good. In addition, foundations should never be created exclusively to run a business enterprise, as is the case in German law (*Stiftungunternehmen*).[16]

In one author's view, founders should have the right to recover assets at dissolution.[17] The distinction between these foundations and one-man corporations would be guaranteed by the fact that in a foundation, the object of the enterprise cannot be changed by the members' will, but is established once and for all in the charter (trusts, in which the beneficiary and the *cestui qui trust* are the same person, are expressly recalled). Another author argues in favor of an absolute "non-distribution constraint" and views business foundations as the expression of an increasing submission of all businesses to State economic planning: structurally, the foundation would be the most functional business form for abiding by State directives.[18]

B. The Category of "Non-Profit Organization"

Only recently, under the influence of the Americans, have Italian scholars endeavored to build up a new category of "non-profit organizations" whose fundamental feature consists of a very strict "non-distribution constraint," whereby the members of the association cannot rely on any kind of restitution, nor on a recurring economic premium in relation to the contribution made by them in entering the association.[19]

The advantage for members cannot be valuable in economic terms, since an economic interest is *in re ipsa* non-existent, and restitution of the share capital would be unlawful. The concept of the non-profit purpose must therefore coincide with the compulsory absence of the distribution of dividends of any sort. Two facts

---

[16] See D. Vittoria, "*Le fondazioni culturali ed il Consiglio di Amministrazione*," in *Riv. dir. Comm.* I (1975), p. 298; *see also* P. Rescigno, "*Fondazione ed impresa*," in *Riv. società* (1967), p. 821.

[17] See R. Costi, "*Fondazione e impresa*," in *Riv. dir. civ.* I (1968), p. 1*ff*.

[18] See D. Vittoria, *supra* note 16, at 315, and, more recently, A. Zoppini, *Le fondazioni. Dalle tipicità alla tipologie*, Jovene, Naples (1995).

[19] See G. Ponzanelli, *Le 'non-profit organisations'*, Milan (1985) and more recently, G. Ponzanelli, *Gli enti collettivi senza scopo di lucro*, Torino, Giapp., (2000).

prove that the principle of the "non-distribution constraint" may be regarded as the borderline distinguishing the two sectors of collective organizations. As to the first sector, in the Italian Civil Code, the clause of one of the articles in a charter of a *società* compelling the non-distribution of dividends would certainly be invalidated.[20] As to the second point, when according to its articles of incorporation, a *società* sets aside the dividends for purposes other than the economic interest of the members (culture, charity, assistance), that same *società* must be regarded in every respect as an association.[21]

Such an autonomous category of non-profit organizations, like that recognized in the United States, was not welcomed with enthusiasm. Three principal objections to it have been raised. First, this category derives from an interpretative effort, but does not exist either in the Civil Code or in any other statute. Secondly, the absolute non-distribution constraint, which is imposed even upon those who represent the association, has been strictly criticized by those scholars who would have preferred to distinguish between different types of non-profit organizations. Thirdly, it has been suggested that it would be better to point out the differences among the non-profit organizations than to underline the commonalties within the same category.

At any rate, the non-profit world is composed of a variety of structures with a variety of goals. For example, in the mid-1980s, there was a lively discussion in Italy resulting in the elaboration of a distinction between two types of banking foundations (*fondazioni bancarie*) recently transformed into private foundations. The first recognized the central task of an institutional investor; the second recognized a center of cultural promotion, very similar to that of the large American foundations. As it was very difficult to accept both of these quite different types of banking foundations within the same category, the Italian legislator finally recognized the second type.[22]

Furthermore, in the Italian non-profit system, organizations that belong to the social organizations established under art. 2 of the Italian Constitution exist, since they pursue goals like the promotion of responsibility and solidarity, and they are in this sense not unlike family associations. At the same time, there are non-profit organizations that produce goods and services. For example, social cooperative corporations clearly exist, and respond to the negative results of market failure.

---

[20] *See* G. Ferri, "*Diritto agli utili e diritto al dividendo,*" in *Riv. dir. comm.* I (1963), p. 405.

[21] *See* the Italian Supreme Court, 14 October 1958, no. 3251, in *Foro it.* (1958), I, c. 1617.

[22] *See* G. Ponzanelli, "*Le fondazioni bancarie tra passato, presente e futuro*" (delivered at Cariplo Conference on "Non-Profit Organizations," Stresa, 26-27 October 1995), in *Foro it.* (1996), I, 816*ff.*

A final category is represented by organisms that pursue collateral public aims, such as banking foundations.

V. The Different Cultures of the "Non-Profit World": Reform Proposals for the Italian System

The growth of the "non-profit world" has provoked lively discussion about the opportunity for reforming the present discipline of non-profit organizations.[23]

A. A Review of the Discipline Provided by the Civil Code

It is useful to offer a brief survey of the rules applicable to non-profit organizations. Article 16 of the Civil Code requires that articles of incorporation of both foundations and registered associations include a statement of purpose, articulating the object of their activity, the conditions for the admission of new members, and the mode of winding up the non-profit organization and distributing its assets. All these features of the organization may therefore only be modified upon subsequent approval of the same government authority that approved the original articles of incorporation.

Article 2 of the "enforcement rules" of the Code gives the same authority the right to deny incorporation if the initial working capital is not adequate to the purpose of the organization. This rule guarantees prospective creditors perhaps even more than the business corporation's requirement of a starting capital of at least 200 million lire.

Article 17 of the Code forbids foundations and registered associations from receiving goods by will or donation and from purchasing real estate without government permission. The rule, aimed at avoiding mortmain, has been viewed as an obstacle or even a sign of the legislator's opposition to business associations and foundations. In response, however, scholars argue that ownership of real property is seldom a necessary condition for the running of a business (with the obvious exception of construction enterprises; this article was abrogated by law no. 127 of 15 May 1997, art. 13).[24]

---

[23] *See* comment by G. Ponzanelli, *"Gli enti colletivi senza scopo di lucro nell'attesa della riforma,"* in *Giur. comm.* I (1995), p. 515*ff.*

[24] *See* D. Vittoria, *"L'abrogazione dell'art. 17 c.c.: l'incidenza sull'assetto normativo degli enti del I libro del Codice Civile,"* in *Contratto Impresa* (1998), p. 331*ff.*

Article 18 regulates directors' liability in registered associations in a way that may be construed as slightly less stringent than liability in business corporations. More importantly, directors may be sued only by the association, through members' general meetings. In business corporations, a creditors' action and an individual action by members or third parties are also possible. The reader should, however, be aware that the former action is allowed substantially only in cases of insolvency, and therefore always promoted by the receiver together with the corporation's action, to substantially no different effect. As for the individual action, it does not at all resemble derivative action; instead, it is restricted to damages directly caused to the member or third party that do not affect the corporation (mostly the dissemination of false information to prospective members and creditors). Liability standards for directors are therefore probably inadequate for business activities, but they fit in a system in which even the liability of corporate directors is quite narrow.

Article 20 provides for the approval of the annual budget through general meetings of the members, but does not require its publication. Article 21 establishes the "one man-one vote" principle. In the first convocation, members must decide by a majority of five percent; in the second convocation, only with a majority of those present. A special majority is required for changing art. 9. Resolutions taken in the general meeting may be appealed by members, directors, and the general attorney, and, if against public order, also by the government.

Membership may not be sold nor transferred to others in any way, unless permitted by the articles of incorporation. There are no rights of appraisal for members exiting from the association (arts. 24 and 37). Some authors argue that this rule is not compulsory for unregistered associations because the unlimited liability of those acting upon the organization's behalf could constitute a sufficient guarantee for creditors. Members are free to withdraw from the association. Exclusion from registered associations is allowed only on "serious grounds."

Article 31 states that upon dissolution, assets must be distributed according to the articles of incorporation or the general meeting's resolution, or if both are silent, by the government. As we have seen, it is open to debate whether distribution to members is allowed. Unregistered associations are regulated, according to art. 37, by the members' agreements. It is a matter of debate whether the Code articles relating to registered associations should be applied directly or by analogy.

The courts seem to require the existence of a general meeting of members and a board of directors. Whether these associations must be open to new members or may be organized as a closed group is debated. The association is liable to third parties with the common fund resulting from members' contributions. Those who act in the name of the association are also personally liable.

Foundations are subject to continuous governmental control of directors' activities. The authority may void their resolutions when they are contrary to law or to the foundation's charter. It may dismiss directors and substitute them with a *commissario straodinario*, ("extraordinary commissioner") if they have acted against the law or the charter. It may coordinate or unify the activity of several foundations. It may wind up or transform the foundation if its purpose has been achieved, or has become either impossible to achieve or of marginal use, or if the assets are inadequate to the achievement of the foundation's goals.

With regard to both associations and foundations running a business, the courts have by now agreed to subject them to bankruptcy laws whenever the enterprise qualifies under the bankruptcy law, irrespective of the purpose (ideal or economic, egoistic or altruistic) pursued by the organization.

B. The Need for Reform

The discipline provided by the Italian Civil Code as analyzed above has been judged inadequate with regard to the new reality of the non-profit world. The administrative controls in particular run contrary to the Constitution's provisions regarding institutional pluralism, and have also proved to be a less than efficient means of using economic resources. It is for this reason that new rules must be found.

Nowadays, the two main aspects examined are the control over such organizations (particularly the opportunity to switch from administrative to juridical controls) and the applicable rules in the event that a business enterprise is to be carried on by the organization. In the latter case, the problem would be whether or not to apply the bankruptcy rules normally applicable to for-profit corporations.

With respect to the incorporation of a non-profit organization, law no. 59 of 15 March 1997 has granted the government the power to implement new rules in order to fulfill legal requirements. This power has recently been exercised through the enactment of presidential decree no. 161 of 10 February 2000. Now the *Prefetto* (the local administration authority) alone will evaluate whether or not the stated organizational purpose is possible and lawful.[25] Two results have been achieved in this way. First, the shifting of the process of incorporation from the Rome bureaucracy to provincial officers will save an enormous quantity of time. Secondly, the power of the State administration will be greatly reduced.

It is clear that the discipline of non-profit organizations should comply with the

---

[25] *See* M.V. de Giorgi, G. Ponzanelli & A. Zoppini, *Il riconoscimento delle persone giuridiche*, Ipsoa, Milano, (2001).

diverse aims of these organizations; different rules for different kinds of organizations would probably function more efficiently. The risk in this case would be the excessive growth of legislation and, at the same time, a heavy burden on an Italian public administration that has hardly achieved fame in Europe for its efficiency. But this is a risk worth running in order to enhance the various social and economic functions fostered by the presence of non-profit organizations in the society.

Our suggestion, then, is twofold. First, to sketch out a simple discipline-framework common to all non-profit organizations and based on the "non-distribution constraint" principle. This is not an unknown principle in our system, although it is negatively qualified (as non-distribution income). Secondly, we propose that a simple and clearly detailed set of rules be elaborated which are able to qualify the function of non-profit organizations, as well as another set of simple and clear fiscal rules. D. Preite, an acute and sorely missed legal observer who dealt with the non-profit sector in his brilliant 1988 book, divided the non-profit world into three categories.[26]

The first category is characterized by: strict rules of non-distribution constraint; the prohibition of reimbursement of the fund to the members; equal protection rules among the members; controls over the changes in by-laws; and a privileged fiscal drag (provided that the net income is entirely reinvested). The second category is characterized by much more generous fiscal legislation that requires a stricter system of controls, and that complies with principles stated in a discipline-framework (*see* law no. 266 of 11 August 1991, on volunteerism). The third category of non-profit organizations is one that greatly respects private freedom within the limits of non-distribution constraint.

It is now clear that a large percentage of Italian professors agree that the Civil Code is in need of modification with respect to this area of the law. But these scholars hold quite different views as to how to proceed. The debate sustained over the past ten years reflects three main cultural perspectives.

The Catholic approach recommends a policy offering extensive support to non-profit organizations, in compliance with art. 2 of the Italian Constitution. This thesis is based on the idea that society precedes the State, and not vice versa, both in time and in dignity. From this point of view, society is an autonomous entity, where people "in action" are closer to the needs of individuals. The State should support society. This is what the sociological approach would call the "subsidiary principle," as recently re-stated by the Pope in his encyclical *Centesimus annus:*

---

[26] D. Preite, *Destinazione dei risultati nei contratti associativi*, Milan (1988).

"A higher order of society must not interfere with the workings of a lower order of society, depriving it of its natural abilities. On the contrary, the first should support the second as necessary, and help it to cooperate with other social entities in order to achieve the public good." Therefore, the government should support the self-organization process of non-profit organizations, with rules and policies that can aid their activities. For this reason, there should be almost no economic or political control over the non-profit organization.

According to the second theory, government should direct and encourage private organizations operating in our society, as they are not able to promote themselves. This thesis, based on the pluralistic idea of social entities, allows some economic controls, but no political interference.

Finally, there are those who support the philosophy of "respecting the rules," who maintain that in order to comply with the equal protection rule, there cannot be any political or economic immunity in favor of non-profit organizations (nor against for-profit organizations). The only possible immunity would be fiscal, provided that the privileged entity pursued public aims.

The next step toward reform is to gather all the different opinions regarding non-profit organizations and work out solutions to the problems noted above. If we succeed, we may even be able to change Professor F. Fukuyama's negative opinion of Italy. In his recent book on social virtue and prosperity, Fukuyama maintains that Italy, along with China, France, and South Korea, suffers from a very low level of social "trust" – in other words, the belief that each individual member of the community observes the same rules and shares the same values.[27] As well, these populations tend to manifest "low social stock," in the sense that they find it difficult to work together to achieve common aims. Lastly, they have a low spontaneous "sociability," *i.e.* the skill to create new kinds of organized groups: cultural, entertainment-based, entrepreneurial, religious, trade and welfare unions, and so on. Fukuyama's essay evokes the images offered by Alexis de Tocqueville; we hope that in the future, North Americans visiting Italy might be just as surprised as the young French aristocrat was when he first visited the United States of America.

---

[27] F. Fukuyama, *Trust: The Social Virtues and the Creation of Prosperity*, Free Press, New York (1995).

Labor Law

Luca Nogler[1]

I. Two Introductory Remarks

In 1992, reflecting on collective agreements in the legal systems of the European Community's nations, Lord Wedderburn remarked:

> We need a new word. That has never bothered our language nor should it hold up our labor law. Perhaps we could describe the doctrine as *inderogability*. (The word has the advantage of being less barbarous than "subsidiarity.") Not all systems apply the doctrine of inderogability in precisely the same way, but it is central to many different European traditions just as its absence is critical to ours.[2]

To overcome the same difficulty in describing continental labor law systems in England, Sir Otto Kahn-Freund suggested a Latin term:

> Legislation laying down minimum standards for conditions of employment is generally mandatory, *jus cogens*. Obviously legislation on maximum hours of work, on severance pay, on holidays with pay, etc., cannot be contracted out by the individual contract of employment. Its object is to protect the employee. If it was open to him – especially in a (to him) unfavorable labor market – as an individual to bargain away these rights, he would be often unprotected.[3]

---

[1] Professor of Comparative Labor Law, University of Trento.

[2] Wedderburn, "Inderogability, Collective Agreements, and Community Law," *Industrial LJ* 245 (1992), p. 250.

[3] O. Kahn-Freund, *Collective Bargaining and Legislation*, in *Ius Privatum Gentium, Festschrift für Max Rheinstein zum 70 Geburtstag*, 5 July 1969, J.B. Mohr (1969), p. 1030.

Jeffrey S. Lena and Ugo Mattei (eds.), *Introduction to Italian Law*, 357-394
©2002 Kluwer Law International. Printed in the Netherlands.

Given such definitional challenges, it is useful to begin this chapter by describing two particularly significant principles in the evolution of Italian legal system (and certain other civil law systems): the inderogability and the invalidity of waivers and transactions concerning workers' rights derived from mandatory legal rules. We will then briefly introduce the actors and sources of Italian labor law and examine some trends in the relationship between labor law and the labor market.

A. The Inderogability and the Invalidity of Waivers and Transactions Concerning Workers' Rights from Mandatory Legal Rules

Italian labor law is permeated by a natural tendency to formulate and enforce an ever-growing number of imperative and highly legalistic norms and rules for worker protection,[4] norms which the parties to the contract cannot validly set aside to the detriment of the economically weaker party. Traditionally, the justification for this approach to labor market regulation is that an employment contract is not an "ordinary" contract due to the inequality of bargaining power. That is the ground for the legislative protection of the weaker party and for the implementation of an inderogability system. The analysis of inderogability is a good point of departure to begin to describe Italian labor law for at least two reasons. First, it governs the relation between the most important sources of employment law: (i) the relationship between statutory law and the individual contract of employment; (ii) the relationship between statutory law and collective contracts; and (iii) the relationship between collective contracts and individual contracts of employment. Given this fact, it seems appropriate to consider each of these relations separately in our introduction. Secondly, inderogability is the most important legal explanation for the conflict-ridden Italian system of labor relations.

1. The Relationship Between Statutory Law and the Individual Contract of Employment

Existing labor legislation covers nearly all aspects of the employer-employee relationship. This considerable volume of statutory law can be set aside by the individual employment contract only if its content is more favorable to the employee. If the parties to the individual agreements contract out to the detriment of employees (unilateral inderogability *in peius*), their agreement is ineffective and the relationship is automatically regulated by statutory terms.

---

[4] *See* M. Pedrazzoli (ed.), *Codice dei lavori*, Giuffrè, Milan (2001).

But what does "detriment" mean?

Article 2 of legislative decree no. 61 of 25 February 2000 provides that written individual agreements concerning the terms of employment and the distribution of working hours must be specified in relation to day, week, month, and year. For part-time employment, sometimes a flexible distribution is allowed, which may vary between a minimum and maximum calculated in relation to an annual parameter. These individual regulations are incompatible with the legal provision. Yet what happens when the employer pays for the time in which the employee is waiting on call? Is it to the detriment of the employee because it is considered time off, or is it more favorable (for example, to his employment opportunities)? Article 13 of the Workers' Statute (WS) of 1970 provides that an employee must be assigned duties equivalent to the last ones actually performed and that any agreement to the contrary is void. But what if, *quid iuris*, the individual parties agree to assign the employee to lower (not equivalent) duties to prevent a dismissal for organizational reasons? Italian courts tend to give two different answers. In the case of part-time work, the individual agreement is considered detrimental to the employee. By contrast, in the case of full-time work, it is acceptable to assign the worker "lower duties." In practice, the distinction between detriment and non-detriment remains uncertain.

2. The Relationship Between Statutory Law and Collective Contracts

Article 40 WS consolidates the principle that collective rules take precedence over statutory norms unless the latter are more favorable to the employer. Traditionally, legislation fixes the minimum standard of employee protection, but collective bargaining partners can nevertheless agree on higher standards. Therefore, having a correct view of legal regulation in some issues of Italian labor law means knowing its statutory rules, its case law, and its collective contracts rules.

Yet in special cases, labor legislation can be set aside by collective agreements to the detriment of employees. As Otto Kahn-Freund noted, in these cases "collective bargaining here acquires a new function: added to its contractual and codifying functions is its 'permissive' effect, the effect of creating an exception to legal norm."[5] This model of "controlled deregulation" was the Italian way to achieve flexibility in the 1980s and early 1990s.

Part-time work provides an example of this policy, because part-time work legislation delegates to collective contracts the power to introduce the possibility of variable working-hours arrangements (*see* art. 3 of legislative decree no. 61 of

---

[5]   O. Kahn-Freund, *supra* note 3, at 1031.

2000). Statutory law does not directly adopt a deregulation policy on this matter, but simply legitimates the collective bargaining to fix the quantity of part-time contracts. Another example is art. 5 of law no. 903 of 9 December 1977 (today abrogated by art. 17 of law no. 25 of 5 February 1999), which granted to collective bargaining the power to set aside the ban on night work for women employed in the manufacturing industry. This is by no means uncommon in the legislation of the 1980s and 1990s,[6] and demonstartes a regulatory crisis of the State that has utilized collective bargaining for the regulation and implementation of labor market public policy.

3. The Relationship Between Collective Contracts and Individual Contracts of Employment

We have just noted that in Italy, as in the majority of the member States of the European Union, the most important instruments for fashioning employment relations, apart from statutes, are collective agreements. In this system, collective agreements are contracts concluded between a trade union and one or more employers or, more frequently, an employers' association.[7] Collective contract rules concerning the employment relationship have an automatic and compulsory effect on individual contracts of employment.

a. Automatic Effect on Individual Contracts of Employment

The automatic effect is typical of all labor law systems of the Western legal tradition: they agree on the application of collective terms "as between the individual employers and the employees in the absence of an agreement to the contrary between them."[8] But there is no convergence on the legal rules that govern this automatic effect. In Italy, according to a doctrine proposed by Gino Giugni, the individual employment contract does not incorporate the collective rules that are applied by the judge. This means that Italian courts use collective contract rules as sources of the *regula iuris* of the single case (the normative function of collective bargaining). In other systems, as in the common law, the employment contract incorporates the terms of the collective agreement. The employer cannot displace them through

---

[6] *See*, for example, legislation on solidarity agreements, part-time, temporary employment, training and work employment, strike in essential public services, temporary employment agencies. Many of these statutory rules will be discussed in greater detail below.

[7] *See*, generally, G. Giugni, *Diritto sindacale*, Cacucci, Bari (2001), p. 130.

[8] O. Kahn-Freund, "Introduction," in O. Kahn-Freund (ed.), *Labour Relations and the Law. A Comparative Study*, Stevens & S. Brown & Co. (1965), p. 11.

company collective bargaining, but only by a new contract with the employee. The truth is that incorporation into individual contracts is typical of an individualistic and static approach, while the no-incorporation rule promotes collective bargaining. Finally, because employees and employers are, according to the *Verbandstheorie*, third parties, and because the general principle maintains that "a contract affects third parties in the case provided by statute" (art. 1372 CC), it is important to note that such statute is to be found, in my view, in art. 2113 CC, discussed *infra*.[9]

b. Compulsory Effect on Individual Contracts of Employment

In many continental systems (Germany, France, Spain, and Italy, for example), the State has also assigned to collective rules a compulsory effect on individual contracts of employment. Collective contracts take precedence over individual agreements, unless the latter are more favorable to the employee. But in Italy, for an extended period after World War II the "inderogabillity" of collective contracts was judicially mandated. In fact, prior to 1973, courts used art. 2077 CC, which provides that the terms of the individual contract are "substituted by those of the corporate collective contract, unless they contain conditions more favorable to the worker." The point is that in the Fascist era, art. 2077 CC regulated corporative collective contracts as a source of law with effect *erga omnes* and delegated to the (public) parties this law-making power. By contrast, private parties to the new collective agreements concluded after World War II exercise the liberty of collective bargaining guaranteed by art. 39 of the Italian Constitution of 1948 (*see infra*, part III A 2), and they conclude contracts binding only on workers and employers adhering to the negotiating parties. That is why it is impossible to reason by analogy. This difficulty inherent in trying to justify the "inderogability" of the collective rules was ultimately solved by the legislator in 1973 by the passage of law no. 533 of 11 August which introduced into the Civil Code a "new" text of art. 2113 CC that explicitly provides for the "inderogability" of collective contracts. The dominant view in Italy since 1973 is that the "inderogability" of collective contracts is recognized in the "new" art. 2113 CC, and that the binding force of collective rules is governed by the provision that "a contract binds the parties not only as to what expressly provides but also as to all consequences deriving from it by statute" (art. 1374 CC), and by art. 1339 CC, which provides for the automatic insertion of the terms imposed by law, even in place of contrary terms included by the parties themselves.

---

[9] *See* L. Nogler, *Saggio sull' efficacia regolativa del contratto collettivo*, Cedam, Padua (1997), pp. 162-63.

B. The Actors and Sources of Italian Labor Law

It is worth noting that today, many scholars in Italy, as in some other continental systems, criticize the principle of "inderogability." Nevertheless, that "inderogability" is an obstacle to the employment of workers remains to be proved, in my view.[10] It is interesting to note, however, that the substantive legal protection offered to workers by the "inderogability" of labor law is certainly not effective if legislation does not provide a second general principle. This second principle invalidates waivers and transactions concerning workers' rights derived from imperative norms of statutes or collective agreements that are decided without the assistance of the unions or of the judge. In Italy, the prohibition of compromises in which workers give up their rights is also regulated by art. 2113 CC. The avoidance of such waivers and compromise settlements must, under penalty of forfeiture, be instituted within six months from the date of termination of the employment relationship, or from the date of the waiver or compromise settlement, if these occurred after the termination of the employment. In addition, the employee can avoid such settlements with any written document, even extra-judicial, capable of making his intent known.[11]

II. The Actors of Italian Labor Law

A. The Individual Parties (Employees and Employers)

1. Employees

A labor market does not exist as such. It is always seen, described, and classified through the eyes of the observer and the observer's conceptual framework. Characteristic of the conceptual framework of Italian labor law is the division of workers into two categories: *subordinati* (subordinate) and *autonomi* (self-employed). The governing paradigm (in the sense suggested by Thomas Kuhn) of the Italian labor law of the last seventeen years was that the object of labor law legislation was to protect only the subordinate workers, because only this class of workers is in a weakened position.[12]

---

[10] On inderogability, *see* P. Ichino, *Il lavoro e il mercato*, Mondadori, Milan (1996).

[11] *See*, generally, E. Ghera, *Diritto del lavoro. Il rapporto di lavoro*, Cacucci, Bari (2000), p. 419.

[12] But *see* now M. Pedrazzoli, *Lavoro* sans phase *e ordinamento dei lavori. Ipotesi sul lavoro autonomo*, *Riv. italiana di diritto del lavoro*, I (1998), 10, holding that today, self-employment

This fundamental assumption is now subject to challenge because the importance of self-employment is increasing rapidly. According to data collected by the National Statistical Institute (*Istat*) in April 1999, some 28 percent of the 20,692,000 workers in Italy are self-employed. The recent growth in the number of self-employed workers may be associated with an employment shift from the manufacturing to the services sector. At the same time, in dramatic contrast to the changes stimulated by the industrial revolution (which drove workers out of the home and into the factory), the current technological revolution has created an opportunity for the return of market work to the home (as in freelance work and teleworking).[13] Today, it is also clear that the self-employed sector constitutes a very heterogeneous group of workers. Some of them are as weak as the *subordinati*, while others are undoubtedly powerful actors in the labor market. For the first group, the paradigm of the Italian labor law of the last 17 years means a lack of job security, a lack of income security, and an absence of entitlements and other benefits associated with employment. Despite all the changes that have occurred since 1942, Italian labor law largely remains a body of law applicable only to the *subordinati*. In other words, the fact that the historical distinction of workers is now empirically collapsing does not alter the "legal fact" that today's labor law is still the law of the class of subordinate workers. This is why art. 2094 CC – which defines "subordinate employee" as "the person who binds himself, for remuneration, to cooperate in the undertaking by contributing his intellectual or manual work, in the service and under the management of the entrepreneur" – remains the most important legal rule and the "gatekeeper"[14] of Italian labor law.

Generally speaking and according to the case law of the Labor Division of the Italian Supreme Court, the employment relationship only exists where one person, the employer (*datore di lavoro*), has sufficient control over the work to be done by another, the *subordinato* employee. The concept of *subordinazione* (subordination) was created by Ludovico Barassi, the father of modern concept of the employment contract. The problem here is that this traditional concept of subordination developed in the context of traditional manufacturing industries is no longer adequate to address the changes that have taken place in the labor market in the past three decades.

Ultimately, there are three different forms of judicial reasoning employed to

---

must be considered as a field of application of labor law, as it was originally. *See also* A. Perulli, *Il Lavoro Autonomo*, Giuffrè, Milan (1996).

[13] *See* L. Gaeta, P. Pascuzzi (eds.), *Telelavoro e Diritto*, Giapichelli, Turin (1998).

[14] M. Pedrazzoli, *Democrazia industriale e subordinazione*, Giuffrè, Milan (1985), p. 35.

define the relation between worker and employer. First, the basic method of reasoning is to identify subordination analytically and anticipate its essential elements. On this basis, the interpretation and application of art. 2094 CC by the judge should follow a logical path based on the identity between the practical case and the typical situation abstractly described by the same art. 2094 CC. This logical path is called *sussunzione* in Italian. Consider, for example, the leading "pony express" case, which not surprisingly involved a new form of labor arising within the service sector. A transportation company entered into day-to-day contracts with young workers for delivery services and provided each delivery person with a motor scooter and a radio. The radio was necessary for communication with all the pony express workers along the delivery route. Additionally, the contract indisputably specified that the single pony express "rider" was not compelled to respond to the delivery's order, nor to return to work the next day. The Labor Division of the Supreme Court argued that subordination involved the following elements: (i) the employer's use of the power to give precise instructions; (ii) the employer's disciplinary power; and the fact that that the worker is (iii) personally and (iv) continually compelled to perform the job. In the absence of two of the elements (precise instructions and duration), the pony express worker was not found to be "subordinate."[15]

Secondly, some lower courts have suggested reliance on a typological approach, which is based on a general evaluation of the elements of subordination, not all of which may necessarily be present in any single case. Under this approach, the presence of a majority of these elements is sufficient to qualify the relationship as subordinate.[16] Indeed, since there is no further specification as to the qualification procedure (the "majority" criteria), this method risks becoming an exaltation of the judge's intuition. Furthermore, by employing this method, we continue to follow the logic of subsumption, though here the major premise (the idea of subordination) is defined by utilizing an open number of elements.

Finally, to avoid such risks, some scholars[17] – and in the end the Labor Division

---

[15] *See* Cassazione no. 7608 of 10 July 1991, *Massimario di giurisprudenza del lavoro* (1991), p. 506; *Tribunale Milano* of 10 October 1987, *Lavoro* 80 (1987); P. Ichino, *Il contratto di lavoro*, I, Giuffrè, Milan, (2000), p. 269.

[16] Reference to case law based on the typological approach may be found in L. Manghini, *Subordinazione e Dintorni: Itinerari della Giurisprudenza* 21 *Quaderna di Diritto del Lavoro e delle Relazioni Industriali*, p. 143 (1999).

[17] *See* L. Mengoni, "*Il contratto industriale di lavoro*," in *Giornale di diritto del lavoro e relazioni industriali* (2000), p. 193; L. Nogler, "*Metodo tipologico e qualificazione dei rapporti di lavoro subordinato*," in *Riv. Italiana di diritto del lavoro* (1990), I, p. 182.

of the Supreme Court as well – came to rely upon a functional method which defines the case on the grounds of the relations among its single elements, selecting them according to the principle of fitness for possessing the same function. Such a method sets the principle of identity as a guide for the subsumption against the principle of equivalence. For example, the Penal Division of the Supreme Court has established that pony express work is subordinate both because the performance is organized by the employer (even in the absence of specific instructions), and because subordination derives from the way in which the work is organized rather than according to the way the work is regulated by the individual contract.[18]

2. Employers

In the Italian legal context, the English term "employer" corresponds to the term *datore di lavoro*, or "the person *giving* work," and derives from the Italian translation of the German *Arbeitgeber*. The German term suggests that the employer is not a creditor who dominates his employee, but is rather a "giver of work" who is performing a socially useful function. Unfortunately, the Italian legislator does not define the technical legal meaning of the term *datore di lavoro*. The term is currently defined only by, and for the application of, particular statutes. For example, according to the evidence that in a large organization the functions of the employer are divided among the supervisors, managers, president, and stockholders, art. 2 of law no. 626 of 19 September 1994, defined the term as any person who is part of an employment relationship or who is responsible for the enterprise. Yet determining who is the employer is left to the application of other statutes, and so this definition proves unsuitable. In a market in which the group and the holding company is the most important legal form used by employers, and in which the relation between employer and employee is no longer primarily characterized by face-to-face relations, the employees are frequently *à la recherche de l'employer perdu*.

B. The Social Partners (Trade Unions and Employers' Organizations)

The structure of Italian trade unions is marked by ideological fragmentation. Shortly after the World War II, the single non-party trade union confederation established

---

[18] *See* Cassazione no. 5671, of 14 April 1989, *Massimario giurisprudenza del lavoro* (1989), p. 159; at last *see* Cass. s.u. no. 379, of 30 June 1999, *Notiziario di giurisprudenza del lavoro* (2000), p. 21; an overview of the case law can be found in L. Nogler, "*La doppia nozione giuslavoristica di parasubordinazione,*" in *Massimario giurisprudenza del lavoro* (2000), p. 1032.

in 1944 divided into three individual, ideologically defined confederations. The *Confederazione generale italiana lavoratori* (*Cgil*), under the influence of the left-wing parties, had 5,211,568 members in 1996, of which just over 52 percent were retired. In the same year, the Catholic *Confederazione italiana sindacati dei lavoratori* (*Cisl*) had 3,837,104 members, of which just over 43 percent were retired. Finally, the social-democratic *Unione italiana lavoratori* (*Uil*) had 1,593,615 members in 1996, of which 24 percent were retired. Union unity has been a recurrent theme since the end of World War II. After the freeze of the 1980s,[19] the 1990s collapse of those parties which had dominated the political scene eliminated some of the traditional grounds for the split among the unions – especially those of an ideological nature. A new attempt to formalize unity between the trade union organizations was made in 1991, when the confederations agreed on the reform of plan-level union representation structures, which were renamed as *rappresentanze sindacali unitarie* (*see infra*, part III B 3). This agreement was officially recognized in the tripartite accord of 23 July 1993 (*see infra*, part III D), and subsequently in the interconfederal agreement between the social parties of 20 December 1993.

Union membership in Italy (excluding the large numbers of retired members) has shown great historical variation. The rate of unionization peaked at approximately 49.02 percent in 1977. Since then, unionization has steadily declined. In 1996, approximately 36 percent of the Italian labor force was represented by trade unions.[20] There was a marked decline in the level of union organization, above all in the public sector, where grassroots unions operating on a sectional basis (the *Comitati di base-Cobas*) had sprung up parallel to the existing confederations, challenging them. In addition, new trade unions aligned with the *Lega Nord* and the extreme right have emerged. Finally, in recent years there have been some cases of so-called "pirate collective agreements," made by unions existing only in a small part of the national territory, which provide terms and conditions worse than those

---

[19] Following some initial experience in company-level bargaining in the early 1960s, the trade unions rediscovered unity of action in the period of collective mobilization inaugurated during the "hot autumn" of 1969, when the plant-level workers' councils gave impetus to the unitary process. Although full unification was not achieved, a *Cgil-Cisl-Uil* Federation was instituted in 1972 as a step towards union unity. This unitary phase began to crumble during the period when fighting inflation was the top priority, and then ended abruptly in 1984, when *Cgil* refused to sign a new central agreement on the reorganization of the so-called *scala mobile* (sliding scale) mechanism for pay indexing. This break did not prevent attempts at unity of action during the 1980s.

[20] *See* G. Della Rocca, "*Il sindacato*," in G.P. Cella & T. Treu (eds.), *Le nuove relazioni industriali, Il Mulino* (1998), p. 113.

obtained through the collective agreements made by the most representative unions. According to most scholars, they are unlawful because of the "no trade union" stance of their parties.

At present, the employers' association system is organized according to economic sectors. The *Confindustria*, established in 1911 and having around 131,150 members (employing approximately four million workers), is the organization representing manufacturing and service enterprises in Italy, and is also the most powerful organization of employers; *Confcommercio* and *Confesercenti* (258,000 members), representing the commercial sector; and *Confagricoltura* (676,000 members) and *Coldiretti* (1,028,000 members) representing agriculture. Small firms are represented by *Confabi* (with 30,000 members employing 850,000 workers). Public employers (*e.g.*, State ministerial departments, Regions, municipalities, public hospitals, and schools) have their own association: the Agency for Bargaining Representation (*Agenzia per la rappresentanza negoziale*), a new institution set up by art. 50 of legislative decree no. 29 of 3 February 1993 in order to represent the public party in collective bargaining.

Finally, it is important to note that there is no law in Italy concerning the formation and function of labor market organizations. Case law provides individual members with certain rights protecting them against actions by their organization, such as unwarranted expulsion. Nevertheless, today there is undoubtedly a disparity between trade union power in the labor market and the quality of its internal democracy.

C. The State

To begin, the function of passing labor legislation is distributed between parliament and the government. The Republican Constitution gives much attention to the procedure for Parliament's promulgation of legislation and provides to each House the possibility of utilizing various procedures. The fact is that recent legislation in the field has increasingly become a matter of governmental instruments having the force of law. Emergency executive decrees (*decreti legge*) are subject to conversion by parliamentary act within 60 days, and legislative decrees (*decreti legislativi*) are adopted by the government on the basis of parliamentary law delegating legislative power to the government. The Constitution deals with the issue of the governmental decree power very carefully. Even so, the government tended in the 1980s to apply emergency decrees as an almost ordinary instrument of law-making, particularly in the field of labor law. In the early 1990s, the Constitutional Court stopped the practice of repeating those emergency decrees not converted into law within 60 days. The new trend in labor relations lawmaking is the frequent use of the delegation of legislative power to the government. Such delegation needs to be preceded by a parliamentary act, and the new procedure is the approval by parliament of a single act containing several delegations to the government. Finally, an advisory organ to parliament and to the government is the National Economic and Labor Council (*Consiglio nazionale dell'economia e del lavoro*), which is composed, according to the provisions of art. 99 of the Constitution and of law no. 936 of 30 December 1986, of experts and representatives of productive branches, so that their views are properly taken into consideration. The council undertakes research, gives advice to the government, makes recommendations to it, retains the right to propose legislation, and may contribute to the drafting of economic and social laws according to the principles, set forth by law no. 936 of 1986.

The Ministry of Labor and Social Insurance has the overall responsibility to draft, apply,[21] and monitor this labor legislation. Equally important is the role of several independent authorities in the shaping and administration of labor law. These agencies are today more diverse and numerous than at any previous time in the rather short history of Italian labor law. These agencies have several important functions. First, the *Commissione di garanzia*, or Guarantee Commission for the Implementation of the Regulation on Strikes in Fundamental Service, is appointed by Parliament, and has the task of helping social partners arrive at an agreement on strikes in essential public services (*see infra*, part III A 5); to evaluate whether the rules set by collective agreements (or by codes of practice, or by employers) are adequate with respect to provisions of statutory principles; and to promote the application of sanctions against unions for breach of the law no. 146 of 12 June 1990. Secondly, there are the two agencies in the field of equal opportunity: the National Commission for Equality and Equal Opportunities, which was established by law no. 164 of 22 June 1990, and the National Committee for Equality (or Italian Ministry of Labor's Equal Opportunities Committee: *Comitato nazionale per l'attuazione dei principi di parità di trattamento ed uguaglianza di opportunità tra lavoratori e lavoratrici*), established by art. 5 of law no. 125 of 1991. Finally, legislative decree no. 675 of 1996 introduced the Guarantee of Privacy (*Garante per la privacy*).

Pursuant to art. 5 of the Constitution, some of the functions normally carried out at the national level in other countries have been decentralized in Italy into 20

---

[21] Regarding the statutory instruments of single Ministers, law no. 400 of 1988 established that they can be adopted only on the basis of an explicit attribution of normative power by the legislator to the Ministry, and has furthermore extended the system of control of legitimacy, already applied to the government's measures, to these instruments.

regional administrations. Landmark legislation in 1977 and 1997 (art. 1 of law no. 59 of 15 March 1997) delegated and transferred many subjects in the field of labor law to the regional administrations. In particular, in 1997 Parliament and the government delegated to the Regions, within the limits fixed by law, the legislative and administrative functions related to job system (*see infra*, part III B 1) and active labor market policies, including supervision of the application of labor rules, the conciliation of disputes before the local labor offices (*see* legislative decree no. 469 of 23 December 1997),[22] the conciliation of local collective labor disputes of rights and interests and, finally, the information about labor markets and the relations with the European Union's organs. In the administration of these functions, particular tasks are entrusted to the provincial labor market policy office (*commissione provinciale per le politiche del lavoro*), the tripartite regional labor committee (*commissione regionale tripartita*), the employment centers (*centri per l'impiego*), the institutional board (*organismo istituzionale*) and the regional board having drafting functions (*struttura regionale*). Regions will transfer to these new organs the functions that are managed today by a disparate group of committees.

III. The Sources of Italian Labor Law

The six essential sources of Italian labor law are: constitutional law; statute law; ILO conventions and European Community law; collective bargaining and concertation agreements; individual contracts of employment; and case law.

A. Constitutional Law

The Italian Constitution of 1947[23] includes a long list of employment rights, longer than any of European Union member. While a detailed study of these fundamental social rights is impossible, we will broadly sketch the socio-economic rights in the Constitutional system.

Italy is also party to a number of international human rights Conventions that guarantee socio-economic rights, including the European Convention on Human Rights of 4 November 1950 (ratified by law no. 848 of 4 August 1955); the European Social Charter of 18 October 1961 (ratified by law no. 929 of 3 July 1965); the International Covenant on Economic, Social and Cultural Rights of 16 December

---

[22] On this important legislative decree, *see I servizi per l'impiego tra pubblico e privato*, Utet, Torino (1999).

[23] The Constitution actually came into force on 1 January 1948.

1966 (ratified by law no. 881 of 25 October 1977); the Convention on the Elimination of All Forms of Racial Discrimination of 7 March 1966 (ratified by law no. 654 of 3 October 1975); the Convention on the Elimination of Discrimination against Women of 18 December 1979 (ratified by law no. 132 of 14 March 1985); and the Community Charter of Fundamental Social Rights of 9 December 1989.

In Italy, courts have maintained an activist approach to applying the Constitution to labor relations. In a series of decisions in the 1950s, the Supreme Court stated that the majority of constitutional employment rights (for example, freedom of expression, the right to a fair wage,[24] to equal treatment between women and men or between juveniles and adults, the right to strike or to engage in union activity, and the right to privacy) are "directly enforceable law" that can form the basis for a legal claim in court.[25] The balance of these rights with other fundamental rights of the employer,[26] of other employees or of third parties is a matter of legislation and also of case law (primarily of the Constitutional Court[27]). The legislator took this approach only at the beginning of 1970s with passage of the Workers' Statute. An example of legislation that balances two fundamental employees' rights – the right to public health and the right to privacy (art. 2 Const.) of workers infected with the HIV virus or suffering from AIDS – is law no. 135 of 5 June 1990, which prohibits HIV testing of employees. In 1994, the Constitutional Court declared this prohibition unconstitutional for jobs that involved a serious risk of infection.[28]

For many labor rights, particularly in the area of welfare law, there is also a so-called "second dimension," because aspects of them need to be clarified by

---

[24] *See* Corte di Cassazione no. 1184 of 1951 and no. 461 of 1952. Since the 1960s, the Italian Supreme Court has held that art. 36 is also directly enforceable against collective bargaining (*see* Corte di Cassazione no. 636 of 1960).

[25] There is also incoherence to the courts' willingness to impose constitutional values on employment relationships. In fact, according to the Italian Supreme Court, the direct enforceability of the fundamental right to human dignity (art. 2 Const.) is based on art. 2087 CC and on the general principle of fairness and good faith (art. 1175 CC) and can give arise only to damages.

[26] The most important employers' fundamental right is protected by art. 41 Const., which expressly guarantees freedom in economic affairs as the basis of business life, provided that its exercise is not "in conflict with public policy and does not infringe safety, freedom and human rights."

[27] The Constitutional Court started to operate in 1956, and began its work by eliminating outworn or irrelevant statutes and institutions, mainly from the Fascist era and no longer compatible with the new constitutional order.

[28] *See* Corte Costituzionale no. 218, 1994.

constantly changing legislation. This area of individual social rights includes the right to the protection of health (art. 32 Const.); the right to professional or vocational training (art. 35 Const.); the right to assistance (art. 38 Const.); the right to adequate insurance in case of accident, illness, disability, old age, and involuntary unemployment (art. 38 Const.); the right to education and vocational training of disabled workers (art. 30 Const; *see also infra*, part III B 1); the right to a maximum number of daily working hours (art. 36 Const.); the right to a weekly day of rest and to paid annual holidays (art. 36 Const.); and finally, the right of workers to participate in management (art. 46 Const.). Notably, there is no implementing labor legislation on the latter important matter.

More generally, the constitutional background of labor market regulation is found in art. 35 Const., which provides that the Republic "safeguards labor in all its forms and methods of execution." Toward this purpose, "it promotes and encourages international agreements, and organizations calculated to confirm and regulate the rights of labor" (*see infra*, part III C). The Republic provides for "freedom to emigrate, save for limitations prescribed by statute in the general interest, and for the protection of Italian labor abroad." In this context, it should be also noted that art. 4 Const. provides that the Republic recognizes the right of all citizens to work and promotes conditions that will effectuate this right. It is clear that the measures adopted by the Italian Republic to achieve this "right to work" fall within the realm of economic and social policy rather than individual rights and obligations.[29]

Furthermore, in relation to fundamental social rights that are directly enforceable, the Constitutional Court and labor courts adopt an expansive, value-based interpretation of constitutional employment rights. For example, the Constitutional Court held in a 1974 decision that political strikes called to protest a government policy are legal – *i.e.* the strike only suspends the contract of employment – if the policy in question is directly related to workers' conditions. On the other hand, the Italian Supreme Court has held that the word "strike" and its attendant concept are to be employed "in the meaning that they bear in ordinary language adopted in their surrounding social setting." This reflects the potential of the judge to control the way in which the strike is carried out in practice. The Court, which tried on several occasions to determine the limits of the right to strike, finally held that only other constitutional rights – for example, the freedom of economic initiative (art. 41 Const.) – justify limiting the individual's right to strike. Lastly, the Constitutional Court approach is today consolidated by art. 1 of law no. 146 of 12 June 1990 on

---

[29] *See* Corte Costituzionale no. 268 of 30 June 1994, *Foro it.* (1994), I, 2307.

strikes in essential services. This law establishes the general principle that the exercise of the right to strike in essential services must be "balanced" against the exercise of the individual rights listed by law (life, health and safety, liberty, freedom of movement, social assistance, security, education, and freedom of communication; *see infra*, part III A 3).

1. Wages

Article 36 Const. provides that "an employed person is entitled to wages in proportion to the quantity and quality of his work, and in any case sufficient to provide him and his family with a free and dignified living." Italian labor courts (*see infra*, part III E) have assumed an activist stance in applying this norm to employment relationships, but the "two principal players" – the Italian Supreme Court (*Corte di Cassazione*) and the Constitutional Court (*Corte Costituzionale*) – have adopted fundamentally different approaches to the interpretation of art. 36. The Constitutional Court has found that art. 36 Const. contains two different principles on wages: the principle of sufficient wage and the principle of proportionality of wage. The Supreme Court, on the other hand, has determined that the principle of "fair wage" (the Court's terminology) is a unified concept. While the Constitutional Court applies art. 36 Const. with respect to statutory norms and the Supreme Court with respect to the employment relationship, the different views of these two "players" have no consequence for employment law.

Apart from the minimum income (*reddito minimo garantito*) relating to the at-risk areas of the country (*see* legislative decree no. 237 of 18 June 1998), in Italy, as opposed to the United States, there is no minimum wage legislation. Wages are a typical subject of collective bargaining and it is the case law on fair wage that fixes the wage rates normally on the basis of collective contracts.

2. The Principles of Equal Treatment

There are three different principles of equal treatment in the Constitution. First, under art. 3 Const., all citizens are vested with equal social status and are equal before the law, without distinction as to sex, race, language, religion, political opinion, or personal or social conditions. This rule is understood only in the sense of equality before the law.[30] While the mere guarantee of normative equality does

---

[30] *See* Corte di Cassazione no. 10282 of 1 December 1994, *Massimario giurisprudenza del lavoro* (1994), p. 688; Corte di Cassazione no. 1444 of 5 March 1986, *Foro it.* (1986), I, p. 3051*ff*; Corte di Cassazione no. 513 of 29 January 1985), *Rivista italiana di diritto del lavoro* (1985), II, p. 732.

not eliminate social inequality, art. 3 Const. also provides that it is the responsibility of the Republic to remove all obstacles of an economic or social nature which, by limiting the freedom and equality of citizens, prevent the full development of the individual and the participation of all workers in the political, economic, and social organizations of the country. Consequently, the main instrument for eliminating discrimination on the basis of race, religion, ethnicity, or national origin is art. 44 Const. or legislative decree no. 286 of 25 July 1998. In cases of discrimination in employment, it is also possible to use art. 15 WS.

Secondly, art. 37 Const. provides that "female labor enjoys equal rights and the same wages for the same work as male labor. Conditions of work must make it possible for them to fulfill their essential family duties and provide for the adequate protection of mothers and children." The principle of equal treatment was specified only by law no. 903 of 1977. This statute called for the absolute prohibition of any form of discrimination on the basis of gender or relating to "access to jobs, whatever the hiring procedures may be and whatever the sector or branch of activity." The law further prohibits any reference being made to "marriage, family or pregnancy status and to pre-selection methods through the press or to any other advertising form that indicates a particular sex as a vocational pre-requisite." Besides, law no. 125 of 1991 provided for equal opportunities between men and women by means of affirmative action. In particular, these so-called positive actions aim at: (i) eliminating inequalities in school education and vocational training, access to employment, and career advancement; (ii) eliminating conditions and factors relating to the organization and division of tasks which adversely affect women in the areas of training, career advancement, and economic treatment; (iii) promoting the integration of women into activities and sectors where they are under-represented (particularly in high-tech jobs and positions of responsibility); (iv) and promoting the balance between family and professional responsibilities, and a better division of these responsibilities between the sexes. The most important legal example of differential measures in favor of women provided by the legislation is art. 6 of law no. 236 of 1993, concerning contractual obligations for employers to avoid, in collective dismissals, laying off a greater percentage of female workers in comparison to those who work in the same firm with the same duties, as well as actions in favor of working mothers during "mobility."[31] This so-called "reverse discrimination"

---

[31] The aim of "mobility" is to facilitate the vocational reintegration of surplus workers when companies themselves are unable to guarantee the continuation of the employment contract. These workers may be registered in the "mobility list." The legislation accords priority to listed workers when the employer recruits workers with the same qualifications and also offers incentives to employers recruiting listed workers.

instigated a new type of employment litigation, and recently, two significant decisions by the European Court of Justice (17 October 1995, no. 450/93 and 11 November 1997 no. 409/95) have prompted renewed discussion of this theme. The solution to the conflicting interests of minorities (women) and non-minorities (men) is based on the opinion by the ECJ guaranteeing to non-minority members that there will be no automatic finding of "reverse discrimination." The employer's comparison of workers (for example, in deciding whom to promote) will not be based upon ordinarily discriminatory characteristics (for example, seniority).

Finally, art. 37 Const. guarantees equal pay for equal work between young and adult workers. "Equal work" here means "equal classification" and not "equal performance."[32] Constitutional law protects individuals against employee selections, discharges, classifications, and compensations, among other practices, on the simple basis of age. The remedy is the extension of the better treatment to the employee discriminated against.

3. The Trade Union Right and the Right to Strike

a. The Trade Union Right

The trade union right, is a composite right including the individual rights to join a trade union or not, and the collective right of union activity (including the right to collective bargaining), and is protected by art. 39 Const. ("Freedom in the organization of trade unions is affirmed"). The same article also provides in its second part that "no compulsion may be imposed on trade unions except that of registering at local or central offices according to the provisions of the statute" and that "a condition of registration is that the statutes of the unions sanction an internal organization on a democratic basis." Registered trade unions "have a legal status" and "may, being represented in proportion to the number of their registered members, negotiate collective labor contracts having compulsory value for all persons belonging to the categories to which the said agreements refer." In spite of this, Italian legislation has never provided a system by which the unions can register. As Federico Mancini has shown, the registering system of art. 39 Const. is typical of a corporative state.[33]

---

[32] See Cassazione no. 2571 of 19 April 1984, *Repertorio del Foro it.* (1984), *Lavoro (rapporto)*, no. 751.

[33] See F. Mancini, "*Liberta' sindacale e contratto collettivo 'erga omnes'*," in *Riv. Trimestrale di Diritto e Procedura Civile* (1963), p. 580 *et seq.*

A collective contract that provides that only union members are permitted to work, or which requires the employer to hire only employees who are members of the union, is outlawed under art. 39 Const. Also outlawed is the union security form in which the employer recognizes the union as the bargaining representative for its members only. These provisions do not frequently appear in Italian collective contracts in any case. In my view, the judicial rule that employees and employers not belonging to the unions that have concluded the collective contract are never legally bound by the contract rules, should instead be grounded in the individual trade union's right guaranteed by art. 39 Const.[34] Not all scholars agree with this rule.

b. The Individual's Right to Strike

The individual's right to strike (*diritto di sciopero*) is provided by art. 40 Const. ("The right to strike is exercised within the sphere of the statutes concerning the subject"). The article bears a striking resemblance to that of the Preamble to the Constitution of the Fourth French Republic of 1946 ("The right to strike is exercised within the framework of laws which govern it"). As a right, the strike only suspends the employment relationship and it is not possible for the employer to use disciplinary powers, including dismissal. As distinguished from the German approach, Italian law does not provide a corresponding right to lock employees out or to undertake other kinds of hostile action. If the employer locks out his employees, he has to pay their wages and there is no loss of seniority.

The only statute concerning the right to strike is law no. 146 of 12 June 1990, as amended in 2000 (law no. 83 of 11 April).[35] This law regulates strikes in essential public services, through a complex procedure based on a network of different sources (codes of practice unilaterally adopted by trade unions, collective bargaining, unilateral regulations and instructions issued by employers). The law only gives a definition of essential services ("all activities which are functional to the fulfillment of the fundamental personal interests and rights of citizens as recognized by the Constitution"), and an open-ended list includes sectors ranging from energy production and distribution to transport, health services, school, television, the judicial system, banks, and telecommunications. In these services, the exercise of the right to strike must be "balanced" against the exercise of the individual rights

---

[34] *See* L. Nogler, *Saggio sull'efficacia regolativa del contratto collettivo*, Cedam, Padua (1997), p. 150.

[35] *See* P. Pascucci (ed.), *La nuova disciplina dello sciopero nei servizi essenziali*, Ipsoa, Milan (2000); *Il conflitto collettivo nei servizi essenziali*, Utet, Torino (2001).

of citizens. The Guarantee Commission for the Implementation of the Regulation of Strikes in Fundamental Service (*see supra*, part II C) evaluates the rules regarding minimum levels of service set by collective agreements, by codes of practice, or by employers, and this evaluation constitutes the ground for the special sanctions provided under the law no. 146 of 1990. Despite this complex statutory regulation, the problem of strikes in the most conflict-plagued public services (the railway and airline sectors) is still under discussion in Italy, because in these sectors only partial agreements have been signed, and these have not been judged adequate by the Commission.

B. Statutory Law

In keeping with legal positivism, Italy has gone much further in adopting positive law norms in the labor law area than has the United States. But unfortunately, in Italy the statutory regulations of the employment contract and the employment relationship generally are not consolidated in a *code du travail*. A considerable number of different matters have been regulated separately. One may identify three broad areas of statutory regulation. First, the so-called labor market entry system, which includes job placement, compulsory employment, and the conclusion of an employment (subordinate) contract; secondly, legislation regarding the employment relationship and the main obligations of the parties to an employment contract; and thirdly, the legislation regarding union-management relations.

1. The Labor Market Entry System and Compulsory Employment

Initially (under law no. 264 of 29 April 1949 and art. 34 of law no. 300 of 20 May 1970), employers were required to apply to public employment agencies whenever they needed unqualified workers, and they were bound to employ the workers proposed to them. This public job system was inefficient, and it is considered to be the main source of the low (and still falling) job mobility levels in Italy. These local public employment agencies provided "no training and no information on job vacancies."[36] Recently, art. 10 of legislative decree no. 469 of 1997 (*see also supra*, part II C) provided, for the first time and as a consequence of an important decision of the European Court of Justice, the possibility to establish private job agencies.

---

[36] *See* R. Faini, G. Galli & P. Gennari, *An Empirical Puzzle: Falling Migrations and Growing Unemployment Differentials among Italian Regions*, European Univ. Institute: EUI Working Papers (1996), p. 7.

Today, under law no. 608 of 1997, there are no restrictions on the freedom of the employers to choose a contractual partner. In cases of compulsory employment of particularly disadvantaged groups of workers, the employer must choose the partner from among members of these groups. Disadvantaged workers are those who have been registered for more than two years in the employment exchange lists governed by the public employment agencies, or those who are selected by the regional employment commissions (*commissioni regionali per l'impiego*).[37] If the employer's organization has more than ten employees, the employer must reserve twelve percent of all new positions for disadvantaged people. In addition, law no. 68 of 12 March 1999 governs the compulsory employment of disabled people in the public and private sectors.[38] It applies to organizations employing, respectively, between 15 and 35 workers, between 36 and 50 workers, and more than 50 workers. The first group of employers must hire one disabled worker. The second two and the third must hire disabled workers to work in seven percent of the overall positions of employment at the firm. In order to benefit from these legal provisions, disabled people must register at the local employment center (*see supra*, part II C, *ufficio provinciale del lavoro e della massima occupazione*). The special technical commission (*comitato technico*) of the provincial labor market office is charged with overseeing the register and its sub-classifications. Employers obligated to employ disabled people must forward a request for the staff they need to the provincial employment office. Applicants must be selected from the names on the list, but only employers of the first group are free to choose either the persons they feel are best suited to the work or those most specialized. The employers of the second and third groups are free to choose only 50 and 60 percent of their disabled workers respectively. Many commentators have noted a negative attitude toward these matters among employers, who are also reluctant to bear the extra costs of employing disabled people. Law no. 68 of 12 March also contains some specific measures to promote the integration of disabled workers and extends the quota system to include people with psychological impairments. In recent years there have been numerous unsuccessful attempts in Parliament to reform the quota system.

Only after the conclusion of an employment contract (with or without a disadvantaged worker) must the employer communicate it to the public employment

---

[37] *See* art. 25 of law no. 223 of 23 July 1991.

[38] *See* M. Cinelli, P. Sandulli, (eds.), *Diritto al lavoro dei disabili*, Giappichelli, Torino (2000). The "disabled" category includes war disabled, civilian war disabled, those disabled through military or public service, disabled civilians, deaf and dumb individuals, persons with mental handicaps, and working-age persons affected by various physical, sensory, or psychic handicaps.

agencies and present a document stating the terms of employment to the employee. The terms must specify the job, working time, paid leaves, remuneration, social benefits, and any applicable collective contracts.[39]

2. The Employment Relationship

This overview of Italian legislation on the employment relationship is divided into three broad categories: the types of employment (subordinate) contracts, the obligations of the parties, and the termination of the relationship. It is important to note that after the so-called "privatization" and "contractualization" of the public employment relationships provided by the Civil Service Reform of 1993 (legislative decree no. 29), there remain only marginal regulatory differences between the employment relationship under a private employer and that under a public employer.

a. The Types of Employment (Subordinate) Contracts

There has been much debate recently over the issue of workforce flexibility. The so-called "non-standard" forms of employment include temporary work, job-sharing, part-time work, interim work, short-term contracts, home employment and teleworking.[40]

Law no. 230 of 1962 strictly controls employment contracts for fixed periods of time, allowing them only in very limited situations such as for specified seasonal activities and for temporary replacement of an absent employee whose job security is guaranteed. In the 1980s, as a response to the economic crisis, there was a growing trend in Italy toward greater flexibility in the use of fixed-term contracts. Some liberalization has occurred, including the introduction of the possibility to hire temporary workers on a seasonal basis. In 1987, art. 23 of law no. 56 of 28 February deregulated the determination of situations in which it is permitted to use fixed-term contracts in collective contracts. Finally, the whole subject matter of employment contracts for fixed periods has been deregulated by legislative decree no. 368 of 2001, according to which termination is possible for all reasons related to "technical, production, organization and subordination factors," a flexible and far-reaching clause, to say the least. In addition, arts. 1-11 of law no. 196 of 24 June 1997 stipulated for the first time that, subject to the acceptance by the Minister

---

[39] *See* Legislative Decree no. 152 of 26 May 1997, which implemented Council Directive 91/533 on the employer's obligation to inform employees of the conditions applicable to the contract or employment relationship of 14 October 1991.

[40] *See supra* note 11.

of Labor, private temporary-employment agencies can be started.[41] The interim worker is legally bound to these agencies, but it is the user-firm that benefits from the work performed. Collective contracts can fix the percentage of interim workers and the situations in which interim work is permitted.

Recently, legislative decree no. 61 of 25 February 2000 reformed part-time employment regulation. Part-time employment is defined as work for fewer hours every day (horizontal part-time employment) or for alternative periods in the week, in the month or in the year (vertical part-time employment). The contract for part-time employment is stipulated in writing, and includes the distribution of working hours – flexible clauses setting the distribution of working time can be introduced only by collective agreements. Collective agreements play an important role in the organization of working hours. Job sharing is considered a variation of part-time work because it implies the stipulation of two contracts of employment for two job performances carried out by two different workers.

b. The Obligations of the Parties

The employers' most important legal duties are the payment of wages and the guarantee of safety and health at work (*see infra*, part III C). Under article 2099 CC, the remuneration of an employee can be established either on a time or piece-work basis,[42] by participation in company profits[43] or its products, on a commission basis, or by payments in kind (fringe benefits). Furthermore, an employee shall be paid in the amount determined by collective contracts in the manner and within the periods that are customary in the place where the work is performed. Only in the absence of collective rules or an individual agreement between employer and employee is the remuneration established by the court.

Employees also have obligations. What tasks can rightly be assigned to the employee is of particular importance. We find the answer to this crucial question in the Civil Code and in the Workers' Statute of 1970 (*see also infra*, part III B 3).

---

[41] *See* M. Biagi (ed.), *Mercati e rapporti di lavoro*, Giuffrè (1997) and F. Liso, U. Carabelli, *Il lavoro Temporaneo*, Angeli, Milan (2000).

[42] Article 2100 CC provides that an employee shall be remunerated on a piecework basis when, by reason of the organization of the work, he is bound to observe a certain production rate, or when his services are evaluated on the basis of the results of measuring the period of production.

[43] In this case, the worker's share in the profits shall be based on the undertaking's net profits and, where undertakings are required to publish their balances sheets, on the basis of the net profits as shown on a balance sheet that has been duly approved and published (*see* art. 2102).

The provisions stated therein reflect a traditional model of an institutionalized adversarial relationship with rigid and highly legalistic categories of activity. While adopted to ensure objective treatment by employers, these rules undoubtedly limit management's discretion in production changes. In the Workers' Statute, the employer's powers of direction, defined by art. 2104 CC as the power to give "instructions for the performance and discipline of work," is founded on a new basis. Article 13 WS provides that employees must be assigned to the duties for which they have been engaged, or those corresponding to the higher category which may have subsequently attained, or to the duties equivalent to the last ones actually performed, without any reduction in remuneration. In addition, employers must assign the employees' duties in consideration of workers' rights to health and safety (art. 4 of legislative decree no. 626 of 19 September 1994). An employee assigned to higher duties is entitled to treatment corresponding to the work performed, and, after a period established in the collective contract, such an assignment becomes final, unless it was made in order to substitute for an absent employee who has a right to return to the position. On the one hand, this rigid job structure has undoubtedly made it difficult for firms to reallocate workers to more productive uses as need arises. On the other hand, the adversarial logic of the Workers' Statute was also favorable to employers. For example, art. 7 of the Workers' Statute regulated the employer's powers to discipline employees (defined by art. 2106 CC), a feature that is incompatible with the general private law principle of equality between the parties to a contract, and also with art. 1455 CC, which provides that minor negligent breaches of contract are insignificant and that non-performance must be serious in order to give rise to liability.

Other matters relating to obligations of employees are *where*, *when*, and *how* the work is to be performed. The duration of work is a matter for the individual contract of employment. Consequently, the employer cannot reduce working hours, with a correspondent reduction in pay, without the employee's consent (except in the cases expressly provided by statutory law: *e.g.*, solidarity collective agreements). In addition, under arts. 2110 and 2111 CC, workers may be permitted to remain away from their jobs for a limited period of time without loss of seniority and benefit coverage and with reinstatement rights. Leave may be granted in case of accident, sickness, pregnancy, and maternity. On the other hand, the distribution of working hours in the day or week is, in the absence of an agreement, typically subject to the power of the employer, but collective agreements often contain clarifying restraints. Secondly, as to the question of where the work is to be performed, the dominant view is that it is first and foremost a matter for the individual employment contract, and that the employer is able to decide where the work is to be performed only in the absence of a contractual provision. It is also important to note that under the Workers' Statute, the employee cannot be transferred from one productive unit to another, except for justifiable technical, organizational, and productive reasons (art. 13). Lastly, there is the question of *how* work is to be performed. The Civil Code provides that an employee shall act with that diligence required by the nature of the services he renders in the interest of the undertaking (*interesse dell'impresa*; *see also infra*, part III E). Moreover, an employee cannot engage in business, either for his own account or for the account of third persons, in competition with his employer. Nor can he disclose information pertaining to the organization and to methods of production of the undertaking; nor can he use it in such a manner as may be prejudicial to the undertaking itself (art. 2105).

c. The Termination of the Relationship

The Civil Code, which was adopted under the influence of the "corporativist" thinking of the fascist period and the effects of its *Carta del lavoro* (probably the most successful product of Italian labor law thinking from an international perspective),[44] has traditionally recognized that employment relationships are terminable at will by either party: "each of the parties of an employment contract may withdraw from the contract with no time limit, by giving notice in the terms and in the manner" established by collective rules, by usage, or on equitable basis (art. 2118). Besides, in cases of dismissal for grave misconduct (*giusta causa*) – *i.e.* where a cause arises that does not permit even the provisional continuation of the employment – it is possible to withdraw from the contract even without notice (art. 2119). Protection of workers against unfair dismissal was first regulated by law no. 604 of 15 July 1966 and then by art. 18 of the Workers' Statute of 1970. This legislation was finally enacted in 1990 (law no. 108 of 11 May).[45] Essentially, a worker[46] is unlawfully discharged if termination of the employment relationship occurs without a very considerable cause (*giusta causa*), or a considerable "reason of conduct" (*giustificato motivo soggettivo*), or without "organizational reasons" (*giustificato motivo oggettivo*). Additionally, in cases of dismissal for reasons of

---

[44] The *Carta del lavoro* was adopted in April 1927. It was part of the prolonged enterprise seeking to develop a system of functional representation and to transform Italy into a Corporate State.

[45] *See*, generally, E. Ghera, *supra* note 11, at 333, and O. Mazzotta (ed.) (1999), *I licenziamenti*, Giuffrè, Milan (1999).

[46] The legislation excludes executive employees (*dirigenti*) from the area of application of the statutory protection. Yet a less restrictive regulation has been introduced for them by collective bargaining.

conduct (also called disciplinary dismissal), the employer must first notify the worker of the claimed breach in writing and then wait five days before the actual dismissal. In case of unlawful termination, the solutions vary according to the number of workers of the employer's organization. If there are more than 15, the law guarantees an injunction for reinstatement of the worker and compensation for damages incurred by the wrongful termination; the employment relationship persists and there is no loss of seniority. This protection really halts the effects of the unlawful termination (*tutela reale*). A "small employer" (with 15 or fewer workers) "only" has the obligation to pay compensation for the damages within the limits established by law, or alternatively to re-employ the worker unlawfully discharged. In this second case, which is called compulsory protection (*tutela obbligatoria*), the employment relationship is extinguished with a loss of seniority for the worker. It may be noted that the reinstatement injunction is not applicable with respect to "ideological" organizations such as the trade unions, political parties, or religious orders. Yet the dominant view is that these legal provisions are subject to strict and narrow interpretation. Finally, even in case law, the legal consequences of oral dismissal and dismissal for *giusta causa* without previous notification of the employee's breaches are not clarified.

In all cases of termination of an employment contract, the employee shall be entitled to receive a severance indemnity called "employment termination indemnity." This indemnity is computed by adding, for each year of service, a share equal to (and in any case not higher than) the amount of remuneration due for the year as such, divided by 13.5 (art. 2120 CC).

3. Union-Management Relations

The Worker Statute enacted in 1970 is a basic statute covering union-management relations in Italy, and is still of paramount importance today.[47] The WS represents a *mélange* of foreign and indigenous solutions. The first part of the WS, which protects individual fundamental rights in employment relationships (arts. 1-11 and 14), is the child of the German doctrine of the *Drittwirkung* (literally, "third effect") of constitutional fundamental rights. Secondly, to effectuate union activity, the WS introduced the employers' anti-union activity along the lines of the US model

---

[47] Sweeping amendments to art. 28 were adopted in 1977 (law no. 847 of 8 November), with additional amendments enacted in 1990 (law no. 146 of 12 June); of art. 31 in 1977 (law no. 210 of 9 May) and in 1979 (law no. 384 of 13 August); of art. 15 in 1977 (law no. 903 of 9 December); of art. 18 in 1990 (law no. 108 of 11 May) and finally of art. 11 in 1992 (law no. 359 of 8 August). A referendum held in June 1995 abrogated arts. 26 and (partially) 19 WS.

of employer unfair employment practices (art. 28). Thirdly, and in accordance with the British doctrine of abstention of the law, there are no limits on the bargaining agenda in the WS. Thus, under the Workers' Statute, there are no mandatory subjects of bargaining such as are provided under the National Labor Relations Act in the United States.

Lastly, the WS envisages the *rappresentanze sindacali aziendali*, which are created on the initiative of workers in the most representative union confederations, or alternatively in the unions that have concluded collective contracts applied in the enterprise (art. 19). The WS also provides for unhindered representative trade union activity, including limited rights to time off for union duties (art. 23), and allows representative trade union meetings during work time (art. 20). Delegates are protected against transfer and dismissal (arts. 22 and 18), except in cases of serious misconduct, and unions have a right to office space. Another crucial aspect of WS regulations of union relations is the concept of "representative unions," derived from the French notion of unions *plus représentatives*. It is clear that there exists no single legal concept of the representative union, but instead a variety of concepts relevant to the concrete reasons for which the legislature resorted to selective criteria among unions. In the case of art. 19 WS, the Constitutional Court excludes unions with a restricted professional range of activity (*e.g.* the *Quadri* union, which represents only clerks) from the list of the most representative union confederations, though these do maintain an actual representative power.[48]

Since the interconfederal agreement of December 1993 (*see supra*, part II B), the duties and rights of the *rappresentanze sindacali aziendali* were ascribed to a unitary body, the *rappresentanze sindacali unitarie*. Two thirds of the members of this body are to be elected by all workers (including non-union members) and one third of the members are to be elected or nominated by the national union signatories to the agreement (*Cgil*, *Cisl*, and *Uil*). This body is also recognized as a bargaining agent, in conjunction with the territorial unions affiliated with the national union parties to the agreement. A referendum held in June 1995 has partially abrogated art. 19 WS and the institution of *rappresentanze sindacali aziendali* is now available to all unions that have concluded collective contracts which are applied in the enterprise.

C. ILO Conventions and European Community Law

Except for a short period between 1939 and 1945, Italy has been a permanent member of the International Labor Organization, and, in contrast with the United

---

[48] Corte costituzionale no. 334 (1988).

States, has given its consent to the ratification of numerous Conventions.[49] Once adopted, a Convention must be submitted to the competent authorities for ratification, which in Italy's case is Parliament. The ratification of a Convention involves a commitment by the member State to render its provisions effective within its national legal system, and to provide information to relevant ILO supervisory mechanisms for this purpose. Thus, Conventions cannot affect the rights and duties of persons in Italy unless their provisions have been incorporated into domestic law by legislation. Moreover, even after their incorporation, ILO Conventions create enforceable rights in Italy only if they are *self-executing – i.e.* if the provisions of a Convention appear to be sufficiently precise to confer rights and duties on the parties to an employment relationship. It follows, in the Italian Supreme Court's opinion, that the incorporation of non-self-executing ILO Conventions only binds the State.[50] ILO Conventions are generally not self-executing; thus, they are of secondary importance in legal practice. Furthermore, as the standards of the International Labor Code are mainly a reflection of the achievements of the more advanced industrial countries, established by conventions and recommendations,[51] the ILO's work is not of primary significance in Italy.

More importantly, thanks to the transfer of sovereignty to the European Community, a portion of Italian labor law is in fact based upon European Community labor law. Generally speaking, the most important influence of European Community law on Italian labor law concerns the distribution of information within the workplace and the consultation and participation of workers in the workplace – in other words, the conventions relating to industrial democracy. Council Directives have introduced several information and consultation rights for Italian work councils and unions. For example, part III of Council Directive 77/187 of February 1977 on the safeguarding of employees' rights in the event of transfer of

---

[49] Italy has ratified the following Conventions: 1-4, 6-16, 18, 19, 22, 23, 26-27, 29; 32; 35-40, 42, 44, 45, 48, 52, 53, 55, 58-60, 68, 69, 71, 73, 74, 77-81, 87, 89-92, 94, 95, 96, 97, 98, 99, 100-103, 105, 106, 108, 109, 111, 112, 114, 115; 117-120, 122-124, 127, 129, 132-139, 141-151 and 160. The ILO's Governing Body has decided to shelve a number of Conventions that no longer correspond to current needs and that have become outmoded or obsolete, and Italy has denounced eleven of these ratifications (7, 10, 15, 52, 58, 59, 60, 91, 101, 112 and 123). In the case of the Convention 89, there is presently a conflict between EC and ILO law.

[50] *See* especially Cassazione no. 9459, 14 September 1993, *Riv. italiana di diritto del lavoro* (1994), II, p. 372 and Cassazione no. 1455, 21 May 1973, *Foro it.* (1973), I, 2443.

[51] International Labor Recommendations do not have the binding force of Conventions, and are not subject to ratification. Often, Recommendations are adopted at the same time as Conventions to supplement the latter with additional or more detailed provisions.

undertakings, businesses or parts of businesses, enacted in Italy by law no. 428 of 29 December 1990 and legislative devree no. 18 of 2 February 2001, instated a procedure for dissemination of information and consultation prior to any business transfer. Both old and new employers must inform employee representatives of "the legal, economic and social implications" of the transfer and any "measures envisaged in relation to the employees." The new employer must consult with the employees' representatives concerning any measures affecting employees (such as dismissals or reallocation of employees).

Even the fundamental rule that the employer must give advance notice of "all relevant information" (the number of workers to be dismissed and especially the time period prior to dismissal) concerning collective redundancies to the *rappresentanze sindacali aziendali* and their trade unions (art. 4 of law no. 223 of 23 July 1991) is a result of the transposition of EC law, *i.e.* Council Directive 75/129 of 17 February 1975 on the approximation of the laws of the member States relating to collective redundancies. Under art. 4, the employee representatives also have the right to compel the employer to carry out consultation on the proposed dismissals, in order to try to reach an agreement on strategies for avoiding collective redundancies or reducing the number of workers affected and mitigating the consequences. The most important collective alternative to the redundancy measures is the recourse to part-time work or to work-sharing "solidarity agreements" (regulated by law no. 863 of 1984) that imply: a reduction of working hours with a corresponding loss of remuneration; compromises on the disqualification of redundant workers; the reduction in years of service with pre-retirement; the temporary transfer of the workers from the company in crisis to other companies; or, finally, other forms of concession bargaining in which unions agree to modify, forego, or defer improvements in pay or working conditions in return for job security. The social parties can agree to all of these, as well as other alternatives to the dismissal of redundant workers.

Another example of legislation in the field of industrial democracy is legislative decree no. 626 of 19 September 1994,[52] which implemented the "framework" Council Directive 89/391 of 12 June 1989 on the introduction of measures to encourage improvements in the safety and health of workers. This directive sets certain general

---

[52] The best analysis of this is L. Montuschi (ed.), *Ambiente, salute e sicurezza. Per una gestione integrata dei rischi del lavoro*, Giappichelli (1997). *See also* the *Indagine conoscitiva sulla sicurezza e igiene del lavoro* approved on 22 July 1997 by the *Comitato paritetico delle Commissioni 11a (Lavoro e previdenza sociale) del Senato della Repubblica e XI (Lavoro pubblico e privato) della Camera dei deputati*, a Parliamentary committee.

rules for the protection of workers at their principal place of employment, requiring, for example, consultation with employee representatives. An additional aspect of the process of translating the EC industrial democracy system into national regulatory frameworks is the collective agreement of 27 November 1996 (and now law no. 422 of 29 December 2000), which implemented Council Directive 94/45 of 22 September 1994 on the establishment of the European Work Council.

Italian industrial democracy law is fragmentary and partial because it is addressed principally to the industrial sector and to medium and large enterprises. But it is important to consider that of all member States in the European Union, Italy is traditionally the most conflict-ridden from a labor perspective. According to a survey of the Society for the Promotion of the Swiss Economy, for each group of 1000 Italian workers, 842 days were spent on strike between 1970 and 1996. In Germany there were only 34, and in the United States 245. With the establishment of statutory rights of codetermination supporting the implementation of new strategies in the administration of industrial relations, many companies have advocated the creation of a new, non-adversarial system of relations to facilitate communication, participation, and joint decision-making in order to reduce costs associated with adversarial approaches to problems.

D. Collective Bargaining and Accords

Historically, collective agreements were restricted to the arena of wages (and known as *concordati di tariffe*), but today they cover practically all questions concerning the relationship between employers and employees, and they represent the most important source of Italian labor law.

Post-World War II Italian collective bargaining initially developed at the national level in an environment of voluntarism – reminding us of Hugo Sinzheimer's preference for collective economic self-determination "quite opposed to the country's tradition, and even more pronounced than in other countries."[53] Only in 1959 was temporary law no. 741 created, making agreements binding *erga omnes*. But the Constitutional Court's judgment rendered permanent machinery of this kind unconstitutional. Today, Italian labor legislation does not contain any rule on the extension of the effects of a collective contract to all those employing and employed in a given industry irrespective of their membership in any organization.

Company and workplace bargaining developed in response to the growing

---

[53] T. Treu (ed.), *Labour law and industrial relations in Italy*, Giuffrè, Milan (1998), p. 113. This book is an excellent introduction to Italian Labor Law.

influence of shop-floor representatives, particularly during the late 1960s and the early 1970s. But under the Workers' Statute, an employer's refusal to bargain with the representatives of his or her employees is not considered an anti-union activity. The legislation of the 1980s and 1990s was the first to introduce a group of particular situations in which the employer has an obligation to bargain in good faith.[54]

In the 1960s and 1970s – the last two decades in which mass production dominated production in Italy – employers and employees generally negotiated collective agreements that were highly legalistic, presenting an amalgamation of the pay scales for blue-collar and white-collar workers. The strong compression of all collectively-bargained differentials – the so-called *egualitarismo* – was also the consequence of an agreement between *Cgil-Cisl-Uil* and Confindustria that took full effect in 1977. The symbolic break came in October 1980, when the middle managers, technicians and supervisors rebelled against the unions' line and demonstrated toward a more differentiated and less egalitarian pay and employment policy.

In the late 1970s and early 1980s, Italy was hit severely by the first oil crisis and experienced large-scale unemployment, particularly among women and young men. Inflation was as big a problem as unemployment. The government introduced a number of statutory measures – the most important of which was the "wage compensation fund" (*Cassa Integrazione Guadagni*, 1975) that governed working time reduction by supplemental wages with government benefits. This placed a heavy financial burden on the State.

In the 1990s, Italy had a clear "concertation" procedure that involved the participation of government, trade unions, and organizations representing employers and the tertiary sector. In recent years, this has led to the drafting of four important agreements between the Government and the social partners: the first dates from 31 July 1992 ("Policy on income, combating inflation and labor costs"), the second from 23 July 1993 ("Policy on incomes and employment, contractual issues, labor policies and support for the productive system"), the third from 24 September 1996 ("Agreement for employment"), and the last from 22 December 1998 (the so-called *Patto di Natale*, or "Christmas Agreement," which was subsequently approved by Parliament in January 1999). The agreement of 1993 dismantled the residual index clauses linking nominal wages to prices, and defined two levels of wage bargaining: the national level, at which sectorial minimum wages must now be set with a dynamic link to the targeted inflation rates established by government for subsequent years; and the firm level, at which wage increases must be closely tied to indicators of the firm's performance. In the first five years since 1993, it is

---

[54] *See* C. Zoli, *Gli obblighi a trattare nel sistema dei rapporti collettivi*, Cedam, Padua (1992).

estimated that only 30 percent of the businesses concluded collective agreements at the firm level. In the current context of decreasing inflation, there is less room for an overlapping of raises in pay established by the two bargaining levels. That is why a reform of the 1993 agreement is now on the agenda of social parties and government.

On the other hand, the painful process of the convergence of national macro-economic performances in order to comply with the Maastricht Treaty criteria has finally come to an end. But today's deflationary and restrictive budgetary policies represent two permanent collective choices of the formal or informal concertation procedures governing Italian industrial relations. Concertation is developing spontaneously in Italy, apart from the agreement of 1993. Trade union advocates have proposed that the concertation policy should be given institutional, *i.e.* Constitutional, recognition. Yet today, the non-observance of concertation procedures does not entail judicial sanctions, only political ones.

The economic policy of the government and the social partners of recent years emphasizes the need to improve the productivity and competitiveness of firms. More generally, the arrival of the euro-based monetary system will do away with all possibilities of Italy's use of exchange-rate adjustments to accommodate excessively high or excessively low pay settlements. In a situation of mass unemployment and extremely low prices, there is a risk that excessively low wage settlements will be forged in order to win markets to the detriment of euro-partners. It is very important that euro-partners undertake to abide by a macro-economic criterion of wage determination in the way of European collective agreements. Such concertation, hitherto neglected in the Treaties, is a matter for labor market partners and Community bodies to undertake.

In recent years, a form of local neo-corporatist policy began focusing efforts on the introduction of new and more flexible wage schemes calibrated to the specific conditions of depressed areas. This has been the response to the fact that during the last ten years, the social and economic structure of southern Italy has been characterized by a gradual decrease in entrepreneurial competitiveness, and by industrial crisis. Evidence of the continuous decay in the economic structure is supplied by the increasing unemployment rate (today 21 percent, with more than 50 percent of young people unemployed) and the significant role of informal work continues to play in the economy.

Finally we come to 1990s legislation. Law no. 662 of 23 December 1996[55] distinguishes six forms of local concertation (*strumenti di programmazione negoziata*),

---

[55] *See*, finally, Cipe Resolution of 21 March 1997 and of 22 June 2000.

of which two involve employment relations: the area contract (*contratto d'area*) and the territorial alliance (*patto territoriale*). Each of these is a concertation agreement between public and private bodies with a view to promoting local development in disadvantaged regions of Italy, in accordance with the aims and directives of EC law. Once approval of the concertation agreement has been obtained, the sponsoring bodies name the responsible entity, which formulates requests concerning the allocation of financial resources. In the period between 1995 and 1997, 109 territorial alliances were set up and 49 (concerning approximately eleven million people) have received government approval.

The new conservative Berlusconi government seems to favor the abandonment of concertation, as demonstrated by a white paper presented in October 2001 on labor market regulation. Formal abandonment of concertation would not necessarily imply the abandonment of its informal use.

E. Employment Contract

There must be a contract of employment (*rapporto di lavoro subordinato*), express or implied, for the relationship between employer and employee to exist.

The employment contract may be informal, and the fact that one person provides services for another would seem to raise a presumption that they have contracted for the provision of such services. However, a written agreement is required for certain stipulations – probation,[56] part-time and temporary work, and training-*cum*-work.

The term "employment contract" may be used to denote a fact (*i.e.*, what the parties, expressly or implicitly, have contracted) or the whole set of rules that govern the single employment relationship. This illustrates what Rodolfo Sacco describes as the ambiguity of the term "contract" ("an agreement between two or more parties to create, regulate or terminate an economic legal relationship," according to art. 1321 CC).

---

[56] Unless otherwise provided for by collective rules, the hiring of an employee for a period of probation shall be proved in writing. *See* art. 2096 CC In the case of probation period, the employer and the employee are required, respectively, to consent to and proceed with the experiment that constitutes the object of the probation agreement. During this period, each of the parties can withdraw from the contract without being bound to give notice or to pay an indemnity and without application of the legislation regarding the protection of workers against unfair dismissal (*see supra* part III B 2). However, if probation is established for a minimum required term, the power of withdrawal cannot be exercised before the expiration of such term. Upon completion of the probation period, the employment shall become final.

If the term "contract" is intended to mean an act of the worker's and employer's own volition from which an employment relationship derives, then we can say there is a contractual foundation for the obligation to work and to pay the wage. But we *cannot* say that the contract regulates the employment relationship because regulation of employment relations take place at multiple external levels (via statutes and collective contracts). The relationship between employer and employee in the Italian labor market is uneven and asymmetrical.

However, if the term "contract" is used to denote the rules that govern the employment relationship, it seems correct to say that the "contract" regulates the rights of the parties *inter se*. For example, courts have frequently stated that the employer must explain the reasons behind all acts related to employment relations.[57] This rule results from application of the general private law principle of equality between the parties to a contract. "Contract thinking" also involves the idea that the employee's obligation to obey the orders of his employer is not so extensive as to imply the obligation to obey all commands. If the employer does not ensure safety in the workplace, the employee may disobey him or her and refuse to work. Furthermore, the notion of *interesse dell'impresa*, which serves as a point of reference for a plurality of Civil Code articles (*see*, for example, arts. 2104 and 2109 CC), must be strictly applied to this relationship. This is fundamental above all in cases concerning the employee's duty of loyalty, which therefore persists only in very particular cases in the "no labor" period.

A final example of "contract thinking" in employment law is the judge-made rule that the parties who have made an employment contract are entitled to terminate it. Freedom of contract means the freedom to make contracts but also the freedom to unmake them. This is explicitly recognized by the Civil Code when it lays down the general principle that contracts are binding on the parties, then adds that they can be dissolved by mutual consent (art. 1372 CC). When the employee and the employer agree to terminate the employment contract, it is not possible for the judge to apply law no. 604 of 1966 or art. 18 WS. This is in marked contrast to the traditional position, still shared by some lower courts, that the termination agreement is always unlawful due to the inequality of bargaining power between employee and employer. Obviously, according to art. 2113 CC, the parties may agree to terminate the contract only for the future and not with retroactive effects.

---

[57] *See* Cassazione no. 2015, 25 February 1988, *Riv. italiana di diritto del lavoro* (1988), II, p. 956.

F. Judge-Made Law

Before focusing our attention on the role of case law, we will first undertake to describe the different ways in which a labor dispute may be solved in Italy. First, except in the agreement between the parties and conciliation before the provincial labor offices, the principal instrument for the solution of labor disputes in Italy is judicial decision-making. Law no. 533 of 1973 permits individual disputes over rights to be decided by arbitration only if this is agreed upon in a collective contract. The sole case of arbitration frequently practiced is provided for by art. 7 WS.

Legislation has stimulated only the conciliation of rights disputes, above all before the provincial labor office. Recently, art. 31 of Legislative Decree no. 80 of 31 March 1998 provides that before an employee or an employer goes to court, he or she has to attempt a conciliation at the provincial labor office. The conciliation board is presided over by the director of the labor office, and is composed of four labor union and four employer representatives nominated by the most representative organizations. The majority of cases are settled by this tripartite board or by conciliation before the court.

If the dispute is not solved by the parties or via conciliation, it can be decided in the private (and also in the public) sector by ordinary courts. The basic law covering judicial labor disputes is the Code of Civil Procedure 1940, as amended in 1973 (law no. 533 of 11 August), and in 1998 (Legislative Decree no. 51 of February 1998). The judicial settlement of labor disputes involves three different courts: the court of first instance, which is the district court (*tribunale*), followed by the appellate court (*corte d'appello*), and finally the Labor Division of the Supreme Court (*sezione lavoro della Corte di cassazione*).

The style used in the decisions of these labor courts is often dogmatic and axiomatic.[58] From a strictly legal point of view, Italian labor law is not based on case law at all. Legislation is theoretically complete in the sense that statutory provisions are supposed to cover every situation with which the labor courts are concerned. It can still be argued that, strictly speaking, case law is not a true source of law in Italy because a judge is not obliged to consider it when coming to a decision. Yet from a practical point of view, the judicial development of law is a very important formant of Italian labor law. In several matters, it is still the most important formant. For example, in the absence of a specific statute, judicial rules

---

[58] *See* M. Taruffo, "*La motivazione della decisione dei giudici*," in T. Treu (ed.), *Sindacato e magistratura nei conflitti di lavoro*, II, *Lo Statuto dei lavoratori: prassi sindacali e motivazioni dei giudici*, Il Mulino, Bologna (1976), p. 100.

govern strikes, collective agreements, and all other cases in which the legislator uses general clauses such as "just cause for dismissal" or "sufficient wages." In these cases, judicial decisions often make reference to the intention of the Parliament, only to disavow the substantial creative role in the interpretation of statutes, and even in the application of collective rules attempting to specify the general clauses used by the legislator. For example, there are several cases of Italian wage legislation in which the calculation of one element of the wage is referred to as the "normal wage," the "global net wage," or simply the "wage." It goes without saying that it is very difficult to lay down a general rule, and that it is the typical function of collective bargaining to specify these general clauses, adapt them to the needs of a particular industry, and fix the basis for wage calculation. Yet in the late 1970s, labor courts played an intrusive role in collective relations and have adopted the so-called principle of *omnicomprensività*, according to which the basis of calculation of any wage item is composed of all the remaining wage items. Only beginning in 1984 did the courts abandon this "expensive" principle and leave room for collective bargaining to regulate the issue.

Courts, especially those of first instance, often take an equitable approach to labor disputes. For example, one recent study conducted in 1998[59] found that local labor market conditions influence the court's decision in dismissal litigation, so that misconduct considered sufficient for a lawful dismissal in a tight labor market may be insufficient under different circumstances. This suggests that higher unemployment rates may increase termination costs through their effect on the court's criteria for reaching a decision. [60]

IV. Labor Law and the Labor Market

The Italian labor market is characterized by lower employment and activity rates (58.1 percent) than the European average: one of the highest percentage of long-

---

[59] *"L'influenza delle condizioni del mercato del lavoro regionale sulle decisioni dei giudici in materia di licenziamenti,"* in *Riv. italiana di diritto del lavoro*, 1998, I, p. 19.

[60] The decisions of labor courts are published in several widely available legal journals. The most important are: *Riv. italiana di diritto del lavoro*; *Massimario della giurisprudenza del lavoro* (cassazione decisions); *Argomenti di diritto del lavoro*; *Il lavoro nella giurisprudenza*; *Riv. giuridica del lavoro e della previdenza sociale*; *Il lavoro nella pubblica amministrazione*; *Riv. critica di diritto del lavoro*; *Notiziario di giurisprudenza del lavoro; Diritto delle relazioni industriali*; *Il Diritto del Lavoro*; *Orientamenti di giurisprudenza del lavoro*.

term unemployment rates in Europe (in April 1999, 11.5 percent of the workforce were unemployed); a prevalence of young people among the unemployed; and a disproportionate distribution of employment opportunities across the country.

From an institutional standpoint, this situation may be viewed as a consequence of the fact that the Italian labor market is too highly regulated and institutionalized. For example, the "colonialization" of the individual employee by public and private power has created an asymmetry between the mobility of firms and the decreased mobility of workers. The population-at-large is a matter of substantial social policy concern because the economic space does not match the social space. This general mismatch has given rise to numerous problems. In Faini, Galli, and Gennari's terminology, the Italian labor market is an "empirical puzzle," because falling internal migration is accompanied by growing differentials in regional unemployment levels. As mentioned above, the low level of mobility in Italy is related to the public employment system. Other relevant factors frequently emphasized include the legal rules restricting employers' control on hiring and firing, the availability of contractual forms permitting temporary work relationships, and, above all, the system of income protection in the case of unemployment. A study by Pietro Ichino (1996) suggests that there is another important aspect that has so far gone unnoticed in this context. As a rule, insiders (*i.e.* those who perform jobs with a high level of legal protection: approximately 9,400,000 workers) do not match the outsiders (*i.e.* those who perform simple jobs in uncertain, flexible employment relationships, or who are unemployed). On the other hand, according to Gordon,[61] it is necessary to avoid overrating the role played by labor law in the evolution of society. Many aspects of existing regulations have been rendered obsolete by new technologies, and this development has been accompanied by a growing individualization of work. In addition, recent trends signal the existence of a crisis. A large part of the secondary segment of the labor market is characterized by irregular or informal work,[62] especially in the South. More than labor legislation, the powerful incentive toward the growth of this informal economy is the high tax rate (including social security) existing in Italy. These facts are mirrored in statistical data collected by *Istat*, which suggests that in Italy only 77.3 percent of the approximately 20 million workers are regular. The rest are black-market workers.

In the coming years, we will see if it is still possible to approach the labor market with the labor law taxonomies of the industrial sectors, or whether the traditional adversarial model that originally developed in the industrial context is coming to an end.

---

[61] Concerning this, *see* R.W. Gordon, "Critical Legal Histories," 36 *Stanford LRev* (1984), p. 57.

[62] *See* A. Bellavista, *Il lavoro sommerso*, Giappichelli, Torino (2000).

V. Selected Bibliography

A. Baylos Grau, B. Caruso, M. D'Antona, S. Sciarra (eds.), *Dizionario di diritto del lavoro comunitario*, Monduzzi, Bologna (1996).

F. Carinci, M. D'Antona, *Il lavoro alle dipendenze delle amministrazioni pubbliche. Commentario*, I-II-III, Milan, Giuffrè (2000).

M. Cinelli, *Diritto della previdenza sociale*, Giappichelli, Torino (1999).

E. Ghera, *Diritto del lavoro. Il rapporto di lavoro*, Cacucci, Bari (2000).

G. Giugni, *Diritto sindacale*, Cacucci, Bari (2001).

M. Grandi, G. Pera (eds.), *Commentario alle leggi sul lavoro*, Cedam, Padova (2001).

P. Ichino, *Il lavoro e il mercato*, Mondadori, Milan (1996).

O. Mazzotta, (ed.), *I licenziamenti*, Giuffrè, Milan, (1999).

M. Pedrazzoli (ed.), *Codice dei lavori*, Giuffrè, Milan (2001).

A. Perulli, *Il lavoro Autonomo*, Giuffrè, Milan (1996).

T. Treu (ed.), *Labour Law and Industrial Relations in Italy*, Giuffrè, Milan (1998).

CHAPTER FIFTEEN

Corporate Governance

Francesco Denozza[1]

This chapter does not attempt to provide a general overview of the Law of
Corporations. I have chosen instead to focus more narrowly on a particularly
important shift in Italian corporation law from a system dominated by corporations
firmly controlled by a close group of shareholders to one in which institutional
investors play an increasingly important role. This is a topic of undeniable
importance and general interest with respect to the development of Italian
corporation law in today's world.

I. The primary characteristics of the Italian legal system with respect to corporations

Until just a few years ago, almost all limited companies were controlled by private
shareholders (*azionisti proprietari*), holding either as individuals or as groups more
than 50 percent of the voting capital.

Another characteristic of the Italian economic system (like other European
economic systems) is that the most important corporations are part of groups often
made up of various corporations that are listed on the Italian stock exchange.
Frequently in the Italian system, large shareholders would join in a sort of syndicate
agreement to control a corporation together. This corporation in turn controls other
corporations, in which a variety of smaller shareholders also invest.

This situation leads to several peculiarities. First, the directors are nominated
by the shareholders, who control the greatest share of each corporation. Management
therefore tends to consider itself more as a fiduciary of the large shareholding
cartels to which it owes its appointment rather than the whole body of shareholders.

---

[1] Professor of Commercial Law, University of Milan. Translated from the Italian original by
    Jeffrey S. Lena.

Jeffrey S. Lena and Ugo Mattei (eds.), *Introduction to Italian Law*, 395-406
©2002 Kluwer Law International. Printed in the Netherlands.

Secondly, there exists a constant conflict of interest between the large shareholders and the managers whom the shareholders have nominated, on the one hand, and the small shareholders (*azionisti risparmiatori*) on the other. The large shareholders, in fact, have an interest in drawing off resources from the corporations in which they have lesser interests (and in which the small shareholders have a greater interest), in order to place those resources in corporations in which the small shareholders have a lower stake than they do. (For example, if shareholder (*socio*) A holds 30 percent of the capital of corporation X and 60 percent of corporation Y, it can be to A's advantage that contracts are entered into between the two corporations which are to the advantage of corporation X and to the disadvantage of corporation Y, with a consequent damage to the creditors and small saving shareholders (*risparmiatori*) who invested in X.) Very few corporations are exposed to takeover, so the market's pressure and stimulus upon the managers is of limited impact.

These peculiarities of the economic system explain the basic characteristics of Italian legislation, characteristics that are in fact common to various other European legal systems. A number of such features are imposed by European directives and they therefore tend to be the same in the other European countries. The regulations covering changes in capital stock, mergers, disclosure, and accounting provide examples.

The first characteristic is the presence of a great number of mandatory rules. Many of these regulations are aimed at protecting the corporate assets against possible abuses by controlling shareholders and their fiduciaries. Examples of how mandatory norms are used include the control over the reduction in the stock of a corporation, corporate accounting procedures, share repurchase, or reciprocal stock repurchase. These regulations above all protect the creditors, but also indirectly protect the minority shareholders.

The second characteristic is the particular attention paid to the rules regarding the liability of the directors of a corporation, particularly with respect to conflicts of interest that arise within groups of corporations, or *gruppi di società*. The entire body of law related to conflicts of interest and the liability of corporate directors is considered part of "public policy," and cannot be contracted around.

The third characteristic derives from the fact that the protection of savings investors (also *risparmiatori*), cannot be entrusted to the market and, in particular, to the mechanisms of the takeover. The protection of savings investors is therefore entrusted to mandatory regulations (as well as to public organs like the *Commissione nazionale per le società e la borsa* (*Consob*), that is, the National Commission for Corporations and Stock Exchange). Among these regulations are rules that guarantee certain intangible individual rights to investors (for example, a preemption right, or *diritto di opzione*).

II. The Present Evolution: Trust in the Market, and its Limits

The situation described in the preceding paragraph appears to be in a state of evolution.

The privatization of companies that had at one time been controlled by the Italian State has often been effectuated through offers of shares to the public. This has created a certain number of important companies that are no longer controlled by a small and closely-knit group of partners. Moreover, the natural growth of certain businesses, and perhaps the decreased ability to obtain financial backing, has augmented the share of capital in the hands of savers and investors.

All things considered, it would appear that the market will play a larger role than it has played in the past. The desire to favor and accelerate an evolution towards a larger role played by the market has inspired the most recent legal reforms covering publicly traded corporations, set forth in *decreto legge* no. 58 of 24 February 1998.

The path taken by the Italian legislator has not, however, been that of reducing the number of mandatory rules, or entrusting the selection of the most efficient rules to the free choice of the investors. Such an approach would have implied a trust in the functions of the financial markets, which is not particularly pronounced in Italy.

The approach of entrusting to the market the role of "controller" of businesses and "selector" of the most efficient rules by which businesses function holds that shareholders who are excluded from actual management of the corporation manifest their approval or disapproval of how a corporation is run through their decision to buy and sell shares. Thus, managers and controlling bodies are placed under continuous control and pressure to improve the quality of the management of the corporation. So the manager who does not keep pace with market demands is penalized through a fall in share value, and ultimately through loss of control of the company (and the manager's job) when the corporation becomes subject to takeover.

An analogous mechanism also ensures that the corporation will adopt by-laws that are the most efficient for and attractive to savers. Its basic premise is that the most efficient contractual conditions emerge not as a consequence of the direct contracting between the interested parties, but rather as an effect of a selective mechanism of the market, nourished by competition between the various persons or entities trying to attract investment capital to their company. Managers (and controlling partners) also compete in the capital markets by adopting efficient corporate by-laws that will engender the approval of savings investors, and hence the acquisition of shares. Those corporations that have by-laws containing provisions not appreciated by the savings investing public will consequently enjoy little investment and will be forced to modify their by-laws to make them more attractive. This is hardly different from what may occur in any other market situation, where the mechanism of competition operates to select the best product (the by-laws containing the most efficient rules) and ultimately leads to the failure of less attractive products (the by-laws containing inefficient rules).

According to this view, actions of the legislator intended to guarantee non-waivable individual rights to the shareholders are considered superfluous and damaging – superfluous because the market already ensures that by-laws include clauses protecting interests that the investors consider essential, and damaging because it runs the risk of uselessly reducing managerial discretion, and thereby potentially rendering the company less efficient.

The credibility of this approach requires reflection upon the function of the market and on the conditions that render the market efficient. In an efficient market, each person making choices needs relatively little information, which can easily be obtained. The person can narrow his decision down from what is often an innumerable number of choices (one may either buy a pound of pears or try one and then decide whether to divide one's choice between apples and pears, and then determine what percentage of each kind of fruit to purchase). The person can also modify his choice at anytime (for example, stop buying apples and start buying pears). And the person may change his mind without suffering too much harm by, for example, selling the pears at their market price, which would normally be rather similar to the purchase price, and then taking the recovered funds to purchase apples, and so on.

In this context, the system continually gathers information regarding the preference of the prospective purchasers and continually adapts itself to purchasers' changing desires.

But not all choices and decisions are able to produce these results. For example, the choice of the investor who acquires shares offered by a corporation that affords wide discretion to its corporate directors does not possess all the positive attributes generally possessed by the consensus to a transaction manifested by a consumer operating in an efficient market. The consensus of the investor refers to a complex aggregate of choices, and a practically unbridgeable gap exists between the information known to the agent and the information necessary to make an adequately considered choice (for not even the most expert of investors can foresee whether the directors' good use of the discretion afforded them will compensate for, or exceed, the poor use of the directors' discretionary powers).

The value of a share could be considered as the product of at least two components: the economic results expected by the company, and the foreseeable effect of the rules related to the management of the company, as provided by law and by the corporate by-laws.

The rules relative to the management of the company affect not only the size of the pie (as a corporation with less rigid rules is more ready to take advantage of opportunities as they arise, and can therefore improve its expectation of economic success), but also the criteria used to determine just how the pie will be divided, because less rigid rules allow managers and the controlling bodies to take for themselves, more or less explicitly, larger shares of the company products. When the products sold in a particular market are complicated, as they are in reality aggregates of diverse and different elements, many special problems may arise.

For example, it may occur (and here I am thinking of a phenomenon well known to the law of antitrust) that the modification of investor preferences on the margin (those who in fact "make" the price) do not reflect changes in the preferences of investors who are infra-marginal, *i.e.*, not on the margin (whereas it is obvious that social welfare, taken as a whole, depends upon the satisfaction of the preferences of all investors, and not simply those of the investors on the margin).

Observing the situation from the perspective of managers and controlling shareholders, one may presume that they would attempt to maximize the aggregate utility derived from the amount of capital that they manage to accumulate from the investors, *in addition to* the utility derived from the degree of discretion afforded to them in management. It is, therefore, possible that they prefer a combination of (i) capital X_1, together with discretion Y_1, than a combination of (ii) $X_2 + Y_2$, in which $X_1 < X_2$ but $Y_1 > Y_2$. (One assumes, obviously, that all other conditions being equal, fewer investors would be willing to invest in a corporation that guarantees too much discretion to managers and controlling shareholders.)

May one say that combination (i), in which smaller savings are attracted to the investment in shares, is more efficient than combination (ii) – and if combination (i) were in fact less efficient than combination (ii), how could this be avoided? Nothing guarantees that this will not result in a situation characterized by negative equilibrium in which managers and controlling shareholders prefer to take a larger slice of a smaller but more certain pie, rather than to give up their privileges in exchange for a potentially larger pie (non-metaphorically, in exchange for a more extensive collection of a larger amount of savings).

It is possible that situations of this sort have, in effect, existed in the past in Italy, when the possibility of obtaining low-interest loans from banks could cause many controlling shareholders to refrain from broadening the shareholder base of their company. Consequently, this situation reduced the risks of takeover and nourished a vicious circle that helps explain the low level of trust that Italy has with respect to the market's ability to control corporations.

III. The Attention of the Italian Legislator to Institutional Investors

Having declined to follow a model of "corporate governance" based upon market-based control, the Italian legislator has sought to create an environment favorable to the development of monitoring activities by institutional investors. The legislator has relied upon a broadening of powers exercised by selected minorities (*i.e.*, shareholders or groups of shareholders who possess a certain number of shares in the capital stock) to accomplish this monitoring. The intent of the legislator is to make it easier for the minority shareholders to control the managers, while at the same time limiting the risk that individual shareholders holding an insignificant percentage of the capital stock (and therefore not substantially interested in the comprehensive fortunes of the corporation) will engage in blackmailing activities.

This is the path that has been followed in regard to one of the most important innovations in this context – the creation of a course of action for director liability that can be initiated by "many shareholders, who are registered for at least six months in the book of shareholders, who represent at least five percent of the social capital, or the smallest percentage established by the articles of incorporation" (art. 129, *decreto legge* 58/1998).

We refer here to an action similar to the shareholders' derivative suit and also analogous to an action permitted under the German legal system. It is entirely novel in the Italian context, which until now has relied on the firmly embedded principle that a shareholders' cause of action for director liability would only be allowed following deliberation and a majority vote of the partners gathered at the stockholders' meeting.

Taking into account that we are dealing here with corporations of substantial size that trade on the stock exchange, the requirement of holding five percent of the capital clearly excludes the possibility that this action can be carried out by small savings shareholders.

This same five percent minimum is also required in order to file a complaint in cases of serious irregularities by the directors. In such cases the court can require inspection of the corporation and the substitution of seated directors with judicial administrators (art. 2409 CC, art. 128 para. 2 of *decreto legislativo* 58/1998).

To repeat, shareholders who represent at least five percent of the capital have the right, under art. 149 para. 1d of *decreto legislativo* 58/1998, to contest the deliberation approving the corporate accounting, and to request a determination of the legitimacy of the consolidated balance sheet.

The system is completed by the rule that affords shareholders representing ten percent of the capital stock the power to ask directors to call a shareholders meeting within 30 days. This permits any group of investors who meet the ten-percent requirement to require the directors to publicly discuss any matter chosen by the inquiring investor at any time. An exception to this rule is that if the judge, likely acting upon request of the directors, determines that the meeting would not be in "the best interests of the corporation," then the judge could order the meeting not held.

Along with this and other regulations that assure certain powers, not just to any shareholder, but exclusively to shareholders who reach a certain level of importance with respect to the corporation as a whole, there exist other regulations that many scholars believe favor an action by institutional investors. We refer here to the rule that for some important resolutions of the shareholders meetings (among which are those addressing merger, spin offs and issuance of stock), has reduced the amount of capital necessary to adopt the resolution, but has required the approval of two thirds of the shares present at the meeting.

The decisions of the small shareholders to participate in the meeting – a decision that in the past could have prevented the achievement of the necessary quorum – thus becomes irrelevant. What becomes relevant, rather, is the position of the shareholders present at the meeting – principally institutional investors (who, one supposes, must participate in such important decisions). Even their simple abstention can be decisive in achieving a favorable two-thirds vote of the stockholders present, which is presently required by the law.

Thus, there are an increasing number of situations in which managers and controlling shareholders cannot limit themselves to merely not displeasing the institutional investors, but must actually receive the positive assent of those investors.

Another area in which Italian scholars have noted the existence of an orientation of the legislator favorable to the development of institutional investment regards laws controlling how individual shareholder-power is exercised. The legislator would appear to have rendered the exercise of certain rights more difficult for the individual investor, thereby creating a negative incentive to invest directly and a positive incentive to entrust the investment of savings to professional investors. An example of such a disincentive is the reduction of the minimum term for the exercise of pre-emption rights from 30 to 15 days. This reduces the amount of time available to make a choice and does not damage a well-informed institutional investor, but can have negative consequences for individual investors who may not be terribly competent.

IV. The Activism of the Institutional Investors: Possibilities and Limitations

As can be seen from the example provided in the preceding paragraph, Italian legislation offers a relatively wide breadth of action to institutional investors, and correlatively creates an incentive to the savings investors to invest through professional intermediaries rather than investing directly.

The Italian legislator would appear to adhere to the notion that institutional investors, given the increasing difficulty (if not impossibility) of demonstrating dissatisfaction towards a poorly managed corporation through the sale of shares, will be required to consider the monitoring of managers and possible conditioning of their choices as a way to defend their investment.

This consideration does not, however, necessarily provide a basis for maintaining that we should expect a significant increase in the level of institutional investor activism, as the legislator apparently has. It provides even less of a basis for maintaining that a way has finally been found to adequately protect the small shareholder, and that the problem is only one of providing institutional investors with adequate instruments to control corporate managers' activities. The emergence of institutional investors poses a much more complex problem.

This category of investor includes various types of entities, which are mostly directed by professional money managers bound by a fiduciary relationship to the investors who have entrusted their savings to them. We therefore find ourselves faced with a classic problem of agency that could be formulated in the following manner: who will require the money manager to undertake the costly and risky steps (those where the probability of failure or poor return on investment are elevated) necessary to control the managers (or the major investors) of the corporation in which they have decided to invest the capital entrusted to them?

Direct intervention by the savings shareholders who have entrusted their capital to the money managers is out of the question, if only for practical reasons. The savings shareholders could punish inefficient money managers by investing their savings elsewhere, but it is hard to imagine them creating monitoring devices to detect and prevent infidelity and laziness.

As far as savers who have invested directly in corporations where institutional investors (the other minority shareholders) are present, they do not have any fiduciary relationship with the money managers considered important from a legal point of view. Any possible influence on their part is therefore hindered by both practical and legal considerations.

The issue becomes all the more complex because the interests of the two groups of savers (those who have invested directly in corporate stock and those who have entrusted their savings to institutional investors) do not necessarily converge.

In this context, there arises a typical collective action problem because a good that has been collectively produced cannot be easily divided in a way that reflects the contribution each has made to its production. This is the case with monitoring activities directed at corporate managers. The "collective" good produced by such activity consists of the superior results obtained through the superior performance of those corporations whose managers were adequately monitored. This good is divided among all shareholders in proportion to the shares they own, rather than in proportion to the contribution each made to the performance of the monitoring activities.

This gives rise to two sets of problems. The first relates to the fact that this configuration of interests can create a strong tendency to exploit the work done by others. Each shareholder can rationally decide not to invest in monitoring activities, hoping that somebody else will, and thereby benefit from the efforts of others without having to pay.

The second set of problems stems from the fact that the peculiarities of collective action offer incentives to those members of the collectivity who decide to employ a system by which they can obtain benefits that they are not forced to share with other members of the collectivity. In Italy, such systems are unfortunately readily accessible. The first such system is that of exploiting the monitoring threat, not in order to force managers or controlling shareholders to behave more diligently or properly (resulting in a benefit for all shareholders), but rather to induce them to barter, exchanging special advantages granted exclusively to the shareholder who promoted monitoring activities for protection from external interference. The second system, which is partly intertwined with the first, consists of using information gathered in the course of performing the monitoring activities (or information provided by managers and controlling shareholders) for their own exclusive benefit.

If money managers are allowed to make use of "collateral" systems of compensation for monitoring activities, that can also be translated into an advantage for savers who have entrusted their savings to them (at least to the degree to which money managers are prevented from actually turning these collateral compensations into personal gain). But the issue of protecting direct savings shareholders remains unresolved, as does the more general issue of effectively monitoring managers and controlling shareholders.

Competition between potential monitors, in which the goal is that of obtaining the most sizeable collateral payments from those who are being monitored, could scarcely be considered a virtuous monitoring mechanism.

At this point in the discussion, there seem to be good reasons to lean towards the introduction of appropriate prohibitions aimed at suppressing any possibility of redundant collateral payments to the exclusive advantage of one or another shareholder. Italian lawmakers seem not to have taken this adequately into account.

On the other hand, if one foregoes (as I think one should) using the possibility of obtaining individual collateral advantages as a potential incentive, the problem reemerges of finding mechanisms capable of inducing institutional investors to sustain the cost of monitoring initiatives that are certain to be difficult and risky, since investments may not match results.

Competition is the mechanism that could potentially solve this problem. If a reasonable, wisely exercised monitoring activity directed at corporate managers enhances the value of stock investments made in the corporations they manage, the money managers who invest resources in monitoring activities should gain net benefits from it. Improved performance of the institution they manage should result, and this should give rise to additional positive results, such as greater inflow of savings, increased savers' satisfaction, and higher salaries for the money managers themselves.

The typical problems associated with collective action briefly outlined above also surface in a different context. The convenience of producing an indivisible collective good (or, in any case, one that cannot be divided in a way that matches the contribution each made to its production) depends on the costs each has to sustain and the advantages each can gain. If, for any of the members of the collectivity under consideration, the share of advantages that will accrue to him is higher than the costs that he will have to sustain individually, it will be to the advantage of this member to bring about the collective good, even if other members engage in opportunistic behavior.

Thus, if an investor has the prospect of appropriating for himself five percent of that greater value that can be assured to the whole of the shares issued through an appropriate monitoring of managers and controlling of shareholders, the investor at issue will still find it convenient to undertake any monitoring activity whose cost is lower than that five percent of the overall benefit that such activity is certain to produce.

If this general consideration is placed in the specific context of relations involving institutional investors, the picture that emerges is anything but linear.

As noted, institutional investors are competitors on the market in which they gather capital from savers. Such competition must be preserved at all costs, because in its absence nothing could induce them to make risky investments in monitoring activities yielding uncertain results. In the absence of aggressive competition between money managers, the managers could find it much more attractive to reach an agreement among themselves aimed at avoiding those activities, which, while potentially advantageous for their clients, may prove to be exacting or dangerous for themselves.

If now we re-examine the position of each money manager, and place it in a context where collateral earnings to the benefit of single shareholders have been excluded or rendered too costly, we immediately realize the specific difficulties that hinder the overcoming of collective action problems. As we said, in order to overcome these problems, it is necessary that the costs be lower than the share of expected benefits for at least one member of the collectivity. Generally speaking, the simplest way to create a favorable cost-benefit ratio is to form coalitions between different members of the groups at issue. In fact, forming a coalition allows costs, which are usually fixed, to be shared without affecting individual earnings (which in our case, nevertheless remain dependent on the shares of stock owned by each).

In the case of institutional investors, who are competing among themselves on the market where they collect private investors' savings, making use of this tool to help reduce costs (*i.e.*, the formation of coalitions) turns out to be especially complex. It is, in fact, a matter of achieving a delicate balance between competitive and cooperative tendencies, which is difficult to imagine happening spontaneously.

Furthermore, one must consider that in the absence of a collaboration and agreement as to how costs should be shared, the institutional investor's initiative turns out to be more costly than that of any shareholder who is not involved in other markets in competitive relationships with other shareholders.

It is evident that in calculating the institutional investor's costs and benefits, adequate space must also be found for the advantage that his competitors, who have invested in the same corporation in which he decides to start a monitoring activity, will gain from benefiting from his activity without incurring costs. Normally, the fact that a partner can gain undeserved benefits from the activity performed by another might be irritating, but it makes no sense as an economic phenomenon that could potentially affect choices dictated by purely rational criteria.

The peculiar relationship existing between institutional investors on capital markets provides that the benefit each can gain by opportunistically exploiting the sacrifices of another does not get configured, as might normally occur, as simply a moral or psychological problem (which is economically irrelevant), but rather as a true "cost" that the agent must necessarily take into account. In their enthusiasm for the actions of institutional investors, Italian lawmakers have failed to take this series of problems into account. In their defense, we may say that one finds the same problems in all legal systems, and no one seems to have found a completely satisfactory solution.

Brief Bibliography

G.F. Campobasso, *Diritto commerciale*, Utet, Torino.

G. Cottino, *Diritto commerciale*, 4 vols., Cedam, Padova:

F. Galgano, *Diritto commerciale*, Zanichelli, Bologna, (1999/2000).

P.G. Jaeger, F. Denozza, *Appunti di diritto commerciale*, Giuffrè, Milano, (2000).

CHAPTER SIXTEEN

Family Law and Succession

Francesco Parisi and Giampaolo Frezza[1]

I. Introduction

The following pages treat the evolution of Italian family law, and to a limited extent the law of succession, from an historical and economic perspective.

In most Western societies, the role of the family and the functions of family law have undergone a dramatic change during the last few decades. Italian law is no exception. Most of the changes in the regulation of the family can be construed as a by-product of the transformation in the economic and social concept of the family that has taken place during the last several decades. During the second half of the twentieth century, women have come to enjoy increased access to and increasingly equal opportunities in the labor market. This has altered the social function of the family, and thereby changed the relative cost of entering into a marriage relationship for the two spouses.

II. A Brief History of Italian Family Law

In the Italian legal system, the core provisions on family law are contained in Book 1 of the Italian Civil Code, entitled "On Persons and On the Family."[2] However, the current regulation of the family is not the product of a monolithic

---

[1]   Francesco Parisi is Professor of Law, George Mason University School of Law and the University of Milan. Professor Parisi is the primary author of parts II, IX, and X of this chapter, and has elaborated the sections on economic analysis. Professor Frezza is Visiting Scholar, George Mason University, School of Law. Professor Frezza is the primary author of the remaining parts.

[2]   The provisions most directly related to the family can be found in Chapter VI *et seq.*

Jeffrey S. Lena and Ugo Mattei (eds.), *Introduction to Italian Law*, 407-430
©2002 Kluwer Law International. Printed in the Netherlands.

piece of legislation. Rather, it originates from a protracted historical evolution, marked by important revolutions in the legal concept of the family.

The original version of the 1942 Civil Code[3] reflected an authoritarian and patriarchal image of the family. The husband was considered the head of the family and made all the decisions for his wife and children. The wife was subordinate to her husband and had less than equal rights in the management of the family. This is not surprising given the drafters' heavy reliance on the pre-existing regulation of the family contained in the 1865 codification, which in turn reflected the principles set out in the 1804 *Code Napoléon*. Both the French and Italian Codes were affected by a conservative cultural heritage; both were underpinned by a pyramid-like concept of social relations in the realm of family law.[4]

The concept of the family embraced by the first European codes stressed its unitary and irreducible nature. Such a concept was the product of an agricultural economy in which the family jointly managed resources and production. The various features of family and succession law can be seen as instrumental to the unitary concept of the family enterprise and the maintenance of concentrated ownership of land to allow for economies of scale. The authority of the husband over the other members of the family can also be viewed as instrumental to the effective leadership of the family enterprise.

The 1942 Civil Code embraced a more dynamic concept of ownership and enterprise, in line with aspects of fascist ideology.[5] In terms of family relations, however, it maintained the authoritarian structure that was contained in the earlier Italian and French codifications. Another important historical factor in the develop-

---

[3] This Code is still in force, although the section on family law has undergone profound changes following the introduction of the Family Law Reform Act of May 19, 1975, no. 151.

[4] For an historical account of Italian family law, *see* Bessone, Alpa, D'Angelo & Ferrando, "*La famiglia nel nuovo diritto*, Bologna (1991); *see also* Bessone, *L'ordinamento costituzionale del diritto di famiglia e le prospettive di evoluzione della società italiana*," in *Dir. fam.* (1976), 217; Bellomo, *La condizione giuridica della donna in Italia. Vicende antiche e moderne*, Turin (1970); Grassetti, "*Famiglia (diritto privato)*," in *Noviss. Dig.*, it. App. di Agg.*, III, Turin (1982), 637*ff*; Barcellona, "*Famiglia (diritto privato)*," in *Enc. Dir.*, XVI, Milan (1967); Bianca, "*Famiglia (diritto di)*," in *Noviss. Dig. It.*, VII, Turin (1961); Ungari, *Il diritto di famiglia in Italia*, Bologna (1975); Bessone & Roppo, *Il diritto di famiglia. Evoluzione storica, principi costituzionali, prospettive di riforma*, Genoa (1975); *id.*, *Il diritto di famiglia. Evoluzione storica, disciplina costituzionale, lineamenti della riforma*, Turin (1979), 320*ff*; Dogliotti, "*Principi della Costituzione e ruolo sociale della famiglia*," in *Dir. fam.* (1977), 1488*ff*.

[5] The dynamic value of ownership and its relation to entrepreneurial incentives are at the core of fascist ideology, which reigned in Italy at the time of the 1942 codification.

ment of family law is the Concordat between the State and the Holy See that was stipulated on 11 February 1929.[6] This international agreement introduced the so-called Concordat marriage, which was a form of religious marriage that paralleled the standard form contemplated in civil legislation. According to the Concordat, religious marriages carried out in the Roman Catholic rite were recognized as having the same legal effect[7] as civil marriages, subject only to a requirement of registration with civil authorities. Thus, family law felected the strong hegemony of Roman Catholic Religion on Italian Society.

In 1948, the principles of family law were radically altered by the enactment of the Constitution of the Italian Republic.[8] Articles 29, 30, and 31 of the Constitution introduced an equal-responsibility model of the family, which was now seen as a social formation based on marriage. Those articles provide as follows:

Article 29 [Marriage]:

The State recognizes the family as a natural association founded on marriage.

(2) Marriage is based on the moral and legal equality of husband and wife, within the limits laid down by the laws for ensuring family unity.

Article 30 [Education]:

(1) It is the duty and right of parents to support, instruct and educate their children, even those born out of wedlock.

(2) The law states the way in which these duties shall be fulfilled should the parents prove incapable.

(3) The law ensures full legal and social protection for children born out of wedlock consistent with the rights of the members of the legitimate family.

(4) The law lays down rules and limitations for ascertaining paternity.

---

[6] The Concordat became part of Italy's internal legal system as law no. 847 on 27 May 1929.

[7] Two forms of marriage are still possible under Italian law; this dual system was retained even after Italy and the Holy See reached an accord modifying the Concordat in 1985, becoming law no. 121 of 25 March 1985, and followed by an Additional Protocol.

[8] In the Italian legal system, the rigidly hierarchical structure of legal sources gives overriding force to the Constitution.

Article 31 [Family]

(1) The Republic facilitates, by means of economic and other provisions, the formation of the family and the fulfillment of the tasks connected therewith, with particular consideration for large families.

(2) [The Republic] safeguards maternity, infancy, and youth, promoting and encouraging institutions necessary for such purposes.

The new constitutional principles triggered a pervasive re-conceptualization of the legal notion of the family. The implementation of the new constitutional principles was carried out with two main instruments: numerous interventions by the Constitutional Court and action by the legislator by the 1975 Family Law Reform Act, which modified most family law norms contained in the Civil Code.

Prior to the 1975 reform, judicial interventions in the field of family law were numerous and unsystematic. In spite of occasional interventions by the Constitutional Court, the underlying concept of the family remained linked to its traditional concept as an indissoluble unit with patriarchal governance. The 1975 reform homogenized the earlier piecemeal case lawdevelopments. The task of reform was far from easy. First, the constitutional principles were difficult to reconcile with the existing legal rules, and radical changes were necessary to effectively implement the new principles. Secondly, the legislator had to account for the quite diverse social views on the family across the nation in order to avoid too drastic a departure from the established understanding of such a fundamental social institution. In many respects, these tasks were successfully carried out.

Implementation of the constitutional principles yielded important changes.[9] It introduced the joint relationship, both personal and patrimonial, between spouses; it raised the age of consent for marriage; it increased the number of recognized causes for the invalidity of marriage; it introduced a default patrimonial regime in which assets of the marriage were legally shared; it introduced a no-fault provision for the separation of spouses; and it assured the equality of children born within and outside the marriage (so-called "legitimate" and "illegitimate" offspring).[10]

---

[9] *See* Bessone, Alpa, D'Angelo & Ferrando, *supra* note 4.

[10] For a critical examination of the Italian reform of family law, *see* Bessone, Dogliotti & Ferrando, *Giurisprudenza del diritto di famiglia*, Milan (1975), 217*ff*, where the reader can find a wealth of bibliographical references; *see also* Montuschi, Romagnoli, Finocchiaro, Dell'oro, Provera, Ferri, Talamanca, Forchielli & Gorla, in Scialoja & Branca (eds.), "*Aggiornamento sulla base della legge di riforma del diritto di famiglia,*" in *Commentario del Codice civile*, Bologna-Rome (1975); Rodotà, "*La riforma del diritto di famiglia alla*

In the midst of this transition, two additional legislative enactments encapsulated the evolving social concept of the family. In spite of the religious dogma of the indissolubility of marriage, popular consensus endorsed the introduction of divorce into the Italian legal system, and in 1970 Italy passed a law allowing for the dissolution of the spousal relationship by cessation of the civil effects of marriage (law no. 898 of 1 December 1970). Another change of equal ideological importance took effect in 1978, with the legalization of voluntary abortion (law no. 184 of 22 May 1978). Both of these reforms which have successfully resisted conservative challenges by means of popular abrogative referendum then considerably affected the evolving legal and social concepts of the family, as discussed in the following sections.

III. Civil and Concordat Marriage under Italian Law

Before addressing the patrimonial system of the family, it may be helpful to make a couple of points about family law.

The Italian matrimonial system distinguishes between marriage intended as a legal act and marriage as a legal relationship. This distinction is usually only of a descriptive nature in the theory of juridical acts. But in the area of family law, it is a useful criterion for understanding the dual matrimonial regime of Italian law. The regulation of marriage as a legal act governs issues of the form and the legal requirements for contracting a valid marriage. The rules governing marriage as a legal relationship address issues related to the personal and patrimonial effects of the marriage between the spouses and with respect to their children.

Two forms of marriage exist under Italian law: civil and Concordat.[11] The distinction between the two relates to the notion of marriage as a legal act. In the case of civil marriage, the act and relationship are both regulated by the Italian family law system. The Concordat marriage is regulated by canon law, while the Italian legal system continues to regulate the relationship. The Concordat marriage, then, is simply a marriage contracted according to canon law but recognized, upon registration with the civil authorities, by the Italian legal system.[12]

---

prova," in *Pol. dir.* (1975), 661; Carraro, "*Il nuovo diritto di famiglia*," in *Riv. dir. civ.*, I (1975), 93; De Cupis, *Postilla sul nuovo diritto di famiglia*, ivi (1975); Barbiera, "*Divorzio e nuovo diritto di famiglia*," in *Dir. fam. e persone* (1976); A. & M. Finocchiaro, *Riforma del diritto di famiglia*, I, Milan (1975).

[11] The Civil Code regulates all aspects of civil marriage.

[12] On the legal significance of Concordat marriage, *see* F. Finocchiaro, "Matrimonio, arts. 79-83," in Scialoja & Branca (eds.), *Commentario del codice civile*, Zanichelli, Bologna-Rome

A triggering factor in the historical evolution of the Concordat marriage was that prior to the political unification of Italy the Catholic Church held a monopoly on the regulation of marriage, at least in the Papal States. This contributed to the consolidation of the social belief that a religious matrimony was necessary for a marriage to be fully valid.

Following territorial unification in 1861 the State denied effective legal recognition of marriages celebrated by the clergy. This denial, however, did not occasion a wholesale replacement of the older religious ceremonies with secular formalities. Catholic Italian citizens (who constituted the vast majority of the population) felt morally compelled to celebrate two marriages to satisfy both the religious and the secular requirements.

The two forms of marriage were independent of one another. One was dictated by the rules of canon law, the other by the Italian Civil Code. Apart from the endorsement of the dogma of indissolubility of marriage, there were few points of contact between the two legal orders. Soon, the unified State and the Holy See found themselves involved in an unpleasant political debate over the regulation of the family.[13]

In 1929, Italy and the Holy See reached an agreement on religious and political fronts: the Concordat guaranteed protection to the Catholic Church and the creation of the Vatican City State guaranteed a physical location and recognized political structure. On the regulation of marriage, the formulation of art. 29 of the Concordat is the origin of the idea of two legal orders regulating two aspects of the same social institution. According to the spirit of the Concordat, the legal act of marriage remained within the domain of canon law, while marriage intended as a legal relationship was to be the subject of Italian civil law. In spite of the theoretical rigor of this distinction, the duality of approach became particularly problematic in cases of marriage annulment.

The later formulation of the Italian Constitution evinces a conscious tension over the matter. Article 7 of the Italian Constitution acknowledged the prior

---

(1971); *id.*, "*I patti lateranensi e i principi supremi dell'ordinamento costituzionale*," in *Giurisprudenza italiana* (1982), 2, 1 (1985). Cardia, "*Una ridefinizione del matrimonio concordatario*," in *Giustizia Civile*, I (1982), 1450; Bellini, "*Matrimoni concordatario e principio di eguaglianza*," in *Rivista diritto civile*, II (1982), 793*ff*; C.M. Bianca, "*Il matrimonio concordatario nella prospettiva civilistica*," in *Rivista di Diritto Civile* (1986), 1-13.

[13] For an interesting comparative discussion of the rise and fall of ecclesiastical jurisdiction over marriage formation, *see* M.A. Glendon, *State Law and Family: Family Law in Transition in the United States and Western Europe*, North-Holland Publishing, Amsterdam (1977), 304-25.

international agreement: "the State and the Catholic Church are, each in its order, independent and sovereign. Their relations are regulated by the Lateran Pacts … " But the constitutional formulation remained mute on the delicate issues arising from the dichotomous manner in which family law was disciplined.

With regard to the civil aspect of family law, scholars and judges engaged in considerable debate over the relevance of the Lateran Pacts in the constitutional system. The discussions became particularly intense on the critical issue of marriage dissolution. Would the Lateran Pacts legally prevent the Italian secular system from allowing the voluntary dissolution of marriage? One school of thought, both scholarly and political, held that the appeal to the Lateran Pacts and to marriage as the basis of the "family" as natural society (art. 29 Const.) had to uphold the legal concept of marriage as an indissoluble bond. On the opposite front, the constitutionalists argued that the Constitution did not prejudice creation of a divorce law.[14]

The problem became relevant when divorce was introduced in 1970. The constitutional legitimacy of divorce, as the Constitutional Court also argued, was said to rest on the Lateran Pacts, which had drawn a distinction between jurisdiction over the validity of the act of marriage and jurisdiction over the relationship. Since it reserved the right to determine the validity of the act according to the canonical order, the State's power to regulate the relationship resulting from the act, including its dissolution, was total.

Law no. 898 of 1 December 1978 on marriage dissolution contains two articles that reflect this mechanism. Article 1 states: "The judge pronounces the dissolution of the marriage contracted under the Civil Code when … there is a certified absence of material or spiritual union between the spouses." Article 2 provides that: "[i]n cases of marriages celebrated by religious rite and registered under the [Italian] law, the judge … having certified the absence of material and spiritual union, … pronounces the cessation of the civil effects of the registration of the marriage." The result was that the marriage under canon law, indissoluble under its own order, became dissoluble under the Italian legal system (though solely with respect to the civil effects of the relationship), if registered and with effect under the law.

The Concordat regime further implies that the relationship aspect of the marriage is governed exclusively by Italian law, the main principles of which can be found in arts. 143, 144, and 147 of the Civil Code, which state:

---

[14] The constitutionalists' argument rested on the absence of a clear position of the Constitutional Assembly, notwithstanding an express discussion of the matter in a special session.

Article 143 [Mutual Rights and Duties of Spouses]:

Through marriage, the husband and wife acquire the same rights and assume the same duties.

A mutual obligation to loyalty, moral and material support, cooperation in the interest of the family and cohabitation derives from the marriage.

Both spouses are bound, each in relation to his own assets and his own ability for professional or household work, to contribute to the needs of the family.

Article 144 [Pattern of Family Life and Residence of Family]:

The spouses agree between them on the pattern of life and fix the residence of the family according to the requirements of both and the superior needs of the family.

Each spouse has the authority to implement the agreed pattern.

Article 147 [Duties to Children]:

Marriage imposes on both spouses the obligation to maintain, educate and instruct the children, taking into account their ability, natural inclination and aspirations.

The duality of this approach is particularly evident when family life breaks down. The approach highlights the difference between the rules governing annulment and those concerning the cessation of the marriage's civil effects. In declaring a marriage null, the judge rules on the validity of the act and eliminates it *ex tunc*, *i.e.* retroactively. On declaration of the cessation of the civil effects, the judge is ruling on the relationship, dissolving it and therefore depriving it of its effects *ex nunc*, *i.e.* with no retroactive effects.[15]

The patrimonial and hereditary aspects of the family are those specifically addressed in the following sections.

---

[15] Conversely, the separation of the spouses has effects neither on the act nor on the relationship, since separation does not dissolve the bond but only eliminates some of the aspects of the personal relationship between the spouses.

IV. The Legal and Patrimonial Structure

At the time when most of the modern European codes were enacted, most societies viewed the family as a hierarchically organized indissoluble unit. In the presence of an indissoluble relationship, incentive problems in the physiological phase of the family are often governed by the informal rules between the spouses, without any end-game problem. In the old regime, the patrimonial rules were thus attentive to the *ex ante* incentive of the spouses, rather than constituting a tool to correct the potential *ex post* opportunism of one spouse. In the Italian legal system, the rules that governed the patrimonial relations between the spouses were indeed only minimally articulated and were instrumental to the older concept of the family.

Once the dogma of indissolubility faded away from the secular concept of the family, the regulation of patrimonial relations between spouses became crucially important. The reformed concept of the family has, as one of its most radical innovations, the introduction of a well-articulated patrimonial regime, enacted through the 1975 Family Law Reform Act.

The original version of the 1942 Italian Civil Code envisioned a system of asset separation. This system was consistent with the value of ownership and enterprise that had inspired the Code, and which could be linked to a tradition dating back to Roman law. Moreover, in the historical period between the 1865 and 1942 codifications, the legal system based on asset separation intensified the wife's inferior economic condition. But as Italian society evolved, the emergence of new social norms and life models, all of them tending to re-evaluate the work of women and the economic importance of their role in the family, highlighted the need for a radical revision of the patrimonial legal regime of the family. With the enactment of the Constitution, the focus of the legal system shifted towards the protection of the person and human personality (art. 2 Const.), together with the formal and substantial application of the principle of equality (art. 3 Const.). These principles were applied to family law in 1975,[16] and led to the proclamation of the moral and legal equality of spouses.

Prior to the 1975 reform, there had been a lively debate on the appropriate domain of a constitutionally-driven reform of family law. The first platform was one of rigorous interpretation of the constitutional norms on the principle of shared responsibility and family unity (art. 29 para. 2 Const.). The conclusion was that marriage brings about not only spiritual union but also material union, and that

---

[16] Other provisions, contained in arts. 29, 30, and 31 Const., played an equally important role in the 1975 revision of family law.

therefore all assets should be viewed as contributions to the realization of one family estate. According to this view, the unitary nature of the family as a natural society founded on marriage required a legal regime based on joint ownership of all assets, with no permitted derogations. The other platform was less radical and more attentive to the historical development of Italian family law. According to this latter approach, economic considerations especially applicable to the case of family entrepreneurial activities dictated a more flexible regime for the patrimonial relations of the family. The historical point of view ultimately prevailed so that, in the absence of other explicit arrangements, the economic system of the family is constituted by the common ownership of assets as a matter of law. This system was believed to be sufficient to protect the wife's position in family administration.

In sum, the Italian family law reform of 1975 introduced the following main principles: it abolished dowry; it shifted the patrimonial system from one based on separate assets to one based on common ownership; and it introduced new rules governing the administration of commonly owned assets.

The Italian legal system opted for a default common ownership regime from which certain derogations were permissible. Such a system is neither obligatory nor universal, since its sphere is restricted. It is binding because no spouse may dissolve it at whim,[17] nor may a spouse acting alone dispose of his or her share. On this latter point, according to a Constitutional Court ruling, spouses do not have individual entitlements to any share, but are joint holders of an entitlement to commonly owned assets.[18]

V. The Current Patrimonial Regime of the Family

The patrimonial system of the family established by law in Italy is based on the common ownership of assets, but spouses may opt for a different regime through mutual assent. In the absence of such an agreement, the family economic system in Italy is one of Common Ownership of Assets as regulated by Section III, Chapter VI, Volume I of the Civil Code (art. 159 CC). Section V, Chapter VI, Volume I of the Civil Code regulates the system of voluntary separation of assets. Marriage agreements opting for the separation of assets may be stipulated at any time, but require a formal public notarial act. The decision to opt for separation of assets may also be declared upon registration of the marriage (*see* arts. 162-66*bis* CC).

---

[17] *See* art. 191 CC.

[18] Constitutional Court, 17 March 1988, no. 311.

The Common Ownership of Assets by Agreement is regulated by Section IV, Chapter VI, Volume I of the Civil Code, arts. 210-14.[19]

A. The Common Ownership of Assets by Law

An analysis of the norms of the Civil Code on the common ownership of assets by law highlights three major categories: assets immediately included in common ownership; common assets *de residuo*; and personal property.

Assets commonly owned include items spouses purchased together or separately during the marriage, excluding individual acquisitions. With respect to businesses owned by spouses prior to their marriage, and still managed by them after marriage, common ownership includes only increases in profits.

Some categories of asset are only included in common ownership upon dissolution of this arrangement.[20] This is known as common ownership *de residuo*. The following assets are included in common ownership on dissolution of this arrangement: gains from assets each spouse individually owned, distributed and were not consumed upon dissolution; proceeds from the separate activities of either spouse, if they have not been consumed upon dissolution; assets designated to a

---

[19] On the patrimonial regime of the family, *see* G. Bonilini & G. Cattaneo (eds.), *Il diritto di famiglia*, II, *Il regime patrimoniale della famiglia*, Utet, Turin (1997), with a rich bibliography; F.D. Busnelli, *"Convenzione matrimoniale,"* in *Enciclopedia del diritto*, X (1962), 512-24; G. Tedeschi, *"Il regime patrimoniale della famiglia,"* in *Trattato Vassalli*, 4th ed., Utet (1963); R. Sacco, in Oppo, Carraro & Trabucchi (eds.), *Commentario alla riforma del diritto di famiglia*, I, Cedam, Padua (1977); E. Russo, *Le convenzioni matrimoniali ed altri saggi sul nuovo diritto di famiglia*, Giuffrè (1983); F. Santosuosso, *"Il regime patrimoniale della famiglia,"* in *Comm. cod. civ.*, I, 1, Turin (1983), 154-326; F. Corsi, *"Il regime patrimoniale della famiglia,"* in *Tratt. dir. civ. e comm.* Cicu-Messineo & Mengoni, II, Giuffrè, Milan (1984); A. & M. Finocchiaro, *Diritto di famigilia*, I Milan (1988); S. Maiorca, *"Regime patrimoniale della famiglia (Disposizioni generali),"* in *Novissimo Digesto Italiano*, App. VII, 76-120; G. Gabrielli, *"Scioglimento parziale della comunione legale fra coniugi, esclusione della comunione di singoli beni e rifiuto preventivo del coacquisto,"* in *Rivista di diritto civile*, I (1988), 341-64; S. Maiorca, *"Regime patrimoniale della famiglia (Disposizioni generali),"* in *Novissimo digesto italiano*, App. VI (1986), 450-504; *id.*, *Separazione di beni tra coniugi*, App. VII, ivi (1987), 76-120; G. Oberto, *"Comunione legale, regimi convenzionali e pubblicità immobiliare,"* in *Riv. diritto civile*, II (1988), 187-230; E. Roppo, *"Convenzioni matrimoniali,"* in *Enciclopedia Giuridica Treccani*, XI (1988), 1-6.

[20] Common ownership is dissolved as a result of the certified absence, death, or presumed death of either spouse; of the annulment, dissolution or cessation of the civil effects of the marriage; of the legal separation of the spouses; of the legal separation of assets; of changes in the patrimonial system by mutual agreement; and of the bankruptcy of either spouse.

business run by either spouse and established during the marriage; and profits from a business established prior to the marriage and unconsumed upon dissolution.

Personal property of spouses includes: assets that a spouse owned before marriage or for which he or she holds usufruct rights; assets acquired after marriage by gift or right of succession when the act of gift or legacy does not specify inclusion in common ownership; assets and accessories for the strictly personal use of either spouse; assets required for running the trade or business of either spouse except those designated to a business included in common ownership; assets obtained by way of compensation for damages, and invalidity pensions or benefits in full or in part; and assets acquired with proceeds from the transfer or sale of personal property, providing there is explicit declaration to this effect at the moment of sale.

Having pinpointed the specific sphere of the joint ownership default rules, there follows a summary of norms governing the administration of commonly owned assets and patrimonial guarantees for such assets. Both spouses have the power of administration of the jointly owned assets and of representation in judicial proceedings relating to such assets. Spouses may jointly pursue activities of extraordinary administration and stipulate contracts for the creation and transfer of usufruct rights. Both also have power of attorney in pertinent judicial proceedings.

Under the Civil Code, joint ownership places certain burdens on both spouses, which include all burdens that accompany the asset at the time of acquisition, all administration charges, all family maintenance costs, the education of children, and obligations contracted together or separately by spouses in the interests of the family.

When a commonly owned asset is insufficient to service debt encumbering the asset, creditors may apply to the personal property of either spouse for up to 50 percent of the debt. This is known as the subordinate liability of personal property. Since the burden of responsibility is only partially shared, this norm is clearly unfair according to the majority opinion. Consider the example of spouses who jointly guarantee a bank loan for a friend. Assume, for example, that this obligation equals 100, while commonly owned assets equal 50. Further assume that one of the spouses has no assets, while the other has a patrimony of 1,000. In this case, the creditor could demand a patrimonial guarantee worth 75 (50 in commonly owned assets plus 25 in personal property of one of the spouses) and not 100, as should be the case according to the general principle of passive solidarity.[21]

---

[21] Note that art. 2740 CC merely establishes that a debtor's liability for the fulfillment of obligations includes all present and future assets.

B. Separation of Assets

Section V, Chapter VI Book I of the Civil Code regulates the separation of assets. Spouses may agree that each of them retains sole ownership of assets acquired during the marriage. In this case, each spouse has the right of usufruct and administration of the asset of which the other has exclusive ownership. A spouse can prove ownership of an asset to the exclusion of the other spouse by any means. Assets for which neither spouse can prove exclusive ownership are the undivided property in equal shares of both spouses.

C. The Common Ownership of Assets by Agreement

By means of an agreement stipulated by a public notarial act, spouses may modify the default system of common ownership of assets that would apply to their patrimonial relations. Article 161 CC requires that such agreements be specific in their content and not merely declaratory of the choice of a different legal regime. The rule clearly guards against opting out of the default legal regime by uninformed spouses. Article 210 CC also specifies that certain personal property can in no event be included in common ownership by agreement. Such property includes assets and accessories for the strictly personal use of either spouse; assets required for running the trade or business of a spouse (except those designated to a business included in common ownership); assets obtained by way of compensation for damages; and invalidity pensions or benefits in full or in part.

VI. Matrimonial Breakdowns and Economic Relationships

The underlying concept of the family as a spousal joint enterprise should be evaluated in light of the absence of an explicit price system within the family. There are no explicit prices to compensate spouses for their respective inputs as managers of the family unit. Services rendered by a spouse for the benefit of others within the family remain unpaid. Likewise, there is no explicit contract regulating the respective tasks of the spouses within the family nor any compensation scheme for the services rendered by each spouse. Like any team production scenario, spouses work as a team, and it is difficult to attribute the product of their joint efforts to the specific input of one or the other. Thus, even the implicit exchange within the family may be incapable of compensating the relative inputs with the marginal value of the respective labor.

Within the family, just as in any collective enterprise, there is a division of labor between the spouses. Such division is the rational consequence of economies derived from specialization and will obtain even in the absence of an initial comparative advantage of one spouse in the production of family services.[22] But as expected, the presence of economies from specialization in a joint output environment may be problematic. In the absence of a price system, the optimal mix of inputs for the well-being of the family may not coincide with the equilibrium mix of input for the two spouses.

The divergence between private and social (*i.e.* family) incentives is exacerbated by the possibility of dissolution of the family union upon the request of one spouse. In the absence of legal rules regulating the "pathological" phase of marriage, each subject will set his or her own value of input in such a way as to equalize marginal private costs and benefits. In the absence of warranties for the case of dissolution of the family unit, the input choices of the spouses will be sub-optimal from the point of view of the family as a whole.

In this setting, the legal regime of the family patrimony can be viewed as designed as a remedy to the risk of *ex post* opportunism of spouses with a finite horizon of individual optimization. This explains why the increased importance of the economic regime of the family is a necessary by-product of the historical decline of the dogma of indissolubility of the family union.[23]

VII. Patrimonial Regime in Case of Separation or Dissolution

Family life may enter a "pathological" phase either temporarily (upon the separation of spouses) or definitively (upon the dissolution of marriage).[24] The 1942 Civil Code regulated family crises solely by the separation of the spouses and, in this regard, reflected the underlying limited domain of private autonomy in family relations.

Legal separation was only permitted in cases explicitly envisioned by the legislator: adultery (also considered penal in nature); voluntary desertion; excessively disturbing behavior; violence; threats; serious injury; the conviction of a spouse to life imprisonment or sentencing to more than five years; and failure by the husband to establish a family domicile.

---

[22] *See* G.S. Becker, *A Treatise on the Family*, Harvard University Press, Cambridge, Mass. (1991), 288.

[23] For a general discussion of the economics of family law, *see* G.S. Becker, *supra* note 22, at 288; *see also* T.H. Schultz (ed.), *Economics of the Family: Marriage, Children and Human Capital*, University of Chicago Press, Chicago (1974), 584; A. Cigno, *Economics of the Family*, Clarendon, Oxford (1991), 212.

[24] Article 149 CC on the dissolution of marriage. Marriage is dissolved by the death of a spouse or by law.

Separation by agreement was originally permitted only upon judicial approval. The 1942 lawmaker had opted for a general approach to the separation of spouses based upon a fault analysis. The system introduced under the reform was markedly different. It allowed no-fault separation, although many courts continued to rule according to a spouse's behavior, which might put the children at risk. Notably, in 1970 the lawmaker also introduced the cessation of the civil effects of marriage and divorce. The Italian legal system does not recognize consensual divorce following an explicit agreement. The Italian system recognizes remedial divorce, which always envisions a judge's ruling and assessment when a relationship lived in *communio omnis vitae* breaks down.

The present inquiry is confined to the sphere of family law, and we will proceed to consider the economic relations between spouses with children in cases of separation or dissolution.

A. Effects of Separation on Patrimonial Relations

The first and most important effect of separation on economic relations is the right to support. The general criterion for the amount of support is related to the economic rationale outlined in the previous section. The support, generally established through a judicial order to pay regular maintenance, is determined to assist both spouses in maintaining the same standard of living that they had enjoyed during the marriage. This criterion is indeed aimed at preventing exploitation by the spouses of asymmetrical, irreversible investments in the family. In turn, this remedy prevents the disruption of the spouse's incentives during family union.[25]

---

[25] On the separation of the spouses and the patrimonial consequences thereof, *see* C.M. Bianca, *La famiglia. Le succesioni*, II, Milan (1982); *see also* P. Zatti & M. Mantovani, *La separazione personale*, Padua (1983); A. & M. Finocchiaro, *Diritto di famiglia*, I, *supra* note 19; F. Santoro Passarelli, *"Note introduttive agli arts. 24 e 28, della novella,"* in Carraro, Oppo & Trambucchi (eds.), *I Commentario alla riforma del diritto di famiglia*, 1, Padua, 215-62; L. Carraro, *"Il nuovo diritto di famiglia,"* in *Rivista di diritto civile*, I (1975), 94*ff*; G. Ferrando, *"Dalla separazione per colpa alla separazione per 'impossibilita' della convivenza,"* in *Proceedings of the Conference on Italian Family Law*, Milan (1976), 55-71; C. Grassetti, *"Scioglimento del matrimonio e separazione personale dei coniugi,"* in Carraro Oppo & Trabucchi (eds.), *Commentario al diritto di famiglia*, I, 1, Padua (1977), 283-314; F. Santosuosso, *"Delle persone e della famiglia. Il matrimonio,"* in *Commentario codice civile*, I, Utet, Turin (1978), 1; Zanetti Vitali, *"Il mutamento del titolo della separazione,"* in *Diritto delle persone e della famiglia*, (1980), 264-314; A. Bargamini, *"Appunti sull'autonomia dei coniugi di disporre l'assetto dei loro rapporti patrimoniali in concomitanza della separazione consensuale e in vista di un futuro divorzio,"* in *Giustizia Civile*, I (1974), 173-76; U.M. Caferra, *"L'assegno*

In decreeing separation, the court provides for the right of the spouse to whom separation is not imputable to receive from the other spouse an amount that is regarded as necessary for their support, if they have no adequate income of their own. Not surprisingly, the liquidated amount depends on the circumstances and the relative incomes of the spouses. The Italian legal system explicitly regulates chargeable separation. In adjudicating separation, the court will, under proper circumstances, determine the at-fault spouse, based upon findings of behavior contrary to fulfillment of marital obligations.

The at-fault spouse is not entitled to maintenance, even if in a state of financial need, but only to alimony. Alimony differs from maintenance in that it is designed to satisfy only the basic financial needs of the claimant, rather than attempting to equalize the standards of life *vis-à-vis* the other spouse.

Regarding the children, the court establishes custody and determines how much the non-custodial spouse should contribute towards their maintenance and education. The court will also rule on the extent and allocation of parental rights over the children.

B. Effects of Dissolution of Marriage on Patrimonial Relations

The legal-economic regime in the event of dissolution of the marriage provides remedies to correct for potential asymmetries between the spouses' investments in the family. The goal is once again aimed at preventing the distortion of the incentives of the spouses over the normal course of their relationship.

With the decline of the dogma of indissolubility of marriage, the spouses' incentives became affected by uncertainty concerning the stability and duration of their relationship. Some long-term choices, such as specialization of one spouse in the rearing of the children, which would be regarded as individually optimal in a no-divorce regime, could become irrational in the presence of uncertainty regarding the duration of the family union. The legal-economic regime of the family aims at correcting this potential misalignment of incentives. Because of the retrospective protection provided by the legal system, spouses can live out their matrimonial union as if it were indissoluble. This protection is designed to induce optimal investments in the family and diversification of the labor inputs of the spouses with differing specializations in professional or domestic activities, as their comparative

---

di mantenimento nel giudizio di separazione dei coniugi," in *Giurisprudenza italiana*, 1 (1977), 1, 1908*ff*; E. Quadri, "*L'adeguamento monetario degli assegni periodici con funzione assistenziale*," in *Giur. it.*, IV (1980), 49*ff*; A. Trabucchi, "*Il nuovo divorzio. Il contenuto e il senso della riforma*," in *Rivista diritto civile*, II (1987), 125-47.

advantages dictate. In this setting, the effects on the dissolution of marriage can be viewed as instrumental to providing a solution to such incentive-compatibility problems.[26]

Other legal-economic effects of the dissolution of marriage include receipt of a divorce allowance and assignment of the family home.

With respect to divorce allowances, the court, in decreeing dissolution or the cessation of the civil effects of the marriage, evaluates various factors: the condition of both spouses; the reasons for the divorce; the personal and financial contribution of each spouse to family administration and to the formation of the estate of each or both; and the current and expected incomes of both spouses. Having assessed all these elements, together with the duration of the marriage, the court will establish the obligation of one of the spouses to provide a periodical allowance to the other when he or she has no adequate financial means and cannot justifiably obtain them. By agreement of the parties, this allowance may also be paid in a lump sum.[27]

---

[26] On the incentive structure of family relationships, *see* M.F. Brinig & S.T. Crafton, "Marriage and Opportunism," 23 *J of Legal Stud* (1994), 869-94; L. Cohen, Marriage, "Divorce, and Quasi-Rents; or, 'I Gave Him the Best Years of My Life'," 16 *J of Legal Stud* (1987), 267-303.

[27] On divorce and its patrimonial consequences between the spouses, *see* M. Dogliotti, *Separazione e divorzio*, Turin (1988); C.M. Bianca, *La nuova disciplina del divorzio. Appendice di aggiornamento*, Milan (1988); L. Barbiera, *Il divorzio dopo la seconda riforma*, Bologna (1988); F. Mosconi, *"Commentario alla riforma del divorzio,"* in *AAVV*, Ipsoa, Milan (1987), 45-49, 147-51; Luminoso, *"La riforma del divorzio: profili di diritto sostanziale,"* in *Rivista giuridica sarda*, II (1987), 591-621; A. Lanzi, *"Commentario alla riforma del divorzio,"* in *AAVV*, Ipsoa, Milan (1987), 33-36, 152-56; E. Cipriani, *"Nuove norme sulla disciplina dei casi di scioglimento del matrimonio,"* in N. Lipari (ed.), *Nuove leggi civili commentate* (1987), 874-93; A. Giusti, *Crisi coniugale e protezione della casa familiare*, ivi, (1986), 850-874, 1023-32; V. Carbone, *"Divorzio accelerato e maggiori tutele per il coniuge debole,"* in *Corriere giuridico* (1987), 727-32; G. Frezza, *"Su alcuni aspetti patrimoniali della separazione e del divorzio,"* in *Giust. Civ.*, I (1994), 540*ff*; Dell'Ongaro, *"Sulla controversa natura dell'assegno di divorzio,"* in *Dir. famiglia* (1974), 635; F. Morozzo Della Rocca, *"Un problema ancora insoluto: la natura dell'attribuzione dell'assegno di divorzio,"* in *Dir. famiglia* (1974), 354; Santosuosso, *"Il divorzio,"* in P. Rescigno (ed.), *Trattato di diritto privato*, vol. 3, Turin (1982), 365; Arrivas, in Arrivas, Guccione & Tortorici (eds.), *Dieci anni di giurisprudenza*, Palermo (1981), 120; Perillo, *"Riflessi patrimoniali del divorzio,"* in *Riv. dir. civ.*, II (1979), 532; Galoppini, *"Divorzio (diritto privato e processuale),"* in *Noviss. Dig. It.*, III, Turin (1982), 100*ff*; De Martino, Protetti' & Taddeucci, *Scioglimento del matrimonio. Commentario alla legge no. 898 del 1970*, Rome (1971), 551; D. Vincenzi Amato, *"I rapporti patrimoniali,"* in P. Rescigno (ed.), Commentario sul divorzio, Milan (1980), 309*ff*. (with special attention to 328); C.M. Udda, *"Sull'indisponibilità del diritto all'assegno di divorzio,"* in *Fam. e dir.* (1995), 14-16; L. Cavallo, *"Sull'indisponibilità dell'assegno di divorzio,"* in *Giust. Civ.*, I

The divorce allowance has an economic function comparable to the maintenance obligation during the separation phase, since it is intended to assist both spouses in maintaining the same standard of living as they enjoyed during the marriage. Both payments maintain optimal incentives during the family union, encouraging optimal investment in the family on the part of the spouses, while minimizing the likelihood of *ex post* opportunism and the exploitation of asymmetrical, irreversible investments in the family.[28]

Assignment of the family home is a major factor in both separation and divorce. In the case of separation, the family home is preferably assigned to the spouse given custody of the children. In the case of divorce, the family home is assigned to the spouse who not only has custody, but with whom the children are likely to live upon reaching the age of majority. In all cases for the purpose of assigning the family home, the judge will evaluate the financial conditions of the spouses and the reasons for their divorce,[29] and will favor the weaker party. The assigned home,

---

(1992), 1241*ff*; A. Trabucchi, "*Assegno di divorzio: attribuzione giudiziale e disponibilità degli interessati*," in *Giur. it.* (1981), I, 1, 1553; L. Barbiera, "*Il divorzio dopo la riforma del diritto di famiglia*," in *Comm. Scialoja-Branca*, Bologna-Roma (1979), sub. art. 149, 387; Santosuosso, "*Il divorzio*," in *Trattato Rescigno*, 3, 2, Turin (1982), 361; E. Quadri, *La nuova legge sul divorzio*, I, *Profili patrimoniali*, Naples (1987), 43*ff*, 71*ff*; C.M. Bianca, *Diritto civile*, II, *La famiglia*, Milan (1989), 208*ff*; and *id.*, "*Commentario al diritto italiano della famiglia*," Oppo, Cian & Trabucchi (eds.), Padua (1993), 358*ff*.

[28] *See* M. Krauskopf, "Recompense for Financing Spouse's Education: Legal Protection for the Marital Investor in Human Captial," 28 *UKanLRev* 379; R.A. Posner, *Economic Analysis of Law*, 2nd ed., Little Brown, Boston (1986), 139-60; L.J. Weitzman, "The Economics of Divorce: Social and Economic Consequences of Property, Alimony and Child Support Awards," 28 *UCLA LRev* (1981), 1181.

[29] On the assignment of the family home, in cases of separation and divorce, *see* A. Finocchiaro, in A. & M. Finocchiaro (eds.), *supra* note 19, vol III, 495*ff*; *id.*, "*Puo' il giudice della separazione assegnare l'abitazione nella casa familiare al coniuge cui non vengono affidati i figli?*," in *Giust. Civ.*, I (1981), 142; *id.*, "*Ancora sul potere del giudice del divorzio di disporre della casa familiare*," in *Giust. Civ.*, I (1982), 703; C. Coccia, "*La casa familiare: qualificazione giuridica e diritti del coniuge*," in *Dir. fam. e pers.* (1985), 722; A. Giusti, *supra* note 28, at 773; R. Amaglini, "*Separazione dei coniugi e assegnazione della casa familiare*," in *Rass. Dir. Civ.* (1982), 2; S. Bartolomucci, "*Casa familiare e attribuzione giudiziale a seguito di separazione personale fra coniugi*," in *Giust. Civ.* (1985), 515, containing ample bibliographic references; A. Belvedere, "*Residenza e casa familiare: riflessioni conclusive*," in *Riv. Crit. Dir. priv.* (1988), 243; G. Tamburrino, *Lineamenti del nuovo diritto di famiglia*, Turin (1978), 277; G. Gabrielli, in Carraro, Oppo & Trabucchi (eds.), *Commentario della riforma del diritto di famiglia*, II (1976), 16; M. Dogliotti, *Separazione e divorzio*, *supra* note 27 at 115*ff*. *See also* C.M. Bianca, *supra* note 27 at 160;

if legally registered, may be sold to a third party under art. 1599 CC. Thus, the assignment of the family home in the case of separation and divorce is considered by Italian judges to serve the interests of children and also as a practical means of guaranteeing fulfillment of the obligation of maintenance. With respect to the patrimonial effects on children, the rules the legislator has introduced resemble those applicable in the case of separation.

VIII. The Family Enterprise

We shall now briefly examine the rules applying to the family enterprise, *i.e.*, whenever two or more members of the same family jointly own and manage a family business.[30]

While the economic relevance of family enterprises has declined with the expansion of the large-scale market economy, it remains important. The family has always been a natural economic organization, not only in terms of collective needs and activities, but also in terms of its capacity to work together in a small-scale economic unit. The family, whether undertaking a formal business activity or not, can be regarded as a sort of firm, with an internal division of labor and implicit norms for the division of the joint product.[31] The legal system provides

---

L. Barbiera, *I diritti patrimoniali dei separati e dei divorziati*, Zanichelli (1995), 45*ff*; E. Quadri, *"La casa familiare nel divorzio,"* in *La nuova legge nel divorzio*, Naples (1988), 201*ff*; *id.*, *"L'attribuzione della casa familiare in sede di divorzio,"* in *Fam. e dir.* (1995), 269; M.G. Ceccherini, *"Tutela del coniuge separato e assegnazione della casa familiare,"* in *Riv. Crit. Dir. Priv.* (1986), 567*ff*; M. Di Nardo, *"Attribuzione giudiziale della casa familiare al coniuge non affidatario della prole,"* in *Nuova Giur. Civ. Commentata*, I (1988), 127; A.M. Marchio, *"Questioni in tema di assegnazione della casa familiare,"* in *Giur. It.* (1987), I, 1, 1294; G. Frezza, *"L'assegnazione della casa familiare al coniuge affidatario della prole,"* in *Giustizia civile* (1996), 725; *id.*, *"Diversa ratio della assegnazione della casa familiare nella separazione e nel divorzio,"* in *Giur. It.* (1996), I, 1, 3*ff*.

[30] On the family enterprise, *see* G. Oppo, *Scritti giuridici*, vol. V, Cedam (1992), with an extensive bibliography. *See also* C.M. Bianca, *Diritto civile*, *supra* note 27 at 308-54; A. & M. Finocchiaro, *Diritto di famiglia*, *supra* note 19; F. Santosuosso, *"Il matrimonio,"* in *Comm. Cod. Civile. Delle persone e della famiglia*, Utet, Turin (1983), 366*ff*; G. Gabrielli, *I rapporti patrimoniali tra i coniugi*, I, Trieste (1981); G. Tamburrino, *Lineamenti del nuovo diritto di famiglia*, Utet, Turin (1978), 239*ff*; C.A. Graziani, *"L'impresa familiare nel nuovo diritto di famiglia. Prime considerazioni,"* in *Nuovo diritto agrario* (1975), 199, 246; *id.*, *"Comunione tacita familiare,"* in *Noviss. Dig. it*, App. II (1981), 191-93.

[31] For an introduction, *see* G.S. Becker, *A Treatise on the Family*, Harvard University Press, Cambridge, Mass. (1991), 288; R.A. Posner, *supra* note 30, at 139-60.

guidelines and constraints for the content of such implicit norms. The case of family businesses is qualitatively analogous. The problems regularly posed by the regulation of the family are exacerbated in the event of a family-run enterprise, given the greater personal investment of each family member in the collective enterprise.

A. Regulation of the Family Enterprise After the 1975 Reform

In the history of the Italian economy, family enterprises have played a relatively important role. Historically, while many legal scholars have analyzed the family-enterprise relationship, there had been relatively little case law or legislative treatment of the matter. The practical matters were eventually treated through a joint reading and application of the corporate law rules contained in the Book 5 of the Civil Code, together with the family law rules contained in the Book 1.

After the 1975 reform of family law, the Italian legal system distinguished three hypotheses: (i) individual enterprise; (ii) marital enterprise; and (iii) family enterprise.

With respect to the case of the *individual business* of a spouse, it is presumed that the assets of the business are managed individually and not by the family in common.[32]

Conversely, *marital business* refers to an enterprise jointly run by both spouses.[33] This category includes businesses managed by both spouses, where it is likely that the *affectio coniugalis* (*i.e.* the implicit norms in effect within the family), prevails over the *societatis* (*i.e.*, the norms that would govern in a purely commercial business enterprise). The application of norms on the common ownership of assets applies.

Finally, the notion of *family enterprise* includes situations in which the spouse's extended family jointly contributes to a common business enterprise. Under art.

---

[32] This applies to the following cases: (i) art. 320 CC para. 5 on the representation and administration of children's assets by their parents establishes that a business enterprise cannot be continued without the authorization of the juvenile court following a ruling by the judge acting as guardian; the judge acting as guardian can consent to the enterprise on a provisional basis until the court rules on the petition; (ii) a business run individually by a spouse (his or her personal property), under the common ownership system; and (iii) common ownership *de residuo* of the assets of a business run individually.

[33] This includes the following cases: (i) under art. 177 (d) CC (businesses run by both spouses and established after the marriage); (ii) under art. 177 para. 2 CC, in the case of businesses belonging to one of the spouses prior to the marriage but then run by both, common ownership concerns only profits and increases in profits.

230*bis* CC, and in the absence of agreements to the contrary, a family member who renders services to the family or in the family enterprise with continuity has a right to maintenance in keeping with the economic status of the family. In proportion to the quantity and quality of the services rendered, he or she may share in profits, and benefit from goodwill. Decisions on the use of profits, as well as those pertaining to the extraordinary course of business, production policy, and close-down, are majority decisions made by the family members participating in the enterprise.[34]

IX. Aspects of Family Succession

Several aspects of Italian succession law also are instrumental in maintaining optimal incentives in relationships between family members and close relatives. The patrimony of the family is regarded as the accumulation of wealth obtained through the joint efforts of family members. The close members of the family unit are regarded as residual claimants of a portion of the family wealth, which constitutes the share of wealth subjected to the regime of forced heirship. In this respect, the law of succession in Italy is highly distinctive from an Anglo-American standpoint, given its special emphasis on the economic unity of the family. The economic unity of the Italian family, protected through forced heirship provisions, is regulated in Book 2 of the Italian Civil Code. The legal system reserves absolute succession rights to a limited group of individuals within the family, which include the surviving spouse, legitimate and illegitimate children, and, in the absence of children, lawful ascendants (*ex.* art. 536 CC).[35]

In the usual textbook presentation of Italian succession law, the estate of the deceased is considered to be made up of two main portions: first, a share that

---

[34] According to the art. 230*bis* CC, in all these settings, the work of a woman is considered equivalent to that of a man. Furthermore, the right of participation is not transferable unless the transfer benefits family members. It can be liquidated in money upon termination of the business for any reason. The payment may be in more than one installment as determined by the court failing agreement.

[35] On succession law issues relevant to the family, *see*, most generally, G. Cian, G. Oppo & A. Trabucchi (eds.), *Commentario del diritto della famiglia*, vol. 5, Padua (1992), with contributions by A. Burdese (arts. 467-69 CC); G. Gabrielli (arts. 536-48 CC); M. Costanza (arts. 566-79 CC); L. Mengoni (arts. 581-85 CC); L. Carraro (art. 594 CC); U. Carnevali (art. 687); G. Benedetti (arts. 692-97 CC); P. Forchiello (arts. 737-51 CC); U. Carnevali (arts. 803-04, 785 CC).

cannot be disposed of and which is reserved by law for the sole benefit of close members of the family; and secondly, a disposable share that is transferred according to the express will of the deceased individual or, in the absence of a valid will, according to the rules of default succession (arts. 565-86 CC).

The non-disposable portion can be claimed by the forced heirs even against the express will of the deceased (arts. 553 through 564 CC). The term "forced heir" is used to refer to an heir who has a right at law to receive a share of the decedent's estate, is taken from M. Bettramo, G. Longo, J. Merryman (eds.), *The Italian Civil Code and Complementary Legislation* (1996). If he or she dies intestate or if the will is found not to be valid, the intestate succession mechanism is triggered so that additional family members may succeed to the disposable portion by law (in intestate succession, the inheritance is devolved to the individual's legitimate and illegitimate descendants, collaterals, other relatives to the sixth degree, and, in the absence of any individual within those categories, to the State).

If the testator has willed (or previously donated) property whose value exceeds the value of the disposable portion, the rights of the forced heirs are regarded as violated. The Italian legal system permits legitimate heirs to reduce the dispositions (and life donations) made in favor of third parties in a sufficient amount to guarantee the full forced heirship value.[36]

Given this premise on family succession, the following paragraphs consider the system of succession in the case of marriage breakdown.

A. Succession in the Case of Separation

Separated spouses are considered on a par with non-separated spouses for the purposes of the succession rules considered above (*i.e.* forced heirship, *ex.* art. 536 CC), which directly apply in favor of the separated spouse. Conversely, the at-fault separated spouse loses his or her rights to succession, and is entitled only to alimony, if any, chargeable to the estate.

---

[36] When the testator disposes of a usufruct or life annuity with income exceeding that of the disposable share, the forced heirs to whom the naked ownership of the disposable portion or part of it has been assigned have the choice of carrying out this provision or abandoning naked ownership of the disposable portion. In the second case the legatee, in taking the abandoned disposable portion, does not acquire the status of heir. The same choice belongs to the forced heirs when the testator has disposed of the naked ownership of a share in excess of the disposable portion. If there is more than one forced heir, unanimous agreement is required for the fulfillment of the testamentary provision. The same rules apply if the usufruct, annuity or naked ownership is disposed of by gift.

Both the separated spouse and the at-fault separated spouse are on the same social security level as regards transferable pensions (although the latter, according to a unanimous court opinion, are not acquired by right of *iure successionis* but rather by *iure proprio*).[37]

B. Succession in the Case of Divorce

The divorcee acquires the right to succession *mortis causa*, which consists of an alimony payment chargeable to the estate. From the social security standpoint, divorced spouses are also entitled to transferable pensions and to a portion of the spouse's retirement lump-sum payments.

With respect to the alimony chargeable to the estate after the death of the obligor, the court may attribute to the spouse previously entitled to the periodical payment of sums of money (under art. 5), and who is in a state of need, a periodical allowance chargeable to the estate. This allowance may be granted after an evaluation of the sums already paid, the extent of financial need, the existence and amount of the survivor's pension, the wealth obtained through inheritance, the number and category of heirs, and their financial status.

The transferable pension applies in the case of the death of a former spouse and in the absence of a surviving spouse possessing the prerequisites for obtaining the pension. The divorced spouse, if he or she has not contracted a new marriage, and

---

[37] On the social security profiles of divorce, with reference to workers' compensation, pension, and liquidation payments, *see* M. Persiani, *"Commento all'art. 38 Cost.,"* in Branca (ed.), *Commentario della Costituzione*, Bologna-Rome (1979), 232*ff*, 239*ff*; F.P. Rossi, "La previdenza sociale," in G. Mazzoni (ed.), *Enc. giur. del lavoro*, IX, Padua (1993), 1*ff*; S. Piccininno, *"Pensione (rapporto di lavoro privato),"* in *Enc. giur. Treccani*, XXII, Rome (1990), 1*ff*; M. Persiani, *Diritto della previdenza sociale*, Rome (1994), 1*ff*; F.P. Rossi, *"Pensione (diritto privato),"* in *Enc. dir.*, XXXII, Milan (1982), 893; M. Persiani, *"La funzione della pensione di reversibilità nella piu' recente giurisprudenza della Corte Costituzionale,"* in *Giur. cost.* (1980), 494*ff*; G. Frezza, *"Coniuge divorziato e trattamento pensionistico di reversibilità,"* in *Giust. Civ.* (1994), 2963; id., *"Diritto del divorziato alla pensione di reversibilità e Convenzioni preventive di Divorzio,"* in *Diritto di famiglia e delle persone* (1996), 15*ff*; E. Quadri, *"Divorzio: verso quale riforma?,"* in *Foro it.* (1987), V, 72*ff*; id., *"Le aspettative pensionistiche: vecchi problemi e nuove soluzioni,"* in *Foro it.* (1988), I, 3523; id., *"Divorzio nel diritto civile e internazionale,"* in *Digesto, Discipline Privatistiche*, VI, Turin (1991), 547*ff*; C. Maggio, *"L'attribuzione della pensione al coniuge divorziato e la novella no. 74 del 1987,"* in *Giur. it.* (1988), I, 1, 473; A. Luminoso, *"La riforma del divorzio: profili di diritto sostanziale (prime impressioni dulla L. 6 marzo 1987, no. 74),"* in *Dir. Famiglia*, II (1988), 457.

providing that he or she is the beneficiary of an allowance under art. 5, has the right to the survivor's pension as long as the pension agreement existed before the divorce decreed was entered.

Finally, if the divorced spouse has not contracted a new marriage, and providing that he or she is the beneficiary of an allowance under art. 5, then he or she is entitled to a percentage of the retirement lump-sum payments owed to the deceased, even if this sum matured after the divorce was decreed.

X. Conclusions

Italian family law has undergone notable transformations since the comprehensive regulation provided by the 1942 Civil Code.[38]

First, family law issues have been subjected to the increasing scrutiny of the Constitutional Court. Since 1948, many ordinary family law issues have gradually acquired constitutional relevance due to their fundamental interrelationship with issues of equality and personal rights of the spouses. Secondly, since 1970, family law has embraced the concept of consecutive marriages (*i.e.* the clear contemplation of divorce in the law treating marriage) and have revised the rules governing the physiological phase of the marriage relationships accordingly. Issues related to custody, child support, and property division have become an integrated and important part of the modern regulation of the family. Additional developments are likely to emerge in the evolution of Italian family law. For example, emerging notions of children's autonomy and the increasing constraints posed on parents' authority are likely to lead toward a re-conceptualization of the traditional notion of individual autonomy within the family.

Finally, the decline of the functional view of family is likely to corrode the understanding of what constitutes a "family" in the modern context. This, in turn, will lead to an expansion of the legal regime of the family, well beyond the traditional domains of family law.

---

[38] For a comparative perspective on the changing role of family law in the United States and Western Europe, *see* M.A. Glendon, *The Transformation of Family Law: State, Law, and Family in the United States and Western Europe*, Chicago University Press, Chicago (1989).

CHAPTER SEVENTEEN

Private International Law

Luca G. Radicati di Brozolo [1]

I. Introduction

This chapter addresses the Italian system of private international law, which here includes the rules on conflicts of laws, conflicts of jurisdiction, and recognition and enforcement of foreign judgments, as well as those on international arbitration.

The analysis is aimed primarily at placing the Italian system in an international context, particularly in light of the recent trends in this area of the law, and will consequently try to focus more on general features rather than on individual rules.[2] My comments presuppose a knowledge of the basics of private international law, and of the main international conventions relevant to the subject, foremost among which are the Brussels Convention of 27 September 1968 on jurisdiction and recognition and enforcement of foreign judgments in civil and commercial matters (the "Brussels Convention") and the "parallel" Lugano Convention of 16 September

---

[1] Professor of Private International Law, Catholic University, Milan.

[2] For recent detailed studies of the subject, *see* Ballarino, *Diritto internazionale privato*, 3rd ed. (1999); Bariatti (ed.), *"Commentario della riforma del sistema italiano di diritto internazionale privato,"* 19 *Nuove leggi civili commentate* 877-1505 (1996); Boschiero, *Appunti sulla riforma del sistema Italiano di diritto internazionale privato* (1996); Gaja (ed.), *La riforma del diritto internazionale e processuale* (1994); Mosconi, *Diritto internazionale privato e processuale*, vol. I (1996), vol. II (1997); Picone, *La riforma del diritto internazionale privato* (1998); Pocar, Treves, Carbone, Giardina, Luzzatto, Mosconi, Clerici, *Commentario del nuovo diritto internazionale privato* (1996); Pocar, *Il nuovo diritto internazionale privato italiano* (1997); Società Italiana di diritto internazionale, *La riforma del diritto internazionale privato italiano* (1997).

Jeffrey S. Lena and Ugo Mattei (eds.), *Introduction to Italian Law*, 431-454
©2002 Kluwer Law International. Printed in the Netherlands.

1988, as well as the Rome Convention of 19 June 1980 on the law applicable to contractual obligations (the "Rome Convention").[3]

II. The Sources

The Italian system of private international law has undergone extensive reform in the past few years. The most sweeping changes have been introduced by law no. 218 of 31 May 1995 (henceforth, the "1995 Law"). This comprehensive statute governs conflicts of laws, the jurisdiction of Italian courts, and the recognition and enforcement of foreign judgments.[4] The 1995 Law, which came into force on 1 September 1995, replaced the previous rules. Conflicts of laws were contained in the preliminary provisions of the Civil Code[5] and jurisdiction and the recognition and enforcement of foreign judgments were contained in the Code of Civil Procedure.[6] These rules dated back to the 1940s, but regarding conflict of laws, they were actually almost identical to the ones contained in the 1865 Civil Code.

The law on international arbitration has also been thoroughly modernized in the context of the general reform of arbitration enacted through law no. 25 of 5 January 1994, which introduced specific rules on arbitration with foreign elements into the Code of Civil Procedure (arts. 832-840).

Italy is a party to a large number of international conventions that set forth uniform rules on conflicts of laws, substantive law, conflicts of jurisdiction and the recognition and enforcement of foreign judgments, and international arbitration.[7]

Moreover, Italy is a member of the European Community. As is increasingly apparent, EC membership is a source of both direct and indirect influence on the member States' private international law systems, primarily because EC membership

---

[3] For an interesting introduction to the general notions of European conflicts law, particularly from the perspective of US lawyers, *see* Reimann, *Conflict of Laws in Western Europe* (1995).

[4] *Gazzetta Ufficiale* No. 128 of 3 June 1995. The text of the 1995 Law is published also in 78 *Riv. di diritto internazionale* 857-874 (1995), and, in an English translation, in 35 *International Legal Materials* 760 (1996). Note that the following subject areas are not discussed in this presentation: adoption; the special conflict rules relating to the law of navigation contained in arts. 5-14 of the *Codice della Navigazione* which have not been affected by the reform; and insolvency.

[5] Articles 17-31.

[6] Articles 2-5 (jurisdiction) and arts. 796-801 regarding foreign judgments.

[7] Foremost among which is the New York Convention of 10 June 1958 on the recognition and enforcement of foreign arbitration awards.

implies participation in of certain international Conventions that are central to these subjects, *i.e.* the Brussels Convention and the Rome Convention.[8] And because conflict rules are contained in European Community legislation on matters such as insurance and consumer contracts, and because the general principles of Community law can influence the application of rules on conflict of laws and of jurisdiction.[9]

III. The General Features of the System

One of the primary aims of the 1995 Law was to modernize the Italian system of private international law particularly in the wake of the reforms in other countries, notably Switzerland, whose law of 18 December 1987 (hereafter the "Swiss Law") provided an important model. The reform also sought to introduce greater harmony with respect to the solutions of the international Conventions to which Italy is a party, most importantly the Brussels Convention. Finally, it was needed to fill the gaps resulting from the declaration of unconstitutionality of a number of conflict rules based on criteria considered no longer acceptable (*e.g.*, the law of the husband with regard to relations between spouses, and of the father with regard to relations between parents and children, which conflicted with the principle of equality of the sexes).

Despite the many novelties introduced by the Brussels Convention from both conceptual and practical viewpoints,[10] on balance the 1995 Law is definitely more of an evolution than a revolution with respect to the previous system.

Among its novel elements worth mentioning is the fact that the 1995 Law deals both with conflicts of law and with what is known in Italy as international civil procedure, *i.e.* jurisdiction and recognition and enforcement of judgments. This seems justified in light of the many common elements between the two subjects and the need for consistent solutions at both levels.

In several respects – particularly with regard to jurisdiction and the enforcement of judgments – the 1995 Law also displays a much greater openness toward foreign

---

[8]   *See* now art. 65 of the EC Treaty as modified by the Amsterdam Treaty of 2 October 1997.

[9]   *See, e.g.*, Radicati di Brozolo, "*L'influence sur les conflits de lois des principes de droit communautaire en matière de liberté de circulation,*" 1993 *Revue critique de droit international privé* 401-424; Radicati di Brozolo, "*Diritto comunitario e regole processuali interne,*" 29 *Riv. di diritto internazionale privato e processuale* 607-614 (1993); *see* Reimann, at 33-34, *supra* note 3 with further references.

[10] Picone, *La riforma del diritto internazionale privato, supra* note 2.

legal systems and solutions. This openness is also a trait of the new rules on international arbitration.

The 1995 Law provides for coordination with international conventions in two ways. First, it contains a provision, art. 2, specifically confirming their supremacy over national law and the requirement that they be interpreted with their international character, and the need for uniform application at the international level to be taken into account. Although it has been labeled merely "narrative," in the sense that it states principles which would apply anyway, this provision may be useful in bringing to the attention of the courts and interested parties the need to take the existence of conventions into account, and to remind judges of their important obligation to apply them. The 1995 Law also contains five provisions that extend the field of application of certain conventions beyond that required by the conventions themselves.[11] The aim of these provisions – which have given rise to an inordinate amount of discussion and to some criticism[12] – is to eliminate frequently unjustified differences of treatment between situations falling respectively under the conventions and outside of them.

Elements of continuity with respect to the old system lie first of all in the fact that the new system still consists of rules, and does not rely on approaches or analyses based on different factors, as is the case with United States conflict-of-laws rules. This is in keeping with the continental European – and in particular Italian – tradition, which tends to favor stability and predictability, as well as the pursuit of the correct solution for broad classes of cases rather than the best solution, which is left to the courts to determine on a case-by-case basis.

Nevertheless, in line with European developments, the hard and fast connecting factors of the past have been abandoned, at least in some cases, and the rules have been built on more flexible criteria aimed at permitting consideration of the specifics of individual cases (notably the principal location of matrimonial life).[13] The 1995 Law contains neither a general "escape clause" (such as art. 15 of the Swiss Law), allowing the judge to depart from the solution mandated by the written rules where these lead to the application of a law which for some reason may be inappropriate,

---

[11] *See* arts. 3, 42, 45, 57 and 59 dealing respectively with the 1968 Brussels Convention (discussed below), the 1961 Hague Convention on the protection of minors, the 1973 Hague Convention on maintenance obligations, the 1980 Rome Convention on the law applicable to contractual relations, and the two Geneva Conventions on bills of exchange and checks.

[12] Salerno (ed.), *Convenzioni internazionali e legge di riforma del diritto internazionale privato* (1997).

[13] Articles 29, 31, 38, and 39.

nor more limited escape clauses for specific categories of cases. In addition, consistent with the broader trend in Europe, in a number of cases the rules are drafted to take directly into account, at the conflicts of law level, the protection of certain substantive interests (for example, *favor filiationis, favor legitimationis*, and the protection of the damaged party).

Continuity with tradition is also apparent in the content of many of the rules, especially in the area of conflicts of law, which for the most part reflect the solutions either spelled out in the written provisions or generally accepted by legal writers and the case law. There are nonetheless several rules for which more modern solutions have been adopted. Moreover, the rules are considerably more numerous than in the past (the 1995 Law contains 74 articles, versus eleven in the previous codification). This allows for most topics to be governed in somewhat greater detail than under the broad rules that they have replaced.

In addition to the greater resort to flexible criteria mentioned above, there has also been an evolution in the nature of the connecting factors used by the rules, both for conflict of laws and conflicts of jurisdiction. Perhaps the most significant evolution in this respect is the fact that the new legislation relies less heavily on nationality than did the old system, which was greatly influenced by the nineteenth-century tradition of P.S. Mancini. Although nationality continues to play a consider-able role, greater emphasis is now placed on domicile. While reflecting the trend that considers domicile a more significant connection than nationality, this emphasis also reflects the changing situation of Italy, which has ceased to be a country of emigration and is now subject to increasing immigrant influxes. Another significant change in the connecting factors – again in keeping with international trends – is the increased role assigned to the will of the parties both in the rules of conflict of laws and in those of conflict of jurisdictions, as well as those on international arbitration. With respect to the conflict of laws, the parties can now influence the applicable law (albeit only within given limits in some cases) in relation not only to contracts, but also to economic relations between spouses (art. 30), succession (art. 46), donations (art. 56), non-contractual liability (art. 62), and products liability (art. 63).

There is also a tendency to use more than one connecting factor for each individual type of situation. Depending on the situation, the applicability of one connecting factor or the other may either be left to the involved parties (such as in the case of relations between spouses, succession, gifts and torts) or governed by strict rules.

Overall, it can probably be said that the new system of private international law is fairly satisfactory, and does not compare too unfavorably with its foreign counterparts. It broadly achieves the aim of modernizing the system and rendering it more understandable, especially to practitioners, while at the same time maintaining a systematic consistency. This is not to say that a number of specific solutions are not beyond criticism, and indeed legal writers have already begun to point out defects and gaps. In more than one instance, a further effort at departing from tradition and old solutions would have been welcome.

IV. Jurisdiction

Given the importance of relations between Italy and the other EC member States, as well as the States which are still parties to the European Free Trade Association, the jurisdiction of Italian courts is governed by the Brussels and Lugano Conventions in a sizeable proportion of international disputes. The remaining rules on jurisdiction are contained in arts. 3-10 of the 1995 Law, as well as in several provisions of this same law dealing with specific subject matters.

These rules have fundamentally changed the perspective of the system, previously based on the postulate that the jurisdiction of Italian courts was universal, and therefore subject only to few limitations. Consistent with that approach, jurisdiction existed whenever the defendant was an Italian national. *Lis alibi pendens* was irrelevant, and the possibility of using a forum selection clause to avoid the jurisdiction of Italian courts was limited.

The new system, which is considerably influenced by the rules of the Brussels Convention, better respects the need to exercise jurisdiction only in the presence of significant contacts with Italy and for coordination with other judicial systems. The rules remain fairly precise and leave courts very little latitude in deciding jurisdictional issues. In particular, there is no place in Italian law for the doctrine of *forum non conveniens*; nor is there a place for other jurisdictional bases recognized in the United States, such as minimum contacts, doing business in the country, or mere presence in the territory. Generally speaking, and despite the inevitable peculiarities and differences on points of detail, the system is in line with the mainstream of continental European conflicts of jurisdiction.

Presently, according to the basic principle, Italian courts may assert jurisdiction whenever the defendant is either domiciled in or is a resident of Italy, with no regard to nationality (art. 3 para. 1). In substance, this applies the *actor sequitur forum rei* principle of the Brussels and Lugano Conventions, although art. 3 also provides for jurisdiction where the defendant has a representative in Italy, within the meaning of art. 77 of the Code of Civil Procedure. Predictably, jurisdiction also exists if it is the object of an agreement or if the defendant does not object to it (art. 4 para. 1).

In addition to the general rule that a defendant may be sued in the forum of his domicile or residence, the 1995 Law lays down several additional rules providing for "special," *i.e.* alternative, *fora*. The first category of such *fora* applies to disputes relating to civil and commercial matters. As is well known, these disputes fall under the Brussels Convention (in the context of intra-European Community relations) and under the parallel Lugano Convention (especially with respect to relations with Switzerland). The rules of these Conventions are by now well known to litigants and to the courts, which apply them consistently, and they have by and large worked satisfactorily. Therefore, also in the interest of avoiding the proliferation of jurisdictional rules, art. 3 para. 1 of the 1995 Law simply incorporates arts. 5-15 of the Brussels Convention. As a result of this incorporation, the jurisdictional criteria of these provisions are likewise declared applicable with regard to civil and commercial disputes where the defendant is domiciled outside of the Community.

These rules of the Brussels Convention therefore now apply to torts, trusts, maintenance, insurance and consumer contracts, as well as general contracts. Among the interesting issues posed with respect to the Brussels Convention is whether it will be possible to request an interpretation of the Convention's rules by the European Court of Justice in cases in which the Convention's rules are applicable as a result of this reference.[14] Another interesting issue is whether Italian courts must abide by the "uniform" interpretation of the Convention's rules, which is mandatory when the Convention is applicable on its own merits, and also when these rules apply as a result of the reference of art. 3.

A further question is whether, in the event of an amendment of the Brussels Convention (such as the one presently under consideration),[15] the jurisdictional criteria applicable to cases falling outside the Convention's scope should be considered to be modified accordingly, or whether the reference in art. 3 is to be interpreted as a reference to a Convention "crystallized" at the time when the 1995 Law came into force. In both cases the reasonable, though not unanimous, answer would seem to be one permitting the survival of the parallelism between the

---

[14] This question has not been rendered totally moot by the judgment of the European Court of Justice of 28 March 1995, *Kleinwort Benson*, C-346/93, in ECJ Reports I-617 (1995): *see* Gaja, "*Il rinvio alla convenzione di Bruxelles*," in Salerno (ed.), *Convenzioni internazionali*, *supra* note 13.

[15] For the latest draft *see* the document of the General Secretariat of the EC Council SN 2581/1/99. The problem referred to in the text might become even more delicate if the Convention were to be replaced by a Regulation under art. 65 of the EC Treaty, following the broadening of the competence of the European Community in matters of private international law.

"general" rules and the rules of the Convention, the desirability of which underlies the reference to the Convention.

The jurisdictional criteria applicable to matters other than civil and commercial ones are somewhat more complicated. Pursuant to the last sentence of art. 3 para. 2, in these cases jurisdiction is determined on the basis of the same criteria which determine the distribution of territorial competence among different domestic courts. This constitutes a departure from the earlier system, under which jurisdictional rules were completely separate from those on territorial competence. From a practical point of view, the solution is rather confusing, especially for foreign lawyers seeking to determine whether Italian courts will have jurisdiction in a given case, since they will have to sort through all the various rules on internal jurisdictional competence that are interspersed throughout Italian legislation. Among the criteria that become applicable as a result of this rule is the domicile of the plaintiff, contemplated by art. 18 of the Code of Civil Procedure. This typically exorbitant forum diverges from the purportedly international spirit of the statute, and there have been scholarly attempts to reduce its scope or even to consider it inapplicable precisely for this reason. In any case, its practical relevance should not be overestimated, if for no other reason than because, at least in some of the cases liable to fall under the general rule laid down by the second sentence of art. 3 para. 2, this rule is inapplicable, owing to the existence of specific rules on jurisdiction contained elsewhere in the 1995 Law.

The 1995 Law contains a number of other provisions dealing with specific classes of cases, some of which confer jurisdiction on Italian courts based on the nationality of the parties (arts. 22, 32, 37, 40, 42, 44, and 50 dealing, respectively, with presumption of death, separation and divorce, affiliation, adoption, protection of minors, and succession). These rules are inspired for the most part by the desire to protect the perceived weaker party, or by the belief that in these classes of cases nationality creates a more significant connection, or by the aim of permitting a parallelism between jurisdiction and applicable law. The same considerations underlie the very broad rule on voluntary jurisdiction (art. 9). Finally, specific rules deal with disputes relating to real property (art. 5 excludes jurisdiction in relation to immovables located outside Italy) and interim measures (art. 10).

The 1995 Law does not deal with jurisdiction with regard to bankruptcy cases; such cases are therefore governed by the rules on domestic competence contained in the bankruptcy law.[16]

---

[16] Salerno, *"Legge di riforma del diritto internazionale privato e giurisdizione fallimentare,"* 34 *Riv. di diritto internazionale privato e processuale* 5-50 (1998).

As to the possibility of excluding the jurisdiction of Italian courts, this is now broadly admitted in favor of foreign courts or arbitration, on condition that the intention of the parties is evidenced in writing and that the dispute relates to "disposable rights" (art. 4 para. 2). This solution is also substantially in accordance with the general trend (and with art. 17 of the Brussels and Lugano Conventions), although the scope of the second exception, drawn from substantive Italian law, is not precisely defined. This might lead to a restrictive interpretation which would contrast with the spirit of the law.

In regard to *lis alibi pendens* and related actions, art. 7 contains two rules that substantially mirror arts. 21 and 22 of the Brussels and Lugano Conventions. In the case of *lis alibi pendens*, the Italian proceedings must be suspended if in the court's opinion the judgment issuing from the foreign proceedings is liable to be recognized in Italy. Proceedings in an Italian court may be resumed if the foreign court declines jurisdiction or if the judgment is not recognized in Italy. Given the difficulties in assessing the likelihood of the recognition of the foreign judgment (*e.g.* in the light of the public policy exception) as well as the time frame involved, the pure and simple extrapolation of a mechanism devised for the homogeneous environment of intra-Community litigation has come under heavy criticism.[17] If the Italian court deems the outcome of the foreign proceedings relevant to the proceedings before it, it is entitled (but not obliged) to suspend them.

V. Conflict of Laws

A. The General Issues

Much like continental textbooks, the 1995 Law's treatment of conflicts of laws begins with a section relating to the general questions of this body of law.[18]

The first of these, art. 13, relates to a centerpiece of traditional scholarly discussion, *i.e. renvoi*, and reverses the previous solution. The reference to another law made by the conflict rules of the foreign law declared applicable by the Italian conflict rule is now taken into account if (i) the *renvoi* is "accepted" by the law so designated (in other words, if that law would be applicable in the case at bar on the basis of its own conflict rules), or if (ii) the *renvoi* leads to the application of Italian

---

[17] Consolo, "*Profili della litispendenza internazionale*," 80 *Riv. di diritto internazionale* 5-77 (1997).

[18] Davì, "*Le questioni generali del diritto internazionale privato nel progetto di riforma*," 73 *Riv. di diritto internazionale* 596 (1990).

law. This new approach – the concrete relevance of which is limited given the small number of cases in everyday practice where issues of *renvoi* actually arise – was considered preferable because it gives greater respect to the harmonization of substantive solutions at the international level. For different reasons, *renvoi* is not taken into account in certain cases, most notably where the conflict rules permit the designation of the applicable law by the parties, in relation to non-contractual obligations and issues of form, and in matters concerning relations between parents and children (in the latter case it can only be taken into account if *renvoi* leads to a substantive solution favorable to the child).

The second general provision deals with the more concretely relevant question of knowledge and evidence of foreign law with regard to which, in the absence of an express rule, the case law was previously divided. Article 14 now unequivocally calls upon the courts to apply foreign law on their own initiative, thereby also obliging them to research the content of foreign rules. This also confirms that foreign law is an issue of law and not of fact, with the further consequence that the erroneous application of foreign law can be raised before the Italian Supreme Court. On the practical side, art. 14 permits the courts to avail themselves of both the instruments provided for by international conventions regarding cooperation in this matter (among which is the London Convention of 7 June 1968) and the assistance of the Ministry of Foreign Affairs and of experts. Since foreign law is law, not fact, it must obviously be applied and interpreted in conformity with the principles prevailing in the relevant foreign legal system (art. 15).

Articles 16 and 17 deal with the classical general exceptions to the application of foreign law, *i.e.*, public policy and mandatory rules. The public policy exception, which requires an analysis of the solution required under the foreign law designated by the conflict rules and a comparison with the basic tenets of the substantive law of the *lex fori*, is no novelty in itself. The novelty is the rule whereby, if the foreign rule is inapplicable because of a contrast with public policy, instead of applying the relevant rules of Italian law, the court must apply the law designated by any other connecting factors applicable in that case (*e.g.*, with regard to a contract, the law of the place of the characteristic performance, if the law chosen by the parties is contrary to public policy).[19] With regard to mandatory rules, art. 17 does nothing more than codify the settled principle that the courts are not to apply the rules of foreign law – regardless of their substantive content – if the subject matter is

---

[19] The same solution, which would apply only in two cases (arts. 28 and 30), is provided for situations in which the judge is unable to ascertain the content of the foreign law rendered applicable by the conflict rules pursuant to art. 14.

governed by a mandatory rule of Italian law. By expressly referring to the mandatory rules of the *lex fori*, this provision appears to reject the solution adopted in art. 7 para. 1, of the Rome Convention (as well as that in art. 19 of the Swiss Law), thereby forbidding the courts from taking into account the mandatory rules of laws other than the *lex fori* and the *lex causae*, even if these have important factual contacts with the situation.

The 1995 Law also contains a provision of particular relevance to conflict situations involving the United States. Pursuant to art. 18, where the Italian conflict rules designate the law of a country with a plurality of legal systems, the applicable law must be identified according to the conflict criteria prevailing in that country. This means that, with specific regard to cases where the connecting factors of the Italian conflict rules point to the United States as the country whose law should be applied, the applicable state law (say, the law of New York state, or the law of California) will be identified by using the American rules governing inter-state conflicts, rather than the Italian rules. The difficulty in this case lies in the fact that in the United States there is no common body of rules governing such conflicts, as each state has its own conflict rules. If the Italian judge were unable to identify the applicable conflict rules, art. 18 para. 2 would require him to apply the rules of the (internal) legal system to which the case is most closely connected.

Unlike the previous system, the new one contains no general provision on form; this subject is dealt with only with regard to the form of specific types of acts (arts. 28; 35 para. 2; 48; 56; 60 para. 2; dealing respectively with marriage, the recognition of natural children, wills, gifts, and agency). In other cases, form is governed by the *lex substantiae*.

The 1995 Law also contains no provision on classification. In all likelihood, this will continue to be made with regard essentially to the *lex fori*, whose rules must nonetheless be interpreted with a certain latitude for this purpose, given the international context. Where the relevant conflict rule is part of an international convention, the principles of interpretation of treaties and the aim of uniformity mandate an autonomous, or at least uniform, classification.

The new rules have for the most part also retained one further feature of the old ones – their bilateral nature. This means that they point indifferently to Italian law or foreign law, depending only on the factual situation considered relevant by the connecting factors applicable in each given instance. Nevertheless, there are traces of other conflict solution methods in the system, including the *lex fori* approach. [20]

---

[20] Picone, *La riforma del diritto internazionale privato*, *supra* note 2.

The system's neutrality is tempered by a provision aimed at dealing with dual citizenship, where citizenship is a connecting factor. Under art. 19 para. 2 of the 1995 Law, when a person is a national both of Italy and of another country, Italian law governs the case. This is a questionable exception to the principle set forth in the same paragraph, and which accords well with international law, whereby regard must be accorded to the nationality most closely connected to the person in question.

Albeit on a somewhat different plane, the system's neutrality is also tempered by the reform's failure to repeal art. 16 of the preliminary provisions of the Civil Code, pursuant to which foreigners enjoy the same civil rights as citizens only on condition of reciprocity. Though its scope is largely limited by international conventions, European Community law, and constitutional guarantees, this much-criticized provision must still be reckoned with.

B. The Individual Conflict Rules

Coming now to the conflict rules in the strict sense, the 1995 Law deals in great detail (arts. 20-50) with the law of persons, of family and personal relations, and of succession. The principal connecting factor remains the national law, although it is now used in a more flexible manner than it was previously, and in many cases may be replaced by a different law identified by means of alternative connecting factors.

With some exceptions, the national law governs most notably the existence, content, and loss of legal capacity – *i.e.*, the ability to hold rights and obligations (art. 25); simultaneous death (art. 22); the legal capacity of natural persons (art. 23); and the rights of personality (such as the right to a name, to privacy, to one's body and one's own image (art. 24)). Article 24 also makes clear that the consequences of the violation of such rights fall under the law governing tort.

With respect to marriage, reference is made to the law of each spouse's nationality to govern their respective capacities and other conditions of entry into marriage, although priority is given to the unmarried status that results from either a decision rendered by an Italian court or a decision which is recognized in Italy (art. 27). The law of nationality also governs the personal relations between spouses when such law is common to both spouses, while in the absence of a common nationality, reference is made to the law of the place where the life of the couple is "prevailingly localized" (art. 29). This flexible criterion, which leaves the courts considerable discretion, is one of the novelties referred to above. The same criteria apply to separation and divorce, with the proviso that these matters fall under Italian law when separation or divorce are not permitted by the applicable foreign law (art. 31).

The second novelty in the context of family relations concerns the economic relations between spouses. While as a general rule these are governed by the law governing personal relations, the married couple is now entitled to choose a different law (art. 30). However, the choice is limited to the law of the country of which at least one of the spouses is a national or a resident, and is possible only if it is valid according to the chosen law or the law of the place where the choice is made. Curiously, the drafters deemed it necessary to include a provision (art. 26) on promises to marry which are today completely irrelevant. Not surprisingly, they are disregarded by other legislation on private international law.

Nationality is also the principal criterion of the rules governing the relations between parents and children (arts. 33-36), but it is the law of the child and not that of the parents which now plays the central role. This is purportedly in deference to substantive considerations, with a view to favoring the interests of the child, as are all the exceptions to this basic rule. The national law is thus in principle called upon to govern affiliation, legitimation, the possibility of recognizing an illegitimate child, and the personal and economic relations between parents and children. If the result is more favorable on the issues of legitimacy, recognition of illegitimate children, or of legitimization, reference must instead be made to the law of either one of the parents.

An even broader approach is taken with regard to adoption, where recourse is made to a multitude of criteria (arts. 38 and 39). These provisions are not very clearly drafted and require, in any case, coordination with the statute governing adoptions,[21] which contains several provisions on international adoptions, and which is specifically declared applicable to adoptions of minors liable to lead to the acquisition of the status of legitimate child.

The protection of minors and maintenance obligations within the family are two of the matters with regard to which the 1995 Law adopts the conflict rules of international Conventions (the 1961 and the 1973 Hague Conventions, respectively) by declaring them applicable even to cases falling outside their scope of application (arts. 42 and 45). In the first case, the reference is somewhat awkward because the 1961 Hague Convention in question had already been revised at the time of entry into force of the law, and thus the entry into force of the new Convention would seem to require a modification of the general conflict rule. The criterion of the nationality of the person requiring protection is called upon again with regard to the protection of adults, but courts are permitted to refer to the *lex fori* where interim measures are needed to protect the person or the assets of a disabled person.

---

[21] Law no. 184 of 1983.

Succession and gifts are treated similarly. Although this is consistent with Italian substantive law, it is somewhat surprising, since gifts notoriously fall under the Rome Convention, and the scope of the provisions on gifts of the 1995 Law thus emerges as rather unclear. Also with respect to these two types of situation, following past tradition, the basic criterion remains the national law of the testator and of the donor (arts. 46 and 56, respectively). In a departure from the previous system, certain concessions are made to the will of the persons involved. Both the testator and the donor are indeed free to choose the law of their country of residence (at the time of death, in the case of wills) to govern the succession and the gift. In order to reduce the chances of invalidity, successions and gifts are considered valid as to form if they conform either to the law governing the substance or to the law of the place where the will or the gift is made. In the case of successions, several other laws may come into play as well (*see* art. 48). With regard to successions, the substantive rules of Italian law protecting certain heirship categories are declared applicable regardless of the governing law, when the testator is Italian and the heirs reside in Italy.

With regard to real rights, art. 51 abides by the previous and universal principle of the *lex rei sitae*. This law governs possession, property, pledges, mortgages, etc. in movables and immovables, and applies both to the acquisition and the loss of the right, save in those cases in which this results from a succession, a family relation, or a contract. Article 51 thus confirms that the relationship giving rise to the real right is subject to its own governing law (typically the law governing the succession or the contract by effect of which the property, possession, or other real right is transferred), while the content of the right is governed by the *lex situs*. The 1995 Law also contains a few new provisions that clarify issues related to real rights formerly plagued by uncertainty. Article 52 deals with real rights in *res in transitu*, declaring these to be subject to the law of the country of destination, which may obviously lead to difficulties where – as is often the case in modern commerce – the destination of the travelling goods changes or is unknown. Article 53 handles *Usucapio* by subjecting it to the law of the *situs* of the good at the end of the period for perfection. Finally, art. 54 provides that rights in non-material goods (trademarks, patents, and other forms of intellectual property) are subjected to the law of the place where they are utilized. The publicity of the acts giving rise to the creation, transfer, or extinction of real right are governed by the law of the State in which the good is located at the moment when the act is made.

With respect to the fundamental issue of the law governing contracts, the 1995 Law can afford to be quite brief, because the subject is comprehensively dealt with in the Rome Convention, which – being a convention *erga omnes* – also governs contracts having no contacts with the other contracting parties of the Convention, or which might be governed by the laws of a non-contracting country. As a result, only a very small number of contracts fall outside the scope of the Rome Convention (*i.e.*, those belonging to the categories listed in art. 1 thereof). It is thus only with these contracts that the 1995 Law was called upon to deal, and it has done this by resorting to the aforementioned technique of incorporation. Article 57 quite simply declares that contractual obligations are "in any case" governed by the Rome Convention. Since the meaning of this provision is often misunderstood, it is worth clarifying that whenever a case falls within the scope of the Rome Convention, the applicability of the latter does not depend on art. 57, which is therefore relevant only to contracts not governed by the Convention.

The Convention's concise treatment of contractual obligations stands in marked contrast to the apparent detail of the 1995 Law on the subject of non-contractual obligations. Six articles (58-63) are now devoted to a number of disparate matters previously considered to fall under a single, very general provision. Article 58 is concerned with unilateral promises (such as promises to pay, recognition of debt, and promises to the public), which it subjects to the law of the country in which they are made public.

Negotiable instruments are dealt with in a long, but rather unsatisfactory provision (art. 59) that considers promissory notes and checks separately from other instruments.[22] The first type of instruments are the object of the last reference of the 1995 Law to international conventions, *i.e.* the 1931 and 1933 Geneva Conflict of Laws Conventions. Since it was not clear whether, with regard to Italy, these Conventions applied to all bills and checks (as the Conventions permit but do not require), art. 59 paras. 1 and 2 explicitly extend their validity across the board. This measure has the advantages of eliminating an unwarranted difference of treatment between bills and checks issued in different places and of rendering applicable considerably detailed (if now perhaps no longer totally satisfactory) conflict rules. With regard to other types of negotiable instrument, art. 59 para. 3 stands by the solution that was previously considered to apply, inasmuch as it declares applicable the law of the place of issue of the instrument. This provision is heavily influenced by the substantive law approach of Italian law to this matter. It gives rise to a problem of coordination with the Rome Convention, since in most countries other than Italy, negotiable instruments are considered to be of a contractual rather than non-contractual nature. In short, one can say that paragraph 3 is overly broad, in that it gives similar treatment to instruments having little in common, even though

---

[22] Radicati di Brozolo, "*La legge regolatrice dei titoli di credito,*" 51 *Banca, borsa e titoli di credito* 434-458 (1998).

a different conflict rule would have been appropriate for some (for instance, shares and bonds, which would be more appropriately governed by the law of the company and the proper law of the loan, respectively). At the same time, it relies on an archaic and inept connecting factor and – like many other rules of the 1995 Law – it is too general because it fails to provide solutions to myriad problems.

Voluntary representation in a professional context is the object of the third provision (art. 60), which stipulates the applicability of the law of the country in which the agent has his place of business – provided, however, that this is known to the third party. In other cases the agents' powers are subject to the law of the country in which they are exercised.

Obligations arising at law (notably *negotiorum gestio*, unjust enrichment, and restitution) are stipulated to be governed by the law of the place in which the facts giving rise to them occur (art. 61). This provision is also archaic and unduly influenced by substantive law (which also stands behind the Italian reservation to art. 10 para. 1e) of the Rome Convention). The provision's most serious flaw lies in the fact that it would seem not to permit an "accessory" connection where these types of obligations are closely connected to other situations (for example, where a claim for restitution arises in the context of a contractual relationship) and would more appropriately be governed by the law governing the "principal" relationship. Perhaps, however, arguments can be found to circumvent the literal application of this rule.[23]

Articles 62 and 63 deal with the delicate issue of the law governing tort, which is notoriously one of the fields of conflicts of laws that have given rise to the most heated discussions and "revolutionary" movements.[24] While remaining faithful to the basic tenets of the traditional Italian approach on this matter, these provisions have introduced a few, albeit not very brave, concessions to more modern trends.

Article 62, which sets forth the general rule, follows the traditional approach of the *lex loci delicti*, but is somewhat more detailed and flexible than the rule it has replaced. First of all, the new rule is more precise with regard to the identification of the *locus delicti*, now clearly identified as the one where the tortious activity has its effects, rather than the (possibly different) one where the action giving rise to liability occurs. This can give rise to a *depeçage*, where the tort has effects in more than one country. The real novelty is that this conflict rule provides for alternative

---

[23] Radicati di Brozolo, "*La ripetizione dell'indebito nel diritto internazionale privato e processuale,*" *Collisio legum, Beiträge zum internationalen Privatrecht für Gerardo Broggini* 421 (1997).

[24] Davì, *La responsabilità extracontrattuale nel nuovo diritto internazionale privato Italiano* (1997).

criteria. In a further instance in which the applicable law can be influenced by the will of the interested party, the damaged party has the option to request the application of the law of the country where the tortious event has occurred. It is not specified when this option is to be made, and whether the choice can be made before the event's occurrence. A further, and probably excessively rigid, exception to the general rule concerns cases where all the parties involved are nationals and residents of the same country, in which case the law of that country is applicable. Article 62 has been criticized because it is too general and seeks to apply to all kinds of tort, while it would perhaps have been more sensible to allow for greater flexibility or to devise specific rules for certain types of torts (such as libel, unfair competition, violation of antitrust rules, violation of rules on insider trading, and other financial legislation).

The 1995 Law does, however, contain a specific provision at least for product liability, which is not subject to the general principle of the *lex loci delicti* (art. 63). In this case the applicable law is chosen by the damaged party, who has the choice between the law of the domicile or the seat of the manufacturer and that of the place of purchase of the good, save in the event that the latter has been put on the market in this country without the consent of the manufacturer, who bears the burden of proof on this point. A small difference between the two provisions lies in the role of the damaged party in determining the governing law: under the general rule, the law of the place of the event is applied by default, unless the damaged party specifically requests the contrary, while under art. 63 the choice would seem to be in the hands of the purchaser.

Finally, the 1995 Law contains a new provision (art. 25) on companies, associations, foundations, and other entities, the conflict rules relating to which used to be the object of considerable debate. The basic criterion is now the place of incorporation, but a special unilateral rule is laid down for companies having the seat of their management in Italy or operating for the most part in Italy. In this case, Italian law applies. Article 25 also sets forth the matters governed by the applicable law in considerable detail, and specifies that the transfer of the corporate seat from one country to another, as well as mergers between companies in different countries, are effective only if permitted by the laws of both countries concerned.

VI. Foreign Judgments

As mentioned, the rules on recognition and enforcement of foreign judgments are among the most innovative of the entire 1995 Law.

The principal novelty of this point is in the adoption of the approach taken by the Brussels and Lugano Conventions, which distinguish between recognition and enforcement of foreign judgments and greatly simplify the procedure. Like arts. 27 and 28 of the Brussels Convention, art. 64 of the 1995 Law provides that foreign judgments are automatically effective in Italy; that is to say, they are effective without the need for a pronouncement of an Italian court, as was normally required under the previous system. This effect is subject to a number of conditions: (i) that the foreign court had jurisdiction according to the principles governing the jurisdiction of Italian courts; (ii) that the defendant had been given proper notice of the proceedings and that there has been no violation of the rights of defense; (iii) that the parties appeared in the proceedings, or that default was properly declared; (iv) that the foreign judgment is final according to the foreign law; (v) that it is not contrary to a judgment of an Italian court; (vi) that there are no proceedings between the same parties having the same subject matter that are pending before an Italian court and have been initiated before the start of the foreign proceedings; and (vii) that the effects of the judgment are not contrary to public policy. These grounds are practically identical to those foreseen by the Brussels Convention. The only elements that do not coincide with the Brussels Convention are those relating to the jurisdiction of the foreign court and to *lis alibi pendens*. This is easily explained by the fact that the Brussels Convention is a "closed" Convention dealing with jurisdiction as well.

An intervention of the Italian courts is required only where the recognition of the foreign judgment is contested (on the assumption that the foreign judgment does not satisfy one or more of the above-mentioned conditions) or where enforcement is sought. In this case "anybody having an interest" (which would not seem to be limited to the party in whose favor the foreign decision was rendered) may request that the court ascertain the existence of the conditions for recognition (art. 67). This mechanism is clearly similar to that of art. 31 of the Brussels Convention, and it likewise rules out any possibility of a revision of the merits of the foreign judgment (previously this was possible if the defendant failed to appear in the foreign proceedings). The difference between the two mechanisms is that under the Brussels Convention, the decision granting enforcement is adopted without hearing the party against whom the judgment is invoked. Adversary proceedings take place only where such decision is contested. Under art. 67 of the 1995 Law, the decision granting enforcement is, instead, adopted only after normal proceedings. Although this is not specified in the Law, it would seem that the competence with respect to these proceedings lies with the Courts of Appeal, which means that they are subject to only one level of judgment on the merits.

In addition to the procedure for recognition of foreign judgments governed by art. 64, the 1995 Law provides for a further mechanism for recognition, limited to matters of the capacity of persons, the existence of family relations, and rights of personality. Under art. 65, foreign decisions (the term used is *provvedimenti*, which would seem to include both judgments of courts and decisions of administrative authorities) on these matters have effect in Italy if they have been issued by the authorities of the State whose law is designated by the Italian conflict rules to govern these matters. This effect is conditional only with respect to Italian public policy and the rights of defense, and not to the further requirements of art. 64. This rule, based on a conflicts of laws approach to recognition, codifies a solution developed by scholars and courts under the previous system in order to permit the automatic recognition of certain foreign judgments notwithstanding the rule which made even recognition conditional upon a decision of the Italian court. This solution is perhaps less necessary now, since automatic recognition is possible under art. 64. Among the numerous problems raised by art. 65 is whether decisions on the matters contemplated by this provision are also susceptible to recognition under art. 64. Under art. 66, the same solution also applies to decisions in non-adversary proceedings (such as those relating to adoptions, declarations of incapacity, etc.).

This new mechanism for the recognition of foreign judgments and decisions (which is revolutionary with respect to the previous system, although it recalls the one applied from 1865 to 1919) has encountered considerable opposition because of its purportedly excessive openness. The contending argument states that automatic recognition and the reduction of the grounds for control on enforcement are acceptable in a closed system based on reciprocity, such as those of the Brussels and Lugano Conventions. But they may be dangerous if applied on a general scale, thereby affording automatic recognition to judgments of countries with potentially very different legal systems and traditions which do not afford the same procedural and substantive guarantees, and which moreover are not bound by reciprocal obligations with regard to Italian judgments.

These arguments, voiced particularly by the Ministry of Justice and the *ufficiali di stato civile* (an office that performs many of the same functions as the "Recorders Office" in the US system), engendered the delay of the entering into force of this part of the Law[25] as well as that of a number of attempts at modifying art. 67. The delicacy of the issue is evinced by the instructions issued by the Ministry of Justice to the *ufficiali di stato civile* with regard to situations in which a foreign judgment or decision is used to support a request for the registration of a matter concerning the status of a natural person. If the *ufficiali di stato civile* have doubts as to the

---

[25] Title IV of the 1995 law on the effects of foreign judgments and acts came into force more than a year after the rest of the law, on 31 December 1996.

compliance of the foreign decision with the conditions for recognition set out in art. 64, they are instructed to submit the matter to the public prosecutor, who will express an opinion based on these doubts. Relying on this opinion, *ufficiale di stato civile* will then decide whether or not to recognize the foreign judgment or decision. If the decision is negative, it will be up to the interested party to commence the proceedings for recognition foreseen by art. 67. Given the difficulty for the *ufficiale di stato civile* and the prosecutor to ascertain the fulfillment of many of the conditions for recognition (especially in the absence of adversary proceedings), in practice there will likely be a tendency to refuse recognition, thereby obliging the parties to seek recourse in the courts under art. 67.

The 1995 Law also contains provisions on the procedure for gathering evidence in Italy in the context of foreign proceedings (arts. 69 and 70), and on the service of process in Italy regarding foreign proceedings in Italy (art. 71).

VII. Arbitration

Like the reform of the rule on conflict of laws and on conflicts of jurisdiction, the reform of the law on international arbitration was aimed at modernizing the system as well as rendering Italy more "arbitration-friendly," in keeping with the trend followed by many other countries.

The rules on international arbitration are contained in two sections of the Code of Civil Procedure, dealing respectively with "international arbitration" in the technical sense (arts. 832-838) and with the recognition and enforcement of foreign awards (arts. 839 and 840).[26] Both sections expressly confirm the applicability of the international conventions to the matter to which Italy is a party.

As a result of the reform, Italian law now deals with three categories of arbitration and award: (i) purely domestic (Italian) arbitration, which is not relevant here; (ii) "international" arbitration, and (iii) foreign arbitration.

A. International Arbitration

The concept of "international" arbitration is new to Italian law. The term "international" arbitration refers to a special category of arbitration, which – like domestic and unlike foreign arbitration – is Italian, in the sense that it is governed by Italian law; the difference with respect to ordinary domestic arbitration is that "inter-

---

[26] Luzzatto, *"L'arbitrato internazionale e i lodi stranieri nella nuova disciplina legislativa italiana,"* 30 *Riv. di diritto internazionale e processuale* 256 (1994).

national" arbitration is governed by a special set of rules giving rise to a considerably more liberal substantive and procedural regime than the one applicable to domestic arbitration.

The introduction of this special regime – which is warranted by the presence of foreign, or international, elements in the underlying relationships – is a response to the general trend aimed at granting parties to international relationships a large degree of freedom regarding both the substantive rules governing their relationship and the means of settlement of the disputes liable to arise. It is also aimed at rendering Italy more attractive as a seat for international arbitration, whose parties traditionally preferred more liberal jurisdictions, such as London, Paris, or Geneva.

Although not explicitly stated, it is implied that the rules on international arbitration apply to what are considered by Italian law to be Italian arbitrations, by reason of the fact that their "seat" is in Italy. This does not mean that the arbitration proceedings must actually be held wholly, or even in part in Italy. Nor does it mean that the award must be rendered in Italian territory. The seat is, in fact, simply the product of a decision of the parties or, failing that, of the arbitrators. This means that the seat of arbitration in Italy (which is thus the unilateral connecting factor rendering Italian arbitration law applicable) coincides with the decision to submit the arbitration to Italian law with regard to procedure.

The applicability of the more liberal regime referred to above is reserved to those arbitrations having their seat in Italy which are "international." For these purposes, an arbitration is considered international (thereby qualifying for submission to the special regime) if one of the parties was not an Italian resident or did not have office in Italy at the time of execution of the arbitration clause, or if a significant (but not necessarily the most significant) portion of the obligations arising from the underlying relationship had to be performed abroad (art. 832). Given the freedom of every State to determine the criteria establishing whether a given arbitration is submitted to its own law, it could of course happen that an arbitration considered an Italian "international" arbitration is also considered by another State to be governed by its own law.

The drafting technique adopted by the legislator is relatively simple. It is stipulated (art. 832) that international arbitration is governed by the rules applicable to domestic arbitration (arts. 806-831), with the exceptions listed in arts. 833-838. In practice, these exceptions are significant because they afford the parties or arbitrators a large degree of freedom in determining both the substantive and the procedural rules governing their arbitration, as is deemed necessary to satisfy the needs of international commerce.

The exceptions in favor of international arbitration concern the formal requirements for the validity of the arbitration clause, the rules applicable to the merits of the dispute, the language of the arbitration, the removal of the arbitrators, the decision, and the annulment of the award.

With respect to the validity of the arbitration clause, art. 833 recognizes the validity of clauses contained in general conditions by declaring the formal requirements set out in the Civil Code inapplicable (arts. 1341 and 1342), and by stipulating simply that the clause contained in such conditions is valid if the parties were, or should have been, aware of it.

On the complex matter of the law applicable to the merits, art. 834 allows the parties to choose the substantive rules to be applied by the arbitrators and to empower the arbitrators to decide *ex aequo et bono*. The reference to "rules" rather than to laws is interpreted as meaning that the parties are also free to designate bodies of rules (such as the *lex mercatoria* or specific trade usages) in lieu of a national law. Failing a choice by the parties, the arbitrators must apply the law to which the relationship is most closely related. This provision, which clearly echoes the Rome Convention, is a direct conflict rule, and does away with the need for the arbitrators to identify a conflict system through which to determine the applicable law. In keeping with the general trend in international arbitration, the last paragraph of art. 834 calls upon the arbitrators to take into account the "indications of the contract and the uses of commerce" as well.

The parties to international arbitrations are also left free to determine the language of the arbitration, as well as the rules on the removal of arbitrators and the adoption of the award (arts. 835-837). The section on international arbitration contains no reference to the procedural rules of the arbitration; more specifically, it does not contain a rule permitting the parties or the arbitrators to govern the matter, as has by now become the norm in international arbitration. However, this freedom is set forth in the rules governing domestic arbitration (art. 816 CCP) and therefore applies also to international arbitration.

Since international arbitrations are Italian arbitrations, they are subject to the Italian procedural regime for annulment of the award (arts. 827-831). However, in this regard too, the system is more liberal than it is with respect to domestic arbitration (art. 838). Unless the parties to international arbitration expressly stipulate the contrary, certain rules applicable to domestic arbitration are not applicable to international arbitration rules. Most notably, the award is not subject to annulment for failure by the arbitrators to correctly apply the rules on the merits and, where the award is annulled on other grounds (*e.g.* invalidity of the arbitration clause, or the failure to follow the principles of due process pursuant to Code of Civil Procedure art. 829), the decision on the merits is not left to the court having declared the nullity of the award.

As a result of these rules, parties to international transactions can now choose to arbitrate under Italian law and yet maintain essentially the same degree of freedom they would have under the arbitration laws of the jurisdictions most commonly associated with international arbitration. In particular, the choice of Italian law affords the parties full recourse to institutionalized arbitration under, for instance, the rules of the International Chamber of Commerce or other such bodies.

B. The Recognition of Foreign Awards

As regards "foreign" arbitrations, a term that includes all arbitrations not governed by Italian law (be they domestic or international), it is obvious that these can be dealt with by Italian law only with regard to the recognition and enforcement of the resulting awards in Italy. Because Italy has been a party to the 1958 New York Convention since it entered into force, this problem no longer raises major issues of principle.

The two new provisions governing this matter (arts. 839 and 840) are thus aimed essentially at providing a more expeditious procedural framework for recognition and enforcement, in keeping with art. III of the New York Convention, which had remained unimplemented in Italian law. Until the reform, recognition and enforcement of foreign awards were subject to normal proceedings before the Court of Appeal, and thus the procedure was considerably more onerous than that required for national awards, contrary to art. III.

The new procedure governed by arts. 839 and 840 of the Code of Civil Procedure is modeled on the one applicable to foreign judgments under the Brussels Convention (at least until the next revision), and now that under arts. 64-67 of the 1995 Law. Under this system, the party intending to avail itself of a foreign award is required to file an application with the President of the competent Court of Appeal, who must declare the award enforceable, subject only to a verification that the dispute could form the object of arbitration and that the award is compatible with public policy. At this stage there is no place for adversary proceedings. As under art. 31 of the Brussels Convention, adversary proceedings are possible only where the decree granting or denying enforcement is contested. The resultant proceedings take place before the Court of Appeal, whose decision to refuse enforcement can be based only on the five well-known grounds set forth in art. V of the New York Convention, which are reproduced almost word-for-word in art. 840. The Court of Appeal may suspend its proceedings if the validity of the award is contested before the courts of the country under whose law the award was rendered.

CHAPTER EIGHTEEN

How to Find the Law

Giovanni Pascuzzi [1]

This chapter provides a brief overview of the ways in which legal information is stored and used in Italy, and where that information can be found.[2] It further provides a brief bibliography of English-language academic sources related to Italian law to assist the reader in further research in the field.

I. Legal Data

The jurist is called upon to solve problems of a legal nature, searching for the law that governs the matter and then applying it. These are two very distinct actions. On the one hand, there is the activity of seeking out the law to apply; on the other, there is the activity of constructing the reasoning that will yield a solution.

The expression "search for the law" denotes complex activities, both conceptual and operational, which present space constraints allow me only to sketch out briefly. I shall therefore restrict my treatment to an examination of the ways in which legal practitioners find the information that they require for their work, and I will deal specifically with legislation, case law and scholarship.

A. How Legal Information Becomes known in the Italian System

If legal information is to perform its role, it must be knowable and readily accessible.

First, in some cases, the legal system requires that certain acts and documents be published for them to have force and effect, and to ensure that legal texts circulate in the society as well. Legislative acts provide an example.

---

[1] Professor of Private Comparative Law, University of Trento.

[2] For more detailed treatment, *see* Pascuzzi, *Cercare il diritto* (book & interactive CD-ROM), Bologna (1998).

Jeffrey S. Lena and Ugo Mattei (eds.), *Introduction to Italian Law*, 455-496
©2002 Kluwer Law International. Printed in the Netherlands.

Secondly, in individual cases before Italian courts, the Italian legal system requires the formal filing of judicial documents and decisions in the *cancelleria*, or records office. Although this process serves the knowledge requirements of the parties to a suit, it does not ensure – and is by no means designed to ensure – the generalized knowability of decisions by the courts. There is, in fact, no official system in Italy for the public disclosure of court decisions corresponding to the publication of "official reports" in the United States. An exception is made for the judgments of the *Corte Costituzionale*, or Constitutional Court, which are treated as State legislative documents, and for the digests of decisions rendered by the *Corte di Cassazione*, the Supreme Court (court of last resort) for most criminal and civil proceedings, which are published by the *Ufficio del Massimario*. The lacunae left by the lack of official reports is filled by means of specialized publications and periodicals containing the texts of judicial pronouncements, edited by private practitioners and publishers.

Thirdly, the authors of scholarly efforts can disseminate their work only by gaining access to the publishing circuit of books and periodicals maintained by a number of prominent legal publishing houses.

Thus those wishing to obtain legal data must consult publications that disseminate legal materials. These publications may be official in character, but they are more frequently produced through the initiative of private individuals or organizations. Some of them contain statutes and regulations, others are concerned with case law, yet others publish scholarly writings. There are also numerous publications that combine materials of different kinds (*e.g.*, scholarship and case law). Some are periodicals, some are books and series, and others are specialized publications serving specialized branches of the law.

B. Paper Editions and Computerized Editions

Traditionally, Italian legal materials – books, periodicals, case law digests, collections of statutes, and the like – are conserved and disseminated in paper form. The advent of computers, however, has revolutionized the situation. It is now possible to consult legal materials not only in paper publications, but also by computer on CD-ROMs, and by accessing online databases.

The first part of this chapter discusses paper editions. The second part describes the types of legal data that can be obtained from CD-ROMs or online.

It should be stressed, however, that the passage from books to bytes in the storage, representation, and dissemination of legislation, case law, and scholarship will have profound repercussions on the workings of the legal system and, more generally, on legal culture.[3]

C. How Legal Information Is Identified

In Italy, legal documents may be distinguished from one another by means of several identifying elements. Legislative documents are distinguished according to (i) the nature of the document (*e.g.*, a State statute, a regional statute, an administrative regulation); (ii) the document's date; (iii) the progressive number, if it is in series; and (iv) its title or rubric. For example, *Legge 24 dicembre 1969, no. 990, Assicurazione obbligatoria della responsabilità civile derivante dalla circolazione dei veicoli a motore*, is a parliamentary statute (*Legge*) of specified description and date.

The following image charts the Italian system of courts from the lower Civil, Criminal and Administrative Courts through first level appeals, the Court of State, Court of Cassazione, the Constitutional Court, and the Court of Justice of the European Union. A judicial document is first distinguished according to the issuing body and the type of act set out in it. The basic system of courts issuing materials is set out below.

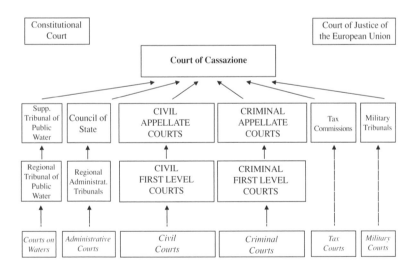

---

[3]   For more detailed treatment, *see* Pascuzzi, *Il diritto fra tomi e bit. Generi letterari e ipertesti*, Padua (1997).

The document is followed by a description of the nature of the judicial act: *sentenza* (judgment), *ordinanza* (ordinance), *decreto* (decree). When left unspecified, such judicial acts are understood to be judgments. The section of the jurisdictional body that has issued the act is also usually specified, along with the date on which the court handed down the decision, and, usually, the number of the names of the parties[4] – for example, *Cassazione 17 gennaio 1994 no. 370*.

Scholarly studies are distinguished by the name of the author, the title of the study, publishing and other typographical information (place and date of publication, publishing house; or if it is a law review, by the title, year, part, and page).

D. How Legal Information Is Cited

When it is necessary to cite a document in a written text, the usual practice is to employ abbreviations.

For legislative documents, these abbreviations essentially refer to the title of the document, as in the following list of examples:

Title	*Abbreviation*	
Costituzione	Cost.	Constitution: The body of fundamental rules and principles.
Codice civile	Cod. civ.	Civil Code: The set of rules on private relations (persons, family, inheritance, property, contracts, torts)
Codice di procedura civile	C.p.c.	Code of civil procedure
Codice penale	C.p.	Criminal Code: The set of rules on crimes.
Codice di procedura penale	C.p.p.	Code of criminal procedure
Legge	L.	A statute passed by the Parliament
Decreto legge	D.l.	An act of the Government with the same force of the statute
Decreto legislativo	D.lgs.	A statute delegated to the Government
Decreto ministeriale	D.m.	An administrative regulation

---

[4] If the name of the party appears immediately after the date, the document is a provision issued by the criminal jurisdiction.

A legislative document with a progressive number can be identified by means of this number and the year of publication – *e.g.*, *legge 990/1969*.

To cite case law, the following abbreviation scheme for jurisdictional bodies is usually adopted:

Body	*Abbreviation*
Corte Costituzionale	Corte cost.
Corte di cassazione	Cass.
Corte d'appello	App.
Tribunale	Trib.
Pretura	Pret.
Consiglio di Stato	Cons. Stato
Tribunale amministrativo regionale	Tar

Judicial documents with a progressive number can be identified by number and year of publication – *e.g.*, *Cass. 370/1994*.

Periodicals that publish legal documents are usually cited in abbreviated form, as in the following examples:

Periodical	*Abbreviation*
Il Foro italiano	Foro it.
Giurisprudenza italiana	Giur. it.
Rivista di diritto processuale	Riv. dir. proc.
Rassegna di diritto civile	Rass. dir. civ.
Giurisprudenza costituzionale	Giur. costit.
Giurisprudenza commerciale	Giur. comm.

A detailed list of the abbreviations used for the most widely circulating periodicals can be found on the opening pages of *Repertorio del Foro italiano* (discussed below).

Finally, it should be pointed out that in Italy there is nothing like the American *Bluebook – A Uniform System of Citation*. There is no set of general rules about the way to cite legal publications, and different authors therefore adopt different citation methods.

E. How Legal Information Is Handled

In the Italian system, as in others, the mass of information that jurists must master is considerably larger today than it was in the past. It is claimed that Italy likely has more than 100,000 statutes. The Supreme Court alone issues more than 15,000 opinions every year, while hundreds of thousands of judgments are entered in the various jurisdictions. A small but substantial proportion of these judgments are published in the more than 200 Italian law journals. And Italian legal experts annually write thousands of books and articles. How can one navigate one's way through this ocean of materials when looking for something specific?

Help is provided by specialized publications designed to facilitate the search for legal information. In these publications, known as digests, all the materials produced in a certain period (usually one year) are catalogued in grids under headings and subheadings, making it possible to handle.

In consulting the heading under which the sought-for item may appear, one finds the identifying elements of the materials (statutes, judgments, essays) that have dealt with the topic in the period of time in question, together with a reference to the book or journal containing the actual text of the document. It is also possible to obtain the information via other sources, such as the name of an author.

These publications – of which the prime examples are the digests of legislation, scholarship and case law are discussed below.

II. Statutes and Regulations

Statutes and regulations usually are texts (comprising one or more sections and articles) produced by a particular subject according to particular procedures. The subjects empowered to enact rules, and the procedures whereby a text becomes a normative text, are set out by the so-called Rules on Rule Production set forth as arts. 70*ff* of the Italian Constitution, under which a text which has been both approved by the two chambers of Parliament (subjects) and promulgated by the President of the Republic (procedures) is to be considered a valid statute of the State.

These constitute the most important source of law in Italy, although they are by no means the only source of law.

It would obviously be beyond the scope of this chapter to undertake detailed discussion of the sources of Italian law. Merely for the sake of classification, I would point out that numerous subjects are empowered to enact normative texts, most notably, the International Community;[5] the European Union; the *Parlamento Italiano* (State Parliament), the *Consigli Regionali* (regional Parliaments); and the *pubblica amministrazione* (public administration).

The sources of law also differ according to the various types of enactments, which are usually of differing legal force and thus give rise to a hierarchy among sources. In descending order of importance the hierarchy is: Constitutional rules, European Community rules, State legislative rules; regional legislative rules; administrative regulations, and *consuetudini*, or customs.

That said, we may now turn to the paper-based means by which legislation is disseminated in Italy.

Publication is a necessary condition for the entry into force of the legislative acts belonging to the various categories envisaged by the Italian legal system. Consequently, knowledge of normative acts is ensured principally by the official publications used by the subjects empowered to enact statutes and regulations. Note, however, that normative acts can also be consulted in periodicals and books published by private practitioners. I shall now discuss the distinction between official and private publications.

A. Official Publications

1. Gazzetta Ufficiale Della Repubblica Italiana

The *Gazzetta Ufficiale* is the official journal of the Italian State. It is published in two parts. The first part consists of several "series." Presently printed are the "General Series;" the "First special series" on the Constitutional Court (published on Wednesdays); the "Second special series" on the European Community (published on Mondays and Thursdays); the "Third special series" on Regional Administration (published on Saturdays); and the "Fourth special series" on Procurement Contracts and Examinations (published on Tuesdays and Fridays).

The first part of the *Gazzetta Ufficiale* publishes several important materials: those legislative acts enacted by the organs of the State (*e.g.*, statutes and decrees with the force of statute); those judicial acts before the Constitutional Court; those acts relative to international treaties signed by Italy; the acts and notices concerning citizens that are publicized for information purposes; those legislative enactments by the regional and autonomous provincial administrations; and the legislative acts of the European Union (*e.g.*, directives and regulations).

---

[5] International treaties signed by Italy are published in the Gazzetta Ufficiale (*see below*, in the text).

The second part of the *Gazzetta Ufficiale*, entitled the *Foglio delle Inserzioni*, contains private notices, such as announcements of corporation meetings.

Consultation of a legislative text is often hampered by two difficulties: first, the frequent references made to the particulars of other legislative provisions; secondly, the need to reconstruct the law in force. To obviate these difficulties, the *Gazzetta Ufficiale* publishes the text of the statutes cited in the footnotes. If a statute or some other legislative act provides for the removal, addition, or replacement of one or more words from a previous statute, the *Gazzetta Ufficiale* reproduces the entire text of the provision resulting from the changes made. The editors highlight these changes by printing them in a different font.

Indices to the *Gazzetta Ufficiale* are published on a monthly basis and in an annual cumulative separate volume. Each of the series into which the *Gazzetta* is currently divided has its own index. There are also indices of *errata corrige*.

In relation to the diverse types of documents published in the various series, there may be a numerical index, a chronological index, or a subject index. The numerical index orders the documents according to the progressive numbering assigned to them. The chronological index arranges them according to the date of issue. The subject index consists of a list of keywords, under which are grouped all the documents relevant to it.

Some of the acts published in the *Gazzetta Ufficiale* are republished in another official collection, the *Raccolta Ufficiale degli atti normativi della Repubblica Italiana*.

2. The Official Bulletins of the Regional Administrations

Each Region of Italy (as well as the Autonomous Provinces of Trento and Bolzano) has its own official publications: official bulletins that publish regional statutes and other legislative acts of a regional scope.

B. Private Publications

The dissemination of legislative documents is also ensured by unofficial publications edited by expert jurists and produced by private publishing houses. Practitioners in search of a legislative text most frequently make use of this type of publication, for several reasons.

The official publications are usually costly, bulky, and difficult to obtain. Moreover, they rarely provide the current text of legislative acts that have been subjected to modifications (a significant exception is the *Gazzetta Ufficiale*'s inclusion of updated or coordinated texts, mentioned above). Further, the random chronological order of the legislative acts contained in official publications makes it impossible to correlate the materials published in the same fascicle or the same volume. It therefore becomes difficult to maintain all the legislative production on any particular matter readily at hand.

Private publications are usually less costly and easier to find, thanks to the distribution networks of specialized publishers. Another popular type of publication consists of collections of laws concerning a specific sector. Non-technically known as *codici* (Codes), these collections contain the norms (statutes, regulations, etc.) governing a particular matter, and they are frequently updated.

Among private publications containing legislative materials, particular mention should be made of periodicals which systematically reproduce the texts published in the *Gazzetta Ufficiale*, most notably: *Lex*, published by Utet, Turin; *La legislazione italiana*, published by Giuffrè, Milan; and *Le Leggi*, published by Zanichelli, Bologna.

1. Codes and Collections of Statutes

The Italian legal system is comprised of five *codici*, or Codes, in the proper sense of the term: the Civil Code, the Penal Code, the Code of Civil Procedure, the Code of Criminal Procedure, and the Code of Navigation. In addition to these are the military codes.

These Codes have been repeatedly modified over the years. Every year, numerous private publishing houses bring out updated editions, usually edited by well-known scholars. A single book often contains several Codes in order to help practitioners in their work.

The term *codice* is also used for volumes containing collections of statutes and regulations relative to a particular branch of law. These publications are extremely useful because they give the practitioner rapid access to the law on a certain matter in an updated version. These works are frequently reprinted in order to take account of changes that have been made. Alternatively, appendices updating the main volume may be published. Also extremely useful are the Codes that reproduce statutes and regulations enacted by the regional administrations.

The retrieval of information from the Codes and collections of statutes and regulations is facilitated by the indices usually included in the volume. One generally finds a chronological index and an analytical index consisting of keywords alongside of which are listed all the relevant statutes, and regulations related to them.

2. Annotated Statutes

Codes and collections of statutes and regulations are also published in editions that juxtapose the texts of individual statutes with scholarly commentary and/or references to relevant case law. These publications (sometimes consisting of several volumes) are prepared by reputable jurists so that practitioners may rapidly determine judicial and/or scholarly opinion on a particular provision.

III. Case Law

The Italian legal system is made up of various jurisdictions largely divided according to subject matter: with constitutional, civil, criminal, administrative, tax, accounting, military and so on. Mention should also be made of the jurisdiction exercised by the European Court of Justice, and by the recently instituted Community Court of First Instance.

Within each jurisdiction (with the obvious exception of constitutional jurisdiction) there are various organs among which judicial powers are divided, according to jurisdiction based upon territory, subject, value, and function.

The only form of publicity for the opinions of the courts envisaged by the Italian legal system is the formality of the *deposito in cancelleria*, or filing in the record office. The only exceptions concern the opinions of the Constitutional Court and of the Supreme Court. The acts of the Constitutional Court are published in the *Raccolta ufficiale delle sentenze e delle ordinanze della Corte costituzionale*, as well as in the *Gazzetta Ufficiale della Repubblica Italiana* and the *Bollettino ufficiale* of the Regions concerned. As regards the Supreme Court, art. 68 of the *Ordinamento giudiziario* (r.d. 30 January 1941 no. 12) created the office known as the *Ufficio del Massimario*, which draws up and circulates the 'official maxims' of the opinions of the court (*see* below III A).

Filing in the record office is certainly not a suitable means of ensuring general knowledge of court decisions, or of the acts issued in exercise of the jurisdictional function. The problem concerns the Supreme Court itself, given that the *Ufficio Massimario* does not publish opinions in their complete form.

The important task of making case law information known and readily accessible is therefore undertaken by case law periodicals compiled, published, and distributed by private organizations. The work of these organizations will be discussed at IV C, after I have illustrated the structure and contents of a jurisdictional act.

A jurisdictional pronouncement is a document, usually 20 or 30 pages in length, which sets out in formal terms various elements identifying the act: the organ issuing the document; the names of the judges who decided the case; the name of the judge who drafted the opinion (the *giudice estensore* or *giudice relatore*); the type of act issued, *i.e.* the judgment, ordinance, or decree; the progressive number assigned to the decision; the date of filing in the record office; the names of plaintiff (*attore*) and defendant (*convenuto*); and the names of the attorneys for the parties.

The largest part of a jurisdictional pronouncement usually consists of the *motivazione*, which is divided into two parts. The first, entitled *Svolgimento del processo* (or also *narrativa*) sets out the facts of the case. The second part, entitled *Motivi della decisione*, states the judge's reasons for reaching that particular decision.

Nowadays not infrequently a useful distinction borrowed from the common law is made between *obiter dictum* and *ratio decidendi* in the *motivazione*. The *ratio decidendi* is the principle of law adopted by the judge to decide the case. *Obiter dicta*, on the other hand, consist of the set of arguments commented upon by the judge, but which do not bear directly upon the decision at hand.

The jurisdictional decision concludes with the so-called *dispositivo* or operative part, which generally consists of a few lines stating the judge's ruling after the *motivazione* has been set out. The *dispositivo* follows the well-known acronym *PQM*, which stands for *per questi motivi*, or "for these reasons,"; with this the argumentative portion of the document concludes.

A. Case Law Periodicals

Every year, probably more than a million judicial decisions are issued in Italy. A large percentage of these decisions remain unpublished, apart from the above-mentioned filing in the record office. A small quantity will be brought to the attention of practitioners by journals specializing in the publication of jurisprudential materials.

The work of the editors employed by these journals can be schematized as follows. Their first task is to select the documents to be published. It is impossible to fix objective criteria by which the publishers attempt to distinguish those documents worth publishing from those of no interest. Among the parameters used are: the authoritativeness of the judicial body issuing the decision; whether the decision reflects a change of opinion; whether it reflects an interpretative conflict worthy of publication; and the novelty or topicality of the issue treated.

The selection stage is followed by the editing of the texts for publication. Substantially all of the text of the act is published, although the pagination does not replicate that of the original.

The text is preceded by a series of notations inserted by the editors. The *testatina*, or heading, which gives the particulars of the document – the issuing jurisdictional body, the type of act adopted, the date of the pronouncement, its number, the name of the president of the judicial panel, the writer of the *motivazione*, the names of the parties, and the defense counsel. Thereafter follow the *neretti*, or summaries of the maxims contained in the case which state the principle of law stated immediately afterwards. The first word indicates the matter to which the maxim refers. Below each summary are the provisions of statutes to which the maxim refers. Thereafter follows the maxim. The maxim reproduces the principle of law applied by the judge in reaching the decision. A judgment may have several maxims if a number of issues have been addressed. Formulation of the maxim is probably the most difficult task performed by the editors of the case law periodicals. The maxim should state the *ratio dicendi* of the judgment – not always an easy matter. In relying on the maxim to determine the "meaning" of the case, it is necessary to bear several things in mind: (i) the maxim is not written by the judge, but rather by persons not directly involved in the decision-making process, and is wholly distinct from the actual opinion; (ii) there is no guarantee of uniformity in the drafting of maxims, though those which issue from the *Ufficio del Massimario* are perhaps most reliable; (iii) the maxim does not have official status; and (iv) the same judgment may be published with different maxims in different periodicals.

Italian cases contain *note redazionali*, or case notes. A maxim usually concludes with a number in brackets. This number refers to a note in which the editors cite the precedents consistent or at variance with the opinion contained in the document and the doctrinal studies published on the topic. In some cases the reference note may be flanked or replaced by a commentary.

The elements just illustrated (which are compiled by the editors) precede the text of the pronouncement by the jurisdictional organ, and the actual text is not always reproduced in its entirety. Sometimes the facts of the case or the part of the *motivazione* deemed irrelevant are omitted.

Locating published cases is made easier by indices, the structure of which tends to be fairly uniform from one journal to another. These indices include the following:

First, an alphabetical index of decisions, which is useful for tracing all the decisions published on a particular matter. This index consists of a grid of alphabetized keywords and sub-keywords under which the materials are catalogued according to the topic treated. Set alongside each item are the *neretti* associated with it; generally, the first word of the *neretto* corresponds to a keyword in the analytical index. Indicated for each *neretto* is the location within the periodical of the document. Second are the chronological indiceswhich help locate the decisions published in a particular year whose identifying elements – issuing body, date, and volume number, for example – are known. Third are the alphabetical indices of the names of the parties. These aid the location of opinions published in a particular year when the names of the parties to the suit are known. Finally, there are the indices of legislative provisions, useful when searching for the cases published in a particular year that have treated specific legislative provisions.

In addition to the above periodicals, dozens of periodicals containing case law materials are published in Italy every year. There are periodicals containing materials from all the jurisdictions, of which perhaps the most notable are the following: *Il Foro italiano*; *Giurisprudenza italiana*; and *Giurisprudenza di merito*.

Specialized journals publish materials concerning a particular branch of law or documents issued in a certain jurisdiction. For example:

Constitutional, civil and commercial case law: *Giurisprudenza costituzionale*; *Giustizia civile*; *Giurisprudenza commerciale*; *Archivio civile*; *Danno e responsabilità*; *Banca, borsa e titoli di credito*; *Contratto e impresa*; *Contratto e impresa/Europa*; *Il Corriere giuridico*; *Il Diritto di famiglia e delle persone*; *Il diritto industriale*; *Il Foro padano*; *Responsabilità civile e previdenza*.

Criminal case law: *Archivio penale*; *Cassazione penale*; *L'indice penale*.

Administrative case law: *Il Consiglio di Stato*; *Il Foro amministrativo*; *I Tribunali Amminstrativi Regionali*.

Tax case law: *Le commissioni tributarie*; *Giurisprudenza delle imposte*; *Rassegna tributaria*.

IV. Scholarly Writings

A. The Literary Genres

The Italian term *dottrina* denotes the body of opinions and analysis produced by scholars of law in the legal-scientific literature, and is best translated by the English word "scholarship."

Literature is the means by which legal culture develops and transmits knowledge. At different times and in different places, the form assumed by the legal literature has complied with paradigms divergent in terms of both content and method. It is for this reason that the Western legal tradition has seen such a wide variety of literary genres.

The following are the most distinctive genres of Italian legal literature:

- The *Monografia*, or monograph, in which the author explores a specific theme or a particular problem, demonstrating his or her scientific maturity in both the originality of the treatment and the coherence of the solutions proposed.

- The *Saggio Monografico*, or Monographic Essay, which is a work more restricted in length and ambition than a monograph, usually published in a scholarly review, but still a sustained exposition.

- The *Trattato*, or Treatise, which is a systematic and detailed exposition of an entire area of law. The *Trattato* usually consists of several volumes written by different authors.

- The *Commentario*, or Commentary, is a relatively uniform article by article analysis of some body of positive law written by several authors, such as Codes, statutes, or regulations. The *Commentario* does not contain the systematic exposition of a specific legal matter or institution, but rather comments on individual provisions of law.

- The *Encylopedia*, usually a multi-volume effort, consists of subject entries arranged in alphabetical order. Each contributor provides a brief but comprehensive description of the subject indicated by the heading. Consultation of an encyclopedia entry is often the simplest way to gain an immediate overview of a topic of interest.

- The *Manuale*, or Manual, is a text that lays out the fundamental elements of a certain subject or discipline, and is usually designed for those addressing the topic for the first time. It is the teaching tool in the Italian educational system most analogous to the American Casebook, though it is not a case-based text.

The *nota redazionale* or Case Note is a literary genre typical of case law periodicals, which conventionally takes the form of an editorial note (unsigned) on a judgment. The Case Note typically makes reference to similar or dissimilar precedents as well as scholarly studies on the issues dealt with by the opinion of the court. It may sometimes be broader in scope and constitute a full-blown article; see also the Casebook, the purpose of which is to reconstruct the opinion of the courts on specific arguments.

B. Scholarly Reviews

Every year thousands of publications belonging to the various genres listed above appear in Italy. This mass of doctrinal material is further increased by the myriad essays, articles, and notes published in legal journals. Among the reviews specializing in the publishing of doctrinal materials are the following:

> *Rivista di diritto civile*
>
> *Rivista trimestrale di diritto pubblico*
>
> *Rivista italiana di diritto e procedura penale*
>
> *Quaderni costituzionali*
>
> *Rivista critica del diritto privato*

Rivista di diritto processuale

Rivista trimestrale di diritto e procedura civile

Sociologia del diritto

Rivista giuridica dell' ambiente

Democrazia e diritto

Il Diritto dell' informazione e dell' informatica

Materiali per una storia della cultura giuridica

Informatica e diritto

C. The Digests of Legislation, Doctrine, and Case Law

In previous sections, I have illustrated the various paper-based instruments for legal research. The quantity of data suggests just how difficult it may be to master this veritable flood of documents. But how can one locate specific information?

One of the most efficient approaches to this challenge is to use a digest of legislation, doctrine, or case law. Private organizations issue these publications in order to make legal periodicals more readily available. I shall illustrate the structure and contents of these information search tools by offering the *Repertorio del Foro italiano* as an example, since it is one of the most accurate and complete digests available.

A digest is a bulky periodical usually comprised of thousands of pages, published annually and consisting of a progressively numbered series of entries. Every year, the digest editors sift through books and journals of legal interest published in Italy. Each published item (statute, case law opinion, scholarly essay, etc.) is associated with one entry in the digest.

For example, if the periodical *Giurisprudenza italiana* publishes an opinion on contracts, the editor will include that opinion under the heading "Contracts in general," such that the entry comprises all the materials on contracts published in legal journals over the course of the year.

However, the digests do not reproduce the texts of documents. Instead, they print the identifying elements of documents, as well as information on the book or periodical in which the texts may be found in their entirety. Therefore, each entry states: (i) for legislative acts: the type of act, its date of issue, its number and title; (ii) for scholarly studies: the author's name, the title of the work, its page run in the review, or, if it has appeared in a book, the publisher, and the place and date of publication; (iii) for case law: the issuing jurisdictional organ, the date of the pronouncement, the number or names of the parties concerned, the maxims of the pronouncement, and the periodicals in which they have been published.

When consulting the *Repertorio*, the first task is to determine the entry in which the documents required have most probably been classified. Selection is simplified by an alphabetical keyword index. Once the relevant entries have been identified, the user will have the necessary legislation, bibliography, and case law available.

A digest is a veritable mine of information. In addition to the methods just outlined, one may obtain information through alternative and more specifically targeted search devices. One such device is the Index of Articles, which is useful for locating documents in the digest relating to a specific legislative provision. A second one is the Chronological Index of Decisions, which shows where judgments may be found in the digest. An additional device is offered by the Index of Authors, which can be used to discover what a certain author has published over the course of the year.

Finally, the Name Index of parties to actions provides quick signposts to specific sections of the digest containing a judgment for which the name of one of the parties is known.

Other publishers produce digests of legislation, doctrine and case law similar to the *Repertorio*, including the *Repertorio generale della Giurisprudenza italiana* published annually by Utet, and the *Repertorio di Giustizia civile* published by Giuffrè.

There is no shortage of other publications in Italy attempting to streamline retrieval of legal information, but these others are more limited in their scope. There are works which contain information only on the legislation in force (*e.g.*, *La legislazione vigente*, published by Utet), or works which catalogue the case law produced on a certain matter (*e.g.*, *Repertorio di giurisprudenza del lavoro*, published by Giuffrè), or again, works which aid the search for scholarly studies published in a certain period (*e.g.*, *Dizionario bibliografico delle riviste giuridiche*, edited by Napoletano, published by Giuffrè).

D. Prompt Information

The frenetic rate at which new legislative texts are produced and the importance of certain opinions requires legal practitioners to acquire information promptly about new material and changes in existent material. Consequently, a number of periodicals are published aimed at rapidly informing practitioners about newly issued legal materials; two prominent examples are *Guida al diritto* (published by the newspaper Il Sole 24 ore) and *Gazzetta giuridica* (published by Giuffrè).

V. Computerized Editions

The law in Italy has not been immune to the sea-change wrought by computers in the gathering and retrieval of information. Despite some institutional conservatism, the jurist's training and working methods are undergoing changes that have already transformed how they work.

A. Online Databases

Jurists have called upon information technology to provide them, above all, with the means to handle and retrieve legal materials more efficiently. Online databases have provided the first responses to this demand, constituting a new model for the storage and transmission of legal data.[6]

Among the most popular Italian online databases are the following:

1. *Italgiure* is the electronic documentation center of the Supreme Court. This consists of a set of archives grouped into: legislation (useful for obtaining information on current legislation in Italy), case law (containing the maxims extracted from decisions issued in the various jurisdictions); international law; scholarship; and the like. *Italguire* is located at the Internet site http://www.giustizia.it/009/09_sub-h.htm and may be consulted through Telnet (193.43.143.70) or by means of *EasyFind*-guided interrogation software. *Italgiure* is a pay-for-use database; those wishing to access the site must take out a subscription and obtain a password. Information on subscription procedures and costs may be obtained from Corte Suprema di Cassazione – Centro Elettronico di Documentazione – Via Damiano Chiesa 24 – 00136 Rome.

2. The Italian Senate also provides a database consisting of various archives of parliamentary sessions, which can be grouped into: archives of bills (useful for those wishing to know what stage a bill has reached in its progress through parliament); archives of the Senate's non-legislative sessions; archives of the Senators' activities, archives of the composition of the Senate and Government; archives of non-legislative acts; and utility archives. The Senate database can be accessed at Internet site http://www.senato.it. The Senate database is also pay-for-use. In order to obtain user permission, one must apply to the Segretario generale del Senato della Repubblica – Piazza Madama 2 – 00186 Rome.

---

[6] For more detailed treatment, *see* Pascuzzi, *Cyberdiritto. Guida alle banche dati italiane e straniere, alla rete Internet e all' apprendimento assistito da calcolatore*, Bologna (1995).

3. The Chamber of Deputies also provides a database consisting of a set of archives concerning parliamentary sessions that may be grouped into: archives of parliamentary sessions; archives of texts; archives of legislation; archives of electoral data; archives of doctrine and bibliography. The Chamber database can be accessed at Internet site http://www.camera.it. The Chamber's information system can be accessed by sending the appropriate request to the Secretary General.

B. CD-ROM

CD-ROMs have recently grown into a substantial branch of the publishing industry. Indeed, several publishing houses market legal works both in paper and CD-ROM versions. For example, the publisher Zanichelli, which for decades has published the journal *Il Foro Italiano* and the case law digest of the same name, has issued the most recent annual editions of these works on CD-ROM.

Today, dozens of CD-ROM legal titles are published in Italy. The following table lists the most important of them: *Codice civile* (Civil Code and complementary laws – *Ipsoa*); *Codici del lavoro* (labour legislation – *Ipsoa*); *Contratti collettivi nazionali di lavoro* (texts of collective labor contracts – *Laserdata*); *Eurodata* (European Community legislation – Cedi); *Giurisprudenza Italiana – Repertorio* (contains issues of the *Repertorio di Giuriprudenza Italiana* – Utet – from 1981 to the present); *Foro Italiano – Repertorio* (contains issues of the *Repertorio del Foro Italiano* – Zanichelli – from 1981 to the present); *Italedi CD-Rom* (Italian administrative jurisprudence – *Italedi*); *Juris data* (contains issues of the *Repertorio di Giustizia Civile* – Giuffrè – since 1979); *Leggi d'Italia* (current texts of Italian statutes – DeAgostini).

C. Other Resources Available on the Internet

A list follows of the Italian institutions that have created websites providing information about their respective fields of interest.

Corte Suprema di Cassazione	*http://www.giustizia.it/009/09_sub-h.htm*
Parlamento Italiano	*http://www.parlamento.it*
Senato	*http://www.senato.it*

Camera	*http://www.camera.it*
Presidenza del Consiglio dei Ministri	*http://die.pcm.it*
Ministero degli Affari Esteri	*http://sigserv1.casaccia.enea.it/MAE*
Ministero dei Beni Culturali e Ambientali	*http://www.beniculturali.it*
Ministero del Commercio con l'Estero	*http://www.mincomes.it*
Ministero delle Finanze	*http://www.finanze.it*
Ministero di Grazie e Giustizia	*http://www.giustizia.it*
Ministero dell'Industria	*http://www.minindustria.it*
Ministero dell'Interno	*http://www.mininterno.it*
Ministero del Lavoro	*http://www.minlavoro.it*
Ministero dei Lavori Pubblici	*http://www.llpp.it*
Ministero della Pubblica Istruzione	*http://www.bdp.it/mpi.htm*
Ministero della Sanità	*http://www.sanita.it*
Ministero del Tesoro	*http://www.tesoro.it*
Ministero dei Trasporti	*http://www.trasportinavigazione.it*
Ministero dell'Università	*http://www.murst.it*
Autorità Garante della Concorrenza e del Mercato	*http://www.agcm.it*
Autorità per l'Informatica nella Pubblica Amministrazione	*http://www.aipa.it*
Banca d'Italia	*http://www.bancaditalia.it*
Istituto di documentazione giuridica del CNR	*http://www.idg.fi.cnr.it*
Unidroit – International Institute for the Unification of Private Law	*http://www.agora.stm.it/unidroit*
Multiaterals Project (International Treaties)	*http://www.tufts.edu/departments/ fletcher/multilaterals.html*

Further information about Italian websites providing information of interest to jurists can be obtained by logging onto the University of Trento Law Faculty website (http://www.jus.unitn.it/services/home.html). This site maintains a constantly updated archive of the most important sources of information of this nature.

D. Legal Journals Online

Electronic legal journals have recently made their appearance on the web; one of the most important is the Cardozo Electronic Law Bulletin (http://gelso.unitn.it/card-adm/).

VI. Bibliography of English Language Sources [7]

The following bibliography attempts to account for the most recent writings on the Italian legal system written in English. We have divided the entries into six sections: private law and civil procedure; commercial law and arbitration; constitutional law, public and administrative law; criminal law and criminal procedure; international and EC law.

The bibliography is thorough, but largely confined to the last two decades of scholarly work in the area, and some selection was necessary. Additional bibliographic material may be obtained by consulting the periodically updated *International Encyclopedia of Comparative Law*. An increasing amount of information is also available through the Internet. The *Cardozo Electronic Law Bulletin* has a page of links dedicated to Italian law on the Web (http://www.gelso.unitn.it/card-adm/it law.html). Another useful site is maintained by the Law Library of the University of California at Berkeley Law School (Boalt Hall), http://www.law.berkeley.edu/library/library.html, which provides access not only to the entire collection at Boalt, but also to a series of secondary links to the holdings of the entire University of California library. Several other legal research libraries provide similar resources. Subscriber-based services such as the H.W. Wilson Company's Index to Legal Periodicals, http://www.silverplatter.com/catalog/wilp.htm, or the Legal Trac service, http://library.albany.edu/databases2/about/legaltrac.html, provide extensive coverage of English-language materials on Italian law. Finally, further coverage of the subject is provided by the *Index to Foreign Legal Periodicals*,

---

[7] This section was compiled by Dott. Barbara Pasa, University of Turin, Dott. Andrea Rossato, University of Trent, and Dott. Stefania Savini, University of Milan. The information contained herein is updated as of July 2001.

T. Reynolds (ed.), University of California Press, http://www.law.berkeley.edu/iflp and by the online version of Mr. Reynolds' *Foreign Law* at http://www.foreignlawguide.com.

Books

Peter C. Alegi, *Business operations in Italy*, Washington (2000).

M. Cappelletti, J.H. Merryman and J.M. Perillo, *The Italian Legal System – An Introduction*, Stanford (1967).

Casilini Libri (ed.), *Italian law publications: a selection 1997-1998: published on the occasion of the IALL 17th annual course, held at UNIDROIT, Rome, 20-24 1998*, Fiesole (1998).

G.L. Certoma, *The Italian Legal System*, London (1985).

Rory O'Connell, *Legal Theory in the Crucible of Constitutional Justice: a Study of Judges and Political Morality in Canada, Ireland and Italy*, Aldershot (2000).

Antonio Gambaro, Alfredo Rabello (eds.), International Congress: *Towards a New European* Ius Commune*: Essays on European, Italian and Israeli Law in Occasion of 50 Years of the EU and the State of Israel*, Jerusalem (1999).

Adelmo Manna, The *CriminalJustice System in Europe and North America: Italy*, Helsinki (2000).

J.H. Merryman, *The Loneliness of the Comparative Lawyer*, Kluwer, The Hague. Boston (1999).

Antonello Miranda, *Introducing the Italian Legal System*, Palermo (1987).

Thomas Reynolds, Arturo A. Flores (eds.), *Foreign Law – Current Sources of Codes and Basic Legislation in Jurisdictions of the World*, Buffalo, Hein (1989) (updated looseleaf).

Tiziano Treu, *Labour Law and Industrial Relations in Italy*, The Hague (1998).

Thomas Glyn Watkin, *The Italian Legal Tradition*, Aldershot Hants (1997).

Private Law and Civil Procedure

Stefano Agostini, "Advertising and Solicitation: A Comparative Analysis of Why Italian and American Lawyers Approach Their Profession Differently," 10 *Temple International and Comparative Law Journal* 329 (1996).

Guido Alpa, "Manufacturer, Importer and Supplier Liability in Italy Before and After the Implementation of the EEC Directive on Damages for Defective Products," 6 *Tulane Civil Law Forum* 233 (1991).

Guido Alpa, "Unjust Damage and the Role of Negligence: Historical Profile," 9 *Tulane European and Civil Law Forum* 147 (1994).

Adalberto Anibaldi, "Inheritance: Dealing With Assets Situated in Italy," 27 *Law Society Journal* 70 (1989).

Roberto Barbalich, "Buying a Property in Italy," 135 *Solicitors Journal* 1218 (1991).

Anita Bernstein and Paul Fanning, "Heirs of Leonardo: Cultural Obstacles to Strict Products Liability in Italy," 27 *Vanderbilt Journal of Transnational Law* 1 (1994).

Barbara Bettelli, "Article 50 Italian Copyright Law: The Outstanding Issue of the Statutory Three-Year Term," 7 *Entertainment Law Review* 283 (1996).

Marino Bin, "Italy: Reform of Maintenance After Divorce," 28 *Journal of Family Law* 542 (1990).

Antonio Braggion, "Protection of Know-How Under Italian Law," 17 *International Business Lawyer* 417 (1989).

Antonio Brancaccio, "The Protection of Human Rights in the Decisions of the Italian Supreme Court of Cassation" (St. John's University School of Law: Rededication Symposia), 70 *St. John's Law Review* 101 (1996).

Richard B. Cappalli, "The Style and Substance of Civil Procedure Reform: Comparison of the United States and Italy," 16 *Loyola of Los Angeles International and Comparative Law Journal* 861 (August 1994).

Domenico Carzo, "A Model of Legal Communication: Succession (Italy)," 6 *Liverpool Law Review* 179 (1984).

Roberto Ceccon, "Arbitration and Intellectual Property in the Italian Legal System," 13 *Journal of International Arbitration* 65 (1996).

Roberta Ceschini, "Divorce Proceedings in Italy: Domestic and International Procedures" (Special Issue on International Family Law), 28 *Family Law Quarterly* 143 (1994).

D.R. Chambers, "The Italian Civil Code Supplement 1969-1978" (book review), 20 *Medicine, Science, and the Law* 74 (1980).

Oscar G. Chase, "Civil Litigation Delay in Italy and the United States," 36 *American Journal of Comparative Law* 41 (1988).

Massimo Cimoli, "Towards a New Italian Design Law," 15 *EIPR: European Intellectual Property Review* 425 (1993).

Gabriel Cuonzo and Julia Holden, "The Evaluation of Damages in Italian Patent Litigation," 15 *EIPR: European Intellectual Property Review* 441 (1993).

Gabriel Cuonzo and Julia Holden, "Patent Litigation in Italy: Recent Procedural Reforms," 22 *International Business Lawyer* 352 (1994).

Gabriel Cuonzo and Julia Holden, "Interlocutory Measures in the Defense of Trademarks in Italy – Strategies and Procedural Techniques in the Light of Recent Legislative Reforms," *Trademark Reporter* 55 (1995).

Gabriele Dara, "Limitation of Authority of Agents and Innocent Third Parties (Italy)," 9 *The Company Lawyer* 227 (1988).

David M. Dobson and Rita Gaudenzi, "Agency and Distributorship Laws in Italy: Guidelines for the Foreign Principal," 20 *International Lawyer* 997 (1986).

David M. Dobson and Vincenzo Sinisi, "Legal Aspects of Property Investment in Italy," 4 *International Law Practicum* 23 (1991).

Richard H. Dreyfuss, "The Italian Law on Strict Products Liability," 17 *New York Law School Journal of International and Comparative Law* 37 (1997).

Maria Rosaria Ferrarese, "Civil Justice and the Judicial Role in Italy. (International Perspectives on Civil Court Reform)," 13 *The Justice System Journal* 168 (1988).

Mario Franzosi, "The Italian Industrial Property Council," 18 *EIPR: European Intellectual Property Review* 471 (August 1996).

Mario Franzosi, "Worldwide Patent Litigation and the Italian Torpedo," 19 *EIPR: European Intellectual Property Review* 382 (1997).

Mario Franzosi and Giustino De Sanctis, "Intellectual and Industrial Property Litigation in Italy: A Change for the Better?" 16 *EIPR: European Intellectual Property Review* 392 (1994).

Mario Franzosi and Vincenzo Jandoli, "A Preliminary Injunction Concerning Unfair Competition in the Alcoholic Beverages Sector in Italy," 18 *EIPR: European Intellectual Property Review* 567 (1996).

Enrico Gabrielli, "Security Over Movables in Italy," *Journal of Business Law* 525 (1992).

Michele Graziadei and Ugo Mattei, "Judicial Responsibility in Italy: A New Statute," 38 *American Journal of Comparative Law* 103 (1990).

Philip Girard, "Why Canada Has No Family Policy: Lessons from France and Italy," 32 *Osgoode Hall Law Journal* 579 (1994).

Lucio Ghia, "Damage Due to Anesthetist's Error (Italy)," 30 *Law Technology* 37 (1997).

Gino Gorla, "Civilian Judicial Decisions – An Historical Account of Italian Style," 20 *Comparative Juridical Review* 3 (1983).

P.C. Hemphill, "The Civil-Law Foundation as a Model for the Reform of Charitable Trusts Law (Great Britain, Italy)," 64 *Australian Law Journal* 404 (1990).

G. Jacobacci, "Italian Trademark Law and Practice and the Protection of Product and Packaging Design," 74 *Trademark Reporter* 418 (1984).

Silvio Martucelli, "An Up-and-Coming Right – The Right of Publicity: Its Birth in Italy and Its Consideration in the United States," 4 *Entertainment Law Review* 109 (1993).

Silvio Martuccelli, "The Right of Publicity Under Italian Civil Law" (Symposium: International Rights of Publicity), 18 *Loyola of Los Angeles Entertainment Law Journal* 543 (1998).

Geoffrey MacCormack, "Italian Law of Contract" (book review), *Scots Law Times* 297 (1992).

Alex Maitland Hudson and Roberto Barbalich, "Succession Law in France and Italy," 135 *Solicitors Journal* 1032 (1991).

Finbarr McAuley, "The Theory of Justification and Excuse: Some Italian Lessons," 35 *American Journal of Comparative Law* 359 (1987).

Antonello Miranda, "Bank's Liability in Contract for the Use of Safe Deposit Box," 10 *The Company Lawyer* 29 (1989).

Paolisa Nebbia, "Judex ex Machina: The Justice of the Peace in the Tragedy of the Italian Civil Process," 17 *Civil Justice Quarterly* 164 (1998).

Douglas L. Parker, "Standing to Litigate 'Abstract Social Interests' in the United States and Italy: Reexamining 'Injury in Fact'," 33 *Columbia Journal of Transnational Law* 259 (1995).

Salvatore Patti, "Environmental Protection in Italy: The Emerging Concept of a Right to a Healthful Environment," 24 *Natural Resources Journal* 535 (1984).

Massimo Pavolini, "Protection of Fictional Characters in the United States and in Italy or 'sei personaggi in cerca di diritto d'autore'," 4 *Entertainment Law Review* 135 (1993).

Giovanni A. Pedde, "Multimedia Works Under Italian Copyright Law and Contractual Process," 9 *Entertainment Law Review* 39 (1998).

David Pugsley, "When in Rome (Italian law)," 20 *Bracton Law Journal* 15 (1988).

Egidio Rinaldi, "Circumstances in Which Proceedings of Bankruptcy Winding-Up May Be Initiated in Italy," 10 *International Business Lawyer* 37 (1982).

Egidio Rinaldi, "Executory Contracts and Leases in Bankruptcy Italy," 10 *International Business Lawyer* 296 (1982).

Roberto Rome and Silvana Sciarra, "The Protection of Employees' Privacy: A Survey of Italian Legislation and Case Law (Worker Privacy: A Ten-Nation Study by the Committee on International Studies of the National Academy of Arbitrators)," 17 *Comparative Labor Law Journal* 91 (1995).

Elisabetta Silvestri, "Alternatives to or Within Formal Procedures in Italy," 8 *Civil Justice Quarterly* 45 (1989).

Charles Stanley Ross, "The Right of Privacy and Restraints on Abortion Under the 'Undue Burden' Test: A Jurisprudential Comparison of Planned Parenthood v. Casey With European Practice and Italian Law," 3 *Indiana International & Comparative Law Review* 199 (1993).

J.G. Starke, "Italian Law of Contract" (book review), 66 *Australian Law Journal* 687 (1992).

Massimo Sterpi, "Preliminary Discovery Procedures, Precautionary Measures and Remedies in Italian Litigation," 84 *Trademark Reporter* 245 (1994).

June M. Stover, "Copyright Protection for Computer Programs in the United Kingdom, West Germany and Italy: A Comparative Overview," 7 *Loyola of Los Angeles International and Comparative Law Journal* 279 (1984).

Pietro Tamburrini, "A Note of Software Protection in Italy" (Special Issue: Software Protection Laws in Europe), 6 *Computer Law & Practice* 119 (1990).

Marina Timoteo, "Italy: Some Recent Judicial Interpretations of Family Law," 33 *University of Louisville Journal of Family Law* 409 (1995).

Vincenzo Varano, "Civil Procedure Reform in Italy" (Symposium: Civil Procedure Reform in Comparative Context), 45 *American Journal of Comparative Law* 657 (1997).

Kenneth William Wedderburn, "Italian Yearbook of Civil Procedure" (book review), 12 *Civil Justice Quarterly* 308 (1993).

Marco Della Vedova, "Italy (Same Words, Different Meanings: English Legalese in Non-English Contracts)," 26 *International Business Lawyer* 419 (1998).

Vincenzo Zeno-Zencovich, "Damage Awards in Defamation Cases: An Italian View," 40 *International and Comparative Law Quarterly* 691 (1991).

Commercial Law, Arbitration

Bruno Bartocci, "The Italian Merger Control Regulation," 39 *Antitrust Bulletin* 541 (1994).

Carlo Bavetta, "More Restrictive Rules on Company Law. (Italy)," 7 *The Company Lawyer* 124 (1986).

Giorgio Bernini, "Domestic and International Arbitration in Italy After the Legislative Reform" (International Commercial Arbitration Issue), 5 *Pace Law Review* 543 (1985).

Patrizio Bianchi and Giuseppina Gualtieri, "Mergers and Acquisitions in Italy and the Debate on Competition Policy," 34 *Antitrust Bulletin* 601 (1989).

Antonio Braggion, "Protection of Know-How Under Italian Law," 17 *International Business Lawyer* 417 (1989).

Marco Brescia, "Corporate Law: New Developments; Italy," 11 *International Business Lawyer* 32 (1983).

Giuseppe Calabi and Marco Frigessi di Rattalma, "Securities Intermediation in Italy," 23 *International Business Lawyer* 73 (1995).

Attilio M. Costabel, "Fundamental Changes in Italian Arbitration Law," *Lloyds Maritime and Commercial Law Quarterly* 440 (1983).

Lorenzo De Angelis, "Changing Corporate Culture: A View From Italy," *Journal of Business Law* 184 (1988).

David C. Donald, "Comments on the Italian Antitrust Law of October 10, 1990," 26 *International Lawyer* 201 (1992).

Mario Franzosi, "Report on the New Trade Mark Law in Italy. (European Community)," 15 *EIPR: European Intellectual Property Review* 220 (1993).

Bruno Gangemi, "Business Law Guide to Italy" (book review), 22 *International Business Lawyer* 237 (1994).

G. Jacobacci, "Italian Trademark Law and Practice and the Protection of Product and Packaging Design," 74 *Trademark Reporter* 418 (1984).

Roberta S. Karmel, "Italian Stock Market Reform," 220 *New York Law Journal* 3 (1998).

John P. Love, "Arbitration: US. Court Stays Plenary Action, Pending Arbitration in Italy, Notwithstanding the Fact that the Agreement to Arbitrate Could Not Be Enforced Under Italian Law," 15 *Journal of Maritime Law and Commerce* 455 (1984).

Piergaetano Marchetti, Filippo Annunziata, Giuseppe Carcano and Marco S. Spolidoro, "A Survey of New Italian Companies Legislation," *Journal of Business Law* 304 (1993).

Jeffrey A. Orr. Brigham, "Can You Bank on It? Italy's Response to the Second Banking Directive of the European Community," *Young University Law Review* 253 (1992).

Bian Battistia Origoni della Croce and Enzo Schiavello, "Italian Mergers Legislation: New Developments," 20 *International Business Lawyer* 427 (1992).

Robert Pennington, "Business Law Guide to Italy" (book review), 8 *Insolvency Law & Practice* 190 (1993).

Raffaele Mauro Petriccione, "Competition Law in Italy: A Consultative Document," 12 *European Law Review* 379 (1987).

Franco Reviglio, "Arbitration and the Enterprise: An Italian Perspective," 44 *Arbitration Journal* 45 (1989).

Egidio Rinaldi, "Bankruptcy Laws Under Review: Italy," 8 *International Business Lawyer* 27 (1980).

Egidio Rinaldi, "Circumstances in Which Proceedings of Bankruptcy Winding-Up May Be Initiated in Italy," 10 *International Business Lawyer* 37 (1982).

Giuseppe L. Rosa, "The Concept of Separate Legal Personality Under Italian Company Law," 10 *International Business Lawyer* 357 (1982).

Mauro Rubino-Sammartano, "Multi Party Arbitration: Disputes Arising From One Or More Contractual Relationship (Italy)," 9 *International Business Lawyer* 436 (1981).

Mauro Rubino-Sammartano, "New International Arbitration Legislation in Italy," 11 *Journal of International Arbitration* 77 (1994).

Eugenio Ruggiero, "The Regulation of Insider Trading in Italy," 22 *Brooklyn Journal of International Law* 157 (1996).

Vincenzo Sinisi, "Second Banking Directive and Italian Legislation," 24 *International Business Lawyer* 538 (1996).

Marco Saverio Spolidoro, "New Italian Antitrust Law," 19 *International Business Lawyer* 506 (1991).

Tim Steele, "Italy: Practical Commercial Law" (book review), 136 *Solicitors Journal* 10 (1992).

Maurizio Traverso, "Italy (Liability of Arbitrators)," 8 *International Business Lawyer* 339 (1980).

Giovanni Ughi, "The Use of Arbitration Clauses in Governing Instruments of Corporate Entities as a Means of Settling Disputes Among Shareholders or Among Companies and Their Shareholders (In Italian Law)," 8 *International Business Lawyer* 189 (1980).

Giovanni M. Ughi, "Attachments and Other Interim Court Remedies. in Support of Arbitration: Italy," 12 *International Business Lawyer* 115 (1984).

Piergiorgio Valente, "Italy Issues New Rules on Corporate Reorganizations," 15 *Tax Notes International* 791 (1997).

Jan A. Van de Yen, Robert L. Van de Water and Bruno Gangemi, "Partnerships Versus Corporations: Why and When to Use Partnerships in the Light of Legal Format and Tax Treatment (Netherlands and Italy)," 8 *International Business Lawyer* 283 (1980).

Claudio Visco, "Public Offerings of Securities and Takeover Bids: The New Italian Code," 20 *International Business Lawyer* 583 (1992).

Claudio Vixco, "Recent Developments in Securities Law: Italy," 20 *International Business Lawyer* 310 (1992).

Criminal Law and Procedure

Elisabetta Addis, "Women's Liberation and the Law on Sexual Violence: The Italian Feminist Debate," 4 *Socialist Review* 105 (1989).

Ennio Amodio and Eugenio Selvaggli, "An Accusatorial System in a Civil Law Country: The 1988 Italian Code of Criminal Procedure (International Criminal Procedure Symposium)," 62 *Temple Law Review* 1211 (1989).

John Andrews, "Pre-Trial Detention. (Recent Decision of the European Commission of Human Rights)," 7 *European Law Review* 79 (1982).

John Andrews, "Trial in Absentia in Italy," 10 *European Law Review* 368 (1985).

Barbara Bettelli, "Audio-Visual Piracy Laws in Italy: Legal Instruments Against Organised Crime," 7 *Entertainment Law Review* 27 (1996).

Nicola Boari, "On the Efficiency of Penal Systems: Several Lessons From the Italian Experience" (12th Annual Conference of the European Association of Law and Economics), 17 *International Review of Law and Economics* 115 (1997).

Renato Breda and Franco Ferracuti, "Alternatives to Incarceration in Italy," 26 *Crime and Delinquency* 63 (1980).

Alberto Cadoppi, "Recent Developments in Italian Constitutional Criminal Law," 28 *Alberta Law Review* 427 (1990).

M. Chiavario, "The Criminal Process in Italy," in M. Delams-Marty (ed.), *The Criminal Process and Human Rights: Towards a European Consciousness* (1995).

Ernesto d'Aloja, "Ethical and Legal Issues of DNA Typing in Forensic Medicine: A Brief Survey on the Italian Situation" (Proceedings of the European Symposium: Ethical and Legal Issues of DNA Typing in Forensic Medicine), 88 *Forensic Science International* 75 (1997).

Louis F. Del Duca, "An Historic Convergence of Civil and Common Law Systems – Italy's New 'Adversarial' Criminal Procedure System," 10 *Dickinson Journal of International Law* 73 (1991).

Torquil D. Erikson, "Confessions in Evidence: A Look at the Inquisitorial System (Great Britain and Italy)," 140 *New Law Journal* 844 (1990).

Amy Jo Everhart, "Predicting the Effect of Italy's Long-Awaited Rape Law Reform on 'the Land of Machismo'," 31 *Vanderbilt Journal of Transnational Law* 671 (1998).

Marco Fabbri, "Theory Versus Practice of Italian Criminal Justice Reform," 77 *Judicature* 211 (1994).

Lawrence J. Fassler, "The Italian Penal Procedure Code: An Adversarial System of Criminal Procedure in Continental Europe," 29 *Columbia Journal of Transnational Law* 245 (1990).

Vincenzo Ferrari, "The Policy of Law and Order in Italy: The Voice of the Power and Its Impact," 9 *International Journal of the Sociology of the Law* 23 (1981).

Stephen P. Freccero, "An Introduction to the New Italian Criminal Procedure," 21 *American Journal of Criminal Law* 345 (1994).

G.V. Giusti, M. Bacci and A. De Luca, "Criminality and Social Control in a Medium Size Town of Central Italy: An Investigation of the Sentences of the Penal Court (1923-1985) and the Court of Assizes (1952-1985) of Terni," 12 *International Journal of Comparative and Applied Criminal Justice* 237 (1988).

Mario Garavelli, "Drug Abuse in Italy and Europe in a Comparative Context" (Italy in Crisis: A Symposium on the Political and Social Aspects of Italian Law), 4 *Indiana International & Comparative Law Review* 277 (1994).

Elisabetta Grande, "Italian Criminal Justice: Borrowing and Resistance," 48 *American Journal of Comparative Law* 22 (2000).

V. Grevi, "The New Italian Code of Criminal Procedure: A Concise Overview," in A. Pizzorusso (ed.), *Italian Studies in Law*, vol. 2 (1994), p. 145.

Daniel Klaidman, "Mob Trial Brings Justice, Italian-Style, to U.S. Court," 15 *Legal Times* 2 (1992).

Monroe Leigh, "Jurisdiction Over Felonies Committed by Citizens Abroad – Admissibility of Evidence Taken Abroad by Investigating Magistrate (Italy)," 77 *American Journal of International Law* 164 (1983).

Konstantinos D. Maglivera, "The Implementation of the 1991 EC Directive on Money Laundering in Germany, Italy and the Netherlands," 8 *International Law Practicum* 89 (1995).

Riccardo Marselli and Marco Vannini, "Estimating a Crime Equation in the Presence of Organized Crime: Evidence From Italy (12th Annual Conference of the European Association of Law and Economics)," 17 *International Review of Law and Economics* 89 (1997).

Jeffrey J. Miller, "Plea Bargaining and Its Analogues Under the New Italian Criminal Procedure Code and in the United States: Towards a New Understanding of Comparative Criminal Procedure," 22 *New York University Journal of International Law and Politics* 215 (1990).

Walter Pakter, "Exclusionary Rules in France, Germany, and Italy," 9 *Hastings International and Comparative Law Review* 1 (1985).

Tamar Pitch, "The Political Use of Laws: The Italian Women's Movement and the Rape Campaign," 7 *ALSA Forum* 139 (1983).

William T. Pizzi and Luca Marafioti, "The New Italian Code of Criminal Procedure: The Difficulties of Building an Adversarial Trial System on a Civil Law Foundation," 17 *The Yale Journal of International Law* 1 (1992).

Gloria Ramakus, "Legal Assistance to the Indigent in Italy and the United States: Does Volunteer Defense Really Work?," 11 *Brooklyn Journal of International Law* 651 (1985).

Antonello E. Scorcu and Roberto Cellini, "Economic Activity and Crime in the Long Run: An Empirical Investigation on Aggregate Data From Italy, 1951-1994," 18 *International Review of Law and Economics* 279 (1998).

Alexander D. Tripp, "Margins of the Mob: A Comparison Of *Reves v. Ernst & Young* with Criminal Association Laws in Italy and France," 20 *Fordham International Law Journal* 263 (1996).

Rachel A. Van Cleave, "An Offer You Can't Refuse? Punishment Without Trial in Italy and the United States: The Search for Truth and an Efficient Criminal Justice System," 11 *Emory International Law Review* 419 (1997).

Karen Wolman, "Italians Try Doing Justice all'Americana," 12 *The National Law Journal* 8 (1990).

Michael Zander, "From Inquisitorial to Adversarial the Italian Experiment," 141 *New Law Journal* 678 (1991).

"Constitutional, Public and Administrative Law, and Labor Law Employment Security Law and Practice in Belgium, Bulgaria, France, Germany, Great Britain, Italy, Japan and the European Communities" (book review), 16 *Comparative Labor Law Journal* 573 (1995).

"Italian Cabinet Forms Plan for Dual Tax on Corporate Earnings," 15 *Tax Notes International* 978 (1997).

Giuliano Amato, "Italy: The Rise and Decline of a System Of Government" (Italy in Crisis: A Symposium on the Political and Social Aspects of Italian Law), 4 *Indiana International & Comparative Law Review* 225 (1994).

Eleonora Andreatta and Giovanni A. Pedde, "Broadcast Regulation in Italy: Debating New Rules to Join the European Audio-Visual Market," 6 *Entertainment Law Review* 7 (1995).

Maria Armanno and Wahe H. Balekjian, "The Reform and Regulation of the Stock Market (Italy)," 8 *The Company Lawyer* 40 (1987).

Antonio Baldassarre, "Structure and Organization of the Constitutional Court of Italy," 40 *Saint Louis University Law Journal* 649 (1996).

Eric Barendt, "The Influence of the German and Italian Constitutional Courts on Their National Broadcasting Systems," *Public Law* 93 (1991).

Anna Bartolacci and Jennifer Gann, "Italy Issues Regulations on New Municipal Tax," 17 *Tax Notes International* 356 (1998).

Franco Basaglia, "Problems of Law and Psychiatry: The Italian Experience," 3 *International Journal of Law and Psychiatry* 17 (1980).

Marco Biagi, "Employee Representational Participation in Italy" (International Colloquium on Labor Law: Models of Employee Representational Participation), 15 *Comparative Labor Law Journal* 155 (1994).

Marco Biagi, "Recession and the Labour Market: Training for Flexibility – The Italian Case in a Comparative Perspective," 15 *Comparative Labor Law Journal* 303 (1994).

Marco Biagi and Tiziano Treu, "Italy's New Law on Promotion of Employment: An Explanation and Summary," 19 *Comparative Labor Law & Policy Journal* 97 (1997).

Guido Bolaffi, "Redesigning Italy: The New Flow of Immigration" (Italy in Crisis: A Symposium on the Political and Social Aspects of Italian Law), 4 *Indiana International & Comparative Law Review* 291 (1994).

Kitty Calavita, "Worker Safety, Law, and Social Change: The Italian Case," 20 *Law and Society Review* 189 (1986).

Nico Calavita, "Urbanization, Public Control of Land Use and Private Ownership of Land: The Development of Italian Planning Law," 16 *The Urban Lawyer* 459 (1984).

Laura Castellucci, "The Tax System of Italy," 10 *Tax Notes International* 547 (1995).

Mario P. Chiti, "The Italian Experience of Regional Government," 4 *Urban Law and Policy* 89 (1981).

David Christensen, "Leaving the Back Door Open: Italy's Response to Illegal Immigration," 11 *Georgetown Immigration Law Journal* 461 (1997).

Francesco Cossiga, "Institutional Reform and Italian Crisis" (Italy in Crisis: A Symposium on the Political and Social Aspects of Italian Law), 4 *Indiana Internationnal & Comparative Law Review* 231 (1994).

Bruno Cova, "Italy's New Broadcasting Law," 2 *Entertainment Law Review* 56 (1991).

Anna Paola Deiana and Paolo Ludovici, "Italy Finally Implements Second VA T Simplification Directive," 15 *Tax Notes International* 1823 (1997).

Patrick Del Duca, "United States, French and Italian Air Pollution Control: Central and Local Relations as a Structural Determinant of Policy," 10 *Loyola of Los Angeles International and Comparative Law Journal* 497 (1988).

Gianaldo Della Rocca, "Land Use Planning in Italy," 2 *International Property Investment Journal* 379 (1985).

Anthony Falzon-McNab, "Reform of the Italian Financial Sector," 12 *The Company Lawyer* 227 (1991).

Bruno Gangemi, "Recent Tax Planning Developments in Italy," 14 *International Business Lawyer* 17 (1986).

Gino Giugni, "Juridification of Italian Labor Relations," 8 *Comparative Labor Law* 309 (1987).

Jeffrey P. Greenbaum, "Italy's EFIM Law – A Never Ending Story," 21 *International Business Lawyer* 478 (1993).

Carlo Guarnieri, Justice and Politics: "The Italian Case in a Comparative Perspective" (Italy in Crisis: A Symposium on the Political and Social Aspects of Italian Law), 4 *Indiana International & Comparative Law Review* 241 (1994).

Riccardo Guastini, "Grounds of Unconstitutionality: The Italian Case" (International Conference on Comparative Constitutional Law), 17 *Cardozo Law Review* 253 (1995).

Giuseppe Guerreri, "Amendments Long Overdue in Italian Code of Navigation," 13 *Air Law* 35 (1988).

Giuseppe Guerreri, "Law no. 274 of 7 July 1988: A Remarkable Piece of Italian Patchwork," 14 *Air Law* 176 (1989).

Mark H. Lazerson, "Labour Conflict Within the Structure of the Law: Dismissals Under the Italian Workers' Charter in Two Plants," 16 *International Journal of the Sociology of the Law* 31 (1988).

Guglielmo Maisto, "Italy Introduces Regional Tax on Productive Activities," 14 *Tax Notes International* 1029 (1997).

Andrea Mauzitti, "Italy's New Rules on the Taxation of Financial Transactions Examined," 6 *Tax Notes International* 371 (1993).

Zaim M. Nedjatigil, "Judicial Control of Administrative Discretion: A Comparative Study (Great Britain, France, Germany, Netherlands, Italy)," 14 *Anglo-American Law Review* 97 (1985).

Marcella Pagano, "Industrial Democracy and Collective Agreements in Italy," *Journal of Business Law* 351 (1983).

Giovanni A. Pedde, "National and International Issues Concerning the New Draft Cinema Law in Italy," 3 *Entertainment Law Review* 171 (1992).

Alessandro Pizzorusso, "Italian and American Models of the Judiciary and of Judicial Review of Legislation: A Comparison of Recent Tendencies," 38 *American Journal of Comparative Law* 373 (1990).

Alessandro Pizzorusso, Vincenzo Vigoriti and G.L. Certoma, "The Constitutional Review of Legislation in Italy" (Constitutional Judicial Review of Legislation: A Comparative Law Symposium), 56 *Temple Law Quarterly* 503 (1983).

Guendalina Ponti, "Regulation of TV Broadcasting Quotas in Italy and the EEC," 4 *Entertainment Law Review* 10 (1993).

Massimo Roccella, "The Reinstatement of Dismissed Employees in Italy: An Empirical Analysis," 10 *Comparative Labor Law Journal* 166 (1989).

Charles Stanley Ross, "Introduction: Italy's Crisis of Justice" (Italy in Crisis: Symposium on the Political and Social Aspects of Italian Law), 4 *Indiana International & Comparative Law Review* 219 (1994).

David Williams Russell, "Refractions of Italy Law: An Indiana Perspective" (Italy in Crisis: A Symposium on the Political and Social Aspects of Italian Law), 4 *Indiana International & Comparative Law Review* 297 (1994).

Lucantonio Salvi, "Italian Immigration: The Albanian Precedent," 16 *The Fletcher Forum of World Affairs* 183 (1992).

Paul A. Smith, "Italy Embarks on Income Tax Reform Initiative," 14 *Tax Notes International* 815 (1997).

Paul A. Smith and Anna Bartolacci, "Italian Supreme Court Interprets Antiabuse Provision," 17 *Tax Notes International* 140 (1998).

Paul A. Smith and Sandra Takyi, "Italian Tax Authorities Announce Procedures for Ruling Requests," 17 *Tax Notes International* 1234 (1998).

Alberto Tampieri, "Recent Trends in Industrial Relations in Italy" (Symposium on International Law), 20 *Hamline Law Review* 621 (1997).

Richard W. Taylor, "The Ombud of South Tirol (Italy, Austria)," 7 *The Ombudsman Journal* 61 (1988).

Tiziano Treu, "Strikes in Essential Services in Italy: An Extreme Case of Pluralistic Regulation," 15 *Comparative Labor Law Journal* 461 (1994).

Francesco Tundo and Fabio Balza, "Recent Tax Developments in Italy," 11 *Tax Notes International* 1083 (1995).

Paola Tranchina, Giuliana Archi and Maurizio Ferrara, "The New Legislation in Italian Psychiatry: An Advanced Law Originating From Alternative Practice," 4 *International Journal of Law and Psychiatry* 181 (1981).

Mary L. Volcansek, "Judicial Review in Italy: A Reflection of the United States?" (Symposium on Judicial Review and Public Policy in Comparative Perspective), 19 *Policy Studies Journal* 127 (1990).

Mary L. Volcansek, "The Judicial Role in Italy: Independence, Impartiality and Legitimacy," 73 *Judicature* 322 (1990).

Kenneth William Wedderburn, "Political Strikes in Italy and Comparative Labour Law," 12 *Industrial Law Journal* 253 (1983).

Kenneth William Wedderburn, "The Italian Workers' Statute -Some British Reflections," 19 *Industrial Law Journal* 154 (1990).

Kenneth William Wedderburn, "Minimum Wage Laws: Comparative Notes From the Italian," 24 *Industrial Law Journal* 251 (1995).

International and EC Law

"The Doctrine of 'Direct Effect': An Infant Disease of Community Law," 8 *European Law Review* 155 (1983).

"Italy: Law on the Exploration and Exploitation of the Mineral Resources of the Deep Seabed (February 20, 1985)," 24 *International Legal Materials* 983 (1985).

Girolamo Abbatescianni, "Recognition of English Judgments in Italy: the Terruzzi Case," 135 *New Law Journal* 179 (1985).

Petrina R. Albulescu, "Prospective Exemptions Under EEC Competition Law: A Proposal," 16 *Law and Policy in International Business* 1137 (1984).

Guido Alpa, "Manufacturer, Importer and Supplier Liability in Italy Before and After the Implementation of the EEC Directive on Damages for Defective Products," 6 *Tulane Civil Law Forum* 233 (1991).

Mads Andenas, "Italian Nationality Requirement and Community Law," 17 *The Company Lawyer* 219 (1996).

Gavin Barrett, "European Law – Mr. Francovich Strikes Again or When Is an Insolvency not an Insolvency?," 18 *Dublin University Law Journal* 157 (1996).

Francesco Basenghi, "Indirect Discrimination: The Italian Choice (Symposium on International Law)," 20 *Hamline Law Review* 603 (1997).

Andrea Bianchi, "US-Italy Extradition Treaty – Challenge Regarding Constitutionality – Protection of Fundamental Human Rights, Including Right to Life – Prohibition of Death Penalty in Requested Party's Constitution –

Inadmissibility of Assurances that Death Penalty Shall not be Imposed or Enforced," 91 *American Journal of International Law* 727 (1997).

Andrea Biondi, "The *Corte di Cassazione* and the Proper Implementation of Community Law," 21 *European Law Review* 485 (1996).

Wm. W. Bishop, "The Italian Yearbook of International Law: Vol. 3, 1977" (book review), 76 *American Journal of International Law* 222 (1982).

Amy Blackwell, "The Humane Society and Italian Driftnetters: Environmental Activists and Unilateral Action in International Environmental Law," 23 *North Carolina Journal of International Law and Commercial Regulation* 313 (1998).

Giovanni Bognetti, "The Role of Italian Parliament in the Treaty-Making Process" (Symposium on Parliamentary Participation in the Making and Operation of Treatises), 67 *Chicago-Kent Law Review* 391 (1991).

Antonio Braggion, "Validity of Multi-Party Arbitration Clauses Under Italian Law and Its Consequences on the Enforcement of Awards Through the 1958 New York Convention," 18 *International Business Lawyer* 412 (1990).

Roberto Caranta, "Judicial Protection Against Member States: A New *Jus Commune* Takes Shape," 32 *Common Market Law Review* 703 (1995).

Roberta Ceschini, "International Marriage and Divorce Regulations and Recognition in Italy" (Special Symposium on International Marriage and Divorce Regulation and Recognition), 29 *Family Law Quarterly* 567 (1995).

George Cumming, "*Andrea Francovich v. the Italian Republic; Danila Bonifaci et al. v. the Italian Republic* (Wages Due From Bankrupt Companies)," *Journal of Business Law* (1992) 610-614.

Peter Anthony Curran, "Italian Legislation on Deep Sea Mining," 20 *Journal of World Trade Law* 713 (1986).

Luigi Daniele, "Italy and EEC Law in 1990," 16 *European Law Review* 417 (1991).

Mark E. DeWitt, "Extradition Enigma: Italy and Human Rights vs. American and the Death Penalty," 47 *Catholic University Law Review* 535 (1998).

J. Dutheil de la Rochere, "Member State Liability for Infringement of European Community Law," 11 *Tulane European and Civil Law Forum* 18 (1996).

Gordon H. Downie, "New Right to Damages in Community Law," 37 *Journal of the Law Society of Scotland* 424 (1992).

Augusto Fantozzi and Andrea Manganelli, "An Analysis of Italy's Implementing Legislation for the EC Parent/Subsidiary Directive," 6 *Tax Notes International* 698 (1993).

Franco Ferrari, "Uniform Law of International Sales: Issues of Applicability and Private International Law (Italy)," 15 *Journal of Law and Commerce* 159 (1995).

Giorgio Gaja, "National Courts. (*S.p.a. Comavicola v. Amministrazione delle finanze dello Stato*)," 19 *Common Market Law Review* 455 (1982).

Giorgio Gaja, "New Developments in a Continuing Story: The Relationship Between EEC Law and Italian Law," 27 *Common Market Law Review* 83 (1990).

Andrea Giardina, "Court Decisions in Italy Interpreting and Implementing the New York Convention," 7 *Journal of International Arbitration* 77 (1990).

Alberto Giampieri and Giovanni Nardulli, "Enforceability of International Documentary Letters of Credit: An Italian Perspective," 27 *International Lawyer* 1013 (1993).

David R. Gilmour, "The Enforcement of Community Law by the Commission in the Context of State Aids: The Relationship Between Articles 93 and 169 and the Choice of Remedies," 18 *Common Market Law Review* 63 (1981).

Dorothy A. Gillies, "Individuals and EEC Directives," *Juridical Review* 283 (1992).

Paolo Girolami, "Implementation of the Second Company Law Directive (Italy)," 8 *European Law Review* 266 (1983).

Sheila M. Greene, "The Italian Practice of International Law" (book review), 15 *International Lawyer* 175 (1981).

Christopher Greenwood, "Effect of EC Directives in National Law (*Marleasing SA v. La Comercial Internacional de Alimentacion SA*; *Francovich v. Italian Republic*)," 51 *Cambridge Law Journal* 3 (1992).

Stefano Guiso-Gallisay, "Italian Tax Implications of European Economic and Monetary Union," 17 *Tax Notes International* 329 (1998).

Wendy Huey, "International Litigation: United States and Italy FCN Treaty and ICJ Jurisdiction Over Disputes," 32 *Harvard International Law Journal* 236 (1991).

John Temple Lang, "New Legal Effects Resulting From the Failure Under European Community Law: The *Frankovich* Judgment," 16 *Fordham International Law Journal* 1 (1992).

Antonio La Pergola, "Italy and European Integration: A Lawyer's Perspective" (Italy in Crisis: A Symposium on the Political and Social Aspects of Italian Law), 4 *Indiana International & Comparative Law Review* 259 (1994).

Antonio La Pergola and Patrick Del Duca, "Community Law, International Law and the Italian Constitution," 79 *American Journal of International Law* 598 (1985).

Guglielmo Maisto, "Italy Implements EC Parent/Subsidiary Directive on Taxation of Cross-Border Dividends," 6 *Tax Notes International* 635 (1993).

Carlo Mastellone, The Judicial Application of Community Law in Italy, 1976-1980, 19 *Common Market Law Review* 153 (1982).

Paolo Mengozzi, "A View From Italy on Judicial Cooperation Between Italy and the United States: The 1982 Mutual Assistance Treaty and the 1983 Extradition Treaty," 18 *New York University Journal of International Law and Politics* 813 (1986).

Paolo Mengozzi, "The Influence of Italian Constitutional and European Community Law on Italian Conflict of Laws" (XIV International Conference of the International Association of Jurists, Italy-USA), 37 *Saint Louis University Law Journal* 365 (1993).

Jackie Minor, "Enforcing the Environment Directives (European Economic Community)," 8 *European Law Review* 64 (1983).

Miguel Montana i Mora, "European Community Law – Legal Status of International Agreements Within the Community Legal Order – General Agreement on Tariffs and Trade – Lome Conventions," 91 *American Journal of International Law* 152 (1997).

Gian Battista Origoni della Croce, "Choice of Substantive Law: The 1994 Italian Reform," 25 *International Business Lawyer* 161 (1997).

Jeffrey A. Orr. Brigham, "Can You Bank on It? Italy's Response to the Second Banking Directive of the European Community," *Young University Law Review* 253 (1992).

Andrew G. Paton and Rosanna Grosso, "The Hague Convention on the Law Applicable to Trusts and on Their Recognition: Implementation in Italy," 43 *International and Comparative Law Quarterly* 654 (1994).

Angelo Pesce, "Protection of Sellers in Transnational Sales: Beyond Letters of Credit (Italy)," 10 *International Business Lawyer* 331 (1982).

Raffaele Mauro Petriccione, "Italy: Supremacy of Community Law Over National Law," 11 *European Law Review* 320 (1986).

Raffaele Petriccione, "Italy: A New Mechanism for the Implementation of Community Law," 14 *European Law Review* 456 (1989).

Maurizio Ragazzi, "Italy – The Holy See: Agreement to Amend the 1929 Lateran Concordat," 24 *International Legal Materials* 1589 (1985).

Robert A. Rosen, "The Seveso Directives – Catastrophic Releases" (Italian Implementation of EC Directives, part 1), 11 *Environmental Claims Journal* 123 (1998)

Malcolm Ross, "Article 37: the French and Italian Monopolies," 8 *European Law Review* 407 (1983).

Malcolm Ross, "Beyond *Francovich*," 56 *Modern Law Review* 55 (1993).

Roberta Louise Rubin, "International Agreements: Two *Treaties Between the United States and Italy*," 26 *Harvard International Law Journal* 601 (1985).

Henry G. Schermers, "The Scales in Balance: National Constitutional Court v. Court of Justice," 27 *Common Market Law Review* 97 (1990).

Joseph J. Simeone, "The Recognition and Enforceability of Foreign Country Judgments" (XIVInternational Conference of the International Association of Jurists, Italy-USA), 37 *Saint Louis University Law Journal* 341 (1993).

Mario Siragusa and Giuseppe Scassellati-Sforzolini, "Italian and EC Competition Law: A New Relationship Reciprocal Exclusivity and Common Principles," 29 *Common Market Law Review* 93 (1992).

Anthony Sistilli, "Italy: Enforcement of Foreign Judgments," 24 *International Business Lawyer* 542 (1996).

Fiona Smith and Lorna Woods, "Causation in *Francovich*: The Neglected Problem," 46 *International and Comparative Law Quarterly* 925 (1997).

Josephine Steiner, "From Direct Effects to *Francovich*: Shifting Means of Enforcement of Community Law," 18 *European Law Review* 3 (1993).

Elda Turco Bulgherini, "Warsaw Convention and the Italian Constitution," 6 *Air Law* 251 (1981).

Tiziano Treu, "European Unification and Italian Labor Relations" (Symposium: The European Economic Community and 1992), 11 *Comparative Labor Law Journal* 441 (1990).

Gabriella Venturini, "Italy and the United Nations: Membership, Contribution, and Proposals for Reform" (Symposium on International Law), 20 *Hamline Law Review* 627 (1997).

Mary L. Volcansek, "Impact of Judicial Policies in the European Community: the Italian Constitutional Court and European Community Law," 42 *Western Political Quarterly* 569 (1989).

Derrick Wyatt, "Compatibility of Italian Rules on Customs Agents With Articles 30 and 52 (EEC)," 5 *European Law Review* 480 (1980).

Jurisprudence, Legal History, Legal Research, Legal Profession, and other law-related issues

"Conflict and Control: Law and Order in Nineteenth-Century Italy" (book review), 14 *Law and Social Inquiry* 217 (1989).

"Italian Legal Information Retrieval" (book review), 43 *Computers and Law* 20 (1985).

"The Italian Legal System" (book review), 135 *New Law Journal* 543 (1985).

"The Italian Legal System" (book review, 5), 129 *Solicitors Journal* 521 (1985).

Mark Benney, "Gramsci on Law, Morality, and Power," II *International Journal of the Sociology of the Law* 191 (1983).

Sarah R. Blanshei, "Criminal Justice in Medieval Perugia and Bologna," 1 *Law and History Review* 251 (1983).

Ottavio Campanella, "The Italian Legal Profession," 19 *Journal of the Legal Profession* 59 (1994).

Roberta Ceschini, "The Role of Women in the Italian Legal System" (Symposium: The Comparative International Role of Women Attorneys in Law and Society), 12 *Georgia State University Law Review* 431 (1996).

Constantino Ciampi and Deirdre Exell Pirro, "Legal Informatics in Italy," 34 *Computers and Law* 2 (1982).

Jeremy Cooper, "Legal Services in Italy," 130 *New Law Journal* 143 (1980).

Louis F. Del Duca, "The Expanding Role of International and Comparative Law Studies – An Overview of the Italian Legal System," 88 *Dickinson Law Review* 221 (1984).

Jerrold F. Elkin, "Application of the 'Open City' Concept to Rome 1942-1944," 22 *Air Force Law Review* 188 (1981).

Gino Gorla, "A Decision of the Rota Fiorentina of 1780 on Liability for Damages Caused by the 'Ball Game'," 21 *Comparative Juridical Review* 103 (1984).

Thomas Kuehn, "'As if Conceived Within a Legitimate Marriage': A Dispute Concerning Legitimation in Quattrocento Florence," 29 *American Journal of Legal History* 275 (1985).

Roberto A. Jacchio, "Consulting Italian Commercial Lawyers," 135 *Solicitors Journal* 751 (1991).

Laura Ikins Stern, "Inquisition Procedure and Crime in Early Fifteenth Century Florence," 8 *Law and History Review* 297 (1990).

Ugo Mattei and P.G. Monateri, "Faculty Recruitment in Italy: Two Sides of the Moon" (Selecting Minds Symposium), 41 *American Journal of Comparative Law* 427 (1993).

Peter Meijes Tiersma, "Rites of Passage: Legal Ritual in Roman Law and Anthropological Analogues" (Special Issue on Customary Law and Related Essays), 9 *Journal of Legal History* 3 (1988).

Luigi Moccia, "The Italian Legal System" (book review), 35 *International and Comparative Law Quarterly* 749 (1986).

W. Keith Percival, "Maffeo Vegio and the Prelude to Juridical Humanism," 6 *Journal of Legal History* 179 (1985).

K. W. Ryan, "The Italian Legal System" (book review), 11 *Sydney Law Review* 176 (1986).

Giorgio Sacerdoti, "The Italian Legal System" (book review), 80 *American Journal of International Law* 406 (1986).

Albert J. Schmidt, "Crime, Society and the Law in Renaissance Italy" (book review), 15 *Law and History Review* 164 (1997).

Christiane Serkis Bischof, "Legal Databases in France, Switzerland and Italy," 21 *International Journal of Legal Information* 7 (1993).

Claire D.C. Spirou, "English, French, German and Italian Language Materials Relating to Greek Law: A Selected and Annotated Bibliography," 17 *International Journal of Legal Information* 10 (1989).

Daniela Tiscornia, "Meta-Reasoning in Law: A Computational Model," 4 *Journal of Law and Information Science* 368 (1993).

James Q. Whitman, "The Lawyers Discover the Fall of Rome (in 13th century Bologna)," 9 *Law and History Review* 191 (1991).

James Q. Whitman, "Law, Family and Women: Toward a Legal Anthropology of Renaissance in Italy" (book review), 12 *Law and History Review* 185 (1994).

Marvin E. Wolfgang, "Crime and Punishment in Renaissance Florence," 81 *Journal of Criminal Law and Criminology* 567 (1990).

Index